Readings in
Ancient History

CONTENTS

Near Eastern Civilizations   *1*

 1. The Epic of Gilgamesh   5
 2. The Epic of the Flood   12
 3. The Reforms of Urukagina   16
 4. Poem of the Righteous Sufferer   20
 5. The Dialogue of Pessimism   23
 6. The Shamash Hymn   25
 7. The Laws of Hammurabi   28
 8. The Instruction of Ptah-hotep   36
 9. The Edwin Smith Surgical Papyrus   39
10. The Prophecy of Nefer-rohu   43
11. Romantic Poetry   45
12. A Dispute over Suicide   49
13. The Negative Confession   52
14. Hymn to the Aton   54
15. An Egyptian–Hittite Treaty   58
16. The Old Testament   60
     A. Earliest Relations Between Man and God   61
     B. Hebrew Origins   66
     C. Bondage and Deliverance   68
     D. The Sinai Covenant   72
     E. The Song of Deborah   76
     F. The People Demand a King   79

	G.	The United Kingdom of Israel	81
	H.	Jeremiah: Prophet of the New Covenant	87
	I.	Second Isaiah: Monotheism and Universalism	92
	J.	Job: A Perplexed Sufferer	96
	K.	The Song of Songs	99
	L.	Ecclesiastes: The Meditations of a Skeptic	102
	M.	The Wisdom of Solomon	105

Greek Civilization

109

17.	Homer, The Iliad		113
18.	Hesiod, Works and Days		129
19.	Early Greek Lyric Poetry		135
	A. Archilochus	136	
	B. Mimnermus	137	
	C. Sappho	138	
	D. Theognis	139	
	E. Anacreon	141	
20.	Solon: The Athenian New Deal		143
21.	Pisistratus: The Rise of Tyranny at Athens		150
22.	Lycurgus: The Spartan Totalitarian System		153
23.	Herodotus, History of the Persian Wars		160
24.	Thucydides: The Failure of Sparta		176
25.	Pericles' Funeral Oration		179
26.	The Old Oligarch		184
27.	Thucydides, History of the Peloponnesian War		189
	A. The Revolt of Mitylene	190	
	B. The Corcyrean Revolution	194	
	C. The Melian Dialogue	196	
	D. The Sicilian Expedition	201	
28.	Socrates		207
	A. The Socratic Method	209	
	B. The Apology of Socrates	211	
29.	Plato		216
	A. The Theory of Ideas	217	
	B. The Spiritual Life	221	
30.	Aristotle		223
	A. The Nicomachean Ethics	224	
	1. The Subject of the Ethics	224	
	2. The Definition of Happiness	226	
	3. Intellectual and Moral Virtue	227	

　　　4.　Moral Virtue and the Doctrine of the Mean　229
　　　5.　Intellectual Virtue: The Ideal Life　231
　　　6.　The Need of Legislation: Transition to the
　　　　　Politics　233
　　B.　The Politics　234
　　　1.　Nature, Origin, and Purpose of the State　235
　　　2.　A Criticism of Communism　237
　　　3.　Good and Bad Constitutions　238
　　　4.　The Ideal State: Its True Object　240
　　　5.　The Ideal State: Education　241
　　　6.　The Practicable State: The Best Constitution　243
　　　7.　The Practicable State: Causes of Revolutions　245
　　　8.　The Practicable State: Preserving
　　　　　Constitutions　246
31.　Demosthenes vs. Isocrates　248
　　A.　Demosthenes, First Philippic　249
　　B.　Isocrates, Address to Philip　252
　　C.　Demosthenes, On the Crown　257
32.　Plutarch: Alexander the Great　261
33.　Hellenistic Philosophy: The Cynic Counter-Culture　266
34.　Hellenistic Literature: Theocritus　270
　　A.　Idyl XI　271
　　B.　Idyl XV　273
35.　Hellenistic Science: Archimedes　277

Roman Civilization　281

36.　Polybius, The Constitution of the Roman Republic　285
37.　Livy: The Foreign Policy of the Roman Republic　291
38.　Cato the Elder　296
39.　Tiberius Gracchus　301
40.　Gaius Gracchus　309
41.　The Conspiracy of Catiline　316
42.　Julius Caesar: The Man and the Statesman　323
43.　The Assassination of Julius Caesar　334
44.　Cicero　339
　　A.　Advocate of Property Rights and the Status Quo　340
　　B.　Champion of Liberty　345
　　C.　The Laws　350
45.　The Poetry of Catullus　356
46.　Lucretius, On the Nature of Things　360

47. Augustus' Reconstruction of the Roman World   *371*

    A.   Dio Cassius, Roman History   372

    B.   Tacitus, Annals   379

48. The Pax Romana   *382*

    A.   Tacitus, Histories   383

    B.   Tacitus, Agricola   384

49. Capitalism in the Early Empire   *386*

    A.   Petronius, The Satyricon   387

    B.   Emergency Measures to Deal with Depression   396

        1.   *Apollonius of Tyana and the Grain Dealers*   396

        2.   *State Regulation of Grain Dealers and Bakers*   398

50. Juvenal: The Emancipated Women of the Early Empire   *399*

51. Marcus Aurelius, To Himself   *402*

52. Apuleius, The Golden Ass   *406*

53. The New Testament   *410*

    A.   The Teachings of Jesus   410

        1.   *John the Baptist and the Sermon on the Mount*   411

        2.   *Parables of the Kingdom*   415

        3.   *Jesus' Instructions to His Disciples*   417

    B.   The Work of Paul   421

        1.   *Paul's Address to the Athenians*   421

        2.   *Paul's Epistles*   422

           a.   *Paul's Answer to Intellectuals*   423

           b.   *Faith and the Law*   424

           c.   *Flesh and the Spirit*   426

           d.   *The Resurrection of Christ and the Faithful*   427

           e.   *Predestination*   428

           f.   *Love*   429

54. Christianity and Greco-Roman Thought   *430*

    A.   Justin, Apology   431

    B.   Tertullian, Against Heretics   432

    C.   St. Augustine, Confessions   433

55. The Persecution of Christians   *445*

    A.   Pliny, Letters   446

    B.   Tertullian, Apology   448

56. The Reforms of Diocletian   *456*

    A.   Administrative Reorganization   457

    B.   Edict of Prices   459

57. Tacitus, Germania   *461*

58. Ausonius: Twilight in the Roman West   *467*

Readings in
Ancient History

Near Eastern Civilizations

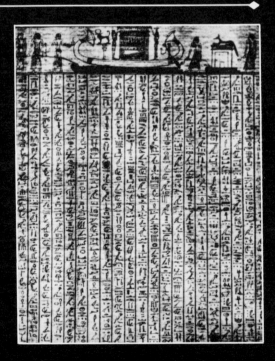

"The Book of the Dead" — Egyptian papyrus roll.
Photo courtesy of University of Chicago Oriental Institute.

Is there a thing whereof men say,
"See, this is new"? It
Hath been already, in the ages
Which were before us.

— ECCLESIASTES 1:10

The readings in this section deal mainly with the religious development of the peoples of the ancient Near East. Their political, social, and economic progress was curtailed by a despotic though usually benevolent collectivism which left little room for the emergence of individualism and freedom. Their thought remained closely tied to religion and found expression predominately in religious forms. Their religious progress, on the other hand, is significant not only because of the obvious heritage it left to later civilizations, but also because its pattern of growth provides the first illustration of a complete development from lower to higher forms of belief and practice. The three phases of this development, and the changing values of life which accompanied them, can be summarized as follows.

The earliest period in the history of a civilization is commonly called a heroic age because the values for which men strive and which give meaning to their lives are connected with a life of heroic action on earth. Material success and the prestige which comes from the accomplishment of notable deeds are the paramount goals of life, and a person's success is measured by glory or fame as a hero. The boast of a nobleman of the Old Kingdom of Egypt, "I filled an office which made my reputation in this Upper Egypt. Never before had the like been done in this Upper Egypt," reflects the same outlook on life as the words of the valorous Sumerian hero Gilgamesh, who could not be deterred from combat with a fierce dragon: "If I fall, I shall have established my fame. 'Gilgamesh fell, they will say, in combat with terrible Huwawa.'"

When we turn to the religious beliefs of this first, or heroic, age of the Near Eastern civilizations, we find that they shared the same materialistic interest in this earthly life. Death, which cut short the exciting life of action, was dreaded as the worst of evils. To offset this catastrophe, people either sought some means of prolonging their earthly existence and avoiding the final journey to what the Sumerians called the "land of no return," or they conceived of life after death as a copy and a continuation of their happy existence on earth. The relationship between mortals and the gods, who were cut from the same heroic pattern as mortals, was purely material and premoral — premoral in the sense that rewards and punishments meted out by the gods had nothing as yet to do with the kind of conduct that was based upon man's love for his fellow man. Religion was on a materialistic cash basis: people believed that the more they gave to the gods in the form of sacrifices, the more they would be rewarded. This close reciprocal relationship was viewed as completely satisfactory to both parties, and this fact is the main theme of man's earliest religious literature. "Well tended are men, the cattle of god," states an early Egyptian text, "he made heaven and earth according to their desire."

The values of the heroic age and their accompanying religious beliefs and practices did not continue forever. In each of the civilizations we shall examine time brought changes which resulted in a collapse of the old order. Largely as a result of what is often called a "time of trouble" — a term for social calamity which was first used by the ancient Hebrews — old practices and beliefs were swept away amid political, economic, and social disintegration. "No sudden change of outward affairs," wrote Boethius in the sixth century A.D. as he viewed the collapse of his Roman world, "can ever come without some up-heaval in the mind." The ancient Near Eastern civilizations were affected in the same fashion by similar disastrous events. As a result, they turned away from the gods who no longer seemed to answer the petitions of the sacrifice, and they rejected the pursuits and values of the heroic age. People lamented their sad lot in a new age empty of the old values; and while some sought a temporary refuge by immersing themselves in worldly pleasures, others turned to the task of constructing a stable and meaningful life with new values.

The values of this new way of life were moral values, for it was discovered that the only way to restore order and stability to society was by laying stress upon right conduct by its members. A life of justice and righteousness, in-spired by a love for one's fellows and a golden rule, became the goal for which to strive. Religion reflected this profound change in the values of life, and there arose moral religions in which rewards and punishments from the gods were thought to be based solely upon human conduct. The contrast between the old and the new in religion, the premoral and the moral, was put in one short sentence by an Egyptian sage who witnessed the collapse of the Old Kingdom and reflected upon that disaster: "More acceptable [to the gods] is the virtue of the upright man than the ox of him that doeth inequity." The prophet Micah proclaimed the same moral view at a similar moment in the development of Hebrew religious beliefs: "What does the Lord require of thee, but to do justly, and love kindness, and to walk humbly with thy God?"

These are the main religious, and closely related intellectual, developments discernible in the literature of the ancient Near Eastern civilizations. They form a pattern that is repeated in the histories of later civilizations, giving the words of the Hebrew author of Ecclesiastes meaning beyond their time.

I

The Epic of Gilgamesh

The Sumerian heroic age

Folk epics are impersonal accounts of heroic deeds composed in a simple and forceful meter. They were at first unwritten, transmitted by minstrels who chanted them to the accompaniment of a musical instrument. They form the early literature of many civilizations and are of great interest not only for the tales they tell but also for the institutions and ideas which they describe.

The Sumerians were the first people to produce epic tales of semi-legendary heroes, the most famous of whom was Gilgamesh, ruler of the city-state of Uruk (or Erech) about 2700 B.C. About 2000 B.C., or somewhat later, an unknown Babylonian collected some of the Gilgamesh stories, together with other tales, and wove them into a new whole. The following selections are from this Babylonian Epic of Gilgamesh.

The theme which gives unity to the varied heroic adventures described in the Epic of Gilgamesh is that of death — the sudden realization that death will cut short the glorious career of the great hero and the frantic but unsuccessful search for some means of living forever. The story opens with an account of the friction between Gilgamesh and the nobles of Uruk, who claim that their ruler is acting tyrannically. (Their complaint that Gilgamesh drafted their sons to serve in his army is described in a separate epic tale; their charge in the tale below that he mistreated their wives and daughters is probably pure propaganda.) The nobles appeal to the gods for aid, with the result that Enkidu is created by Aruru, the mother goddess, to check Gilgamesh's tyranny. Gilgamesh sends a harlot to tame Enkidu's barbarous nature before he is brought to Uruk, where the two heroes fight to a draw and thereafter become fast friends. Together they set out on dangerous adventures, slaying the terrible monster Huwawa who guards the Cedar Forest for the storm-god Enlil, insulting the goddess Ishtar who falls in love with Gilgamesh — love that here, as elsewhere in the epic, contains no romantic element — and destroying the awesome Bull of Heaven sent by the angered Ishtar to kill Gilgamesh. When next Enkidu dies as the result of Enlil's displeasure over the slaying of Huwawa, Gilgamesh is panic-stricken by the sudden realization of the stark reality of death. His life is henceforth dominated by the one aim of finding everlasting life. This leads him to search out Utnapishtim, the one man to whom the gods

From *Ancient Near Eastern Texts Relating to the Old Testament*, ed. James B. Pritchard, 3rd rev. ed. with Supplement, pp. 73–75, 78–79, 84–85, 87, 89–90, 96. Copyright © 1969 by Princeton University Press. Reprinted by permission of Princeton University Press. Translated by E. A. Speiser.

have granted immortality, in order to learn from him the secret of eternal life. The remainder of the epic incorporates the story of the Flood (see Selection 2), which originally existed as an independent tale. Utnapishtim relates how he obtained eternal life as a reward for the deeds he performed at the time of the Flood. But this unique event cannot be duplicated. As a parting gift to the dejected Gilgamesh, Utnapishtim tells him of the Plant of Life that grows on the bottom of the sea and renews the life of him who eats it. But once again Gilgamesh's hopes are ended when the Plant of Life is stolen from him by a snake. The epic ends with Gilgamesh's bitter lament over the failure of his quest; though snakes may hereafter slough off their old skins and eternally renew their youth, the sad lot of man is old age and death.

> He who saw everything to the ends of the land,
> Who all things experienced, considered all! . . .
> Two-thirds of him is god, one third of him is human. . . .
> The onslaught of his weapons verily has no equal.
> By the drum are aroused his companions.

Gilgamesh's despotic behavior leads to the creation of Enkidu.

> The nobles of Uruk are gloomy in their chambers:
> "Gilgamesh leaves not the son to his father;
> Day and night is unbridled his arrogance.
> Yet this is Gilgamesh, the shepherd of Uruk.
> He should be our shepherd: strong, stately, and wise!
> Gilgamesh leaves not the maid to her mother,
> The warrior's daughter, the noble's spouse!"
> The gods hearkened to their plaint,
> The gods of heaven, Uruk's lords . . .
> The great Aruru they called:
> "Thou, Aruru, didst create Gilgamesh;
> Create now his double;
> His stormy heart let him match.
> Let them contend, that Uruk may have peace!" . . .
> Aruru washed her hands,
> Pinched off clay and cast it on the steppe.
> On the steppe she created valiant Enkidu, . . .
> Shaggy with hair is his whole body,
> He is endowed with head hair like a woman. . . .
> He knows neither people nor land; . . .
> With the gazelles he feeds on grass,
> With the wild beasts he jostles at the watering-place,
> With the teeming creatures his heart delights in water. . . .

Having heard of the animal-like Enkidu, Gilgamesh sends a harlot to civilize him and bring him to Uruk.

The lass beheld him, the savage-man,
The barbarous fellow from the depths of the steppe: ...
The lass freed her breasts, bared her bosom,
And he possessed her ripeness.
She was not bashful as she welcomed his ardor.
She laid aside her cloth and he rested upon her.
She treated him, the savage, to a woman's task,
As his love was drawn unto her.
For six days and seven nights Enkidu comes forth,
Mating with the lass.
After he had had his fill of her charms,
He set his face toward his wild beasts.
On seeing him, Enkidu, the gazelles ran off,
The wild beasts of the steppe drew away from his body.
Startled was Enkidu, as his body became taut,
His knees were motionless — for his wild beasts had gone.
Enkidu had to slacken his pace — it was not as before;
But he now had wisdom, broader understanding.
Returning, he sat at the feet of the harlot.
He looks up at the face of the harlot,
His ears attentive, as the harlot speaks;
The harlot says to him, to Enkidu:
"Thou art wise, Enkidu, art become like a god!
Why with the wild creatures dost thou roam over the steppe?
Come, let me lead thee to ramparted Uruk,
To the holy temple, abode of Anu and Ishtar,
Where lives Gilgamesh, accomplished in strength,
And like a wild ox lords it over the folk."
As she speaks to him, her words find favor,
His heart enlightened, he yearns for a friend. ...
Enkidu says to her, to the harlot:
"Up, lass, escort thou me,
To the pure sacred temple, abode of Anu and Ishtar,
Where lives Gilgamesh, accomplished in strength,
And like a wild ox lords it over the folk.
I will challenge him and will boldly address him,
I will shout in Uruk: 'I am he who is mighty! ...' "
The nobles rejoiced:
"A hero has appeared
For the man of proper mien!
For Gilgamesh, the godlike,
His equal has come forth." ...

Enkidu and Gilgamesh meet and battle to a draw.

They met in the Market-of-the-Land.
Enkidu barred the gate with his foot,
Not allowing Gilgamesh to enter.
They grappled each other, butting like bulls,
They shattered the doorpost, as the wall shook.
As Gilgamesh bent the knee — his foot on the ground —
His fury abated and he turned away. . . .
They kissed each other
And formed a friendship. . . .

Enkidu quails at the prospect of fighting the monstrous Huwawa, guardian of the Cedar Forest, and Gilgamesh reassures him with a reminder of the heroic meaning of life.

Gilgamesh opened his mouth, saying to Enkidu:
"In the forest resides fierce Huwawa.
Let us, me and thee, slay him,
That all evil from the land we may banish! [. . .]
Enkidu opened his mouth, saying to Gilgamesh:
"I found it out, my friend, in the hills,
As I was roaming with the wild beasts.
For ten thousand leagues extends the forest.
Who is there that would go down into it?
Huwawa — his roaring is the flood-storm,
His mouth is fire, his breath is death!
Why dost thou desire to do this thing?
An unequal struggle is tangling with Huwawa." . . .
Gilgamesh opened his mouth, saying to Enkidu:
"Who, my friend, is superior to death?
Only the gods live forever in the sun.
As for mankind, numbered are their days;
Whatever they achieve is but the wind!
Even here thou art afraid of death.
What of thy heroic might?
Let me go then before thee,
Let thy voice call to me, 'Advance, fear not!'
Should I fall, I shall have made me a name:
'Gilgamesh' — they will say — 'against fierce Huwawa
Has fallen!' Long after
My offspring has been born in my house, [. . .]
Thus calling to me, thou hast grieved my heart.
My hand I will poise and will fell the cedars.
A name that endures I will make for me! . . ."

Having slain Huwawa, Gilgamesh next scornfully rejects the goddess Ishtar's offer of love, and she forces the gods to create the Bull of Heaven to punish his insolence.

Ishtar was enraged and mounted to heaven.
Forth went Ishtar before Anu, her father,
To Antum, her mother, she went and said:
"My father, Gilgamesh has heaped insults upon me! . . ."
Anu opened his mouth to speak,
Saying to glorious Ishtar:
"But surely thou didst invite [. . .],"
Ishtar opened her mouth to speak,
Saying to Anu, her father:
"My father, make me the Bull of Heaven that he smite Gilgamesh. . . .
If thou dost not make me the Bull of Heaven,
I will smash the doors of the nether world,
I will [. . .],
I will raise up the dead eating and alive,
So that the dead shall outnumber the living!" . . .

The heroes slay the Bull of Heaven and again insult Ishtar.

Up leaped Enkidu, seizing the Bull of Heaven by the horns,
The Bull of Heaven hurled his foam in his face,
Brushed him with the back of his tail. . . .
Between neck and horns he thrust his sword.
When they had slain the Bull, they tore out his heart,
Placing it before Shamash.
They drew back and did homage before Shamash.
The two brothers sat down.
Then Ishtar mounted the wall of ramparted Uruk,
Sprang on the battlements, uttering a curse:
"Woe unto Gilgamesh because he insulted me
By slaying the Bull of Heaven!"
When Enkidu heard this speech of Ishtar,
He tore loose the right thigh of the Bull of Heaven
And tossed it in her face:
"Could I but get thee, like unto him
I would do unto thee.
His entrails I would hang at thy side!" . . .
In the Euphrates they washed their hands,
They embraced each other as they went on,
Riding through the market street of Uruk.
The people of Uruk are gathered to gaze upon them.
Gilgamesh to the lyre maidens of Uruk
Says these words:
"Who is most splendid among the heroes?
Who is most glorious among men?"
"Gilgamesh is most splendid among the heroes,
Gilgamesh is most glorious among men."

By means of a dream, Enkidu learns two things: that the gods have decided he must die as punishment for the insolent behavior of the two heroes, and that the land of the dead is a most dismal place.

> Gilgamesh in his palace holds a celebration.
> Down lie the heroes on their beds of night.
> Also Enkidu lies down, a dream beholding.
> Up rose Enkidu to relate his dream,
> Saying to his friend:
> "My friend, why are the great gods in council? . . .
> My friend, I saw a dream this night:
> The heavens moaned, the earth responded;
> [. . .] I stood alone.
> [. . .] his face was darkened. . . .
> Looking at me, he leads me to the House of Darkness,
> The abode of Irkalla,
> To the house which none leave who have entered it,
> On the road from which there is no way back,
> To the house wherein the dwellers are bereft of light,
> Where dust is their fare and clay their food.
> They are clothed like birds, with wings for garments,
> And see no light, residing in darkness.
> In the House of Dust, which I entered,
> I looked at rulers, their crowns put away;
> I saw princes, those born to the crown,
> Who ruled the land from the days of yore. . . ."

Enkidu dies, and the reality of death as the common lot of all mankind — even fearless heroes — strikes home to Gilgamesh. The remainder of the epic deals with his attempt to find everlasting life, a quest that all tell him is hopeless. In the following selection, Gilgamesh is talking to a barmaid who gives him sage advice.

> "He who with me underwent all hardships —
> Enkidu, whom I loved dearly,
> Who with me underwent all hardships —
> Has now gone to the fate of mankind!
> Day and night I have wept over him.
> I would not give him up for burial —
> In case my friend should rise at my plaint —
> Seven days and seven nights,
> Until a worm fell out of his nose.
> Since his passing I have not found life,
> I have roamed like a hunter in the midst of the steppe.
> O ale-wife, now that I have seen thy face,
> Let me not see the death which I ever dread."

The ale-wife said to him, to Gilgamesh:
"Gilgamesh, whither rovest thou?
The life thou pursueth, thou shalt not find.
When the gods created mankind,
Death for mankind they set aside,
Life in their own hands retaining.
Thou, Gilgamesh, let full be thy belly,
Make thou merry by day and by night.
Of each day make thou a feast of rejoicing,
Day and night dance thou and play!
Let thy garments be sparkling fresh,
Thy head be washed; bathe thou in water.
Pay heed to the little one that holds on to thy hand,
Let thy spouse delight in thy bosom!
For this is the task of mankind!" ...

Gilgamesh next searches out Utnapishtim, the immortal hero of the Flood
(Selection 2), who also cannot help him. The dejected Gilgamesh is about to
depart when he is told of the Plant of Life — his last and most disappointing
hope.

His spouse says to him, to Utnapishtim the Faraway:
"Gilgamesh has come hither, toiling and straining.
What wilt thou give him that he may return to his land?"
At that he, Gilgamesh, raised up his pole,
To bring the boat nigh to the shore.
Utnapishtim says to him, to Gilgamesh:
"Gilgamesh, thou hast come hither, toiling and straining.
What shall I give thee that thou mayest return to thy land?
I will disclose, O Gilgamesh, a hidden thing,
And about a plant I will tell thee:
This plant, like the buckthorn is [...].
Its thorns will prick thy hands just as does the rose.
If thy hands obtain the plant, thou wilt attain life."
No sooner had Gilgamesh heard this, ...
He tied heavy stones to his feet.
They pulled him down into the deep and he saw the plant.
He took the plant, though it pricked his hands.
He cut the heavy stones from his feet.
The sea cast him up upon its shore.
Gilgamesh says to him, to Urshanabi, the boatman:
"Urshanabi, this plant is a plant apart,
Whereby a man may regain his life's breath.
I will take it to ramparted Uruk. . . .
Its name shall be 'Man Becomes Young in Old Age.'
I myself shall eat it

And thus return to the state of my youth."
After twenty leagues they broke off a morsel,
After thirty more leagues they prepared for the night.
Gilgamesh saw a well whose water was cool.
He went down into it to bathe in the water.
A serpent snuffed the fragrance of the plant;
It came up from the water and carried off the plant,
Going back to shed its slough.
Thereupon Gilgamesh sits down and weeps,
His tears running down over his face.
He took the hand of Urshanabi, the boatman:
"For whom, Urshanabi, have my hands toiled?
For whom is being spent the blood of my heart?
I have not obtained a boon for myself.
For the serpent have I effected a boon!"

2

The Epic of the Flood

The Babylonian Noah

Archaeologists have discovered evidence of great floods in the Tigris-Euphrates valley, one of which left a deposit of sediment eight feet deep. Undoubtedly one such disastrous flood became the historical basis for a Sumerian flood epic, fragments of which have survived. It told how a Sumerian Noah, Ziusudra, warned beforehand by the god Ea of the intention of the gods "to destroy the seed of mankind" by a flood, built a ship and embarked upon it with his household, his possessions, and all types of living things. Because Ziusudra had thus "perceived the secret of the gods," they decided to give him "life like a god" and so made him one with themselves.

The later Babylonians incorporated the flood story into their composite Epic of Gilgamesh. When the yearning for everlasting life takes hold of Gilgamesh after the death of his friend Enkidu, he searches out Ziusudra, whom the Babylonians called Utnapishtim, to gain from him the secret of eternal life. Utnapishtim tells him his story, and it is this more complete Babylonian ver-

From "The Epic Of Gilgamesh." Tablet XI, based on the translation in Morris Jastrow, *The Civilization of Babylonia and Assyria* (Philadelphia: J. B. Lippincott Company, 1915), pp. 445–52. Reprinted by permission.

sion that is given in part below. The striking similarities with the later Hebrew story are quite evident, but the great gulf between them needs to be emphasized: the Hebrew version has been completely moralized. In the Hebrew account the Flood is sent because of sin, and the hero is saved because he is righteous. In the Sumero-Babylonian version the hero is saved out of mere favoritism and the gods send the Flood, as we learn from a separate account, because their sleep has been disturbed: "oppressive has become the clamor of mankind, by their uproar they prevent sleep." Above all, the one supreme righteous God of the Hebrews contrasts with the gang of weak, quarrelsome, greedy gods who "cowered like dogs" in the presence of the Flood and who later "like flies gathered around the sacrificer."

Gilgamesh speaks to him, to Utnapishtim, the far-removed:
"I gaze at thee, Utnapishtim!
Thy appearance is not different. As I am, so art thou. . . .
Tell me how thou didst enter into the assembly of the gods and secure
    [eternal] life."
Utnapishtim said to him, to Gilgamesh:
"I will reveal to thee, Gilgamesh, a secret story,
And the decision of the gods I will tell thee.
The city Shuruppak, a city which thou knowest,
The one that lies on the Euphrates,
That city was old, as were the gods thereof,
When the great gods decided to bring a flood over it. . . .

THE GOD EA WARNS UTNAPISHTIM

"The lord of brilliant vision, Ea, was with them.
He repeated their decision to the reed-hut.
'Reed-hut, reed-hut, wall, wall,
Reed-hut, hear! Wall, give ear!
O man of Shuruppak, son of Ubara-Tutu,
Break up this house, build a ship,
Abandon your property, seek life!
Bring into the ship seed of all living things!
The ship that thou shalt build,
Let its dimensions be measured, so that
Its breadth and length be made to correspond.
On a level with the deep, provide it with a covering.'
I understood and spoke to Ea, my lord:
'The command of my lord which thou hast commanded,
As I have understood it, I will carry out.
But what shall I answer the city — the people and the elders?'
Ea opened his mouth and spoke:
'As answer thus speak to them:
Know that Enlil [god who rules all Sumer] has conceived hatred towards
    me,

So that I can no longer dwell in your city.
On Enlil's territory I dare no longer set my face.
Therefore, I go to the Deep to dwell with Ea, my lord.
Over you he will cause blessings to rain down.' . . .

THE SHIP IS BUILT AND LOADED

"On the fifth day, I designed its outline.
Its walls were ten *gar* [120 cubits] high;
Ten *gar* the measure of its width.
I determined its shape and drew it.
I gave it six decks.
I divided (the superstructure?) into seven parts.
Its interior I divided into nine sections.
Water-plugs I constructed in the interior.
I selected a punting-pole and added accessories.
Six measures of asphalt I poured on the outer wall.
Three measures of pitch I poured on the inner wall. . . .
All that I had I loaded on her.
All that I had of silver I loaded on her.
All that I had of gold I loaded on her.
All that I had of living beings of all kinds I loaded on her.
I brought to the ship all my family and household;
Cattle of the field, beasts of the field, all the workmen I brought on
    board. . . .

THE FLOOD

"As morning dawned,
There arose on the firmament of heaven black clouds;
Adad thundered therein; . . .
Adad's roar reaches to heaven,
All light is changed to darkness. . . .
For one day the hurricane raged,
Storming furiously, . . .
Coming like a combat over men.
Brother sees not brother,
And from heaven people cannot be recognized.

"THE GODS ARE TERRIFIED"

"The gods are terrified by the deluge,
They flee and mount to the heaven of Anu;
The gods cowered like dogs in an enclosure.
Ishtar cries aloud like one in birth throes,
The mistress of the gods howls aloud:
'The former days are turned to clay. . . .
My people are like fish, they fill the sea.'

All of the Anunnaki gods weep with her;
The gods sit down, depressed and weeping. . . .

THE FLOOD SUBSIDES

"Six days and nights
The storm and flood continued to sweep over the land.
When the seventh day approached, the storm and flood ceased the combat,
After having fought like warriors. . . .
I looked at the day and the roar had quieted down,
And all mankind had returned to clay.
The landscape was level as a flat roof.
I opened a window and light fell on my face,
I bowed down and sat and wept,
Tears flowed over my face.
I looked in all directions of the sea.
At a distance of twelve miles an island appeared.
On Mount Nisir the ship stood still.
Mount Nisir held the ship so that it could not move.
One day, two days, Mount Nisir held the ship fast. . . .
When the seventh day arrived,
I sent forth a dove, letting it free.
The dove went hither and thither;
Not finding a resting place, it came back.
I sent forth a swallow, letting it free.
The swallow went hither and thither.
Not finding a resting place, it came back.
I sent forth a raven, letting it free.
The raven went and saw the decrease of the waters.
It ate, croaked, but did not turn back.
Then I let all out to the four regions and brought an offering.
I brought a sacrifice on the mountain top.
Seven and seven cult jars I arranged.
Beneath them I strewed reeds, cedarwood and myrtle.
The gods smelled the odor,
The gods smelled the sweet odor.
The gods like flies gathered around the sacrificer.

THE GODS QUARREL

"As soon as [Ishtar] the mistress of the gods arrived, . . .
'Ye gods . . . I will remember these days — never to forget them.
Let the gods come to the sacrifice,
But let not Enlil come to the sacrifice,
Because without reflection he brought on the flood,
And decreed destruction for my people.'
As soon as Enlil arrived,
He saw the ship, and Enlil was enraged,

Filled with anger at the gods.
'Who now has escaped with his life?
No man was to survive the destruction!'
Ninib opened his mouth and spoke,
Spoke to the warrior Enlil,
'Who except Ea can plan any affair?
Ea indeed knows every order.'
Ea opened his mouth and spoke,
Spoke to the warrior Enlil:
'Thou art the leader and warrior of the gods.
But why didst thou, without reflection, bring on the flood?
On the sinner impose his sin,
On the transgressor impose his transgression,
But be merciful not to root out completely, be considerate not to
    destroy altogether! . . .
I did not reveal the secret of the great gods,
I sent Utnapishtim a dream and he understood the secret of the gods.
Now take counsel for him.'

UTNAPISHTIM IS GRANTED ETERNAL LIFE

"Enlil mounted the ship,
Took hold of my hand and led me up,
Led me up and caused my wife to kneel at my side,
Touched our foreheads, stepped between us and blessed us.
'Hitherto Utnapishtim was a man;
Now Utnapishtim and his wife shall be on a level with the gods.
Utnapishtim shall dwell in the distance, at the mouth of the rivers.'
Then they took me and settled me at the mouth of the rivers."

3

The Reforms of Urukagina

"He established freedom."

While Greek political experience was so rich and varied that it has been said with pardonable exaggeration that the Greeks "invented politics," that of ancient Mesopotamia is commonly said to have been limited to an unvarying despotism that was total and not benevolent, whose subjects knew only "the

From Urukagina Cones B–C. [Editor's translation.]

language of the whip." There is good evidence, however, that not only were many of these despots exceptionally benevolent, but also that ancient Mesopotamia experienced forms of government other than despotism.[1]

The greatest political achievement of the Greeks was democracy, which never developed in Mesopotamia or elsewhere in the ancient Near East. But before the Greeks attained democracy they had experienced three other major types of government, which they called monarchy, oligarchy, and tyranny. These three constitutional forms did develop in Mesopotamia.

The Greeks called their earliest form of government monarchy because of the prominent part played by the warleader, as shown in the Homeric epics. But because the power of this early monarch was greatly limited — his actions had to be approved by an aristocratic council of nobles and, in moments of crisis such as war, by a popular assembly of all arms-bearing men — modern scholars prefer the term "primitive monarchy," or even "primitive democracy." Primitive monarchy was followed by oligarchy ("rule of the few") when the council of nobles succeeded in eliminating both the king and the popular assembly. In time, discontent with the oppressive rule of the oligarchs caused the common people, both peasantry and rising middle class, to support the rise of usurping despots called "tyrants," a non-Greek word meaning "boss" or "chief" that was borrowed from the Orient.

That primitive monarchy was also the earliest form of government in Mesopotamia is revealed in a number of epic tales. In the Epic of Gilgamesh, for example, the nobles of Uruk resent Gilgamesh's "arrogance," and they seek to curtail his arbitrary actions by setting up Enkidu as anti-king. Again, Enkidu in a dream sees "the great gods in council," an illustration of the way in which men attribute to the gods in heaven institutions similar to their own on earth. An independent Gilgamesh tale describes how Gilgamesh circumvented the opposition of his council to his proposal for a preventive war against the ruler of Kish. He is described as turning to the "convened assembly of the men of his city," who readily supported him and upbraided the nobles:

> O ye who are raised with the sons of the king,
> O ye who press the donkey's thigh . . .
> Do not submit to the house of Kish,
> let us smite it with weapons.[2]

There is also evidence that the nobles of Uruk ultimately resorted to the use of force, severely wounded Gilgamesh, and drove him into temporary exile.

Gilgamesh was the last of the Sumerian primitive monarchs whose exploits were celebrated in epics. Thereafter, for more than a century, priest-dominated

[1] See Nels Bailkey, "Early Mesopotamian Constitutional Development," *American Historical Review*, LXXII (1967), 1211–36.
[2] "Gilgamesh and Agga," tr. S. N. Kramer in *Ancient Near Eastern Texts Relating to the Old Testament*, ed. James B. Pritchard, 3rd rev. ed. with Supplement. (Copyright © 1969 by Princeton University Press), pp. 45–46. Reprinted by permission of Princeton University Press.

aristocratic councils ruled the Sumerian city-states through weak and compliant magistrates called ensi-gar's, "governors installed (by a superior)." But from roughly 2550 B.C., when true historical sources first become relatively abundant, to about 2350 B.C., when Sargon of Akkad conquered Sumer, dissatisfaction with oligarchic rule led intermittently to the rise of tyrants in the Greek sense of the term. Best known among these lugal's (literally "great [gal] man [lu]," a term used also in the sense of "master" and usually translated "king") was Urukagina, who usurped power as "lugal of Lagash" about 2400 B.C. and promulgated so many reforms in the interest of the oppressed common people that he has been called the first social reformer in history.

Urukagina's inscriptions, selections from which follow, begin with a description of the abuses which "since time immemorial," or so it seemed, had been undermining the original "divinely decreed way of life." It is Urukagina's view that all the leading elements in society — priests, administrators, powerful men, and even the ensi ("governor") and his family — were guilty of acting each "for his own benefit." Particularly noteworthy among the many resulting abuses — partly because the same evil inspired Hesiod's demand for social justice at a parallel moment in Greek history (see Selection 18 on page 129) and partly because Urukagina seems to have taken greatest pride in eradicating it — was the seizure of the property and even the persons of debtors by temple officials working in collusion with corrupt judges (mashkim).[3] Of special interest, also, is Urukagina's use of a contract theory of government to justify both his usurpation of power and his reforms: he made a "covenant" with Ningirsu, patron god of Lagash, and he carried out Ningirsu's instructions.

"THE PRACTICES OF FORMER DAYS"

Since time immemorial, since the seedcorn (first) sprouted forth, the head boatman had the boats in charge for his own benefit, the head shepherd had the asses in charge for his own benefit, the head shepherd had the sheep in charge for his own benefit, the head fisherman had the fishing places in charge for his own benefit. The incantation-priest measured out the barley rent (to his own advantage). . . .

The [temple] oxen of the gods plowed the gardens of the ensi; the gardens and the cucumber fields of the ensi were in the best fields of the gods; the asses and oxen of the priests were taken away (by the ensi). The barley rations [income] of the priests were administered by the men of the ensi. . . .

In the garden of a humble person a priest could cut a tree or carry away its fruit. When a dead man was placed in the tomb, it was necessary to deliver in his name seven jars of beer and 420 loaves of bread. The uh-mush priest received one-half gur [about fourteen gallons] of barley, one garment, one turban, and one bed. The priest's assistant received one-fourth gur of barley. . . .

---

[3] The operation of this abuse is not described by Urukagina, apparently because it was so well known; the details have been reconstructed from contemporary documents by Ferris J. Stephens, "Notes on Some Economic Texts of the Time of Urukagina," Revue d'Assyriologie, XLIX (1955), 129–30, 132–35.

The workingman was forced to beg for his bread; the youth was forced to work in the *a-zar-la*.

The houses of the *ensi*, the fields of the *ensi*, the houses of the *ensi's* wife, the fields of the *ensi's* wife, the houses of the *ensi's* children, the fields of the *ensi's* children — all were joined together side by side.

Everywhere from border to border there were the priest-judges [*mash-kim*]. . . .

Such were the practices of former days.

"HE FREED THE INHABITANTS OF LAGASH"

When the god Ningirsu, the warrior of the god Enlil, granted the *lugal*-ship of Lagash to Urukagina, picking him out of the entire population, he [Ningirsu] enjoined upon him (the restoration of) the divinely decreed way of life of former days. He [Urukagina] carried out the instructions of his divine *lugal*, Ningirsu.

He removed the head boatman in charge of the boats. He removed the head shepherd in charge of the asses and sheep. He removed the head fisherman from the fishing places. He removed the head of the storehouse from his responsibility of measuring out the barley ration to the incantation-priests. . . . He removed the palace official in charge of collecting the *il*-tax from the priests.

The houses of the *ensi* and the fields of the *ensi* were restored to the god Ningirsu. The houses of the *ensi's* wife and the fields of the *ensi's* wife were restored to the goddess Bau. The houses of the *ensi's* children and the fields of the *ensi's* children were restored to the god Shulshaggana.

Everywhere from border to border no one spoke further of priest-judges [*mashkim*].

When a dead man was placed in the tomb, (only) three jars of beer and eighty loaves of bread were delivered in his name. The *uh-mush* priest received one bed and one turban. The priest's assistant received one-eighth *gur* of barley. . . .

The youth was not required to work in the *a-zar-la*; the workingman was not forced to beg for his bread. The priest no longer invaded the garden of a humble person.

He (also) decreed: If a good ass is born to a client and his overseer says to him, "I will buy if from you," then if he wishes to sell it he will say, "Pay me what pleases me"; but if he does not wish to sell, the overseer must not force him. If the house of a powerful man is next to the house of a client, and if the powerful man says to him, "I wish to buy it," then if he wishes to sell he will say, "Pay me in silver as much as suits me," or "Reimburse me with an equivalent amount of barley"; but if he does not wish to sell, the powerful man must not force him.

CONCLUSION

He [Urukagina] freed the inhabitants of Lagash from usury, burdensome controls, hunger, theft, murder, and seizure (of their property and persons). He established freedom. The widow and the orphan were no longer at the mercy of the powerful man: for them has Urukagina made his covenant with Ningirsu.

—4—

Poem of the Righteous Sufferer

The Babylonian Job

Ancient Mesopotamian literature shows the eventual rejection of the premoral beliefs and practices that are described in epic tales (see Selections 1 and 2) and early hymns. The following lines from a hymn to the great Sumerian god Enlil reflect the once close relationship between gods and mortals that was based upon material considerations of "gifts of sacrifice":

> Oh Enlil, lord that knowest fate, who of thyself art glorious in Sumer,
> Father Enlil, lord of lands,
> Father Enlil, lord of unerring word,
> Father Enlil, shepherd of the dark headed people, . . .
> Father Enlil, with song majestically we come, the presents of the
>   ground are offered to thee as gifts of sacrifice. . . .
> Father Enlil, accept the sacred offerings, the many offerings.[1]

Other hymns, however, are filled with lamentation over the loss of this once stable and profitable relationship. They generally lay the blame on the gods who have decided, states one typical text, "to bring on other days, annihilate the plan and — while the storms foamed like a flood — subvert the ways of Sumer." [2]

The "Poem of the Righteous Sufferer," which exists in both Sumerian and Babylonian versions (selections from the latter are given below), apparently re-

From *Babylonian Wisdom Literature*, tr. W. G. Lambert (Oxford: 1960), pp. 31, 35, 39, 41, 59, 61. Reprinted by permission of The Clarendon Press.

[1] *Sumerian and Babylonian Psalms*, tr. Stephen Langdon (London, 1909), pp. 278–79.
[2] Quoted in Henri Frankfort *et al.*, *The Intellectual Adventure of Ancient Man* (Chicago: University of Chicago Press, 1946), p. 197.

flects the beginning of this great change in outlook. It tells of a man who has lost his prosperous and exalted position and suffers from ever-increasing afflictions despite his strict adherence to established religious practices — sacrifices, supplications, incantations, and magic. (His religiosity clearly seems to be ceremonial and cultic rather than ethical.) Forsaken by gods and men, he moves from perplexity and doubt to blank despair. The greater part of the poem, however, is a defense of the whole system of traditional doctrine and ritual. It glorifies Marduk, the great god of Babylon, who restored the sufferer to happiness and prosperity. In the conclusion, only a few lines of which are given here, the implied answer to skepticism is that the evils which afflict the pious are only temporary.

"WHAT STRANGE CONDITIONS EVERYWHERE!"

My god has forsaken me and disappeared,
My goddess has failed me and keeps at a distance.
The benevolent angel who walked beside me has departed,
My protecting spirit has taken to flight, and is seeking someone else.
My strength is gone; my appearance has become gloomy;
My dignity has flown away, my protection made off. . . .
The king, the flesh of the gods, the sun of his peoples,
His heart is enraged with me, and cannot be appeased.
The courtiers plot hostile action against me,
They assemble themselves and give utterance to impious words. . . .
They combine against me in slander and lies.
My lordly mouth have they held as with reins,
So that I, whose lips used to prate, have become like a mute.
My sonorous shout is reduced to silence,
My lofty head is bowed down to the ground,
Dread has enfeebled my robust heart. . . .
If I walk the street, ears are pricked;
If I enter the palace, eyes blink.
My city frowns on me as an enemy;
Indeed my land is savage and hostile.
My friend has become foe,
My companion has become a wretch and a devil. . . .
As I turn round, it is terrible, it is terrible;
My ill luck has increased, and I do not find the right.
I called to my god, but he did not show his face,
I prayed to my goddess, but she did not raise her head.
The diviner with his inspection has not got to the root of the matter,
Nor has the dream priest with his libation elucidated my case.
I sought the favour of the *zaqiqu*-spirit, but he did not enlighten me;
And the incantation priest with his ritual did not appease the divine
    wrath against me.
What strange conditions everywhere!
When I look behind, there is persecution, trouble.

"PRAYER WAS DISCRETION, SACRIFICE MY RULE"

Like one who has not made libations to his god,
Nor invoked his goddess at table,
Does not engage in prostration, nor takes cognizance of bowing down;
From whose mouth supplication and prayer is lacking,
Who has done nothing on holy days, and despised sabbaths,
Who in his negligence has despised the gods' rites,
Has not taught his people reverence and worship,
But has eaten his food without invoking his god,
And abandoned his goddess by not bringing a flour offering,
Like one who has grown torpid and forgotten his lord,
Has frivolously sworn a solemn oath by his god, like such an one do I
    appear.
For myself, I gave attention to supplication and prayer:
To me prayer was discretion, sacrifice my rule.
The day for reverencing the god was a joy to my heart;
The day of the goddess's procession was profit and gain to me.
The king's prayer — that was my joy,
And the accompanying music became a delight for me.
I instructed my land to keep the god's rites,
And provoked my people to value the goddess's name.
I made praise for the king like a god's,
And taught the populace reverence for the palace.
I wish I knew that these things were pleasing to one's god!

"WHO KNOWS THE WILL OF THE GODS?"

What is proper to oneself is an offence to one's god,
What in one's own heart seems despicable is proper to one's god.
Who knows the will of the gods in heaven?
Who understands the plans of the underworld gods?
Where have mortals learnt the way of a god?
He who was alive yesterday is dead today.
For a minute he was dejected, suddenly he is exuberant.
One moment people are singing in exaltation,
Another they groan like professional mourners.
Their condition changes like opening and shutting the legs.
When starving they become like corpses,
When replete they vie with the gods.
In prosperity they speak of scaling heaven,
Under adversity they complain of going down to hell.
I am appalled at these things; I do not understand their significance....

CONCLUSION: "MARDUK RESTORED ME"

The Lord took hold of me,
The Lord set me on my feet,
The Lord gave me life,

He rescued me from the pit,
He summoned me from destruction,
[. . .] he pulled me from the Hubur river,[1]
[. . .] he took my hand. . . .
Marduk, he restored me. . . .
The Babylonians saw how Marduk restores to life,
And all quarters extolled his greatness: . . .
Mortals, as many as there are, give praise to Marduk!

5

The Dialogue of Pessimism

All is vanity

That the skepticism and doubt which were responsible for the "Poem of the Righteous Sufferer" could lead to complete pessimism and a denial of all values is revealed in the remarkable Babylonian text known as the "Dialogue of Pessimism." The message of this work is starkly simple — all human activity is vain and worthless, and only death is attractive.

The text is in the form of a dialogue between a master and his servant in which the master first enthusiastically proposes and then, after reflection, despondently rejects the pursuit of the various major values that at one time had given meaning to life. The servant discreetly agrees with his master's vacillating proposals and, in each instance, first describes the significance which the proposed activity originally contained and then concludes with a deeply pessimistic account of the fruitlessness of the contemplated action.

Seven of the poem's eleven stanzas are presented below. Noteworthy is the fact that even the excitements of banqueting and romantic love are proposed and found wanting. We know that the ancient Mesopotamians developed an interest in such excitements. Unfortunately, except for some parallels to the Biblical Song of Songs, only the titles or first lines of a number of their love songs have survived: "How do I long for pleasure," "By night I thought of thee," "The bosom of a female friend is a jar of sweetness," "My love is a lamp illuminating the shadows [of life]."

The rejection of romantic love as a value — a value neatly expressed in the last of the titles just quoted — makes the unknown author of the "Dialogue of

Based on the translation by Stephen Langdon, "Babylonian Wisdom," *Babyloniaca*, VII (1922), 197–208.

[1] The river of death in the underworld.

Pessimism" a contemporary, philosophically speaking, of the modern writer whose essay, "Love — or the Life and Death of a Value," concludes that romantic love "no longer is the ultimate self-justifying value which once it was.... Many other things we have come to doubt ... but in the general wreck the wreck of love is conspicuous and typical." [2]

"Servant, hearken unto me." "Yes, my lord, yes."
"Hasten, summon me the chariot and hitch it up; to the palace I will ride."
"Drive quickly, my lord, drive quickly, the king [. . .] will give thee and they shall be thine. . . .'"
"No, servant, I unto the palace will not drive."
"Drive not, my lord, drive not. Unto a place whence one cometh not up he will send thee. In a land which thou knowest not he will let thee be seized. Day and night will he cause thee to see misery."

"Servant, hearken unto me." "Yes, my lord, yes."
"I will institute rebellion."
"So do, my lord, so do. If thou institutest not rebellion, what happiness is thine? Who will give to thee that thou fillest thy stomach?"
"No, servant, rebellion will I not institute."
"Do it not, my lord, do it not. The man who institutes rebellion, he is slain or he is flayed. Or he is blinded, or seized and thrown into prison."

"Servant, hearken unto me." "Yes, my lord, yes."
"Hasten, order me water for my hands, give it me and I will make sacrifice unto my god."
"Do it, my lord, do it. The man that maketh sacrifice unto his god, glad is his heart, loan upon loan he maketh."
"No, servant, sacrifice unto my god will I not make."
"Do it not, my lord, do it not. Wilt thou teach god that he run after thee like a dog? . . ."

"Servant, hearken unto me." "Yes, my lord, yes."
"A benefit unto my land I will do."
"So do, my lord, so do. The man who doeth a benefaction unto his land findeth benefaction in the bowl of Marduk."
"No, servant, a benefaction unto my land I will not do."
"Do it not, my lord, do it not. Ascend thou unto the ruins of cities, go to those of old; behold the skulls of the later and the former ones: who is now an evildoer, who is now a benefactor?"

"Servant, hearken unto me." "Yes, my lord, yes."
"Hasten, order me water for my hands, give it me and I will dine."

[2] Joseph Wood Krutch, The Modern Temper: A Study and a Confession (New York: Harcourt, Brace & World, 1929), pp. 72–73.

"Dine, my lord, dine. To dine repeatedly is the opening of the heart. With him that dines in happiness and with washed hands will Shamash walk."

"No, servant, I will not partake of the feast."

"Dine not, my lord, dine not. Fasting and eating, thirsting and drinking come to every man."

"Servant, hearken unto me." "Yes, my lord, yes."

"I will love a woman."

"So love, my lord, so love. The man who loves a woman forgets woe and misery."

"No, servant, a woman will I not love."

"Do not love, my lord, do not love. A woman is a pit, a slough, a pitfall; a woman is a sharp iron sword which cutteth the neck of a man."

"Servant, hearken unto me." "Yes, my lord, yes."

"Now then, what is good?"

"To break my neck and thy neck, to fall into the river — that is good. Who is tall enough to ascend unto heaven? Who is broad enough to encompass the earth?"

"No, servant, I will slay thee and cause thee to go before me."

"And my lord would not want to live even three days after me."

6

The Shamash Hymn

Moral religion and social justice

By the time of the reformer Urukagina of Lagash, as we have seen (Selection 3), the fact of human suffering had produced a high level of social consciousness in Sumer. From at least that time onward, ideals of social justice not only motivated the domestic policies of rulers but also were regarded as the basis for the rewards and punishments which the gods bestowed on mankind. Thus, for example, a hymn to the goddess Nanshe of Lagash honors her as the guarantor of justice who "searches the heart of the people" in order to punish those "walking in transgression," who "knows the oppression of man over man,

From *Babylonian Wisdom Literature*, tr. W. G. Lambert (Oxford: 1960), pp. 127–137. Reprinted by permission of The Clarendon Press.

is the orphan's mother, ... who cares for the widow, who seeks out justice for the poorest ... brings the refugee to her lap, finds shelter for the weak." [1]

But it was the sun-god Utu, called Shamash by the Babylonians, who emerged from relative obscurity to become the god of justice par excellence. The following lines from the great two-hundred-line Babylonian hymn to Shamash, considered the noblest example of Mesopotamian lyric poetry and worthy of being compared with the best of the Hebrew psalms, reveal Shamash to have achieved such a position of importance that the Igigi and Anunnaki gods (the great gods of the Upperworld and the Underworld) humble themselves before him. He is even seen as a universal god who receives the worship of men in foreign lands. It is also noteworthy that as the guardian of the moral order Shamash is particularly concerned with the plight of the weak and the oppressed and with the malpractices of businessmen. The evident emphasis placed on business activity is a reflection of the known fact that large numbers of enterprising capitalists flourished during the Old Babylonian period (roughly 2000–1600 B.C.).

> Shamash, at your arising mankind bows down,
> [. . .] every land.
> Illuminator, dispeller of darkness of the vault of the heavens,
> Who sets aglow the beard of light, the corn field, the life of the land.
> Your splendour covers the vast mountains,
> Your fierce light fills the lands to their limits.
> You climb to the mountains surveying the earth,
> You suspend from the heavens the circle of the lands.
> You care for all the peoples of the lands,
> And everything that Ea [god of wisdom], king of the counsellors, had
>   created is entrusted to you.
> Whatever has breath you shepherd without exception,
> You are their keeper in upper and lower regions.
> Regularly and without cease you traverse the heavens,
> Every day you pass over the broad earth. . . .
> In the underworld, you care for the counsellors of Kusu, the Anunnaki,
> Above, you direct all the affairs of men,
> Shepherd of that beneath, keeper of that above,
> You, Shamash, direct, you are the light of everything. . . .
> Among all the Igigi there is none who toils but you,
> None who is supreme like you in the whole pantheon of gods.
> At your rising the gods of the land assemble;
> Your fierce glare covers the land.
> Of all the lands of varied speech,
> You know their plans, you scan their way.
> The whole of mankind bows to you,
> Shamash, the universe longs for your light. . . .

[1] Samuel N. Kramer, *The Sumerians: Their History, Culture, and Character* (Chicago: University of Chicago Press, 1963), pp. 124–25.

You stand by the traveller whose road is difficult,
To the seafarer in dread of the waves you give [. . .]
It is you who patrol the unseen routes,
You constantly tread paths which confront Shamash alone.
You save from the storm the merchant carrying his capital,
The [. . .] who goes down to the ocean you equip with wings.
You point out settling-places to refugees and fugitives,
To the captive you point out routes that only Shamash knows. . . .
A man who covets his neighbor's wife
Will [. . .] before his appointed day.
A nasty snare is prepared for him [. . .]
Your weapon will strike at him, and there will be none to save him. . . .
You give the unscrupulous judge experience of fetters,
Him who accepts a present and yet lets justice miscarry you make bear
     his punishment.
As for him who declines a present, but nevertheless takes the part of
     the weak,
It is pleasing to Shamash, and he will prolong his life. . . .
What is he benefited who invests money in unscrupulous trading mis-
     sions?
He is disappointed in the matter of profit and loses his capital.
As for him who invests money in distant trading missions and pays one
     shekel per [. . .],
It is pleasing to Shamash, and he will prolong his life.
The merchant who practises trickery as he holds the balances,
Who uses two sets of weights, thus lowering the [. . .],
He is disappointed in the matter of profit and loses his capital.
The honest merchant who holds the balances and gives good weight —
Everything is presented to him in good measure [. . .]
The merchant who practises trickery as he holds the corn measure,
Who weighs out loans of corn by the minimum standard, but requires
     a large quantity in repayment,
The curse of the people will overtake him before his time,
If he demanded repayment before the agreed date, there will be guilt
     upon him. . . .
The honest merchant who weighs out loans of corn by the maximum
     standard, thus multiplying kindness,
It is pleasing to Shamash, and he will prolong his life.
He will enlarge his family, gain wealth,
And like the water of a never failing spring his descendants will never
     fail. . . .
The progeny of evil-doers will fail.
Those whose mouth says "No" — their case is before you.
In a moment you discern what they say;
You hear and examine them; you determine the lawsuit of the wronged.
Every single person is entrusted to your hands;

You manage their omens; that which is perplexing you make plain.
You observe, Shamash, prayer, supplication, and benediction,
Obeisance, kneeling, ritual murmurs, and prostration.
The feeble man calls you from the hollow of his mouth,
The humble, the weak, the afflicted, the poor,
She whose son is captive constantly and unceasingly confronts you. . . .
Which are the mountains not clothed with your beams?
Which are the regions not warmed by the brightness of your light?
Brightener of gloom, illuminator of darkness,
Dispeller of darkness, illuminator of the broad earth, . . .

—7—
The Laws of Hammurabi

"To further the welfare of the people"

The last major period (roughly 2000–1600 B.C.) in the early history of Meso-potamia is commonly called the Old Babylonian period because of the impor-tance of the First Dynasty of Babylon, and especially of Hammurabi (ca. 1792–1750 B.C.), the outstanding member of that dynasty. Known also as the Era of Warring States, this turbulent period was characterized by political in-stability, chronic economic depression, and extremes of wealth and poverty. Incessant wars to maintain the balance of power, fought by continually shifting coalitions of city-states, beset the land together with resurgent oligarchy. Tem-porary respite from the latter evil was at times provided by strong rulers, but, with the exception of Hammurabi, who temporarily united all of Mesopotamia under the sway of Babylon, hardly more than locally.

Of major interest are the social reforms promulgated by these stronger rulers of the Old Babylonian period. In broad reference to their work as social reformers, these rulers commonly employed the phrase first used, as we have seen, by Urukagina, "I have established freedom," meaning the removal of abuses from the oppressed and the restoration and safeguarding of their rights. In part, these reformers viewed social justice as a return to what Urukagina had called "the divinely decreed way of life of former days," or what was now termed kittum, "truth," the fixed and invariable body of law upon which society had been founded, the creation of the gods who had entrusted it to the ruler's care. But greater emphasis was placed on a new, dynamic type of

Based on the translation by Robert F. Harper, *The Code of Hammurabi* (Chicago: The Uni-versity of Chicago Press, 1904).

law that had emerged as a supplement to kittum. Called misharum, literally "rightings" and hence translated "equity," "justice," or "righteousness," this new law was of human origin, the work of a true legislator. Promulgated as "judgments" and "decisions" of the ruler, these misharu-acts sought to alleviate the injustices produced by the economic and social dislocations of the Old Babylonian period for which kittum had no specific remedy. The distinction between these two types of law, which are found in all civilizations, was briefly stated by Hammurabi in calling himself "the king of justice (misharum), to whom Shamash has committed truth (kittum)."

While many misharu-acts consisted only of seisachtheias — Solon of Athens' term meaning "throwing off the burdens" (see Selection 20) — which proclaimed the remission of various obligations, including indebtedness, and, at times, the freeing of persons enslaved for debt, others comprised extensive collections of remedial legislation. The best known and only virtually complete example of the latter "codes" (there are four from the Old Babylonian period and one from the preceding Third Dynasty of Ur) is that of Hammurabi. Its prologue and epilogue set forth the divine commission which Hammurabi received from the gods to secure the general welfare, while the nearly three hundred individual laws, touching on a wide variety of abuses, justify Hammurabi's claim of having acted "like a real father to his people . . . [who] has established prosperity . . . and given good government to the land."

PROLOGUE

When the lofty Anu, king of the Anunnaki gods, and Enlil, lord of heaven and earth, he who determines the destiny of the land, committed the rule of all mankind to Marduk, the chief son of Ea; when they made him great among the Igigi gods; when they pronounced the lofty name of Babylon; when they made it famous among the quarters of the world and in its midst established an everlasting kingdom whose foundations were firm as heaven and earth — at that time, Anu and Enlil named me, Hammurabi, the exalted prince, the worshiper of the gods, to cause justice to prevail in the land, to destroy the wicked and the evil, to prevent the strong from oppressing the weak, to go forth like the sun over the black-headed people, to enlighten the land and to further the welfare of the people. Hammurabi, the shepherd named by Enlil, am I, who brought about plenty and abundance; . . . obedient to the mighty Shamash; . . . who rebuilt Ebabbar for Shamash, his helper; . . . the powerful king, the sun of Babylon, who caused light to go forth over the lands of Sumer and Akkad; the king who caused the four quarters of the world to render obedience; the favorite of Ishtar, am I.

When Marduk sent me to rule the people and to bring help to the country, I established law and justice in the language of the land and promoted the welfare of the people. At that time (I decreed):

THE ADMINISTRATION OF JUSTICE

1. If a man bring an accusation against another man, charging him with murder, but cannot prove it, the accuser shall be put to death.

3. If a man bear false witness in a case, or does not establish the testimony that he has given, if that case be a case involving life, that man shall be put to death.

4. If he bear (false) witness concerning grain or money, he shall himself bear the penalty imposed in that case.

5. If a judge pronounce a judgment, render a decision, deliver a verdict duly signed and sealed, and afterward alter his judgment, they shall call that judge to account for the alteration of the judgment which he has pronounced, and he shall pay twelve-fold the penalty in that judgment; and, in the assembly, they shall expel him from his seat of judgment, and with the judges in a case he shall not take his seat.

PROPERTY

9. If a man who has lost anything find that which was lost in the possession of (another) man, and the man in whose possession the lost property is found say, "It was sold to me, I purchased it in the presence of witnesses"; and the owner of the lost property say, "I will bring witnesses to identify my lost property"; if the purchaser produce the seller who has sold it to him and the witnesses in whose presence he purchased it, and the owner of the lost property produce witnesses to identify his lost property, the judges shall consider their evidence. The witnesses in whose presence the purchase was made and the witnesses to identify the lost property shall give their testimony in the presence of god. The seller shall be put to death as a thief; the owner of the lost property shall recover his loss; the purchaser shall recover from the estate of the seller the money which he paid out.

10. If the purchaser does not produce the seller who sold it to him and the witnesses in whose presence he purchased it, and if the owner of the lost property produces witnesses to identify his lost property, the purchaser shall be put to death as a thief. The owner of the lost property shall recover his lost property.

11. If the (alleged) owner of the lost property does not produce witnesses to identify his lost property, he has attempted fraud, he has stirred up strife, he shall be put to death.

22. If a man practice robbery and is captured, that man shall be put to death.

23. If the robber is not captured, the man who has been robbed shall, in the presence of god, make an itemized statement of his loss, and the city and the governor in whose province and jurisdiction the robbery was committed shall compensate him for whatever was lost.

24. If it be a life (that is lost), the city and governor shall pay one mina [about one pound] of silver to his heirs.

IRRIGATION

53. If a man neglects to maintain his dike and does not strengthen it, and a break is made in his dike and the water carries away the farmland, the man in

whose dike the break has been made shall replace the grain which has been damaged.

54. If he is not able to replace the grain, they shall sell him and his goods, and the farmers whose grain the water has carried away shall divide (the results of the sale).

55. If a man opens his canal for irrigation and neglects it and the water carries away an adjacent field, he shall pay out grain on the basis of the adjacent field.

56. If a man opens up the water and the water carries away the improvements of an adjacent field, he shall pay out ten *gur* of grain per *bur* [of damaged land].

LOANS AND INTEREST

88. If a merchant lends grain at interest, for one *gur* [300 *sila*] he shall receive one hundred *sila* as interest [33⅓ per cent]; if he lends money at interest, for one shekel of silver he shall receive one-fifth of a shekel as interest [20 per cent].

90. If a merchant increases the interest on grain above one hundred *sila* for one *gur*, or the interest on silver above one-fifth of a shekel (per shekel), and takes this interest, he shall forfeit whatever he lent.

94. If a merchant lends grain or silver at interest and when he lends it at interest he gives silver by the small weight and grain by the small measure but when he gets it back he gets silver by the large weight and grain by the large measure, that merchant shall forfeit whatever he lent.

REGULATION OF TRADE

104. If a merchant give to an agent grain, wool, oil, or goods of any kind with which to trade, the agent shall write down the value and return (the money) to the merchant. The agent shall take a sealed receipt for the money which he gives to the merchant.

105. If the agent is careless and does not take a receipt for the money which he has given to the merchant, the money not receipted for shall not be placed to his account.

108. If a wine seller does not take grain for the price of a drink but takes money by the large weight, or if she makes the measure of drink smaller than the measure of grain, they shall call that wine seller to account and throw her into the water.

109. If bad characters gather in the house of a wine seller and she does not arrest those bad characters and bring them to the palace, that wine seller shall be put to death.

110. If a priestess who is not living in a convent opens a wine shop or enters a wine shop for a drink, they shall burn that woman.

111. If a wine seller has given sixty *sila* of drink on credit, at the time of harvest she shall receive fifty *sila* of grain.

117. If a man be in debt and sell his wife, son, or daughter, or bind them over to service, for three years they shall work in the house of their purchaser or master; in the fourth year they shall be given their freedom.

118. If he bind over to service a male or female slave and let the time (of redemption) expire and the merchant transfers or sells such slave, there is no cause for complaint.

MARRIAGE AND THE FAMILY

128. If a man takes a wife and does not arrange a contract for her, that woman is not a wife.

129. If the wife of a man is caught lying with another man, they shall bind them and throw them into the water. If the husband of the woman wishes to spare his wife, then the king shall spare his servant.

131. If a man has accused his wife but she has not been caught lying with another man, she shall take an oath in the name of god and return to her house.

136. If a man deserts his city and flees and afterwards his wife enters into another house, if that man returns and wishes to take back his wife, the wife of the fugitive shall not return to her husband because he hated his city and fled.

138. If a man wishes to put away his wife who has not borne him children, he shall give her money to the amount of her marriage price and he shall make good to her the dowry which she brought from her father's house and then he may put her away.

141. If the wife of a man who is living in his house set her face to go out and play the part of a fool, neglecting her house and belittling her husband, they shall call her to account; and if her husband says, "I have put her away," he may let her go. On her departure nothing shall be given to her for her divorce. If her husband says, "I have not put her away," her husband may marry another woman. The first woman shall dwell in the house of her husband as a maidservant.

142. If a woman hates her husband and says, "You may not have me," the city council shall inquire into her case; and if she has been careful and without reproach and her husband has been going about and greatly belittling her, that woman has no blame. She may take her dowry and go to her father's house.

143. If she has not been careful but has gadded about, neglecting her house and belittling her husband, they shall throw that woman into the water.

145. If a man takes a wife and she does not present him with children and he sets his face to take a concubine, that man may take a concubine and bring her into his house. That concubine shall not rank with his wife.

146. If a man takes a wife and she gives a maidservant to her husband, and that maidservant bears children and afterwards claims equal rank with her mistress; because she has borne children, her mistress may not sell her, but she may reduce her to bondage and count her among the slaves.

150. If a man gives to his wife a field, garden, house, or goods and delivers to her a sealed deed, after (the death of) her husband her children cannot

enter a claim against her. The mother may will her estate to her son whom she loves, but to an outsider she may not.

159. If a man, who has brought a gift to the house of his father-in-law and has paid the marriage price, look with longing upon another woman and say to his father-in-law, "I will not take your daughter," the father of the daughter shall take to himself whatever was brought to him.

160. If a man has brought a gift to the house of his father-in-law and has paid the marriage price and the father of the daughter say, "I will not give you my daughter," he shall double the amount that was brought to him and return it.

162. If a man takes a wife and she bears him children and that woman dies, her father may not lay claim to her dowry. Her dowry belongs to her children.

165. If a man presents a field, garden, or house to his favorite son and writes for him a sealed deed, after the father dies, when the brothers divide (the estate), he shall take the present which the father gave him, but otherwise they shall divide the goods of the father's estate equally.

168. If a man set his face to disinherit his son and say to the judges, "I will disinherit my son," the judges shall inquire into his record, and if the son has not committed a crime sufficiently grave to cut him off from sonship, the father may not cut off his son from sonship.

170. If a man's wife bear him children and his maidservant bear him children, and the father during his lifetime says to the children which the maidservant bore him, "My children," and reckon them with the children of his wife, after the father dies the children of the wife and the children of the maidservant shall divide the goods of the father's estate equally. The son of the wife shall have the right of choice at the division.

ADOPTION

185. If a man take in his own name a young boy as a son and rear him, one may not bring claim for that adopted son.

191. If a man, who has taken a young boy as a son and reared him, establish his own house and acquire children, and set his face to cut off the adopted son, that son shall not go off empty-handed. The father who reared him shall give to him of his goods one-third the portion of a son and then he shall go. He may not give to him (any portion) of field, garden, or house.

PERSONAL INJURY AND MANSLAUGHTER

195. If a son strike his father, they shall cut off his hand.

196. If a man destroy the eye of another man, they shall destroy his eye.

197. If he break another man's bone, they shall break his bone.

198. If he destroy the eye of a client or break the bone of a client, he shall pay one mina of silver.

199. If he destroy the eye of a man's slave or break a bone of a man's slave, he shall pay one-half his price.

200. If a man knock out a tooth of a man of his own rank, they shall knock out his tooth.

201. If he knock out a tooth of a client, he shall pay one-third mina of silver.

206. If a man strike another man in a quarrel and wound him, he shall swear, "I struck him without intent," and he shall pay for the physician.

207. If he die as the result of the blow, he shall swear (as above), and if the man was a free man, he shall pay one-half mina of silver.

208. If he was a client, he shall pay one-third mina of silver.

PHYSICIAN'S FEES AND MALPRACTICE

215. If a physician operate on a man for a severe wound with a bronze lancet and save the man's life, or if he open an abscess (in the eye) of a man with a bronze lancet and save that man's eye, he shall receive ten shekels of silver.

216. If he be a client, he shall receive five shekels.

217. If he be a man's slave, the owner of the slave shall give two shekels of silver to the physician.

218. If a physician operate on a man for a severe wound with a bronze lancet and cause the man's death, or open an abscess (in the eye) of a man with a bronze lancet and destroy the man's eye, they shall cut off his hand.

219. If a physician operate on a slave of a client for a severe wound with a bronze lancet and cause his death, he shall restore a slave of equal value.

221. If a physician set a broken bone for a man or cure a sprained tendon, the patient shall give five shekels of silver to the physician.

222. If he be a client, he shall give three shekels of silver.

223. If he be a man's slave, the owner of the slave shall give two shekels of silver to the physician.

BUILDING REGULATIONS

228. If a builder build a house for a man and complete it, he shall give him two shekels of silver per *sar* of house as his fee.

229. If a builder build a house for a man and does not make its construction sound, and the house which he has built collapses and causes the death of the owner of the house, that builder shall be put to death.

233. If a builder build a house for a man and does not make its construction sound, and a wall cracks, that builder shall strengthen that wall at his own expense.

WAGE REGULATIONS

257. If a man hire a field laborer, he shall pay him eight *gur* of grain per year.

258. If a man hire a herdsman, he shall pay him six *gur* of grain per year.

268. If a man hire an ox to thresh, twenty *sila* of grain is its [daily] hire.

269. If a man hire an ass to thresh, ten *sila* of grain is its hire.

271. If a man hire oxen, a wagon, and a driver, he shall pay 180 *sila* of grain per day.

273. If a man hire a laborer, from the beginning of the year until the fifth month he shall pay six *she* of silver per day; from the sixth month till the end of the year he shall pay five *she* of silver per day.

274. If a man hire an artisan, the [daily] wage of a [potter?] is five *she* of silver; the wage of a bricklayer is five *she* of silver; the wage of a tailor is five *she* of silver; the wage of a stonecutter is [. . .] *she* of silver; the wage of a jeweller is [. . .] *she* of silver; the wage of a smith is [. . .] *she* of silver; the wage of a carpenter is four *she* of silver; the wage of a leather worker is [. . .] *she* of silver; the wage of a basketmaker is [. . .] *she* of silver; the wage of a builder is [. . .] *she* of silver.

EPILOGUE

(These are) the just laws which Hammurabi, the wise king, established and by which he gave the land stable support and good government. Hammurabi, the perfect king, am I. I was not careless, nor was I neglectful of the black-headed people, whose rule Enlil presented and Marduk delivered to me. . . .

The great gods called me, and I am the guardian shepherd whose scepter is just and whose beneficient shadow is spread over my city. In my bosom I carried the people of the land of Sumer and Akkad; under my protection they prospered; I governed them in peace; in my wisdom I sheltered them.

In order that the strong might not oppress the weak, that justice be given to the orphan and the widow, in Babylon, the city whose turrets Anu and Enlil raised, in Esagila, the temple whose foundations are firm as heaven and earth, for the pronouncing of judgments in the land, for the rendering of decisions for the land, and to give justice to the oppressed, my weighty words I have written upon my monument, and in the presence of my image as king of justice have I estab.ished it.

The king who is preeminent among kings am I. My words are precious, my wisdom is unrivaled. By the command of Shamash, the great judge of heaven and earth, may I make justice to shine forth on the land. By the order of Marduk, my lord, may no one efface my statues, may my name be remembered with favor in Esagila forever.

Let any oppressed man, who has a cause, come before my image as king of justice! Let him read the inscription on my monument! Let him give heed to my weighty words! And may my monument enlighten him as to his cause and may he understand his case! May he set his heart at ease! (and he will exclaim): "Hammurabi indeed is a ruler who is like a real father to his people; he has given reverence to the words of Marduk, his lord; he has obtained victory for Marduk in north and south; he has made glad the heart of Marduk, his lord; he has established prosperity for the people for all time and given good government to the land." . . .

In the days that are yet to come, for all future time, may the king who is in the land observe the words of justice which I have written upon my monument! May he not alter the judgments of the land which I have pronounced, or the decisions of the country which I have rendered! May he not efface my statues! If that man have wisdom, if he wish to give his land good government, let him give attention to the words which I have written upon my monument! And may this monument enlighten him as to procedure and administration, the judgments which I have pronounced, and the decisions which I have rendered for the land! And let him rightly rule his black-headed people; let him pronounce judgments for them and render for them decisions! Let him root out the wicked and the evil from his land! Let him promote the welfare of his people!

Hammurabi, the king of justice, to whom Shamash has committed truth, am I. My words are weighty; my deeds are unrivaled; only to the fool are they vain; to the wise they are worthy of every praise.

8

The Instruction of Ptah-hotep

Early material values

The values pursued in a heroic age ordinarily are found described in folk epics (see Selections 1 and 17). Egypt has left us no epics, but the same zest for worldly success and fame can be seen in texts inscribed within the tombs of the kings and nobles of the Old Kingdom (2700–2200 B.C.). The "Instruction of Ptah-hotep," the author of which lived around 2450 B.C. and was the vizier of a Fifth Dynasty pharaoh, is an outstanding example of this early type of literary expression. It consists of precepts addressed to the vizier's son instructing the young man in rules of behavior leading to worldly success. These early precepts reflect no concern for a life beyond the grave, nor do they emphasize mankind's dependence upon the gods. No moral principles of good and evil are involved; right and wrong are equivalent to what works and makes for success and what does not.[1]

In this text, therefore, the term maat, usually translated "justice," should be viewed in the more static sense of "norm," "path," "tradition," "truth," "correctness," referring to that which is customary and accepted because it has always worked. Ptah-hotep has no doubts about the value and eternity of maat,

Based on the translation by F. L. Griffith in *A Library of the World's Best Literature*, XIII, 5329–5340.

[1] "The high achievements of the Old Kingdom were attained by an amoral people, or rather by a people whose morals were pragmatic and materialistic." John A. Wilson, *The Burden of Egypt* (Chicago: University of Chicago Press, 1951), p. 110.

the creation of the gods which can be handed down from father to son like property: "A great thing is maat, enduring and surviving; it has not been upset since the time of its creator... it endureth long, and a man can say, 'It is the property of my father.'" But we shall see that this materialistic conception of maat did not outlast the Old Kingdom; it was undermined by the total disorder produced by a time of troubles — the Feudal Age or First Intermediate Period — and men were forced to redefine maat and create a new foundation for conduct in positive moral principles of justice and righteousness.

PREFACE: ROYAL APPROVAL

The mayor and vizier Ptah-hotep said: "O king, my lord, years come on, old age is here, decrepitude arrives, weakness is renewed. . . . Let it be commanded of your servant to make a staff of old age: let my son be set in my place. Let me tell him the sayings of those who obeyed, the conduct of them of old, of them who listened to the gods. . . .

Said the majesty of this god [the king]: "Instruct him in the sayings of the past. . . . Speak to him, for no one is born wise."

TITLE AND AIM

Beginning of the maxims of good words spoken by the . . . mayor and vizier, Ptah-hotep, teaching the ignorant to know according to the standard of good words, expounding the profit to him who shall listen to it, and the injury to him who shall transgress it. He said to his son:

INTELLECTUAL SNOBBERY

Be not arrogant because of your knowledge, and be not puffed up because you are a learned man. Take counsel with the ignorant as with the learned, for the limits of art cannot be reached, and no artist is perfect in his skills. Good speech is more hidden than the precious greenstone, and yet it is found among slave girls at the millstones. . . .

LEADERSHIP AND "MAAT"

If you are a leader, commanding the conduct of many, seek out every good aim, so that your policy may be without error. A great. thing is truth [maat], enduring and surviving; it has not been upset since the time of Osiris. He who departs from its laws is punished. It is the right path for him who knows nothing. Wrongdoing has never brought its venture safe to port. Evil may win riches, but it is the strength of truth that it endures long, and a man can say, "I learned it from my father." . . .

CONDUCT AS A GUEST AT TABLE

If you are a guest at the table of one who is greater than you, take what he offers as it is set before you. Fix your gaze upon what is before you, and pierce not your host with many glances, for it is an abomination to force your attention upon him. Speak not to him until he calls, for no one knows what may be offensive; speak when he addresses you, for then your words will give satisfaction. Laugh when he laughs; that will please him, and then whatever you do will please him. . . .

PATIENCE WITH SUPPLIANTS

If you are a leader be kind in hearing the speech of a suppliant. Treat him not roughly until he has unburdened himself of what he was minded to tell you. The complainant sets greater store by the easing of his mind than by the accomplishment of that for which he came. As for him who deals roughly with a petition, men say, "Why, pray, has he ignored it?" Not all that men plead for ever comes to pass, but to listen kindly soothes the heart.

RELATIONS WITH WOMEN

If you wish to prolong friendship in a house into which you enter as master, brother or friend, or any place that you enter, beware of approaching the women. No place in which that is done prospers. There is no wisdom in it. A thousand men are turned aside from their own good because of a little moment, like a dream, by tasting which death is reached. . . . He who fails because of lusting after women, no plan of his will succeed.

GREED

If you want your conduct to be good, free from every evil, then beware of greed. It is an evil and incurable sickness. No man can live with it; it causes divisions between fathers and mothers, and between brothers of the same mother; it parts wife and husband; it is a gathering of every evil, a bag of everything hateful. A man thrives if his conduct is right. He who follows the right course wins wealth thereby. But the greedy man has no tomb. . . .

MARRIAGE

If you are prosperous you should establish a household and love your wife as is fitting. Fill her belly and clothe her back. Oil is the tonic for her body. Make her heart glad as long as you live. She is a profitable field for her lord. . . .

CONDUCT IN COUNCIL

If you are a worthy man sitting in the council of his lord, confine your attention to excellence. Silence is more valuable than chatter. Speak only when you know you can resolve difficulties. He who gives good counsel is an artist, for speech is more difficult than any craft. . . .

BEHAVIOR IN CHANGED CIRCUMSTANCES

If you are now great after being humble and rich after being poor in the city that you know, do not boast because of what happened to you in the past. Be not miserly with your wealth, which has come to you by the god's gift. You are no different from another to whom the same has happened.

OBEDIENCE TO A SUPERIOR

Bend your back to him who is over you, your superior in the administration; then your house will endure by reason of its property, and your reward will come in due season. Wretched is he who opposes his superior, for one lives only so long as he is gracious. . . .

EXHORTATION TO LISTEN

If you listen to my sayings, then all your affairs will go forward. They are precious; their memory goes on in the speech of men because of their excellence. If each saying is carried on, they will never perish in this land. . . .

If the son of a man accepts what his father says, no plan of his will fail. . . . Failure follows him who does not listen. He who hears is established; he who is a fool is crushed. . . .

A son who hears is a follower of Horus: there is good for him who listens. When he reaches old age and attains honor, he tells the like to his children, renewing the teaching of his father. Every man teaches as he has acted. He speaks to his children so that they may speak to their children. . . .

CONCLUSION

May you succeed me, may your body be sound, may the king be well pleased with all that is done, and may you spend many years of life! It is no small thing that I have done on earth; I have spent one hundred and ten years of life, which the king gave me, and with rewards greater than those of the ancestors, by doing right for the king until death.

---9---

The Edwin Smith
Surgical Papyrus

Thought divorced from myth

The Edwin Smith Surgical Papyrus is of considerable significance for the intellectual history of mankind. As noted by the translator, James H. Breasted, "Here we find the first scientific observer known to us, and in this papyrus we have the earliest known scientific document." The unknown author, who lived sometime during the Old Kingdom, has written a treatise on surgery in which

Reprinted from *The Edwin Smith Surgical Papyrus*, tr. James Henry Breasted, I, pp. 429–30, 432–33, 437–39, 449–50, 455–56, by permission of the University of Chicago Press. The University of Chicago Press, Chicago, Illinois, 1930.

he inductively draws conclusions from a body of observed facts. In seeking causes, he has separated the natural from the supernatural and is concerned only with the former. And in prescribing treatment he resorts to the use of magic in only one of the forty-eight cases described. A truly scientific attitude is further illustrated in fourteen of the cases he has classified as ailments "not to be treated" but nevertheless has fully described because of their intrinsic interest.

Cases 1 and 8 in particular highlight the remarkable scientific character of this treatise. The physician who "measures to the heart" and "its vessels" by taking the pulse (Case 1) has recognized the relation of the heart to the other parts of the body and has approached the concept of the circulation of the blood. And in Case 8 there is clear insistence that the unknown and mysterious cause of the fracture and partial paralysis in question is not to be considered supernatural ("something entering from outside" as "the breath of an outside god") but natural ("something which his flesh engenders").

The promise of this text was destined to be short-lived, however; with few exceptions, thought in ancient Egypt and in the whole ancient Near East remained in bondage to religion. It is one of the glories of the ancient Greeks that they were the first to make permanent the emancipation of thought from myth.

CASE 1. A WOUND IN THE HEAD PENETRATING TO THE BONE

Examination. If thou examinest a man having a wound in his head, penetrating to the bone of his skull, but not having a gash, thou shouldst palpate his wound: shouldst thou find his skull uninjured, not having a perforation, a split, or a smash in it,

Diagnosis. Thou shouldst say regarding him: "One having a wound in his head, while his wound does not have two lips, [. . .] nor a gash, although it penetrates to the bone of his head. An ailment which I will treat."

Treatment. Thou shouldst bind it with fresh meat the first day and treat afterward with grease, honey and lint every day until he recovers.

Explanatory Gloss A. As for: "Thou examinest a man," it means counting any one [. . .] like counting things with a bushel. For examining is like one's counting a certain quantity with a bushel, or counting something with the fingers, in order to know [. . .]. It is measuring things . . . in order to know the action of the heart. There are canals in it [the heart] to every member. Now if the priests of Sekhmet or any physician put his hands or his fingers upon the head, upon the back of the head, upon the two hands, upon the pulse, upon the two feet, he measures to the heart, because its vessels are in the back of the head and in the pulse; and because its pulsation is in every vessel of every member. He says "measure" regarding his wound because of the vessels to his head and to the back of his head and to his two feet [. . .] his heart in order to recognize the indications which have arisen therein; meaning to measure it in order to know what is befalling therein.

CASE 4. A GAPING WOUND IN THE HEAD PENETRATING TO THE BONE
AND SPLITTING THE SKULL

Examination. If thou examinest a man having a gaping wound in his head, penetrating to the bone, and splitting his skull, thou shouldst palpate his wound. Shouldst thou find something disturbing therein under thy fingers, and he shudders exceedingly, while the swelling which is over it protrudes, he discharges blood from both his nostrils and from both his ears, he suffers with stiffness in his neck, so that he is unable to look at his two shoulders and his breast,

Diagnosis. Thou shouldst say regarding him: "One having a gaping wound in his head, penetrating to the bone, and splitting his skull; while he discharges blood from both his nostrils and from both his ears, and he suffers with stiffness in his neck. An ailment with which I will contend."

Treatment. Now when thou findest that the skull of that man is split, thou shouldst not bind him, but moor him at his mooring stakes until the period of his injury passes by. His treatment is sitting. Make for him two supports of brick, until thou knowest he has reached a decisive point. Thou shouldst apply grease to his head, and soften his neck therewith and both his shoulders. Thou shouldst do likewise for every man whom thou findest having a split skull.

Explanatory Gloss A. As for: "Splitting his skull," it means separating shell from shell of his skull, while fragments remain sticking in the flesh of his head, and do not come away.

Explanatory Gloss C. As for: "Until thou knowest he has reached a decisive point," it means until thou knowest whether he will die or he will live; for he is a case of "an ailment with which I will contend."

Explanatory Gloss D [from Case 3]. As for: "Moor him at his mooring stakes," it means putting him on his customary diet, without administering to him a prescription.

CASE 8. COMPOUND COMMINUTED FRACTURE OF THE SKULL DISPLAYING
NO VISIBLE EXTERNAL INJURY

Examination. If thou examinest a man having a smash of his skull, under the skin of his head, while there is nothing at all upon it, thou shouldst palpate his wound. Shouldst thou find that there is a swelling protruding on the outside of that smash which is in his skull, while his eye is askew because of it, on the side of him having that injury which is in his skull; and he walks shuffling with his sole, on the side of him having that injury which is in his skull,

Diagnosis[1]. Thou shouldst distinguish him from one whom something entering from outside has smitten, but simply as one the head of whose shoulder-fork is not released, as well as one whose nails have fallen into the middle of his

---

[1] Translation emended by John A. Wilson, *The Burden of Egypt* (Chicago: University of Chicago Press, 1951), p. 57.

hand, while he discharges blood from his nostrils and his ears, and he suffers a stiffness in his neck. An ailment not to be treated.

Treatment. His treatment is sitting, until he gains color, and until thou knowest he has reached the decisive point.

Second Examination. Now as soon as thou findest that smash which is in his skull like those corrugations which form on molten copper, and something therein throbbing and fluttering under thy fingers like the weak place of an infant's crown before it knits together — when it has happened there is no throbbing and fluttering under thy fingers, until the brain of his skull is rent open — and he discharges blood from both his nostrils and both his ears, and he suffers with stiffness in his neck,

Second Diagnosis. An ailment not to be treated.

Explanatory Gloss A. As for: "A smash in his skull under the skin of his head, there being no wound at all upon it," it means a smash of the shell of his skull, the flesh of his head being uninjured.

Explanatory Gloss B. As for: "He walks shuffling with his sole," he [the surgeon] is speaking about his walking with his sole dragging, so that it is not easy for him to walk, when it (the sole) is feeble and turned over, while the tips of his toes are contracted to the ball of his sole, and they [the toes] walk fumbling the ground. He [the surgeon] says: "He shuffles," concerning it.

Explanatory Gloss C. As for: "One whom something entering from outside has smitten" on the side of him having this injury, it means one whom something entering from outside presses, on the side of him having this injury.

Explanatory Gloss D. As for: "Something entering from outside," it means the breath of an outside god or death; not the intrusion of something which his flesh engenders.

Explanatory Gloss E. As for: "One the head of whose shoulder-fork is not released, as well as one whose nails have fallen into the middle of his hand," it means that he says: "One to whom the head of his shoulder-fork is not given, and one who does not fall with his nails in the middle of his palm."

CASE 35. A FRACTURE OF THE CLAVICLE

Examination. If thou examinest a man having a break in his collar-bone, and thou shouldst find his collar-bone short and separated from its fellow,

Diagnosis. Thou shouldst say concerning him: "One having a break in his collar-bone. An ailment which I will treat."

Treatment. Thou shouldst place him prostrate on his back, with something folded between his two shoulder-blades; thou shouldst spread out with his two shoulders in order to stretch apart his collar-bone until that break falls into its place. Thou shouldst make for him two splints of linen, and thou shouldst apply one of them both on the inside of his upper arm and the other on the under side of his upper arm. Thou shouldst bind it with *ymrw*, and treat it afterward with honey every day, until he recovers.

The Prophecy of Nefer-rohu

Time of troubles and Messianism

The anarchy of the Egyptian Feudal Age, or First Intermediate Period (2200–2050 B.C.), brought to an end the seemingly eternal orderliness and serenity of life which had characterized the Old Kingdom. "Woe is me for the misery of this time" is the recurrent refrain found in the texts of the new period. Although the "Prophecy of Nefer-rohu" purports to be a Fourth Dynasty text foretelling the collapse of the Old Kingdom, it is really one of many expressions of dismay and bewilderment felt by the Egyptians as they viewed the overturn of their old world which, in retrospect, appeared to have been a veritable golden age. A typical "time of trouble" is described, characterized by collapse of the central government, foreign invasion, and social revolution. A simple explanation is found for these calamitous events, but it is one destined to revolutionize religious beliefs: the sun-god Re, the supreme god of the Old Kingdom, has turned away and no longer cares for mankind. The resulting bewilderment and beginnings of disbelief was well expressed in another text of the same period: "If I knew where god is, then would I make offerings to him."

Nefer-rohu does not stop with mere lamentation over the evils of his time; he goes on to prophesy the coming of a king — Ameni, short for Amenemhet I (1991–1962 B.C.), the first pharaoh of the Twelfth Dynasty — who will restore the lost golden age with its stability and security. Since the Egyptians of the Old Kingdom had viewed their kings as gods sojourning on earth, James H. Breasted has concluded that such prophecies of the return of a heaven-sent king to rule Egypt represent "Messianism nearly 1500 years before it appeared among the Hebrews."

What the lector-priest Nefer-rohu said, that wise man of the east, . . . as he brooded over what was to happen in the land. . . .

"I SHOW THEE THE LAND TOPSY-TURVY"

Reconstruct, O my heart, how thou bewailest this land in which thou didst begin! To be silent is repression. Behold, there is something about which men speak as terrifying, for, behold, the great man is a thing passed away in the land where thou didst begin. Be not lax; behold, it is before thy face! Mayest

From *Ancient Near Eastern Texts Relating to the Old Testament*, ed. James B. Pritchard, 3rd rev. ed. with Supplement, pp. 444–46. Copyright © 1969 by the Princeton University Press. Reprinted by permission of the Princeton University Press. Translated by John A. Wilson.

thou rise up against what is before thee, for, behold, although great men are concerned with the land, what has been done is as what is not done. Re must begin the foundation of the earth over again. The land is completely perished, so that no remainder exists, so that not even the black of the nail survives from what was [the "Black Land" of Egypt] . . . .

Foes have arisen in the east, and Asiatics have come down into Egypt. . . . No protector will listen. . . . Men will enter into the fortresses. Sleep will be banished from my eyes, as I spend the night wakeful. The wild beasts of the desert will drink at the rivers of Egypt and be at their ease on their banks for lack of some one to scare them away.

This land is helter-skelter, and no one knows the result which will come about, which is hidden from speech, sight, or hearing. The face is deaf, for silence confronts. I show thee the land topsy-turvy. That which never happened has happened. Men will take up weapons of warfare, so that the land lives in confusion. Men will make arrows of metal, beg for the bread of blood, and laugh with the laughter of sickness. There is no one who weeps because of death; there is no one who spends the night fasting because of death; but a man's heart pursues himself alone. Dishevelled mourning is no longer carried out today, for the heart is completely separated from it. A man sits in his corner, turning his back while one man kills another. I show thee the son as a foe, the brother as an enemy, and a man killing his own father.

Every month is full of "Love me!," and everything good has disappeared. The land is perished, as though laws were destined for it: the damaging of what had been done, the emptiness of what had been found, and the doing of what had not been done. Men take a man's property away from him, and it is given to him who is from outside. I show thee the possessor in need and the outsider satisfied. He who never filled for himself now empties. Men will treat fellow citizens as hateful, in order to silence the mouth that speaks. If a statement is answered, an arm goes out with a stick, and men speak with: "Kill him!" The utterance of speech in the heart is like a fire. Men cannot suffer what issues from a man's mouth.

The land is diminished, but its administrators are many; bare, but its taxes are great; little in grain, but the measure is large, and it is measured to overflowing.

Re separates himself from mankind. If he shines forth, it is but an hour. No one knows when midday falls, for his shadow cannot be distinguished. . . .

I show thee the land topsy-turvy. The weak of arm is now the possessor of an arm. Men salute respectfully him who formerly saluted. I show thee the undermost on top, turned about in proportion to the turning about of my belly. Men live in the necropolis. The poor man will make wealth. . . . It is the paupers who eat the offering-bread, while the servants jubilate. The Heliopolitan nome, the birthplace of every god, will no longer be on earth.

"A KING WILL COME"

Then it is that a king will come, belonging to the south, Ameni, the triumphant, his name. He is the son of a woman of the land of Nubia; he is one born in Upper Egypt. He will take the White Crown; he will wear the Red Crown; he will unite the Two Mighty Ones; he will satisfy the Two Lords with what they desire. . . .

Rejoice, ye people of his time! The son of a man will make his name forever and ever. They who incline toward evil and who plot rebellion have subdued their speech for fear of him. The Asiatics will fall to his sword, and the Libyans will fall to his flame. The rebels belong to his wrath, and the treacherous of heart to the awe of him. The uraeus-serpent which is on his brow stills for him the treacherous of heart.

There will be built the Wall of the Ruler — life, prosperity, health! — and the Asiatics will not be permitted to come down into Egypt that they might beg for water in the customary manner, in order to let their beasts drink. And justice will come into its place, while wrongdoing is driven out. Rejoice, he who may behold this and who may be in the service of the king!

The learned man will pour out water for me, when he sees what I have spoken come to pass.

II

Romantic Poetry

Wine, women, and song

The collapse of the Old Kingdom produced an upheaval in the mind — the old standards, values, and beliefs no longer seemed to fit the times and were rejected. In a manner characteristic of the romantic revolt against established standards of taste and value which occurs at times in all civilizations, an Egyptian of the Feudal Age wrote: "Would I had phrases that are not known, utterances that are strange, in new language that hath not been used, free from repetition; not an utterance which hath grown stale, which men of old have already spoken." [1]

The following texts have been selected to illustrate the romantic individualism in thought and feeling which arose by the end of the Feudal Age to replace the universally accepted norms of the preceding Old Kingdom. The hedonistic "Song of the Harper" (late Feudal Age or early Middle Kingdom) advises grasping the sensual pleasures of today and rejecting the wisdom of Old Kingdom sages, which in the skeptical eyes of the singer seems as worth-

---

[1] Quoted in T. Eric Peet, A *Comparative Study of the Literatures of Egypt, Palestine, and Mesopotamia,* The Schweich Lectures of the British Academy, 1929, p. 120.

less an attempt at permanence as the efforts of the pyramid builders. The songs celebrating romantic love come to us in their present form from the New Kingdom, but it can be assumed on the basis of their content that they originated as a type during the same age and as a product of the same forces as the "Song of the Harper."

SONG OF THE HARPER

"Make holiday!"

One generation passes away
And others remain in its place
Since the time of the ancestors.
The gods[1] that were aforetime
Rest in their pyramids;
Nobles and glorified likewise
Are buried in their pyramids.
They that built houses,
Their places are no more;
What has been done with them?
I have heard the sayings of Imhotep and Djedefhor,
With whose words men still speak so much;
What are their places?
Their walls have crumbled,
Their places are no more,
As if they had never been.
None cometh from thence
That he might tell their circumstances,
That he might tell their needs
And content our heart
Until we have reached the place
Whither they have gone.
May thy heart be cheerful
To permit the heart to forget
The making of funerary services for thee.
Follow thy desire while thou livest!
Put myrrh upon thy head,
Clothe thyself in fine linen,
Anoint thee with the genuine wonders
Which are the god's own.
Increase yet more thy happiness,

Reprinted from the "Songs of the Harpers," tr. Miriam Lichtheim, *Journal of Near Eastern Studies*, IV (1945), pp. 192–193. By permission of The University of Chicago Press.

[1] The pharaohs of the Old Kingdom.

And let not thy heart languish;
Follow thy desire and thy good,
Fashion thine affairs on earth
After the command of thy heart.
That day of lamentation will come to thee,
When the Still of Heart[2] does not hear their lamentation,
And mourning does not deliver a man from the netherworld.
Make holiday!
Do not weary thereof!
Lo, none is allowed to take his goods with him,
Lo, none that has gone has come back!

LOVE SONGS

"She is more to me than the collected writings"

"A SICKNESS HAS INVADED ME"

Seven days to yesterday I have not seen the sister,
    And a sickness has invaded me.
My body has become heavy,
    Forgetful of my own self.
If the chief of physicians come to me,
    My heart is not content with their remedies;
The lector priests, no way out is in them —
    My sickness will not be probed.

To say to me: "Here she is!" is what will revive me;
    Her name is what will lift me up;
The going in and out of her messengers
    Is what will revive my heart.
More beneficial to me is the sister than any remedies;
    She is more to me than the collected writings.

My health is her coming in from outside:
    When I see her, then I am well.
If she opens her eye, my body is young again;
    If she speaks, then I am strong again;
When I embrace her, she drives evil away from me —
    But she has gone forth from me for seven days!

From *Ancient Near Eastern Texts Relating to the Old Testament*, ed. James B. Pritchard, 3rd rev. ed. with Supplement, pp. 468–69. Reprinted by permission of the Princeton University Press. Copyright © 1969 by Princeton University Press. Translated by John A. Wilson.

[2] Osiris, god of the netherworld.

"HER LOVE MAKETH ME MIGHTY" [1]

The love of my sister is beyond the river;
The arm of the Nile is between us, and a crocodile lurketh on the bank.
Yet will I plunge into the depths of the water; I will walk on the flood;
My courage is high on the stream; the water is earth to my feet.
'Tis her love that maketh me mighty: that is my magic which smiteth
    the crocodile.
I behold how my sister cometh, and my heart is in gladness.
Mine arms open wide to embrace her; my heart exulteth within me: for
    my lady hath come to me [. . .]
She kisseth me, she openeth her lips to me: then am I joyful even
    without beer [. . .]
Oh that I were but her Nubian slave girl, her companion;
Then might I behold the fairness of her limbs!
Would that I might be my sister's launderer, if for but a single month;
Then could I wash the sweet oil from her headcloth —
A labor of love would it be: that would I do without pay!

"THAT WHICH MAKETH MY HEART LIVE"

My brother hath gone forth;
He careth not for my love;
My heart standeth still within me.

Behold, honeyed cakes in my mouth,
They are turned into salt;
Even mead, that sweet thing,
In my mouth is as the gall of a bird!

The breath of thy nostrils alone
Is that which maketh my heart live.
I found thee! Amon grant thee unto me,
Eternally and for ever!

Trans. W. Max Müller

"I AM YOUR BEST GIRL" [2]

I am your best girl:
I belong to you like an acre of land

---

[1] Reprinted from *When Egypt Ruled the East* by George Steindorff and Keith C. Seele, p. 125. By permission of The University of Chicago Press. Copyright 1942 by the University of Chicago.

[2] Translated by William Kelly Simpson, William Kelly Simpson, ed., *The Literature of Ancient Egypt: An Anthology of Stories, Instructions, and Poetry,* New Edition, pp. 308–309. Copyright © 1972 by Yale University. Reprinted by permission of the Yale University Press.

which I have planted
with flowers and every sweet-smelling grass.

Pleasant is the channel through it
which your hand dug out
for refreshing ourselves with the breeze,
a happy place for walking
with your hand in my hand.

My body is excited, my heart joyful,
at our traveling together.

Hearing your voice is pomegranate wine,
for I live to hear it,
and every glance which rests on me
means more to me than eating and drinking.

I 2

A Dispute Over Suicide

The denial of all values

The realization that romantic excitements are not permanently satisfying and
lead only to despair is the message of this remarkable text — also called the
"Dialogue of the Man Weary of Life" — from the early Middle Kingdom.
The author uses the literary device of a conversation with his soul (ba) which,
in the lost beginning of the document, had tried to dissuade him from suicide
by refusing to accompany him to the hereafter ("the West"). It is a reflection
on the nature of the times that the only constructive argument given by the
man's soul is to urge him to forget his troubles in the pursuit of sensual enjoyment. The man answers pessimistically (first poem) that to follow such advice
would have as its only result the giving of a bad odor to his name. To this
argument that sensual pleasure is without value he adds a vivid description
(second poem) of the intolerable character of life in his time, and he concludes

From *Ancient Near Eastern Texts Relating to the Old Testament*, ed. James B. Pritchard,
3rd rev. ed. with Supplement, pp. 405–406. Reprinted by permission of the Princeton University Press. Copyright © 1969 by Princeton University Press. Translated by John A. Wilson.

with a moving argument (third poem) in favor of death as a welcome release from the weariness of life.

I opened my mouth to my soul, that I might answer what it had said: "This is too much for me today, that my soul no longer talks with me. It is really too great to be exaggerated. It is like abandoning me. Let not my soul go away; it should wait for me because of [. . .] There is no competent person who deserts on the day of misfortune. Behold, my soul wrongs me, but I do not listen to it, dragging myself toward death before I come to it and casting myself upon the fire to burn myself up. . . . My soul is stupid to try to win over one wretched over life and delay me from death before I come to it. Make the West pleasant for me! Is that so bad? Life is a circumscribed period: even the trees must fall. . . . My wretchedness is heavy. . . ."

My soul opened its mouth to me, that it might answer what I had said: ". . . Listen to me. Behold, it is good for men to listen. Pursue the happy day and forget care! . . ."

I opened my mouth to my soul, that I might answer what it had said:

FIRST POEM

Behold, my name will reek through thee
    More than the stench of bird-droppings
    On summer days, when the sky is hot.
Behold, my name will reek through thee
    More than a fish-handler
    On the day of the catch, when the sky is hot.
Behold, my name will reek through thee
    More than the stench of bird-droppings,
    More than a covert of reeds with waterfowl.
Behold, my name will reek through thee
    More than the stench of fishermen,
    More than the stagnant pools which they have fished. . . .
Behold, my name will reek through thee
    More than a married woman
    Against whom a lie has been told because of a man. . . .

SECOND POEM

To whom can I speak today?
    One's fellows are evil;
    The friends of today do not love.
To whom can I speak today?
    Hearts are rapacious:
    Every man seizes his fellow's goods.
To whom can I speak today?
    The gentle man has perished,
    But the violent man has access to everybody.

To whom can I speak today?
>Even the calm of face is wicked;
>Goodness is rejected everywhere.

To whom can I speak today?
>Though a man should arouse wrath by his evil character,
>He only stirs everyone to laughter, so wicked is his sin.

To whom can I speak today?
>Men are plundering;
>Every man seizes his fellow's goods.

To whom can I speak today?
>The foul fiend is an intimate,
>But a brother, with whom one worked, has become an enemy.

To whom can I speak today?
>No one thinks of yesterday;
>No one at this time acts for him who has acted. . . .

To whom can I speak today?
>There are no righteous;
>The land is left to those who do wrong. . . .

To whom can I speak today?
>I am laden with wretchedness
>For lack of an intimate friend.

To whom can I speak today?
>The sin which treads the earth,
>It has no end.

THIRD POEM

Death is in my sight today
>Like the recovery of a sick man,
>Like going out into the open after a confinement.

Death is in my sight today
>Like the odor of myrrh
>Like sitting under an awning on a breezy day.

Death is in my sight today
>Like the odor of lotus blossoms,
>Like sitting on the bank of drunkenness.

Death is in my sight today
>Like the passing away of rain,
>Like the return of men to their houses from an expedition.

Death is in my sight today
>Like the clearing of the sky,
>Like a man fowling thereby for what he knew not.

Death is in my sight today
>Like the longing of a man to see his house again,
>After he has spent many years held in captivity.

⚬————— I3 —————⚬

The Negative Confession

Moral religion and a blessed hereafter

While some people were seeking to escape from reality by immersing them-selves in sensual pleasures (see Selection 11), others were pursuing a course that ultimately led to the reestablishment of a stable society with new values. This movement continued to place emphasis upon maat, but the meaning of the concept had changed; new wine was put into the old bottle.

In a world become topsy-turvy, the old idea of maat as "norm," "tradition," or "path" became meaningless. Maat came instead to be used in the sense of "righteousness" and "justice." (Compare Mesopotamian kittum and misharum in the introduction to Selection 7.) It is understandable that in the midst of the evil conditions of the Feudal Age there should arise a demand for a new order of society, based upon the new definition of maat, in which every person from peasant to pharaoh would be conscious of his duty to promote social justice through righteous dealing with his fellow men. "Now this is the com-mand," reads the Egyptian version of the golden rule that now appeared, " 'Do to the doer to cause that he do.' " Typical of many other expressions of this new view of maat is the boast of a nobleman of the Feudal Age who proudly tells us that he was one "who rescued the widow and supported the suffering, who buried the aged and nourished the child, who sustained alive his city in famine, and who fed it when there was nothing, who gave to it without dis-crimination therein, so that its great ones were like its little ones." So, too, the pharaoh Amenemhet I, that messiah foretold in the "Prophecy of Nefer-rohu" (see page 43), was described in his day as one who "cast out unrighteousness, ... because he so greatly loved righteousness (maat)." [1]

This new emphasis upon moral conduct in daily living produced a cor-responding change in religious beliefs. As if to emphasize further the desir-ability of righteous living, the gods were moralized; they now punished the evildoer and rewarded the righteous, and the ultimate reward was the promise of a felicitous afterlife in a heavenly hereafter called the "West." We are told just what could be hoped for — especially by the common man — when one reached the "West": "There must be in heaven the field of the blessed, an ideal land where there is no wailing and nothing evil; where barley grows four

---

From *The Book of the Dead According to the Theban Recension*, tr. E. A. Wallis Budge, Ch. CXXV.

[1] The quotations are from John A. Wilson, *The Burden of Egypt* (Chicago: University of Chicago Press, 1951), p. 121, and James H. Breasted, *The Dawn of Conscience* (New York: Charles Scribner's Sons, 1939), pp. 203, 214.

cubits high, and spelt [emmer wheat] seven ells high; where, even better, one has to do no work in the field oneself, but can let others take care of it." [2]

Beginning in the Middle Kingdom and continuing through the New Kingdom, a multitude of texts, collectively called the Book of the Dead, deal with this search for eternal happiness for the dead. One of these texts, usually called the "Negative Confession," describes the deceased standing before Osiris, the god of justice who judges the dead in the Hall of Double Justice in the underworld, and proclaiming his moral purity. The following example of "counting up character," as this ceremony was called, is from the tomb of Nu, a high official during the Eighteenth Dynasty (1570–1305 B.C.).

The following shall be said when the overseer of the palace, the chancellor-in-chief, Nu, triumphant, cometh forth into the Hall of Double Maati so that he may be separated from every sin which he hath done and may behold the faces of the gods. The Osiris Nu, triumphant, saith:

Homage to thee, O Great God [Osiris], Lord of Double Maati, I have come to thee, O my Lord, I have brought myself hither that I may behold thy beauties. I know thee, and I know thy name, and I know the names of the two and forty gods who exist with thee in this Hall of Double Maati, who live as warders of sinners and who feed upon their blood on the day when the lives of men are taken into account in the presence of the god Un-nefer [Osiris]: in truth, "Lord of Justice" is thy name. In truth I have come to thee, and I have brought *maat* to thee, and I have expelled wickedness for thee.

1. I have not done evil to mankind.
2. I have not oppressed the members of my family.
3. I have not wrought evil in the place of right and truth.
4. I have had no knowledge of worthless men.
5. I have not wrought evil. . . .
7. I have not brought forward my name for exaltation to honors.
8. I have not ill-treated servants.
9. I have not belittled a god.
10. I have not defrauded the oppressed one of his property.
11. I have not done that which is an abomination unto the gods.
14. I have made no man to suffer hunger.
15. I have made no one to weep.
16. I have done no murder.
17. I have not given the order for murder to be done for me.
18. I have not inflicted pain upon mankind.
22. I have not committed fornication.
26. I have not encroached upon the fields of others.
27. I have not added to the weights of the scales [to cheat the seller].
28. I have not misread the pointer of the scales [to cheat the buyer].

[2] Quoted in George Steindorff and George Hoyningen-Huene, *Egypt* (New York: J. J. Augustin, 1943), p. 23.

29. I have not carried away the milk from the mouths of children.
30. I have not driven away the cattle which were upon their pastures.
33. I have not turned back water at the time [when it should flow].
34. I have not cut a cutting in a canal of running water.
37. I have not driven off the cattle from the property of the gods.
38. I have not obstructed a god in his procession.
   I am pure! I am pure! I am pure! I am pure!

I4

Hymn to the Aton

Religious reform and monotheism

The high moral and ethical content which Egyptian religion acquired during
the Middle Kingdom became obscured during the New Kingdom as the various
priesthoods successfully sought after power and wealth. The priests of the
supreme god Amon vied with the god-king for power, and those of Osiris
venally stressed outward forms and paid only lip service to the moral content
of their popular funerary religion. A monument to this latter development is
the Book of the Dead, largely composed of formulas, often magical, which
were sold by the priests to guarantee to the deceased access to the hereafter
without regard for his sins. Even the "Negative Confession" was sold as a
magical spell with instructions for use which guaranteed that "for him on
whose behalf this book was made, . . . He cannot be held back at the door of
the West, but he shall be ushered in with the Kings of Upper and Lower
Egypt, and he shall be in the retinue of Osiris. Right and true a million times!"

This common development in the history of religion produced in Egypt an
equally common reaction — a reformer arose who challenged the power of
the priests and taught a more exalted type of religion. This was the pharaoh
Amenhotep IV (1369–1353 B.C.) of the Eighteenth Dynasty, who ignored the
military and administrative problems of the Egyptian empire to concentrate
upon religious reform. He changed his name from Amenhotep, "Amon is
satisfied," to Akhenaton, "He who is serviceable to the Aton," and his magnificent hymn to the Aton, the sun disc, as the source of all life is not only

From *Ancient Near Eastern Texts Relating to the Old Testament*, ed. James B. Pritchard,
3rd rev. ed. with Supplement, pp. 370–71. Reprinted by permission of the Princeton University Press. Copyright © 1969 by Princeton University Press. Translated by John A. Wilson.

filled with profound religious feeling, but also for the first time in the history of religion expresses a belief in a sole god of the universe.

Akhenaton's reformed religion did not last beyond his own lifetime. A powerful combination of forces compelled his weak successor, the well-known Tutankhamen, to renounce the new teaching. The priests of the old cults bitterly resented the domination they had lost at the hands of the man they called "the criminal"; the army leaders were ever ready to revolt against a king who neglected Egypt's imperial interests in Palestine and Syria; and the great mass of the people longed for the solace of the blessed hereafter, promised them by the condemned Osiris cult and not contained in the intellectualized teaching of the reformer-king.

The long-range effect of the triumph of priestism upon Egyptian culture is reflected in a new version of the "Song of the Harper" (see page 46) found in the tomb of a wealthy priest who died not more than a generation after "the heretic," as some called Akhenaton. As the following excerpt shows, it condemns the old secular songs for "extolling the earthly" and glorifies death and the land of the dead. It might well serve as the epitaph of Egyptian civilization.

> I have heard those songs that are in the tombs of old
> And what they relate in extolling the earthly
> And in belittling the land of the dead.
> Wherefore is the like done to the land of eternity,
> The just and fair that holds no terror? . . .
> As for the span of earthly affairs,
> It is the manner of a dream.
> One says, "welcome safe and sound"
> To him who has reached the West.[1]

Thou appearest beautifully on the horizon of heaven,
Thou living Aton, the beginning of life!
When thou art arisen on the eastern horizon,
Thou has filled every land with thy beauty.
Thou art gracious, great, glistening, and high over every land;
Thy rays encompass the lands to the limit of all that thou hast made:
As thou art Re, thou reachest to the end of them;
Thou subduest them for thy beloved son.
Though thou art far away, thy rays are on earth;
Though thou art in their faces, no one knows thy going.

When thou settest in the western horizon,
The land is in darkness, in the manner of death.
They sleep in a room, with heads wrapped up,
Nor sees one eye the other.

---

[1] Reprinted from the "Songs of the Harper," tr. Miriam Lichtheim, *Journal of Near Eastern Studies*, IV (1945), p. 197. By permission of The University of Chicago Press.

All their goods which are under their heads might be stolen,
But they would not perceive it.
Every lion is come forth from his den;
All creeping things, they sting.
Darkness is a shroud, and the earth is in stillness,
For he who made them rests in his horizon.

At daybreak, when thou arisest on the horizon,
When thou shinest as the Aton by day,
Thou drivest away the darkness and givest thy rays.
The Two Lands are in festivity every day,
Awake and standing upon their feet,
For thou hast raised them up.
Washing their bodies, taking their clothing,
Their arms are raised in praise at thy appearance.
All the world, they do their work. . . .

Creator of seed in women,
Thou who makest fluid into man,
Who maintainest the son in the womb of his mother,
Who soothest him with that which stills his weeping,
Thou nurse even in the womb,
Who givest breath to sustain all that he has made!
When he descends from the womb to breathe
On the day when he is born,
Thou openest his mouth completely,
Thou suppliest his necessities.
When the chick in the egg speaks within the shell,
Thou givest him breath within it to maintain him.
When thou hast made him his fulfillment within the egg, to break it,
He comes forth from the egg to speak at his completed time;
He walks upon his legs when he comes forth from it. . . .

How manifold it is, what thou hast made!
They are hidden from the face of man.
O sole god, like whom there is no other!
Thou didst create the world according to thy desire,
Whilst thou wert alone:
All men, cattle, and wild beasts,
Whatever is on earth, going upon its feet,
And what is on high, flying with its wings.

The countries of Syria and Nubia, the land of Egypt,
Thou settest every man in his place,
Thou suppliest their necessities:

Everyone has his food, and his time of life is reckoned.
Their tongues are separate in speech,
And their natures as well;
Their skins are distinguished,
As thou distinguishest the foreign peoples.
Thou makest a Nile in the underworld,
Thou bringest it forth as thou desirest
To maintain the people of Egypt
According as thou madest them for thyself,
The lord of all of them, wearying himself with them,
The lord of every land, rising for them,
The Aton of the day, great of majesty.

All distant foreign countries, thou makest their life also,
For thou hast set a Nile in heaven,
That it may descend for them and make waves upon the mountains,
Like the great green sea,
To water their fields in their towns.
How effective they are, thy plans, O lord of eternity!
The Nile in heaven, it is for the foreign peoples
And for the beasts of every desert that go upon their feet;
While the true Nile comes from the underworld for Egypt. . . .

Thou art in my heart,
And there is no other that knows thee
Save thy son [Akhenaton],
For thou hast made him well-versed in thy plans and in thy strength.

The world came into being by thy hand,
According as thou hast made them.
When thou hast risen they live,
When thou settest they die.
Thou art lifetime thy own self,
For one lives only through thee.

Eyes are fixed on beauty until thou settest.
All work is laid aside when thou settest in the west.
But when thou risest again,
Everything is made to flourish for the king, . . .
Since thou didst found the earth
And raise them up for thy son,
Who came forth from thy body:
the King of Upper and Lower Egypt, . . . Akh-en-Aton, . . . and the
Chief Wife of the King . . . Nefert-iti, living and youthful forever and
ever.

I5

An Egyptian-Hittite Treaty

Imperialism and international diplomacy

The pharaohs of the Nineteenth Dynasty undertook to save the Egyptian empire from the decline which had resulted from Akhenaton's preoccupation with religious reform. Ramses II (1290–1224 B.C.) was successful in restoring Egyptian control in Palestine and southern Syria, but in so doing he came into conflict with the Hittite empire, which was expanding southward from its center in Asia Minor. After a stubborn struggle which ended in a draw, both sides accepted a treaty of peace and alliance, the earliest international treaty in existence (about 1270 B.C.). The treaty is a complex one, with provisions for nonaggression, mutual aid against attack, and extradition of political fugitives. Both Hittite and Egyptian versions of the treaty exist, and it is interesting to observe that each of the rival kings, Ramses II and Hattusilis III, sought to save face by claiming to have assented to the appeal of the other for peace. The Egyptian version, selections from which follow, is the more blunt: Hattusilis sent messengers to "beg peace" from Ramses, "who makes his boundary where he will in every land."

Copy of the tablet of silver which the great chief of Hatti, Hattusilis, caused to be brought to Pharaoh by the hand of his messenger Tartesub and his messenger Ramose, in order to beg peace from the Majesty of Usi-ma-Re-setpen-Re, son of Re, Ramesse-mi-Amun [Ramses II], bull of rulers, who makes his boundary where he will in every land. . . .

PEACE AND BROTHERHOOD

Behold, Hattusilis, the great chief of Hatti, has made himself in a treaty with [Ramses], the great ruler of Egypt, beginning with this day, to cause to be made good peace and good brotherhood between us forever; and he is in brotherhood with me and at peace with me, and I am in brotherhood with him and at peace with him forever.

And since Muwattallis, the great chief of Hatti, my brother, hastened after his fate, and Hattusilis took his seat as great chief of Hatti on the throne of his father; behold I have become with Ramesse-mi-Amun, the great ruler of Egypt,

From S. Langdon and A. H. Gardiner, "The Treaty of Alliance between Hattusilis, King of the Hittites, and the Pharaoh Ramesses II of Egypt," tr. A. H. Gardiner, *Journal of Egyptian Archaeology*, VI (1920), 186 ff. Reprinted by permission of the Egypt Exploration Society.

we being together in our peace and our brotherhood; and it is better than the peace and the brotherhood of formerly, which was in the land.

Behold I, being the great chief of Hatti, am with Ramesse-mi-Amun, the great ruler of Egypt, in good peace and good brotherhood.

And the children of the children of the great chief of Hatti shall be in brotherhood and at peace with the children of the children of Ramesse-mi-Amun, the great ruler of Egypt; they being in our policy of brotherhood and our policy of peace.

And the land of Egypt with the land Hatti shall be at peace and in brotherhood like us forever; and hostilities shall not be made between them forever.

MUTUAL NONAGGRESSION

And the great chief of Hatti shall not trespass into the land of Egypt forever to take aught from it; and [Ramses], the great ruler of Egypt, shall not trepass into the land of Hatti to take aught from it forever. . . .

MUTUAL DEFENSE

And if another enemy come to the lands of [Ramses], the great ruler of Egypt, and he send to the great chief of Hatti saying, "Come with me as help against him"; the great chief of Hatti shall come to him, the great chief of Hatti shall slay his enemy.

But if it be not the desire of the great chief of Hatti to come, he shall send his troops and his chariotry and shall slay his enemy.

Or if Ramesse-mi-Amun, the great ruler of Egypt, become incensed against servants of his, and they do another offense against him, and he go to slay his enemy; the great chief of Hatti shall act with him to destroy everyone against whom they shall be incensed.

The corresponding provision regarding Hatti follows.

EXTRADITION OF FUGITIVES

If any great man flee from the land of Egypt and he come to the lands of the great chief of Hatti; or a town or a district . . . belonging to the lands of Ramesse-mi-Amun, the great ruler of Egypt, and they come to the great chief of Hatti: the great chief of Hatti shall not receive them. The great chief of Hatti shall cause them to be brought to [Ramses], the great ruler of Egypt, their lord, on account of it.

Or if one [common] man or two men who are unknown flee . . . and they come to the land of Hatti, they shall be brought to Ramesse-mi-Amun, the great ruler of Egypt.

The corresponding provision regarding Hittite fugitives follows.

IMMUNITY OF FUGITIVES

If one man flee from the land of Egypt, or two, or three, and they come to the great chief of Hatti, the great chief of Hatti shall seize them and shall cause them to be brought back to [Ramses], the great ruler of Egypt. But as for the man who shall be brought to Ramesse-mi-Amun, the great ruler of Egypt, let not his crime be charged against him, let not his house, his wives or his children be destroyed, let him not be killed, let no injury be done to his eyes, to his ears, to his mouth or to his legs, let not any crime be charged against him.

The corresponding provision regarding Hittite fugitives follows.

DIVINE WITNESSES

As for these words of the treaty made by the great chief of Hatti with Ramesse-mi-Amun, the great ruler of Egypt, in writing upon this tablet of silver; as for these words, a thousand gods, male gods and female gods of those of the land of Hatti, together with a thousand gods, male gods and female gods of those of the land of Egypt — they are with me as witnesses hearing these words. . . .

As to these words which are upon this tablet of silver of the land of Hatti and of the land of Egypt, as to him who shall not keep them, a thousand gods of the land of Hatti and a thousand gods of the land of Egypt shall destroy his house, his land and his servants. But he who shall keep these words which are on this tablet of silver, be they Hatti, or be they Egyptians, and who do not neglect them, a thousand gods of the land of Hatti and a thousand gods of the land of Egypt will cause him to be healthy and to live, together with his houses and his land and his servants.

16

The Old Testament

Hebrew views on God and on history

The Holy Writ of Israel, the Old Testament of the Christian Bible, is a huge anthology of folk tales, historical chronicles, the utterances of men possessed of deep religious insight, love lyrics, and skeptical wisdom literature. Final approval of its present content was given about 90 A.D. by the rabbis at the Council of Jamnia in Palestine.

The Old Testament is a record of Hebrew experience, and the ideas distilled from that experience, during a period of nearly two thousand years that began about 1800 B.C. with Abraham's entry into the land of Canaan. Much that the Hebrews experienced and expressed can also be seen in the literature of Mesopotamia and Egypt, but in their views on God and on history the Hebrews broke with the thought of the ancient Near East.

The gods of Mesopotamia and Egypt — sun-gods, earth gods, storm-gods, and so on — were immanent in nature. The Hebrews, however, distinguished completely between God and nature, placing God entirely outside of the physical universe. He was the Creator who stood above and apart from what He had created; as the psalmist expressed it, "The heavens declare the glory of God; and the firmament showeth his handiwork" (Psalm 19:1). This view of God as the Creator of all things everywhere inevitably led to monotheism and, equally important, to the view that mortals, since they stood apart from God, had free will and were therefore responsible for their own failures. To the Hebrews, history was the story of the clash of God's will with the will of mortals, but since God was righteous and ruled all, he employed these clashes to mold human life to His purpose.

Accordingly, while other ancient peoples viewed history as an endless recurrence of cycles leading nowhere, the Hebrews, with the exception of the author of the Book of Ecclesiastes, understood history as moving in a straight line from a beginning to an end, in accordance with God's purpose for the good of all men and women. "It is the work of a personal divine will, contending with the foolish, stubborn wills of men, promising and warning, judging and punishing and destroying, yet sifting, saving, and abundantly blessing those found amenable to discipline and instruction." [1] This essentially optimistic view of history as the story of progress to better things was passed on to Christianity and, after being divested of its theological underpinnings, to modern Western civilization.

Many of the selections from the Old Testament that follow are from the King James Version of the Bible, first published in 1611, which the late John Livingston Lowes called "the noblest monument of English prose." "Its phraseology," he wrote, "has become part and parcel of our common tongue. ... Its rhythms and cadences, its turns of speech, its familiar imagery, its very words are woven into the texture of our literature.... The English of the Bible ... is characterized not merely by a homely vigor and pithiness of phrase but also a singular nobility of diction and by a rhythmic quality which is, I think, unrivalled in its beauty."

◆ A ◆ EARLIEST RELATIONS BETWEEN MAN AND GOD

The earliest Hebrew views on the relationship between man and God are found in the early chapters of Genesis, the first book of the Pentateuch (the first five books of the Old Testament), whose earliest strand, according to modern Biblical scholars, was composed by a great Hebrew historian during

---

[1] Millar Burrows, "Ancient Israel," in The Idea of History in the Ancient Near East, ed. Robert C. Dentan (New Haven: Yale University Press, 1955), p. 128.

the reign of Solomon. This tenth-century historian prefaced his account of Hebrew origins, which begins with Abraham; with a number of early folk tales that have their parallels in the folklore of other peoples. The particular purpose for which these stories were used is clear; they were viewed as incidents in the history of sin and punishment which left early man at odds with his Creator. and his fellow men.

THE GARDEN OF EDEN

And the Lord God formed man of the dust of the ground, and breathed into his nostrils the breath of life; and man became a living soul.

And the Lord God planted a garden eastward in Eden; and there he put the man whom he had formed. And out of the ground made the Lord God to grow every tree that is pleasant to the sight, and good for food; the tree of life also in the midst of the garden, and the tree of knowledge of good and evil. . . .

And the Lord God commanded the man, saying, Of every tree of the garden thou mayest freely eat: But of the tree of knowledge of good and evil, thou shalt not eat of it: for in the day that thou eatest thereof thou shalt surely die.

And the Lord God said, It is not good that the man should be alone; I will make him a help meet for him. . . . And the Lord God caused a deep sleep to fall upon Adam, and he slept; and he took one of his ribs, and closed up the flesh instead thereof. And the rib, which the Lord God had taken from man, made he a woman, and brought her unto the man. . . . Therefore shall a man leave his father and mother, and shall cleave unto his wife: and they shall be one flesh. And they were both naked, the man and his wife, and were not ashamed.

Now the serpent was more subtile than any beast of the field which the Lord God had made. And he said unto the woman, Yea, hath God said, Ye shall not eat of every tree of the garden? . . . Ye shall not surely die: For God doth know that in the day ye eat thereof, then your eyes shall be opened, and ye shall be as gods, knowing good and evil.

And when the woman saw that the tree was good for food, and that it was pleasant to the eyes, and a tree to be desired to make one wise, she took of the fruit thereof, and did eat, and gave also unto her husband with her; and he did eat. And the eyes of them both were opened, and they knew that they were naked; and they sewed fig leaves together, and made themselves aprons.

And they heard the voice of the Lord God walking in the garden in the cool of the day: and Adam and his wife hid themselves from the presence of the Lord God amongst the trees of the garden. And the Lord God called unto Adam, and said unto him, Where art thou?

And he said, I heard thy voice in the garden, and I was afraid, because I was naked; and I hid myself.

From Genesis 2, 3, 6–9, 11; the King James Version of the Bible.

And he said, Who told thee that thou wast naked? Hast thou eaten of the tree, whereof I commanded thee that thou shouldest not eat?

And the man said, The woman whom thou gavest to be with me, she gave me of the tree, and I did eat.

And the Lord God said unto the woman, What is this that thou hast done? And the woman said, The serpent beguiled me, and I did eat.

And the Lord God said unto the serpent, Because thou hast done this, thou art cursed above all cattle, and above every beast of the field; upon thy belly shalt thou go, and dust shalt thou eat all the days of thy life. . . .

Unto the woman he said, I will greatly multiply thy sorrow and thy conception; in sorrow thou shalt bring forth children; and thy desire shall be to thy husband, and he shall rule over thee.

And unto Adam he said, Because thou hast hearkened unto the voice of thy wife, and hast eaten of the tree, . . . cursed is the ground for thy sake; in sorrow shalt thou eat of it all the days of thy life; Thorns also and thistles shall it bring forth to thee; and thou shalt eat the herb of the field: In the sweat of thy face shalt thou eat bread, till thou return unto the ground; for out of it wast thou taken; for dust thou art, and unto dust shalt thou return. . . .

And the Lord God said, Behold, the man is become as one of us, to know good and evil: and now, lest he put forth his hand, and take also of the tree of life, and eat, and live for ever: Therefore the Lord God sent him forth from the garden of Eden, to till the ground from whence he was taken. So he drove out the man: and he placed at the east of the garden of Eden cherubim, and a flaming sword which turned every way, to keep the way of the tree of life. . . .

THE MARRIAGE OF THE SONS OF GOD

And it came to pass, when men began to multiply on the face of the earth, and daughters were born unto them, That the sons of God saw the daughters of men that they were fair; and they took them wives of all which they chose. And the Lord said, My Spirit shall not always strive with man, for that he also is flesh: yet his days shall be a hundred and twenty years. There were giants in the earth in those days; and also after that, when the sons of God came in unto the daughters of men, and they bare children to them, the same became mighty men which were of old, men of renown.

THE STORY OF THE FLOOD

And God saw that the wickedness of man was great in the earth, and that every imagination of the thoughts of his heart was only evil continually. And it repented the Lord that he had made man on the earth, and it grieved him at his heart. And the Lord said, I will destroy man whom I have created from the face of the earth; both man, and beast, and the creeping thing, and the fowls of the air; for it repenteth me that I have made them. But Noah found grace in the eyes of the Lord. . . .

And God looked upon the earth, and, behold, it was corrupt; for all flesh had corrupted his way upon the earth. And God said unto Noah, The end of all flesh is come before me; for the earth is filled with violence through them; and, behold, I will destroy them with the earth. Make thee an ark of gopher wood; rooms shalt thou make in the ark, and shalt pitch it within and without with pitch. And this is the fashion which thou shalt make it of: The length of the ark shall be three hundred cubits, the breadth of it fifty cubits, and the height of it thirty cubits. A window shalt thou make to the ark, and in a cubit shalt thou finish it above; and the door of the ark shalt thou set in the side thereof; with lower, second, and third stories shalt thou make it.

And, behold, I, even I, do bring a flood of waters upon the earth, to destroy all flesh, wherein is the breath of life, from under heaven; and every thing that is in the earth shall die. But with thee will I establish my covenant; and thou shalt come into the ark, thou, and thy sons, and thy wife, and thy sons' wives with thee. And of every living thing of all flesh, two of every sort shalt thou bring into the ark, to keep them alive with thee; they shall be male and female. . . . And take thou unto thee of all food that is eaten, and thou shalt gather it to thee; and it shall be for food for thee, and for them. Thus did Noah; according to all that God commanded him, so did he.

And the Lord said unto Noah, Come thou and all thy house into the ark; for thee have I seen righteous before me in this generation. . . .

And it came to pass after seven days, that the waters of the flood were upon the earth. In the six hundredth year of Noah's life, in the second month, the seventeenth day of the month, the same day were all the fountains of the great deep broken up, and the windows of heaven were opened. And the rain was upon the earth forty days and forty nights . . . and the Lord shut him in. And the flood was forty days upon the earth; and the waters increased, and bare up the ark, and it was lifted up above the earth. And the waters prevailed, and were increased greatly upon the earth; and the ark went upon the face of the waters. And the waters prevailed exceedingly upon the earth; and all the high hills, that were under the whole heaven, were covered. Fifteen cubits upward did the waters prevail; and the mountains were covered.

And all flesh died that moved upon the earth, both of fowl, and of cattle, and of beast, and of every creeping thing that creepeth upon the earth, and every man: All in whose nostrils was the breath of life, of all that was in the dry land, died. . . . and Noah only remained alive, and they that were with him in the ark. And the waters prevailed upon the earth a hundred and fifty days.

And God remembered Noah, and every living thing, and all the cattle that was with him in the ark: and God made a wind to pass over the earth, and the waters assuaged. The fountains also of the deep and the windows of heaven were stopped, and the rain from heaven was restrained. And the waters returned from off the earth continually: . . . And the ark rested . . . upon the mountains of Ararat. . . .

And it came to pass at the end of forty days, that Noah opened the window of the ark which he had made: And he sent forth a raven, which went forth to and fro, until the waters were dried up from the earth. Also he sent forth a dove from him, to see if the waters were abated from off the face of the ground.

But the dove found no rest for the sole of her foot, and she returned unto him into the ark; for the waters were on the face of the whole earth. Then he put forth his hand, and took her, and pulled her in unto him into the ark.

And he stayed yet other seven days; and again he sent forth the dove out of the ark. And the dove came in to him in the evening, and lo, in her mouth was an olive leaf plucked off: so Noah knew that the waters were abated from off the earth. And he stayed yet other seven days, and sent forth the dove, which returned not again unto him any more.

. . . and Noah removed the covering of the ark, and looked, and, behold, the face of the ground was dry. . . . And God spake unto Noah, saying, Go forth of the ark, thou, and thy wife, and thy sons, and thy sons' wives with thee. Bring forth with thee every living thing that is with thee, . . . that they may breed abundantly in the earth, and be fruitful, and multiply upon the earth. And Noah went forth, and his sons, and his wife, and his sons' wives with him: Every beast, every creeping thing, and every fowl, and whatsoever creepeth upon the earth, after their kinds, went forth out of the ark.

And Noah builded an altar unto the Lord; and took of every clean beast, and of every clean fowl, and offered burnt offerings on the altar. And the Lord smelled a sweet savor; and the Lord said in his heart, I will not again curse the ground any more for man's sake; for the imagination of man's heart is evil from his youth; neither will I again smite any more every thing living, as I have done. While the earth remaineth, seedtime and harvest, and cold and heat, and summer and winter, and day and night shall not cease.

And God blessed Noah and his sons, and said unto them, Be fruitful, and multiply, and replenish the earth. . . .

And the sons of Noah, that went forth of the ark, were Shem, and Ham, and Japheth: and Ham is the father of Canaan. These are the three sons of Noah: and of them was the whole earth overspread. . . .

THE TOWER OF BABEL

And the whole earth was of one language, and of one speech. And it came to pass, as they [the descendants of Noah] journeyed from the east, that they found a plain in the land of Shinar; and they dwelt there. And they said one to another, Go to, let us make brick, and burn them thoroughly. And they had brick for stone, and slime had they for mortar. And they said, Go to, let us build us a city, and a tower, whose top may reach unto heaven; and let us make us a name, lest we be scattered abroad upon the face of the whole earth.

And the Lord came down to see the city and the tower, which the children of men builded. And the Lord said, Behold, the people is one, and they have all one language; and this they begin to do: and now nothing will be restrained from them, which they have imagined to do. Go to, let us go down, and there confound their language, that they may not understand one another's speech. So the Lord scattered them abroad from thence upon the face of all the earth: and they left off to build the city. Therefore is the name of it called Babel; because the Lord did there confound the language of all the earth: and from thence did the Lord scatter them abroad upon the face of all the earth.

◆ B ◆ HEBREW ORIGINS

The patriarchs

In the Old Testament the name "Hebrew" is first applied to the wandering patriarch Abraham (Abram), a ninth-generation descendant of Shem who was one of Noah's three sons and considered to be the progenitor of the Semites. The nomadic character of the early Hebrews, described in several places in the Old Testament, is confirmed by references made in Mesopotamian documents of the early second millenium B.C. to nomads called "Habiru," a word phonetically identical with "Hebrew" and meaning wanderer or outsider. When the Hebrews finally settled and became a nation, they took the name "Israelites" ("Children of Israel"), just as other Habiru groups became known as Moabites, Ammonites, Edomites, and Midianites.

The following selections from the Book of Genesis describe the two most important episodes in the patriarchal history of the Hebrews: the wandering of Abraham and his family (about 1800 B.C.) from Ur in Sumer to the promised land of Canaan, and the descent into Egypt (about 1700 B.C.) of a group of Hebrews who followed the call of Joseph, son of Jacob (also called Israel) and great-grandson of Abraham. Modern scholars attribute Joseph's rise to power in Egypt, and the hospitable reception of his father's people there, to the presence of the mainly Semitic Hyksos, who had conquered Egypt about 1710 B.C.

ABRAHAM, THE FIRST PATRIARCH

Now these are the generations of Terah: Terah begat Abram, Nahor, and Haran; and Haran begat Lot. And Haran died before his father Terah in the land of his nativity, in Ur of the Chaldees. And Abram and Nahor took them wives; the name of Abram's wife was Sarai; and the name of Nahor's wife, Milcah, the daughter of Haran, the father of Milcah, and the father of Iscah. But Sarai was barren, she had no child.

And Terah took Abram his son, and Lot the son of Haran his son's son, and Sarai his daughter-in-law, his son Abram's wife; and they went forth with them from Ur of the Chaldees, to go unto the land of Canaan; and they came unto Haran, and dwelt there. And the days of Terah were two hundred and five years; and Terah died in Haran.

Now the Lord had said unto Abram, Get thee out of thy country, and from thy kindred, and from thy father's house, and unto a land that I will show thee: And I will make of thee a great nation, and I will bless thee, and make thy name great; and thou shalt be a blessing; And I will bless them that bless thee, and curse him that curseth thee; and in thee shall all families of the earth be blessed.

So Abram departed, as the Lord had spoken unto him; and Lot went with him: and Abram was seventy and five years old when he departed out of Haran.

From Genesis 11–12, 46–47; the King James Version of the Bible.

And Abram took Sarai his wife, and Lot his brother's son, and all their substance that they had gathered, and the souls that they had gotten in Haran; and they went forth to go into the land of Canaan; and into the land of Canaan they came. And Abram passed through the land unto the place of Shechem, unto the plain of Moreh. And the Canaanite was then in the land.

And the Lord appeared unto Abram, and said, Unto thy seed will I give this land; and there builded he an altar unto the Lord, who appeared unto him. And he removed from thence unto a mountain on the east of Beth-el and pitched his tent, having Beth-el on the west, and Hai on the east; and there he builded an altar unto the Lord, and called upon the name of the Lord. And Abram journeyed, going on still toward the south. . . .

JOSEPH: THE MIGRATION TO EGYPT

And Israel took his journey with all that he had, and came to Beer-sheba, and offered sacrifices unto the God of his father Isaac. And God spake unto Israel in the visions of the night, and said, Jacob, Jacob. And he said, Here am I. And he said, I am God, the God of thy father: fear not to go down into Egypt; for I will there make of thee a great nation, I will go down with thee into Egypt; and I will also surely bring thee up again: and Joseph shall put his hand upon thine eyes.

And Jacob rose up from Beer-sheba: and the sons of Israel carried Jacob their father, and their little ones, and their wives, in the wagons which Pharaoh had sent to carry him. And they took their cattle, and their goods, which they had gotten in the land of Canaan, and came into Egypt, Jacob and all his seed with him: His sons, and his sons' sons with him, and his sons' daughters, and all his seed brought he with him into Egypt. . . . All the souls that came with Jacob into Egypt, which came out of his loins, besides Jacob's sons' wives, all the souls were threescore and six; . . .

And he sent Judah before him unto Joseph, to direct his face unto Goshen; and they came into the land of Goshen. And Joseph made ready his chariot, and went up to meet Israel his father, to Goshen, and presented himself unto him; and he fell on his neck, and wept on his neck a good while. And Israel said unto Joseph, Now let me die, since I have seen thy face, because thou art yet alive.

And Joseph said unto his brethren, and unto his father's house, I will go up, and show Pharaoh, and say unto him, My brethren, and my father's house, which were in the land of Canaan, are come unto me; And the men are shepherds, for their trade hath been to feed cattle; and they have brought their flocks, and their herds, and all that they have. And it shall come to pass, when Pharaoh shall call you, and shall say, What is your occupation? That ye shall say, Thy servants' trade hath been about cattle from our youth until now, both we, and also our fathers: that ye may dwell in the land of Goshen; for every shepherd is an abomination unto the Egyptians.

Then Joseph came and told Pharaoh, and said, My father and my brethren, and their flocks, and their herds, and all that they have, are come out of the land of Canaan, and, behold, they are in the land of Goshen. And he took some of his brethren, even five men, and presented them unto Pharaoh. And Pharaoh said unto his brethren, What is your occupation? And they said unto Pharaoh, Thy servants are shepherds, both we, and also our fathers. They said moreover unto Pharaoh, For to sojourn in the land are we come; for thy servants have no pasture for their flocks; for the famine is sore in the land of Canaan; now, therefore, we pray thee, let thy servants dwell in the land of Goshen.

And Pharaoh spake unto Joseph, saying, Thy father and thy brethren are come unto thee: The land of Egypt is before thee; in the best of the land make thy father and brethren to dwell; in the land of Goshen let them dwell: and if thou knowest any men of activity among them, then make them rulers over my cattle.

And Joseph brought in Jacob his father, and set him before Pharaoh: and Jacob blessed Pharaoh. And Pharaoh said unto Jacob, How old art thou? And Jacob said unto Pharaoh, The days of the years of my pilgrimage are a hundred and thirty years; few and evil have the days of the years of my life been, and have not attained unto the days of the years of the life of my fathers in the days of their pilgrimage. And Jacob blessed Pharaoh, and went out from before Pharaoh.

And Joseph placed his father and his brethren, and gave them a possession in the land of Egypt, in the best of the land, in the land of Rameses, as Pharaoh had commanded. And Joseph nourished his father, and his brethren. and all his father's household, with bread, according to their families.

◆ C ◆ BONDAGE AND DELIVERANCE

The Hebrews in Egypt experienced a sudden reversal of their fortunes after about 1570 B.C. when the first pharaoh of the Eighteenth Dynasty succeeded in ousting the Hyksos. Under a pharaoh "which knew not Joseph" the Hebrews became state slaves and were forced to build fortress-cities in the Delta. After approximately a century and a half of oppression, God called on Moses to be his instrument in freeing the Hebrews from bondage. In answer to Moses' request, God tells him that his name is YHWH, a form of the verb "to be" that is usually written Yahweh or Jehovah (in most English translations of the Old Testament the word "Lord" is substituted). Shortly after 1300 B.C., Moses led the "mixed multitude" in a dramatic escape across the Sea of Reeds (erroneously translated "Red Sea"), a shallow estuary of the Gulf of Suez, and into "the wilderness" of Sinai.

BONDAGE IN EGYPT

And Joseph died, and all his brethren, and all that generation. And the children of Israel were fruitful, and increased abundantly, and multiplied, and waxed exceeding mighty, and the land was filled with them.

From Exodus 1–3, 6, 12–14; the King James Version of the Bible.

Now there arose up a new king over Egypt, which knew not Joseph. And he said unto his people, Behold the people of the children of Israel are more and mightier than we: Come on, let us deal wisely with them; lest they multiply, and it come to pass that, when there falleth out any war, they join also unto our enemies, and fight against us, and so get them up out of the land. Therefore they did set over them taskmasters to afflict them with their burdens. And they built for Pharaoh treasure cities, Pithom and Raamses. But the more they afflicted them, the more they multiplied and grew. And they were grieved because of the children of Israel. And the Egyptians made the children of Israel to serve with rigor; And they made their lives bitter with hard bondage, in mortar, and in brick, and in all manner of service in the field; all their service, wherein they made them serve, was with rigor. . . .

GOD'S CALL TO MOSES

And it came to pass in process of time, that the king of Egypt died: and the children of Egypt sighed by reason of the bondage, and they cried, and their cry came up unto God by reason of the bondage. And God heard their groaning, and God remembered his covenant with Abraham, with Isaac, and with Jacob. And God looked upon the children of Israel, and God had respect unto them.

Now Moses kept the flock of Jethro his father-in-law, the priest of Midian: and he led the flock to the back side of the desert, and came to the mountain of God, even to Horeb. And the Angel of the Lord appeared unto him in a flame of fire out of the midst of a bush: and he looked, and, behold, the bush burned with fire, and the bush was not consumed. And Moses said, I will now turn aside, and see this great sight, why the bush is not burnt.

And when the Lord saw that he turned aside to see, God called unto him out of the midst of the bush, and said, Moses, Moses. And he said, Here am I. And he said, Draw not nigh hither: put off thy shoes from off thy feet; for the place whereon thou standest is holy ground. Moreover he said, I am the God of thy father, the God of Abraham, the God of Isaac, and the God of Jacob. And Moses hid his face, for he was afraid to look upon God.

And the Lord said, I have surely seen the affliction of my people which are in Egypt, and have heard their cry by reason of their taskmasters; for I know their sorrows; and I am come down to deliver them out of the hand of the Egyptians, and to bring them out of that land unto a good land and a large, unto a land flowing with milk and honey; unto the place of the Canaanites, and the Hittites, and the Amorites, and the Perizzites, and the Hivites, and the Jebusites. Now, therefore, behold the cry of the children of Israel is come unto me: and I have also seen the oppression wherewith the Egyptians oppress them. Come now therefore, and I will send thee unto Pharaoh, that thou mayest bring forth my people the children of Israel out of Egypt.

And Moses said unto God, Who am I, that I should go unto Pharaoh, and that I should bring forth the children of Israel out of Egypt? And he said, Certainly I will be with thee; and this shall be a token unto thee, that I have sent thee: When thou has brought forth the people out of Egypt, ye shall serve God upon this mountain.

And Moses said unto God, Behold when I come unto the children of Israel, and shall say unto them, the God of your fathers hath sent me unto you; and they shall say to me, What is his name? What shall I say unto them?

And God said unto Moses, I AM THAT I AM: Thus shalt thou say unto the children of Israel, I AM hath sent me unto you. And God said moreover unto Moses, Thus shalt thou say unto the children of Israel, The Lord God of your fathers, the God of Abraham, the God of Isaac, and the God of Jacob, hath sent me unto you: this is my name for ever, and this is my memorial unto all generations. . . .

And I am sure that the king of Egypt will not let you go, no, not by a mighty hand. And I will stretch out my hand, and smite Egypt with all my wonders which I will do in the midst thereof: and after that he will let you go. And I will give this people favor in the sight of the Egyptians; and it shall come to pass that, when ye go, ye shall not go empty: But every woman shall borrow of her neighbor, and of her that sojourneth in her house, jewels of silver, and jewels of gold, and raiment: and ye shall put them upon your sons and upon your daughters; and ye shall spoil the Egyptians. . . .

And God spake unto Moses, and said unto him, I am the Lord: And I appeared unto Abraham, unto Isaac, and unto Jacob, by the name of God Almighty; but by my name JEHOVAH was I not known to them. And I have also established my covenant with them to give them the land of Canaan, the land of their pilgrimage, wherein they were strangers. . . .

THE ESCAPE

Now the sojourning of the children of Israel, who dwelt in Egypt, was four hundred and thirty years. And it came to pass at the end of the four hundred and thirty years, even the selfsame day it came to pass, that all the hosts of the Lord went out from the land of Egypt. It is a night to be much observed unto the Lord for bringing them out from the land of Egypt: this is that night of the Lord to be observed of all the children of Israel in their generations. . . .

And it came to pass, when Pharaoh had let the people go, that God led them not through the way of the land of the Philistines, although that was near; for God said, Lest peradventure the people repent when they see war, and they return to Egypt: But God led the people about, through the way of the wilderness of the Red Sea: and the children of Israel went up harnessed out of the land of Egypt. And Moses took the bones of Joseph with him: for he had straitly sworn the children of Israel, saying, God will surely visit you; and ye shall surely carry up my bones away hence with you. And they took their journey from Succoth, and encamped in Etham, in the edge of the wilderness. And the Lord went before them by day in a pillar of a cloud, to lead them the way; and by night in a pillar of fire, to give them light; to go by day and night. . . .

And it was told the king of Egypt that the people fled: and the heart of

Pharaoh and his servants was turned against the people, and they said, Why have we done this, that we have let Israel go from serving us? And he made ready his chariot, and took his people with him: And he took six hundred chosen chariots, and all the chariots of Egypt, and captains over every one of them. And the Lord hardened the heart of Pharaoh king of Egypt, and he pursued after the children of Israel: and the children of Israel went out with a high hand. But the Egyptians pursued after them, all the horses and chariots of Pharaoh, and his horsemen, and his army, and overtook them encamping by the sea. . . .

And when Pharaoh drew nigh, the children of Israel lifted up their eyes, and, behold, the Egyptians marched after them; and they were sore afraid: and the children of Israel cried out unto the Lord. And they said unto Moses, Because there were no graves in Egypt, hast thou taken us away to die in the wilderness? Wherefore hast thou dealt thus with us, to carry us forth out of Egypt? Is not this the word that we did tell thee in Egypt, saying, Let us alone, that we may serve the Egyptians? For it had been better for us to serve the Egyptians, than that we should die in the wilderness.

And Moses said unto the people, Fear ye not, stand still, and see the salvation of the Lord, which he will show to you today: for the Egyptians whom ye have seen today, ye shall see them no more for ever. The Lord shall fight for you, and ye shall hold your peace. . . .

And the Angel of God, which went before the camp of Israel, removed and went behind them; and the pillar of the cloud went from before their face and stood behind them: And it came between the camp of the Egyptians and the camp of Israel; and it was a cloud and darkness to them, but it gave light by night to these: so that the one came not near the other all the night. And Moses stretched out his hand over the sea; and the Lord caused the sea to go back by a strong east wind all that night, and made the sea dry land, and the waters were divided. And the children of Israel went into the midst of the sea upon the dry ground: and the waters were a wall unto them on their right hand, and on their left. And the Egyptians pursued, and went in after them to the midst of the sea, even all Pharaoh's horses, his chariots, and his horsemen. And it came to pass, that in the morning watch the Lord looked unto the host of the Egyptians through the pillar of fire and of the cloud, and troubled the host of the Egyptians, And took off their chariot wheels, that they drave them heavily: so that the Egyptians said, Let us flee from the face of Israel; for the Lord fighteth for them against the Egyptians.

And the Lord said unto Moses, Stretch out thine hand over the sea, that the waters may come again upon the Egyptians, upon their chariots and upon their horsemen. And Moses stretched forth his hand over the sea, and the sea returned to his strength when the morning appeared; and the Egyptians fled against it; and the Lord overthrew the Egyptians in the midst of the sea. And the waters returned, and covered the chariots, and the horsemen, and all the host of Pharaoh that came into the sea after them; there remained not so much as one of them. But the children of Israel walked upon dry land in the midst of the sea; and the waters were a wall unto them on their right hand, and on their left.

Thus the Lord saved Israel out of the hand of the Egyptians; and Israel saw the Egyptians dead upon the seashore. And Israel saw that great work which the Lord did upon the Egyptians: and the people feared the Lord, and believed the Lord, and his servant Moses.

◆ D ◆ THE SINAI COVENANT

Because it led to the formation of the nation of Israel, the Hebrews looked upon their deliverance from bondage in Egypt as the decisive divine act in their history. The sequel to the Exodus was the Sinai pact or covenant between Yahweh and the nation of Israel, which replaced the older covenants made with individual patriarchs like Abraham. From this time on the Israelites considered themselves the chosen people of the Lord, Who would protect them in return for obedience to His law.

Like an eagle bearing its young on its wings, Yahweh brought the people to Mount Sinai for the purpose of announcing, through Moses, the laws of the covenant. These laws are of two types, absolute and conditional. Absolute law is best illustrated by the Decalogue, or Ten Commandments: it expresses unconditional demands and general principles. Conditional law, on the other hand, is case law such as we have seen in the Code of Hammurabi: its object is the detailed regulation of society — if or when a certain circumstance occurs, then a specific legal consequence will follow. Most of the many laws of the Covenant Code, which follows the Decalogue, are of this conditional type. Because they reflect a settled agricultural rather than a nomadic life, most scholars conclude that they are from a period several centuries later than Moses and the Decalogue. They bear the stamp of the later settled life in Palestine, where Babylonian cultural influences — including law — had long been felt. This is thought to explain certain similarities between the Covenant Code and the Code of Hammurabi.

On the third new moon after the people of Israel had gone forth out of the land of Egypt, on that day they came into the wilderness of Sinai. . . . and there Israel encamped before the mountain. And Moses went up to God, and the Lord called him out of the mountain, saying, "Thus you shall say to the house of Jacob, and tell the people of Israel: You have seen what I did to the Egyptians, and how I bore you on eagles' wings and brought you to myself. Now therefore, if you will obey my voice and keep my covenant, you shall be my

From Exodus 19–24; the Revised Standard Version of the Bible, copyright 1946 and 1952. Reprinted by permission of the National Council of the Churches of Christ.

own possession among all peoples; for all the earth is mine, and you shall be to me a kingdom of priests and a holy nation. These are the words which you shall speak to the children of Israel.". . .

And the Lord said to Moses, "Go to the people and consecrate them today and tomorrow, and let them wash their garments, and be ready by the third day; for on the third day the Lord will come down upon Mount Sinai in the sight of all the people. And you shall set bounds for the people round about, saying, 'Take heed that you do not go up into the mountain or touch the border of it; whoever touches the mountain shall be put to death; no hand shall touch him, but he shall be stoned or shot; whether beast or man, he shall not live.' When the trumpet sounds a long blast, they shall come up to the mountain." So Moses went down from the mountain to the people, and consecrated the people; and they washed their garments. And he said to the people, "Be ready by the third day; do not go near a woman."

On the morning of the third day there were thunders and lightnings, and a thick cloud upon the mountain, and a very loud trumpet blast, so that all the people who were in the camp trembled. Then Moses brought the people out of the camp to meet God; and they took their stand at the foot of the mountain. And Mount Sinai was wrapped in smoke, because the Lord descended upon it in fire; and the smoke of it went up like the smoke of a kiln, and the whole mountain quaked greatly. And as the sound of the trumpet grew louder and louder, Moses spoke, and God answered him in thunder. And the Lord came down upon Mount Sinai, to the top of the mountain; and the Lord called Moses to the top of the mountain, and Moses went up. . . .

THE TEN COMMANDMENTS

And God spoke all these words, saying,

"I am the Lord your God, who brought you out of the land of Egypt, out of the house of bondage.

"You shall have no other gods before me.

"You shall not make yourself a graven image, or any likeness of anything that is in heaven above, or that is in the earth beneath, or that is in the water under the earth; you shall not bow down to them or serve them; for I the Lord your God am a jealous God, visiting the iniquity of the fathers upon the children of the third and the fourth generation of those who hate me, but showing steadfast love to thousands of those who love me and keep my commandments.

"You shall not take the name of the Lord your God in vain; for the Lord will not hold him guiltless who takes his name in vain.

"Remember the sabbath day, to keep it holy. Six days you shall labor, and do all your work; but the seventh day is a sabbath to the Lord your God; in it you shall not do any work, you, or your son, or your daughter, or your manservant, or your maidservant, or your cattle, or the sojourner who is within your gates; for in six days the Lord made heaven and earth, the sea, and all that is in them, and rested the seventh day; therefore the Lord blessed the sabbath day and hallowed it.

"Honor your father and your mother, that your days may be long in the land which the Lord your God gives you.

"You shall not kill.

"You shall not commit adultery.

"You shall not steal.

"You shall not bear false witness against your neighbor.

"You shall not covet your neighbor's house; you shall not covet your neighbor's wife, or his manservant, or his maidservant, or his ox, or his ass, or anything that is your neighbor's.". . .

SUNDRY LAWS OF THE COVENANT CODE

"Now these are the ordinances which you shall set before them. When you buy a Hebrew slave, he shall serve six years, and in the seventh he shall go out free, for nothing. If he comes in single, he shall go out single; if he comes in married, then his wife shall go out with him. If his master gives him a wife and she bears him sons and daughters, the wife and her children shall be her master's and he shall go out alone. But if the slave plainly says, 'I love my master, my wife, and my children; I will not go out free,' then his master shall bring him to God, and he shall bring him to the door or the doorpost; and his master shall bore his ear through with an awl; and he shall serve him for life.

"When a man sells his daughter as a slave, she shall not go out as the male slaves do. If she does not please her master, who has designated her for himself, then he shall let her be redeemed; he shall have no right to sell her to a foreign people, since he has dealt faithlessly with her. If he designates her for his son, he shall deal with her as with a daughter. If he takes another wife to himself, he shall not diminish her food, her clothing, or her marital rights. And if he does not do these three things for her, she shall go out for nothing, without payment of money.

"Whoever strikes a man so that he dies shall be put to death. But if he did not lie in wait for him, but God let him fall into his hand, then I will appoint for you a place to which he may flee. But if a man willfully attacks another to kill him treacherously, you shall take him from my altar, that he may die.

"Whoever strikes his father or his mother shall be put to death.

"Whoever steals a man, whether he sells him or is found in possession of him, shall be put to death.

"Whoever curses his father or his mother shall be put to death.

"When men quarrel and one strikes the other with a stone or with his fist and the man does not die but keeps his bed, then if the man rises again and walks abroad with his staff, he that struck him shall be clear; only he shall pay for the loss of his time, and shall have him thoroughly healed.

"When a man strikes his slave, male or female, with a rod and the slave dies under his hand, he shall be punished. But if the slave survives a day or two, he is not to be punished; for the slave is his money.

"When men strive together, and hurt a woman with child, so that there is a miscarriage, and yet no harm follows, the one who hurt her shall be fined, according as the woman's husband shall lay upon him; and he shall pay as the judges determine. If any harm follows, then you shall give life for life, eye for eye, tooth for tooth, hand for hand, foot for foot, burn for burn, wound for wound, stripe for stripe. . . .

"When a man causes a field or vineyard to be grazed over, or lets his beast loose and it feeds in another man's field, he shall make restitution from the best in his own field and in his own vineyard. . . .

"For every breach of trust, whether it is for ox, for ass, for sheep, for clothing, or for any kind of lost thing, of which one says, 'That is it,' the case of both parties shall come before God; he whom God shall condemn shall pay double to his neighbor. . . .

"If a man seduces a virgin who is not betrothed, and lies with her, he shall give the marriage present for her, and make her his wife. If her father utterly refuses to give her to him, he shall pay money equivalent to the marriage present for virgins.

"You shall not permit a sorceress to live. . . .

"You shall not wrong a stranger or oppress him, for you were strangers in the land of Egypt. You shall not afflict any widow or orphan. If you do afflict them, and they cry out to me, I will surely hear their cry; and my wrath will burn, and I will kill you with the sword, and your wives shall become widows and your children fatherless.

"If you lend money to any of my people with you who is poor, you shall not be to him as a creditor, and you shall not exact interest from him. If ever you take your neighbor's garment in pledge, you shall restore it to him before the sun goes down; for that is his only covering, it is his mantle for his body; in what else shall he sleep? And if he cries to me, I will hear it, for I am compassionate. . . .

"The first-born of your sons you shall give to me. You shall do likewise with your oxen and with your sheep: seven days it shall be with its dam; on the eighth day you shall give it to me. . . .

"Three times in the year you shall keep a feast to me. You shall keep the feast of unleavened bread; as I commanded you, you shall eat unleavened bread for seven days at the appointed time in the month of Abib, for in it you came out of Egypt. None shall appear before me empty-handed. You shall keep the feast of harvest, of the first fruits of your labor, of what you sow in the field. You shall keep the feast of ingathering at the end of the year, when you gather in from the field the fruit of your labor. Three times in the year shall all your males appear before the Lord God. . . .

"The first of the first fruits of your ground you shall bring into the house of the Lord your God.

"You shall not boil a kid in its mother's milk. . . ."

Moses came and told the people all the words of the Lord and all the ordinances; and all the people answered with one voice, and said, "All the words which the Lord has spoken we will do." And Moses wrote all the words of the Lord.

◆ E ◆ THE SONG OF DEBORAH

"So perish all thine enemies, O Lord!"

The Pentateuch's account of Hebrew history is reduced to capsule form in an ancient liturgy preserved in Deuteronomy (26:5–10):

> A wandering Aramean was my father; and he went down into Egypt and sojourned there, few in number; and there he became a nation, great, mighty, and populous. And the Egyptians treated us harshly, and afflicted us, and laid upon us hard bondage. Then we cried to the Lord the God of our fathers, and the Lord heard our voice, and saw our affliction, our toil, and our oppression; and the Lord brought us out of Egypt with a mighty hand and an outstretched arm, with great terror, with signs and wonders; and he brought us into this place and gave us this land, a land flowing with milk and honey. And behold, now I bring the first of the fruit of the ground, which thou, O Lord hast given me.

Following their arrival in the promised land of Canaan around the middle of the thirteenth century B.C., the Israelites joined with their Hebrew brethren in the land to form a loose confederation of twelve tribes. The confederacy was held together by a common religious tie — the covenant with Yahweh. Its center was the sanctuary at Shechem (later moved to Shiloh) where the Ark of the Covenant, a chest containing the stone tablets upon which the Ten Commandments were engraved, was housed in a tent. In times of danger, resulting from frequent wars with the strong Canaanite cities, the tribes joined together under war leaders, called judges, to face the common foe.

The long struggle between the Israelites and the Canaanites reached a climax in the last half of the twelfth century B.C., when a coalition of Canaanite kings made a final attempt to stop Israelite expansion. The Canaanite forces were commanded by Sisera, who "had nine hundred chariots of iron, and oppressed the people of Israel cruelly for twenty years" (Judges 4:3). About 1125 B.C. a resounding Israelite victory destroyed Sisera's powerful forces and marked the end of united Canaanite resistance to Israel. The Song of Deborah, one of the oldest passages in the Old Testament, is a poetic account of this final battle written, it is thought, by a contemporary. The scene of the battle was the Valley of Jezreel, a narrow pass on the main north–south caravan artery which was as important for the economic life of ancient Israel as the Gulf of Aqabah is for modern Israel. The Canaanite fortress of Megiddo blocked this vital lifeline with the result that, in the words of the poet, "caravans ceased and travelers kept to the byways."

Inspired by the woman Deborah, and led by the hero Barak ("Lightning"), the Israelites (some tribes refused to participate) routed Sisera's forces, whose chariots became mired in mud after the river Kishon providentially overflowed. Although the poet touches often on the fierce Israelite passion for

Judges 5; the Revised Standard Version of the Bible, copyright 1946 and 1952. Reprinted by permission of the National Council of the Churches of Christ.

victory, he is also at times objective, and there is bitter pathos in his account of Sisera's mother peering through a window for a son who will never return. And while the poet praises the magnificent feat performed by the people and their leaders, he does not let us forget that the victory was in reality another of Yahweh's triumphs.

Then sang Deborah and Barak the son of Abinoam on that day:
"That the leaders took the lead in Israel,
    that the people offered themselves willingly,
    bless the Lord!

"Hear, O kings; give ear, O princes;
    to the Lord I will sing,
    I will make melody to the Lord, the God of Israel.

"Lord, when thou didst go forth from Seir,
    when thou didst march from the region of Edom,
the earth trembled,
    and the heavens dropped,
    yea, the clouds dropped water.
The mountains quaked before the Lord,
    yon Sinai before the Lord, the God of Israel.

"In the days of Shamgar, son of Anath,
    in the days of Jael, caravans ceased
    and travelers kept to the byways.
The peasantry ceased in Israel, they ceased
    until you arose, Deborah,
    arose as a mother in Israel.
When new gods were chosen,
    then war was in the gates.
Was shield or spear to be seen
    among forty thousand in Israel?
My heart goes out to the commanders of Israel
    who offered themselves willingly among the people.
    Bless the Lord.

"Tell of it, you who ride on tawny asses,
    you who sit on rich carpets
    and you who walk by the way.
To the sound of musicians at the watering places,
    there they repeat the triumphs of the Lord,
    the triumphs of his peasantry in Israel.

"Then down to the gates marched the people of the Lord.

"Awake, awake, Deborah!
    Awake, awake, utter a song!
Arise, Barak, lead away your captives,
    O son of Abinoam.

"Then down marched the remnant of the noble;
    the people of the Lord marched down for him against the mighty.
From Ephraim they set out thither into the valley,
    following you, Benjamin, with your kinsmen;
from Machir marched down the commanders,
    and from Zebulun those who bear the marshal's staff;
the princes of Issachar came with Deborah,
    and Issachar faithful to Barak;
    into the valley they rushed forth at his heels.
Among the clans of Reuben
    there were great searchings of heart.
Why did you tarry among the sheepfolds,
    to hear the piping for the flocks?
Among the clans of Reuben
    there were great searchings of heart.

"Gilead stayed beyond the Jordan;
    and Dan, why did he abide with the ships?
Asher sat still at the coast of the sea,
    settling down by his landings.
Zebulun is a people that jeopardied their lives to the death;
    Naphtali too, on the heights of the field.

"The kings came, they fought;
    then fought the kings of Canaan,
at Taanach, by the waters of Megiddo;
    they got no spoils of silver.
From heaven fought the stars,
    from their courses they fought against Sisera.
The torrent Kishon swept them away,
    the onrushing torrent, the torrent Kishon.
    March on, my soul, with might!

"Then loud beat the horses' hoofs
    with the galloping, galloping of his steeds.

"Curse Meroz, says the angel of the Lord,
    curse bitterly its inhabitants,
because they came not to the help of the Lord,
    to the help of the Lord against the mighty.

"Most blessed of women be Jael,
     the wife of Heber the Kenite,
     of tent-dwelling women most blessed.
He asked water and she gave him milk.
     she brought him curds in a lordly bowl.
She put her hand to the tent peg
     and her right hand to the workmen's mallet;
she struck Sisera a blow,
     she crushed his head,
     she shattered and pierced his temple.
He sank, he fell,
     he lay still at her feet;
at her feet he sank, he fell;
     where he sank, there he fell dead.

"Out of the window she peered,
     the mother of Sisera gazed through the lattice:
'Why is his chariot so long in coming?
     Why tarry the hoofbeats of his chariots?'
Her wisest ladies make answer,
     nay, she gives answer to herself,
'Are they not finding and dividing the spoil? —
     A maiden or two for every man;
spoil of dyed stuffs for Sisera,
     spoil of dyed stuffs embroidered,
     two pieces of dyed work embroidered for my neck as spoil?'

"So perish all thine enemies, O Lord!
     But thy friends be like the sun as he rises in his might."

And the land had rest for forty years.

◆ F ◆ THE PEOPLE DEMAND A KING

"To govern us like all the nations"

The ineffectiveness of the loose Israelite tribal confederacy in the face of danger — to be noted even in the Song of Deborah with its curses directed at those tribes that refused to join in the battle at Megiddo — became fully apparent in the eleventh century. By that time the Philistines, who shortly after 1200 B.C. had settled along the coast of what is now called the Gaza Strip, were threatening to conquer all of Palestine. Israel's fortunes reached their

From I Samuel 8; the Revised Standard Version of the Bible, copyright 1946 and 1952. Reprinted by permission of the National Council of the Churches of Christ.

lowest ebb around 1050 B.C. when the Philistines destroyed the central sanctuary of the confederacy at Shiloh and carried away the Ark of the Covenant as a trophy of war. The resulting demand of the people for a more effective type of centralized government was reinforced by the prevalence of injustice under the weak rule of judges. "In those days," we read in Judges 17:6, "there was no king in Israel; every man did what was right in his own eyes." This desire to end lawlessness is touched on in the following selection, in which the great prophet-judge Samuel, before reluctantly giving in to the demand of the people for a king, presents the conservative argument against strong, centralized government.

When Samuel became old, he made his sons judges over Israel. . . . Yet his sons did not walk in his ways, but turned aside after gain; they took bribes and perverted justice.

Then all the elders of Israel gathered together and came to Samuel at Ramah, and said to him, "Behold, you are old and your sons do not walk in your ways; now appoint for us a king to govern us like all the nations." But the thing displeased Samuel when they said, "Give us a king to govern us." And Samuel prayed to the Lord. And the Lord said to Samuel, "Hearken to the voice of the people in all that they say to you; for they have not rejected you, but they have rejected me from being king over them. According to all deeds which they have done to me, from the day I brought them up out of Egypt even to this day, forsaking me and serving other gods, so they are also doing to you. Now then, hearken to their voice; only, you shall solemnly warn them, and show them the ways of the king who shall reign over them."

So Samuel told all the words of the Lord to the people who were asking a king from him. He said, "These will be the ways of the king who will reign over you: he will take your sons and appoint them to his chariots and to be his horsemen, and to run before his chariots; and he will appoint for himself commanders of thousands and commanders of fifties, some to plow his ground and to reap his harvest, and to make his implements of war and the equipment of his chariots. He will take your daughters to be perfumers and cooks and bakers. He will take the best of your fields and vineyards and olive orchards and give them to his servants. He will take the tenth of your grain and of your vineyards and give it to his officers and to his servants. He will take your menservants and maidservants, and the best of your cattle and your asses, and put them to his work. He will take the tenth of your flocks, and you shall be his slaves. And in that day you will cry out because of your king, whom you have chosen for yourselves; but the Lord will not answer you in that day."

But the people refused to listen to the voice of Samuel; and they said, "No! but we will have a king over us, that we also may be like all the nations, and that our king may govern us and go out before us and fight our battles." And when Samuel had heard all the words of the people, he repeated them in the ears of the Lord. And the Lord said to Samuel, "Hearken to their voice, and make them a king." Samuel then said to the men of Israel, "Go every man to his city."

◆G◆ THE UNITED KINGDOM OF ISRAEL

"A great name, like the name of the great ones of the earth"

The beginning of the Hebrew monarchy under Saul (1020–1000 B.C.) were not auspicious. The prey of his own moody nature, jealous of the fame of the boy-hero David, and plagued by tribal disloyalty and the opposition of Samuel and the conservatives, Saul died tragically in his last unsuccessful battle with the Philistines. During the reign of the popular David (1000–961 B.C.), both the foreign and the domestic problems of Israel were solved. The Philistines were defeated and restricted to a narrow coastal plain, and among Israel's other neighbors, from the Gulf of Aqabah in the south to the Euphrates in the north, only the Phoenicians were not subdued. Tribal independence was greatly weakened when David established a national capital and a centralized administration at Jerusalem, a Canaanite stronghold which he captured despite the boast of its inhabitants that even "the blind and the lame" could defend it. Royal administrators replaced the elders and judges of the confederacy period, and a census of all Israel was taken, to be used as a basis for military service, taxes, and forced labor. David shrewdly provided a religious sanction for the new monarchy by transferring with great pomp and ceremony the Ark of the Covenant to Jerusalem, and by building a royal shrine — the forerunner of Solomon's great Temple — which he placed in the hands of an official priesthood. Thus was established the doctrine of the divine origin of David's monarchy and that of his successors.

David's son Solomon (961–922 B.C.) completed the work of his father in establishing an oriental type of centralized monarchy. Tribal loyalties were further weakened by the division of Israel into twelve administrative districts, which did not always correspond to the old tribal territories. Each district was supervised by a royal official, who was also responsible for provisioning the royal household during one month of the year. The construction of the Temple, together with a palace complex, government buildings, and "store cities," required the frequent levying of taxes and an oppressive program of forced labor. The "chariot cities" served to protect the trade that flowed through Palestine from such places as Egypt, Arabia, Phoenicia, and Cilicia (Kue). In cooperation with the Phoenicians, Solomon built a trading fleet to exploit the Red Sea area, and the "hard questions" which the Queen of Sheba travelled a thousand miles from southwest Arabia to put to Solomon are thought to have been connected with Solomon's monopoly of trade in this area.

Yet as Samuel had foretold when he sought to dissuade the people from their desire to have a king, the price of monarchy was high — limitations on

From II Samuel 5–8; I Kings 4–6, 9–11; the Revised Standard Version of the Bible, copyright 1946 and 1952. Reprinted by permission of the National Council of the Churches of Christ.

freedom and exploitation by a despot. The resentment caused by Solomon's oppressive policies led to a revolution at his death which split the kingdom into two parts: Israel (or Ephraim) in the north and Judah in the south. Threatened by the rise of new great empires, these two weak kingdoms were to have little rest before Israel fell to the Assyrians (722 B.C.) and Judah to the Chaldeans (586 B.C.). Unlike the northern Israelites, the Judeans, or Jews, survived their exile in Babylonia and returned to their homeland after Cyrus the Persian conquered Babylon (539 B.C.) and liberated them. From the turmoil of these years rose the great Hebrew prophets of doom and righteousness, who saw the history of their people as one of stubborn rebellion against "the one eternal, living God [who] is working out his own sovereign purpose for the good of his creatures, first for his chosen people, and through them for the rest of mankind." [1]

"DAVID REIGNED OVER ALL ISRAEL"

Then all the tribes of Israel came to David at Hebron, and said, "Behold, we are your bone and flesh. In times past when Saul was king over us, it was you that led out and brought in Israel; and the Lord said to you, 'You shall be shepherd of my people Israel, and you shall be prince over Israel.'" So all the elders of Israel came to the king at Hebron; and King David made a covenant with them at Hebron before the Lord, and they anointed David king over Israel. David was thirty years old when he began to reign, and he reigned forty years. . . .

And the king and his men went to Jerusalem against the Jebusites, the inhabitants of the land, who said to David, "You will not come in here, but the blind and the lame will ward you off" — thinking, "David cannot come in here." Nevertheless David took the stronghold of Zion, that is, the city of David. . . . And David built the city round about from the Millo inward. And David became greater and greater, for the Lord, the God of hosts, was with him.

And Hiram king of Tyre sent messengers to David, and cedar trees, also carpenters and masons who built David a house. And David perceived that the Lord had established him king over Israel, and that he had exalted his kingdom for the sake of his people Israel. . . .

So David went and brought up the ark of God . . . to the city of David with rejoicing; and when those who bore the ark of the Lord had gone six paces, he sacrificed an ox and a fatling. And David danced before the Lord with all his might; and David was girded with a linen ephod. So David and all the house of Israel brought up the ark of the Lord with shouting, and with the sound of the horn. . . .

Now when the king dwelt in his house, and the Lord had given him rest from all his enemies round about, the king said to Nathan the prophet, "See now, I dwell in a house of cedar, but the ark of God dwells in a tent." And

---

[1] Millar Burrows, "Ancient Israel," in *The Idea of History in the Ancient Near East*, ed. Robert C. Dentan (New Haven: Yale University Press, 1955), p. 128.

Nathan said to the king, "Go, do all that is in your heart; for the Lord is with you."

But that same night the word of the Lord came to Nathan, "Go and tell my servant David, 'Thus says the Lord: Would you build me a house to dwell in? I have not dwelt in a house since the day I brought up the people of Israel from Egypt to this day, but I have been moving about in a tent for my dwelling. In all places where I have moved with all the people of Israel, did I speak a word with any of the judges of Israel, whom I commanded to shepherd my people Israel, saying, "Why have you not built me a house of cedar?" Now therefore thus you shall say to my servant David, 'Thus says the Lord of hosts, I took you from the pasture, from following the sheep, that you should be prince over my people Israel; and I have been with you wherever you went, and have cut off all your enemies from before you; and I will make you a great name, like the names of the great ones of the earth. And I will appoint a place for my people Israel, and will plant them, that they may dwell in their own place, and be disturbed no more; and violent men shall afflict them no more, as formerly, from the time that I appointed judges over my people Israel; and I will give you rest from all your enemies. Moreover the Lord declares to you that the Lord will make you a house. When your days are fulfilled and you lie down with your fathers, I will raise up your son after you, who shall come forth from your body, and I will establish his kingdom. He shall build a house for my name, and I will establish the throne of his kingdom for ever. I will be his father, and he shall be my son. When he commits iniquity, I will chasten him with the rod of men; but I will not take my steadfast love from him, as I took it from Saul, whom I put away from before you. And your house and your kingdom shall be made sure for ever before me; your throne shall be established for ever.' " In accordance with all these words, and in accordance with all this vision, Nathan spoke to David. . . .

After this David defeated the Philistines and subdued them, and David took Methegh-ammah out of the hand of the Philistines.

And he defeated Moab, . . . And the Moabites became servants to David and brought tribute.

David also defeated Hadadezer the son of Rehob, king of Zobah, as he went to restore his power at the river Euphrates. And David took from him a thousand and seven hundred horsemen, and twenty thousand foot soldiers; and David hamstrung all the chariot horses, but left enough for a hundred chariots. And when the Syrians of Damascus came to help Hadadezer king of Zobah, David slew twenty-two thousand men of the Syrians. Then David put garrisons in Aram of Damascus; and the Syrians become servants to David and brought tribute. And the Lord gave victory to David wherever he went. . . .

When Toi king of Hamath heard that David had defeated the whole army of Hadadezer, Toi sent his son Joram to King David, to greet him, and to congratulate him; for Hadadezer had often been at war with Toi. And Joram brought with him articles of silver, of gold, and of bronze; these also King David dedicated to the Lord, together with the silver and gold which he dedicated from all the nations he subdued, from Edom, Moab, the Ammonites, the

Philistines, Amalek, and from the spoil of Hadadezer the son of Rehob, king of Zobah.

And David won a name for himself. When he returned, he slew eighteen thousand Edomites in the valley of Salt. And he put garrisons in Edom; throughout all Edom he put garrisons, and all the Edomites became David's servants. And the Lord gave victory to David wherever he went.

So David reigned over all Israel; and David administered justice and equity to all his people. . . .

"KING SOLOMON: HIS HIGH OFFICIALS"

King Solomon was king over all Israel, and these were his high officials: Azariah the son of Zadok was the priest; Elihoreph and Ahijah the sons of Shisha were secretaries; Jehoshaphat the son of Ahilud was recorder; Benaiah the son of Jehoiada was in command of the army; Zadok and Abiathar were priests; Azariah the son of Nathan was over the officers; Zabud the son of Nathan was priest and king's friend; Ahishar was in charge of the palace; and Adoniram the son of Abda was in charge of the forced labor.

Solomon had twelve officers over all Israel, who provided food for the king and his household; each man had to make provision for one month in the year. These were their names: Ben-hur, in the hill country of Ephraim; Ben-deker, in Makaz . . . .

Solomon's provision for one day was thirty measures of fine flour, and sixty measures of meal, ten fat oxen, and twenty pasture-fed cattle, a hundred sheep, besides harts, gazelles, roebucks, and fatted fowl. For he had dominion over all the region west of the Euphrates from Tiphsah to Gaza, over all the kings west of the Euphrates; and he had peace on all sides round about him. And Judah and Israel dwelt in safety, from Dan even to Beer-sheba, every man under his vine and under his fig tree, all the days of Solomon. . . .

"THE HOUSE SOLOMON BUILT FOR THE LORD"

Now Hiram king of Tyre sent his servants to Solomon, when he heard that they had anointed him king in place of his father; for Hiram always loved David. And Solomon sent word to Hiram," You know that David my father could not build a house for the name of the Lord his God because of the warfare with which his enemies surrounded him, until the Lord put them under the soles of his feet. But now the Lord my God has given me rest on every side; there is neither adversary nor misfortune. And so I purpose to build a house for the name of the Lord my God, as the Lord said to David my father, 'Your son, whom I will set upon your throne in your place, shall build the house of my name.' Now therefore command that cedars of Lebanon be cut for me; and my servants will join your servants, and I will pay you for your services such wages as you set; for you know that there is no one among us who knows how to cut timber like the Sidonians."

When Hiram heard the words of Solomon, he rejoiced greatly, and said, "Blessed be the Lord this day, who has given to David a wise son to be over this great people." . . . So Hiram supplied Solomon with all the timber of cedar and cypress that he desired, while Solomon gave Hiram twenty thousand cors of wheat as food for his household, and twenty thousand cors of beaten oil. Solomon gave this to Hiram year by year. And the Lord gave Solomon wisdom, as he promised him; and there was peace between Hiram and Solomon; and the two of them made a treaty.

King Solomon raised a levy of forced labor out of all Israel; and the levy numbered thirty thousand men. And he sent them to Lebanon, ten thousand a month in relays; they would be a month in Lebanon and two months at home; Adoniram was in charge of the levy. Solomon also had seventy thousand burden-bearers and eighty thousand hewers of stone in the hill country, besides Solomon's three thousand three hundred chief officers who were over the work, who had charge of the people who carried on the work. At the king's command, they quarried out great, costly stones in order to lay the foundation of the house with dressed stones. So Solomon's builders and Hiram's builders and the men of Gebal did the hewing and prepared the timber and the stone to build the house.

In the four hundred and eightieth year after the people of Israel came out of the land of Egypt, in the fourth year of Solomon's reign over Israel, in the month of Ziv, which is the second month, he began to build the house of the Lord. The house which King Solomon built for the Lord was sixty cubits long, twenty cubits wide, and thirty cubits high. . . . He was seven years in building it. . . .

"SOLOMON EXCELLED ALL KINGS IN RICHES AND WISDOM"

King Solomon built a fleet of ships at Ezion-geber, which is near Eloth on the shore of the Red Sea, in the land of Edom. And Hiram sent with the fleet his servants, seamen who were familiar with the sea, together with the servants of Solomon; and they went to Ophir, and brought from there gold, to the amount of four hundred and twenty talents; and they brought it to King Solomon.

Now when the queen of Sheba heard of the fame of Solomon concerning the name of the Lord, she came to test him with hard questions. She came to Jerusalem with a very great retinue, with camels bearing spices, and very much gold, and precious stones; and when she came to Solomon, she told him all that was on her mind. And Solomon answered all her questions; there was nothing hidden from the king which he could not explain to her. And when the queen of Sheba had seen all the wisdom of Solomon, the house that he had built, the food of his table, the seating of his officials, and the attendance of his servants, their clothing, his cupbearers, and his burnt offerings which he offered at the house of the Lord, there was no more spirit in her.

And she said to the king, "The report was true which I heard in my own land of your affairs and of your wisdom, but I did not believe the reports until I came and my own eyes had seen it; and, behold, the half was not told me; your wisdom and prosperity surpass the report which I heard. Happy are your wives! Happy are these servants, who continually stand before you and hear your wisdom! Blessed be the Lord your God, who has delighted in you and set you on the throne of Israel! Because the Lord loved Israel for ever, he has made you king, that you may execute justice and righteousness." Then she gave the king a hundred and twenty talents of gold, and a very great quantity of spices, and precious stones; never again came such an abundance of spices as these which the queen of Sheba gave to King Solomon. . . .

And King Solomon gave to the queen of Sheba all that she desired, whatever she asked besides what was given her by the bounty of King Solomon. So she turned and went back to her own land, with her servants.

Now the weight of gold that came to Solomon in one year was six hundred and sixty-six talents of gold, besides that which came from the traders and from the traffic of the merchants, and from all the kings of Arabia and from the governors of the land. King Solomon made two hundred large shields of beaten gold; . . . The king also made a great ivory throne, and overlaid it with the finest gold. The throne had six steps, and at the back of the throne was a calf's head, and on each side of the seat were arm rests and two lions standing beside the arm rests, while twelve lions stood there, one on each end of a step on the six steps. The like of it was never made in any kingdom. All King Solomon's drinking vessels were of gold, and all the vessels of the House of the Forest of Lebanon were of pure gold; none were of silver, it was not considered as anything in the days of Solomon. For the king had a fleet of ships of Tarshish at sea with the fleet of Hiram. Once every three years the fleet of ships of Tarshish used to come bringing gold, silver, ivory, apes, and peacocks.

Thus King Solomon excelled all the kings of the earth in riches and in wisdom. And the whole earth sought the presence of Solomon to hear his wisdom, which God had put into his mind. Every one of them brought his present, articles of silver and gold, garments, myrrh, spices, horses, and mules, so much year by year.

And Solomon gathered together chariots and horsemen; he had fourteen hundred chariots and twelve thousand horsemen, whom he stationed in the chariot cities and with the king in Jerusalem. And the king made silver as common in Jerusalem as stone, and he made cedar as plentiful as the sycamore of the Shephelah. And Solomon's import of horses was from Egypt and Kue, and the king's traders received them from Kue at a price. A chariot could be imported from Egypt for six hundreds shekels of silver, and a horse for a hundred and fifty; and so through the king's traders they were exported to all the kings of the Hittites and the kings of Syria.

"SOLOMON DID WHAT WAS EVIL IN THE SIGHT OF THE LORD"

Now King Solomon loved many foreign women: the daughter of Pharaoh, and Moabite, Ammonite, Edomite, Sidonian, and Hittite women, from the nations concerning which the Lord had said to the people of Israel, "You shall not enter into marriage with them, neither shall they with you, for surely they will turn away your heart after their gods"; Solomon clung to these in love. He had seven hundred wives, princesses, and three hundred concubines; and his wives turned away his heart. For when Solomon was old his wives turned away his heart after other gods; and his heart was not wholly true to the Lord his God, as was the heart of David his father. For Solomon went after Ashtoreth the goddess of the Sidonians, and after Milcom the abomination of the Ammonites. So Solomon did what was evil in the sight of the Lord, and did not wholly follow the Lord, as David his father had done. Then Solomon built a high place for Chemosh the abomination of Moab, and for Molech the abomination of the Ammonites, on the mountain east of Jerusalem. And so he did for all his foreign wives, who burned incense and sacrificed to their gods.

And the Lord was angry with Solomon, because his heart had turned away from the Lord, the God of Israel, who had appeared to him twice, and had commanded him concerning this thing, that he should not go after other gods; but he did not keep what the Lord commanded. Therefore the Lord said to Solomon, "Since this has been your mind and you have not kept my covenant and my statutes which I have commanded you, I will surely tear the kingdom from you and will give it to your servant. Yet for the sake of David your father I will not do it in your days, but I will tear it out of the hand of your son. However I will not tear away all the kingdom; but I will give one tribe to your son, for the sake of David my servant and for the sake of Jerusalem which I have chosen."

◆H◆ JEREMIAH: PROPHET OF THE NEW COVENANT

Between roughly 750 and 550 B.C., what is called the "prophetic revolution" raised the religion of the Hebrews to new heights. The great prophets who arose during these two centuries "spoke for" (from the Greek word prophetes) Yahweh in condemning social injustice and the general unfaithfulness of the people of Israel and Judah to the covenant with Yahweh. "I am filled with power," proclaimed Micah, "with the Spirit of the Lord, and with justice and might, to declare to Jacob his transgression, and to Israel its sin" (3:8). Amos, the first of these "literary" prophets, was a peasant shepherd of Judah who travelled to the northern kingdom of Israel to denounce the greed, violence, luxury, and idolatry that flourished there and to predict, as a consequence, the destruction of that kingdom by Assyria, called by Isaiah "the rod of Yahweh's anger." Driven back to the south, Amos became the first of the prophets to write down his message of Yahweh's demand for social justice and adherence to his covenant. Amos' successors among the prophets of the eighth century, Hosea, Micah, and Isaiah, elaborated on the same message which Micah summed up in a statement often cited as the essence of all higher religion: "He has showed you, O man, what is good; and what does the Lord require of you but to do justice, and to love kindness, and to walk humbly with your God?" (6:8)

From Jeremiah 7–8, 18, 23, 31; the Revised Standard Version of the Bible, copyright 1946 and 1952. Reprinted by permission of the National Council of the Churches of Christ.

One of the greatest of the prophets — so great that later generations of Jews referred to him as The Prophet — was Jeremiah. His career (626–586 B.C.) coincided with the troubled era that ended with the Babylonian exile of the Jews. As illustrated by the following selections, Jeremiah's teachings in part echo those of the eighth-century prophets in condemning social injustice, "burnt offerings and sacrifices," and going "after other gods." Like Isaiah before him, Jeremiah affirms that Yahweh will save a "remnant" of his dispersed people and will raise up a king of the House of David to "execute justice and righteousness in the land." Such prophecies of the coming of a Messiah, "the Anointed One," were to sustain the hopes of the Jews for centuries and were also to prepare the way for Jesus.

But Jeremiah's most profound expression of hope is his preaching of a "new covenant" between God and his people. God destroys and overthrows, but he also builds anew; he is like the potter who reworks the clay of a spoiled vessel into something new and better. The old vessel was the covenant announced by Moses, which bound the nation as a whole. It failed because it became overlaid with ritual and ceremony formalized by priests and centered in the Temple. According to Jeremiah, God now demanded a new covenant not with the nation but with each individual. External conformity is useless; what is needed is a moral and spiritual renewal on the part of each individual. Religion is now a matter of a man's own heart and conscience. Such teachings brought Jeremiah into conflict with the priests: "How can you say, 'We are wise, and the law of the Lord is with us'? But, behold, the false pen of the scribes has made it into a lie." Ultimately, however, his teachings made it possible for non-Jews to accept Judaism since they placed no stress on nationality or race. We know that Jesus admired Jeremiah above all other prophets, and his Sermon on the Mount was a profound expression of the new concept that God's law is written upon the individual heart rather than upon tablets of stone.

"AMEND YOUR WAYS AND YOUR DOINGS"

The word that came to Jeremiah from the Lord: "Stand in the gate of the Lord's house, and proclaim there this word, and say, Hear the word of the Lord, all you men of Judah who enter these gates to worship the Lord. Thus says the Lord of hosts, the God of Israel, Amend your ways and your doings, and I will let you dwell in this place. Do not trust in these deceptive words: 'This is the temple of the Lord, the temple of the Lord, the temple of the Lord.'

"For if you truly amend your ways and your doings, if you truly execute justice one with another, if you do not oppress the alien, the fatherless or the widow, or shed innocent blood in this place, and if you do not go after other gods to your own hurt, then I will let you dwell in this place, in the land that I gave of old to your fathers for ever.

"Behold, you trust in deceptive words to no avail. Will you steal, murder, commit adultery, swear falsely, burn incense to Baal, and go after other gods that you have not known, and then come and stand before me in this house, which is called by my name, and say, 'We are delivered!' — only to go on doing all these abominations? Has this house, which is called by my name, become a den of robbers in your eyes? Behold, I myself have seen it, says the Lord. Go now to my place that was in Shiloh, where I made my name dwell at first, and see what I did to it for the wickedness of my people Israel. And now, because you have done all these things, says the Lord, and when I spoke to you persistently you did not listen, and when I called you, you did not answer, therefore I will do to the house which is called by my name, and in which you trust, and to the place which I gave to you and to your fathers, as I did to Shiloh. And I will cast you out of my sight, as I cast out all your kinsmen, all the offspring of Ephraim.

"As for you, do not pray for this people, or lift up cry or prayer for them, and do not intercede with me, for I do not hear you. Do you not see what they are doing in the cities of Judah and in the streets of Jerusalem? The children gather wood, the fathers kindle fire, and the women knead dough, to make cakes for the queen of heaven; and they pour out drink offerings to other gods, to provoke me to anger. Is it I whom they provoke? says the Lord. Is it not themselves, to their own confusion? Therefore thus says the Lord God: Behold, my anger and my wrath will be poured out on this place, upon man and beast, upon the trees of the field and the fruit of the ground; it will burn and not be quenched."

Thus says the Lord of hosts, the God of Israel: "Add your burnt offerings to your sacrifices, and eat the flesh. For in the days that I brought them out of the land of Egypt, I did not speak to your fathers or command them concerning burnt offerings and sacrifices. But this command I gave them, 'Obey my voice, and I will be your God, and you shall be my people; and walk in all the way that I command you, that it may be well with you.' But they did not obey or incline their ear, but walked in their own counsels and the stubbornness of their evil hearts, and went backward and not forward. From the day that your fathers came out of the land of Egypt to this day, I have persistently sent all my servants the prophets to them, day after day; yet they did not listen to me, or incline their ear, but stiffened their neck. They did worse than their fathers.

"So you shall speak all these words to them, but they will not listen to you. You shall call to them, but they will not answer you. And you shall say to them, 'This is the nation that did not obey the voice of the Lord their God, and did not accept discipline; truth has perished; it is cut off from their lips. . . .'

"You shall say to them, Thus says the Lord:
When men fall, do they not rise again?
    If one turns away, does he not return?
Why then has this people turned away
    in perpetual backsliding?
They hold fast to deceit,
    they refuse to return.

I have given heed and listened,
    but they have not spoken aright;
no man repents of his wickedness,
    saying, 'What have I done?'
Every one turns to his own course,
    like a horse plunging headlong into battle.
Even the stork in the heavens
    knows her times;
and the turtledove, swallow, and crane
    keep the time of their coming;
but my people know not
    the ordinance of the Lord.

"How can you say, 'We are wise,
    and the law of the Lord is with us'?
But, behold, the false pen of the scribes
    has made it into a lie.
The wise men shall be put to shame,
    they shall be dismayed and taken;
lo, they have rejected the word of the Lord,
    and what wisdom is in them?
Therefore I will give their wives to others
    and their fields to conquerors,
because from the least to the greatest
    every one is greedy for unjust gain;
from prophet to priest
    every one deals falsely. . . ."

"LIKE THE CLAY IN THE POTTER'S HAND"

The word that came to Jeremiah from the Lord: "Arise, and go down to the potter's house, and there I will let you hear my words." So I went down to the potter's house, and there he was working at his wheel. And the vessel he was making of clay was spoiled in the potter's hand, and he reworked it into another vessel, as it seemed good to the potter to do.

Then the word of the Lord came to me: "O house of Israel, can I not do with you as this potter has done? says the Lord. Behold, like the clay in the potter's hand, so are you in my hand, O house of Israel. If at any time I declare concerning a nation or a kingdom, that I will pluck up and break down and destroy it, and if that nation, concerning which I have spoken, turns from its evil, I will repent of the evil that I intended to do to it. And if at any time I declare concerning a nation or a kingdom that I will build and plant it, and if it does evil in my sight, not listening to my voice, then I will repent of the good which I had intended to do to it. Now, therefore, say to the men of Judah and the inhabitants of Jerusalem: 'Thus says the Lord, Behold I am shaping evil against you and devising a plan against you. Return, every one from his evil way, and amend your ways and your doings.'

"But they say, 'That is in vain! We will follow our own plans, and will every one act according to the stubbornness of his evil heart.' " . . .

"Woe to the shepherds who destroy and scatter the sheep of my pasture!" says the Lord. Therefore thus says the Lord, the God of Israel, concerning the shepherds who care for my people: "You have scattered my flock, and have driven them away, and you have not attended to them. Behold, I will attend to you for your evil doings, says the Lord. Then I will gather the remnant of my flock out of all the countries where I have driven them, and I will bring them back to their fold, and they shall be fruitful and multiply. I will set shepherds over them who will care for them, and they shall fear no more, nor be dismayed, neither shall any be missing, says the Lord.

"Behold, the days are coming, says the Lord, when I will raise up for David a righteous Branch, and he shall reign as king and deal wisely, and shall execute justice and righteousness in the land. In his days Judah will be saved, and Israel will dwell securely. And this is the name by which he will be called: 'The Lord is righteousness.'

"Therefore, behold, the days are coming, says the Lord, when men shall no longer say, 'As the Lord lives who brought up the people of Israel out of the land of Egypt,' but 'As the Lord lives who brought up and led the descendants of the house of Israel out of the north country and out of all the countries where he had driven them.' Then they shall dwell in their own land." . . .

"Behold, the days are coming, says the Lord, when I will sow the house of Israel and the house of Judah with the seed of man and the seed of beast. And it shall come to pass that as I have watched over them to pluck up and break down, to overthrow, destroy, and bring evil, so I will watch over them to build and to plant, says the Lord. In those days they shall no longer say:

> 'The fathers have eaten sour grapes,
> and the children's teeth are set on edge.'

But every one shall die for his own sin; each man who eats sour grapes, his teeth shall be set on edge.

"Behold, the days are coming, says the Lord, when I will make a new covenant with the house of Israel and the house of Judah, not like the covenant which I made with their fathers when I took them by the hand to bring them out of the land of Egypt, my covenant which they broke, though I was their husband, says the Lord. But this is the covenant which I will make with the house of Israel after those days, says the Lord: I will put my law within them, and I will write it upon their hearts; and I will be their God, and they shall be my people. And no longer shall each man teach his neighbor and each his brother, saying 'Know the Lord,' for they shall all know me, from the least of them to the greatest, says the Lord; for I will forgive their iniquity, and I will remember their sin no more."

◆ I ◆ SECOND ISAIAH: MONOTHEISM AND UNIVERSALISM

During the Exile there lived in Babylonia an unknown prophet, referred to by scholars as Second Isaiah, who published his prophecies (they begin with chapter 40 of the Book of Isaiah) soon after Cyrus the Persian captured Babylon in 539 B.C. and liberated the Judean exiles. He has been called "the greatest thinker . . . and perhaps the greatest poet the Hebrew genius ever produced." His purpose was to "sing unto the Lord a new song," proclaiming that Israel has been purified and enlightened by suffering and is now ready to guide the world to the worship of the one, eternal, and supreme God whose rule extends to "all the ends of the earth." These themes of a single God and His universal rule were implicit in the writings of earlier prophets, but in Second Isaiah they are expanded and deepened. The view of Israel as the suffering servant of Yahweh, "despised and rejected of men," who would lead the world to redemption in the true God, was interpreted by Christians as a prophecy of the role of Jesus.

"THERE IS NO OTHER GOD BESIDES ME"

Remember these things, O Jacob,
    and Israel, for you are my servant;
I formed you, you are my servant;
    O Israel, you will not be forgotten by me.
I have swept away your transgressions like a cloud,
    and your sins like a mist;
return to me, for I have redeemed you. . . .

Thus says the Lord, your Redeemer,
    who formed you from the womb:
"I am the Lord, who made all things,
    who stretched out the heavens alone,
    who spread out the earth — Who was with me? —
who frustrates the omens of liars,
    and makes fools of diviners;
who turns wise men back,
    and makes their knowledge foolish;
who confirms the word of his servant,
    and performs the counsel of his messengers;
who says of Jerusalem, 'She shall be inhabited,'
    and of the cities of Judah, 'They shall be built,
    and I will raise up their ruins';
who says to the deep, 'Be dry.

From Isaiah 44–45, 48–49, 53; the Revised Standard Version of the Bible, copyright 1946 and 1952. Reprinted by permission of the National Council of the Churches of Christ.

I will dry up your rivers';
who says of Cyrus, 'He is my shepherd,
    and he shall fulfill all my purpose';
saying of Jerusalem, "She shall be built,'
    and of the temple, 'Your foundation shall be laid.' "

Thus says the Lord to his anointed, to Cyrus,
    whose right hand I have grasped,
to subdue nations before him
    and ungird the loins of kings,
to open doors before him
    that gates may not be closed:
"I will go before you
    and level the mountains,
I will break in pieces the doors of bronze
    and cut asunder the bars of iron,
I will give you the treasures of darkness
    and the hoards in secret places,
that you may know that it is I, the Lord,
    the God of Israel, who call you by your name.
For the sake of my servant Jacob,
    and Israel my chosen,
I call you by your name,
    I surname you, though you do not know me.
I am the Lord, and there is no other,
    besides me there is no God;
    I gird you, though you do not know me,
that men may know, from the rising of the sun
    and from the west, that there is none besides me;
    I am the Lord and there is no other.
I form light and create darkness,
    I make weal and create woe,
    I am the Lord, who do all these things. . . .

"Woe to him who strives with his Maker,
    an earthen vessel with the potter!
Does the clay say to him who fashions it, 'What are you making'?
    or 'Your work has no handles'?
Woe to him who says to a father, 'What are you begetting?'
    or to a woman, 'With what are you in travail?' "
Thus says the Lord,
    the Holy One of Israel, and his Maker:
"Will you question me about my children,
    or command me concerning the work of my hands?
I made the earth,
    and created man upon it;

it was my hands that stretched out the heavens,
    and I commanded all their host.
I have aroused him in righteousness,
    and I will make straight all his ways;
he shall build my city
    and set my exiles free,
not for price or reward,"
    says the Lord of hosts. . . .

For thus says the Lord,
who created the heavens
    (he is God!),
who formed the earth and made it
    (he established it;
he did not create it a chaos,
    he formed it to be inhabited!) : . . .
"Assemble yourselves and come,
    draw near together,
    you survivors of the nations!
They have no knowledge
    who carry about their wooden idols,
and keep on praying to a god
    that cannot save.
Declare and present your case;
    let them take counsel together!
Who told this long ago?
    Who declared it of old?
Was it not I, the Lord?
    And there is no other god besides me,
a righteous God and a Savior;
    there is none besides me.

"Turn to me and be saved,
    all the ends of the earth!
    For I am God, and there is no other.
By myself I have sworn,
    from my mouth has gone forth in righteousness
    a word that shall not return:
'To me every knee shall bow,
    every tongue shall swear.' ". . .

"A LIGHT TO THE NATIONS"

Go forth from Babylon, flee from Chaldea,
    declare this with a shout of joy, proclaim it,
send it forth to the end of the earth;
    say, "The Lord has redeemed his servant Jacob!". . .

Listen to me, O coastlands,
    and hearken, you peoples from afar.
The Lord called me from the womb,
    from the body of my mother he named my name.
He made my mouth like a sharp sword,
    in the shadow of his hand he hid me;
he made me a polished arrow,
    in his quiver he hid me away.
And he said to me, "You are my servant,
    Israel, in whom I will be glorified."
But I said, "I have labored in vain,
    I have spent my strength for nothing and vanity;
yet surely my right is with the Lord,
    and my recompense with my God."

And now the Lord says,
    who formed me from the womb to be his servant,
to bring Jacob back to him,
    and that Israel might be gathered to him,
for I am honored in the eyes of the Lord,
    and my God has become my strength —
he says:
"It is too light a thing that you should be my servant
    to raise up the tribes of Jacob
    and to restore the preserved of Israel;
I will give you as a light to the nations,
    that my salvation may reach to the end of the earth." . . .

THE SUFFERING SERVANT

Who has believed what we have heard?
    And to whom has the arm of the Lord been revealed?
For he grew up before him like a young plant,
    and like a root out of dry ground;
he had no form or comeliness that we should look at him,
    and no beauty that we should desire him.
He was despised and rejected by men;
    a man of sorrows, and acquainted with grief;
and as one from whom men hide their faces
    he was despised and we esteemed him not.

Surely he has borne our griefs
    and carried our sorrows;
yet we esteemed him stricken,
    smitten by God, and afflicted.
But he was wounded for our transgressions,
    he was bruised for our iniquities;

upon him was the chastisement that made us whole,
>   and with his stripes we are healed.
All we like sheep have gone astray;
>   we have turned every one to his own way;
and the Lord has laid on him
>   the iniquity of us all.

He was oppressed, and he was afflicted,
>   yet he opened not his mouth;
like a lamb that is led to the slaughter,
>   and like a sheep that before its shearers is dumb,
>   so he opened not his mouth.
By oppression and judgment he was taken away;
>   and as for his generation, who considered
that he was cut off out of the land of the living,
>   stricken for the transgression of my people?
And they made his grave with the wicked
>   and with a rich man in his death,
although he had done no violence,
>   and there was no deceit in his mouth.

Yet it was the will of the Lord to bruise him;
>   he has put him to grief; . . .
>   he shall see the fruit of the travail of his soul and be satisfied;
by his knowledge shall the righteous one, my servant,
>   make many to be accounted righteous;
>   and he shall bear their iniquities.
Therefore I will divide him a portion with the great,
>   and he shall divide the spoil with the strong;
because he poured out his soul to death,
>   and was numbered with the transgressors;
yet he bore the sin of many,
>   and made intercession for the transgressors.

◆ J ◆ JOB: A PERPLEXED SUFFERER

The Book of Job, whose author is thought by some scholars to have lived in the sixth century B.C., has much in common with its Babylonian counterpart, the "Poem of the Righteous Sufferer." Both question a divine governance of the world that produces unmerited suffering, and both resolve their questions in favor of orthodoxy. But the Hebrew story is the product of a higher level of religious belief, and its vastly superior literary form has made it one of the world's

From Job 3, 10, 14, 23, 24, 38, 40, 42; the King James Version of the Bible.

great classics. Its conclusion is also more profound than the Babylonian; it contains the same message found in Second Isaiah, that suffering need not be the result of sin, but can be a part of God's purpose to test and enlighten man.

"LET THE DAY PERISH WHEREIN I WAS BORN"

Let the day perish wherein I was born, and the night in which it was said, There is a man child conceived. Let that day be darkness; let not God regard it from above, neither let the light shine upon it. . . .

Why died I not from the womb? why did I not give up the ghost when I came out of the belly? . . . For now should I have lain still and been quiet, I should have slept; then had I been at rest; There the wicked cease from troubling; and there the weary be at rest. . . .

Wherefore is light given to him that is in misery, and life unto the bitter in soul; Which long for death, but it cometh not; and dig for it more than for hid treasures; Which rejoice exceedingly, and are glad, when they can find the grave? Why is light given to a man whose way is hid, and whom God hath hedged in? . . .

"I AM FULL OF CONFUSION"

My soul is weary of my life; I will leave my complaint upon myself; I will speak in the bitterness of my soul. . . .

If I be wicked, woe unto me; and if I be righteous, yet will I not lift up my head. I am full of confusion; therefore see thou mine affliction; For it increaseth. Thou huntest me as a fierce lion: and again thou showest thyself marvelous upon me. . . .

Are not my days few? cease then, and let me alone, that I may take comfort a little, Before I go whence I shall not return, even to the land of darkness and the shadow of death, without any order, and where the light is darkness. . . .

Man that is born of a woman is of few days, and full of trouble. He cometh forth like a flower, and is cut down: he fleeth also as a shadow, and continueth not. . . .

For there is hope of a tree, if it be cut down, that it will sprout again, and that the tender branch thereof will not cease. . . . But man dieth, and wasteth away: yea, man giveth up the ghost, and where is he? As the waters fail from the sea, and the flood decayeth and drieth up; So man lieth down, and riseth not: till the heavens be no more, they shall not awake, nor be raised out of their sleep.

If a man die, shall he live again? all the days of my appointed time will I wait, till my change come. . . . The waters wear the stones: thou washest away the things which grow out of the dust of the earth; and thou destroyest the hope of man.

"OH THAT I KNEW WHERE I MIGHT FIND HIM!"

Even today is my complaint bitter: my stroke is heavier than my groaning. Oh that I knew where I might find him! that I might come even to his seat! I would order my cause before him, and fill my mouth with my arguments. . . .

Behold, I go forward, but he is not there; and backward, but I cannot perceive him: On the left hand, where he doth work, but I cannot behold him: he hideth on the right hand, that I cannot see him. . . .

Why, seeing times are not hidden from the Almighty, do they that know him not see his days? Some remove the landmarks; they violently take away flocks, and feed thereof. They drive away the ass of the fatherless, they take the widow's ox for a pledge. They turn the needy out of the way: the poor of the earth hide themselves together. . . .

Men groan from out of the city, and the soul of the wounded crieth out: yet God layeth not folly to them. They are of those that rebel against the light; they know not the ways thereof, nor abide in the paths thereof. . . . And if it be not so now, who will make me a liar, and make my speech nothing worth? . . .

"THE LORD ANSWERED JOB"

Then the Lord answered Job out of the whirlwind, and said, Who is this that darkeneth counsel by words without knowledge? Gird up now thy loins like a man; for I will demand of thee, and answer thou me.

Where wast thou when I laid the foundations of the earth? declare, if thou hast understanding. Who hath laid the measures thereof, if thou knowest? or who hath stretched the line upon it? Whereupon are the foundations thereof fastened? or who laid the corner stone thereof; when the morning stars sang together, and all the sons of God shouted for joy? . . .

Hast thou entered into the springs of the sea? or hast thou walked in the search of the depth? Have the gates of death been opened unto thee? or hast thou seen the doors of the shadow of death? Hast thou perceived the breadth of the earth? declare if thou knowest it all. . . .

Shall he that contendeth with the Almighty instruct him? he that reproveth God, let him answer it. . . .

"JOB ANSWERED THE LORD AND SAID, I REPENT"

Then Job answered the Lord, and said, I know thou canst do every thing, and that no thought can be hidden from thee. Who is he that hideth counsel without knowledge? therefore have I uttered that I understood not; things too wonderful for me, which I knew not. . . . I have heard of thee by the hearing of the ear; but now mine eye seeth thee; Wherefore I abhor myself, and repent in dust and ashes. . . .

So the Lord blessed the latter end of Job more than his beginning: for he had fourteen thousand sheep, and six thousand camels, and a thousand yoke of oxen, and a thousand she asses. He had also seven sons and three daughters. . . . And in all the land were no women found so fair as the daughters of Job: and their father gave them inheritance among their brethren. After this lived Job a hundred and forty years, and saw his sons, and his sons' sons, even four generations. So Job died, being old and full of days.

◆ K ◆ THE SONG OF SONGS

Poetry of love

The Song of Songs, also called the Song of Solomon, is regarded by many as a lyric dialogue on the subject of love between a maiden and a youth. This view was first expressed in the third century A.D. by the great Christian scholar Origen, who called it a "nuptial poem composed in dramatic form." The Hebrew compilers of the Old Testament, however, viewed it as an allegory of the love of Israel for God, and Christians have continued this allegorical interpretation, changing it to the mutual love of Christ and His Church.

THE MAIDEN

Let him kiss me with the kisses of his mouth:
    for thy love is better than wine.
Because of the savor of thy good ointments
    thy name is as ointment poured forth,
    therefore do the virgins love thee.
Draw me, we will run after thee: . . .

I am black, but comely, O ye daughters of Jerusalem,
    as the tents of Kedar,
    as the curtains of Solomon.
Look not upon me, because I am black,
    because the sun hath looked upon me:
my mother's children were angry with me;
they made me the keeper of the vineyards;
    but mine own vineyard have I not kept. . . .

A bundle of myrrh is my well-beloved unto me;
he shall lie all night betwixt my breasts.

THE YOUTH

Behold, thou art fair, my love;
    behold, thou art fair;
    thou hast doves' eyes.

THE MAIDEN

Behold, thou art fair, my beloved,
    yea, pleasant; also our bed is green.
The beams of our house are cedar,
    and our rafters of fir.

From The Song of Solomon 1–5; the King James Version of the Bible.

I am the rose of Sharon,
and the lily of the valleys.

THE YOUTH

As the lily among thorns,
So is my love among the daughters.

THE MAIDEN

As the apple tree among the trees of the wood,
so is my beloved among the sons.
I sat down under his shadow with great delight,
and his fruit was sweet to my taste.
He brought me to the banqueting house,
and his banner over me was love.
Stay me with flagons,
comfort me with apples:
for I am sick of love.
His left hand is under my head,
and his right hand doth embrace me.
I charge you, O ye daughters of Jerusalem,
by the roes, and by the hinds of the field,
that ye stir not up, nor awake my love, till he please.

The voice of my beloved!
behold, he cometh leaping upon the mountains,
skipping upon the hills.
My beloved is like a roe or a young hart:
behold, he standeth behind our wall,
he looketh forth at the windows,
showing himself through the lattice.
My beloved spake, and said unto me,
Rise up, my love, my fair one,
and come away.
For, lo, the winter is past,
the rain is over and gone;
The flowers appear on the earth;
the time of the singing of birds is come,
and the voice of the turtle is heard in our land:
The fig tree putteth forth her green figs,
and the vines with the tender grape give a good smell.
Arise, my love, my fair one,
and come away.
. . . let me see thy countenance,
for sweet is thy voice,
and thy countenance is comely.

Take us the foxes,
 the little foxes, that spoil the vines:
 for our vines have tender grapes. . . .

By night on my bed I sought him whom my soul loveth:
 I sought him, but I found him not. . . .

THE YOUTH

Behold, thou art fair, my love;
 behold, thou art fair;
thou hast doves' eyes within thy locks:
 thy hair is as a flock of goats, that appear from mount Gilead.
Thy teeth are like a flock of sheep that are even shorn,
 which came up from the washing;
 whereof every one bears twins, and none is barren among them.
Thy lips are like a thread of scarlet,
 and thy speech is comely:
thy temples are like a piece of a pomegranate within thy locks.
Thy neck is like the tower of David builded for an armory,
 whereon there hang a thousand bucklers,
 all shields of mighty men.
Thy two breasts are like two young roes that are twins,
 which feed among the lilies.
Until the day break, and the shadows flee away,
I will get me to the mountain of myrrh,
 and to the hill of frankincense.
Thou art all fair, my love;
 there is no spot in thee. . . .

THE MAIDEN

I sleep, but my heart waketh:
it is the voice of my beloved that knocketh, saying,
 Open to me, my sister, my love, my dove, my undefiled:
 for my head is filled with dew,
 and my locks with the drops of the night.
My beloved put in his hand by the hole of the door,
 and my bowels were moved for him.
I rose up to open to my beloved;
 and my hands dropped with myrrh,
 and my fingers with sweet smelling myrrh,
 upon the handles of the lock.
I opened to my beloved;
 but my beloved had withdrawn himself, and was gone:
 my soul failed when he spake:
 I sought him, but could not find him;
 I called him, but he gave me no answer.

The watchmen that went about the city found me.
   they smote me,
   they wounded me;
   the keepers of the walls took away my veil from me.

I charge you, O ye daughters of Jerusalem,
   if you find my beloved, that ye tell him,
   that I am sick of love.

◆L◆ ECCLESIASTES: THE MEDITATIONS OF A SKEPTIC

Isolated but monumental among the several examples of wisdom literature in the Old Testament is Ecclesiastes (Greek for the Hebrew Koheleth, the "preacher"), written perhaps between 250 and 200 B.C. It is thought by many to reflect the influence of Greek thought upon educated Jews during the Hellenistic Age following Alexander's conquests. The insistence that "all the works that are done . . . [are] vanity and a striving after wind," that the world is ruled by chance, and that pleasure is mankind's highest good, is in harmony with Epicurean philosophy (see Selection 46). Yet there are also ample grounds for viewing Ecclesiastes as a product of Hebrew thought and maintaining that "his type of mind and his methods are intimately a part of the questioning mood that had been at home in Israel for many centuries." The skepticism of Ecclesiastes goes much deeper than that of Job, and we know that many rabbis questioned whether it and the Song of Songs should be included in the Old Testament. But the tradition that Ecclesiastes was written by Solomon, together with its short orthodox conclusion, resulted in its being included in the Old Testament canon. The conclusion reiterates the fundamental tenet of Judaism, "Fear God, and keep his commandments," and it cautions the reader not to take the work seriously, for "of making many books there is no end, and much study is a weariness of the flesh."

"ALL IS VANITY"

Vanity of vanities, saith the Preacher,
   vanity of vanities; all is vanity.
What profit hath a man of all his labor
   which he taketh under the sun?
One generation passeth away, and another generation cometh:
   but the earth abideth for ever.
The sun also ariseth, and the sun goeth down,
   and hasteth to his place where he arose.

From Ecclesiastes 1, 3, 8–9, 12; the King James Version of the Bible.

The wind goeth toward the south
    and turneth about unto the north:
it whirleth about continually,
    and the wind returneth again according to his circuits.
All the rivers run into the sea; yet the sea is not full:
    unto the place from whence the rivers come, thither they return
        again.

All things are full of labor;
    man cannot utter it:
the eye is not satisfied with seeing,
    nor the ear filled with hearing.

The thing that hath been, it is that which shall be;
    and that which is done is that which shall be done:
    and there is no new thing under the sun.
Is there any thing whereof it may be said, See, this is new?
    it hath been already of old time, which was before us. . . .

That which is crooked cannot be made straight:
    and that which is wanting cannot be numbered. . . .
And I gave my heart to know wisdom, and to know madness and folly:
    I perceived that this also is vexation of spirit.
For in much wisdom is much grief:
    and he that increaseth knowledge increaseth sorrow. . . .

THE TRANSIENCE OF LIFE

To every thing there is a season, and a time to every purpose under the
heaven:

            A time to be born,
                and a time to die;
            a time to plant,
                and a time to pluck up that which is planted;

            A time to kill,
                and a time to heal;
            a time to break down,
                and a time to build up;

            A time to weep,
                and a time to laugh;
            a time to mourn,
                and a time to dance;

A time to cast away stones,
     and a time to gather stones together;
a time to embrace,
     and a time to refrain from embracing;

A time to get,
     and a time to lose;
a time to keep,
     and a time to cast away;

A time to rend,
     and a time to sew;
a time to keep silence,
     and a time to speak;

A time to love,
     and a time to hate;
a time of war,
     and a time of peace. . . .

"MAN HATH NO PREEMINENCE ABOVE A BEAST"

What profit hath he that worketh in that wherein he laboreth? I have seen the travail, which God hath given to the sons of men to be exercised in it. . . . For that which befalleth the sons of men befalleth beasts; even one thing befalleth them: as the one dieth, so dieth the other; yea, they have all one breath; so that a man hath no preeminence above a beast: for all is vanity. All go unto one place; all are of the dust, and all turn to dust again. Who knoweth the spirit of man that goeth upward, and the spirit of the beast that goeth downward to the earth? Wherefore I perceive that there is nothing better, than that a man should rejoice in his own works; for that is his portion: for who shall bring him to see what shall be after him? . . .

"NO BETTER THAN TO EAT, DRINK, AND BE MERRY"

Then I commended mirth, because a man hath no better thing under the sun, than to eat, and to drink, and to be merry: for that shall abide with him of his labor the days of his life, which God giveth him under the sun. . . .

For to him that is joined to all the living there is hope: for a living dog is better than a dead lion. For the living know that they shall die: but the dead know not any thing, neither have they any more a reward; for the memory of them is forgotten. . . .

Go thy way, eat thy bread with joy, and drink thy wine with a merry heart; for God now accepteth thy works. Let thy garments be always white; and let thy head lack no ointment. Live joyfully with the wife whom thou lovest all the days of the life of thy vanity, which he hath given thee under the sun, all the days of thy vanity: for that is thy portion in this life, and in thy labor which thou takest under the sun. Whatsoever thy hand findeth to do, do it with thy might; for there is no work, nor device, nor knowledge, nor wisdom, in the grave, whither thou goest.

I returned, and saw under the sun, that the race is not to the swift, nor the battle to the strong, neither yet bread to the wise, nor yet riches to men of understanding, nor yet favor to men of skill; but time and chance happeneth to them all. For man also knoweth not his time: as the fishes that are taken in an evil net, and as the birds that are caught in the snare; so are the sons of men snared in an evil time, when it falleth suddenly upon them. . . .

"THE CONCLUSION OF THE WHOLE MATTER"

And moreover, because the Preacher was wise, he still taught the people knowledge; yea, he gave good heed, and sought out, and set in order many proverbs. The Preacher sought to find out acceptable words: and that which was written was upright, even words of truth. . . .

And further, by these, my son, be admonished: of making many books there is no end; and much study is a weariness of the flesh.

Let us hear the conclusion of the whole matter: Fear God, and keep his commandments: for this is the whole duty of man. For God shall bring every work into judgment, and every secret thing, whether it be good, or whether it be evil.

◆ M ◆ THE WISDOM OF SOLOMON

Resurrection of the dead

The Apocrypha (Greek for "obscure") is a collection of Jewish writings produced after the Babylonian Exile at the end of the sixth century B.C. that are not considered inspired and therefore authoritative. While Protestants have followed the Jewish view, the Roman Catholic Church, since 1546 A.D., has declared them canonical, that is, inspired and authoritative. They are particularly valuable in illustrating the development of Jewish religious beliefs during the three or four centuries before the birth of Jesus. Extreme oppression under Seleucid rulers during the second century B.C. intensified the growth of a new type of literature known as apocalyptic (Greek for "revelation") in which the hopes of the faithful were fortified by visions of a glorious future encompassing such beliefs as a divine Messianic kingdom, a last judgment, and the resurrection of the dead. The books of Daniel in the Old Testament and Revelation in the New Testament are filled with such predictions. A well-known example from the Book of Daniel states that "there shall be a time of trouble, such as never was since there was a nation even to that same time: and at that time thy people shall be delivered, every one that shall be found written in the book. And many of them that sleep in the dust of the earth shall awake, some to everlasting life, and some to shame and everlasting contempt" (12:1–2).

Abridged from The Wisdom of Solomon 2–3, 5; the King James Version of the Bible.

The Wisdom of Solomon, written in Greek probably during the last half of the first century B.C., is a book of the Apocrypha that teaches the resurrection of the dead. This concept contrasts with the negative view of the afterlife found generally in the Old Testament and mentioned in the above selections from Job and Ecclesiastes. In addition to elaborating on the view quoted above from the Book of Daniel, the Wisdom of Solomon is thought to reflect Platonic dualism of body and soul when it states (9:15) that "the corruptible body presseth down the soul, and the earthly tabernacle weigheth down the mind that museth upon many things." (Compare Plato's views in Selection 29B.)

"THE UNGODLY SAID"

For the ungodly said, reasoning with themselves, but not aright, Our life is short and tedious, and in the death of a man there is no remedy: neither was there any man known to have returned from the grave. For we are born at all adventure: and we shall be hereafter as though we have never been: for the breath in our nostrils is as smoke, and a little spark in the moving of our heart: Which being extinguished, our body shall be turned into ashes, and our spirit shall vanish as the soft air, For our time is a very shadow that passeth away; and after our end there is no returning: for it is fast sealed, so that no man cometh again.

Come on therefore, let us enjoy the good things that are present: and let us speedily use the creatures like as in youth. Let us fill ourselves with costly wine and ointments: and let no flower of the spring pass by us: Let us crown ourselves with rosebuds, before they be withered: Let none of us go without his part of our voluptuousness: let us leave tokens of our joyfulness in every place: for this is our portion, and our lot is this.

Let us oppress the poor righteous man, let us not spare the widow, nor reverence the ancient gray hairs of the aged.

Therefore let us lie in wait for the righteous; because he is not for our turn, and he is clean contrary to our doings: he upbraideth us with our offending the law, and objecteth to our infamy the transgressings of our education. He professeth to have the knowledge of God: and he calleth himself the child of the Lord. He was made to reprove our thoughts. He is grievous unto us even to behold: for his life is not like other men's, his ways are of another fashion. We are esteemed of him as counterfeits: he abstaineth from our ways as from filthiness: he pronounceth the end of the just to be blessed, and maketh his boast that God is his father.

Let us see if his words be true: and let us prove what shall happen in the end to him. For if the just man be the son of God, he will help him, and deliver him from the hand of his enemies. Let us examine him with despitefulness and torture, that we may know his meekness, and prove his patience.

"GOD CREATED MAN TO BE IMMORTAL"

Such things they did imagine, and were deceived: for their own wickedness hath blinded them. As for the mysteries of God, they knew them not: neither hoped they for the wages of righteousness, nor discerned a reward for blameless souls.

For God created man to be immortal, and made him to be an image of his own eternity. Nevertheless through envy of the devil came death into the world: and they that do hold of his side do find it.

But the souls of the righteous are in the hand of God, and there shall no torment touch them. In the sight of the unwise they seemed to die: and their departure is taken for misery. And their going from us to be utter destruction: but they are in peace. For though they be punished in the sight of men, yet is their hope full of immortality. And having been a little chastised, they shall be greatly rewarded: for God proved them, and found them worthy for himself. As gold in the furnace hath he tried them, and received them as a burnt offering.

They that put their trust in him shall understand the truth: and such as be faithful in love shall abide with him: for grace and mercy is to his saints, and he hath care for his elect. But the ungodly shall be punished according to their own imaginations, which have neglected the righteous, and forsaken the Lord.

For the hope of the ungodly is like dust that is blown away with the wind; like as the smoke which is dispersed here and there with a tempest, and passeth away as the remembrance of a guest that tarrieth but a day. But the righteous live for evermore.

Let us remember that we should not
disregard the experience of ages.

— ARISTOTLE (see p. 238)

Greek Civilization

109

"Woman Playing the Flute" — in the Louvre.
Photo courtesy of Alinari.

King of Lydia, as God has given the Greeks
a moderate proportion of other things,
so likewise has He favored them with
a democratic spirit and a liberal kind of wisdom.

— PLUTARCH, *Solon*

The statement quoted above was addressed by Solon, a sixth-century B.C. Athenian statesman, to Croesus, the oriental despot who ruled over Lydia in Asia Minor. It well illustrates the contrast in character and achievement which distinguishes the civilization of the Greeks from those of the ancient Near East. No longer among the Greeks is thought dominated by an all-powerful priesthood and inextricably tied to religion, nor is individualism continually suppressed by despotism and collectivism. The Greeks achieved a freedom of thought and action — the "democratic spirit and a liberal kind of wisdom" of Plutarch's quotation — which was never achieved and never understood in the ancient Orient. We can, therefore, easily understand the bewilderment of Croesus as he listened to the words of his Greek guest, and Plutarch adds that Solon "was dismissed, having given Croesus some pain, but no instruction."

It would be a mistake to think that the Greek view and practice of life was an expression of qualities uniquely inherent in the Greek people or that it was a continuous and permanent possession. Such generalizations lead to the dilemma faced by one modern scholar who, having described Homer as a typical manifestation of the Greek genius, was forced to conclude that Plato was, unfortunately, non-Greek. Both Homer and Plato appear as "typical" Greeks when each is seen as the product of a different period in the long course of Hellenic development. Hellenic civilization underwent change through time, until the conquests of Alexander the Great produced a fusion of Greek and oriental elements which so changed its character that thereafter it is called "Hellenistic."

During the Hellenic period of their history, from about 1200 B.C. to the Macedonian conquest of Greece in 338 B.C., the Greeks developed many ideas and institutions which were new to the ancient world. These achievements can perhaps best be explained as the varied and rich response of a gifted people to a more complex and changing historical environment than had existed in the ancient Near East. Though largely new, the Greek experience was not to be entirely unique, for we can find much of it duplicated in the course of our own Western civilization. As many historians — notably Arnold Toynbee — have pointed out, the Greeks went over much of the same ground before us. For this reason some historians find it both possible and significant to divide Hellenic history into the same three phases that distinguish our Western civilization — medieval, renaissance, and modern.

The Greek Middle Ages began around 1200 B.C. with the mass migration into Greece of the uncultured Dorian Greeks, whose presence engulfed the Mycenaean and Minoan centers of Aegean civilization — Greece's "ancient history"— and ushered in some four centuries of decline. The ideas and institutions of this age, which have much in common with those found in our own early Middle Ages, are described in the epics of Homer, who lived toward the end of the period. About 750 B.C. a revival began during which all aspects of the civilization took on new forms and produced what can be called the Greek Renaissance. Starting with an economic revival that brought a renewal of city life and the expansion of the Greek world through colonization, it went on to produce revolutionary changes in society, culture, and religion which correspond to those which characterize our own Renaissance and Reformation.

By the middle of the fifth century B.C., the ideas and institutions of the Hellenic world had developed to the point where we can find much in them that is distinctly modern. In the economic area, the increasing "industrialization" of the Greek city-states made "international" trade imperative for prosperity, but that trade was handicapped by the "national" rivalries of the city-states, which led to frequent wars, economic depression, and class struggle. The resulting loss of economic and political stability was accompanied by a paralyzing cultural ferment, all of which led Aristophanes, acutely aware at the end of the fifth century of the crisis of his civilization, to declare that "Chaos is king, having overthrown Zeus." The decline went on far into the fourth century B.C., until the continued failure of the Greeks to solve their "modern" problems culminated in their subjection to the Macedonian despots, Philip and Alexander. Greeks of a later age, looking back upon the events of their civilization's decline, found the cause to lie primarily in their own shortcomings, as is indicated by a saying quoted by Plutarch:

> Greece to herself doth a barbaran grow,
> Others could not, she doth herself o'erthrow.

17

Homer, The Iliad

The Greek heroic age

In addition to its well-deserved fame as one of the great classics of world literature, the Iliad is an historical document of great significance for an understanding of the earliest period of Hellenic civilization (Hellenic civilization was preceded by what is now called the "first Greek cvilization" — the Mycenaean age
which reached its apex on the Greek mainland between 1400 and 1200 B.C.
after the first wave of Greek immigrants, the Achaeans, had assumed leadership
of the advanced Aegean civilization whose center had been the island of Crete.)
In his account of the siege of Troy, Homer deals with an actual historical event
that occurred during the period of Achaean Greek expansion into Asia Minor
near the close of the Mycenaean age. Although he lived some four hundred
years later, Homer knew of this event through the many folk songs and tales
which celebrated the deeds of the Achaean heroes of these early migrations,
but in collecting and molding these stories about a central theme, he embellished them with detailed descriptions of ideas and institutions which were
essentially those of his own day. Here, as always, great literature reflects contemporary life.

Homer's account of the values of life, the religious beliefs and practices,
and the political, economic, and social institutions of his day — probably
around 800 B.C. — are those of a typical heroic age. The ideals for which men
strive are the products of heroic valor; men seek the prize of imperishable fame
through hardship, struggle, and even death. The denial of honor due to a preeminent warrior is the greatest of human tragedies, and the wrath of Achilles —
the theme of the Iliad — is the result of such a denial. The gods possess all the
traits of humans, with Zeus asserting his superiority through threats of violence
when he is not the undignified victim of the plots of his wife and the other
deities. Gods mingle freely with mortals and aid their favorites, who have pro-
pitiated them with sacrifices and with prayers that are usually childishly selfish
petitions for some material reward. Hades, the abode of the dead, is a subterranean land of dust and darkness, and Achilles, as Homer tells us in the Odyssey, would rather be the slave of the lowest man on earth than be king in
Hades. Society is clearly aristocratic, and the common man puts in an appearance only to be reviled and beaten when he dares to question his betters. Yet
the common man has certain political rights as a member of the popular assembly that is summoned whenever a crisis arises, such as war, which requires his
participation. Two other institutions of government described by Homer are

From Bks. I, II, VI, XII, XVIII, XXII, based on the translation by Samuel Butler.

the king and his council. The king is hardly more than a chief among his peers, his fellow nobles who sit in the council to advise him and to check his every attempt to exercise arbitrary power. Economic conditions are those of a simple and self-sufficient agricultural economy with group rather than private ownership of land.

Agamemnon, ruler of Mycenae and leader of the Achaean host, is compelled to restore the captive Chryseis to her father, but in retaliation takes from Achilles the lovely Briseis. Achilles, enraged, vows he will fight no more for Agamemnon and through his mother, the sea nymph Thetis, secures the aid of Zeus for the Trojans. This provokes the wrath of the goddess Hera.

Sing, O goddess, the anger of Achilles, son of Peleus, that brought countless ills upon the Achaeans. Many a brave soul did it send hurrying down to Hades, and many a hero did it yield a prey to dogs and vultures, for so were the counsels of Zeus fulfilled from the day on which the son of Atreus, king of men, and great Achilles first fell out with one another.

And which of the gods was it that set them on to quarrel? It was the son of Zeus and Leto; for he was angry with the king and sent a pestilence upon the host to plague the people, because the son of Atreus had dishonored Chryses, his priest. Now Chryses had come to the ships of the Achaeans to free his daughter and had brought with him a great ransom. Moreover, he bore in his hand the sceptor of Apollo wreathed with a suppliant's wreath, and he besought the Achaeans, but most of all, the two sons of Atreus, who were their chiefs.

"Sons of Atreus," he cried, "and all other Achaeans, may the gods who dwell in Olympus grant you to sack the city of Priam and to reach your homes in safety; but free my daughter and accept a ransom for her in reverence to Apollo, son of Zeus."

On this the rest of the Achaeans with one voice were for respecting the priest and taking the ransom that he offered; but not so Agamemnon, who spoke fiercely to him and sent him roughly away. "Old man," said he, "let me not find you tarrying about our ships, nor yet coming hereafter. Your scepter of the god and your wreath shall profit you nothing. I will not free her. She shall grow old in my house at Argos far from her own home, busying herself with her loom and visiting my couch. So go, and do not provoke me or it shall be the worse for you."

The old man feared him and obeyed. Not a word he spoke, but went by the shore of the sounding sea and prayed apart to King Apollo whom lovely Leto had borne. "Hear me," he cried, "O god of the silver bow, that protectest Chryses and holy Cilla and rulest Tenedos with thy might, hear me, O thou of Sminthe! If I have ever decked your temple with garlands or burned you thighbones in fat of bulls or goats, grant my prayer and let your arrows avenge these my tears upon the Danaans."

Thus did he pray, and Apollo heard his prayer. He came down furious from the summits of Olympus, with his bow and his quiver upon his shoulder, and the arrows rattled on his back with the rage that trembled within him. He sat himself down away from the ships with a face as dark as night, and his silver bow rang death as he shot his arrow in the midst of them. First he smote their mules and their hounds, but presently he aimed his shafts at the people themselves, and all day long the pyres of the dead were burning.

For nine whole days he shot his arrows among the people, but upon the tenth day Achilles called them in assembly — moved thereto by Hera, who saw the Achaeans in their death throes and had compassion upon them. Then, when they were got together, he rose and spoke among them.

"Son of Atreus," said he, "I deem that we should now turn roving home if we would escape destruction, for we are being cut down by war and pestilence at once. Let us ask some priest or prophet, or some reader of dreams (for dreams, too, are of Zeus) who can tell us why Phoebus Apollo is so angry, and say whether it is for some vow that we have broken, or hecatomb that we have not offered, and whether he will accept the savor of lambs and goats without blemish, so as to take away the plague from us."

With these words he sat down, and Calchas, son of Thestor, wisest of augurs, who knew things past present and to come, rose to speak. He it was who had guided the Achaeans with their fleet to Ilium, through the prophesyings with which Phoebus Apollo had inspired him. With all sincerity and good will he addressed them thus: . . .

"The god," he said, "is angry neither about vow nor hecatomb, but for his priest's sake, whom Agamemnon had dishonored, in that he would not free his daughter nor take a ransom for her. Therefore has he sent these evils upon us and will yet send others. He will not deliver the Danaans from this pestilence till Agamemnon has restored the girl without fee or ransom to her father and has sent a holy hecatomb to Chryses. Thus we may perhaps appease him."

With these words he sat down, and Agamemnon rose in anger. His heart was black with rage, and his eyes flashed fire as he scowled on Calchas and said: "Seer of evil, you never yet prophesied smooth things concerning me, but have ever loved to foretell that which was evil. You have brought me neither comfort nor performance; and now you come seeking among the Danaans, and saying that Apollo has plagued us because I would not take a ransom for this girl, the daughter of Chryses. I have set my heart on keeping her in my own house, for I love her better even than my own wife, Clytemnestra, whose peer she is alike in form and feature, in understanding and accomplishments. Still I will give her up if I must, for I would have the people live, not die; but you must find me a prize instead, or I alone among the Argives shall be without one. This is not well; for you behold, all of you, that my prize is to go elsewhither."

And Achilles answered: "Most noble son of Atreus, covetous beyond all mankind, how shall the Achaeans find you another prize? We have no common store from which to take one. Those we took from the cities have been awarded; we cannot disallow the awards that have been made already. Give this girl, therefore, to the god, and if ever Zeus grants us to sack the city of Troy we will requite you three and fourfold."

Then Agamemnon said: "Achilles, valiant though you be, you shall not thus outwit me. You shall not overreach and you shall not persuade me. Are you to keep your own prize, while I sit tamely under my loss and give up the girl at your bidding? Let the Achaeans find me a prize in fair exchange to my liking, or I will come and take your own, or that of Ajax or of Odysseus; and he to whomsoever I may come shall rue my coming. But of this we will take thought hereafter; for the present, let us draw a ship into the sea, and find a crew for her expressly; let us put a hecatomb on board, and let us send Chryseis also. Further, let some chief man among us be in command, either Ajax, or Idomeneus, or yourself, son of Peleus, mighty warrior that you are, that we may offer sacrifice and appease the anger of the god."

Achilles scowled at him and answered: "You are steeped in insolence and lust of gain. With what heart can any of the Achaeans do your bidding, either on foray or in open fighting? I came not warring here for any ill the Trojans had done me. I have no quarrel with them. They have not raided my cattle or my horses, or cut down my harvests on the rich plains of Phthia; for between me and them there is a great space, both mountain and sounding sea. We have followed you, Sir Insolence! for your pleasure, not ours — to gain satisfaction from the Trojans for your shameless self and for Menelaus. You forget this, and threaten to rob me of the prize for which I have toiled, and which the sons of the Achaeans have given me. Never when the Achaeans sack any rich city of the Trojans do I receive so good a prize as you do, though it is my hands that do the better part of the fighting. When the sharing comes, your share is far the largest, and I, forsooth, must go back to my ships, take what I can get and be thankful, when my labor of fighting is done. Now, therefore, I shall go back to Phthia; it will be much better for me to return home with my ships, for I will not stay here dishonored to gather gold and substance for you."

And Agamemnon answered: "Fly if you will, I shall make you no prayers to stay you. I have others here who will do me honor, and above all Zeus, the lord of counsel. There is no king here so hateful to me as you are, for you are ever quarrelsome and ill-affected. What though you be brave? Was it not heaven that made you so? Go home, then, with your ships and comrades to lord it over the Myrmidons. I care neither for you nor for your anger; and thus will I do: since Phoebus Apollo is taking Chryseis from me, I shall send her with my ship and my followers, but I shall come to your tent and take your own prize, Briseis, that you may learn how much stronger I am than you are, and that another may fear to set himself up as equal or comparable with me."

The son of Peleus was furious, and his heart within his shaggy breast was divided whether to draw his sword, push the others aside, and kill the son of Atreus, or to restrain himself and check his anger. . . .

"Wine-bibber," he cried, "with the face of a dog and the heart of a hind, you never dare to go out with the host in fight, nor yet with our chosen men in ambuscade. You shun this as you do death itself. You had rather go round and rob his prizes from any man who contradicts you. You devour your people, for you are king over a feeble folk; otherwise, son of Atreus, henceforward you would insult no man. Therefore I say, and swear it with a great oath — nay, by this my scepter, which shall sprout neither leaf nor shoot, nor bud anew from the day on which it left its parent stem upon the mountains — for the ax stripped it of leaf and bark, and now the sons of the Achaeans bear it as judges and guardians of the decrees of heaven — so surely and solemnly do I swear that hereafter they shall look fondly for Achilles and shall not find him. In the day of your distress, when your men fall dying by the murderous hand of Hector, you shall not know how to help them and shall rend your heart with rage for the hour when you offered insult to the bravest of the Achaeans."

With this the son of Peleus dashed his gold-bestudded scepter on the ground and took his seat, while the son of Atreus was beginning fiercely from his place upon the other side. Then uprose smooth-tongued Nestor, the facile speaker of the Pylians, and the words fell from his lips sweeter than honey. Two generations of men born and bred in Pylos had passed away under his rule, and he was now reigning over the third. With all sincerity and good will, therefore, he addressed them thus:

"Of a truth," he said, "a great sorrow has befallen the Achaean land. Surely Priam with his sons would rejoice, and the Trojans be glad at heart if they could hear this quarrel between you two, who are so excellent in fight and counsel. I am older than either of you; therefore be guided by me. Moreover, I have been the familiar friend of men even greater than you are, and they did not disregard my counsels. . . . Therefore, Agamemnon, though you be strong, take not this girl away, for the sons of the Achaeans have already given her to Achilles; and you, Achilles, strive not further with the king, for no man who by the grace of Zeus wields a scepter has like honor with Agamemnon. You are strong and have a goddess for your mother, but Agamemnon is stronger than you, for he has more people under him. Son of Atreus, check your anger, I implore you; end this quarrel with Achilles, who in the day of battle is a tower of strength to the Achaeans."

And Agamemnon answered: "Sir, all that you have said is true, but this fellow must needs become our lord and master: he must be lord of all, king of all, and captain of all, and this shall hardly be. Granted that the gods have made him a great warrior, have they also given him the right to speak with railing?"

Achilles interrupted him. "I should be a mean coward," he cried, "were I to give in to you in all things. Order other people about, not me, for I shall obey no longer. Furthermore I say — and lay my saying to your heart — I shall fight neither you nor any man about this girl, for those that take were those also that gave. But of all else that is at my ship you shall carry away nothing by force. Try, that others may see; if you do, my spear shall be reddened with your blood."

When they had quarreled thus angrily, they rose, and broke up the assembly at the ships of the Achaeans. The son of Peleus went back to his tents and ships with the son of Menoetius and his company, while Agamemnon drew a vessel into the water and chose a crew of twenty oarsmen. He escorted Chryseis on board and sent moreover a hecatomb for the god. And Odysseus went as captain. . . .

But Agamemnon did not forget the threat that he had made Achilles and called his trusty messengers and squires, Talthybius and Eurybates. "Go," said he, "to the tent of Achilles, son of Peleus. Take Briseis by the hand and bring her hither; if he will not give her I shall come with others and take her — which will press him harder." . . .

ACHILLES ASKS HIS GODDESS MOTHER FOR AID

Then Achilles went all alone by the side of the hoar sea, weeping and looking out upon the boundless waste of waters. He raised his hands in prayer to his immortal mother. "Mother," he cried, "you bore me doomed to live but for a little season. Surely Zeus, who thunders from Olympus, might have made that little glorious. It is not so. Agamemnon, son of Atreus, has done me dishonor, and has robbed me of my prize by force."

As he spoke he wept aloud, and his mother heard him where she was sitting in the depths of the sea hard by the old man, her father. Forthwith she rose as it were a gray mist out of the waves, sat down before him as he stood weeping, caressed him with her hand, and said, "My son, why are you weeping? What is it that grieves you? Keep it not from me, but tell me, that we may know it together." . . .

Achilles drew a deep sigh and said: "You know it; why tell you what you know well already? . . . Help your brave son, therefore, if you are able. Go to Olympus, and if you have ever done him service in word or deed, implore the aid of Zeus. Ofttimes in my father's house have I heard you glory in that you alone of the immortals saved the son of Cronus from ruin, when the others, with Hera, Poseidon, and Pallas Athene would have put him in bonds. It was you, goddess, who delivered him by calling to Olympus the hundred-handed monster whom gods call Briareus, but men Aegaeon, for he is stronger even than his father. When, therefore, he took his seat all-glorious beside the son of Cronus, the other gods were afraid, and did not bind him. Go, then, to him, remind him of all this, clasp his knees, and bid him give succor to the Trojans. Let the Achaeans be hemmed in at the sterns of their ships, and perish on the seashore, that they may reap what joy they may of their kind, and that Agamemnon may rue his blindness in offering insult to the foremost of the Achaeans."

Thetis wept and answered: "My son, woe is me that I should have borne or suckled you. Would indeed that you had lived your span free from all sorrow at your ships, for it is all too brief; alas, that you should be at once short of life and long of sorrow above your peers. Woe, therefore, was the hour in which I bore you. Nevertheless, I will go to the snowy heights of Olympus, and tell this tale to Zeus, if he will hear our prayer. Meanwhile stay where you are with your ships, nurse your anger against the Achaeans, and hold aloof from fight. For Zeus went yesterday to Oceanus to a feast among the Ethiopians, and the other gods went with him. He will return to Olympus twelve days hence. I will then go to his mansion paved with bronze and will beseech him, nor do I doubt that I shall be able to persuade him."

A SACRIFICE

On this she left him, still furious at the loss of her that had been taken from him. Meanwhile Odysseus reached Chryse with the hecatomb. . . . He gave the girl over to her father, who received her gladly, and they ranged the holy hecatomb all orderly round the altar of the god. They washed their hands and took up the barley meal to sprinkle over the victims, while Chryses lifted up his hands and prayed aloud on their behalf. "Hear me," he cried, "O god of the silver bow, that protectest Chryse and holy Cilla, and rulest Tenedos with thy might! Even as thou didst hear me aforetime when I prayed, and didst press hardly upon the Achaeans, so hear me yet again, and stay this fearful pestilence from the Danaans."

Thus did he pray, and Apollo heard his prayer. When they had done praying and sprinkling the barley meal, they drew back the heads of the victims and killed and flayed them. They cut out the thighbones, wrapped them round in two layers of fat, set some pieces of raw meat on top of them, and then Chryses laid them on the wood fire and poured wine over them, while the young men stood near him with five-pronged spits in their hands. When the thighbones were burned and they had tasted the inward meats, they cut the rest up small, put the pieces upon the spits, roasted them till they were done, and drew them off: then, when they had finished their work and the feast was ready, they ate it, and every man had his full share, so that all were satisfied. As soon as they had had enough to eat and drink, pages filled the mixing bowl with wine and water and handed it round, after giving every man his drink offering. Thus all day long the young men worshipped the god with song, hymning him and chanting the joyous paean, and the god took pleasure in their voices. . . .

But Achilles abode at his ships and nursed his anger. He went not to the honorable assembly, and sallied not forth to fight, but gnawed at his own heart, pining for battle and the war cry.

LIFE AMONG THE GODS

Now after twelve days the immortal gods came back in a body to Olympus, and Zeus led the way. Thetis was not unmindful of the charge her son had laid upon her, so she rose from under the sea and went through great heaven with early morning to Olympus, where she found the mighty son of Cronus sitting all alone upon its topmost ridges. She sat herself down before him, and with her left hand seized his knees, while with her right she caught him under the chin, and besought him, saying:

"Father Zeus, if I ever did you service in word or deed among the immortals, hear my prayer, and do honor to my son, whose life is to be cut short so early. King Agamemnon has dishonored him by taking his prize and keeping her. Honor him then yourself, Olympian lord of counsel, and grant victory to the Trojans, till the Achaeans give my son his due and load him with riches in requital."

Zeus sat for a while silent, and without a word, but Thetis still kept firm hold of his knees, and besought him a second time. "Incline your head," said she, "and promise me surely, or else deny me — for you have nothing to fear — that I may learn how greatly you disdain me."

At this Zeus was much troubled and answered: "I shall have trouble if you set me quarreling with Hera, for she will provoke me with her taunting speeches; even now she is always railing at me before the other gods and accusing me of giving aid to the Trojans. Go back now, lest she should find out. I will consider the matter, and will bring it about as you wish. See, I incline my head that you may believe me. This is the most solemn token that I can give to any god. I never recall my word, or deceive, or fail to do what I say, when I have nodded my head."

As he spoke, the son of Cronus bowed his dark brows, and the ambrosial locks swayed on his immortal head, till vast Olympus reeled.

When the pair had thus laid their plans, they parted — Zeus to his own house, while the goddess quitted the splender of Olympus, and plunged into the depths of the sea. The gods rose from their seats, before the coming of their sire. Not one of them dared to remain sitting, but all stood up as he came among them. There, then, he took his seat. But Hera, when she saw him, knew that he and the old merman's daughter, silver-footed Thetis, had been hatching mischief, so she at once began to upbraid him. "Trickster," she cried, "which of the gods have you been taking into your counsels now? You are always settling matters in secret behind my back, and have never yet told me, if you could help it, one word of your intentions."

"Hera," replied the sire of gods and men, "you must not expect to be informed of all my counsels. You are my wife, but you would find it hard to understand them. When it is proper for you to hear, there is no one, god or man, who will be told sooner, but when I mean to keep a matter to myself, you must not pry nor ask questions."

"Dread son of Cronus," answered Hera, "what are you talking about? I? Pry and ask questions? Never. I let you have your own way in everything. Still, I have a strong misgiving that the old merman's daughter Thetis has been talking you over, for she was with you and had hold of your knees this selfsame morning. I believe, therefore, that you have been promising her to give glory to Achilles, and to kill much people at the ships of the Achaeans."

"Wife," said Zeus, "I can do nothing but you suspect me and find it out. You will take nothing by it, for I shall only dislike you the more, and it will go harder with you. Granted that it is as you say; I mean to have it so. Sit down and hold your tongue as I bid you, for if I once begin to lay my hands about you, though all heaven were on your side it would profit you nothing."

On this Hera was frightened, so she curbed her stubborn will and sat down in silence. But the heavenly beings were disquieted throughout the house of Zeus, till the cunning workman Hephaestus began to try and pacify his mother Hera. "It will be intolerable," said he, "if you two fall to wrangling and setting heaven in an uproar about a pack of mortals. If such ill counsels are to prevail, we shall have no pleasure at our banquet. Let me then advise my mother — and she must herself know that it will be better — to make friends with my dear father Zeus, lest he again scold her and disturb our feast. If the Olympian Thunderer wants to hurl us all from our seats, he can do so, for he is far the strongest, so give him fair words, and he will then soon be in a good humor with us."

As he spoke, he took a double cup of nectar and placed it in his mother's hand. "Cheer up, my dear mother," said he, "and make the best of it. I love you dearly, and should be very sorry to see you get a thrashing; however grieved I might be, I could not help you, for there is no standing against Zeus. Once before when I was trying to help you, he caught me by the foot and flung me from the heavenly threshold. All day long from morn till eve, was I falling, till at sunset I came to ground in the island of Lemnos, and there I lay, with very little life left in me, till the Sintians came and tended me."

Hera smiled at this, and as she smiled she took the cup from her son's hands. Then Hephaestus drew sweet nectar from the mixing bowl, and served it round among the gods, going from left to right; and the blessed gods laughed out a loud applause as they saw him bustling about the heavenly mansion.

Thus through the livelong day to the going down of the sun they feasted, and everyone had his full share, so that all were satisfied. Apollo struck his lyre, and the Muses lifted up their sweet voices, calling and answering one another. But when the sun's glorous light had faded, they went home to bed, each in his own abode, which lame Hephaestus with his consummate skill had fashioned for them. So Zeus, the Olympian lord of thunder, hied him to the bed in which he always slept; and when he had got on to it he went to sleep, with Hera of the golden throne by his side.

Zeus, keeping his promise, tricks Agamemnon with a dream into imagining he can capture Troy at once. Agamemnon craftily tests the spirit of his men by telling them that Zeus has bidden him give up the siege. Athene, sent by Hera, inspires Odysseus to oppose the plan, and he incites the host to continue the struggle.

THE LYING DREAM

Now the other gods and the armed warriors on the plain slept soundly, but Zeus was wakeful, for he was thinking how to do honor to Achilles and destroy much people at the ships of the Achaeans. In the end he deemed it would be best to send a lying dream to King Agamemnon. So he called one to him and said to it: "Lying Dream, go to the ships of the Achaeans, into the tent of Agamemnon, and say to him word for word as I now bid you. Tell him to get the Achaeans instantly under arms, for he shall take Troy. There are no longer divided counsels among the gods. Hera has brought them to her own mind, and woe betides the Trojans."

The dream went when it had heard its message, and soon reached the ships of the Achaeans. It sought Agamemnon, son of Atreus, and found him in his tent wrapped in a profound slumber. It hovered over his head in the likeness of Nestor, son of Neleus, whom Agamemnon honored above all his councilors. . . .

The dream then left him, and he thought of things that were surely not to be accomplished. He thought that on that same day he was to take the city of Priam, but he little knew what was in the mind of Zeus, who had many another hard-fought fight in store alike for Danaans and Trojans. Then presently he woke, with the divine message still ringing in his ears, so he sat upright, and put on his soft shirt so fair and new, and over this his heavy cloak. He bound his sandals on to his comely feet, and slung his silver-studded sword about his shoulders; then he took the imperishable staff of his father and sallied forth to the ships of the Achaeans.

MEETING OF THE KING'S COUNCIL

The goddess Dawn now wended her way to vast Olympus that she might herald day to Zeus and to the other immortals, and Agamemnon sent the criers round to call the people in assembly; so they called them and the people gathered thereon. But first he summoned a meeting of the elders at the ship of Nestor, king of Pylos, and when they were assembled he laid a cunning counsel before them.

"My friends," said he, "I have had a dream from heaven in the dead of night, and its face and figure resembled none but Nestor's. It stood beside me and addressed me. . . .

He then sat down, and Nestor, the prince of Pylos, with all sincerity and good will addressed them thus: "My friends," said he, "princes and councilors of the Argives, if any other man of the Achaeans had told us of this dream we should have declared it false, and would have had nothing to do with it. But he who has seen it is the foremost man among us; we must therefore set about getting the people under arms."

MEETING OF THE POPULAR ASSEMBLY

With this he led the way from the assembly, and the other sceptered kings rose with him in obedience to the word of Agamemnon; but the people pressed forward to hear. They swarmed like bees that sally from some hollow cave and flit in countless throng among the spring flowers, bunched in knots and clusters; even so did the mighty multitude pour from ships and tents to the assembly, and range themselves upon the wide-watered shore, while among them ran Wildfire Rumor, messenger of Zeus, urging them ever to the fore. Thus they gathered in a pell-mell of mad confusion, and the earth groaned under the tramp of men as the people sought their places. Nine heralds went crying about among them to stay their tumult and bid them listen to the kings, till at last they were got into their several places and ceased their clamor. Then King Agamemnon rose, holding his scepter. . . .

AGAMEMNON TESTS THE GREEKS' SPIRIT

"My friends," he said, "heroes, servants of Ares, the hand of heaven has been laid heavily upon me. Cruel Zeus gave me his solemn promise that I should sack the city of Priam before returning, but he has played me false, and is now bidding me go ingloriously back to Argos with the loss of much people. Such is the will of Zeus, who has laid many a proud city in the dust, as he will yet lay others, for his power is above all. . . . Nine of Zeus' years are gone. The timbers of our ships have rotted; their tackling is sound no longer. Our wives and little ones at home look anxiously for our coming, but the work that we came hither to do has not been done. Now, therefore, let us all do as I say: let us sail back to our own land, for we shall not take Troy."

With these words he moved the hearts of the multitude, so many of them as knew not the cunning counsel of Agamemnon. They surged to and fro like the waves of the Icarian Sea, when the east and south winds break from heaven's clouds to lash them; or as when the west wind sweeps over a field of corn and the ears bow beneath the blast, even so were they swayed as they flew with loud cries towards the ships, and the dust from under their feet rose heavenward. They cheered each other on to draw the ships into the sea; they cleared the channels in front of them; they began taking away the stays from underneath them, and the welkin rang with their glad cries, so eager were they to return.

Then surely the Argives would have returned after a fashion that was not fated. But Hera said to Athene, "Alas, daughter of aegis-bearing Zeus, unwearriable, shall the Argives fly home to their own land over the broad sea, and leave Priam and the Trojans the glory of still keeping Helen, for whose sake so many of the Achaeans have died at Troy, far from their homes? Go about at once among the host, and speak fairly to them, man by man, that they draw not their ships into the sea."

Athene was not slack to do her bidding. Down she darted from the topmost summits of Olympus, and in a moment she was at the ships of the Achaeans. There she found Odysseus, peer of Zeus in counsel, standing alone. He had not as yet laid a hand upon his ship, for he was grieved and sorry; so she went close to him and said, "Odysseus, noble son of Laertes, are you going to fling yourselves into your ships, and be off home to your own land in this way? Will you leave Priam and the Trojans the glory of still keeping Helen, for whose sake so many of the Achaeans have died at Troy, far from their homes? Go about at once among the host, and speak fairly to them, man by man, that they draw not their ships into the sea."

Odysseus knew the voice as that of the goddess: he flung his cloak from him and set off to run. His servant Eurybates, a man of Ithaca, who waited on him, took charge of the cloak, whereon Odysseus went straight up to Agamemnon and received from him his ancestral, imperishable staff. With this he went about among the ships of the Achaeans.

Whenever he met a king or chieftain, he stood by him and spoke him fairly. "Sir," said he, "this flight is cowardly and unworthy. Stand to your post, and bid your people also keep their places. You do not yet know the full mind of Agamemnon; he was sounding us, and ere long will visit the Achaeans with his displeasure. We were not all of us at the council to hear what he then said. See to it lest he be angry and do us a mischief; for the pride of kings is great and the hand of Zeus is with them."

THE LOT OF THE COMMON MAN

But when he came across any common man who was making a noise, he struck him with his staff and rebuked him, saying: "Sirrah, hold your peace, and listen to better men than yourself. You are a coward and no soldier; you are nobody either in fight or council; we cannot all be kings; it is not well that there should be many masters; one man must be supreme — one king to whom the son of scheming Cronus has given the scepter of sovereignty over you all."

Thus masterfully did he go about among the host, and the people hurried back to the assembly from their tents and ships with a sound as the thunder of surf when it comes crashing down upon the shore, and all the sea is in an uproar.

The rest now took their seats and kept to their own several places, but Thersites still went on wagging his unbriddled tongue — a man of many words, and those unseemly; a monger of sedition, a railer against all who were in authority, who cared not what he said, so that he might set the Achaeans in a laugh. He was the ugliest man of all those that came before Troy — bandy-legged, lame of one foot, with his two shoulders rounded and hunched over his chest. His head ran up to a point, but there was little hair on the top of it. Achilles and Odysseus hated him worst of all, for it was with them that he was most wont to wrangle. Now, however, with a shrill squeaky voice he began heaping his abuse on Agamemnon. The Achaeans were angry and disgusted, yet nonetheless he kept on brawling and bawling at the son of Atreus.

"Agamemnon," he cried, "what ails you now, and what more do you want? Your tents are filled with bronze and with fair women, for whenever we take a town we give you the pick of them. Would you have yet more gold, which some Trojan is to give you as ransom for his son, when I or another Achaean has taken him prisoner? Or is it some young girl to hide away and lie with? It is not well that you, the ruler of the Achaeans, should bring them into such misery. Weakling cowards, women rather than men, let us sail home, and leave this fellow here at Troy to stew in his own meeds of honor, and discover whether we were of any service to him or no. Achilles is a much better man than he is, and see how he has treated him — robbing him of his prize and keeping it himself. Achilles takes it meekly and shows no fight; if he did, son of Atreus, you would never again insult him."

Thus railed Thersites, but Odysseus at once went up to him and rebuked him sternly. "Check your glib tongue, Thersites," said he, "and babble not a word further. Chide not with princes when you have none to back you. There is no viler creature come before Troy with the sons of Atreus. Drop this chatter about kings, and neither revile them nor keep harping about going home. We do not yet know how things are going to be, nor whether the Achaeans are to return with good success or evil. How dare you gibe at Agamemnon because the Danaans have awarded him so many prizes? I tell you, therefore — and it shall surely be — that if I again catch you talking such nonsense, I will either forfeit my own head and be no more called father of Telemachus, or I will take you, strip you stark naked, and whip you out of the assembly till you go blubbering back to the ships."

On this he beat him with his staff about the back and shoulders till he dropped and fell a-weeping. The golden scepter raised a bloody weal on his back, so he sat down frightened and in pain, looking foolish as he wiped the tears from his eyes. The people were sorry for him, yet they laughed heartily, and one would turn to his neighbor, saying: "Odysseus has done many a good thing ere now in fight and council, but he never did the Argives a better turn than when he stopped this fellow's mouth from prating further. He will give the kings no more of his insolence." . . .

HECTOR'S FAREWELL — HUMANS AS THEY REALLY ARE

When he [Hector, the Trojan commander] had gone through the city and had reached the Scaean gates through which he would go out on to the plain, his wife came running towards him, Andromache, daughter of great Eëtion who ruled in Thebe under the wooded slopes of Mount Placus, and was king of the Cilicians. His daughter had married Hector, and now came to meet him with a nurse who carried his little child in her bosom — a mere babe, Hector's darling son, and lovely as a star. Hector had named him Scamandrius, but the people called him Astyanax ["King of the city"] for his father stood alone as chief guardian of Ilium.

Hector smiled as he looked upon the boy, but he did not speak, and Andromache stood by him weeping and taking his hand in her own. "Dear husband," said she, "your valor will bring you to destruction. Think on your infant son, and on my hapless self who ere long shall be your widow — for the Achaeans will set upon you in a body and kill you. It would be better for me, should I lose you, to lie dead and buried, for I shall have nothing left to comfort me when you are gone, save only sorrow. I have neither father nor mother now. Achilles slew my father when he sacked Thebe, the goodly city of the Cilicians. He slew him, but did not for very shame despoil him. When he had burned him in his wondrous armor, he raised a barrow over his ashes and the mountain nymphs, daughters of aegis-bearing Zeus, planted a grove of elms about his tomb. I had seven brothers in my father's house, but on the same day they all went within the house of Hades. Achilles killed them as they were with their sheep and cattle. My mother — her who had been queen of all the land under Mount Placus — he brought hither with the spoil, and freed her for a great sum, but the archer-queen Artemis took her in the house of your father. Nay, Hector — you who to me are father, mother, brother, and dear husband

— have mercy upon me: stay here upon this wall; make not your child fatherless, and your wife a widow. . . ."

And Hector answered: "Wife, I too have thought upon all this, but with what face should I look upon the Trojans, men or women, if I shirked battle like a coward? I cannot do so: I know nothing save to fight bravely in the forefront of the Trojan host and win renown alike for my father and myself. Well do I know that the day will surely come when mighty Ilium shall be destroyed with Priam and Priam's people, but I grieve for none of these — not even for Hecuba, nor King Priam, nor for my brothers many and brave who may fall in the dust before their foes — for none of these do I grieve as for yourself when the day shall come on which some one of the Achaeans shall rob you forever of your freedom, and bear you weeping away. It may be that you will have to ply the loom in Argos at the bidding of a mistress, or to fetch water from the springs Messeïs or Hypereia, treated brutally by some cruel taskmaster; then will one say who sees you weeping, 'She was wife to Hector, the bravest warrior among the Trojans during the war before Ilium.' On this your tears will break forth anew for him who would have put away the day of captivity from you. May I lie dead under the barrow that is heaped over my body ere I hear your cry as they carry you into bondage."

He stretched his arms towards his child, but the boy cried and nestled in his nurse's bosom, scared at the sight of his father's armor, and at the horsehair plume that nodded fiercely from his helmet. His father and mother laughed to see him, but Hector took the helmet from his head and laid it all gleaming upon the ground. Then he took his darling child, kissed him, and dandled him in his arms, praying over him the while to Zeus and to all the gods. "Zeus," he cried, "grant that this child may be even as myself, chief among the Trojans: let him be not less excellent in strength, and let him rule Ilium with his might. Then may one say of him as he comes from battle, 'The son is far better than the father.' May he bring back the bloodstained spoils of him whom he has laid low, and let his mother's heart be glad."

With this he laid the child again in the arms of his wife, who took him to her own soft bosom, smiling through her tears. As her husband watched her his heart yearned towards her and he caressed her fondly, saying: "My own wife, do not take these things too bitterly to heart. No one can hurry me down to Hades before my time, but if a man's hour is come, be he brave or be he coward, there is no escape for him when he has once been born. Go, then, within the house, and busy yourself with your daily duties, your loom, your distaff, and the ordering of your servants; for war is man's matter, and mine above all others of them that have been born in Ilium."

He took his plumed helmet from the ground, and his wife went back again to her house, weeping bitterly and often looking back towards him.

THE ECONOMY OF THE HOMERIC AGE

. . . even so was Sarpedon fain to attack the [Greek] wall and break down its battlements. Then he said to Glaucus, son of Hippolochus: "Glaucus, why in Lycia do we receive especial honors as regards our place at table? Why are the choicest portions served us and our cups kept brimming, and why do men look up to us as though we were gods? Moreover, we hold a large estate by the banks of the river Zanthus, fair with orchard lawns and wheat-growing land; it becomes us, therefore, to take our stand at the head of all the Lycians and bear the brunt of the fight, that one may say to another, 'Our princes in Lycia eat the fat of the land and drink the best of wine, but they are fine fellows; they fight well and are ever at the front in battle.' My good friend, if, when we were once out of this fight, we could escape old age and death thenceforward and forever, I should neither press forward myself nor bid you do so, but death in ten thousand shapes hangs ever over our heads, and no man can elude him. Therefore, let us go forward and either win glory for ourselves or yield it to another." . . .

The Argives on their part got their men in fighting order within the wall, and there was a deadly struggle between them. The Lycians could not break through the wall and force their way to the ships, nor could the Danaans drive the Lycians from the wall now that they had once reached it. As two men, measuring rods in hand, quarrel about the boundaries in a common field, and stickle for their rights though they be but in a mere strip, even so did the battlements now serve as a bone of contention, and they beat one another's round shields for their possession. . . .

The god Hephaestus forges and decorates new armor for Achilles who, having seen the Greeks routed and his friend Patroclus slain by Hector, has decided to reenter the fray. The scene on Achilles' shield further illustrates Homeric economy.

First he shaped the shield so great and strong, adorning it all over and binding it round with a gleaming circuit in three layers; and the baldric was made of silver. He made the shield in five thicknesses, and with many a wonder did his cunning hand enrich it. . . .

He wrought also two cities, fair to see and busy with the hum of men. . . . the people were gathered in assembly, for there was a quarrel, and two men were wrangling about the blood money for a man who had been killed, the one saying before the people that he had paid damages in full and the other that he had not been paid. Each was trying to make his own case good, and the people took sides, each man backing the side that he had taken; but the heralds kept them back, and the elders sat on their seats of stone in a solemn circle, holding the staves which the heralds had put into their hands. Then they rose and each in his turn gave judgment, and there were two talents laid down, to be given to him whose judgment should be deemed the fairest. . . .

He wrought also a fair fallow field, large and thrice ploughed already. Many men were working at the plough within it, turning their oxen to and fro, furrow after furrow. Each time that they turned on reaching the headland a man would come up to them and give them a cup of wine, and they would go back to their furrows looking forward to the time when they should again reach the headland. The part that they had ploughed was dark behind them, so that the field, though it was of gold, still looked as if it were being plowed — very curious to behold.

He wrought also a chieftain's demesne, and the reapers were reaping with sharp sickles in their hands. Swathe after swathe fell to the ground in a straight line behind them, and the binders bound them in bands of twisted straw. There were three binders, and behind them there were boys who gathered the cut corn in armfuls and kept on bringing them to be bound. Among them all the chieftain stood by in silence and was glad. The servants were getting a meal ready under an oak, for they had sacrificed a great ox and were busy cutting him up, while the women were making a porridge of much white barley for the laborers' dinner. . . .

THE DEATH OF HECTOR: FATE AND HADES

Achilles came up to him [Hector] as it were Ares himself, plumed lord of battle. From his right shoulder he brandished his terrible spear of Pelian ash, and the bronze gleamed around him like flashing fire or the rays of the rising sun. Fear fell upon Hector as he beheld him and he dared not stay longer where he was, but fled in dismay from before the gates, while Achilles darted after him at his utmost speed. As a mountain falcon, swiftest of all birds, swoops down upon some cowering dove — the dove flies before him but the falcon with a shrill scream follows close after, resolved to have her — even so did Achilles make straight for Hector with all his might, while Hector fled under the Trojan wall as fast as his limbs could take him. . . .

All the gods watched them, and the sire of the gods and men was the first to speak. "Alas," said he, "my eyes behold a man who is dear to me being pursued round the walls of Troy. My heart is full of pity for Hector, who has burned the thighbones of many a heifer in my honor, at one while on the crests of many-valleyed Ida, and again on the citadel of Troy; and now I see noble Achilles in full pursuit of him round the city of Priam. What say you? Consider among yourselves and decide whether we shall now save him or let him fall, valiant though he be, before Achilles, son of Peleus."

Then Athene said, "Father, wielder of the lightning, lord of cloud and storm, what mean you? Would you pluck this mortal, doomed long ago by fate, out of the jaws of death? Do as you will, but we others shall not be of a mind with you."

And Zeus answered, "My child, Trito-born, take heart. I did not speak in full earnest, and I will let you have your way. Do without let or hindrance as you are minded." . . .

Achilles was still in full pursuit of Hector . . . and when the two were now close to one another great Hector was the first to speak. "I will no longer fly you, son of Peleus," said he, "as I have been doing hitherto. Three times have I fled round the mighty city of Priam, without daring to withstand you, but now, let me either slay or be slain, for I am in the mind to face you. Let us, then, give pledges to one another by our gods, who are the fittest witnesses and guardians of all covenants; let it be agreed between us that if Zeus vouchsafes me the longer stay and I take your life, I am not to treat your dead body in any unseemly fashion, but when I have stripped you of your armor, I am to give up your body to the Achaeans. And do you likewise."

Achilles glared at him and answered: "Fool, prate not to me about covenants . . . . you shall now pay me in full for the grief you have caused me on account of my comrades whom you have killed in battle." He poised his spear as he spoke and hurled it. . . .

Hector with his dying breath then said: "I know you what you are, and was sure that I should not move you, for your heart is hard as iron; look to it that I bring not heaven's anger upon you on the day when Paris and Phoebus Apollo, valiant though you be, shall slay you at the Scaean gates."

When he had thus said the shrouds of death enfolded him, whereon his soul went out of him and flew down to the house of Hades, lamenting its sad fate that it should enjoy youth and strength no longer. But Achilles said, speaking to the dead body, "Die; for my part I will accept my fate whensoever Zeus and the other gods see fit to send it."

As he spoke he drew his spear from the body and set it on one side; then he stripped the bloodstained armor from Hector's shoulders while the other Achaeans came running up to view his wondrous strength and beauty; and no one came near him without giving him a fresh wound. Then would one turn to his neighbor and say, "It is easier to handle Hector now than when he was flinging fire on to our ships" — and as he spoke he would thrust his spear into him anew.

18

Hesiod, Works and Days

Changing times bring on a moral order

The world of Hesiod as seen in his partly autobiographical Works and Days, written about 700 B.C., is a far different world from that described by Homer. The primitive monarchy of the Iliad, under which the common man had rights as a member of the popular assembly, has been replaced by an oligarchy of nobles which oppresses the lower classes. Hesiod was himself a commoner who had suffered from the rapacity of the nobility. His evil brother Perses had connived with the "bribe-swallowing" aristocratic judges to deprive him of much

Reprinted by permission of the publishers and The Loeb Classical Library from Hugh G. Evelyn-White's translation of Hesiod, Works and Days, lines 1–41, 106–342, 361–382 (Cambridge, Mass.: Harvard University Press).

of his rightful share in their father's small estate, and was now threatening him with another lawsuit. To Hesiod all this was symbolic of the nature of the time of troubles in which he lived, an "age of iron" in which there was little or no justice or happiness. He saw the history of man as one of progressive degeneration through five distinct ages — from an ideal golden age in a faraway past to the present harsh age of "black iron."

Hesiod's mythological account of the five ages of man is a good example of his mingling of fable with fact in an effort to give meaning to the realities of his time and explain their origin. So also is his short fable of the hawk and the nightingale which trenchantly presents the general truth that in an "age of iron" might makes right. Noteworthy also is his personification of justice (dikē) as a goddess who once lived among men but who has long since fled to Mt. Olympus. As Dikē, Goddess of Justice, she sits there beside her father Zeus, who, following her instructions, rewards the just on earth and punishes the unjust. Hesiod's moral seems clear: even though justice has left the earth and exists as an ideal in heaven, it continues to be concerned about human affairs.

Thus, despite Hesiod's gloomy concern with present evils, his viewpoint is essentially optimistic in that he looks ahead to a new and better future. He is the impassioned prophet of a new moral religious order in which Zeus, as an ethical force, demands and rewards only righteous conduct, and in which a new rational ideal of moderation — including work, a form of "strife in moderation" and no longer considered ignoble by gods and men — replaces the aristocratic valor of Homer's day as the chief virtue or "Goodness" of man. As has been noted in the earlier history of the peoples of the ancient Near East, so now in Greece an age of confusion has brought forth a demand for a social conscience and a moral order. In Hesiod's words, "Only when he has suffered does the fool learn."

INVOCATION IN PRAISE OF A MORALIZED ZEUS

Muses of Pieria who give glory through song, come hither, tell of Zeus your father and chant his praise. Through him mortal men are famed or unfamed, sung or unsung alike, as great Zeus wills. For easily he makes strong, and easily he brings the strong man low; easily he humbles the proud and raises the obscure, and easily he straightens the crooked and blasts the proud — Zeus who thunders aloft and has his dwelling most high. Attend thou with eye and ear, and make judgments straight with righteousness. And I, Perses, would tell of true things.

TWO KINDS OF STRIFE: THE IDEAL OF MODERATION

So, after all, there was not one kind of Strife alone, but all over the earth there are two. As for the one, a man would praise her when he came to understand her; but the other is blameworthy: and they are wholly different in nature. For one fosters evil war and battle, being cruel: her no man loves; but perforce, through the will of the deathless gods, men pay harsh Strife her honor due. But the other is . . . far kinder to men. She stirs up even the shiftless to toil; for a man grows eager to work when he considers his neighbor, a rich man who hastens to plough and plant and put his house in good order; and neighbor vies with his neighbor as he hurries after wealth. This Strife is wholesome for men. And potter is angry with potter, and craftsman with craftsman, and beggar is jealous of beggar and minstrel of minstrel.

Perses, lay up these things in your heart, and do not let that Strife who delights in mischief hold your heart back from work, while you peep and peer and listen to the wrangles of the court-house. Little concern has he with quarrels and courts who has not a year's victuals laid up betimes, even that which the earth bears, Demeter's grain. When you have got plenty of that, you can raise disputes and strive to get another's goods. But you shall have no second chance to deal so again: nay, let us settle our dispute here with true judgment which is of Zeus and is perfect. For we had already divided our inheritance, but you seized the greater share and carried it off, greatly swelling the glory of our bribe-swallowing lords who love to judge such a cause as this. Fools! They know not how much more the half is than the whole, nor what great advantage there is in mallow and asphodel ["cheese and crackers"]. . . .

THE FIVE AGES OF MAN

Or if you will, I will sum you up another tale well and skillfully — and do you lay it up in your heart — how the gods and mortal men sprang from one source.

First of all the deathless gods who dwell on Olympus made a golden race of mortal men who lived in the time of Cronos when he was reigning in heaven. And they lived like gods without sorrow of heart, remote and free from toil and grief: miserable age rested not on them; but with legs and arms never failing they made merry with feasting beyond the reach of all evils. When they died, it was as though they were overcome with sleep, and they had all good things; for the fruitful earth unforced bare them fruit abundantly and without stint. They dwelt in ease and peace upon their lands with many good things, rich in flocks and loved by the blessed gods.

But after the earth had covered this generation — they are called pure spirits dwelling on the earth, and are kindly, delivering from harm, and guardians of mortal men; for they roam everywhere over the earth, clothed in mist and keep watch on judgments and cruel deeds, givers of wealth; for this royal right also they received — then they who dwell on Olympus made a second generation which was of silver and less noble by far. It was like the golden race neither in body nor in spirit. A child was brought up at his good mother's side an hundred years, an utter simpleton, playing childishly in his own home. But when they were full grown and were come to the full measure of their prime, they lived only a little time and that in sorrow because of their foolishness, for they could not keep from sinning and from wronging one another, nor would they serve the immortals, nor sacrifice on the holy altars of the blessed ones as it is right for men to do wherever they dwell. Then Zeus the son of Cronos was angry and put them away, because they would not give honor to the blessed gods who live on Olympus.

But when earth had covered this generation also — they are called blessed spirits of the underworld by men, and, though they are of second order, yet honor attends them also — Zeus the Father made a third generation of mortal men, a brazen race, sprung from ash-trees; and it was in no way equal to the silver age, but was terrible and strong. They loved the lamentable works of Ares and deeds of violence; they ate no bread, but were hard of heart like adamant, fearful men. Great was their strength and unconquerable the arms which grew from their shoulders on their strong limbs. Their armor was of bronze, and their houses of bronze, and of bronze were their implements: there was no black iron. These were destroyed by their own hands and passed to the dank house of chill Hades, and left no name: terrible though they were, black Death seized them, and they left the bright light of the sun.

But when earth had covered this generation also, Zeus the son of Cronos made yet another, the fourth, upon the fruitful earth, which was nobler and more righteous, a god-like race of hero-men who are called demi-gods, the race before our own, throughout the boundless earth. Grim war and dread battle destroyed a part of them, some in the land of Cadmus at seven-gated Thebe when they fought for the flocks of Oedipus, and some, when it had brought them in ships over the great sea gulf to Troy for rich-haired Helen's sake: there death's end enshrouded a part of them. But to the others father Zeus the son of Cronos gave a living and an abode apart from men, and made them dwell at the ends of earth. And they live untouched by sorrow in the Islands of the Blessed along the shore of deep swirling Ocean, happy heroes for whom the grain-giving earth bears honey-sweet fruit flourishing thrice a year, far from the deathless gods, and Cronos rules over them; for the father of men and gods released him from his bonds. And these last equally have honor and glory.

And again far-seeing Zeus made yet another generation, the fifth, of men who are upon the bounteous earth.

Thereafter, would that I were not among the men of the fifth generation, but either had died before or been born afterwards. For now truly is a race of iron, and men ever rest from labor and sorrow by day, and from perishing by night; and the gods shall lay sore trouble upon them. But, notwithstanding, even these shall have some good mingled with their evils. And Zeus will destroy this race of mortal men also when they come to have grey hair on the temples at their birth. The father will not agree with his children, nor the children with their father, nor guest with his host, nor comrade with comrade; nor will brother be dear to brother as aforetime. Men will dishonor their parents as they grow quickly old, and will carp at them, chiding them with bitter words, hard-hearted they, not knowing the fear of the gods. They will not repay their aged parents the cost of their nurture, for might shall be their right: and one man will sack another's city. There will be no favor for the man who keeps his oath or for the just or for the good; but rather men will praise the evil-doer and his violent dealing. Strength will be right and reverence will cease to be; and the wicked will hurt the worthy man, speaking false words against him, and will swear an oath upon them. Envy, foul-mouthed, delighting in evil, with scowling face, will go along with wretched men one and all. And then Aidos [Reverence] and Nemesis [Retribution], with their sweet forms wrapped in white robes, will go from the wide-pathed earth and forsake mankind to join the company of the deathless gods: and bitter sorrows will be left for mortal men, and there will be no help against evil.

And now I will tell a fable for princes who themselves understand. Thus said the hawk to the nightingale with speckled neck, while he carried her high up among the clouds, gripped fast in his talons, and she pierced by his crooked talons, cried pitifully. To her he spoke disdainfully: "Miserable thing, why do you cry out? One far stronger than you now holds you fast, and you must go wherever I take you, songstress as you are. And if I please I will make my meal of you, or let you go. He is a fool who tries to withstand the stronger, for he does not get the mastery and suffers pain besides his shame." So said the swiftly flying hawk, the long-winged bird.

THE NEW MORAL ORDER

But you, Perses, listen to right and do not foster violence; for violence is bad for a poor man. Even the prosperous cannot easily bear its burden, but is weighed down under it when he has fallen into delusion. The better path is to go by on the other side towards justice; for [Dikē, Goddess of] Justice beats Outrage when she comes at length to the end of the race. But only when he has suffered does the fool learn this. For Oath keeps pace with wrong judgments. There is a noise when Justice is being dragged in the way where those who devour bribes and give sentence with crooked judgments take her. And she, wrapped in mist, follows to the city and haunts of the people, weeping, and bringing mischief to men, even to such as have driven her forth in that they did not deal straightly with her.

But they who give straight judgments to strangers and to the men of the land, and go not aside from what is just, their city flourishes, and the people prosper in it; Peace, the nurse of children, is abroad in their land, and all-seeing Zeus never decrees cruel war against them. Neither famine nor disaster ever haunt men who do true justice; but light-heartedly they tend the fields which are all their care. The earth bears them victual in plenty, and on the mountains the oak bears acorns upon the top and bees in the midst. Their woolly sheep are laden with fleeces; their women bear children like their parents. They flourish continually with good things, and do not travel on ships, for the grain-giving earth bears them fruit.

But for those who practice violence and cruel deeds far-seeing Zeus, the son of Cronos, ordains a punishment. Often even a whole city suffers for a bad man who sins and devises presumptuous deeds, and the son of Cronos lays great trouble upon the people, famine and plague together, so that the men perish away, and their women do not bear children, and their houses become few, through the contriving of Olympian Zeus. And again, at another time, the son of Cronos either destroys their wide army, or their walls, or else makes an end of their ships on the sea.

You princes, mark well this punishment you also; for the deathless gods are near among men and mark all those who oppress their fellows with crooked judgments, and reck not the anger of the gods. For upon the bounteous earth Zeus has thrice ten thousand spirits, watchers of mortal men, and these keep watch on judgments and deeds of wrong as they roam, clothed in mist, all over the earth. And there is virgin Justice, the daughter of Zeus, who is honored and reverenced among the gods who dwell on Olympus, and whenever anyone hurts her with lying slander, she sits beside her father, Zeus the son of Cronos, and tells him of men's wicked heart, until the people pay for the mad folly of their princes who, evilly minded, pervert judgment and give sentence crookedly. Keep watch against this, you princes, and make straight your judgments, you who devour bribes; put crooked judgments altogether from your thoughts.

He does mischief to himself who does mischief to another, and evil planned harms the plotter most. . . .

But you, Perses, lay up these things within your heart and listen now to right, ceasing altogether to think of violence. For the son of Cronos has ordained this law for men, that fishes and beasts and winged fowls should devour one another, for right is not in them; but to mankind he gave right which proves far the best. . . .

A NEW DEFINITION OF GOODNESS: WORK AND WEALTH

To you, foolish Perses, I will speak good sense. Badness can be got easily and in shoals: the road to her is smooth, and she lives very near us. But between us and Goodness the gods have placed the sweat of our brows: long and steep is the path that leads to her, and it is rough at the first; but when a man has reached the top, then indeed she is easy, though otherwise hard to reach.

That man is altogether best who considers all things himself and marks what will be better afterwards and at the end; and he, again, is good who listens to a good adviser; but whoever neither thinks for himself nor keeps in mind what another tells him, he is an unprofitable man. But do you at any rate, always remembering my charge, work, high-born Perses, that Hunger may hate you, and venerable Demeter richly crowned may love you and fill your barn with food; for Hunger is altogether a meet comrade for the sluggard. Both gods and men are angry with a man who lives idle, for in nature he is like the stingless drones who waste the labor of the bees, eating without working; but let it be your care to order your work properly, that in the right season your barns may be full of victual. Through work men grow rich in flocks and substance, and working they are much better loved by the immortals. Work is no disgrace: it is idleness which is a disgrace. But if you work, the idle will soon envy you as you grow rich, for fame and renown attend on wealth. And whatever be your lot, work is best for you, if you turn your misguided mind away from other men's property to your work and attend to your livelihood as I bid you. An evil shame is the needy man's companion, shame which both greatly harms and prospers men: shame is with poverty, but confidence with wealth.

Wealth should not be seized: god-given wealth is much better; for if a man take great wealth violently and perforce, or if he steal it through his tongue, as often happens when gain deceives men's sense and dishonor tramples down honor, the gods soon blot him out and make that man's house low, and wealth attends him only for a little time. Alike with him who does wrong to a suppliant or a guest, or who goes up to his brother's bed and commits unnatural sin in lying with his wife, or who infatuately offends against fatherless children, or who abuses his old father at the cheerless threshold of old age and attacks him with harsh words, truly Zeus himself is angry, and at the last lays on him a heavy requittal for his evil doing. But do you turn your foolish heart altogether away from these things, and, as far as you are able, sacrifice to the deathless gods purely and cleanly, and burn rich meats also, and at other times propitiate them with libations and incense, both when you go to bed and when the holy light has come back, that they may be gracious to you in heart and spirit, and so you may buy another's holding and not another yours.

. . . He who adds to what he has, will keep off bright-eyed hunger; for if you add only a little to a little and do this often, soon that little will become great. What a man has by him at home does not trouble him: it is better to have your stuff at home, for whatever is abroad may mean loss. It is a good thing to draw on what you have; but it grieves your heart to need something and not to have it, and I bid you mark this. Take your fill when the cask is first opened and when it is nearly spent, but midways be sparing: it is poor saving when you come to the lees.

Let the wage promised to a friend be fixed; even with your brother smile — and get a witness; for trust and mistrust, alike ruin men.

Do not let a flaunting woman coax and cozen and deceive you: she is after your barn. The man who trusts womankind trusts deceivers.

There should be an only son, to feed his father's house, for so wealth will increase in the home; but if you leave a second son you should die old. Yet Zeus can easily give great wealth to a greater number. More hands means more work and more increase.

If your heart within you desires wealth, do these things and work with work upon work.

19

Early Greek Lyric Poetry

Individualism emergent

Additional evidence of the course taken by Greek culture after the Homeric Age is found in the poetry of the seventh and sixth centuries B.C. These poets belong to a different age, and they respond to different needs. Hesiod, in his Works and Days, had been the first Greek poet to turn from the impersonal narration of great deeds, in the manner of Homer, to the expression of his own individual experience. In the following opening lines from his other long poem, the Theogony, which traces the history of the divine government of the universe to the point where it culminates in the benevolent monarchy of Zeus, Hesiod describes the new role of poetry as the expression of a deep personal reaction to life. His view anticipates the later doctrine of Aristotle's Poetics that has ever remained an important element in art criticism — a work of art is the product of a sensitive person's attempt to purge himself of, and thereby gain relief from, the intense emotions aroused within him by significant personal experience.

> Oh, blessed is the man
> Whome'er the Muses love! Sweet is the voice
> That from his lips flows ever. Is there one
> Who hides some grief in his wounded mind
> And mourns with aching heart? . . . Straight he feels
> His sorrow stealing in forgetfulness:
> Nor of his griefs remembers aught: so soon
> The Muses' gift has turned his woes away.

The poets who follow Hesiod intensify this exploration of purely individual experience. With the old way of life now lost, and living amidst the upheaval caused by political, social, and spiritual change, these poets express in new literary forms a corresponding turbulence of beliefs and emotions. They reject old values, cry out in pain over life's woes, sing gaily of romantic love and flowing wine, and lament the inevitable coming of old age.

◆ A ◆ ARCHILOCHUS

The poetry of Archilochus of Paros (early seventh century B.C.) illustrates clearly the complete change in conditions and in poetic expression that has come about since the bygone Homeric Age. The illegitimate son of an aristocratic father and a slave mother, he became an outcast and a wanderer over land and sea. His poetry — perhaps the first of its type — reflects an exultant individualism that holds firm in the face both of the loss of old values and the storm and stress of the new times.

THE LOST SHIELD

> The foeman glories in my shield;
> I left it in the battle-field;
> I threw it down beside the wood,
> Unscathed by scars, unstained by blood:
> And let him glory, since from death

Escaped, I keep my forfeit breath.
I soon may find, at little cost,
As good a shield as that I've lost.

Trans. J. H. Merivale

O HEART, BE STRONG

O heart, my heart, by hopeless woes oppressed,
Rise up, take guard, offer the foe your breast!
Stand firmly where the spears of battle fly;
But, if you conquer, never glorify
Yourself, nor, overcome, lie down and wail
At home. In joys take joy, and if you fail,
Grieve not too much, but know what fortunes men assail.

◆B◆ MIMNERMUS

In the poetry of Mimnermus of Colophon in Asia Minor (late seventh century B.C.), the earlier exuberant individualism of Archilochus is replaced by a note of sadness for the briefness of youth and joy. The romantic joy of living is still proclaimed, but it is tempered by a touch of melancholic world-weariness.

YOUTH AND AGE

Oh what is life by golden love unblest?
Better be mine the grave's eternal rest.
The furtive kiss, soft pledge and genial tie,
Are flowers of youth, that passing smile and die:
Old age succeeds, and dulls each finer sense,
When all we hope, at most, is reverence.
Age brings misfortune clearer to our sight,
Damps every joy and dims the cheerful light,
And scatters frowns, and thins the silvery hair,
Hateful to youth, unlovely to the fair.

Trans. Robert Bland

LIKE THE LEAVES

We, like the leaves of many-blossomed Spring,
When the sun's rays their sudden radiance fling
In growing strength, on earth, a little while,
Delighted, see youth's blooming flowerets smile.
Not with that wisdom of the Gods endued,

To judge aright of evil and of good.
Two Fates, dark-scowling, at our side attend;
Of youth, of life, each points the destined end,
Old age and death: the fruit of youth remains
Brief, as the sunshine scattered o'er the plains:
And when these fleeting hours have sped away,
To die were better than to breathe the day.
A load of grief the burdened spirit wears;
Domestic troubles rise; penurious cares;
One with an earnest love of children sighs;
The grave is opened and he childless dies:
Another drags in pain his lingering days,
While slow disease upon his vitals preys.
Nor lives there one, whom Jupiter on high
Exempts from years of mixt calamity.

Trans. C. A. Elton

◆ C ◆ SAPPHO

Sappho lived at the end of the seventh century B.C. in Mitylene on the island of Lesbos, where she conducted a school for girls. She is the first and perhaps the greatest of all women poets. Her theme is love and loveliness, and no one has ever explored this theme with deeper passion, more delicate grace and simplicity in the choice of words, richer imagination, or greater beauty.

I CANNOT WEAVE

Oh, my sweet mother, 'tis in vain,
    I cannot weave as once I wove,
So 'wildered is my heart and brain
    With thinking of that youth I love.

Trans. Thomas Moore

THE MOON IS SET

The silver moon is set;
    The Pleiades are gone;
Half the long night is spent, and yet
    I lie alone.

Trans. J. H. Merivale

LOVE RENDS ME

Lo, Love once more my soul within me rends
Like wind that on the mountain oak descends.

Trans. John Addington Symonds

FAIR HELEN, ALL FOR LOVE

She, who the beauty of mankind
Excelled, fair Helen, all for love
The noblest husband left behind;
Afar, to Troy she sailed away,
Her child, her parents, clean forgot;
The Cyprian[1] led her far astray
Out of the way, resisting not.

FLOWER GIRL

Here, fairest Rhodope, recline,
And 'mid thy bright locks intertwine,
With fingers soft as softest down,
The verdant parsley crown.
The Gods are pleased with flowers that bloom
And leaves that shed divine perfume,
But, if ungarlanded, despise
The richest offered sacrifice.

Trans. J. H. Merivale

◆D◆ THEOGNIS

Theognis of Megara, near Athens, was a sixth-century aristocrat who filled his verse with outraged bitterness towards the lower classes and their tyrant leaders (see Selection 21), under whom he suffered confiscation of property and exile. Although he claims to be no narrow reactionary "leaguing with the proud and arbitrary few" but a moderate who will "incline to neither side," Theognis expresses the ultra-conservative viewpoint on social and political change; to him the nobles are always "good" and the commoners are always "base."

"A DISCONTENTED CRY FILLS ALL THE EARTH"

This is Theognis, the Megarian poet,
So celebrated and renowned in Greece!
Yet some there are, forsooth, I cannot please;
Nor ever could contrive, with all my skill,
To gain the common liking and goodwill
Of these my fellow-citizens. — No wonder!
Not even he, the god that wields the thunder,

"Fair Helen, All for Love" is from A. R. Burn, *The Lyric Age of Greece* (New York: St. Martin's Press, Inc., 1961), p. 236. Reprinted by permission of St. Martin's Press, Inc., and Edward Arnold, Ltd.

[1] Aphrodite.

The sovereign all-wise, almighty Jove,
Can please them with his government above:
Some call for rainy weather, some for dry,
A discontented and discordant cry
Fills all the earth, and reaches to the sky, . . .
To rear a child is easy, but to teach
Morals and manners is beyond our reach;
To make the foolish wise, the wicked good,
That science never yet was understood.
The sons of Aesculapius, if their art
Could remedy a perverse and wicked heart,
Might earn enormous wages! . . .

"OUR COMMON PEOPLE ARE NO MORE THE SAME"

Our commonwealth preserves its former frame,
Our common people are no more the same:
They that in skins and hides were rudely dressed,
Nor dreamt of law, nor sought to be redressed
By rules of right, but in the days of old
Flocked to the town, like cattle to the fold,
Are now the brave and wise; and we the rest,
Their betters nominally, once the best,
Degenerate, debased, timid, mean!
Who can endure to witness such a scene? . . .

"I INCLINE TO NEITHER SIDE"

I walk by rule and measure, and incline
To neither side, but take an even line;
Fix'd in a single purpose and design.
With learning's happy gifts to celebrate,
To civilize and dignify the state:
Not leaguing with the discontented crew,
Nor with the proud and arbitrary few. . . .
Waste not your efforts, struggle not, my friend,
Idle and old abuses to defend:
Take heed! the very measures that you press
May bring repentance with their own success.

"ZEUS, I MARVEL AT THY WAYS"

Blessed, almighty Zeus! With deep amaze
I view the world; — and marvel at thy ways!
All our devices, every subtle plan,
Each secret act, and all the thoughts of man,
Your boundless intellect can comprehend!
On your award our destinies depend.
How can you reconcile it to your sense

Of right and wrong, thus loosely to dispense
Your bounties on the wicked and the good?
How can your laws be known or understood?
When we behold a man faithful and just,
Humbly devout, true to his word and trust,
Dejected and oppressed; — whilst the profane,
And wicked and unjust, in glory reign,
Proudly triumphant, flushed with power and gain,
What inference can human reason draw?
How can we guess the secret of the law,
Or choose the path approved by power divine? . . .
Not to be born — never to see the sun —
No worldly blessing is a greater one!
And the next best is speedily to die,
And lapt beneath a load of earth to lie!

"LONGING AGAIN TO VIEW THIS LAND OF MINE"

You, great Apollo, with its walls and towers
Fenc'd and adorn'd of old this town of ours! . . .
Yet much I fear the faction and the strife,
Throughout our Grecian cities, raging rife,
And their wild councils. But do thou defend
This town of ours, our founder and our friend!
Wide have I wander'd, far beyond the sea,
Even to the distant shores of Sicily,
To broad Euboea's plentiful domain,
With the rich vineyards in its planted plain;
And to the sunny wave and winding edge
Of fair Eurotas, with its reedy sedge;
Where Sparta stands in simple majesty,
Among her manly rulers, there was I!
Greeted and welcom'd (there and everywhere)
With courteous entertainment, kind and fair;
Yet still my weary spirit would repine,
Longing again to view this land of mine.

Trans. J. H. Frere

◆ E ◆ ANACREON

The story goes that Anacreon of Teos in Asia Minor died at the ripe old age of eighty-five by choking on a grape seed found in his wine — a fitting death for a voluptuary whose only aim in life was to "enjoy the day" and be "a devotee of Bacchus decently." In Anacreon's verse, Greek lyric poetry has lost the power and genuine depth of feeling that Archilochus had expressed almost two centuries earlier; the developing Greek genius was turning to other forms of literary expression, notably the drama.

THE THEME I SING

Give me the harp of epic song,
Which Homer's finger thrilled along;
But tear away the sanguine string,
For war is not the theme I sing.
Proclaim the laws of festal right,
I'm monarch of the board tonight;
And all around shall brim as high,
And quaff the tide as deep as I.
And when the cluster's mellowing dews
Their warm enchanting balm infuse,
Our feet shall catch the elastic bound,
And reel us through the dance's round.
Great Bacchus! we shall sing to thee,
In wild but sweet ebriety;
Flashing around such sparks of thought,
As Bacchus could alone have taught.
  Then, give the harp of epic song,
Which Homer's finger thrilled along;
But tear away the sanguine string,
For war is not the theme I sing.

Trans. Thomas Moore

LET US THE FESTAL HOURS BEGUILE

I care not for the idle state
Of Persia's king, the rich, the great:
I envy not the monarch's throne,
Nor wish the treasured gold my own.
But oh! be mine the rosy wreath,
Its freshness o'er my brow to breathe;
Be mine the rich perfumes that flow,
To cool and scent my locks of snow.
Today I'll haste to quaff my wine,
And if tomorrow comes, why then —
I'll haste to quaff my wine again.
And thus while all our days are bright,
Let us the festal hours beguile
With mantling cup and cordial smile;
And shed from each new bowl of wine
The richest drop on Bacchus' shrine.
For Death may come, with brow unpleasant,

May come, when least we wish him present,
And beckon to the sable shore,
And grimly bid us — drink no more!

Trans. Thomas Moore

20

Solon: The Athenian New Deal

Later Greeks looked back upon Solon as the greatest of statesmen and the wisest of men. Such renown was well deserved. He was called upon to save Athens at a moment of severe crisis in 594 B.C. when. civil war between an oppressed peasantry and an avaricious aristocracy was beginning to threaten the destruction of the state. The crisis had been long preparing. During the seventh century the Athenian nobility had steadily reduced the power of the king to the point where they could finally eliminate him altogether. His powers were taken over by noble magistrates, called archons, who were the dependable agents of the aristocratic Council of the Areopagus. The old Homeric popular assembly sank into virtual oblivion, and the lower classes suffered oppression in the manner described by Hesiod. Most of them lost their lands, many became share-croppers, and a large number were finally reduced to debt-slavery. About 632 B.C. Cylon sought unsuccessfully to capitalize on the discontent of the lower classes to make himself tyrant. This event appears to have frightened the nobility into compromising by allowing an archon named Draco in 621 B.C. to put into written form the hitherto unwritten customary laws. This was to prevent the aristocratic magistrates from administering the laws unjustly after the manner of the judges who, as described by Hesiod, "devour bribes and give crooked decisions." The lower classes found this compromise unsatisfactory, and the class struggle continued unabated.

Solon's economic and political reforms aimed at a compromise between the two parties whose names reveal that Athenian politics was grounded upon conflicting economic interests. The Plain, composed of aristocratic landowners holding the fertile land in the valleys, was the ultra-conservative party opposed to all change, while the Hill, the party of discontented hillbillies, share-croppers, and the lower class in the city, demanded a radical redivision of the landed

From Plutarch, *Parallel Lives*, "Solon," based on the translation by John Dryden and A. H. Clough.

wealth. A third party, called the Shore and composed of fishermen and the beginnings of a merchant class, was as yet too feeble to play an independent part in politics.

It is worth noting that Solon's reforms were linked with the new religious ideal of justice and the new rational ideal of moderation, both expounded earlier by Hesiod. "My spirit commands me to teach the Athenians," Solon declared in the poetry he wrote to justify his reforms, and this motivating spirit was the product of the new ethical religion of Zeus and Dikē, Goddess of Justice. The Athenians must be taught that greed and injustice are pushing their city towards disaster, for "they do not preserve the venerable foundations of Dikē, who in her silence knows all the past and all the present, but does not fail to come in time to punish." To avoid the ruin which such punishment brings, the opposing factions must learn that "the hardest thing of all is to recognize the invisible Mean of judgment, which alone contains the limits of all things." They must, in other words, compromise their differences by accepting the middle-of-the-road reforms of Solon.

The following account of the economic and political reforms of Solon is taken from the "Life of Solon," one of the series of biographies in Plutarch's Parallel Lives of famous Greeks and Romans. Plutarch, who died about 127 A.D., was educated at Athens, lectured on philosophy at Rome, held political office in Greece, and finally retired to his birthplace, the small town of Chaeronea in central Greece, to devote the rest of his life to writing and teaching. His chief interest was in moral philosophy, a fact clearly evident in his Lives where the emphasis is upon the delineation of character. As a moralist, Plutarch believed that the course of history was determined by the actions of great men, and not by economic or other forces. His Lives have enjoyed great popularity, particularly during those times when an upsurge of the human spirit has produced an optimistic outlook that finds Plutarch's idealistic view of men congenial. Thus the Renaissance humanist Montaigne could write in his essay "Of the Education of Boys": "Through the medium of histories he will hold converse with the great souls of the best ages. . . . What profit will he not reap, to that end, by reading the Lives of our Plutarch!"

THE REVOLUTIONARY SITUATION AT ATHENS

13. The Athenians, now that Cylon's sedition was over and those polluted by blood-guilt had gone into banishment, fell into their old quarrels about the form of government, there being as many different parties as there were geographical diversities in the country. The Hill quarter favored an extreme democracy, the Plain an extreme oligarchy, and the Shore stood for a mixed form of government and opposed the other two parties, thus preventing either of them from prevailing. At that time, too, the disparity between rich and poor had reached its height. The city was on the brink of revolution, and the only way to stop disorder and achieve stability seemed to be by changing to a tyranny. All the common people were in debt to the rich. They either tilled their land for them, paying them a sixth of the produce and were therefore called Hectemorii

and Thetes, or they pledged their bodies to raise money and could be seized by their creditors and either enslaved at home or sold to foreigners. Some (for no law forbade it) were forced to sell their children or go into exile to avoid the harshness of their creditors. The most and the bravest of them, however, began to band together and encourage one another not to submit to injustice but to choose a leader, liberate the enslaved debtors, redivide the land, and change the form of government.

SOLON REFUSES ABSOLUTE POWER

14. At this point the wiser among the Athenians began to think of Solon. They knew that he, more than anyone else, was not implicated in the troubles of the time, that he had not joined in the extortions of the rich or been involved in the privations of the poor. Therefore they urged him to come forward and settle the differences. Phanias the Lesbian, however, maintains that in order to save his city, Solon played a trick upon both parties by secretly promising the poor a division of the land and the rich security for their debts. But Solon himself says that he entered politics reluctantly, being afraid of the greediness of one party and the arrogance of the other. He was chosen archon, however, after Philombrotus, and empowered to act as arbitrator and lawgiver, the rich consenting because he was wealthy and the poor because he was honest. There was a saying of his current before the election to the effect that when things are equal there never can be war, and this pleased both the rich and the poor, the first assuming him to mean an equality based on merit and achievement, the second an equality based on the counting of votes. Consequently, there were great hopes on both sides and their leaders repeatedly pressed Solon to establish a tyranny and manage the city freely according to his pleasure. There were also many citizens, belonging to neither party, who saw that it would be difficult to bring about change by debate and legislation and who therefore were willing to have one wise and just man placed at the head of the state. Some also say that Solon received this oracle from Apollo:

> Take the mid-seat, and be the vessel's guide;
> Many in Athens are upon your side.

But most of all his close friends chided him for rejecting absolute power only because of the name of tyrant, without considering that the virtues of the man who seized such power would at once transform it into a lawful sovereignty. Euboea, they argued, had found this true of Tynnondas, and now Mitylene had made Pittacus its tyrant.

None of these arguments could shake Solon's resolution. He replied to his friends, we are told, that it was true that tyranny was a fine spot, but there was no way down from it, and in one of his poems he writes to Phocus:

> That I spared my land,
> And withheld from usurpation and from violence my hand,

And forbore to fix a stain and a disgrace on my good name,
I regret not; I believe that it will be my chieftest fame.

From this it is clear that he was a man of great repute even before he drafted his laws. As for the ridicule that was heaped upon him for refusing to be a tyrant, he has written these words:

Solon surely was a dreamer, and a man of simple mind;
When the gods would give him fortune, he of his own will declined;
When the net was full of fishes, over-heavy thinking it,
He declined to haul it up, through want of heart and want of wit.
Had but I that chance of riches and of tyranny, for one day,
I would give my skin for flaying, and my house to die away.

15. Thus he makes the multitude and the unscrupulous speak of him. Yet, though he refused to be a tyrant, he was not at all mild in his handling of public affairs, and his legislation was not the product of a feeble spirit. He did not make concessions to the powerful or tailor his laws to please the voters. Where things were well before, he attempted no remedy or change for fear lest by turning everything upside down and disorganizing the state he might be too weak to restore it to a workable condition. But what he thought he could effect by persuasion or by the force of his authority, this he did, as he himself says, "With force and justice working in harmony." And so when he was later asked if he had left the Athenians the best laws that could be enacted, he replied, "The best they would accept."

ECONOMIC REFORMS

Later writers note that the Athenians have a way of disguising the ugliness of things by giving them endearing and innocent names, calling harlots, for example, "companions," taxes "contributions," a garrison a "guard," and the jail the "chamber." Solon seems to have been the first to use this device when he called cancelling debts *seisactheia*, a "disburdenment." For the first of his enactments decreed that existing debts should be forgiven and that in the future no one could accept the body of a debtor as security. Though writers such as Androtion maintain that Solon relieved the poor not by cancelling debts but by reducing the interest on them, which so pleased the people that they called not only this humanitarian act *seisactheia*, but also the enlargement of measures and the rise in the value of money which took place at this time. For Solon fixed the value of the mina at one hundred drachmas, whereas before it had contained only seventy-three. In this way, although the amount of the payment remained the same, its value was less, which proved a considerable benefit to the debtors and no loss to the creditors. But most writers agree that it was the removal of all debt that was called *seisactheia*, which is supported by Solon's poems in which he prides himself that

The mortgage stones that covered her, by me
Removed — the land that was a slave is free.

He adds that some of those who had been seized for debt were brought back
from foreign countries where

so far their lot to roam,
They had forgot the language of their home;

And some he says he set free "Who here in shameful servitude were held."

This undertaking is said to have involved him in the greatest trouble of his
life. When he had decided to abolish debts and was considering the best arguments and the proper moment for it, he told his closest friends, Conon, Clinias,
and Hipponicus, that he would not touch the land but intended only to abolish debts. They promptly took advantage of this confidence and anticipated
Solon's decree by borrowing large sums of money and buying up big estates.
Then, when the decree was enacted, they kept their properties but refused to
pay their creditors. This affair brought upon Solon great suspicion and dislike,
as though he himself had not been the victim of a trick but was a party to the
fraud. However, he soon stopped this suspicion by his well-known sacrifice of
five talents; for it was discovered that he had lent this amount (some, among
them Polyzelus the Rhodian, say fifteen talents) and was the first to comply
with his own law and cancel the debt. His friends, on the other hand, were
ever after called *chreocopidae*, or "swindlers."

16. His policy pleased neither party, however. The rich were angry on account of their money, and the poor even more so because Solon had not
divided the land or, as Lycurgus had done [see Selection 22], reduced all men
to equality. But Lycurgus was an eleventh-generation descendant of Heracles
and had reigned many years in Sparta. . . . Solon, on the other hand, could not
go to such extreme in his constitution, since he was a man of modest fortune
and had been chosen by the people. Yet he made full use of his power, relying
on the good will of the citizens and their confidence in him. Nevertheless he
offended many, who looked for different results, as he declares in these words:

Formerly they boasted of me vainly; with averted eyes
Now they look askance upon me; friends no more, but enemies.

And yet had any other man, he adds, received the same power,

He would not have forborne, nor let alone,
But made the fattest of the milk his own.

POLITICAL REFORMS

Soon, however, seeing the value of his policy, they laid aside their complaints,
offered a public sacrifice — which they called the Seisactheia — and appointed

Solon to reform the constitution and draft a code of laws. They gave him full power over everything — magistracies, assemblies, courts, and councils. He had authority to decide the property qualifications and times of meeting of each of these bodies, and also to preserve or dissolve any existing institution as he saw fit.

17. First, then, he repealed all of Draco's laws, except those concerning homicide, because they were too severe and their penalties too heavy. For death was the penalty for almost all offenses, so that even those convicted of idleness were put to death, and those who stole a cabbage or an apple suffered the same punishment as those who committed sacrilege or murder. This is why Demades, in later times, became famous when he said that Draco's laws were written not in ink but in blood. Draco himself, when asked why he made death the punishment for most offenses, replied that the minor ones deserved it, and no heavier penalty was left for major crimes.

18. Next, Solon wished to continue the magistracies in the hands of the rich, but to give the people a share in the rest of the government, which they had never before enjoyed, and he therefore took a census of every citizen's property. Those who were worth five hundred measures of dry and liquid goods he placed in the first class and called them Pentacosiomedimni. The second class was composed of those who could afford a horse, or were worth three hundred measures, and they were called Knights. The third class, whose income was 200 measures, was called Zeugitae. All the rest of the citizens were called Thetes; they were not admitted to any office but could attend the assembly and act as jurors. This last privilege at first seemed of little worth, but later became very important because almost every dispute came before them as jurors. Even in the cases which Solon assigned to the jurisdiction of a magistrate, he also allowed the right of appeal to a popular court. In addition, it is said that he purposely was obscure and ambiguous in the wording of his laws in order to increase the power of the popular courts; for since the parties to a dispute could not settle it according to the letter of the law, they had to place it before the jurors, who thus became in a sense masters of the laws. Solon himself mentions this equality in the following lines:

> Such power I gave the people as might do,
> Abridged not what they had, nor lavished new,
> Those that were great in wealth and high in place
> My counsel likewise kept from all disgrace.
> Before them both I held my shield of might,
> And let not either touch the other's right.

Desiring to further protect the common people, Solon gave every citizen the right of bringing suit on behalf of anyone who had suffered injury. If a man was assaulted and suffered violence or injury, any who wished and was able to do so could prosecute the offender. He intended by this to accustom the citizens, as members of the same body, to feel and sympathize with one another's injuries. We are told of a saying of Solon's relating to this law. Being asked what city was best governed, he replied, "That city where those who have not been wronged try to punish the offender as much as those who have been wronged."

19. He organized the Council of the Areopagus to be composed of those who had held the annual office of archon, which meant that he was also a member. He then observed that the people, now free from debt, were becoming uneasy and bold, and he therefore formed another Council of Four Hundred, composed of a hundred men from each of the four tribes. This council was to inspect all matters before they were presented to the people, and was not to allow any matter to be brought before the popular assembly without its approval. He made the upper council, or Areopagus, the supervisor and guardian of the laws, thinking that the city, held by these two councils like anchors, would be less likely to be tossed by tumults, and the people would be more tranquil. . . .

20. Among Solon's other laws, one is very peculiar and surprising — it disfranchises any citizen who remains neutral in a revolution. Evidently he did not want anyone to remain apathetic or indifferent to the public good, safeguarding his private affairs while congratulating himself for having no concern for the distresses of his country. One should promptly join the good and righteous cause, assist it and share its dangers, rather than wait in safety to see which side wins. . . .

OTHER ECONOMIC REFORMS

22. Solon observed that the city was filling up with people who streamed from all areas into Attica for greater security of living, and at the same time he realized that most of the country was poor and unproductive, and that sea traders send no goods to those who can give them nothing in exchange. Therefore he turned the attention of the citizens to manufactures. He made a law that no son was obliged to support his father unless he had been taught a trade. . . . and seeing that the soil of Attica was scarcely rich enough to maintain those who tilled it and was incapable of feeding an idle and leisured multitude, he sought to dignify all trades and ordered the Council of the Areopagus to inquire how every man made a living and to punish those who had no occupation. . . .

24. Of the products of the soil, Solon allowed only oil to be exported, and those who exported any other product were to be solemnly cursed by the archon, or else were to pay a hundred drachmas into the public treasury. . . . His law concerning naturalized citizens is of doubtful wisdom, because he permitted the naturalization only of those who had been permanently exiled from their country or who came with their families to ply a trade. This he did, we are told, not to discourage all immigrants but rather to invite these particular types with the sure hope of their becoming citizens. He also thought that those who had been forced to leave their country, or who had left it for a particular purpose, would prove to be more faithful citizens.

21

Pisistratus: The Rise of Tyranny in Athens

Solon's admonition that "the hardest thing of all is to recognize the invisible Mean of judgment" was borne out by the developments in Athens after Solon departed from the city, leaving his reforms on trial. His compromise legislation satisfied neither contending party, and strife broke out anew. The nobles were bitter over the weakening of their privileged economic and political position, and the commoners found that debt-cancellation afforded no permanent solution for their economic plight and that the political concessions meant little or nothing in the face of want. The factional strife that resulted paralyzed the state — no magistrates could be elected in 590 or 580 B.C. — and finally led in 560 to the tyranny of Pisistratus, a famed military hero, as the champion of the Hill party with its radical program of redivision of the land. To Solon this was "the retribution of Zeus" which in his verses he had foretold would descend upon the Athenians if they did not learn the lesson of moderation and compromise: "From the clouds come snow and hail, thunder follows the lightning, and by powerful men the city is brought low and the people in its ignorance comes into the power of a despot."

The following account, which Plutarch fittingly attached to the end of his "Life of Solon," is one of the clearest expositions to be found in history of the technique used by ambitious men to acquire dictatorial powers, and, what is even more significant, of the avoidable conditions which, again and again throughout history, have led to dictatorship. In our modern world, beginning with the French Revolution and continuing to the present day, the land-hunger of an oppressed peasantry has contributed to revolution and to the rise of dictators. Unfortunately, as Solon sadly noted in his reference to "the people in its ignorance comes into the power of a despot," not many people in history have had the wisdom to forsee the probability of such disastrous results of the failure to achieve moderate reform.

THE RENEWAL OF CLASS STRUGGLE

29. During Solon's absence the Athenians were again divided into factions. Lycurgus headed the Plain, Megacles the son of Alcmaeon the Shore, and

From Plutarch, *Parallel Lives*, "Solon," based on the translation by John and William Langhorne (Solon's poetry translated by John Dryden).

Pisistratus the Hill. Among the latter was the multitude of laboring people whose enmity was directed at the rich. Hence it was that though the city did observe Solon's laws, all factions expected a revolution and wanted a different form of government, not to obtain equality but with a view to be gainers by the change and to dominate those who differed from them.

While matters stood thus Solon arrived at Athens. He was revered and honored by all, but because of his great age he had neither the strength nor spirit to act or speak in public as he had done. He, therefore, appealed in private to the heads of the factions and endeavored to appease and reconcile them. Pisistratus seemed more amenable than the rest. He had an affable and engaging manner, was a great friend of the poor, and behaved with generosity even to his enemies. He counterfeited so successfully the good qualities which nature had denied him that he gained more credit than those who actually possessed them. He was thought to be cautious and law-abiding, zealous for equality and the present government, and opposed to all who clamored for a change. On these points he deceived most people, but Solon soon discovered his real character and was the first to discern his insidious designs. Yet he did not completely break with him but endeavored to soften him and advise him better, declaring both to him and to others that if ambition could be banished from his soul and he could be cured of his desire for absolute power, there would not be a man better disposed to virtue or a more worthy citizen of Athens.

About this time Thespis began to develop tragedy and the novelty of the thing attracted many spectators, although this was before any prize was given in competition. Solon, who was always willing to listen and to learn, and now in his old age was more inclined to anything that might divert and entertain, even wine and song, went to see Thespis act in his own play, as was the custom of the ancient poets. After the performance, he asked Thespis if he was not ashamed to tell so many lies before so many people. Thespis answered that there was no harm in speaking and acting that way in a play. To which Solon exclaimed, striking the ground violently with his staff: "If we encourage such make-believe as this, we shall soon find it in our contracts and agreements."

THE TECHNIQUE OF ESTABLISHING TYRANNY

30. Soon afterwards, Pisistratus deliberately wounded himself and drove in a chariot to the market place where he tried to arouse the people by telling them that his enemies had plotted to kill him because of his political views. When the multitude loudly expressed their indignation, Solon came up and said to him: "Son of Hippocrates, you act Homer's Odysseus very badly; for he wounded himself to deceive his enemies, but you have done it to mislead your countrymen."

After this the people were ready to fight for Pisistratus, and at a general assembly Ariston made a motion that a bodyguard of fifty club-bearers should be assigned to him. Solon formally opposed it with many arguments similar to those he has left us in his poems:

You dote upon the words of a wily man.
True, you are singly each a crafty soul,
But all together make one empty fool.

But when he saw the poor become riotous and determined to support Pisistratus, while the rich out of fear declined to oppose him, Solon left the assembly, saying that he was wiser than the one party in discerning the plot, and braver than the other, which understood what was happening but was afraid to oppose a tyrant. So the people passed the decree and did not limit the number of guards which Pisistratus employed, but allowed him to keep as many as he pleased until at last he seized the Acropolis.

SOLON REPROVES THE ATHENIANS

When this had been done and the city was in great confusion, Megacles immediately took flight with the rest of the Alcmaeonidae family. But Solon, though he was now very old and had none to support him, appeared in public and addressed the citizens, both upbraiding them for their stupidity and cowardice, and exhorting and encouraging them not to surrender their liberty. Then it was that he spoke those memorable words, that it would have been easier for them to repress the advance of tryranny and prevent its establishment, but now that it was established and fully grown it would be more glorious to destroy it. However, finding that no one had the courage to support him, he returned to his own house and placed his weapons at the street door with these words: "I have done all in my power to defend my country and its laws."

This was his last public effort. Though some urged him to fly, he took no notice of their advice but continued to write poems in which he reproached the Athenians:

> If now you suffer, do not blame the Powers,
> For they are good, and all the fault was ours,
> All the strongholds you put into his hands,
> And now his slaves must do what he commands.

31. Many of his friends, alarmed at this, told him the tyrant would certainly put him to death for it and asked him to what he trusted that he went to such imprudent lengths. He answered: "To my old age." However, when Pisistratus had fully established himself he paid court to Solon. He treated him with kindness and respect and invited him to his house, until Solon actually became his adviser and approved many of his acts. He retained most of Solon's laws, observing them himself and compelling his friends to do so. For example, when he was accused of murder after he had become tyrant, he appeared in due form before the court of the Areopagus to defend himself, but his accuser did not appear. He also added some laws of his own, one of which provides that persons maimed in war should be maintained at public expense.

22

Lycurgus: The Spartan Totalitarian System

The Greeks traditionally regarded Lycurgus, the "Solon" of Sparta (Lacedae-mon), as having forged, sometime in the ninth century B.C., the famed totali-tarian system which made Sparta an armed camp, culturally and economically stagnant, and with the individual completely subordinated to the power of the state. Many modern scholars, however, regard Lycurgus as hardly more than a legend, and they look upon the peculiar Spartan political and social institutions as Sparta's unique answer to the problems which confronted other Greek states during the seventh and sixth centuries B.C.

Until late in the seventh century, Sparta's development had paralleled that of the rest of Greece. She was culturally advanced, being famed as a center for poets, musicians, and painters. Her nobles had achieved a monopoly of govern-ment by the establishment of annual aristocratic magistrates, called ephors, whose powers drastically curtailed those of the kings. Plagued by the twin problems of overpopulation and land hunger, she had also begun to send colonists abroad when, about 740 B.C., she hit upon a simpler solution — the conquest of the fertile plains of neighboring Messenia, whose inhabitants were eventually reduced to serfdom. When the Messenian serfs (helots) revolted around 650 B.C., it took nearly two decades of bitter fighting to crush the up-rising. Complicating this crisis was the demand of the Spartan commoners for land division and political equality.

Fearful lest popular discontent would lead, as elsewhere in Greece, to the rise of a tyrant, and fully aware of the ever-present threat of the helots, who outnumbered their masters ten to one, the Spartan aristocrats moved success-fully to deal with both dangers. A popular assembly was created with the right to elect the ephors and approve or veto the proposals of the aristocratic council; the land was redivided among all citizens; and a new system of education and training was inaugurated which, in the words of Plutarch, "accustomed the citizens to have neither the will nor the ability to lead a private life, but, like bees, to be organic parts of their community, clinging together around their leader, forgetting themselves in their enthusiastic patriotism, and belonging wholly to their country."

Some scholars are of the opinion that if Lycurgus "the lawgiver" was a his-torical person, he probably played the same role in Sparta that Solon played at

From Plutarch, *Parallel Lives*, "Lycurgus," based on the translation by Aubrey Stewart and George Long.

Athens — a mediator between commoners and aristocrats whose political and economic reforms sought (successfully in the case of Lycurgus) to provide an alternative to tyranny. The social reforms that made Sparta a totalitarian state came somewhat later and were attributed to Lycurgus.

The fullest ancient accounts of the "Lycurgan" system are The Constitution of the Lacedaemonians by Xenophon (d. ca. 355 B.C.) and the "Life of Lycurgus" by Plutarch. Selections from Plutarch's more vivid anecdotal account are presented here.

1. With regard to Lycurgus the lawgiver there is nothing whatever that is undisputed; his birth, his travels, his death, and, above all, his legislation, have all been related in various ways. Even the dates given for his birth are not in agreement.... However, in spite of these discrepancies I shall endeavor, by following the least inconsistent accounts and the best known authorities, to write the history of his life....

ECONOMIC REFORMS

8. The . . . boldest of Lycurgus' reforms was the redistribution of the land. Great inequalities existed in this regard, with the result that many poor and needy people had become a burden to the state while wealth was concentrated in a very few hands. Lycurgus abolished all pride, envy, crime, and luxury, which flowed from those old and terrible evils of riches and poverty, by inducing all landowners to offer their estates for redistribution and by prevailing upon all citizens to live on equal terms with equal incomes. They were to strive only to surpass one another in courage and virtue, there being henceforth no social inequalities among them except as praise or blame can create....

Each man's allotment of land was large enough to produce annually seventy medimni of barley for himself and twelve for his wife, with oil and wine in proportion. He thought this would be sufficient because it was enough to maintain them in health, and they needed nothing more. It is said that some years later, as he was returning from a journey through the country at harvest time and saw the sheaves of grain lying in equal parallel rows, he smiled and said to his companions that all Laconia seemed as if it had just been divided among many brothers.

9. He desired to distribute movable property also, in order completely to do away with inequality; but, seeing that actually to take away these things would be a most unpopular measure, he managed to end all avarice by a different method. First, he abolished the use of gold and silver money and made iron money alone legal, and this he made of great size and weight and of so small value that the equivalent for ten minae required a large store-room and a yoke of oxen to transport it. As soon as this happened, many types of crime became unkown in Lacedaemon. For who would steal, or take as a bribe or as plunder, a mass of iron which he could not conceal, which no one envied him for possessing, and which he could not even cut up and make use of? For the hot iron was, it is said, quenched in vinegar so as to make it useless by rendering it brittle and hard to work.

After this he ordered a general expulsion of the workers in unnecessary trades. Indeed, most of them would have left the country anyway when the old currency came to an end, since they could not sell their wares. The iron money had no value and could not be carried elsewhere in Greece, where it was regarded as ridiculous. Nor could it be used for the purchase of foreign trumpery, and so no cargo was shipped to a Laconian port, no sophists came into the country, no vagabond soothsayers, no panderers, no goldsmiths or silversmiths, since there was no money to pay them with. Luxury, thus cut off from all encouragement, gradually became extinct. The rich were on the same footing with other people, as they could not spend their money but were forced to keep it idle at home. . . .

10. Wishing still more to attack luxury and remove the desire for riches, he introduced . . . the most admirable of his reforms, that of the common dining-table. Here the men were to meet and dine together on a fixed allowance of food instead of eating in their own homes, lolling on expensive couches at rich tables, fattened like beasts in private by the hands of servants and cooks, and undermining their health by indulgence to excess in every bodily desire, long sleep, warm baths, and much rest, as though they required a sort of daily nursing like sick people. . . . Men were not even allowed to dine previously at home and then come to the public table; the others would watch him who did not eat or drink with them and reproach him as a weakling, too effeminate to eat the rough common fare. . . .

SPARTAN EDUCATION AND TRAINING

13. Lycurgus did not establish any written laws; indeed, this is distinctly forbidden by one of the so-called Rhetras [decrees]. He thought that the principles of most importance for the prosperity and honor of the state would remain most securely fixed if implanted in the citizens by habit and training, as they would then be followed from choice rather than necessity; for his method of education made each of them into a lawgiver like himself. The trifling conventions of everyday life were best left undefined by hard-and-fast laws, so that they might from time to time receive corrections or additions from men educated in the spirit of the Lacedaemonian system. On this education the whole scheme of Lycurgus' laws depended. . . .

14. Considering education to be the most important and the noblest work of a lawgiver, he began at the very beginning by regulating marriages and the birth of children. . . . He strengthened the bodies of the girls by exercise in running, wrestling, and hurling the discus or the javelin, in order that their children might spring from a healthy source and so grow up strong, and that they themselves might have strength to easily endure the pains of childbirth. He did away with all seclusion and retirement for women, and ordained that girls, no less than boys, should go naked in processions, and dance and sing at festivals in the presence of the young men. There the jokes they made about certain youths were sometimes of great value as reproofs of ill-conduct, while, on the other hand, by reciting verses written in praise of the deserving they inspired great ambition and thirst for distinction in the young men. For he who

had been praised by the maidens for his valor went away congratulated by his friends, while the raillery which they used in sport and jest was as sharp as a serious reproof, especially as the kings and elders were present at these festivals along with all the other citizens.

This nakedness of the maidens had in it nothing disgraceful. It was done modestly, not licentiously, and it produced habits of simplicity and taught them to desire good health and beauty of body, and to love honor and courage no less than the men. This it was that made them speak and think as Gorgo, the wife of Leonidas, is said to have done. Some foreign lady, it seems, said to her, "You Spartan women are the only ones who rule men." She answered, "Yes, for we are the only ones who give birth to men."

15. . . . Furthermore, it was allowable for a respectable man, if he admired a virtuous mother of fine children who was married to someone else, to induce her husband to permit him to have access to her in order, as it were, to sow seed in a fertile field and obtain a fine son from a healthy stock. Lycurgus did not view children as belonging to their parents, but as the property of the state, and therefore he desired his citizens to be born of the best possible parents. Besides, he noticed the inconsistency and folly of the rest of mankind: they are willing to pay money or use their influence with the owners of well-bred stock to obtain a good breed of horses or dogs, but they lock up their women in seclusion and permit them to have children by no one but themselves, even though they be mad, decrepit, or diseased. It is as though the good or bad qualities of children did not depend entirely upon their parents and did not affect the parents more than anyone else. . . .

16. A father had not the right of bringing up his offspring but had to carry it to a place called Lesche, where the elders of the tribes sat in judgment upon the child. If they thought it well-built and strong, they ordered the father to rear it and they assigned it one of the nine thousand plots of land; but if it was meanlooking or misshapen, they sent it away to the place called Exposure, a glen at the foot of Mount Taygetus, for they considered that a child who did not start out healthy and strong would be handicapped in its own life and of no value to the state. . . .

Nor was each man allowed to bring up and educate his son as he chose, but as soon as the children were seven years old Lycurgus took them from their parents and enrolled them in companies. Here they lived and ate in common and shared their play and work. One of the noblest and bravest men of the state was appointed superintendent of the boys, and they themselves in each company chose the wisest and bravest as captain. They looked to him for orders, obeyed his commands, and endured his punishments, so that even in childhood they learned to obey. The older men watched them at their play, and by instituting fights and trials of strength, accurately learned which were the bravest and strongest. They learned to read and write, because that is necessary, but all the rest of their education was meant to teach them to obey with cheerfulness, to endure hardship, and to win battles. As they grew older their training became more severe. Their heads were closely shorn and they were taught to walk barefooted and to play naked. They wore no tunic after their twelfth year, but received one garment for all the year round. They were necessarily dirty, as they had no warm baths and ointments, except on certain days as a luxury. They slept together in troops and companies on beds of rushes which they had picked with their own hands on the banks of the Eurotas, for they were not allowed to use a knife for that purpose. In winter they mixed a thistledown called lycophon with the rushes, as it is thought to possess some warmth.

17. . . . [They are taught to steal, bringing to their captain] what they steal from the gardens and from the men's dining-tables, where they creep in very cleverly and cautiously; for if one is caught he is severely whipped for stealing carelessly and clumsily. They also steal food from those who are asleep or off their guard. Whoever is caught is punished by flogging and starvation. Their meals are purposely scanty in order that they may exercise their ingenuity and daring in obtaining more. . . .

18. The boys steal with such earnestness that there is a story of one who had taken a fox's cub and hidden it under his cloak, and, though his entrails were being torn out by the claws and teeth of the beast, persevered in concealing it until he died. . . .

19. The boys were taught to use a sarcastic yet graceful style of speaking, and to compress much thought into few words. Lycurgus made the iron money have little value for its great size, but on the other hand he made their speech short and compact, yet full of meaning, by teaching the young, after long periods of silent listening, to speak sententiously and to the point. For those who allow themselves much licence in speech seldom say anything memorable. When some Athenian jeered at the small Spartan swords, saying that jugglers on the stage could easily swallow them, King Agis answered, "And yet with these little daggers we can generally reach our enemies.". . .

20. . . . One may also judge their character by their jokes; for they are taught never to talk at random, nor to utter a syllable that does not contain some thought. For example, when one of them was invited to hear a man imitate the nightingale, he answered, "I have heard the original." . . .

"THEY LIVED AS IF IN A CAMP"

24. The training of the Spartan youth continued till their manhood. No one was permitted to live according to his own pleasure, but they lived in the city as if in a camp, with a fixed diet and fixed public duties, thinking themselves to belong not to themselves but to their country. Those who had no other duty either looked after the young and taught them what was useful, or themselves learned such things from the old. For ample leisure was one of the blessings with which Lycurgus provided his countrymen, since they were absolutely forbidden to practice any mechanical craft, and moneymaking and business were unnecessary because wealth was disregarded and despised. The Helots tilled the soil and produced the usual crops for them. Indeed, a Spartan who was at Athens while the courts were sitting and learned that some man had been fined for idleness and was leaving the court in sorrow accompanied by his grieving friends, asked to be shown the man who had been punished for

gentlemanly behavior. So slavish did they deem it to labor at a trade and in business. . . .

27. . . . In Sparta nothing was left without regulation, but with all the necessary acts of life Lycurgus mingled some ceremony which might enkindle virtue or discourage vice; indeed, he filled his city with examples of this kind, by which the citizens were insensibly molded and impelled towards honorable pursuits. For this reason he would not allow citizens to leave the country at pleasure to wander in foreign lands, where they would contract strange habits and learn to imitate the untrained lives and ill-regulated institutions to be found abroad. Also, he banished from Lacedaemon all strangers who were there for no useful purpose; not, as Thucydides says, because he feared they might imitate his constitution and learn something serviceable for the improvement of their own countries, but rather for fear that they might teach the people some mischief. Strangers introduce strange ideas, and these could lead to subversive discussions and political views which would jar with the established constitution, like discord in music. Therefore he thought that it was more important to keep bad habits from entering the city than it was to keep out the plague.

THE KRYPTEIA AND THE HELOTS

28. In all this we cannot find any traces of the injustice and unfairness which some complain of in the laws of Lycurgus, which they say are excellent to produce courage but less so for justice. The secret service, called *Krypteia*, if indeed it is one of the institutions of Lycurgus as Aristotle says, may have given Plato also this view of the man and his system. The *Krypteia* operated in this way: The magistrates at intervals sent out the most discreet of the young soldiers into different parts of the country, equipped only with daggers and food. In the daytime they concealed themselves in unfrequented spots and lay quiet, but at night they came down into the roads and killed every Helot they found. And often they would move through the fields and slay the strongest and bravest Helots they could find. Also, as Thucydides mentions his *History of the Peloponnesian War*, those Helots who were especially honored by the Spartans for their valor were crowned as free men and taken to the temples with rejoicings; but in a short time they all disappeared, more than two thousand of them, in such a way that no man, either then or afterwards, could tell how they perished. Aristotle says that the Ephors, when they first take office, declare war against the Helots in order that it may be lawful to destroy them. And other harsh treatment was inflicted upon them; for example, they were compelled to drink much unmixed wine and then were brought into the public dining-halls to show the young men what drunkenness was. . . .

LYCURGUS' LAWS APPROVED BY HEAVEN

29. When the men of the city were thoroughly imbued with the spirit of his institutions and the newly constituted state was strong enough to operate and preserve itself, then, as Plato says of the Deity, that he was pleased with

the world he had created after it first began to live and move, so it was with Lycurgus. He admired the spectacle of his laws in operation and, as far as human wisdom would permit, he desired to leave it eternal and unchangeable. He therefore assembled all the citizens and told them that the city was now well provided with material for happiness and virtue, but that he would not bestow upon them the most valuable gift of all until he had consulted with Heaven. It was therefore their duty to abide by the already established laws and to change and alter nothing until he had returned from Delphi, and then he would do whatever the god commanded. They all agreed and bade him depart. After making the kings and elders and then the rest of the citizens swear that they would keep the present constitution until he returned, he set out for Delphi.

Upon reaching the temple he sacrificed to the god and inquired whether his laws were sufficient to provide prosperity and happiness for his country. Receiving answer from the oracle that his laws were excellent and the state would become famous if it kept the constitution of Lycurgus, he wrote down this prophecy and sent it to Sparta. But he himself, after offering a second sacrifice to the god and embracing his friends and his sons, resolved never to release his countrymen from their oath by putting an end to his own life. Though life was still pleasant, he had reached an age when it seemed time to go to his rest after having so excellently arranged all his people's affairs. He departed by starvation, as he thought that even the death of a true statesman ought to be of service to the state, not insignificant but recognized as a virtuous act. His death came in the fullness of time, after he had done an excellent work, and it was left as the guardian of all the good that he had done because the citizens had sworn that they would abide by his constitution until he returned to them. Nor was he deceived in his expectations, for his state was by far the most celebrated in Greece for good government at home and renown abroad during a period of five hundred years. . . .

CONCLUSION

30. . . . I am amazed at those who say that the Lacedaemonians "knew how to obey, but not how to rule," and as proof quote the saying of King Theopompus. When told that the safety of Sparta lay in her kings knowing how to rule, he replied: "No, it lies in her citizens knowing how to obey." But people do not obey unless rulers know how to command. . . .

31. . . . Seeing that, in states as in individuals, happiness is derived from virtue and concord, Lycurgus directed all his efforts to implant in his countrymen feelings of honor, self-reliance, and self-control. These were also taken as the basis of their constitutions by Plato, Diogenes, Zeno, and all who have written with any success upon this subject. But they have left mere dissertations; Lycurgus produced an inimitable constitution, . . . showing them the spectacle of an entire city acting like philosophers, and thereby obtained for himself a greater reputation than that of any other Greek legislator at any period.

23

Herodotus, History of The Persian Wars

East vs. West

If history be defined as an "honest attempt first to find out what happened, then to explain why it happened," Herodotus (ca. 484–ca. 425 B.C.) deserves to be called "the father of history." His forerunners in this endeavor were the logographers — "writers of tales [logoi]" — who arose during the late sixth century B.C. in Greek Asia Minor (where Herodotus was born) and in their lost works assembled a multitude of disarrayed facts on such diverse subjects as geneology, local history, and geography. Herodotus was also a collector of facts and a teller of tales, but he went far beyond the logographers in the broad scope and unifying theme of his investigations — the clash of two rival cultures which culminated in the Persian Wars — and in his concern for causation. All this is clearly stated in his very first sentence, which could well serve as the title to his great work of narrative history: "The researches [historia] of Herodotus of Halicarnassus, here set down, that the deeds of men may not be forgotten, and that the great and noble actions of the Greeks and Asiatics may not lose their fame; and, especially, the causes of the war between them."

The theme that gives unity to Herodotus' History is the age-old conflict between East and West, which began with the Trojan War and ended with Xerxes' colossal attempt to conquer Greece in 480 B.C., just a generation before Herodotus' prime. Ten years earlier, the hoplites of Athens (Herodotus' adopted city) had humbled Xerxes' father Darius by pushing into the sea at Marathon the expeditionary force that the Great King had sent across the Aegean to punish the Athenians for aiding the abortive revolt of the Greek cities in Persian Asia Minor. Now Xerxes had readied a combined land and sea operation (according to Herodotus, it ultimately totaled 2,317,610 men and 1,207 warships) and was intent on ending for all time the troublesome meddling of the free Greeks in Persian affairs. By the time the Persians were ready to cross from Asia to Europe on two remarkable pontoon bridges thrown across the mile-wide Hellespont, thirty-one Greek states had put aside their petty quarrels and formed a confederation for the defense of their liberty against an alien despotism.

The following selections from Book VII of Herodotus' History begin with

From Bk. VII, Chs. 8–10, 19–21, 33–37, 44–46, 56, 60, 100–105, 131–33, 138–39, 145–47, 175, 184, 201–205, 207–13, 219–26, 228, based on the translation by George Rawlinson.

some of the preparatory activities of Xerxes and the Greeks and end with the initial clash between the two armies at the narrow pass between sea and mountain at Thermopylae, where a hastily assembled Greek advance force of around 7,000 men met defeat. Although "too little and too late" sums up the Greek effort at Thermopylae, the courageous fight-to-the-death of Leonidas and his small band of Spartans and Thespians has caused it to become celebrated as one of the most glorious defeats in all history. It was followed by two great Greek victories that brought Xerxes' invasion to an inglorious end: a naval battle off Salamis in which the Greek fleet, under Athenian leadership, routed the Persian fleet and forced its return to Asia; and a land battle the following year (479 B.C.) at Plataea where the superb skill and spirit of the Spartan hoplites (commanded by Pausanias, on whose subsequent career see Selection 24), dispersed and slaughtered the enemy until, in the words of Herodotus, "of 300,000 troops, less the 40,000 who fled . . . , not 3,000 escaped."

Many scholars have maintained that Herodotus' acceptance of the greatly exaggerated estimates of the size of the Persian land forces discredits him as a historian. Others, however, noting that the History was designed to be read aloud to festival audiences, have argued that he uses these figures because they had become part of Greek tradition and because they were in keeping with the epic sweep and grandeur of his stated purpose — "that the great and noble actions of the Greeks and Asiatics may not lose their fame." Furthermore, such huge figures suited Herodotus' view of causation in history. They underlay his explanation of why a few tiny Greek states were able to defeat a mighty empire that stretched across three thousand miles and commanded the resources of forty-six nations — to Herodotus, as to all Greeks, overweening pride (hubris) inevitably leads to destruction (atē) because "god tolerates pride in none but himself."

DEBATE AT THE PERSIAN COURT

After Egypt was subdued, Xerxes, being about to take in hand the expedition against Athens, called together an assembly of the noblest Persians, to learn their opinions, and to lay before them his own designs. So, when the men were met, the king spoke thus to them:

". . . What need have I to tell you of the deeds of Cyrus and Cambyses, and my own father Darius, how many nations they conquered, and added to our dominions? You know right well what great things they achieved. But for myself, I will say, that from the day on which I mounted the throne, I have not ceased to consider by what means I may rival those who have preceded me in this post of honor, and increase the power of Persia as much as any of them. And truly I have pondered upon this, until at last I have found out a way whereby we may at once win glory, and likewise get possession of a land which is as large and as rich as our own — nay, which is even more varied in the fruits it bears — while at the same time we obtain satisfaction and revenge. For this cause I have now called you together, that I may make known to you what I design to do. My intent is to throw a bridge over the Hellespont and march an army through Europe against Greece, that thereby I may obtain vengeance from the Athenians for the wrongs committed by them against the Persians and against my father. Your own eyes saw the preparations of Darius against these men; but death came upon him, and balked his hopes of revenge. In his behalf, therefore, and in behalf of all the Persians, I undertake the war, and pledge myself not to rest till I have taken and burnt Athens, which has dared, unprovoked, to injure me and my father. Long since they came to Asia with Aristagoras of Miletus, who was one of our slaves, and entering Sardis, burnt its temples and its sacred groves; again, more lately, when we made a landing upon their coast under Datis and Artaphernes, how roughly they handled us [at Marathon] you do not need to be told. For these reasons, therefore, I am bent upon this war; and I see likewise therewith united no few advantages. Once let us subdue this people, and those neighbors of theirs who hold the land of Pelops the Phrygian, and we shall extend the Persian territory as far as God's heaven reaches. The sun will then shine on no land beyond our borders; for I will pass through Europe from one end to the other, and with your aid make of all the lands which it contains one country. For thus, if what I hear be true, affairs stand: The nations whereof I have spoken, once swept away, there is no city, no country left in all the world, which will venture so much as to withstand us in arms. By this course then we shall bring all mankind under our yoke, alike those who are guilty and those who are innocent of doing us wrong. For yourselves, if you wish to please me, do as follows: When I announce the time for the army to meet together, hasten to the muster with a good will, every one of you; and know that to the man who brings with him the most gallant array I will give the gifts which our people consider the most honorable. This then is what you have to do. But to show that I am not self-willed in this matter I lay the business before you, and give you full leave to speak your minds upon it openly."

Xerxes, having so spoken, held his peace.

Whereupon Mardonius took the word, and said:

"Of a truth, my lord, you surpass, not only all living Persians, but likewise those yet unborn. Most true and right is each word that you have now uttered; but best of all your resolve, not to let the Ionians who live in Europe — a worthless crew — mock us any more. It were indeed a monstrous thing if, after conquering and enslaving the Sacae, the Indians, the Ethiopians, the Assyrians, and many other mighty nations, not for any wrong that they had done us, but only to increase our empire, we should then allow the Greeks, who have done us such wanton injury, to escape our vengeance. What is it that we fear in them? — not surely their numbers? — not the greatness of their wealth? We know the manner of their battle — we know how weak their power is; already have we subdued their children who dwell in our country, the Ionians, Aeolians, and Dorians. I myself have had experience of these men when I marched against them by the orders of your father; and though I went as far as Macedonia, and came but a little short of reaching Athens itself, yet not a soul ventured to come out against me to battle. And yet, I am told, these very Greeks are wont to wage wars against one another in the most foolish way, through sheer perversity and doltishness. . . . Who then will dare, O king, to meet you in arms, when you come with all Asia's warriors at your back, and with all her ships? For my part I do not believe the Greek people will be so foolhardy. Grant, however, that I am mistaken herein, and that they are foolish enough to meet us in open fight; in that case they will learn that there are no such soldiers in the whole world as we. Nevertheless let us spare no pains; for nothing comes without trouble, but all that men acquire is got by painstaking."

When Mardonius had in this way softened the harsh speech of Xerxes, he too held his peace.

The other Persians were silent, for all feared to raise their voice against the plan proposed to them. But Artabanus, the son of Hystaspes, and uncle of Xerxes, trusting to his relationship, was bold to speak:

"O king, it is impossible, if no more than one opinion is uttered, to make choice of the best: a man is forced then to follow whatever advice may have been given him; but if opposite speeches are delivered, then choice can be exercised. . . . You say that you will bridge the Hellespont, and lead your troops through Europe against Greece. Now suppose some disaster befall you by land or sea, or by both. It may be even so, for the men are reputed valiant. Indeed one may measure their prowess from what they have already done; for when Datis and Artaphernes led their huge army against Attica, the Athenians singly defeated them. But grant they are not successful on both elements. Still, if they man their ships, and defeating us by sea, sail to the Hellespont, and there destroy our bridge, that, sire, were a fearful hazard. . . . See how god with his lightning always smites the bigger animals, and will not allow them to wax insolent, while those of a lesser bulk chafe him not. How likewise his bolts fall ever on the highest houses and the tallest trees. So plainly does he love to bring down everything that exalts itself. Thus often a mighty host is discomfited by a few men, when god in his jealousy sends fear or storm from heaven, and they perish in a way unworthy of them. For god tolerates pride in none but himself. Again, hurry always brings about disasters, from which huge sufferings are wont to arise; but in delay lie many advantages, not apparent (it may be) at first sight, but such as in course of time are seen of all. Such then is my counsel, O king. . . ."

THE PERSIAN ARMY IS MUSTERED

After Xerxes had thus determined to go forth to war, . . . straightway all the Persians who were come together departed to their several governments, where each displayed the greatest zeal, on the faith of the king's offers. For all hoped to obtain for themselves the gifts which had been promised. And so Xerxes gathered together his host, ransacking every corner of the continent.

Reckoning from the recovery of Egypt, Xerxes spent four full years in collecting his host, and making ready all things that were needful for his soldiers. It was not till the close of the fifth year that he set forth on his march, accompanied by a mighty multitude. For of all the armaments whereof any mention has reached us, this was by far the greatest; insomuch that no other expedition compared to this seems of any account. . . . For was there a nation in all Asia which Xerxes did not bring with him against Greece? Or was there a river, except those of unusual size, which sufficed for his troops to drink? One nation furnished ships; another was arrayed among the foot-soldiers; a third had to supply horses; a fourth, transports for the horses and men likewise for the service; a fifth, ships of war towards the bridges; a sixth, ships and provisions. . . .

Xerxes [having led his army to Sardis] made preparations to advance to Abydos, where the bridge across the Hellespont from Asia to Europe was lately finished. Midway between Sestos and Madytus in the Hellespontine Chersonese, and right over against Abydos, there is a rocky tongue of land which runs out for some distance into the sea. . . . Towards this tongue of land then, the men to whom the business was assigned, carried out a double bridge from Abydos; and while the Phoenicians constructed one line with cables of white flax, the Egyptians in the other used ropes made of papyrus. Now it is about a mile across from Abydos to the opposite coast. When, therefore, the channel had been bridged successfully, it happened that a great storm arising broke the whole work to pieces, and destroyed all that had been done.

So when Xerxes heard of it, he was full of wrath, and straightway gave orders that the Hellespont should receive three hundred lashes, and that a pair of fetters should be cast into it. Nay, I have even heard it said, that he bade the branders take their irons and therewith brand the Hellespont. It is certain that he commanded those who scourged the waters to utter, as they lashed them, these barbarian and wicked words: "You bitter water, your lord lays on you this punishment because you have wronged him without a cause, having suffered no evil at his hands. But King Xerxes will cross you, whether you will or not. Well do you deserve that no man should honor you with sacrifice; for you are of a truth a treacherous and unsavory river." While the sea was thus punished by his orders, he likewise commanded that the overseers of the work should lose their heads.

Then they, whose business it was, executed the unpleasing task laid upon them; and other master-builders were set over the work, who accomplished it in the way which I will now describe.

They joined together triremes and fifty-oared ships, 360 to support the bridge on the side of the Black Sea, and 314 to sustain the other; and these they placed at right-angles to the Sea, and in the direction of the current of the Hellespont, relieving by these means the tension of the shore cables. Having joined the vessels, they moored them with anchors of unusual size, that the vessels of the bridge towards the Black Sea might resist the winds which blow from within the straits, and that those of the more western bridge facing the Aegean, might withstand the winds which set in from the south and from the southeast. . . . When the bridge across the channel was thus complete, trunks of trees were sawn into planks, which were cut to the width of the bridge, and these were laid side by side upon the tightened cables, and then fastened on the top. This done, brushwood was brought, and arranged upon the planks, after which earth was heaped upon the brushwood, and the whole trodden down into a solid mass. Lastly a bulwark was set up on either side of this causeway, of such a height as to prevent the beasts of burden and the horses from seeing over it and taking fright at the water.

And now when all was prepared . . . , then at length the host, having first wintered at Sardis, began its march towards Abydos, fully equipped, on the first approach of spring. At the moment of departure, the sun suddenly quitted his seat in the heavens, and disappeared, though there were no clouds in sight, but the sky was clear and serene. Day was thus turned into night; whereupon Xerxes, who saw and remarked the prodigy, was seized with alarm, and sending at once for the Magians, inquired of them the meaning of the portent. They replied, "God is foreshowing to the Greeks the destruction of their cities; for the sun foretells for them and the moon for us." So Xerxes, thus instructed, proceeded on his way with great gladness of heart. . . .

Arrived here [Abydos], Xerxes wished to look upon all his host; so, as there was a throne of white marble upon a hill near the city, which they of Abydos had prepared beforehand, by the king's bidding, for his especial use, Xerxes took his seat on it, and gazing thence upon the shore below, beheld at one view all his land forces and all his ships. While thus employed, he felt a desire to behold a sailing-match among his ships, which accordingly took place, and was won by the Phoenicians of Sidon, much to the joy of Xerxes, who was delighted alike with the race and with his army.

And now, as he looked and saw the whole Hellespont covered with the vessels of his fleet, and all the shore and every plain about Abydos as full as could be of men, Xerxes congratulated himself on his good fortune; but after a little while, he wept.

Then Artabanus, the king's uncle (the same who at the first so freely spoke his mind to the king, and advised him not to lead his army against Greece), when he heard that Xerxes was in tears, went to him, and said, "How different, sire, is what you are now doing, from what you did a little while ago! Then you congratulated yourself, and now you weep."

"There came upon me," he replied, "a sudden pity, when I thought of the shortness of man's life, and considered that of all this host, so numerous as it is, not one will be alive when a hundred years are gone by." . . .

As soon as Xerxes had reached the European side, he stood to contemplate his army as they crossed under the lash. And the crossing continued during seven days and seven nights, without rest or pause. It is said that here, after Xerxes had made the passage, a Hellespontian exclaimed, "Why, O Zeus, do you, in the likeness of a Persian man, and with the name of Xerxes instead of your own, lead the whole race of mankind to the destruction of Greece? It would have been as easy for you to destroy it without their aid!" . . .

What the exact number of the troops of each nation was I cannot say with certainty — for it is not mentioned by anyone — but the whole land army together was found to amount to 1,700,000 men. The manner in which the numbering took place was the following. A body of ten thousand men was brought to a certain place, and the men were made to stand as close together as possible; after which a circle was drawn around them, and the men were let go: then where the circle had been, a fence was built about the height of a man's middle; and the enclosure was filled continually with fresh troops, till the whole army had in this way been numbered. When the numbering was over, the troops were drawn up according to their several nations. . . .

DEMARATUS' PRAISE OF SPARTA

Now when the numbering and marshalling of the host was ended . . . Xerxes . . . sent for [the Spartan exile] Demaratus the son of Ariston, who had accompanied him in his march upon Greece, and addressed him thus:

"Demaratus, it is my pleasure at this time to ask you certain things which I wish to know. You are a Greek, and, as I hear from the other Greeks with whom I converse, no less than from your own lips, you are a native of a city which is not the meanest or the weakest in their land. Tell me, therefore, what do you think? Will the Greeks lift a hand against us? My own judgment is, that even if all the Greeks and all the barbarians of the west were gathered together in one place, they would not be able to abide my onset, not being really of one mind. But I would like to know what you think."

Thus Xerxes questioned; and the other replied in his turn, "O king, do you wish me to give you a true answer, or do you wish for a pleasant one?"

Then the king bade him speak the plain truth, and promised that he would not on that account hold him in less favor than heretofore. So Demaratus, when he heard the promise, spoke as follows, "O king, since you bid me at all risks speak the truth, and not say what will one day prove me to have lied to you, thus I answer. Want has at all times been a fellow-dweller with us in our land, while Valor is an ally whom we have gained by dint of wisdom and strict laws. Her aid enables us to drive out want and escape tyranny. Brave are all the Greeks who dwell in any Dorian land, but what I am about to say does not concern all, but only the Lacedaemonians. First then, come what may, they will never accept your terms, which would reduce Greece to slavery; and further, they are sure to join battle with you, though all the rest of the Greeks should submit to your will. As for their numbers, do not ask how many they are, that their resistance should be a possible thing; for if one thousand of them should take the field, they will meet you in battle, and so will any number, be it less than this, or be it more."

When Xerxes heard this answer of Demaratus, he laughed and answered, "What wild words, Demaratus! One thousand men join battle with such an army as this! Come then, will you — who were once, as you say, their king — engage to fight this very day with ten men? I think not. And yet, if all your fellow citizens be indeed such as you say they are, you ought, as their king, by your own country's usages, to be ready to fight with twice the number. If then each one of them be a match for ten of my soldiers, I may well call upon you to be a match for twenty. So would you assure the truth of what you have now said. If, however, you Greeks, who vaunt yourselves so much, are of a truth men like those whom I have seen about my court, as you, Demaratus, and the others with whom I converse, if, I say, you are really men of this sort and size, how is the speech that you have uttered more than a mere empty boast? For, to go to the very verge of likelihood, how could one thousand men, or ten thousand, or even fifty thousand, particularly if they were all alike free, and not under one lord, how could such a force, I say, stand against an army like mine? Let them be five thousand, and we shall have more than one thousand men to each one of theirs. If, indeed, like our troops, they had a single master, their fear of him might make them courageous beyond their natural bent, or they might be urged by lashes against an enemy which far outnumbered them. But left to their own free choice, assuredly they will act differently. For my own part, I believe, that if the Greeks had to contend with the Persians only, and the numbers were equal on both sides, the Greeks would find it hard to stand their ground. We too have among us such men as those of whom you spoke — not many indeed, but still we possess a few. For instance, some of my body-guard would be willing to engage singly with three Greeks. But this you did not know, and therefore it was you talked so foolishly."

Demaratus answered him, "I knew, O king, at the outset, that if I told you the truth, my speech would displease your ears. But as you required me to answer you with all possible truthfulness, I informed you what the Spartans will do. And in this I speak not from any love that I bear them — for you know what my love towards them is likely to be at the present time, when they have robbed me of my rank and my ancestral honors, and made me a homeless exile, whom your father received, bestowing on me both shelter and sustenance. What likelihood is there that a man of understanding should be unthankful for kindness shown him, and not cherish it in his heart? For myself, I pretend not to cope with ten men, or with two, nay, had I the choice, I would rather not fight even with one. But, if need appeared, or if there were any great cause urging me on, I would contend with right good-will against one of those persons who boast themselves a match for any three Greeks. So likewise the Lacedaemonians, when they fight singly, are as good men as any in the world, and when they fight in a body, are the bravest of all. For though they be free men, they are not in all respects free; Law is the master whom they own, and this master they fear more than your subjects fear you. Whatever it commands they do; and its commandment is always the same: it forbids them to flee in battle, whatever the number of their foes, and requires them to stand firm, and either to conquer or die. If in these words, O king, I seem to you to speak foolishly, I am content from this time forward evermore to hold my peace. I had not now spoken unless compelled by you. But I pray that all may turn out according to your wishes."

Such was the answer of Demaratus, and Xerxes was not angry with him at all, but only laughed, and sent him away with words of kindness. After this interview . . . Xerxes started with his army, and marched upon Greece through Thrace. . . .

ATHENS THE SAVIOR OF GREECE

At this time the heralds who had been sent into Greece to require submission to the king returned to the camp, some of them empty-handed, others with earth and water. Among the number of those from whom earth and water were brought, were the Thessalians, Dolopians, Enianians, Perrhaebians, Locrians, Magnetians, Malians, Achaeans of Phthiotis, Thebans, and Boeotians generally, except those of Plataea and Thespiae. These are the nations against whom the Greeks that had taken up arms to resist the barbarians swore the oath, which ran thus, "From all those of Greek blood who delivered themselves up to the Persians without necessity, when their affairs were in good condition, we will take a tithe of their goods, and give it to the god at Delphi." So ran the words of the Greek oath.

King Xerxes had sent no heralds either to Athens or Sparta to ask earth and water, for a reason which I will now relate. When Darius some time before sent messengers for the same purpose, they were thrown, at Athens, into the pit of punishment, at Sparta into a well, and bidden to take therefrom earth and water for themselves, and carry it to their king. On this account Xerxes did not send to ask them. . . .

To return, however, to my main subject, the expedition of the Persian king, though it was in name directed against Athens, it threatened really the whole of Greece. And of this the Greeks were aware some time before, but they did not all view the matter in the same light. Some of them had given the Persian earth and water, and were bold on this account, deeming themselves thereby secured against suffering hurt from the barbarian army; while others, who had refused compliance, were thrown into extreme alarm. For whereas they considered all the ships in Greece too few to engage the enemy, it was plain that the greater number of states would take no part in the war, but warmly favored the Persians.

And here I feel constrained to deliver an opinion, which most men, I know, will dislike, but which, as it seems to me to be true, I am determined not to withhold. Had the Athenians, from fear of the approaching danger, quitted their country, or had they without quitting it submitted to the power of Xerxes, there would certainly have been no attempt to resist the Persians by sea; in which case, the course of events by land would have been the following. Though the Peloponnesians might have carried ever so many breastworks across the Isthmus, yet their allies would have fallen off from the Lacedaemonians, not by voluntary desertion, but because town after town must have been taken by the fleet of the barbarians; and so the Lacedaemonians would at least have stood alone, and, standing alone, would have displayed prodigies of valor, and died nobly. Either they would have done this, or else, before it came to that extremity, seeing one Greek state after another embrace the cause of the Persians, they would have come to terms with King Xerxes; and thus either way Greece would have been brought under Persia. For I cannot understand of what possible use the walls across the Isthmus could have been, if the King had had the mastery of the sea. If then a man should now say that the Athenians were the saviors of Greece, he would not exceed the truth. For they truly held the scales, and whichever side they espoused must have carried the day. They too it was who, when they had determined to maintain the freedom of Greece, roused up that portion of the Greek nation which had not gone over to the

Persians, and so, next to the gods, they repulsed the invader. Even the terrible oracles which reached them from Delphi, and struck fear into their hearts, failed to persuade them to fly from Greece. They had the courage to remain faithful to their land, and await the coming of the foe. . . .

ACTIONS OF THE GREEK CONFEDERACY

The Greeks who were well affected to the Grecian cause, having assembled in one place, and there consulted together, and interchanged pledges with each other, agreed that, before any other step was taken, the feuds and enmities which existed between the different nations should first of all be appeased. Many such there were; but one was of more importance than the rest, namely, the war which was still going on between the Athenians and the Aeginetans. When this business was concluded, understanding that Xerxes had reached Sardis with his army, they resolved to dispatch spies into Asia to take note of the king's affairs. At the same time they determined to send ambassadors to the Argives, and conclude a league with them against the Persians; while they likewise dispatched messengers to Gelo, the son of Deinomenes, in Sicily, to the people of Corcyra, and to those of Crete, exhorting them to send help to Greece. Their wish was to unite, if possible, the entire Greek name in one, and so to bring all to join in the same plan of defense, inasmuch as the approaching dangers threatened all alike. Now the power of Gelo was said to be very great, far greater than that of any single Grecian people.

So when these resolutions had been agreed upon, and the quarrels between the states made up, first of all they sent into Asia three men as spies. These men reached Sardis, and took note of the king's forces, but, being discovered, were examined by order of the generals who commanded the land army, and, having been condemned to suffer death, were led out to execution. Xerxes, however, when the news reached him, disapproving the sentence of the generals, sent some of his body-guard with instructions, if they found the spies still alive, to bring them into his presence. The messengers found the spies alive, and brought them before the king, who, when he heard the purpose for which they had come, gave orders to his guards to take them round the camp, and show them all the footmen and all the horse, letting them gaze at everything to their heart's content; then, when they were satisfied, to send them away unharmed to whatever country they desired.

For these orders Xerxes gave afterwards the following reasons. "Had the spies been put to death," he said, "the Greeks would have continued ignorant of the vastness of his army, which surpassed the common report of it; while he would have done them a very small injury by killing three of their men. On the other hand, by the return of the spies to Greece, his power would become known; and the Greeks," he expected, "would make surrender of their freedom before he began his march, by which means his troops would be saved all the trouble of an expedition." This reasoning was like to that which he used upon another occasion. While he was staying at Abydos, he saw some corn-ships, which were passing through the Hellespont from the Black Sea, on their way to Aegina and the Peloponnese. His attendants, hearing that they were the enemy's, were ready to capture them, and looked to see when Xerxes would give the signal. He, however, merely asked, "Whither are the ships bound?" and when they answered, "For your foes, master, with corn on board," "We too are bound thither," he rejoined, "laden, among other things, with corn. What harm is it, if they carry our provisions for us?"

GREEKS AND PERSIANS AT THERMOPYLAE

The Greeks . . . considered where they should fix the war, and what places they should occupy. The opinion which prevailed was, that they should guard the pass of Thermopylae; since it was narrower than the Thessalian defile, and at the same time nearer to them. Of the pathway, by which the Greeks who fell at Thermopylae were intercepted, they had no knowledge, until, on their arrival at Thermopylae, it was revealed to them by the Trachinians. This pass then it was determined that they should guard, in order to prevent the barbarians from penetrating into Greece through it; and at the same time it was resolved that the fleet should proceed to Artemisium, in the region of Histiacotis; for as those places are near to one another, it would be easy for the fleet and army to hold communication. . . . This was the sea force brought by the king from Asia, and it amounted in all to 517,610 men. The number of the foot soldiers was 1,700,000; that of the horsemen 80,000; to which must be added the Arabs who rode on camels, and the Libyans who fought in chariots, whom I reckon at 20,000. The whole number, therefore, of the land and sea forces added together amounts to 2,317,610 men. Such was the force brought from Asia, without including the camp followers, or taking any account of the provision-ships and the men whom they had on board. . . .

King Xerxes pitched his camp in the region of Malis called Trachinia, while on their side the Greeks occupied the pass which the Greeks in general call Thermopylae (the Hot Gates); but which the natives and those who dwell in the neighbourhood call Pylae (the Gates). Here then the two armies took their stand; the one master of all the region lying north of Trachis, the other of the country extending southward of that place to the verge of the continent.

The Greeks who at this spot awaited the coming of Xerxes were the following: From Sparta, three hundred men-at-arms: from Arcadia, one thousand Tegeans and Mantineans, five hundred of each people; one hundred twenty Orchomenians, from the Arcadian Orchomenus; and one thousand from other cities: from Corinth, four hundred men: from Phlius, two hundred: and from Mycenae eighty. Such was the number from the Peloponnese. There were also present, from Boeotia, seven hundred Thespians and four hundred Thebans.

Besides these troops, the Locrians of Opus and the Phocians had obeyed the call of their countrymen, and sent, the former all the force they had, the latter one thousand men. For envoys had gone from the Greeks at Thermopylae among the Locrians and Phocians, to call on them for assistance, and to say, "They were themselves but the vanguard of the host, sent to precede the main body, which might every day be expected to follow them. The sea was in good keeping, watched by the Athenians, the Aeginetans, and the rest of the fleet. There was no cause why they should fear; for after all the invader was not a god but a man who was liable to misfortunes from the very day of his birth, and those greater in proportion to his own greatness. The assailant therefore, being only a mortal, must needs fall from his glory." Thus urged, the Locrians and the Phocians had come with their troops to Trachis.

The various nations had each captains of their own under whom they served; but the one to whom all especially looked up, and who had the command of the entire force, was the Lacedaemonian, Leonidas. . . . He had now come to Thermopylae, accompanied by the three hundred men which the law assigned him, whom he had himself chosen from among the citizens, and who were all of them fathers with sons living. On his way he had taken the troops from Thebes, whose number I have already mentioned, and who were under the command of Leontiades the son of Eurymachus. The reason why he made a point of taking troops from Thebes and Thebes only was, that the Thebans were strongly suspected of being well inclined to the Persians. Leonidas therefore called on them to come with him to the war, wishing to see whether they would comply with his demand, or openly refuse, and disclaim the Greek alliance. They, however, though their wishes leant the other way, nevertheless sent the men. . . .

The Greek forces at Thermopylae, when the Persian army drew near to the entrance of the pass, were seized with fear, and a council was held to consider about a retreat. It was the wish of the Peloponnesians generally that the army should fall back upon the Peloponnese, and there guard the Isthmus. But Leonidas, who saw with what indignation the Phocians and Locrians heard of this plan, gave his voice for remaining where they were, while they sent envoys to the several cities to ask for help, since they were too few to make a stand against an army like that of the Persians.

While this debate was going on, Xerxes sent a mounted spy to observe the Greeks, and note how many they were, and what they were doing. He had heard, before he came out of Thessaly, that a few men were assembled at this place, and that at their head were certain Lacedaemonians, under Leonidas, a descendant of Heracles. The horseman rode up to the camp, and looked about him, but did not see the whole army; for such as were on the further side of the wall (which had been rebuilt and was now carefully guarded) it was not possible for him to behold; but he observed those on the outside, who were encamped in front of the rampart. It chanced that at this time the Lacedaemonians held the outer guard, and were seen by the spy, some of them engaged in gymnastic exercises, others combing their long hair. At this the spy greatly marvelled, but he counted their number, and when he had taken accurate note of everything, he rode back quietly; for no one pursued after him, or paid any heed to his visit. So he returned, and told Xerxes all that he had seen.

Upon this, Xerxes, who had no means of surmising the truth — namely, that the Spartans were preparing to do or die manfully — but thought it laughable that they should be engaged in such employments, sent and called to his presence Demaratus the son of Ariston, who still remained with the army. When he appeared, Xerxes told him all that he had heard, and questioned him concerning the news, since he was anxious to understand the meaning of such behavior on the part of the Spartans. Then Demaratus said, "I spoke to you, O king, concerning these men long since, when we had but just begun our march upon Greece; you, however, only laughed at my words, when I told you of all this, which I saw would come to pass. Earnestly do I struggle at all times to speak truth to you, sire; and now listen to it once more. These men have come to dispute the pass with us, and it is for this that they are now making ready. It is their custom, when they are about to hazard their lives, to adorn their heads with care. Be assured, however, that if you can subdue the men who are here and the Lacedaemonians who remain in Sparta, there is no other nation in all the world which will venture to lift a hand in their defense. You have now to deal with the first kingdom and town in Greece, and with the bravest men."

Then Xerxes, to whom what Demaratus said seemed altogether to surpass belief, asked further, "How is it possible for so small an army to contend with mine?"

"Oh king," Demaratus answered, "let me be treated as a liar, if matters fall not out as I say."

THE FIGHTING BEGINS

But Xerxes was not persuaded any the more. Four whole days he allowed to go by, expecting that the Greeks would run away. When, however, he found on the fifth that they were not gone, thinking that their firm stand was mere impudence and recklessness, he grew wroth, and sent against them the Medes and Cissians, with orders to take them alive and bring them into his presence. Then the Medes rushed forward and charged the Greeks, but fell in vast numbers: others however took the places of the slain, and would not be beaten off, though they suffered terrible losses. In this way it became clear to all, and especially to the king, that though he had plenty of men, he had but very few soldiers. The struggle, however, continued during the whole day.

Then the Medes, having met so rough a reception, withdrew from the fight; and their place was taken by the band of Persians under Hydarnes, whom the king called his Immortals: they, it was thought, would soon finish the business. But when they joined battle with the Greeks, it was with no better success than the Median detachment — things went much as before — the two armies fighting in a narrow space, and the barbarians using shorter spears than the Greeks, and having no advantage from their numbers. The Lacedaemonians fought in a way worthy of note, and showed themselves far more skillful in fight than their adversaries, often turning their backs, and making as though they were all flying away, on which the barbarians would rush after them with much noise and shouting, when the Spartans at their approach would wheel round and face their pursuers, in this way destroying vast numbers of the enemy. Some Spartans likewise fell in these encounters, but only a very few. At last the Persians, finding that all their efforts to gain the pass availed nothing, and that whether they attacked by divisions or in any other way, it was to no purpose, withdrew to their own quarters.

During these assaults, it is said that Xerxes, who was watching the battle, thrice leaped from the throne on which he sat, in terror for his army.

Next day the combat was renewed, but with no better success on the part of the barbarians. The Greeks were so few that the barbarians hoped to find them disabled, by reason of their wounds, from offering any further resistance; and so they once more attacked them. But the Greeks were drawn up in detachments according to their cities, and bore the brunt of the battle in turns, all except the Phocians, who had been stationed on the mountain to guard the pathway. So when the Persians found no difference between that day and the preceding, they again retired to their quarters.

Now, as the king was at a loss, and knew not how he should deal with the emergency, Ephialtes, the son of Eurydemus, a man of Malis, came to him and was admitted to a conference. Stirred by the hope of receiving a rich reward at the king's hands, he had come to tell him of the pathway which led across the mountain to Thermopylae; by which disclosure he brought destruction on the band of Greeks who had there withstood the barbarians. . . .

LEONIDAS DISMISSES THE ALLIES

The Greeks at Thermopylae received the first warning of the destruction which the dawn would bring on them from the seer Megistias, who read their fate in the victims as he was sacrificing. After this deserters came in, and brought the news that the Persians were marching round by the hills: it was still night when these men arrived. Last of all, the scouts came running down from the heights, and brought in the same accounts, when the day was just beginning to break. Then the Greeks held a council to consider what they should do, and here opinions were divided: some were strong against quitting their post, while others contended to the contrary. So when the council had broken up, part of the troops departed and went their ways homeward to their several states; part however resolved to remain, and to stand by Leonidas to the last.

It is said that Leonidas himself sent away the troops who departed, because he was concerned for their safety, but thought it unseemly that either he or his Spartans should quit the post which they had been especially sent to guard. For my own part, I incline to think that Leonidas gave the order, because he perceived the allies to be out of heart and unwilling to encounter the danger to which his own mind was made up. He therefore commanded them to retreat, but said that he himself could not draw back with honor; knowing that, if he stayed, glory awaited him, and that Sparta in that case would not lose her prosperity. For when the Spartans, at the very beginning of the war, sent to consult the oracle concerning it, the answer which they received from the priestess was that either Sparta must be overthrown by the barbarians, or one of her kings must perish. The prophecy was delivered in hexameter verse, and ran thus:

Oh! ye men who dwell in the streets of broad Lacedaemon,
Either your glorious town shall be sacked by the children of Perseus,
Or, in exchange, must all through the whole Laconian country

Mourn for the loss of a king, descendent of great Heracles.
He cannot be withstood by the courage of bulls or of lions,
Strive as they may; he is mighty as Zeus; there is nought that shall stay
   him,
Till he have got for his prey your king, or your glorious city.

The remembrance of this answer, I think, and the wish to secure the whole glory for the Spartans, caused Leonidas to send the allies away. This is more likely than that they quarrelled with him, and took their departure in such unruly fashion.

To me it seems no small argument in favor of this view, that the seer also who accompanied the army, Megistias, the Acarnanian, said to have been of the blood of Melampus, and the same who was led by the appearance of the victims to warn the Greeks of the danger which threatened them, received orders to retire (as it is certain he did) from Leonidas, that he might escape the coming destruction. Megistias, however, though bidden to depart, refused, and stayed with the army; but he had an only son present with the expedition, whom he now sent away.

So the allies, when Leonidas ordered them to retire, obeyed him and forthwith departed. Only the Thespians and the Thebans remained with the Spartans, and of these the Thebans were kept back by Leonidas as hostages, very much against their will. The Thespians, on the contrary, stayed entirely of their own accord, refusing to retreat, and declaring that they would not forsake Leonidas and his followers. So they abode with the Spartans, and died with them. Their leader was Demophilus, the son of Diadromes.

THE LAST HEROIC ACT

At sunrise Xerxes made libations, after which he waited until the time when the market-place is wont to fill, and then began his advance. Ephialtes had instructed him thus, as the descent of the mountain is much quicker, and the distance much shorter, than the way round the hills, and the ascent. So the barbarians under Xerxes began to draw nigh; and the Greeks under Leonidas, as they now went forth determined to die, advanced much further than on previous days, until they reached the more open portion of the pass. Hitherto they had held their station within the wall, and from this had gone forth to fight at the point where the pass was the narrowest. Now they joined battle beyond the defile, and carried slaughter among the barbarians, who fell in heaps. Behind them the captains of the squadrons, armed with whips, urged their men forward with continual blows. Many were thrust into the sea, and there perished; a still greater number were trampled to death by their own soldiers; no one heeded the dying. For the Greeks, reckless of their own safety and desperate, since they knew that, as the mountain had been crossed, their destruction was nigh at hand, exerted themselves with the most furious valor against the barbarians.

By this time the spears of the greater number were all shivered, and with their swords they hewed down the ranks of the Persians; and here, as they strove, Leonidas fell fighting bravely, together with many other famous Spartans, whose names I have taken care to learn on account of their great worthiness, as indeed I have those of all the three hundred. There fell too at the same time very many famous Persians: among them, two brothers of Xerxes. . . .

And now there arose a fierce struggle between the Persians and the Lacedaemonians over the body of Leonidas, in which the Greeks four times drove back the enemy, and at last by their great bravery succeeded in bearing off the body. This combat was scarcely ended when the Persians with Ephialtes approached; and the Greeks, informed that they drew nigh, made a change in the manner of their fighting. Drawing back into the narrowest part of the pass, and retreating even behind the cross wall, they posted themselves upon a hillock, where they stood all drawn up together in one close body, except only the Thebans. The hillock whereof I speak is at the entrance of the pass, where the stone lion stands which was set up in honor of Leonidas. Here they defended themselves to the last, such as still had swords using them, and the others resisting with their hands and teeth; till the barbarians, who in part had pulled down the wall and attacked them in front, in part had gone round and now encircled them upon every side, overwhelmed and buried the remnant left beneath showers of missile weapons.

Thus nobly did the whole body of Lacedaemonians and Thespians behave, but nevertheless one man is said to have distinguished himself above all the rest, to wit, Dieneces the Spartan. A speech which he made before the Greeks engaged the Persians, remains on record. One of the Trachinians told him, "Such was the number of the barbarians, that when they shot forth their arrows the sun would be darkened by their multitude." Dieneces, not at all frightened at these words, but making light of the Persian numbers, answered, "Our Trachinian friend brings us excellent tidings. If the Persians darken the sun, we shall have our fight in the shade." . . .

The slain were buried where they fell; and in their honor, nor less in honor of those who died before Leonidas sent the allies away, an inscription was set up, which said:

> Here did four thousand men from Pelops' land
> Against three hundred myriads bravely stand.

This was in honor of all. Another was for the Spartans alone:

> Go, stranger, and to Lacedaemon tell
> That here, obedient to her laws, we fell.

This was for the Lacedaemonians. The seer had the following:

> The great Megistias' tomb you here may view,
> Whom slew the Medes, fresh from Spercheius' fords.
> Well the wise seer the coming death foreknew,
> Yet scorned he to forsake his Spartan lords.

24

Thucydides: The Failure of Sparta

"Of the arts of peace they knew nothing." — Aristotle

The Spartan system was widely admired in Greece, particularly by aristocrats, and, after democracies began to falter, by many intellectuals as well. Since Plutarch's idealized account (Selection 22) reflects this admiration, it needs to be balanced by a more objective description of the actualities of the Spartan way of life. In Thucydides' brilliant account of the moral breakdown and miserable death of the Spartan royal regent and general Pausanias, the renowned victor over the Persians in the last great battle (479 B.C.) of the Persian Wars, we are given an insight into how Sparta's system of education and training, narrowly military and often brutalizing, failed to produce leaders capable of coping with problems in the larger world outside Sparta. It is but one of several known instances from the fifth and fourth centuries which show Spartans degenerating when removed from the rigid discipline of the barracks-like life of their homeland.

I, 94. Meanwhile [after the Battle of Plataea, 479 B.C.] Pausanias, son of Cleombrotus, was sent out from Lacedaemon as commander-in-chief of the Hellenes, with twenty ships from Peloponnese. With him sailed the Athenians with thirty ships, and a number of the other allies. They made an expedition against Cyprus and subdued most of the island, and afterwards against Byzantium, which was in the hands of the Persians, and compelled it to surrender. This event took place while the Spartans were still supreme.

95. But the violence of Pausanias had already begun to be disagreeable to the Hellenes, particularly to the Ionians and the newly liberated populations. These resorted to the Athenians and requested them as their kinsmen to become their leaders, and to stop any attempt at violence on the part of Pausanias. . . . In the meantime the Lacedaemonians recalled Pausanias for an investigation of the reports which had reached them. Manifold and grave accusations had been brought against him by Hellenes arriving in Sparta; and, to all appearance, there had been in him more of the mimicry of a despot than of the attitude of a general. As it happened, his recall came just at the time when the hatred which he had inspired had induced the allies to desert him, the soldiers from Peloponnese excepted, and to range themselves by the side

From Thucydides, *History of the Peloponnesian War*, tr. Richard Crawley.

of the Athenians. On his arrival at Lacedaemon, he was censured for his private acts of oppression, but was acquitted on the heaviest counts and pronounced not guilty; it must be known that the charge of Medism [support of Persia] formed one of the principal, and to all appearance one of the best-founded articles against him. The Lacedaemonians did not, however, restore him to his command, but sent out Dorkis and certain others with a small force; they found the allies no longer inclined to concede to them the supremacy. Perceiving this they departed, and the Lacedaemonians did not send out any to succeed them. They feared for those who went out a deterioration similar to that observable in Pausanias; besides, they desired to be rid of the Persian war, and were satisfied of the competency of the Athenians for the position, and of their friendship at the time towards themselves.

128. ... After Pausanias the Lacedaemonian had been recalled by the Spartans from his command in the Hellespont, and had been tried by them and acquitted, not being again sent out in a public capacity, he took a galley of Hermione on his own responsibility, without the authority of the Lacedaemonians, and arrived as a private person in the Hellespont. He came ostensibly for the Hellenic war, really to carry on his intrigues with the King [Xerxes], which he had begun before his recall, being ambitious of reigning over Hellas. The circumstance which first enabled him to lay the King under an obligation, and to make a beginning of the whole design was this. Some connections and kinsmen of the King had been taken in Byzantium, on its capture from the Persians, when he was first there, after the return from Cyprus. These captives he sent off to the King without the knowledge of the rest of the allies, the account being that they had escaped from him. He managed this with the help of Gongylus, an Eretrian, whom he had placed in charge of Byzantium and the prisoners. He also gave Gongylus a letter for the King, the contents of which were as follows, as was afterwards discovered: "Pausanias, the general of Sparta, anxious to do you a favor, sends you these his prisoners of war. I propose also, with your approval, to marry your daughter, and to make Sparta and the rest of Hellas subject to you. I may say that I think I am able to do this, with your cooperation. Accordingly if any of this please you, send a safe man to the sea through whom we may in future conduct our correspondence."

129. This was all that was revealed in the writing, and Xerxes was pleased with the letter ... and sent ... the following answer: "Thus saith King Xerxes to Pausanias. For the men whom you have saved for me across the sea from Byzantium, an obligation is laid up for you in our house, recorded forever; and with your proposals I am well pleased. Let neither night nor day stop you from diligently performing any of your promises to me, neither for cost of gold nor of silver let them be hindered, nor yet for number of troops, wherever it may be that their presence is needed; but with Artabazus, an honorable man whom I send you, boldly advance my objects and yours, as may be most for the honor and interest of us both."

130. Before held in high honor by the Hellenes as the hero of Plataea, Pausanias, after the receipt of this letter, became prouder than ever, and could no longer live in the usual style, but went out of Byzantium in a Persian dress,

was attended on his march through Thrace by a bodyguard of Medes and Egyptians, kept a Persian table, and was quite unable to contain his intentions, but betrayed by his conduct in trifles what his ambition looked one day to enact on a grander scale. He also made himself difficult of access, and displayed so violent a temper to every one without exception that no one could come near him. Indeed, this was the principal reason why the confederacy went over to the Athenians.

131. The above-mentioned conduct, coming to the ears of the Lacedaemonians, occasioned his first recall. And after his second voyage out in the ship of Hermione, without their orders, he gave proofs of similar behavior. Besieged and expelled from Byzantium by the Athenians, he did not return to Sparta; but news came that he had settled at Colonae in the Troad, and was intriguing with the barbarians, and that his stay there was for no good purpose; and the Ephors, now no longer hesitating, sent him a herald and a scytale [coded message] with orders to accompany the herald or be declared a public enemy. Anxious above everything to avoid suspicion, and confident that he could quash the charge by means of money, he returned a second time to Sparta. At first thrown into prison by the Ephors (whose powers enable them to do this to the king), he soon compromised the matter and came out again, and offered himself for trial to any who wished to institute an inquiry concerning him.

132. ... But by his contempt of the laws and imitation of the barbarians, he gave grounds for much suspicion of his being discontented with things established; all the occasions on which he had in any way departed from the regular customs were passed in review, and it was remembered that he had taken upon himself to have inscribed on the tripod at Delphi, which was dedicated by the Hellenes as the first-fruits of the spoil of the Persians, the following couplet:

> Persia defeated, great Pausanias raised
> This monument, that Apollo might be praised.

At the time the Lacedaemonians had at once erased the couplet, and inscribed the names of the cities that had aided in the overthrow of the barbarian and dedicated the offering. Yet it was considered that Pausanias had here been guilty of a grave offense, which, interpreted by the light of the attitude which he had since assumed, gained a new significance, and seemed to be quite in keeping with his present schemes. Besides, they were informed that he was even intriguing with the Helots; and such indeed was the fact, for he promised them freedom and citizenship if they would join him in insurrection, and would help him to carry out his plans to the end. Even now, mistrusting the evidence even of the Helots themselves, the Ephors would not consent to take any decided step against him; in accordance with their regular custom towards themselves, namely, to be slow in taking any irrevocable resolve in the matter of a Spartan citizen, without indisputable proof. At last, it is said, the person who was going to carry to Artabazus the last letter for the King, a man of Argilus, once the favorite and most trusty servant of Pausanias, turned informer. Alarmed by the reflection that none of the previous messengers had ever returned, having counterfeited the seal, in order that, if he found himself mistaken in his surmises, or if Pausanias should ask to make some correction, he might not be discovered, he undid the letter, and found the postscript that he had suspected — an order to put him to death.

On being shown the letter the Ephors now felt more certain. . . . (134) . . . It is reported that, as he was about to be arrested in the street, he saw from the face of one of the Ephors what he was coming for; another, too, made him a secret signal, and betrayed it to him from kindness. Setting off with a run for the temple of the goddess of the Brazen House, the enclosure of which was near at hand, he succeeded in taking sanctuary before they took him, and entering into a small chamber, which formed part of the temple, to avoid being exposed to the weather, lay still there. The Ephors, for the moment distanced in the pursuit, afterwards took off the roof of the chamber, and having made sure that he was inside, shut him in, barricaded the doors, and staying before the place, reduced him by starvation. When they found that he was on the point of expiring, just as he was, in the chamber, they brought him out of the temple, while the breath was still in him, and as soon as he was brought out he died. They were going to throw him into the Kaiadas, where they cast criminals, but finally decided to inter him somewhere near.

25

Pericles' Funeral Oration

An idealized view of Athenian democracy and imperialism

No finer expression of the ideals of democracy exists than the famous Funeral Oration delivered by Pericles in honor of the Athenians who fell fighting Sparta during the first year (431 B.C.) of the Peloponnesian War. Like Lincoln's Gettysburg Address, which resembles it closely and with which it is frequently compared, it is considered one of the greatest speeches in literature. Pericles appeals to the patriotism of his listeners, confronted by the crisis of a great war, by describing the superior qualities and advantages of their democracy as a heritage won for them by their ancestors and worthy of any sacrifice to preserve. He emphasizes as the outstanding feature of their democracy — and,

From Thucydides, *History of the Peloponnesian War*, tr. Alfred Zimmern in *The Greek Commonwealth: Politics and Economics in Fifth-Century Athens*, 4th ed. (Oxford: 1924), pp. 202–209. Reprinted by permission of The Clarendon Press.

we can add, of any democracy — the harmonious blending of opposite tendencies in politics, economics, and culture which it contains. This is perhaps the finest expression of the Greek ideal of a mean between extremes. All this is described in sharp contrast to the rigid totalitarianism of Sparta, which regulated every detail of the citizen's existence. It is to be noted that an outstanding example of this happy blending of control and freedom in all phases of life was the Athenian acceptance of the leadership of Pericles as the recognized superior individual voted into power by the people to "lead them," as Thucydides noted, "instead of being led by them."

Pericles extends the same argument, that order and liberty are compatible, to justify the existence of the Athenian Empire, which had emerged after the Persian Wars to fill the vacuum left by the failure of Spartan leadership in Greek affairs (see Selection 24). It had unified and brought peace and prosperity to half of the Greek world, but it was at present under attack by Sparta and its allies as the "tyrant city" that had extinguished the liberties of many Greek states and was now threatening the remainder. Pericles' reply to this charge is an idealized rationalization of the need to replace the anarchy of narrow city-state "nationalism" with an international organization under Athenian leadership in order to achieve the political and economic well-being similar to that hoped for by those people today who speak of "one world." The goal sought is freedom from fear and want, and such is the meaning of Pericles' inspired conception of Athenian imperialism: "We secure our friends not by accepting favors but by doing them.... We are alone among mankind in doing men benefits, not in calculations of self-interest, but in the fearless confidence of [bringing] freedom. In a word I claim that our city as a whole is an education to Greece. . . ."

We shall see that both Periclean ideals of democracy and international organization failed to be accomplished. This failure marks the beginning of the end of the Greek world.

The Funeral Oration is contained in Thucydides' History of the Peloponnesian War, on which see pp. 189–206.

THE SPIRIT, CONSTITUTION, AND MANNERS OF ATHENS

II, 36. My first words shall be for our ancestors; for it is both just to them and seemly that on an occasion such as this our tribute of memory should be paid them. For, dwelling always in this country, generation after generation in unchanging and unbroken succession, they have handed it down to us free by their exertions. So they are worthy of our praises; and still more so are our fathers. For they enlarged the ancestral patrimony by the Empire which we hold today and delivered it, not without labor, into the hands of our own generation; while it is we ourselves, those of us who are now in middle life, who consolidated our power throughout the greater part of the Empire and secured the city's complete independence both in war and peace.

Of the battles which we and our fathers fought, whether in the winning of our power abroad or in bravely withstanding the warfare of barbarian or Greek at home, I do not wish to say more: they are too familiar to you all. I wish rather to set forth the spirit in which we faced them, and the constitution and manners with which we rose to greatness, and to pass from them to the dead; for I think it not unfitting that these things should be called to mind at today's solemnity, and expedient too that the whole gathering of citizens and strangers should listen to them.

37. For our government is not copied from those of our neighbors: we are an example to them rather than they to us. Our constitution is named a démocracy, because it is in the hands not of the few but of the many. But our laws secure equal justice for all in their private disputes, and our public opinion welcomes and honors talent in every branch of achievement, not for any sectional reason but on grounds of excellence alone. And as we give free play to all in our public life, so we carry the same spirit into our daily relations with one another. We have no black looks or angry words for our neighbor if he enjoys himself in his own way, and we abstain from the little acts of churlishness which, though they leave no mark, yet cause annoyance to whoso notes them. Open and friendly in our private intercourse, in our public acts we keep strictly within the control of law. We acknowledge the restraint of reverence; we are obedient to whomsoever is set in authority, and to the laws, more especially to those which offer protection to the oppressed and those unwritten ordinances whose transgression brings shame.

38. Yet ours is no work-a-day city only. No other provides so many recreations for the spirit — contests and sacrifices all the year round, and beauty in our public buildings to cheer the heart and delight the eye day by day. Moreover, the city is so large and powerful that all the wealth of all the world flows in to her, so that our own Attic products seem no more homelike to us than the fruits of the labors of other nations.

39. Our military training too is different from our opponents'. The gates of our city are flung open to the world. We practice no periodical deportations, nor do we prevent our visitors from observing or discovering what an enemy might usefully apply to his own purposes. For our trust is not in the devices of material equipment, but in our own good spirits for battle.

So too with education. They toil from early boyhood in a laborious pursuit after courage, while we, free to live and wander as we please, march out none the less to face the self-same dangers. . . .

40. We are lovers of beauty without extravagance, and lovers of wisdom without unmanliness. Wealth to us is not mere material for vainglory but an opportunity for achievement; and poverty we think it no disgrace to acknowledge but a real degradation to make no effort to overcome. Our citizens attend both to public and private duties, and do not allow absorption in their own various affairs to interfere with their knowledge of the city's. We differ from other states in regarding the man who holds aloof from public life not as "quiet" but as useless; we decide or debate, carefully and in person, all matters of policy, holding, not that words and deeds go ill together, but that acts are foredoomed to failure when undertaken undiscussed. For we are noted for being at once adventurous in action and most reflective beforehand. Other men are bold in ignorance, while reflection will stop their onset. But the bravest are

surely those who have the clearest vision of what is before them, glory and danger alike, and yet notwithstanding go out to meet it.

APOLOGY FOR ATHENIAN IMPERIALISM

In doing good, too, we are the exact opposite of the rest of mankind. We secure our friends not by accepting favors but by doing them. And so we are naturally more firm in our attachments: for we are anxious, as creditors, to cement by kind offices our relation towards our friends. If they do not respond with the same warmness it is because they feel that their services will not be given spontaneously but only as the repayment of a debt. We are alone among mankind in doing men benefits, not on calculations of self-interest, but in the fearless confidence of freedom. (41.) In a word I claim that our city as a whole is an education to Greece, and that her members yield to none, man by man, for independence of spirit, many-sidedness of attainment, and complete self-reliance in limbs and brain.

That this is no vainglorious phrase but actual fact the supremacy which our manners have won us itself bears testimony. No other city of the present day goes out to her ordeal greater than ever men dreamed; no other is so powerful that the invader feels no bitterness when he suffers at her hands, and her subjects no shame at the indignity of their dependence. Great indeed are the symbols and witnesses of our supremacy, at which posterity, as all mankind today, will be astonished. We need no Homer or other man of words to praise us; for such give pleasure for a moment, but the truth will put to shame their imaginings of our deeds. For our pioneers have forced a way into every sea and every land, establishing among all mankind, in punishment or beneficence, eternal memorials of their settlement.

THE WORTHY DEAD

Such then is the city for whom, lest they should lose her, the men whom we celebrate died a soldier's death: and it is but natural that all of us, who survive them, should wish to spend ourselves in her service. (42.) That, indeed, is why I have spent many words upon the city. I wished to show that we have more at stake than men who have no such inheritance, and to support my praise of the dead by making clear to you what they have done. For if I have chanted the glories of the city it was these men and their like who set hand to array her. With them, as with few among Greeks, words cannot magnify the deeds that they have done. Such an end as we have here seems indeed to show us what a good life is, from its first signs of power to its final consummation. For even where life's previous record showed faults and failures it is just to weigh the last brave hour of devotion against them all. There they wiped out evil with good and did the city more service as soldiers than they did her harm in private life. There no hearts grew faint because they loved riches more than honor; none shirked the issue in the poor man's dreams of wealth. All these they put aside to strike a blow for the city. Counting the quest to avenge her honor as the most glorious of all ventures, and leaving Hope, the uncertain goddess, to send them what she would, they faced the foe as they drew near him in the strength of their own manhood; and when the shock of battle came, they chose rather to suffer the uttermost than to win life by weakness. So their memory has escaped the reproaches of men's lips, but they bore instead on their bodies the marks of men's hands, and in a moment of time, at the climax of their lives, were rapt away from a world filled, for their dying eyes, not with terror but with glory.

43. Such were the men who lie here and such the city that inspired them. We survivors may pray to be spared their bitter hour, but must disdain to meet the foe with a spirit less triumphant. Let us draw strength, not merely from twice-told arguments — how fair and noble a thing it is to show courage in battle — but from the busy spectacle of our great city's life as we have it before us day by day, falling in love with her as we see her, and remembering that all this greatness she owes to men with the fighter's daring, the wise man's understanding of his duty, and the good man's self-discipline in its performance — to men who, if they failed in any ordeal, disdained to deprive the city of their services, but sacrificed their lives as the best offerings on her behalf. So they gave their bodies to the commonwealth and received, each for his own memory, praise that will never die, and with it the grandest of all sepulchers, not that in which their mortal bones are laid, but a home in the minds of men, where their glory remains fresh to stir to speech or action as the occasion comes by. For the whole earth is the sepulcher of famous men; and their story is not graven only on stone over their native earth, but lives on far away, without visible symbol, woven into the stuff of other men's lives. For you now it remains to rival what they have done and, knowing the secret of happiness to be freedom and the secret of freedom a brave heart, not idly to stand aside from the enemy's onset. For it is not the poor and luckless, as having no hope of prosperity, who have most cause to reckon death as little loss, but those for whom fortune may yet keep reversal in store and who would feel the change most if trouble befell them. Moreover, weakly to decline the trial is more painful to a man of spirit than death coming sudden and unperceived in the hour of strength and enthusiasm.

ADVICE TO THE SURVIVORS

44. Therefore I do not mourn with the parents of the dead who are here with us. I will rather comfort them. For they know that they have been born into a world of manifold chances and that he is to be accounted happy to whom the best lot falls — the best sorrow, such as is yours today, or the best death, such as fell to these, for whom life and happiness were cut to the selfsame measure. I know it is not easy to give you comfort. I know how often in the joy of others you will have reminders of what was once your own, and how men feel sorrow, not for the loss of what they have never tasted, but when something that has grown dear to them has been snatched away. But you must keep a brave heart in the hope of other children, those who are still of age to bear them. For the newcomers will help you to forget the gap in your own circle, and will help the city to fill up the ranks of its workers and its soldiers. For no man is fitted to give fair and honest advice in council if he has not, like

his fellows, a family at stake in the hour of the city's danger. To you who are past the age of vigor I would say: count the long years of happiness so much gain to set off against the brief space that yet remains, and let your burden be lightened by the glory of the dead. For the love of honor alone is not staled by age, and it is by honor, not, as some say, by gold, that the helpless end of life is cheered.

45. I turn to those amongst you who are children or brothers of the fallen, for whom I foresee a mighty contest with the memory of the dead. Their praise is in all men's mouths, and hardly, even for supremest heroism, you will be adjudged to have achieved, not the same but a little less than they. For the living have the jealousy of rivals to content with, but the dead are honored with unchallenged admiration.

If I must also speak a word to those who are now in widowhood on the powers and duties of women, I will cast all my advice into one brief sentence. Great will be your glory if you do not lower the nature that is within you — hers greatest of all whose praise or blame is least bruised on the lips of men.

46. I have spoken such words as I had to say according as the law prescribes, and the graveside offerings to the dead have been duly made. Henceforward the city will take charge of their children till manhood: such is the crown and benefit she holds out to the dead and to their kin for the trials they have undergone for her. For where the prize is highest, there, too, are the best citizens to contend for it.

And now, when you have finished your lamentation, let each of you depart.

26

The Old Oligarch

A realistic view of Athenian democracy and imperialism

Some few years after the death of Pericles (429 B.C.), an unknown Athenian oligarch wrote a political pamphlet, On the Constitution of Athens, which contains a sarcastic attack upon the Athenian democracy and its empire. It balances the idealized picture given in Pericles' Funeral Oration with a realistic and penetrating description of the shortcomings of Athenian democracy and the self-interested economic basis of its imperialism. The Old Oligarch's views are in some part valid for the Periclean age, but are especially pertinent to the decade following the death of Pericles when, due largely to the crisis of the war, passion triumphed over wisdom in the making of policy and demagogues,

Reprinted from *The Old Oligarch, Being the Constitution of the Athenians Ascribed to Xenophon*, tr. James A. Petch (Oxford, n.d.). By permission of Basil Blackwell & Mott, Ltd.

who played on the emotions and cupidity of the masses, replaced the courageous and far-sighted statesmen of the stamp of Pericles as leaders of the
democracy. (A vivid example of this development that may have been witnessed by the Old Oligarch in person is given in Selection 27A.) Although he
wrote with the bitterness and exaggeration of a narrow partisan, much of the
Old Oligarch's criticism of the character of the Athenian masses and the motives of their imperialism seems justified.

"RASCALS FARE BETTER THAN GOOD CITIZENS"

I, 1. As for the constitution of the Athenians, their choice of this type of
constitution I do not approve, for in choosing thus they chose that rascals
should fare better than good citizens. This then is why I do not approve. However, this being their decision, I shall show how well they preserve their constitution, and how well otherwise they are acting where the rest of Greece
thinks that they are going wrong.

2. First of all then I shall say that at Athens the poor and the commons
seem justly to have the advantage over the wellborn and the wealthy; for it is
the commons which mans the fleet and has brought the state her power, and
the steersmen and the boatswains and the shipmasters and the lookout-men
and the ship-builders — these have brought the state her power much rather
than the infantry and the well-born and the good citizens. This being so it
seems just that all should have a share in offices filled by lot or by election, and
that any citizen who wishes should be allowed to speak. (3.) Then in those
offices which bring security to the whole commons if they are in the hands of
good citizens, but if not ruin, the commons desires to have no share. They do
not think that they ought to have a share through the lot in the supreme commands or in the cavalry commands, for the commons realizes that it reaps
greater benefit by not having these offices in its own hands, but by allowing
men of standing to hold them. All those offices however whose end is pay and
family benefits the commons does seek to hold.

4. Secondly, some folk are surprised that everywhere they give the advantage to rascals, the poor, and the democrats rather than to good citizens. This
is just where they will be seen to be preserving the democracy. For if the poor
and the common folk and the worse elements are treated well, the growth of
these classes will exalt the democracy; whereas if the rich and the good citizens
are treated well the democrats strengthen their own opponents.

5. In every land the best element is opposed to democracy. Among the
best elements there is very little license and injustice, very great discrimination
as to what is worthy, while among the commons there is very great ignorance,
disorderliness and rascality; for poverty tends to lead them to what is disgraceful, as does lack of education and the ignorance which befalls some men as a
result of lack of means.

6. It may be said that they ought not to have allowed everyone in turn to
make speeches or sit on the Council, but only those of the highest capability
and quality. But in allowing even rascals to speak they are also very well advised. For if the good citizens made speeches and joined in deliberations, good

would result to those like themselves and ill to the democrats. As it is, anyone who wants, a rascally fellow maybe, gets up and makes a speech, and devises what is to the advantage of himself and those like him. (7.) Someone may ask how such a fellow would know what is to the advantage of himself or the commons. They know that this man's ignorance, rascality and goodwill are more beneficial than the good citizen's worth, wisdom, and ill will.

8. From such procedure then a city would not attain the ideal, but the democracy would be best preserved thus. For it is the wish of the commons not that the state should be well ordered and the commons itself in complete subjection, but that the commons should have its freedom and be in control; disorderliness is of little consequence to it. From what you consider lack of order come the strength and the liberty of the commons itself. (9.) If on the other hand you investigate good order, first of all you will see that the most capable make laws for them; then the good citizens will keep the rascals in check and will deliberate on matters of state, refusing to allow madmen to sit on the Council or make speeches or attend the general assemblies. Such advantages indeed would very soon throw the commons into complete subjection.

"LICENSE ALLOWED TO SLAVES AND ALIENS"

10. The license allowed to slaves and aliens at Athens is extreme and a blow is forbidden there, nor will a slave make way for you. I shall tell you why this is the custom of the country. If it were legal for a slave or an alien or a freedman to be beaten by a freeman, you would often have taken the Athenian for a slave and struck him; for the commons there does not dress better than the slaves and the aliens, and their general appearance is in no way superior. (11.) If anyone is surprised also at their allowing slaves, that is some of them, to live luxuriously and magnificently there, here too they would be seen to act with wisdom. In a naval state slaves must serve for hire, that we may receive the fee for their labor, and we must let them go free. Where there are rich slaves it is no longer profitable that my slave should be afraid of you. In Sparta my slave is afraid of you. If your slave is afraid of me there will be a danger even of his giving his own money to avoid personal risks. (12.) This then is why we placed even slaves on a footing of equality with free men; and we placed aliens on a footing of equality with citizens because the state has need of aliens, owing to the number of skilled trades and because of the fleet. For this reason then we were right to place even the aliens on a footing of equality. . . .

"THE ALLIES ARE SLAVES"

14. As for the allies, that the Athenians leave home and, as it is thought, bring false accusations against the good citizens and hate them — they know that the ruler cannot help but be hated by the ruled, and that if the rich and the good citizens in the various cities have control the rule of the commons at Athens will be very short-lived. This then is why they disfranchise the good citizens, rob them of their wealth, drive them into exile, or put them to death, while they exalt the rascals. The good citizens of Athens protect the good

citizens in the allied cities, realizing that it is to their own advantage always to protect the best elements in the various cities. (15.) It might be suggested that the ability of the allies to pay tribute is the strength of Athens. The democrats think it more advantageous that each individual Athenian should possess the wealth of the allies and the allies only enough to live on, and continue working without having the power to conspire.

16. The commons of Athens is also thought to be ill-advised in compelling the allies to travel to Athens to have their law-suits tried. They meet this criticism by reckoning up all the benefits to the Athenian commons that this involves: first of all the receipt of pay out of the court fees all the year round; then while remaining at home without sending out ships they manage the allied cities, and protect the party of the commons while they ruin their opponents in the courts. If each of the allies tried their law-suits at home, out of hatred for Athenians they would have destroyed those of their own people most friendly to the Athenian commons. (17.) In addition the commons of Athens gains the following advantages from having the allied law-suits tried at Athens. First the five per cent duty levied at the Peiraeus brings more in to the state; (18.) next, anyone who has a lodging-house is more prosperous, and so is the man who has a couple of hacks or a slave for hire; then the heralds are more prosperous as a result of the visits of the allies. Above all this, if the allies did not come to Athens for their law-suits they would honor only those Athenians who leave home — the generals, the naval commanders, and envoys. As it is, all the allies individually must fawn upon the Athenian commons, realizing that they must come to Athens and appear as defendant or prosecutor before the commons and the commons alone, for that forsooth is the law at Athens; and in the law-courts they must make supplications and grasp so-and-so by the hand as he enters. This then is why the allies are rather in the position of slaves of the Athenian commons. . . .

CONTROL OF THE SEA

II, 3. Of such mainland states as are subject to Athenian rule the large are in subjection because of fear, the small simply because of need; there is not a city which does not require both import and export trade, and it will not have that unless it is subject to the rulers of the sea. . . .

7. If there is any need to mention less important facts too, command of the sea and contact with the different people of different countries were the first means of introducing luxurious ways of living. The delicacies of Sicily, Italy, Cyprus, Egypt, Lydia, Pontus, the Peloponnese, in fact of any country, all converge upon one point as a result of the command of the sea. (8.) Then hearing every tongue they adopted a phrase from this tongue and a phrase from that. The Greeks as a whole enjoy a language, a way of life, and a general appearance which is rather their own, the Athenians a hotch-potch of those of all the Greeks and foreigners. . . .

11. They alone can possess the wealth of Greeks and foreigners. If a city is rich in shipbuilding timber where will it dispose of it unless it win the consent of the ruler of the sea? What if some city is rich in iron or bronze or

cloth? Where will it dispose of it unless it win the consent of the ruler of the sea? These however are just the very things of which my ships are made — somebody's wood, somebody's iron, somebody's bronze, somebody's cloth and somebody's wax. (12.) Moreover they will not allow our rivals to take their goods elsewhere or (if they try) they will not use the sea. I pass my time in idleness, and because of the sea I have all these products of the earth, whereas no other single city has two of these commodities; the same city does not possess both timber and cloth, but where cloth is plentiful the country is flat and treeless, nor do bronze and iron come from the same city, nor does one city possess two or three of the other commodities, but one has one, another has another. . . .

DEMOCRACIES ARE IRRESPONSIBLE

17. Again oligarchical states must abide by their alliances and their oaths. If they do not keep to the agreement penalties can be exacted from the few who made it. But whenever the commons makes an agreement it can lay the blame on the individual speaker or proposer, and say to the other party that it was not present and does not approve what they know was agreed upon in full assembly; and should it be decided that this is not so, the commons has discovered a hundred excuses for not doing what they may not wish to do. If any ill result from a decision of the commons it lays the blame on a minority for opposing and working its ruin, whereas if any good results they take the credit to themselves.

18. They do not allow caricature and abuse of the commons, lest they should hear themselves evilly spoken of, but they do allow you to caricature any individual you wish to. They well know that generally the man who is caricatured is not of the commons or of the crowd, but someone rich or well-born or influential, and that few of the poor and democrats are caricatured, and they only because they are busy-bodies and try to overreach the commons; so they are not angry when such men are caricatured either.

19. I say then that the commons at Athens realizes which citizens are good citizens and which rascals. With this knowledge they favor those who are friendly and useful to them, even if they are rascals, whereas they hate rather the good citizens. For they do not believe that their worth exists for the good but for the ill of the commons. Conversely, certain men who in fact belong to the commons are not democratic by nature. (20.) I pardon the commons itself its democracy, for it is pardonable that everyone should seek his own interest. But the man who is not of the commons yet chose to live in a democratic rather than in an oligarchical state sought opportunity for wrongdoing, and realized that it was more possible for his wickedness to go unnoticed in a democratic state than in an oligarchical.

RECAPITULATION

III, 1. The type of the constitution of the Athenians I do not approve, but as they saw fit to be a democracy in my opinion they preserve their democracy well by employing the means I have pointed out. . . .

10. The Athenians are also thought to be ill advised because they take sides with the worst elements in cities divided by faction. They do this with good reason. If they sided with the better elements they would not side with those who hold the same opinions as themselves, for in no city is the better element well inclined to the commons, but in each the worse element is well inclined to the commons; like favors like. This then is why the Athenians side with the elements akin to themselves.

27

Thucydides, History of the Peloponnesian War

The statesman's handbook

"My history has been composed to be an everlasting possession, not the show-piece of an hour," wrote Thucydides (no doubt with reference to Herodotus) in the introduction to his history of the great war (431–404 B.C.) between the Athenian Empire and the Spartan League. Posterity has ever been in agreement with this appraisal. He knew that this war, in which he was a participant, represented a momentous crisis to which the political and economic development of the Greek world had led. His aim was to analyze this first "world war" in order to acquire an exact knowledge of the facts that would be useful to future statesmen confronted by a like situation; in similar situations, Thucydides insisted, like causes are always followed by like effects. "I shall be content," he wrote of his History, "if it is judged useful by all who wish to study the plain truth of the events which have happened, and which will according to human nature recur in much the same way."

This emphasis upon "the plain truth of the events which have happened" is the foundation for Thucydides' reputation as a great historian. He is, far more than Herodotus, the first critical writer of history and his standard of scientific objectivity with regard to facts has never been surpassed. In this respect he was a true son of his age, the last half of the fifth century B.C. During the previous century and a half, Greek thought had divorced itself from religion and mythmaking and by substituting reason and experience had culminated in the critical thinking of the Sophists, who were Thucydides' teachers. This new viewpoint with its emphasis upon observed facts had produced also in Thucydides' day the new science of medicine. It is not mere coincidence that the two contemporaries, Hippocrates in medicine and Thucydides in history, were the champions of the scientific approach in their respective fields. Hippocrates' famous aphorism, "Every disease has a natural cause, and without natural causes nothing ever happens," is echoed by Thucydides in his History: "As for my narrative, it is not derived from any chance source, nor have I trusted to my own impressions only. It rests partly on my own experiences and things which I have seen with my own eyes, partly on the witness of others, which I have verified by the severest and most minute tests possible. This has been laborious; for eye-witnesses had not always the same tale to tell of identical events; sometimes, too, memory served badly, or there was prejudice in one direction or another."

What makes Thucydides' History so pertinent to us is the fact that the crisis in the Greek world which he described is basically similar to that confronting modern Europe — and even the whole world — in our own day. Now, as then, the underlying problem is the need for international trade by commercial and industrial states whose economies have outgrown their narrow national boundaries; economic internationalism requires a corresponding political internationalism. In the Greek world the only answer found for this problem was the internationalism of the Athenian Empire which formed a union of the eastern half of the Greek world and maintained the freedom of the seas in order to promote and insure a flourishing inter-state trade. We have seen in Pericles' Funeral Oration an idealized rationalization of the stern economic necessity for the Athenian Empire, but this view of Athens as "an education to Greece" was unacceptable to other Greek states which, led by Sparta, feared the expanding "tyrant city" as a danger to their own independence. In the words of Thucydides, "The real but unavowed cause I consider to have been the growth of the power of Athens, and the alarm which it inspired in Sparta; this made war inevitable."

In the modern world the answer to this problem of international order vs. national sovereignty is still being sought. Will the history of modern Europe, one may ask, be a repetition of that of the Greek states which, incapable of uniting, so weakened themselves by wars and depressions that in the end they fell victim to an outside power? Thucydides' masterly analysis of his own times was written to serve as a handbook for future generations possessed of the wit to profit by the lessons of the Greek example.

◆ A ◆ THE REVOLT OF MITYLENE

"Democracy is incapable of empire."

In 428 B.C., one year after the death of Pericles, occurred an event that reveals the character of Athenian democracy when stripped of Periclean idealism and statesmanship. The island of Lesbos, encouraged by Sparta and led by the oligarchs of its chief city, Mitylene, withdrew from its alliance with Athens.

From Thucydides, *History of the Peloponnesian War*, tr. Richard Crawley.

This revolt — for so the Athenians saw it — was crushed and the Athenian assembly voted to make an example of Lesbos in order to discourage future rebellions within the Empire. A ship was sent with orders to the Athenian commander on Lesbos to put to death all the men of Mitylene and sell the women and children into slavery. "The next day," reports Thucydides, "there was a feeling of repentance; they reflected that the decree was cruel and indiscriminate, to slay a whole city and not the guilty only." The debate was reopened, and the speech delivered on the occasion by Cleon, the promoter of the original policy of frightfulness, is given below in Thucydides' version. It is a typical example of Thucydides' use of speeches as a means of penetrating behind the facts to reveal and interpret the character and motives of both individuals and states. He admitted his inability to give verbatim reports of what was said, explaining that "the speeches have been composed as it seemed to me each speaker would say what was most necessary about the various situations, keeping as close as possible to the general intent of what actually was said."

Cleon represents the new type of democratic leader, "the most violent of the citizens," says Thucydides, given to using "unmeasured language" to inflame the passions of the people. He prided himself on being a practical man — he was a leather manufacturer — who distrusted intellectuals of Pericles' type. Though cynically brutal, his convictions were honestly held, and he had enough of statesman-like courage to oppose the views of his audience. His description of the fickleness of the Athenian populace was warranted. By a narrow margin the assembly reversed itself and sent another order which arrived in the nick of time to halt the wholesale massacre of the Mitylenians.

The question posed here by Thucydides — Is democracy capable of running an empire? — is a recurrent one. The Romans, as we shall see, faced it, and its modern version — Is democracy capable of world leadership? — faces Americans today.

"YOUR EMPIRE IS A DESPOTISM"

III, 37. "I have often before now been convinced that a democracy is incapable of empire, and never more so than by your present change of mind in the matter of Mitylene. Fears or plots being unknown to you in your daily relations with each other, you feel just the same with regard to your allies, and never reflect that the mistakes into which you may be led by listening to their appeals, or by giving way to your own compassion, are full of danger to yourselves, and bring you no thanks for your weakness from your allies; entirely forgetting that your empire is a despotism and your subjects disaffected conspirators, whose obedience is insured not by your suicidal concessions, but by the superiority given you by your own strength and not their loyalty. The most alarming feature in the case is the constant change of measures with which we appear to be threatened, and our seeming ignorance of the fact that bad laws which are never changed are better for a city than good ones that have no authority; that unlearned loyalty is more serviceable than quick-witted insubordination; and that ordinary men usually manage public affairs better than their more gifted fellows. The latter are always wanting to appear wiser than the laws, and to overrule every proposition brought forward, thinking that they cannot show their wit in more important matters, and by such behavior too often ruin their country; while those who mistrust their own cleverness are content to be less learned than the laws, and less able to pick holes in the speech of a good speaker; and being fair judges rather than rival athletes, generally conduct affairs successfully. These we ought to imitate, instead of being led on by cleverness and intellectual rivalry to advise your people against our real opinions.

"THE PERSONS TO BLAME"

38. "For myself, I adhere to my former opinion, and wonder at those who have proposed to reopen the case of the Mitylenians, and who are thus causing a delay which is all in favor of the guilty, by making the sufferer proceed against the offender with the edge of his anger blunted; although where vengeance follows most closely upon the wrong, it best equals it and most amply requites it. I wonder also who will be the man who will maintain the contrary, and will pretend to show that the crimes of the Mitylenians are of service to us, and our misfortunes injurious to the allies. Such a man must plainly either have such confidence in his rhetoric as to adventure to prove that what has been once for all decided is still undetermined, or be bribed to try to delude us by elaborate sophisms. In such contests the state gives the rewards to others, and takes the dangers for herself. The person to blame are you who are so foolish as to institute these contests; who go to see an oration as you would to see a sight, take your facts on hearsay, judge of the practicability of a project by the wit of its advocates, and trust for the truth as to past events not to the fact which you saw more than to the clever strictures which you heard; the easy victims of new-fangled arguments, unwilling to follow received conclusions; slaves to every new paradox, despisers of the commonplace; the first wish of every man being that he could speak himself, the next to rival those who can speak by seeming to be quite up with their ideas by applauding every hit almost before it is made, and by being as quick in catching an argument as you are slow in foreseeing its consequences; asking, if I may so say, for something different from the conditions under which we live, and yet comprehending inadequately those very conditions; very slaves to the pleasure of the ear, and more like the audience of a rhetorician than the council of a city.

"DELIBERATE AND WANTON AGGRESSION"

39. "In order to keep you from this, I proceed to show that no one state has ever injured you as much as Mitylene. I can make allowance for those who revolt because they cannot bear our empire, or who have been forced to do so by the enemy. But for those who possessed an island with fortifications; who could fear our enemies only by sea, and there had their own force of galleys to protect them; who were independent and held in the highest honor by you — to act as these have done, this is not revolt — revolt implies oppression; it is deliberate and wanton aggression; an attempt to ruin us by siding with our bitterest enemies; a worse offense than a war undertaken on their own account

in the acquisition of power. The fate of those of their neighbors who had already rebelled and had been subdued, was no lesson to them; their own prosperity could not dissuade them from affronting danger; but blindly confident in the future, and full of hopes beyond their power though not beyond their ambition, they declared war and made their decision to prefer might to right, their attack being determined not by provocation but by the moment which seemed propitious. . . . Our mistake has been to distinguish the Mitylenians as we have done: had they been long ago treated like the rest, they never would have so far forgotten themselves, human nature being as surely made arrogant by consideration, as it is awed by firmness. Let them now therefore be punished as their crime requires, and do not, while you condemn the aristocracy, absolve the people. This is certain, that all attacked you without distinction, although they might have come over to us, and been now again in possession of their city. But no, they thought it safer to throw in their lot with the aristocracy and so joined their rebellion! Consider therefore! if you subject to the same punishment the ally who is forced to rebel by the enemy, and him who does so by his own free choice, which of them, think you, is there that will not rebel upon the slightest pretext; when the reward of success is freedom, and the penalty of failure nothing so very terrible? We meanwhile shall have to risk our money and our lives against one state after another; and if successful, shall receive a ruined town from which we can no longer draw the revenue upon which our strength depends; while if unsuccessful, we shall have an enemy the more upon our hands, and shall spend the time that might be employed in combating our existing foes in warring with our own allies.

"THREE FAILINGS MOST FATAL TO EMPIRE"

40. "No hope, therefore, that rhetoric may instill or money purchase, of the mercy due to human infirmity must be held out to the Mitylenians. Their offense was not involuntary, but of malice and deliberate; and mercy is only for unwilling offenders. I therefore now as before persist against your reversing your first decision, or giving way to the three failings most fatal to empire — pity, sentiment, and indulgence. . . . To sum up shortly, I say that if you follow my advice you will do what is just towards the Mitylenians, and at the same time expedient; while by a different decision you will not oblige them so much as pass sentence upon yourselves. For if they were right in rebelling, you must be wrong in ruling. However, if right or wrong, you determine to rule, you must carry out your principle and punish the Mitylenians as your interest requires; or else you must give up your empire and cultivate honesty without danger. Make up your minds, therefore, to give them like for like; and do not let the victims who escaped the plot be more insensible than the conspirators who hatched it; but reflect what they would have done if victorious over you, especially as they were the aggressors. . . . Punish them as they deserve, and teach your other allies by a striking example that the penalty of rebellion is death. Let them once understand this and you will not have so often to neglect your enemies while you are fighting with your own confederates." Such were the words of Cleon.

◆ B ◆ THE CORCYREAN REVOLUTION

"Civil war gave birth to every kind of iniquity"

Although the Peloponnesian War began as an attempt on the part of Sparta and its allies in western Greece to destroy the Athenian Empire and put an end to the emerging economic and political unification of the Greek world under Athenian leadership, it soon became a struggle between the two rival ideologies of democracy and oligarchy throughout the Greek world.

The genesis of the Spartan League lay in Sparta's fear that democratic ideas would undermine its totalitarian regime by inspiring revolt among the great mass of subject peoples over whom a small minority of Spartans ruled. To keep democracy and equalitarian ideas as far away as possible, the Spartans created an "iron curtain" by joining forces with the aristocrats in neighboring states and providing them with military aid to establish and maintain oligarchic regimes of their own. The Spartan League was thus a confederation of oligarchic governments devoted to maintaining the status quo and the political subjugation of the common people. The Athenians used the same technique in reverse in extending and holding their empire. Being a democracy, Athens favored and maintained in power the democratic elements in its allied states, and these, in constant fear of their own aristocratic fellow-citizens, welcomed Athenian friendship and leadership. (See Selection 26.)

The Peloponnesian War involved, therefore, a struggle between two opposed ideologies, and it was inevitable that both sides should seek to use the smoldering class hatreds existing in every state as a weapon in the conflict. The Spartan-inspired and oligarchic-led revolt of Lesbos from Athens has already been noted. A more famous example concerned the island of Corcyra, modern Corfu, located off the northwestern coast of Greece. The Athenians had earlier engineered an alliance with the democratic government of Corcyra, and as this state was well within the Spartan sphere of influence, the event was one of several incidents in Athenian expansion causing the fear which originally motivated Sparta to declare war. Finally, in 427 B.C., the Spartan League intrigued with the oligarchic party at Corcyra and a bloody civil war resulted. Both Athens and Sparta sent aid to their respective factions, but the democrats won the day and proceeded to liquidate all who were suspected of oligarchic sympathies. This and similar events inspired Thucydides to write the following brilliant analysis of the psychology of class war and its evil effects.

III, 82. Such was the pitch of savagery reached by the revolution; and it made the greater impression because it was the first of such incidents. Later, practically the whole Greek world was affected; there was a struggle everywhere between the leaders of the democratic and oligarchic parties, the former wishing to secure the support of Athens, the latter that of Lacedaemon. In peace there

From Thucydides, *The History of the Peloponnesian War*, ed. R. W. Livingstone (Oxford: 1943), pp. 189–192. Reprinted by permission of The Clarendon Press.

would have been neither the desire nor the excuse for appealing to them, but the war gave both sides, if they wished for a revolution, a ready chance to invoke outside help in order to injure their opponents and to gain power. Revolution brought on the cities of Greece many calamities, such as exist and will exist till human nature changes, varying in intensity and character with changing circumstances. In peace and prosperity states and individuals are governed by higher ideals because they are not involved in necessities beyond their control, but war deprives them of their easy existence and is a rough teacher that brings most men's dispositions down to the level of their circumstances.

So civil war broke out in the cities, and the later revolutionaries, with previous examples before their eyes, devised new ideas which went far beyond earlier ones, so elaborate were their enterprises, so novel their revenges. Words changed their ordinary meanings and were construed in new senses. Reckless daring passed for the courage of a loyal partisan, far-sighted hesitation was the excuse of a coward, moderation was the pretext of the unmanly, the power to see all sides of a question was complete inability to act. Impulsive rashness was held the mark of a man, caution in conspiracy was a specious excuse for avoiding action. A violent attitude was always to be trusted, its opponents were suspect. To succeed in a plot was shrewd, it was still more clever to divine one: but if you devised a policy that made such success or suspicion needless, you were breaking up your party and showing fear of your opponents. In fine, men were applauded if they forestalled an injury or instigated one that had not been conceived. Ties of party were closer then those of blood, because a partisan was readier to take risks without asking why; for the basis of party association was not an advantage consistent with the laws of the state but a self-interest which ignored them, and the seal of their mutual good faith was complicity in crime and not the divine law. If a stronger opponent made a fair proposal, it was met with active precautions and not in a generous spirit. Revenge was more prized than self-preservation. An agreement sworn to by either party, when they could do nothing else, was binding as long as both were powerless, but the first side to pluck up courage, when they saw an opening and an undefended point, took more pleasure in revenge on a confiding enemy than if they had achieved it by an open attack; apart from considerations of security, a success won by treachery was a victory in a battle of wits. Villainy is sooner called clever than simplicity good, and men in general are proud of cleverness and ashamed of simplicity.

"THE CAUSE OF ALL THESE EVILS WAS LOVE OF POWER"

The cause of all these evils was love of power due to ambition and greed, which led to rivalries from which party spirit sprung. The leaders of both sides used specious phrases, championing a moderate aristocracy or political equality for the masses. They professed to study public interests but made them their prize, and in the struggle to get the better of each other by any means committed terrible excesses and went to still greater extremes in revenge. Neither justice nor the needs of the state restrained them, their only limit was the caprice of the hour, and they were prepared to satisfy a momentary rivalry by the unjust condemnation of an opponent or by a forcible seizure of power. Religion meant nothing to either party, but the use of fair phrases to achieve a criminal end was highly respected. The moderates were destroyed by both parties, either because they declined to cooperate or because their survival was resented.

83. So civil war gave birth to every kind of iniquity in the Greek world. Simplicity, the chief ingredient in a noble nature, was ridiculed and disappeared, and society was divided into rival camps in which no man trusted his fellow. There was no reconciling force — no promise binding, no oath that inspired awe. Each party in its day of power despairing of security was more concerned to save itself from ruin than to trust others. Inferior minds were as a rule the more successful; aware of their own defects and of the intelligence of their opponents, to whom they felt themselves inferior in debate, and by whose versatility of intrigue they were afraid of being surprised, they struck boldly and at once. Their enemies despised them, were confident of detecting their plots and thought it needless to effect by violence what they could achieve by their brains, and so were taken off guard and destroyed.

84. It was in Corcyra that most of these crimes were first perpetrated: the reprisals taken by subjects when their hour came on rulers who had governed them oppressively; the unjust designs of those who wished to escape from a life of poverty and who were stung by passion and covetous of their neighbors' wealth; the savage and pitiless excesses of those with whom greed was not a motive, but who were carried away by undisciplined rage in the struggle with their equals.

In the chaos of city life under these conditions human nature, always rebellious against the law and now its master, was delighted to display its uncontrolled passions, its superiority to justice, its hostility to all above itself; for vengeance would not have been set above religion, or gain above justice, had it not been for the fatal power of envy. But in their revenges men are reckless of the future and do not hesitate to annul those common laws of humanity on which everyone relies in the hour of misfortune for his own hope of deliverance, they forget that in their own need they will look for them in vain.

◆C◆ THE MELIAN DIALOGUE

"The strong do what they can and the weak submit."

In 416 B.C. the Athenians demanded the submission of Melos, the one island-state in the south Aegean that had remained both outside her empire and neutral up to this point in the war. When the Melians refused to surrender, they were overpowered after a six-month's siege and all the men were slaughtered and the women and children enslaved. This incident would be historically unimportant but for the dialogue which Thucydides presents as having oc-

From *Thucydides, The History of the Peloponnesian War,* ed. R. W. Livingstone (Oxford: 1943), pp. 266–274. Reprinted by permission of The Clarendon Press.

curred between the Melians and the Athenian envoys who brought the original demand for submission. Far removed from the idealism of Pericles, the Athenians here justify their empire solely on the grounds of power — power which accepts no limitation from either religion, or justice, or even, in contrast with the earlier Mitylenian revolt, pity. It is a classic example of Thucydides' use of speeches to comment upon the facts and draw universal principles from them. In this masterpiece of political commentary he eternalizes the conflict of the two irreconcilable principles of might and right.

V, 84. The next summer the Athenians made an expedition against the isle of Melos. The Melians are a colony of Lacedaemon that would not submit to the Athenians like the other islanders, and at first remained neutral and took no part in the struggle, but afterwards, upon the Athenians using violence and plundering their territory, assumed an attitude of open hostility. The Athenian generals encamped in their territory with their army, and before doing any harm to their land sent envoys to negotiate. These the Melians did not bring before the people, but told them to state the object of their mission to the magistrates and the council; the Athenian envoys then said:

85. *Athenians.* "As we are not to speak to the people, for fear that if we made a single speech without interruption we might deceive them with attractive arguments to which there was no chance of replying — we realize that this is the meaning of our being brought before your ruling body — we suggest that you who sit here should make security doubly sure. Let us have no long speeches from you either, but deal separately with each point, and take up at once any statement of which you disapprove, and criticize it."

86. *Melians.* "We have no objection to your reasonable suggestion that we should put our respective points of view quietly to each other, but the military preparations which you have already made seem inconsistent with it. We see that you have come to be yourselves the judges of the debate, and that its natural conclusion for us will be slavery if you convince us, and war if we get the better of the argument and therefore refuse to submit."

87. *Ath.* "If you have met us in order to make surmises about the future, or for any other purpose than to look existing facts in the face and to discuss the safety of your city on this basis, we will break off the conversations; otherwise, we are ready to speak."

88. *Mel.* "In our position it is natural and excusable to explore many ideas and arguments. But the problem that has brought us here is our security, so, if you think fit, let the discussion follow the line you propose."

89. *Ath.* "Then we will not make a long and unconvincing speech, full of fine phrases, to prove that our victory over Persia justifies our empire, or that we are now attacking you because you have wronged us, and we ask you not to expect to convince us by saying that you have not injured us, or that, though a colony of Lacedaemon, you did not join her. Let each of us say what we really think and reach a practical agreement. You know and we know, as practical men, that the question of justice arises only between parties equal in strength, and that the strong do what they can, and the weak submit."

90. *Mel.* "As you ignore justice and have made self-interest the basis of discussion, we must take the same ground, and we say that in our opinion it is in your interest to maintain a principle which is for the good of all — that anyone in danger should have just and equitable treatment and any advantage, even if not strictly his due, which he can secure by persuasion. This is your interest as much as ours, for your fall would involve you in a crushing punishment that would be a lesson to the world."

91. *Ath.* "We have no apprehensions about the fate of our empire, if it did fall; those who rule other peoples, like the Lacedaemonians, are not formidable to a defeated enemy. Nor is it the Lacedaemonians with whom we are now contending: the danger is from subjects who of themselves may attack and conquer their rulers. But leave that danger to us to face. At the moment we shall prove that we have come in the interest of our empire and that in what we shall say we are seeking the safety of your state; for we wish you to become our subjects with least trouble to ourselves, and we would like you to survive in our interests as well as your own."

92. *Mel.* "It may be your interest to be our masters: how can it be ours to be your slaves?"

93. *Ath.* "By submitting you would avoid a terrible fate, and we should gain by not destroying you."

94. *Mel.* "Would you not agree to an arrangement under which we should keep out of the war, and be your friends instead of your enemies, but neutral?"

95. *Ath.* "No: your hostility injures us less than your friendship. That, to our subjects, is an illustration of our weakness, while your hatred exhibits our power."

96. *Mel.* "Is this the construction which your subjects put on it? Do they not distinguish between states in which you have no concern, and peoples who are most of them your colonies, and some conquered rebels?"

97. *Ath.* "They think that one nation has as good rights as another, but that some survive because they are strong and we are afraid to attack them. So, apart from the addition to our empire, your subjection would give us security: the fact that you are islanders (and weaker than others) makes it the more important that you should not get the better of the mistress of the sea."

98. *Mel.* "But do you see no safety in our neutrality? You debar us from the plea of justice and press us to submit to your interests, so we must expound our own, and try to convince you, if the two happen to coincide. Will you not make enemies of all neutral Powers when they see your conduct and reflect that some day you will attack them? Will not your action strengthen your existing opponents, and induce those who would otherwise never be your enemies to become so against their will?"

99. *Ath.* "No. The mainland states, secure in their freedom, will be slow to take defensive measures against us, and we do not consider them so formidable as independent island powers like yourselves, or subjects already smarting under our yoke. These are most likely to take a thoughtless step and bring themselves and us into obvious danger."

100. *Mel.* "Surely then, if you are ready to risk so much to maintain your empire, and the enslaved peoples so much to escape from it, it would be criminal cowardice in us, who are still free, not to take any and every measure before submitting to slavery?"

101. *Ath.* "No, if you reflect calmly: for this is not a competition in heroism between equals, where your honor is at stake, but a question of self-preservation to save you from a struggle with a far stronger Power."

102. *Mel.* "Still, we know that in war fortune is more impartial than the disproportion in numbers might lead one to expect. If we submit at once, our position is desperate; if we fight, there is still a hope that we shall stand secure."

103. *Ath.* "Hope encourages men to take risks; men in a strong position may follow her without ruin, if not without loss. But when they stake all that they have to the last coin (for she is a spendthrift), she reveals her real self in the hour of failure, and when her nature is known she leaves them without means of self-protection. You are weak, your future hangs on a turn of the scales; avoid the mistake most men make, who might save themselves by human means, and then, when visible hopes desert them, in their extremity turn to the invisible — prophecies and oracles and all those things which delude men with hopes, to their destruction."

104. *Mel.* "We too, you can be sure, realize the difficulty of struggling against your power and against Fortune if she is not impartial. Still we trust that Heaven will not allow us to be worsted by Fortune, for in this quarrel we are right and you are wrong. Besides, we expect the support of Lacedaemon to supply the deficiencies in our strength, for she is bound to help us as her kinsmen, if for no other reason, and from a sense of honor. So our confidence is not entirely unreasonable."

105. *Ath.* "As for divine favor, we think that we can count on it as much as you, for neither our claims nor our actions are inconsistent with what men believe about Heaven or desire for themselves. We believe that Heaven, and we know that men, by a natural law, always rule where they are stronger. We did not make that law nor were we the first to act on it; we found it existing, and it will exist forever, after we are gone; and we know that you and anyone else as strong as we are would do as we do. As to your expectations from Lacedaemon and your belief that she will help you from a sense of honor, we congratulate you on your innocence but we do not admire your folly. So far as they themselves and their national traditions are concerned, the Lacedaemonians are a highly virtuous people; as for their behavior to others, much might be said, but we can put it shortly by saying that, most obviously of all people we know, they identify their interests with justice and the pleasantest course with honor. Such principles do not favor your present irrational hopes of deliverance."

106. *Mel.* "That is the chief reason why we have confidence in them now; in their own interest they will not wish to betray their own colonists and so help their enemies and destroy the confidence that their friends in Greece feel in them."

107. *Ath.* "Apparently you do not realize that safety and self-interest go together, while the path of justice and honor is dangerous; and danger is a risk which the Lacedaemonians are little inclined to run. . . . (111) Here experience may teach you like others, and you will learn that Athens has never abandoned a siege from fear of another foe. You said that you proposed to discuss the safety of your city, but we observe that in all your speeches you have never said a word on which any reasonable expectation of it could be founded. Your strength lies in deferred hopes; in comparison with the forces now arrayed against you, your resources are too small for any hope of success. You will show a great want of judgment if you do not come to a more reasonable decision after we have withdrawn. Surely you will not fall back on the idea of honor, which has been the ruin of so many when danger and disgrace were staring them in the face. How often, when men have seen the fate to which they were tending, have they been enslaved by a phrase and drawn by the power of this seductive word to fall of their own free will into irreparable disaster, bringing on themselves by their folly a greater dishonor than fortune could inflict! If you are wise, you will avoid that fate. The greatest of cities makes you a fair offer, to keep your own land and become her tributary ally: there is no dishonor in that. The choice between war and safety is given you; do not obstinately take the worse alternative. The most successful people are those who stand up to their equals, behave properly to their superiors, and treat their inferiors fairly. Think it over when we withdraw, and reflect once and again that you have only one country, and that its prosperity or ruin depends on one decision."

112. The Athenians now withdraw from the conference; and the Melians, left to themselves, came to a decision corresponding with what they had maintained in the discussion, and answered, "Our resolution, Athenians, is unaltered. We will not in a moment deprive of freedom a city that has existed for seven hundred years; we put our trust in the fortune by which the gods have preserved it until now, and in the help of men, that is, of the Lacedaemonians; and so we will try and save ourselves. Meanwhile we invite you to allow us to be friends to you and foes to neither party, and to retire from our country after making such a treaty as shall seem fit to us both."

113. Such was the answer of the Melians. The Athenians broke up the conference saying, "To judge from your decision, you are unique in regarding the future as more certain than the present and in allowing your wishes to convert the unseen into reality; and as you have staked most on, and trusted most in, the Lacedaemonians, your fortune, and your hopes, so will you be most completely deceived."

114. The Athenian envoys now returned to the army; and as the Melians showed no signs of yielding the generals at once began hostilities, and drew a line of circumvallation round the Melians . . . . and besieged the place. . . .

116. Summer was now over . . . and the siege was now pressed vigorously; there was some treachery in the town, and the Melians surrendered at discretion to the Athenians, who put to death all the grown men whom they took, and sold the women and children for slaves; subsequently they sent out five hundred settlers and colonized the island.

•D• THE SICILIAN EXPEDITION

"Most glorious to the victors, most calamitous to the conquered."

Thucydides' History of the Peloponnesian War has often been called a tragedy for it deals with the fall of a great empire. The historian's narrative is thus most powerful when describing the ill-fated Sicilian expedition of 415–413 B.C., where the tragedy reaches its climax. The purpose of the expedition was to use economic pressure to bring Sparta and its allies to their knees by conquering the source of much of their food supply and markets on the populous island of Sicily. This accomplished, the Athenians believed that they would be strong enough, as Thucydides reports, "to conquer the whole world." The blame for the failure of the project can be laid to the stupidity of the Athenian masses who appointed, against his will, a virtuous but timid and incompetent old general named Nicias to head the expedition. This is the view of Thucydides, who saw the disaster as a product of the low quality of Athenian leadership since the halcyon days under Pericles, when "what was nominally a democracy became in his hands government by the first citizen. With Pericles' successors it was different. More on a level with one another, and each grasping at supremacy, they ended by committing even the conduct of state affairs to the whims of the multitude. This, as might have been expected in a large imperial state produced a host of blunders, among them the Sicilian expedition. . . ."

In the following selections the mingled feelings of pride and apprehension among the citizens as they see the expedition off are contrasted with the pathos of the tragic fate of the beaten army and the arrival of the news of the disaster at Athens.

MOTIVES OF THE ATHENIANS

VI, 24. . . . All alike fell in love with the enterprise. The older men thought that they would either subdue the places against which they were to sail, or at all events, with so large a force, meet with no disaster; those in the prime of life felt a longing for foreign sights and spectacles, and had no doubt that they should come safe home again; while the idea of the common people and the soldiery was to earn wages at the moment, and make conquests that would supply a never-ending fund of pay for the future. With this enthusiasm of the majority, the few that liked it not feared to appear unpatriotic by holding up their hands against it, and so kept quiet. . . .

THE DEPARTURE

30. After this the departure for Sicily took place, it being now about midsummer. Most of the allies, with the corn transports and the smaller craft and the rest of the expedition, had already received orders to muster at Corcyra, to cross the Ionian sea from thence in a body to the Iapygian promontory. But

From Thucydides, *History of the Peloponnesian War*, tr. Richard Crawley.

the Athenians themselves, and such of their allies as happened to be with them, went down to Piraeus upon a day appointed at daybreak, and began to man the ships for putting out to sea. With them also went down the whole population, one may say, of the city, both citizens and foreigners; the inhabitants of the country each escorting those that belonged to them, their friends, their relatives, or their sons, with hope and lamentation upon their way, as they thought of the conquests which they hoped to make, or of the friends whom they might never see again, considering the long voyage which they were going to make from their country. Indeed, at this moment, when they were now upon the point of parting from one another, the danger came more home to them than when they voted for the expedition; although the strength of the armament, and the profuse provision which they remarked in every department, was a sight that could not but comfort them. As for the foreigners and the rest of the crowd, they simply went to see a sight worth looking at and passing all belief.

TWO YEARS LATER, THE INACTION OF NICIAS BEFORE SYRACUSE,
THE CHIEF SICILIAN CITY, RESULTS IN A REVERSAL OF ROLES —
THE BESIEGERS BECOME THE BESIEGED

VII, 50. . . . The Athenian generals seeing a fresh army come to the aid of the enemy, and that their own circumstances, far from improving, were becoming daily worse, and above all distressed by the sickness of the soldiers, now began to repent of not having removed before; and Nicias no longer offering the same opposition, except by urging that there should be no open voting, they gave orders as secretly as possible for all to be prepared to sail out from the camp at a given signal. All was at last ready, and they were on the point of sailing away, when an eclipse of the moon, which was then at the full, took place. Most of the Athenians, deeply impressed by this occurrence, now urged the generals to wait; and Nicias, who was somewhat over-addicted to divination and practices of that kind, refused from that moment even to take the question of departure into consideration, until they had waited the thrice nine days prescribed by the soothsayers. . . .

WITH THE ATHENIANS NOW COMPLETELY SURROUNDED, THE ONLY HOPE
LAY IN BREAKING OUT OF THE HARBOR TO THE OPEN SEA

71. Meanwhile the two armies on shore, while victory hung in the balance, were a prey to the most agonizing and conflicting emotions; the natives thirsting for more glory than they had already won, while the invaders feared to find themselves in even worse plight than before. The all of the Athenians being set upon their fleet, their fear for the event was like nothing they had ever felt; while their view of the struggle was necessarily as checkered as the battle itself. Close to the scene of action and not all looking at the same point at once, some saw their friends victorious and took courage, and fell to calling upon heaven not to deprive them of salvation, while others who had their eyes turned

upon the losers, wailed and cried aloud, and, although spectators, were more overcome than the actual combatants. Others, again, were gazing at some spot where the battle was evenly disputed; as the strife protracted without decision, their swaying bodies reflected the agitation of their minds, and they suffered the worst agony of all, ever just within reach of safety or just on the point of destruction. In short, in that one Athenian army as long as the seafight remained doubtful there was every sound to be heard at once, shrieks, cheers, "We win," "We lose," and all the other manifold exclamations that a great host would necessarily utter in great peril; and with the men in the fleet it was nearly the same; until at last the Syracusans and their allies after the battle had lasted a long while, put the Athenians to flight, and with much shouting and cheering chased them in open rout to the shore. The naval force, one one way, one another, as many as were not taken afloat, now ran ashore and rushed from on board their ships to their camp; while the army, no more divided, but carried away by one impulse, all with shrieks and groans deplored the event, and ran down, some to help the ships, others to guard what was left of their wall, while the remaining and most numerous part already began to consider how they should save themselves. Indeed, the panic of the present moment had never been surpassed. . . . now the Athenians had no hope of escaping by land, without the help of some extraordinary accident. . . .

WITH ESCAPE BY SEA SHUT OFF, AND PREPARATIONS TO BREAK OUT
BY LAND COMPLETED, THE PATHETIC LOT
OF THE EXPEDITION IS SURVEYED

75. After this, Nicias and Demosthenes now thinking that enough had been done in the way of preparation, the removal of the army took place upon the second day after the seafight. It was a lamentable scene, not merely from the single circumstance that they were retreating after having lost all their ships, their great hopes gone, and themselves and the state in peril; but also in leaving the camp there were things most grievous for every eye and heart to contemplate. The dead lay unburied, and each man as he recognized a friend among them shuddered with grief and horror; while the living whom they were leaving behind, wounded or sick, were to the living far more shocking than the dead, and more to be pitied than those who had perished. These fell to entreating and bewailing until their friends knew not what to do, begging them to take them and loudly calling to each individual comrade or relative whom they could see, hanging upon the necks of their tent-fellows in the act of departure, and following as far as they could, and when their bodily strength failed them, calling again and again upon heaven and shrieking aloud as they were left behind. So that the whole army being filled with tears and distracted after this fashion found it not easy to go, even from an enemy's land, where they had already suffered evils too great for tears and in the unknown future before them feared to suffer more. Dejection and self-condemnation were also rife among them. Indeed they could only be compared to a starved-out town, and that no small one, escaping; the whole multitude upon the march being not less than

forty thousand men. All carried anything they could which might be of use, and the heavy infantry and troopers, contrary to their wont, while under arms carried their own victuals, in some cases for want of servants, in others through not trusting them; as they had long been deserting and now did so in greater numbers than ever. Yet even thus they did not carry enough, as there was no longer food in the camp. Moreover their disgrace generally, and the universality of their sufferings, however to a certain extent alleviated by being borne in company, were still felt at the moment a heavy burden, especially when they contrasted the splendor and glory of their setting out with the humiliation in which it had ended. For this was by far the greatest reverse that ever befell an Hellenic army. They had come to enslave others, and were departing in fear of being enslaved themselves; they had sailed out with prayer and paeans, and now started to go back with omens directly contrary; travelling by land instead of by sea, and trusting not in their fleet but in their heavy infantry. Nevertheless the greatness of the danger still impending made all this appear tolerable.

76. Nicias seeing the army dejected and greatly altered, passed along the ranks and encouraged and comforted them as far as was possible under the circumstances, raising his voice still higher and higher as he went from one company to another in his earnestness, and in his anxiety that the benefit of his words might reach as many as possible:

77. "Athenians and allies, even in our present position we must hope on, since men have ere now been saved from worse straits than this; and you must not condemn yourselves too severely either because of your disasters or because of your present unmerited sufferings. I myself who am not superior to any of you in strength — indeed you see how I am in my sickness — and who in the gifts of fortune am, I think, whether in private life or otherwise, the equal of any, am now exposed to the same danger as the meanest among you; and yet my life has been one of much devotion towards the gods, and of much justice and without offense towards men. I have, therefore, still a strong hope for the future, and our misfortunes do not terrify me as much as they might. Indeed we may hope that they will be lightened: our enemies have had good fortune enough; and if any of the gods was offended at our expedition, we have been already amply punished. Others before us have attacked their neighbors and have done what men will do without suffering more than they could bear; and we may now justly expect to find the gods more kind, for we have become fitter objects for their pity than their jealousy. And then look at yourselves, mark the numbers and efficiency of the heavy infantry marching in your ranks, and do not give way too much to despondency, but reflect that you are yourselves at once a city wherever you sit down, and that there is no other in Sicily that could easily resist your attack, or expel you when once established. The safety and order of the march is for yourselves to look to; the one thought of each man being that the spot on which he may be forced to fight must be conquered and held as his country and stronghold. Meanwhile we shall hasten on our way night and day alike, as our provisions are scanty; and if we can reach some friendly place of the Sicels, whom fear of the Syracusans still keeps true to us,

you may forthwith consider yourselves safe. A message has been sent on to them with directions to meet us with supplies and food. To sum up, be convinced, soldiers, that you must be brave, as there is no place near for your cowardice to take refuge in, and that if you now escape from the enemy, you may all see again what your hearts desire, while those of you who are Athenians will raise up again the great power of the state, fallen though it be. Men make the city and not walls or ships without men in them." . . .

HALF OF THE ATHENIAN FORCES UNDER DEMOSTHENES HAVING BEEN FORCED TO SURRENDER, THE REST UNDER NICIAS COME TO THE SAME END

84. As soon as it was day Nicias put his army in motion, pressed as before, by the Syracusans and their allies, pelted from every side by their missiles, and struck down by their javelins. The Athenians pushed on for the Assinarus, impelled by the attacks made upon them from every side by a numerous cavalry and the swarm of other arms, fancying that they should breathe more freely if once across the river, and driven on also by their exhaustion and craving for water. Once there they rushed in, and all order was at an end, each man wanting to cross first, and the attacks of the enemy making it difficult to cross at all; forced to huddle together, they fell against and trod down one another, some dying immediately upon the javelins, others getting entangled together and stumbling over the articles of baggage, without being able to rise again. Meanwhile the opposite bank, which was steep, was lined by the Syracusans, who showered missiles down upon the Athenians, most of them drinking greedily and heaped together in disorder in the hollow bed of the river. The Peloponnesians also came down and butchered them, especially those in the water, which was thus immediately spoiled, but which they went on drinking just the same, mud and all, bloody as it was, most even fighting to have it.

85. At last, when many dead now lay piled one upon another in the stream, and part of the army had been destroyed at the river, and the few that escaped from thence cut off by the cavalry, Nicias surrendered himself to Gylippus, whom he trusted more than he did the Syracusans, and told him and the Lacedaemonians to do what they liked with him, but to stop the slaughter of the soldiers. . . .

TREATMENT OF THE PRISONERS

86. The Syracusans and their allies now mustered and took up the spoils and as many prisoners as they could, and went back to the city. The rest of their Athenian and allied captives were deposited in the quarries, this seeming the safest way of keeping them; but Nicias and Demosthenes were butchered, against the will of Gylippus, who thought that it would be the crown of his triumph if he could take the enemy's generals to Lacedaemon. . . .

87. The prisoners in the quarries were at first hardly treated by the Syracusans. Crowded in a narrow hole, without any roof to cover them, the heat of the sun and the stifling closeness of the air tormented them during the day,

and then the nights, which came on autumnal and chilly, made them ill by the violence of the change; besides, as they had to do everything in the same place for want of room, and the bodies of those who died of their wounds or from the variation in the temperature, or from similar causes, were left heaped together one upon another, intolerable stenches arose; while hunger and thirst never ceased to afflict them, each man during eight months having only half a pint of water and a pint of corn given him daily. In short, no single suffering to be apprehended by men thrust into such a place was spared them. For some seventy days they thus lived all together, after which all, except the Athenians and any Siceliots or Italiots who had joined in the expedition, were sold. The total number of prisoners taken it would be difficult to state exactly, but it could not have been less than seven thousand.

This was the greatest Hellenic achievement of any in this war, or, in my opinion, in Hellenic history; at once most glorious to the victors, and most calamitous to the conquered. They were beaten at all points and altogether; all that they suffered was great; they were destroyed, as the saying is, with a total destruction, their fleet, their army — everything was destroyed, and few out of many returned home. Such were the events in Sicily.

THE NEWS ARRIVES AT ATHENS

VIII, 1. When the news was brought to Athens, for a long while they disbelieved even the most respectable of the soldiers who had themselves escaped from the scene of action and clearly reported the matter, a destruction so complete not being thought credible. When the conviction was forced upon them, they were angry with the orators who had joined in promoting the expedition, just as if they had not themselves voted it, and were enraged also with the reciters of oracles and soothsayers, and all other omen-mongers of the time who had encouraged them to hope that they should conquer Sicily. Already distressed at all points and in all quarters, after what had now happened, they were seized by a fear and consternation quite without example. It was grievous enough for the state and for every man in his proper person to lose so many heavy infantry, cavalry, and able-bodied troops, and to see none left to replace them; but when they saw, also, that they had not sufficient ships in their docks, or money in the treasury, or crews for the ships, they began to despair of salvation. They thought that their enemies in Sicily would immediately sail with their fleet against Piraeus, inflamed by so signal a victory; while their adversaries at home, redoubling all their preparations, would vigorously attack them by sea and land at once, aided by their own revolted confederates. Nevertheless, with such means as they had, it was determined to resist to the last, and to provide timber and money, and to equip a fleet as they best could, to take steps to secure their confederates and above all Euboea, to reform things in the city upon a more economical footing, and to elect a board of elders to advise upon the state of affairs as occasion should arise. In short, as is the way of a democracy, in the panic of the moment they were ready to be as prudent as possible.

28

Socrates

Philosophy shifts from nature to man

The history of Greek philosophy falls broadly into two divisions, one beginning with Thales of Miletus about 600 B.C., and the other with Socrates of Athens (469–399 B.C.) almost two hundred years later. The pre-Socratic thinkers, usually termed natural philosophers, turned their attention almost exclusively to the world of nature and sought to understand its origin and meaning. They rejected the naive and fantastic fables of Homer and Hesiod and looked for causes not in the gods but in nature itself. Heraclitus (late sixth century B.C.) spoke for the whole group when he rejected the traditional lore with the proud boast, "I have sought for myself." Thus the early Greek philosophers progressed beyond the limits reached by the speculative thinkers of the ancient Near East and are rightly credited with being the first to establish the independence of philosophy by separating thought from religion and myth.

The detached curiosity of these philosophers first led them to seek out and identify the one element that was the primordial stuff out of which the manifold variety of the universe had been formed. No agreement was reached by the various investigators who segregated and championed as the primary material or first cause of all things such elements as water, air, or fire. A second problem arose naturally out of this original preoccupation with the material substance of the universe: the problem of change. How could something be and still change? Some denied the reality of change, others the reality of being. This controversy led to a further problem: the problem of knowledge. How can something be knowable if it changes from moment to moment? The method of finding truth was thus called into question. To replace the now questioned evidence of the senses, appeal was made to reason and there followed a great emphasis upon deductive logic as a technique for expounding and proving various theories on the origin and nature of the universe. But these proofs were not satisfying, and the cumulative effect of two centuries of philosophical speculation was the growing conviction that neither sense experience nor human reason could find truths which could be universally accepted.

This individualism and skepticism in thought coincided in the last half of the fifth century B.C. with the economic and political crisis that produced the Peloponnesian War, and the interaction of these various factors brought Greek thought to the dead end represented by the teachings of the Sophists. These highly critical thinkers largely turned their attention to man and society and away from fruitless speculations about the physical world. All religious, ethical, and political values fell before their attack: the gods were invented as "a clever devise of some prehistoric statesman as a means of preventing crime"; "justice is simply the interest of the stronger." All agreed in interpreting the famous dictum of Protagoras, "man is the measure of all things," to mean that truth and morality were relative and individual matters, and many went on to accept the extreme skepticism regarding truth formulated by Gorgias: "Nothing exists; if anything did exist, it could not be known; if a man should chance to apprehend it, it would still be a secret: he would be unable to communicate it to his fellows."

Into this intellectual and spiritual vacuum stepped Socrates. His place in the history of philosophy rests upon his success in reversing the destructive trend of Greek thought and constructing the foundation upon which Plato and Aristotle later built their philosophical systems. Like the Sophists, Socrates refused to spend time investigating the physical world, and Plato reports his reason: "I have no leisure for such enquiries; shall I tell you why? I must first know myself, as the inscription at Delphi says; it would be absurd to be curious about what is no business of mine, while I don't know my own self." In other words, because Greek thought had reasoned all traditional values out of existence, the resulting void of meaning demanded his attention. It is therefore the world within man that concerns Socrates, or, as he preferred to call it, the care of the soul. ("What shall it profit a man, if he gain the whole world, and lose his own soul?" is Jesus' more familiar statement of the problem.) To Socrates the soul is identified with the mind of man; it is the seat of reason and capable of finding the ethical truths which will restore meaning and value to life. He did not doubt that such truths could be found, and that they would be universally accepted. If people would place themselves under the rule of reason, they would recognize and desire what is good and true, for the nature of goodness and truth is such that all who recognize it will want it; all evil and error are the products of ignorance. This is the meaning of his well-known statements that "virtue is knowledge" and "nobody errs willingly."

To remove ignorance and to demonstrate that if people will think strenuously and honestly they will find themselves in agreement on what is true and good, Socrates developed the famous method that has since borne his name and made him recognized as one of the world's great teachers. The Socratic method employs the two devices of examination and exhortation, with emphasis upon the former. Exhortation to seek wisdom can have little effect so long as men are satisfied with the beliefs they hold, so Socrates felt compelled to go about cross-examining men, using the dialectical technique of question and answer to demonstrate the inadequacies of their beliefs — the inconsistencies, the half-truths, and the errors. Only after the ground has been prepared in this fashion can the seed planted by exhortation grow into fruit. But the destruction involved in preparing the ground brought upon Socrates the charge of radicalism and subversion, and at the age of seventy he was put to death on the charge of teaching atheism and corrupting the young. His optimistic belief in the existence of eternal moral truths and the search for them was left to his most famous pupil, Plato, and to posterity.

◆ A ◆ THE SOCRATIC METHOD

"The unexamined life is not worth living."

Plato's Dialogues, our chief source for understanding the personality and work of Socrates, owe their origin and form to the question-and-answer method of Socrates which they imitate. In the two selections which follow, Plato portrays Socrates in the act of describing to his friends the nature, purpose, and results of his method. Socrates calls it a "rough" method, for in no other way can he remove that great barrier to intellectual growth he terms the "spirit of conceit," itself the product of "great prejudices and harsh notions." He also calls it a type of "midwifery" in that it assists the mind in giving birth to ideas but does not itself produce them. Eternal truths exist, Socrates believes, and his method is a technique for the right use of reason to discover them. This means the use of inductive reasoning, and Aristotle credits Socrates with being the founder of inductive logic. The naive and superficial views of the examinee serve as hypotheses which are tested by reference to specific facts known to be true. The contradictions which result force the revision or abandonment of the original hypotheses and make possible movement in the direction of valid hypotheses and ultimate agreement on fundamental truths.

"A ROUGH AND A SMOOTH METHOD"

There is a rough and a smooth method in intellectual education. There is a time-honored mode which our fathers commonly practiced towards their sons, and which is still adopted by many — either of roughly reproving their errors, or of gently advising them; these two methods may be correctly described as admonition. But some thinkers appear to have arrived at the conclusion that all ignorance is involuntary, and that no one who thinks himself wise is willing to learn anything in the subjects in which he believes himself clever, and that the admonitory sort of instruction gives much trouble and does little good. So they set to work to eradicate the spirit of conceit in another way. They cross-examine a man's words, when he thinks that he is talking sense but really is not, and easily convict him of inconsistencies in his opinions; these they then place side by side, and show that they contradict one another. He, seeing this, is angry with himself, and grows gentle towards others, and thus is entirely delivered from great prejudices and harsh notions, in a way which is most amusing to the hearer, and produces the most lasting good effect on the person who is the subject of the operation. For as the physician considers that the body will receive no benefit from taking food until internal obstacles have been removed, so the purifier of the soul is conscious that his patient will receive no benefit from the application of knowledge until he is

From R. W. Livingstone, ed., *Plato: Selected Passages* (tr. Benjamin Jowett), The World's Classics (1940), pp. 19–21. Reprinted by permission of The Clarendon Press.

refuted, and from refutation learns modesty; he must be purged of his prejudices first and made to think that he knows only what he knows, and no more. For all these reasons, Theaetetus, we must admit that refutation is the greatest and chiefest of purifications, and he who has not been refuted, though he be the King of Persia himself, is in an awful state of impurity; he is uneducated and ugly just where purity and beauty are essential to happiness.

(*Sophist*, 229f.)

"DIRE ARE THE PANGS"

My art is like that of midwives, but differs from theirs, in that I attend men and not women, and I look after their souls when they are in labor, and not after their bodies: and the triumph of my art is in thoroughly examining whether the thought which the mind of a young man brings forth is a phantom and a lie, or a fruitful and true birth. And like the midwives, I am barren, and the reproach often made against me, that I ask questions of others and have not the wit to answer them myself, is very just — the reason is, that the god compels me to be a midwife, but does not allow me to have children. So I myself am not at all wise, nor have I any invention or child of my own soul to show, but those who talk with me profit. Some of them appear dull enough at first, but afterwards, as our acquaintance ripens, if God is gracious to them, they all make astonishing progress; and this in the opinion of others as well as in their own. It is quite clear that they never learned anything from me; all that they master and discover comes from themselves. But to me and the god they owe their delivery. And the proof of my words is, that many of them in their ignorance, either in their self-conceit despising me, or falling under the influence of others, have gone away too soon; and have not only lost by an ill upbringing the children of whom I had previously delivered them, but have had subsequent miscarriages owing to evil associates, prizing lies and shams more than the truth; and they have at last ended by seeing themselves, as others see them, to be great fools. Dire are the pangs which my art is able to arouse and to allay in those who consort with me, just like the pangs of women in childbirth; night and day they are full of perplexity and travail which is even worse than that of the women. So much for them. And there are others, Theaetetus, who come to me apparently having nothing in them; and as I know that they have no need of my art, I coax them into marrying some one, and by the grace of God I can generally tell who is likely to do them good. Many of them I have given away to Prodicus, and many to other inspired sages. I tell you this long story, friend Theaetetus, because I suspect, as indeed you seem to think yourself, that you are in labor — great with some conception. Come then to me, who am a midwife's son and myself a midwife, and do your best to answer the questions which I will ask you. And if I expose your first-born, because I discover upon inspection that the conception which you have formed is a blind shadow, do not quarrel with me on that account, as women do when their first children are taken from them. For I have actually known some who were ready to bite me when I deprived them of a darling folly, they did not see that I acted from goodwill, not knowing that no god is the enemy of man; neither am I their enemy in all this, but it would be wrong for me to admit falsehood, or to stifle the truth.

(Theatetus, 150f.)

◆B◆ THE APOLOGY OF SOCRATES

"I am that gadfly which God has attached to the state."

In addition to being one of the most moving pieces in the history of world literature, written as it was under the emotional impact of the great wrong done to Socrates, Plato's Apology is also the shortest and clearest description of the character and meaning of Socrates' work. It was in 399 B.C., five years after the fall of the Athenian Empire, that the Athenians brought Socrates to trial on the triple charge of denying the state gods, introducing new divinities, and corrupting the youth. Socrates' accusers, made frantic by the collapse of the old political, economic, and spiritual order of things, were aware only of his skeptical and critical attitude and saw it as symbolic of the progressive degeneration of Athenian life so evident since the death of Pericles.

The situation contained the elements of great tragedy. Both Socrates and his accusers sought the regeneration of Athenian society. The former, however, insisted on the necessity of criticism to raze the collapsing structure in order to build anew while the latter feared criticism as the subversive evil that had brought them so low and would, if unchecked, destroy the little that remained. Two eternally opposed viewpoints in the history of mankind thus faced one another; neither side could compromise, and the result was inevitable.

Plato was present at the trial, and his version of Socrates' speech before the court falls into three parts. Socrates first defends himself against the charge that he is either a Sophist or a philosopher of nature and so a promoter of influences subversive to the welfare of the state. He describes himself as the "gadfly" of the state seeking to sting men into mental activity by opening their eyes to their own ignorance and thereby promoting "wisdom and truth and the greatest improvement of the soul." After a small majority of sixty of the 501 judges find Socrates guilty of the charges, he next exercises his right under Athenian law of proposing a lighter penalty than the sentence of death urged by his accusers. His ironic suggestion (not included in the following selection) that he deserves to be supported at public expense as a reward for his service to the state, and at the worst should pay only a small fine, further antagonizes his judges and he is condemned to death. In the final part of his speech, Socrates discourses on the significance of his case and speculates on death and the afterlife.

From *Dialogues of Plato*, tr. Benjamin Jowett (3rd ed., 1875).

How you, O Athenians, have been affected by my accusers, I cannot tell; but I know that they almost made me forget who I was — so persuasively did they speak; and yet they have hardly uttered a word of truth. . . .

I will begin at the beginning, and ask what is the accusation which has given rise to the slander of me, and in fact has encouraged Meletus to prefer this charge against me. Well, what do the slanderers say? They shall be my prosecutors, and I will sum up their words in an affidavit: "Socrates is an evil-doer, and a curious person, who searches into things under the earth and in heaven, and he makes the worse appear the better cause; and he teaches the aforesaid doctrines to others." Such is the nature of the accusation: it is just what you have yourselves seen in the comedy of Aristophanes, who has introduced a man whom he calls Socrates, going about and saying that he walks in air, and talking a deal of nonsense concerning matters of which I do not pretend to know either much or little — not that I mean to speak disparagingly of anyone who is a student of natural philosophy. I should be very sorry if Meletus could bring so grave a charge against me. But the simple truth is, O Athenians, that I have nothing to do with physical speculations. . . .

"WHAT IS THE ORIGIN OF THESE ACCUSATIONS?"

I dare say, Athenians, that some one among you will reply, "Yes, Socrates, but what is the origin of these accusations which are brought against you; there must have been something strange which you have been doing? All these rumors and this talk about you would never have arisen if you had been like other men: tell us, then, what is the cause of them, for we should be sorry to judge hastily of you." Now I regard this as a fair challenge, and I will endeavor to explain to you the reason why I am called wise and have such evil fame. Please to attend then. And although some of you may think that I am joking, I declare that I will tell you the entire truth. Men of Athens, this reputation of mine has come of a certain sort of wisdom which I possess. If you ask me what kind of wisdom, I reply, wisdom such as may perhaps be attained by man, for to that extent I am inclined to believe that I am wise; whereas the persons of whom I was speaking have a superhuman wisdom, which I may fail to describe, because I have it not myself; and he who says that I have, speaks falsely, and is taking away my character. And here, O men of Athens, I must beg you not to interrupt me, even if I seem to say something extravagant. For the word which I will speak is not mine. I will refer you to a witness who is worthy of credit; that witness shall be the God of Delphi — he will tell you about my wisdom, if I have any, and of what sort it is. You must have known Chaerephon; he was early a friend of mine, and also a friend of yours, for he shared in the recent exile of the people, and returned with you. Well, Chaerephon, as you know, was very impetuous in all his doings, and he went to Delphi and boldly asked the oracle to tell him whether — as I was saying, I must beg you not to interrupt — he asked the oracle to tell him whether any one was wiser than I was, and the Pythian prophetess answered, that there was no man wiser. Chaerephon is dead himself; but his brother, who is in court, will confirm the truth of what I am saying.

Why do I mention this? Because I am going to explain to you why I have such an evil name. When I heard the answer, I said to myself, What can the god mean? and what is the interpretation of his riddle? for I know that I have no wisdom, small or great. What then can he mean when he says that I am the wisest of men? And yet he is a god, and cannot lie; that would be against his nature. After long consideration, I thought of a method of trying the question. I reflected that if I could only find a man wiser than myself, then I might go to the god with a refutation in my hand. I should say to him, "Here is a man who is wiser than I am; but you said that I was the wisest." Accordingly I went to one who had the reputation of wisdom, and observed him — his name I need not mention; he was a politician whom I selected for examination — and the result was as follows: When I began to talk with him, I could not help thinking that he was not really wise, although he was thought wise by many, and still wiser by himself; and thereupon I tried to explain to him that he thought himself wise, but was not really wise; and the consequence was that he hated me, and his enmity was shared by several who were present and heard me. So I left him, saying to myself, as I went away: Well, although I do not suppose that either of us knows anything really beautiful and good, I am better off than he is — for he knows nothing, and thinks that he knows; I neither know nor think that I know. In this latter particular, then, I seem to have slightly the advantage of him. Then I went to another who had still higher pretensions to wisdom, and my conclusion was exactly the same. Whereupon I made another enemy of him, and of many others besides him.

Then I went to one man after another, being not unconscious of the enmity which I provoked, and I lamented and feared this: but necessity was laid upon me — the word of God, I thought, ought to be considered first. And I said to myself, Go I must to all who appear to know, and find out the meaning of the oracle. And I swear to you, Athenians, by the dog I swear! — for I must tell you the truth — the result of my mission was just this: I found that the men most in repute were all but the most foolish; and that the others less esteemed were really wiser and better. I will tell you the tale of my wanderings and of the "Herculean" labors, as I may call them, which I endured only to find at last the oracle irrefutable. After the politicians, I went to the poets; tragic, dithyrambic, and all sorts. And there, I said to myself, you will be instantly detected; now you will find out that you are more ignorant than they are. Accordingly, I took them some of the most elaborate passages in their own writings, and asked what was the meaning of them — thinking that they would teach me something. Will you believe me? I am almost ashamed to confess the truth, but I must say that there is hardly a person present who would not have talked better about their poetry than they did themselves. Then I knew that not by wisdom do poets write poetry, but by a sort of genius and inspiration; they are like diviners or soothsayers who also say many fine things, but do not understand the meaning of them. The poets appeared to me to be much in the same case; and I further observed that upon the strength of their poetry they believed themselves to be the wisest of men in other things in which they were not wise. So I departed, conceiving myself to be superior to them for the same reason that I was superior to the politicians.

At last I went to the artisans. I was conscious that I knew nothing at all, as I may say, and I was sure that they knew many fine things; and here I was not mistaken, for they did know many things of which I was ignorant, and in this they certainly were wiser than I was. But I observed that even the good artisans fell into the same error as the poets — because they were good workmen they thought that they also knew all sorts of high matters, and this defect in them overshadowed their wisdom; and therefore I asked myself on behalf of the oracle, whether I would like to be as I was, neither having their knowledge nor their ignorance, or like them in both; and I made answer to myself and to the oracle that I was better off as I was.

This inquisition has led to my having many enemies of the worst and most dangerous kind, and has given occasion also to many calumnies. . . .

There is another thing: young men of the richer classes, who have not much to do, come about me of their own accord; they like to hear the pretenders examined, and they often imitate me, and proceed to examine others; there are plenty of persons, as they quickly discover, who think that they know something, but really know little or nothing; and then those who are examined by them instead of being angry with themselves are angry with me: This confounded Socrates, they say; this villainous misleader of youth! — and then if somebody asks them, Why, what evil does he practice or teach? they do not know, and cannot tell; but in order that they may not appear to be at a loss, they repeat the ready-made charges which are used against all philosophers about teaching things up in the clouds and under the earth, and having no gods, and making the worse appear the better cause; for they do not like to confess that their pretense of knowledge has been detected — which is the truth; and as they are numerous and ambitious and energetic, and are drawn up in battle array and have persuasive tongues, they have filled your ears with their loud and inveterate calumnies. And this is the reason why my three accusers, Meletus and Anytus and Lycon, have set upon me; . . .

"I SHALL OBEY GOD RATHER THAN YOU"

Some one will say: And are you not ashamed, Socrates, of a course of life which is likely to bring you to an untimely end? To him I may fairly answer: There you are mistaken: a man who is good for anything ought not to calculate the chance of living or dying; he ought only to consider whether in doing anything he is doing right or wrong — acting the part of a good man or of a bad. . . . And therefore if you let me go now, . . . if you say to me, Socrates, this time we will not mind Anytus, and you shall be let off, but upon one condition, that you are not to enquire and speculate in this way any more, and that if you are caught doing so again you shall die; if this was the condition on which you let me go, I should reply: Men of Athens, I honor and love you; but I shall obey God rather than you, and while I have life and strength I shall never cease from the practice and teaching of philosophy, exhorting anyone whom I meet and saying to him after my manner: You, my friend — a citizen of the great and mighty and wise city of Athens — are you not ashamed of heaping up the greatest amount of money and honor and reputation, and caring so little about wisdom and truth and the greatest improvement of the soul, which you never regard or heed at all? And if the person with whom I am arguing, says: Yes, but I do care; then I do not leave him or let him go at once; but I proceed to interrogate and examine and cross-examine him, and if I think that he has no virtue in him, but only says that he has, I reproach him with undervaluing the greater, and overvaluing the less.... This is my teaching, and if this is the doctrine which corrupts youth, I am a mischievous person....

And now, Athenians, I am not going to argue for my own sake, as you may think, but for yours, that you may not sin against God by condemning me, who am his gift to you. For if you kill me you will not easily find a successor to me, who, if I may use such a ludicrous figure of speech, am a sort of gadfly, given to the state by God; and the state is a great and noble steed who is tardy in his motions owing to his very size, and requires to be stirred into life. I am that gadfly which God has attached to the state, and all day long and in all places am always fastening upon you, arousing and persuading and reproaching you. You will not easily find another like me, and therefore I would advise you to spare me. I dare say that you may feel out of temper (like a person who is suddenly awakened from sleep), and you think that you might easily strike me dead as Anytus advises, and then you would sleep on for the remainder of your lives, unless God in his care of you sent you another gadfly....

"I PROPHECY TO YOU"

And now, O men who have condemned me, I would fain prophecy to you; for I am about to die, and in the hour of death men are gifted with prophetic power. And I prophecy to you who are my murderers, that immediately after my departure punishment far heavier than you have inflicted on me will surely await you. Me you have killed because you wanted to escape the accuser, and not to give an account of your lives. But that will not be as you suppose: far otherwise. For I say that there will be more accusers of you than there are now; accusers whom hitherto I have restrained: and as they are younger they will be more inconsiderate with you, and you will be more offended at them. If you think that by killing men you can prevent someone from censuring your evil lives, you are mistaken; that is not a way of escape which is either possible or honorable; the easiest and the noblest way is not to be disabling others, but to be improving yourselves. This is the prophecy which I utter before my departure to the judges who have condemned me....

Still I have a favor to ask of them. When my sons are grown up, I would ask you, O my friends, to punish them; and I would have you trouble them, as I have troubled you if they seem to care about riches, or anything, more than about virtue; or if they pretend to be something when they are really nothing — then reprove them, as I have reproved you, for not caring about that for which they ought to care, and thinking that they are something when they are really nothing. And if you do this, both I and my sons will have received justice at your hands.

The hour of departure has arrived, and we go on our ways — I to die, and you to live. Which is better God only knows.

29

Plato

"Turning the eye of the soul toward the light"

The Dialogues of Plato (427–348 B.C.) have always charmed readers with their extraordinary literary beauty and stimulated them by raising fundamental problems in many fields, notably in religion, ethics, and politics. The pupil of Socrates and inheritor of his optimistic view that universal truths exist and can be found, Plato went beyond his master, asserting the existence of universal truths (the Platonic Ideas), and upon them constructed a philosophical system. Known as Idealism, this system has exerted an incalculable influence on the history of Western philosophy and religion. It takes its name from its central doctrine known as the "Theory of Ideas," a metaphysical conception that is extremely difficult to explain simply and adequately. It has been said that Platonists are born and not made, and Plato himself tells us in his Seventh Letter that he was unable to describe his philosophy in ordinary narrative language: "There neither is nor ever will be a treatise of mine on the subject. For it does not admit of exposition like other branches of knowledge; but after much converse about the matter and a life lived together, suddenly a light, as it were, is kindled in one soul by a flame that leaps to it from another, and thereafter sustains itself." It will be understood and accepted only by "some few who are able with a little teaching to find it out for themselves."

Plato's metaphysical doctrine is founded upon the belief that the things which are seen are temporal while the things which are not seen are eternal. These last are the Platonic Ideas, the universal truths which have an independent existence separate from the world of sense experience. All objects perceived by the senses, whether they be material things like horses and chairs, or intangibles like beauty and justice, are all imperfect and transitory manifestations of the only truly real and perfect things, the eternal Ideas. The senses inform us about what is unreal and imperfect, while only the reason, identified by Plato with the soul, can grasp what is perfect and eternal. Confronted by these two worlds, the task of man is to follow the dictates of his reason — or soul — and concern himself as far as possible with the higher and real world, the world of thought or spirit.

Such, in brief, is the doctrine developed by Plato as his answer to the crisis that confronted his civilization — a crisis very similar to our own today — in which the traditional beliefs had been undermined by scientific thought and the material fabric had been rent by war and depression. Its importance for the history of philosophy can be judged by the remark of one scholar that all subsequent philosophy is but a series of footnotes to Plato's writings, and its significance for the history of religion is illustrated by the conversion of St. Augustine to Christianity only after he had been influenced by Platonic philosophy (see Selection 54C). But emphasizing the later influence of Platonic theory should not blind us to the fact that Plato was essentially a practical philosopher whose theories were intended both to serve as guide posts along the road whose goal is the good life for man, and to inspire men to create a state in which that life could be lived. The following lines from his Timaeus give the essence of Plato's whole view which integrates both theory and practice, the ideal and the actual: "God [or the Good, the supreme Idea, the source of all goodness, beauty, and truth] invented and gave us sight to the end that we might behold the courses of intelligence in the heavens and apply them to the courses of our own intelligence which are akin to them, the unperturbed to the perturbed, and that we, learning them and partaking of the natural truth of reason, might imitate the unerring courses of God and regulate our own vagaries."

◆ A ◆ THE THEORY OF IDEAS

The allegory of the cave

Plato frequently employs the language of poetry, using myths and figures of speech to transmit to his readers the profound truths of his idealistic philosophy which, to quote again from his Seventh Letter, "does not admit of exposition like other branches of knowledge." The most famous and brilliant example of Plato's use of this device is the allegory of the cave from the Republic. Its purpose is to illustrate graphically the importance of moving away from the "shadows" of the world of appearances to the world of eternal spiritual realities beyond. This is the realm of the Ideas, the highest of which is the Idea of the Good, here compared with the sun. Like the sun, it causes all things to exist, to be visible, and to become intelligible. The passage also contains evidence of Plato's practical side as a moralist and political thinker. He insists that men who have been converted from error to truth — men who are the true philosophers — despite their understandable reluctance must descend again into the

From the Republic, VII, 514–21 (abridged), tr. Benjamin Jowett.

cave to serve and enlighten their fellow men. Only when this happens will the state be ruled by the best and most intelligent men. "Until philosophers are kings," writes Plato in another passage in the Republic," or the kings and rulers of this world have the spirit of philosophy, until political power and wisdom are united, until those commoner natures, who pursue either the exclusion of the other, stand aside, states will never have rest from their evils — no, nor, I believe, will the human race. . .'."

Behold! human beings living in an underground den, which has a mouth open toward the light and reaching all along the den; here they have been from their childhood, and have their legs and necks chained so that they cannot move, and can only see before them, being prevented by the chains from turning round their heads. Above and behind them a fire is blazing at a distance, and between the fire and the prisoners there is a raised way; and you will see, if you look, a low wall built along the way, like the screen which marionette players have in front of them, over which they show the puppets. And do you see men passing along the wall carrying all sorts of vessels, and statues and figures of animals made of wood and stone and various materials, which appear over the wall? Some of them are talking, others silent.

You have shown me a strange image, and they are strange prisoners.

Like ourselves, I replied; and they see only their own shadows, or the shadows of one another, which the fire throws on the opposite wall of the cave?

True, he said; how could they see anything but the shadows if they were never allowed to move their heads?

And of the objects which are being carried in like manner they would only see the shadows. And if they were able to converse with one another, would they not suppose that they were naming what was actually before them?

Very true.

And suppose further that the prison had an echo which came from the other side, would they not be sure to fancy when one of the passersby spoke that the voice which they heard came from the passing shadows? To them the truth would be literally nothing but the shadows of the images.

And now look again, and see what will naturally follow if the prisoners are released and disabused of their error. At first, when any of them is liberated and compelled suddenly to stand up and turn his neck round and walk and look toward the light, he will suffer sharp pains; the glare will distress him, and he will be unable to see the realities of which in his former state he had seen the shadows; and then conceive someone saying to him, that what he saw before was an illusion, but that now, when he is approaching nearer to being and his eye is turned toward more real existence, he has a clearer vision — what will be his reply? And you may further imagine that his instructor is pointing to the objects as they pass and requiring him to name them — will he not be perplexed? Will he not fancy that the shadows which he formerly saw are truer than the objects which are now shown him?

And if he is compelled to look straight at the light, will he not have a pain in his eyes which will make him turn away to take refuge in the objects of vision which he can see, and which he will conceive to be in reality clearer than the things which are now being shown to him?

And suppose once more, that he is reluctantly dragged up a steep and rugged ascent, and held fast until he is forced into the presence of the sun himself, is he not likely to be pained and irritated? When he approaches the light his eyes will be dazzled, and he will not be able to see anything at all of what are now called realities. He will require to grow accustomed to the sight of the upper world. And first he will see the shadows best, next the reflections of men and other objects in the water, and then the objects themselves; then he will gaze upon the light of the moon and the stars and the spangled heaven; and he will see the sky and the stars by night better than the sun or the light of the sun by day. Last of all he will be able to see the sun, and not mere reflections of him in the water, but he will see him in his own proper place, and not in another; and he will contemplate him as he is. He will then proceed to argue that this is he who gives the seasons and the years, and is the guardian of all that is in the visible world, and in a certain way the cause of all things which he and his fellows have been accustomed to behold.

And when he remembered his old habitation, and the wisdom of the den and his fellow-prisoners, do you not suppose that he would felicitate himself on the change, and pity them? And if they were in the habit of conferring honors among themselves on those who were quickest to observe the passing shadows and to remark which of them went before, and which followed after, and which were together; and who were therefore best able to draw conclusions as to the future, do you think that he would care for such honors and glories or envy the possessors of them? Would he not say with Homer, "Better to be the poor servant of a poor master," and to endure anything, rather than think as they do and live after their manner?

Imagine once more such an one coming suddenly out of the sun to be replaced in his old situation; would he not be certain to have his eyes full of darkness? And if there were a contest, and he had to compete in measuring the shadows with the prisoners who had never moved out of the den, while his sight was still weak, and before his eyes had become steady (and the time which he needed to acquire this new habit of sight might be very considerable), would he not be ridiculous? Men would say of him that up he went and down he came without his eyes; and that it was better not even to think of ascending; and if anyone tried to loose another and lead him up to the light, let them only catch the offender, and they would put him to death.

This entire allegory, you may now append, dear Glaucon, to the previous argument; the prison-house is the world of sight, the light of the fire is the sun, and you will not misapprehend me if you interpret the journey upwards to be the ascent of the soul into the intellectual world according to my poor belief, which, at your desire, I have expressed — whether rightly or wrongly God knows. But, whether true or false, my opinion is that in the world of knowledge the idea of good appears last of all, and is seen only with an effort: and, when seen, is also inferred to the universal author of all things beautiful and right, parent of light, and of the lord of light in this visible world, and the immediate source of reason and truth in the intellectual; and that this is the power upon which he who would act rationally either in public or private life must have his eye fixed.

I agree, he said, as far as I am able to understand you.

Moreover, you must not wonder that those who attain to this beatific vision are unwilling to descend to human affairs; for their souls are ever hastening into the upper world where they desire to dwell; which desire of theirs is very natural, if our allegory may be trusted.

Yes, very natural. . . .

Then the business of us who are the founders of the State will be to compel the best minds to attain that knowledge which has been already declared by us to be the greatest of all — they must continue to ascend until they arrive at the good; but when they have ascended and seen enough we must not allow them to do as they do now.

What do you mean?

I mean that they remain in the upper world: but this must not be allowed; they must be made to descend again among the prisoners in the den, and partake of their labors and honors, whether they are worth having or not.

But is not this unjust? he said; ought we to give them an inferior life, when they might have a superior one?

You have forgotten, my friend, the intention of the legislator, who did not aim at making any one class in the State happy above the rest; the happiness was to be in the whole State, and he held the citizens together by persuasion and necessity, making them benefactors of the State, and therefore benefactors of one another; to this end he created them, not that they should please themselves, but they were to be his instruments in binding up the State.

True, he said, I had forgotten.

Observe, Glaucon, that there will be no injustice in compelling our philosophers to have a care and providence of others; we shall explain to them that in other States, men of their class are not obliged to share in the toils of politics: and this is reasonable, for they grow up at their own sweet will, and the government would rather not have them. Now the wild plant which owes culture to nobody, has nothing to pay for culture. But we have brought you into the world to be rulers of the hive, kings of yourselves and of the other citizens, and have educated you far better and more perfectly than they have been educated, and you are better able to share in the double duty. Wherefore each of you, when his turn comes, must go down to the general underground abode, and get the habit of seeing in the dark; for all is habit; and by accustoming yourselves you will see ten thousand times better than the dwellers in the den, and you will know what the images are, and of what they are images, because you have seen the beautiful and just and good in their truth. And thus the order of our State, and of yours, will be a reality, and not a dream only, as the order of States too often is, for in most of them men are fighting with one another about shadows and are distracted in the struggle for power, which in their eyes is a great good. Whereas the truth is that the State in which the rulers are most reluctant to govern is best and most quietly governed, and the State in which they are most willing, the worst.

Quite true, he replied.

And will our pupils, when they hear this, refuse to share in turn the toils of State, when they are allowed to spend the greater part of their time with one another in the heaven of ideas?

Impossible, he answered; for they are just men, and the commands which we impose upon them are just; there can be no doubt that every one of them will take office as a stern necessity, and not like our present ministers of State.

Yes, my friend, and there lies the point. You must contrive for your future rulers another and a better life than that of a ruler, and then you may have a well-ordered State; for only in the State which offers this, will they rule who are truly rich, not in silver and gold, but in virtue and wisdom, which are the true blessings of life. Whereas if they go to the administration of public affairs, poor and hungering after their own private advantage, thinking that hence they are to snatch the good of life, order there can never be; for they will be fighting about office, and the civil and domestic broils which thus arise will be the ruin of the rulers themselves and of the whole State.

Most true, he replied.

◆ B ◆ THE SPIRITUAL LIFE

Dualism of body and soul

Through the centuries it has been the mystical rather than the practical side of Plato's thought that has exerted the greatest influence. His poetic tendency to exaggerate the distinction between the two worlds of truth and error at times led him to deny the existence of any reality to the material world. This prepared the way for the mystical other-worldliness and the dualism of soul and body which characterized much of later Greco-Roman thought and especially influenced Christianity.

In the following passages from the Phaedo, named for the disciple of Socrates who recounts the story of his master's last hours in prison, Socrates is found welcoming death and arguing for the immortality of the soul and the supremacy of the spiritual life. As this differs from the more realistic picture of Socrates portrayed in the Apology, where Socrates' chief concern is his right to live, it is generally believed that the views expressed are more Platonic than Socratic. Support for this contention is given by Plato himself, who has Phaedo remark that "Plato, if I am not mistaken, was ill" and not present and so unable in this dialogue to give a literal account of what Socrates said.

Phaedo, 66–68, 79, abridged, tr. Benjamin Jowett. From R. W. Livingstone, ed., *Plato: Selected Passages*, The World's Classics (1940), pp. 41–43. Reprinted by permission of The Clarendon Press.

Have we not found a path of thought which seems to bring us and our argument to the conclusion, that while we are in the body, and while the soul is infected with the evils of the body, our desire will not be satisfied? and our desire is of the truth. For the body is a source of endless trouble to us by reason of the mere requirement of food; and is liable also to diseases which overtake and impede us in the search after reality; it fills us full of loves, and lusts, and fears, and fancies of all kinds, and endless nonsense, and in fact takes away from us the power of thinking at all. Whence come wars, and fighting, and factions? whence but from the body and the body's desires? Wars are caused by the love of money, and money has to be acquired for the sake and in the service of the body; and as a result of all these hindrances we have no time to give to philosophy; and, last and worst of all, even if we are at leisure and devote ourselves to some speculation, the body is always breaking in on us, causing turmoil and confusion in our inquiries, and so upsetting us that we are prevented from seeing the truth. Experience has shown us that if we would have pure knowledge of anything we must be quit of the body — the soul in herself must behold things in themselves; and then we shall attain the wisdom which we desire, and of which we say that we are lovers; not while we live, but after death; for if while in company with the body, the soul cannot have pure knowledge, one of two things follows — either knowledge is not to be attained at all, or, if at all, after death. For then, and not till then, the soul will be parted from the body and exist in herself alone.

In this present life, I reckon that we make the nearest approach to knowledge when we have the least possible intercourse or communion with the body, and are not contaminated with the bodily nature, but keep ourselves pure until the hour when God himself is pleased to release us. And so having got rid of the foolishness of the body we shall be pure and hold converse with the pure, and know of ourselves the clear light everywhere, which is no other than the light of truth. If this be true, there is great reason to hope that when I have come to the end of my journey, I shall attain that which has been the pursuit of my life. So I go on my way rejoicing, and not I only, but every other man who believes that his mind is prepared and purified.

True philosophers, Simmias, are always occupied in the practice of dying, and no one finds death so little formidable as they. Look at the matter thus: if they have been in every way at issue with the body, and are wanting to be alone with the soul, when this desire of theirs is granted, how inconsistent would they be if they trembled and repined, instead of rejoicing at their departure to that place where they hope to gain that which in life they desired — and this was wisdom — and at the same time to be rid of the company of their enemy. Many a man has been willing to go to the world below animated by the hope of seeing there an earthly love, or wife, or son, and talking with them. And will a true lover of wisdom, convinced that only in the world below he can worthily enjoin her, still repine at death? Will he not depart with joy? Surely he will, my friend, if he is a true philosopher. For he will have a firm conviction that there, and there only, he can find wisdom in her purity. And if this be true, he would be very absurd, as I was saying, if he were afraid of death. . . .

When the soul uses the body as an instrument of perception, that is to say, when it uses the sense of sight or hearing or some other sense, she is dragged by the body into the region of the changeable, and wanders and is confused; the world spins round her, and she is like a drunkard, when she touches change. But when she contemplates in herself and by herself, then she passes into the other world, the region of purity, and eternity, and immortality, and unchangeableness, which are her kindred, and with them she ever lives, when she is by herself and is not let or hindered; then she ceases from her erring ways, and being in communion with the unchanging is unchanging. And this state of the soul is called wisdom.

30

Aristotle

"The philosophy of human affairs"

Possessing neither the vivid personality of Socrates nor the vision and imagination of Plato, Aristotle (384–322 B.C.) nevertheless has exerted probably a stronger influence upon posterity than either of his two great predecessors. A contemporary of Alexander the Great, he lived at the end of the great period of Greek creative effort and the independent city-state which had nourished the Greek genius. He looked back upon the accomplishments of the past and in a large number of works — forty-six, about three-quarters of which have survived — he collected, classified, and analyzed the intellectual and spiritual heritage of Greece and transmitted it to succeeding civilizations. Much of his philosophy was a continuation of Plato, differing from his master only in degree and emphasis. He systematized scientifically and logically material which Plato in his Dialogues had dealt with only imaginatively and informally. Where Plato poetically described the relationship between the universal Ideas and the transitory world of appearances in a manner that allowed some of his followers to deny the importance of the world of sense impressions, Aristotle insisted that the universal truths, which he called Forms, do not have a separate existence apart from the world of matter. Form transforms matter by giving it meaning and purpose, pattern and character. The object of inquiry is still the discovery of these Forms, but this can be done only by first observing the objects of sense and then discerning inductively their universal characteristics or Forms. From this follows Aristotle's characteristic concern with the world of observed phenomena. He is a practical Platonist, insisting that "theories must be abandoned unless their teachings tally with the indisputable results of observation."

Aristotle's extant writings have the merits and the defects of the scientific mind. They are logical, but hard to read and usually uninspired. Yet what they lack in style is compensated for by illuminating generalizations, most of which, especially in his Ethics and his Politics, are pertinent to our own age.

◆A◆ THE NICOMACHEAN ETHICS

"The proper function of man"

Aristotle's two most influential works, the Ethics and the Politics, are concerned with an investigation of human character and conduct in order to discover and establish the good life for man. Together they constitute the two halves of what is essentially a single treatise on the subject he called the "philosophy of human affairs." The practical goal of this philosophy is the greatest happiness for the greatest number of people. The Ethics discusses the nature of good character, which is the essential ingredient of happiness, while the Politics describes the political institutions and laws which can best produce the greatest amount of good character, and hence the highest degree of happiness. The first work centers its attention on man and the virtues that can make him happy; the second looks to the state as a powerful educative agency necessary for the attainment of the greatest amount of human happiness.

1. *The Subject of the Ethics*

Aristotle tells us at the beginning of the Ethics that the subject of his inquiry, which must be considered a subdivision of political science, is the good for man. He rejects Plato's abstract and universal Idea of Good as being too vague and unreal to have practical value, and maintains that there are many "goods." The good for man is a final end or goal which is always chosen for its own sake. This end is happiness.

I, 1. Every art or applied science and every systematic investigation, and similarly every action and choice, seem to aim at some good; the good, therefore, has been well defined as that at which all things aim. . . .

Since there are many activities, arts, and sciences, the number of ends is correspondingly large: of medicine the end is health, of shipbuilding a vessel, of strategy, victory, and of household management, wealth. In many instances several such pursuits are grouped together under a single capacity: the art of bridle-making, for example, and everything else pertaining to the equipment of a horse are grouped together under horsemanship; horsemanship in turn, along

From Aristotle, *Nicomachean Ethics*, tr. Martin Ostwald, pp. 3–7, 14–18, 29–35, 41–44, 288–293, 295–296, 299, 302 (footnotes omitted). Copyright © 1962 by The Bobbs-Merrill Co., Inc. Reprinted by permission of the publisher.

with every other military action, is grouped together under strategy; and other pursuits are grouped together under other capacities. In all these cases the ends of the master sciences are preferable to the ends of the subordinate sciences, since the latter are pursued for the sake of the former. This is true whether the ends of the actions lie in the activities themselves or, as is the case in the disciplines just mentioned, in something beyond the activities.

2. Now, if there exists an end in the realm of action which we desire for its own sake, an end which determines all our other desires . . . then obviously this end will be the good, that is, the highest good. Will not the knowledge of this good, consequently, be very important to our lives? Would it not better equip us, like archers who have a target to aim at, to hit the proper mark? If so, we must try to comprehend in outline at least what this good is and to which branch of knowledge or to which capacity it belongs.

This good, one should think, belongs to the most sovereign and most comprehensive master science, and politics clearly fits this description. For it determines which sciences ought to exist in states, what kind of sciences each group of citizens must learn, and what degree of proficiency each must attain. We observe further that the most honored capacities, such as strategy, household management, and oratory, are contained in politics. Since this science uses the rest of the sciences, and since, moreover, it legislates what people are to do and what they are not to do, its end seems to embrace the ends of the other sciences. Thus it follows that the end of politics is the good for man. For even if the good is the same for the individual and the state, the good of the state clearly is the greater and more perfect thing to attain and to safeguard. The attainment of the good for one man alone is, to be sure, a source of satisfaction; yet to secure it for a nation and for states is nobler and more divine. In short, these are the aims of our investigation, which is in a sense an investigation of social and political matters. . . .

4. To resume the discussion: since all knowledge and every choice is directed toward some good, let us discuss what is in our view the aim of politics, i.e., the highest good attainable by action. As far as its name is concerned, most people would probably agree: for both the common run of people and cultivated men call it happiness, and understand by "being happy" the same as "living well" and "doing well." But when it comes to defining what happiness is, they disagree, and the account given by the common run differs from that of the philosophers. The former say it is some clear and obvious good, such as pleasure, wealth, or honor; some say it is one thing and others another, and often the very same person identifies it with different things at different times: when he is sick he thinks it is health, and when he is poor he says it is wealth; and when people are conscious of their own ignorance, they admire those who talk above their heads in accents of greatness. Some thinkers used to believe that there exists over and above these many goods another good, good in itself and by itself, which also is the cause of good in all these things. An examination of all the different opinions would perhaps be a little pointless. . . .

7. Let us return again to our investigation into the nature of the good which we are seeking. It is evidently something different in different actions

and in each art: it is one thing in medicine, another in strategy, and another again in each of the other arts. What, then, is the good of each? Is it not that for the sake of which everything else is done? That means it is health in the case of medicine, victory in the case of strategy, a house in the case of building, a different thing in the case of different arts, and in all actions and choices it is the end. For it is for the sake of the end that all else is done. Thus, if there is some one end for all that we do, this would be the good attainable by action; if there are several ends, they will be the goods attainable by action.

Our argument has gradually progressed to the same point at which we were before, and we must try to clarify it still further. Since there are evidently several ends, and since we choose some of these — e.g., wealth, flutes, and instruments generally — as a means to something else, it is obvious that not all ends are final. The highest good, on the other hand, must be something final. Thus, if there is only one final end, this will be the good we are seeking; if there are several, it will be the most final and perfect of them. We call that which is pursued as an end in itself more final than an end which is pursued for the sake of something else; and what is never chosen as a means to something else we call more final than that which is chosen both as an end in itself and as a means to something else. What is always chosen as an end in itself and never as a means to something else is called final in an unqualified sense. This description seems to apply to happiness above all else: for we always choose happiness as an end in itself and never for the sake of something else. Honor, pleasure, intelligence, and all virtue we choose partly for themselves — for we would choose each of them even if no further advantage would accrue from them — but we also choose them partly for the sake of happiness, because we assume that it is through them that we will be happy. On the other hand, no one chooses happiness for the sake of honor, pleasure, and the like, nor as a means to anything at all.

2.   *The Definition of Happiness*

The good for man can only be found by observing man's function. The proper and distinctive function (also called "excellence" and "virtue") of man is the exercise of reason, and this alone can produce happiness. As the seat of reason is in the rational part of the soul, human good or happiness can be defined as "an activity of soul in accordance with excellence or virtue." In other words, the good or happy man is one whose life is guided by the dictates of his reason.

I, 7. To call happiness the highest good is perhaps a little trite, and a clearer account of what it is, is still required. Perhaps this is best done by first ascertaining the proper function of man. For just as the goodness and performance of a flute player, a sculptor, or any kind of expert, and generally of anyone who fulfills some function or performs some action, are thought to reside in his proper function, so the goodness and performance of man would seem to reside in whatever is his proper function. Is it then possible that while a carpenter and a shoemaker have their own proper functions and spheres of action, man as man has none, but was left by nature a good-for-nothing without a function? Should we not assume that just as the eye, the hand, the foot, and in general each part of the body clearly has its own proper function, so man too has some function over and above the functions of his parts? What can this function possibly be? Simply living? He shares that even with plants, but we are now looking for something peculiar to man. Accordingly, the life of nutrition and growth must be excluded. Next in line there is a life of sense perception. But this, too, man has in common with the horse, the ox, and every animal. There remains then an active life of the rational element. The rational element has two parts: one is rational in that it obeys the rule of reason, the other in that it possesses and conceives rational rules. . . .

The proper function of man, then, consists in an activity of the soul in conformity with a rational principle or, at least, not without it. In speaking of the proper function of a given individual we mean that it is the same in kind as the function of an individual who sets high standards for himself: the proper function of a harpist, for example, is the same as the function of a harpist who has set high standards for himself. The same applies to any and every group of individuals: the full attainment of excellence must be added to the mere function. In other words, the function of the harpist is to play the harp; the function of the harpist who has high standards is to play it well. On these assumptions, if we take the proper function of man to be a certain kind of life, and if this kind of life is an activity of the soul and consists in actions performed in conjunction with the rational element, and if a man of high standards is he who performs these actions well and properly, and if a function is well performed when it is performed in accordance with the excellence appropriate to it; we reach the conclusion that the good of man is an activity of the soul in conformity with excellence or virtue, and if there are several virtues, in conformity with the best and most complete.

But we must add "in a complete life." For one swallow does not make a spring, nor does one sunny day; similarly, one day or a short time does not make a man blessed and happy.

3.   Intellectual and Moral Virtue

Human excellence, or virtue, is not of the body but of the soul, and the soul has two parts, the rational and the irrational. Intellectual virtues, such as wisdom and intelligence, are those of the rational part of the soul which alone possesses reason and has its perfection in the contemplative life. Moral virtues, such as liberality and temperance, stem from that part of the irrational side of the soul that is emotional but not vegetative, that does not possess or understand reason but is capable of obedience to reason. It has its perfection in the moral life. Intellectual virtue originates and is fostered by teaching, while moral virtue is created by habit.

I, 13. Since happiness is a certain activity of the soul in conformity with perfect virtue, we must now examine what virtue or excellence is. For such an inquiry will perhaps better enable us to discover the nature of happiness. Moreover, the man who is truly concerned about politics seems to devote special attention to excellence, since it is his aim to make the citizens good and law-abiding. We have an example of this in the lawgivers of Crete and Sparta and in other great legislators. If an examination of virtue is part of politics, this question clearly fits into the pattern of our original plan.

There can be no doubt that the virtue which we have to study is human virtue. For the good which we have been seeking is a human good and the happiness a human happiness. By human virtue we do not mean the excellence of the body, but that of the soul, and we define happiness as an activity of the soul. . . .

Some things that are said about the soul in our less technical discussions are adequate enough to be used here, for instance, that the soul consists of two elements, one irrational and one rational. . . .

Of the irrational element, again, one part seems to be common to all living things and vegetative in nature: I mean that part which is responsible for nurture and growth. We must assume that some such capacity of the soul exists in everything that takes nourishment, in the embryonic stage as well as when the organism is fully developed; for this makes more sense than to assume the existence of some different capacity at the latter stage. The excellence of this part of the soul is, therefore, shown to be common to all living things and is not exclusively human. . . . But enough of this subject: we may pass by the nutritive part, since it has no natural share in human excellence or virtue.

In addition to this, there seems to be another integral element of the soul which, though irrational, still does partake of reason in some way. . . . at any rate, in a mortally strong man it accepts the leadership of reason, and is perhaps more obedient still in a self-controlled and courageous man, since in him everything is in harmony with the voice of reason.

Thus we see that the irrational element of the soul has two parts: the one is vegetative and has no share in reason at all, the other is the seat of the appetites and of desire in general and partakes of reason insofar as it complies with reason and accepts its leadership; it possesses reason in the sense that we say it is "reasonable" to accept the advice of a father and of friends, not in the sense that we have a "rational" understanding of mathematical propositions. That the irrational element can be persuaded by the rational is shown by the fact that admonition and all manner of rebuke and exhortation are possible. If it is correct to say that the appetitive part, too, has reason, it follows that the rational element of the soul has two subdivisions: the one possesses reason in the strict sense, contained within itself, and the other possesses reason in the sense that it listens to reason as one would listen to a father.

Virtue, too, is differentiated in line with this division of the soul. We call some virtues "intellectual" and others "moral": theoretical wisdom, understanding, and practical wisdom are intellectual virtues, generosity and self-control moral virtues. In speaking of a man's character, we do not describe him as wise or understanding, but as gentle or self-controlled; but we praise the wise man, too, for his characteristic, and praiseworthy characteristics are what we call virtues.

II, 1. Virtue, as we have seen, consists of two kinds, intellectual virtue and moral virtue. Intellectual virtue or excellence owes its origin and development chiefly to teaching, and for that reason requires experience and time. Moral virtue, on the other hand, is formed by habit, *ethos*, and its name, *ēthikē*, is therefore derived, by a slight variation, from *ethos*. This shows, too, that none of the moral virtues is implanted in us by nature, for nothing which exists by nature can be changed by habit. For example, it is impossible for a stone, which has a natural downward movement, to become habituated to moving upward, even if one should try ten thousand times to inculcate the habit by throwing it in the air; nor can fire be made to move downward, nor can the direction of any nature-given tendency be changed by habituation. Thus, the virtues are implanted in us neither by nature nor contrary to nature: we are by nature equipped with the ability to receive them, and habit brings this ability to completion and fulfillment. . . .

Moreover, the same causes and the same means that produce any excellence or virtue can also destroy it, and this is also true of every art. It is by playing the harp that men become both good and bad harpists, and correspondingly with builders and all the other craftsmen: a man who builds well will be a good builder, one who builds badly a bad one. For if this were not so, there would be no need for an instructor, but everybody would be born as a good or a bad craftsman. The same holds true of the virtues: in our transactions with other men it is by action that some become just and others unjust, and it is by acting in the face of danger and by developing the habit of feeling fear or confidence that some become brave men and others cowards. The same applies to the appetites and feelings of anger: by reacting in one way or in another to given circumstances some people become self-controlled and gentle, and others self-indulgent and short-tempered. In a word, characteristics develop from corresponding activities. For that reason, we must see to it that our activities are of a certain kind, since any variations in them will be reflected in our characteristics. Hence it is no small matter whether one habit or another is inculcated in us from early childhood; on the contrary, it makes a considerable difference, or, rather, all the difference.

4.   *Moral Virtue and the Doctrine of the Mean*

The chief concern of the Ethics is with moral rather than intellectual virtue, for Aristotle desires to provide for the majority of citizens a practical guide to the happiness to be found in the world of everyday activity. Moral virtue is described in terms of what we would call character. Good character is produced, as has been seen, through the habitual performance of right acts until the power of doing them freely and willingly becomes second nature. But what are right acts? Here Aristotle brings in his famous doctrine of the mean as the rational principle which can and should guide men in determining those acts whose habitual practice will produce moral virtue and so happiness. Acts are right and virtuous when they are means or "medians" lying between two extremes. This is the old Greek doctrine of moderation, or "nothing too much," and it illustrates how moral virtue, though not possessing reason, is nevertheless obedient to reason, without which it would be blind. It is, in Aristotle's words, "defined by a rational principle, such as a man of practical wisdom would use to determine it." Thus bravery, for example, is the rational mean between the two extreme emotions of rashness and cowardice.

II, 6. It is not sufficient, however, merely to define virtue in general terms as a characteristic: we must also specify what kind of characteristic it is. It must, then, be remarked that every virtue or excellence (1) renders good the thing itself of which it is the excellence, and (2) causes it to perform its function well. For example, the excellence of the eye makes both the eye and its function good, for good sight is due to the excellence of the eye. Likewise, the excellence of a horse makes it both good as a horse and good at running, at carrying its rider, and at facing the enemy. Now, if this is true of all things, the virtue or excellence of man, too, will be a characteristic which makes him a good man, and which causes him to perform his own function well. . . .

Of every continuous entity that is divisible into parts it is possible to take the larger, the smaller, or an equal part, and these parts may be larger, smaller, or equal either in relation to the entity itself, or in relation to us. The "equal" part is something median between excess and deficiency. By the median of an entity I understand a point equidistant from both extremes, and this point is one and the same for everybody. By the median relative to us I understand an amount neither too large nor too small, and this is neither one nor the same for everybody. To take an example: . . . if ten pounds of food is much for a man to eat and two pounds little, it does not follow that the trainer will prescribe six pounds, for this may in turn be much or little for him to eat; it may be little for Milo [the wrestler] and much for someone who has just begun to take up athletics. The same applies to running and wrestling. Thus we see that an expert in any field avoids excess and deficiency, but seeks the median and chooses it — not the median of the object but the median relative to us.

If this, then, is the way in which every science perfects its work, by looking to the median and by bringing its work up to that point — and this is the reason why it is usually said of a successful piece of work that it is impossible to detract from it or to add to it, the implication being that excess and deficiency destroy success while the mean safeguards it (good craftsmen, we say, look toward this standard in the performance of their work) — and if virtue, like nature, is more precise and better than any art, we must conclude that virtue aims at the median. I am referring to moral virtue: for it is moral virtue that is concerned with emotions and actions, and it is in emotions and actions that excess, deficiency, and the median are found. Thus we can experience fear, confidence, desire, anger, pity, and generally any kind of pleasure and pain either too much or too little, and in either case not properly. But to experience all this at the right time, toward the right objects, toward the right people, for the right reason, and in the right manner — that is the median and the best course, the course that is a mark of virtue.

Similarly, excess, deficiency, and the median can also be found in actions. Now virtue is concerned with emotions and actions; and in emotions and actions excess and deficiency miss the mark, whereas the median is praised and constitutes success. . . .

We may thus conclude that virtue or excellence is a characteristic involving choice, and that it consists in observing the mean relative to us, a mean which is defined by a rational principle, such as a man of practical wisdom would use to determine it. It is the mean by reference to two vices: the one of excess and the other of deficiency. It is, moreover, a mean because some vices exceed and others fall short of what is required in emotion and in action, whereas virtue finds and chooses the median.

5. Intellectual Virtue: the Ideal Life

To achieve happiness all men must practice those moral virtues which are acquired when the emotional and impulsive functioning of the irrational part of the soul is guided by the rational principle of the Golden Mean. But men whose reason is thus only indirectly and partially employed with the practical and moral concerns of life fall short of complete happiness. The rational part of the soul, as distinct from the irrational part, is the seat of reason, whose speculative activity is the highest faculty of man's nature. Only this pure reason can contemplate the eternal truths found in philosophy, science, art, and theology, and concern with such truths gives the man who is capable of such activity the greatest pleasure and happiness. As Aristotle states elsewhere, "It is only in a secondary sense that the life which accords with other [moral] virtue can be said to be happy; for the activities of such virtue are human, they have no divine [that is, eternal] element." This section of the Ethics reflects the strong influence of Plato, and yet even while praising the life of thought as the ideal life, Aristotle still keeps his feet on the ground and insists that contemplative happiness also requires a certain amount of material goods.

X, 7. Now, if happiness is activity in conformity with virtue, it is to be expected that it should conform with the highest virtue, and that is the virtue of the best part of us. . . . That it is an activity concerned with theoretical knowledge or contemplation has already been stated.

This would seem to be consistent with our earlier statements as well as the truth. For this activity is not only the highest — for intelligence is the highest possession we have in us, and the objects which are the concern of intelligence are the highest objects of knowledge — but also the most continuous: we are able to study continuously more easily than to perform any kind of action. Furthermore, we think of pleasure as a necessary ingredient in happiness. Now everyone agrees that of all the activities that conform with virtue activity in conformity with theoretical wisdom is the most pleasant. At any rate, it seems that (the pursuit of wisdom or) philosophy holds pleasures marvelous in purity and certainty, and it is not surprising that time spent in knowledge is more pleasant than time spent in research. Moreover, what is usually called "self-sufficiency" will be found in the highest degree in the activity which is concerned with theoretical knowledge. Like a just man and any other virtuous man, a wise man requires the necessities of life; once these have been adequately provided, a just man still needs people toward whom and in company with whom to act justly, and the same is true of a self-controlled man, a courageous man, and all the rest. But a wise man is able to study even by himself, and the wiser he is the more is he able to do it. Perhaps he could do it better if he had colleagues to work with him, but he still is the most self-sufficient of all. Again, study seems to be the only activity which is loved for its own sake. . . . it follows that the activity of our intelligence constitutes the complete happiness of man, provided that it encompasses a complete span of life; for nothing connected with happiness must be incomplete.

However, such a life would be more than human. A man who would live it would do so not insofar as he is human, but because there is a divine element within him. This divine element is as far above our composite nature as its activity is above the active exercise of the other (i.e., practical) kind of virtue. So if it is true that intelligence is divine in comparison with man, then a life guided by intelligence is divine in comparison with human life. We must not follow those who advise us to have human thoughts, since we are (only) men, and mortal thoughts, as mortals should; on the contrary, we should try to become immortal as far as that is possible and do our utmost to live in accordance with what is highest in us. For though this is a small portion (of our nature), it far surpasses everything else in power and value. One might even regard it as each man's true self, since it is the controlling and better part. It would, therefore, be strange if a man chose not to live his own life but someone else's.

Moreover, what we stated before will apply here, too: what is by nature proper to each thing will be at once the best and the most pleasant for it. In other words, a life guided by intelligence is the best and most pleasant for man, inasmuch as intelligence, above all else, is man. Consequently, this kind of life is the happiest.

8. . . . A further indication that complete happiness consists in some kind of contemplative activity is this. We assume that the gods are in the highest degree blessed and happy. But what kind of actions are we to attribute to them? Acts of justice? Will they not look ridiculous making contracts with one another, returning deposits, and so forth? Perhaps acts of courage — withstanding terror and taking risks, because it is noble to do so? Or generous actions? . . . If we went through the whole list we would see that a concern with actions is petty and unworthy of the gods. Nevertheless, we all assume that the gods exist and, consequently, that they are active; for surely we do not assume them to be always asleep like Endymion. Now, if we take away action from a living being, to say nothing of production, what is left except contemplation? Therefore, the activity of the divinity which surpasses all others in bliss must be

a contemplative activity, and the human activity which is most closely akin to it is, therefore, most conducive to happiness.

This is further shown by the fact that no other living being has a share in happiness, since they all are completely denied this kind of activity. The gods enjoy a life blessed in its entirety; men enjoy it to the extent that they attain something resembling the divine activity; but none of the other living beings can be happy, because they have no share at all in contemplation or study. So happiness is coextensive with study, and the greater the opportunity for studying, the greater the happiness, not as an incidental effect but as inherent in study; for study is in itself worthy of honor. Consequently, happiness is some kind of study or contemplation.

But we shall also need external well-being, since we are only human. Our nature is not self-sufficient for engaging in study: our body must be healthy and we must have food and generally be cared for. Nevertheless, if it is not possible for a man to be supremely happy without external goods, we must not think that his needs will be great and many in order to be happy; . . .

6. The Need of Legislation: Transition to the Politics

At the end of the Ethics, Aristotle returns to his main subject, moral virtue, and discusses the necessary part to be played by the state whose laws provide the most effective training and environment for the formation of ethical character. This serves as a transition to the Politics, wherein his study of the good life for man is brought to completion.

X, 9. . . . Surely, knowing about excellence or virtue is not enough: we must try to possess it and use it, or find some other way in which we may become good.

Now, if words alone would suffice to make us good, they would rightly "harvest many rewards and great," as Theognis says, and we would have to provide them. But as it is, while words evidently do have the power to encourage and stimulate young men of generous mind, and while they can cause a character well-born and truly enamored of what is noble to be possessed by virtue, they do not have the capacity to turn the common run of people to goodness and nobility. For the natural tendency of most people is to be swayed not by a sense of shame but by fear, and to refrain from acting basely not because it is disgraceful, but because of the punishment it brings. Living under the sway of emotion, they pursue their own proper pleasures and the means by which they can obtain them, and they avoid the pains that are opposed to them. But they do not even have a notion of what is noble and truly pleasant, since they have never tasted it. What argument indeed can transform people like that? To change by argument what has long been ingrained in a character is impossible or, at least, not easy. . . .

... For a man whose life is guided by emotion will not listen to an argument that dissuades him, nor will he understand it. How can we possibly persuade a man like that to change his ways? And in general it seems that emotion does not yield to argument but only to force. Therefore, there must first be a character that somehow has an affinity for excellence or virtue, a character that loves what is noble and feels disgust at what is base.

To obtain the right training for virtue from youth up is difficult, unless one has been brought up under the right laws. To live a life of self-control and tenacity is not pleasant for most people, especially for the young. Therefore, their upbringing and pursuits must be regulated by laws; for once they have become familiar, they will no longer be painful. But it is perhaps not enough that they receive the right upbringing and attention only in their youth. Since they must carry on these pursuits and cultivate them by habit when they have grown up, we probably need laws for this, too, and for the whole of life in general. For most people are swayed rather by compulsion than argument, and by punishments rather than by (a sense of) what is noble. . . .

Is it not, then, our next task to examine from whom and how we can learn to become legislators? . . .

Accordingly, since previous writers have left the subject of legislation un-examined, it is perhaps best if we ourselves investigate it and the general problem of the constitution of a state, in order to complete as best we can our philosophy of human affairs.

◆ B ◆ THE POLITICS

"A state exists for the sake of the good life."

It is often stated that Aristotle in his Politics was blind to the political facts of life in his day in that he ignored the imperial state of the future which Philip and Alexander were creating and dealt only with the political life of the minia-ture city-states whose independent existence was largely over. But this view ignores the fact that the Politics was meant to be a continuation of the Ethics, that the purpose of the state is to promote and maintain the well-being of its citizens, and that this "good and honorable life" would seem to him to be im-possible of achievement in a huge and heterogeneous empire in which people could not act as free citizens participating in a shared life. Although part of what Aristotle writes in the Politics is thus not pertinent to our own world of large nation-states, it remains an excellent summary and interpretation of Greek political experience, and most of its penetrating generalizations on political and social behavior remain valid and illuminating today.

The eight books of the Politics fall into two main divisions, to which

From *The Politics of Aristotle*, translated by Benjamin Jowett, ed. by H. W. C. Davis, 1905. By permission of the Oxford University Press, Oxford.

Book I serves as an introduction. In Books II, III, VII, and VIII, Aristotle gives evidence of the influence of Plato as he describes the characteristics of an ideal state, but in the books thought to have been written last (IV, V, VI), he puts aside considerations of an ideal commonwealth and more realistically deals with practical matters relating to the nature and stability of the existing Greek states of his day. The conclusions reached in this second part of his treatise were supported by the multitude of facts gleaned from his analysis of the constitutions of one hundred and fifty-eight Greek states.

1. *Nature, Origin, and Purpose of the State*

In Book I Aristotle indicates the relationship of the Politics to the Ethics by insisting upon the necessary connection between the state and man's goal of a virtuous and happy life. The state is not an artificial creation, as the Sophists argued, but is the natural culmination of earlier and simpler forms of society, the family and the village, which people naturally and instinctively create in order to satisfy their immediate and elementary wants. But a life of moral virtue and happiness, the highest of their wants, can only be provided by the final manifestation of the "social instinct . . . implanted in all men by nature," namely the state. So "the state comes into existence, originating in the bare needs of life, and continuing in existence for the sake of the good life." The modern concept of man vs. the state would be unthinkable to Aristotle, for "man is by nature a political animal" who can realize his highest ideals only as a member of society.

I, 1. Every state is a community of some kind, and every community is established with a view to some good; for mankind always act in order to obtain that which they think good. But, if all communities aim at some good, the state or political community, which is the highest of all, and which embraces all the rest, aims, and in greater degree than any other, at the highest good. . . .

Governments differ in kind, as will be evident to anyone who considers the matter according to the method which has hitherto guided us. As in other departments of science, so in politics, the compound should always be resolved into the simple elements or least parts of the whole. We must therefore look at the elements of which the state is composed, in order that we may see in what they differ from one another, and whether any scientific distinction can be drawn between the different kinds of rule.

He who thus considers things in their first growth and origin, whether a state or anything else, will obtain the clearest view of them. In the first place (1) there must be a union of those who cannot exist without each other; for example, of male and female, that the race may continue; and this is a union which is formed, not of deliberate purpose, but because, in common with other animals and with plants, mankind have a natural desire to leave behind them an image of themselves. And (2) there must be a union of natural ruler and subject, that both may be preserved. For he who can foresee with his mind is by nature intended to be lord and master, and he who can work with his body is a subject, and by nature a slave; hence master and slave have the same interest. Nature, however, has distinguished between the female and the slave. For she is not niggardly, like the smith who fashions the Delphian knife for many uses; she makes each thing for a single use, and every instrument is best made when intended for one and not for many uses. But among barbarians no distinction is made between women and slaves, because there is no natural ruler among them: they are a community of slaves, male and female. Wherefore the poets say, "It is meet that Hellenes should rule over barbarians"; as if they thought that the barbarian and the slave were by nature one.

Out of these two relationships, between man and woman, master and slave, the family first arises, and Hesiod is right when he says "First house and wife and an ox for the plow," for the ox is the poor man's slave. The family is the association established by nature for the supply of men's everyday wants. . . . But when several families are united, and the association aims at something more than the supply of daily needs, then comes into existence the village. And the most natural form of a village seems to be that of a colony from the family, composed of the children and grandchildren, who are said to be "suckled with the same milk." And this is the reason why Greek states were originally governed by kings; because the Greeks were under royal rule before they came together, as the barbarians still are. . . . Wherefore men say that the Gods have a king, because they themselves either are or were in ancient times under the rule of a king. For they imagine, not only the forms of the Gods, but their ways of life to be like their own.

When several villages are united in a single community, perfect and large enough to be nearly or quite self-sufficing, the state comes into existence, originating in the bare needs of life, and continuing in existence for the sake of a good life. And therefore, if the earlier forms of society are natural, so is the state, for it is the end of them, and the completed nature is the end. For what each thing is when fully developed, we call its nature, whether we are speaking of a man, a horse, or a family. Besides, the final cause and end of the thing is the best, and to be self-sufficing is the end and the best.

Hence it is evident that the state is a creation of nature, and that man is by nature a political animal. And he who by nature and not by mere accident is without a state is either above humanity or below it; he is the "Tribeless, lawless, heartless one," whom Homer denounces — the outcast who is a lover of war; he may be compared to a bird which flies alone. . . .

Thus the state is by nature clearly prior to the family and to the individual, since the whole is of necessity prior to the part; for example, if the whole body be destroyed, there will be no foot or hand, except in an equivocal sense, as we might speak of a stone hand; for when destroyed the hand will be no better than that. But things are defined by their working and power; and we ought not to say that they are the same when they are no longer the same, but only that they have the same name. The proof that the state is a creation of nature and prior to the individual is that the individual, when isolated, is not self-sufficing; and therefore he is like a part in relation to the whole. But he who is unable to live in society, or who has no need because he is sufficient for himself, must be either a beast or a god; he is no part of a state.

A social instinct is implanted in all men by nature, and he who first founded the state was the greatest of benefactors. For man, when perfected, is the best of animals, but when separated from law and justice, he is the worst of all; since armed injustice is the more dangerous, and he is equipped at birth with the arms of intelligence and with moral qualities which he may use for the worst ends. Wherefore, if he have not virtue, he is the most unholy and the most savage of animals, and most full of lust and gluttony. But justice is the bond of men in states, and the administration of justice, which is the determination of what is just, is the principle of order in political society.

2. *A Criticism of Communism*

As a preliminary to his discussion of the ideal state, Aristotle condemns the communism of Plato's utopian Republic. The nub of his argument is that communistic unity runs counter to both human nature and to the nature of the state. People are in the first instance aware of their own private interests, and to deprive them of these would be to create hostility to society and destroy the natural tendency to cooperate with fellow beings in creating the good life through the agency of the state. The greater the degree of individual interests, activities, and possessions, the richer will be the individual's contribution to the community. Aristotle advocates reforms "by good customs and laws," but he condemns the radical who would "disregard the experience of ages" in his extreme haste to remove present evils.

II, 5. Next let us consider what should be our arrangements about property; should the citizens of the perfect state have possessions in common or not? . . .

There is always a difficulty in men living together and having things in common, but especially in their having common property. . . . The present arrangement, if improved as it might be by good customs and laws, would be far better, and would have the advantages of both systems. Property should be in a certain sense common, but, as a general rule, private. For when everyone has his separate interest, men will not complain of one another, and they will make more progress, because everyone will be attending to his own business. Yet among good men, and as regards use, "friends," as the proverb says, "will have all things common." . . . For although every human has his own property, some things he will place at the disposal of his friends, while of others he shares the use of them. . . .

Again, how immeasurably greater is the pleasure, when a man feels a thing to be his own! For love of self is a feeling implanted by nature and not given in vain, although selfishness is rightly condemned. This, however is not mere love of self, but love of self in excess, like the miser's love of money; for all, or almost all, men love money, and other such objects in a measure. Furthermore, there is the greatest pleasure in doing a kindness or service to friends or guests or companions, which can only be done when a man has private property. These advantages are lost by the excessive unification of the state. . . . No one, when men have all things in common, will any longer set an example of liberality or do any liberal action; for liberality consists in the use a man makes of his own property.

Such [communistic] legislation may have a specious appearance of benevolence. Men readily listen to it, and are easily induced to believe that in some wonderful manner everybody will become everybody's friend, especially when someone is heard denouncing the evils now existing in states, suits about contracts, convictions for perjury, flatteries of rich men and the like, which are said to arise out of the possession of private property. These evils, however, are due to a very different cause — the wickedness of human nature. Indeed, we see that there is much more quarreling among those who have all things in common, though there are not many of them when compared with the vast numbers who have private property.

Again, we ought to reckon, not only the evils from which the citizens will be saved, but also the advantages which they will lose. The life which they are to lead appears to be quite impracticable. The error of Socrates must be attributed to the false notion of unity from which he starts. Unity there should be, both of the family and of the state, but in some respects only. For there is a point at which a state may attain such a degree of unity as to be no longer a state, or at which, without actually ceasing to exist, it will become an inferior state, like harmony passing into unison, or rhythm which has been reduced to a single foot. The state, as I was saying, is a plurality, which should be united and made into a community by education. . . . Let us remember that we should not disregard the experience of ages. In the multitude of years these things, if they were good, would certainly not have been unknown. . . .

3. Good and Bad Constitutions

Aristotle's classification of governments has remained standard for nearly 2500 years. His division into six types is based upon his study of Greek political experience, while his criterion for distinguishing between good and bad governments is derived from his views on the nature and purpose of the state. The true end of the state is well-being and happiness, and this is the common interest. Good governments are devoted to the common interest, while bad or "perverted" governments place the selfish interest of a ruling class above "the common good of all."

III, 6. . . . We have next to consider whether there is only one form of government or many; and if many, what they are, and how many; and what are the differences between them.

A constitution is the arrangement of powers in a state, especially of the supreme power, and the constitution is the government. For example, in democracies the people are supreme, but in oligarchies, the few; therefore, we say that the two constitutions are different; and so in other cases.

First let us consider what is the purpose of a state and how many forms of government there are by which human society is regulated. We have already said, earlier in this treatise, when drawing a distinction between household management and the rule of a governor, that man is by nature a political animal. And therefore men, even when they do not require one another's help, desire to live together all the same, and are in fact brought together by their common interests in proportion as they severally attain to any measure of well-being. Well-being is certainly the chief end of individuals and of states. But also, for the sake of mere living, in which there is possibly some noble element, men meet together and maintain the political community, so long as the evils of existence do not heavily overbalance the good. And we all see that men cling to life even in the midst of misfortune, seeming to find in it a natural sweetness and happiness.

The conclusion is evident: governments which have a regard to the common interest are constituted in accordance with strict principles of justice, and are therefore true forms; but those which regard only the interest of the rulers are all defective and perverted forms. For they are despotic, whereas a state is a community of free men.

Having determined these points, we have next to consider how many forms of constitution there are, and what they are; and in the first place what are the true forms, for when they are determined the perversions of them will at once be apparent. The words constitution and government have the same meaning; and the government, which is the supreme authority in states, is necessarily in the hands either of one, or of a few, or of many. The true forms of government, therefore, are those in which the one, or the few, or the many, govern with a view to the common interest; but governments which rule with a view to the private interest, whether of the one, or of the few, or of the many, are perversions. For citizens, if they are truly citizens, ought all to participate in the advantages of a state. We call that form of government in which one rules, and which regards the common interest, kingship or royalty; that in which more than one, but not many, rule, aristocracy. It is so called, either because the rulers are the best men, or because they have at heart the best interest of the state and of the citizens. But when the citizens at large administer the state for the common interest, the government is called by the generic name — constitutional government. And there is a reason for this use of language. One man or a few may excel in virtue; but of virtue there are many kinds. As the number of rulers increases it becomes more difficult for them to attain perfection in every kind, though they may in military virtue, for this is found in the masses. Hence, in a constitutional government the fighting men have the supreme power, and those who possess arms are citizens.

Of the above-mentioned forms, the perversions are as follows: of royalty, tyranny; of aristocracy, oligarchy; of constitutional government, democracy. For tyranny is a kind of monarchy which has in view the interest of the monarch only; oligarchy has in view the interest of the wealthy; democracy, of the needy; none of them the common good of all.

4. *The Ideal State: Its True Object*

The true object of the state is neither trade nor empire nor the prevention of crime nor anything but the good life. By "state" Aristotle does not mean "country," but "government" or "constitution," and the best states are those in which the rulers are best fitted by their possession of moral virtue to rule "in such a manner as to attain the most desirable life." Whether this is to be the rule of one (kingship), or few (aristocracy), or many (constitutionalism), depends upon the nature and temperament of the people. In any case, in an ideal state the laboring and business classes will not be citizens, for "the virtue of a good man is necessarily the same as the virtue of a citizen in a perfect state," and these classes have not the "leisure necessary both for the development of virtue and the performance of political duties."

III, 9. . . . But a state exists for the sake of a good life, and not for the sake of life only. If life only were the object, slaves and brute animals might form a state, but they cannot, for they have no share in happiness or in a life of free choice. Nor does a state exist merely for the sake of alliance and security from injustice, nor yet for the sake of trade and mutual intercourse; for then the Tyrrhenians and the Carthaginians, and all who have commercial treaties with one another, would be citizens of one state. . . . Those who care for good government take into consideration the larger questions of virtue and vice in states. Whence it may be further inferred that virtue must be the serious care of a state which truly deserves the name. Otherwise the community becomes a mere alliance, which differs only in place from alliances of which the members live apart. And law is only a convention, "a surety to one another of justice," as the sophist Lycophron says, and has no real power to make the citizens good and just. . . .

Clearly then a state is not a mere society, having a common place, established for the prevention of crime and for the sake of trade. These are conditions without which a state cannot exist; but all of them together do not constitute a state, which is a community of families and aggregations of families in well-being for the sake of a perfect and self-sufficing life. Such a community can only be established among those who live in the same place and intermarry. Hence arises in states family connections, brotherhoods, common sacrifices, amusements which draw men together. They are created by friendship, for friendship is the motive of society. The end is the good life, and these are the means towards it. And the state is the union of families and villages having for an end a perfect and self-sufficing life, by which we mean a happy and honorable life.

Our conclusion, then, is that political society exists for the sake of noble actions, and not of mere companionship. And they who contribute most to such a society have a greater share in it than those who have the same or a greater freedom or nobility of birth but are inferior to them in political virtue; or than those who exceed them in wealth but are surpassed by them in virtue.

From what has been said it will be clearly seen that all the partisans of different forms of government speak of a part of justice only. . . .

18. We maintain that the true forms of government are three, and that the best must be that which is administered by the best, and in which there is one man, or a whole family, or many persons, excelling in virtue, and both rulers and subjects are fitted, the one to rule, the others to be ruled, in such a manner as to attain the most eligible life. We showed at the commencement of our inquiry that the virtue of the good man is necessarily the same as the virtue of the citizen of the perfect state. Clearly then in the same manner, and by the same means through which a man becomes truly good, he will frame a state which will be truly good whether aristocratical, or under kingly rule, and the same education and the same habits will be found to make a good man and a good statesman and king. . . .

VII, 9. . . . Now, since we are here speaking of the best form of government, and that under which the state will be most happy (and happiness, as has been already said, cannot exist without virtue), it clearly follows that in the state which is best governed the citizens who are absolutely and not merely relatively just men must not lead the life of mechanics or tradesmen, for such a life is ignoble and inimical to virtue. Neither must they be husbandmen, since leisure is necessary both for the development of virtue and the performance of political duties.

5. The Ideal State: Education

Like so much in Aristotle's writings, his discussion of the central importance of public education is pertinent to our modern civilization where state vs. private education has long been a subject of controversy. He also distinguishes between liberal education (he was the first to use the term) and vocational education, and his arguments in favor of the former stem from his all-pervading desire to provide the good life for everyone. It should be noted that what Aristotle terms "music" includes all the arts and literature, or what we today call the "humanities."

VIII, 1. No one will doubt that a lawgiver should direct his attention above all to the education of youth, or that the neglect of education does harm to states. The citizen should be molded to suit the form of government under which he lives. For each government has a peculiar character, which originally formed and which continues to preserve it. The character of democracy creates democracy, and the character of oligarchy creates oligarchy. The better the character, always the better the government.

Now for the exercise of any faculty or art a previous training and practice are required; clearly then they are required for the exercise of virtue. And since the entire state has one end, manifestly education should be one and the same for all, and should be public and not private. It should not be as at present, when everyone looks after his own children separately, and gives them separate instruction of the sort he thinks best. The training in things of common interest should be the same for all. Neither must we suppose that any one of the citizens belongs to himself, for they all belong to the state, and are each of them a part of the state, and the care of each part is inseparable from the care of the whole. In this particular the Spartans are to be praised, for they take the greatest pains about their children, and make education the business of the state.

2. That education should be regulated by law and should be an affair of state is not to be denied; but what should be the character of this public education, and how young persons should be educated, are questions yet to be considered. For men are by no means agreed about the things to be taught, whether we aim at virtue or the best life. Neither is it clear whether education should be more concerned with intellectual or with moral virtue. Existing practice is perplexing; no one knows on what principle we should proceed. Should the useful in life, or should virtue, or should higher knowledge, be the aim of our training? All three opinions have been entertained. Again, about method there is no agreement; for different persons, starting with different ideas about the nature of virtue, naturally disagree about the practice of it.

Undoubtedly children should be taught those useful things that are really necessary, but not all useful things. For occupations are divided into liberal and illiberal, and to young children should be imparted only such kinds of knowledge as will be useful to them without vulgarizing them. Any occupation, art, or science, which makes the body or soul or mind of the free man less fit for the practice or exercise of virtue, is vulgar. Therefore we call those arts vulgar which tend to deform the body, and likewise all paid employments; they absorb and degrade the mind. . . .

3. The customary branches of an education are four, namely, (1) reading and writing, (2) gymnastic exercises, (3) music, to which is sometimes added (4) drawing. Of these, reading, writing, and drawing are regarded as useful for the purposes of life in a variety of ways, and gymnastic exercises are thought to infuse courage. As to music a question may be raised. In our own day most men cultivate it for pleasure, but originally it was included in education because nature herself, as has been often said, requires that we should be able, not only to work well, but to use our leisure well. For, as I must repeat once again, the prime end of all action is leisure. Both are necessary, but leisure is better than labor.

Hence now the question must be asked in good earnest, what ought we to do when at leisure? Clearly we ought not to be always amusing ourselves, for then amusement would be the end of life. . . .

Apparently then there are branches of learning and education which we should study solely with a view to the enjoyment of leisure, and these are to be valued for their own sake; whereas the kinds of knowledge which are useful in business are necessary, and exist for the sake of other things. Therefore our fathers admitted music into education, not on the ground of either its necessity or its utility; for it is not necessary, nor even useful in the same way that reading and writing are useful in wealth getting, in the management of a household, in the acquisition of knowledge, and in political life. Nor is it, like drawing, useful for a more correct judgment of the works of artists, nor again, like gymnastics, does it give health and strength, for neither of these is to be gained from music. There is, however, a use of music for intellectual enjoyment in leisure, which seems indeed to have been the reason of its introduction into education. For music is one of the ways in which, it is thought, a freeman might pass his leisure. . . .

Evidently, then, there is a sort of education in which parents should train their sons, not because it is useful or necessary, but because it is liberal or noble.

6. *The Practicable State: The Best Constitution*

In that part of his Politics which Aristotle seems to have written last (Books IV, V, VI), he turns from a discussion of the ideal state to deal realistically with the subject of practicable constitutions for existing states. "For the best is often unobtainable, and therefore the true lawmaker or statesmen ought to be acquainted . . . with that which is best considering the circumstances." In keeping with his doctrine of the Golden Mean, he defines the best such constitution as one that combines the best features of democracy and oligarchy and rests upon the social foundation of a large middle class. This represents the practicable form of that ideal type of state that Aristotle had called "constitutional government," and is often called today a "republic" as distinct from a "democracy" by those who share Aristotle's fear of the excesses of democracy.

IV, 11. We have now to inquire what is the best constitution for most states, and the best life for most men, neither assuming a standard of virtue which is above ordinary persons, nor an education which is exceptionally favored by nature and circumstances, nor yet an ideal state which is an inspiration only, but having regard to the life in which the majority are able to share, and to the form of government which states in general can attain. . . . If it was truly said in the *Ethics* that the happy life is the life according to unimpeded virtue and that virtue is a mean, then the life which is a mean and a mean attainable by everyone must be best. And the same criteria of virtue and vice are characteristic of cities and of constitutions; for the constitution is in pattern the life of the city.

Now in all states there are three elements; one class is very rich, another very poor, and a third in the mean. It is admitted that moderation and the mean are best, and therefore it will clearly be best to possess the gifts of fortune in moderation; for in that condition of life men are most ready to listen to reason. . . . Those who have too much of the goods of fortune, strength, wealth, friends, and the like, are neither willing nor able to submit to authority. The evil begins at home; for when they are boys, by reason of the luxury in which they are brought up, they never learn, even at school, the habit of obedience. On the other hand, the very poor, who are in the opposite extreme, are too degraded. So that the one class cannot obey, and can only rule despotically; the other knows not how to command and must be ruled like slaves. Thus arises a city, not of freemen, but of masters and slaves, the one despising, the other envying. Nothing can be more fatal to friendship and good fellowship in states than this; for good fellowship starts from friendship. When men are at enmity with one another, they would rather not even share the same path.

But a city ought to be composed, as far as possible, of equals and similars; and these are generally the middle classes. Wherefore a city which is composed of middle-class citizens is necessarily best constituted with respect to what we call the natural elements of a state. And this class of citizens is most secure in a state, for they do not, like the poor, covet their neighbors' goods; nor do others covet theirs, as the poor covet the goods of the rich. And as they neither plot against others nor are themselves plotted against, they pass through life safely. . . .

Thus it is manifest that the best political community is formed by citizens of the middle class, and that those states are likely to be well administered in which the middle class is large, and if possible larger than both the other classes, or at any rate than either singly, for the addition of the middle class turns the scale and prevents either of the extremes from being dominant. Great then is the good fortune of a state in which the citizens have a moderate and sufficient property. For where some possess much and the rest nothing, there may arise an extreme democracy, or a pure oligarchy; or a tyranny may grow out of either extreme — out of either the most rampant democracy or out of an oligarchy. But it is not so likely to arise out of a middle and nearly equal condition. I will explain the reason for this hereafter when I speak of revolutions in states. . . .

Democracies are safer and more permanent than oligarchies, because they have a middle class which is more numerous and has a greater share in the government. For when there is no middle class and the poor greatly exceed in number, troubles arise and the state soon comes to an end. A proof of the superiority of the middle class is that the best legislators have been of a middle rank; for example, Solon, as his own verses testify, and Lycurgus, for he was not a king. . . .

What then is the best form of government, and what makes it the best is evident. Of other states, since we say there are many kinds of democracy and oligarchy, it is not difficult to see which has the first and which the second or any other place in the order of excellence, now that we have determined which is best. For that which is nearest to the best must of necessity be the better, and that which is furthest from it the worse, if we are judging absolutely and not with reference to given conditions. I say "with reference to given conditions," since a particular government may be preferable for some, but another form may be better for others.

7.   The Practicable State: Causes of Revolutions

Aristotle seems to feel that even the best practicable constitution, described above, was too visionary for the Greeks of his day whose governments were actually examples of the worst types of constitutions, either turbulent democracies or selfish oligarchies. He therefore turns his attention to these bad or "perverted" constitutions and realistically describes methods for making them more stable and, equally important, less liable of degenerating into something worse. He turns first to analyze the nature of the danger that constantly threatened the governments of his day — revolution. His account of the causes of revolutions, particularly in democracies, has particular relevance for us today.

V, 1. The design which we proposed to ourselves is now nearly completed. Next in order follow the causes of revolutions in states, how many they are, and what is their nature; what elements work ruin in particular states, and out of what and into what they mostly change; also what methods there are of preserving states generally, or a particular state, and by what means each state may be best preserved: these questions remain to be considered. . . .

2. In considering how dissensions and political revolutions arise, we must first of all ascertain the beginnings and causes of them which affect constitutions generally. They may be said to be three in number; and we have now to give an outline of each. We want to know (1) what is the feeling and (2) what are the motives of those who make them and (3) what causes political disturbances and quarrels. The universal and chief cause of revolutionary feeling has already been mentioned; namely, either the desire for equality, when men think that they are equal to others who have more than themselves; or, the desire for inequality and superiority, when they believe themselves superior and think they have not more but the same or less than their inferiors, pretensions which may or may not be just. Inferiors revolt in order that they may be equal, and equals that they may be superior. Such is the state of mind which creates revolutions.

The motives for making them are the desire for gain and for honor, or the fear of dishonor and loss. The authors of them want to divert punishment or dishonor from themselves or their friends. . . . Other causes are insolence, fear, love of superiority, contempt, disproportionate increase in some part of the state. Causes of another sort are election intrigues, carelessness, neglect about trifles, dissimilarity of elements.

4. In revolutions the occasions may be trifling, but great interests are at stake. . . . Revolutions are accomplished in two ways, by force and by fraud. Force may be applied either at the time of making the revolution or afterwards. Fraud, again, is of two kinds; for (1) sometimes the citizens are deceived into accepting a change of government, and afterwards held in subjection against their will. . . . (2) In other cases the people are persuaded at first, and afterwards, by a repetition of the persuasion, their good will and allegiance are still retained. . . .

5. . . . Revolutions in democracies are often caused by the intemperance of

demagogues, who either in a private capacity report information against rich men until they compel them to combine (for a common danger unites even the bitterest enemies), or else come forward in public and stir up the people against them. The truth of this remark is proved by a variety of examples. At Cos the democracy was overthrown because wicked demagogues arose and the nobles combined. . . . Much in the same manner the democracy at Megara was over-turned [see Selection 19D: Theognis]. There the demagogues drove out many of the nobles in order that they might be able to confiscate their property. At length the exiles, becoming numerous, returned, engaged and defeated the people, and established an oligarchy. . . .

Of old, the demagogue was also a general, and then democracies changed into tyrannies. Most of the ancient tyrants were originally demagogues. They are not so now, but they were then; and the reason is that they were generals and not orators, for oratory had not yet come into fashion. Whereas in our day, when the art of rhetoric has made such progress, orators lead the people. . . . These are the principal causes of revolutions in democracies.

8. *The Practicable State: Preserving Constitutions*

How to preserve existing constitutions from revolution, and even how to cure them of their defects and make them more workable, is the last task which Aristotle sets for himself in the Politics. His views on the preservation of de-mocracy are drawn from his observation of Greek politics, and their evident applicability to our present world indicates how fundamentally similar were the political developments of these specific periods in the history of the two civilizations. At the end, Aristotle returns again to the importance of education. He insists that in a democracy it is fatal to educate people to believe in an extreme and hence "false idea of freedom" which leads men to "think it slavery to live by the rules of the constitution." Respect for law is the funda-mental safeguard of any constitution.

V, 8. We have next to consider what means there are of preserving states in general, and also in particular cases. In the first place, it is evident that if we understand the causes which destroy states, we shall also understand the causes which preserve them; for opposites produce opposites, and destruction is the opposite of preservation.

In all well-organized governments there is nothing which should be more jealousy maintained than the spirit of obedience to law, more especially in small matters; for lawlessness creeps in unperceived and at last ruins the state, just as the constant repetition of small expenses in time eats up a fortune. The change does not take place all at once, and therefore is not observed. The mind is deceived, as by the fallacy which says, "if each part is little, then the whole is little.". . .

VI, 5. The mere establishment of a democracy is not the only or the principal business of the lawgiver, or of those who wish to create such a state, for any state, however badly constituted, may last one, two or three days. A far greater task is the preservation of it. The lawgiver should therefore endeavor to lay a firm foundation according to the principles already described of the preservation and destruction of states. He should guard against the destructive elements, and make laws, written or unwritten, which will contain all measures preservative of states. He must not think that the truly democratic or oligarchic measure is whatever will give the greatest amount of democracy or oligarchy, but what will make them last longest. The demagogues of our own day often get property confiscated in the law-courts in order to please the people. . . .

Now, in the last and worst form of democracy the citizens are very numerous, and can hardly be made to assemble unless they are paid; and to pay them when there are no revenues presses hard upon the upper class, for the money must be obtained by property taxes and confiscations and corrupt practices of the courts, things which have before now overthrown many democracies. . . . Where there are revenues, the demagogues should not be allowed after their fashion to distribute the surplus. The poor are always receiving and always wanting more and more, for such help is like water poured into a leaky cask. Yet the true friend of the people should see that they be not too poor, for extreme poverty lowers the character of the democracy. Measures should also be taken which will give them lasting prosperity, and since this is equally to the interest of all classes, the proceeds of public revenues should be accumulated and distributed among the poor, if possible, in such quantities as may enable them to purchase a little farm, or, at any rate, make a beginning in trade or agriculture. And if this benevolence cannot be extended to all, money should be distributed by tribes or other divisions. . . .

V, 9. . . . But of all the things I have mentioned, that which most contributes to the permanence of constitutions is the adaptation of education to the form of government, and yet in our own day this principle is universally neglected. The best laws, though sanctioned by every citizen of the state, will be of no avail unless the young are trained by habit and education in the spirit of the constitution, if it is democratic, democratically, or if it is oligarchic, oligarchically. For there may be a want of self-discipline in states as well as in individuals. . . .

In democracies of the more extreme type there has arisen a false idea of freedom which is contradictory to the true interests of the state. For two principles are characteristic of democracy, government by the majority and freedom. Men think that what is equal is just, and that equality is the supremacy of the popular will, and that freedom and equality mean doing what a man likes. In such democracies everyone lives as he pleases, or in the words of Euripides, "according to his fancy." But this is all wrong; men should not think it slavery to live according to the rule of the constitution, for it is their salvation.

I have now discussed generally the causes of the revolutions and destruction of states, and the means of their preservation and continuance.

Demosthenes vs. Isocrates

"Nationalism" vs. "Internationalism"

The defeat and destruction of the Athenian Empire in 404 B.C. marked the collapse of the movement towards internationalism in the Greek world. The half-century that followed was characterized by almost continuous warfare punctuated by futile peace conferences as the chief Greek states — Sparta, Thebes, and Athens, aided and abetted by the intervention of Persia in Greek affairs — successfully used the principle of the balance of power to prevent any one state from dominating Greece. The resulting political anarchy interfered disastrously with inter-state trade and produced within the Greek states a continuing economic depression which manifested itself in bitter class strife. The plight of the poor led them to promote radical socialistic attacks on the property of the rich, while the resulting fears of the rich produced in them a reactionary opposition to even moderate reform. Isocrates (436–338 B.C.) noted the bitter and uncompromising character of this class struggle at Athens as he contrasted the conditions of this later period with those that had prevailed during the prosperous days of the Athenian Empire: "In their mutual relations they are so mistrustful and hostile that they fear their fellow citizens more than their enemies; and whereas, during the period of our supremacy, they were united and readily assisted one another, they have now become so unsocial that those who are possessed of wealth would rather throw their property into the sea than assist the needy, while the poor would prefer to take what they want from the rich by force rather than find a treasure."

Unity and stability for the Greek world were finally achieved in 338 B.C., but they were imposed from without by Philip of Macedon and at the point of a sword. All the Greek states, excepting Sparta, were forced into a federal union under Macedonian leadership. Each state retained its local autonomy but was required to renounce the right both to make war on its neighbors and to engage in civil strife at home. No tribute was required, but each state was to supply military assistance for a projected war on Persia which Philip's son Alexander later carried out.

During the critical years preceding Philip's conquest of Greece, the political life of Athens was enlivened by a great debate over foreign policy. Isocrates, the spokesman of the internationalist-minded party, realistically saw that the unification of Greece was the prime necessity of the times; and when the hopelessness of his original plan for a voluntary union became apparent, he turned to Philip and urged him to take the lead in organizing a free and united Greece. But it was the more isolationist and narrowly patriotic party under Demosthenes (384–322 B.C.) that won the day, and Philip had to defeat Athens and its few allies before he could fulfill Isocrates' hopes for a Greece freed from internal strife and Demosthenes' fears of Macedonian "domination of Greece and the end of the honors and rights of our ancestors." The following selections illustrate the nature of the rival arguments in this great debate over foreign policy and suggest analogies which exist between fourth-century Greece and our own times.

✦ A ✦ DEMOSTHENES, FIRST PHILIPPIC

"Athenians, when will you act as becomes you!"

The ambitious, energetic, and shrewd Philip became king of Macedon in 359 B.C., and in less than two years he had transformed a primitive feudal state into a powerful monarchy under his autocratic rule. His permanent national army was the most powerful military machine yet seen in the ancient world. Another result of this national awakening — a phenomenon comparable to the uprisings of colonial peoples throughout the world in our own day — was Philip's conquest of the Greek colonies which had been established along the Macedonian coast during the earlier period of Greek imperialism and Macedonian impotence.

Partly because some of these states were Athenian colonies and allies, and partly because he feared, no doubt rightly, that Philip's ambition would not stop until he had conquered all of Greece, Demosthenes in speech after speech implored the Greeks in general and the Athenians in particular to fight to preserve the free institutions of the city-state from the menace of a military autocracy. The most famous of these speeches, the First Philippic, urged the Athenians to arouse themselves from apathy and prepare for a war which they little realized had already begun. It was delivered in 351 B.C. when Philip was busily intriguing and intervening in various petty wars among northern Greek states. Demosthenes' impassioned appeal went unheeded for the time being, for the Macedonian danger as yet seemed unreal and far away.

"YOUR AFFAIRS ARE AMISS BECAUSE YOU DO NOTHING"

First I say, you must not despair, men of Athens, under your present circumstances, wretched as they are; for that which is worst in the days that are past provides the best hope for the future. What do I mean? That your affairs are amiss, men of Athens, because you do nothing that is needed; for surely if you came into your present predicament while doing all that you should do, we could not then hope for any improvement.

Consider next, what some of you know by report and others know from experience, how powerful the Spartans were not long ago, yet how nobly and

From *First Philippic*, Chs. 2–12, 38–45, 48–50, based on the translation by Charles R. Kennedy.

patriotically you did what was worthy of Athens and undertook the war [378–371 B.C.] against them for the rights of Greece. Why do I remind you of this? To show and convince you, men of Athens, that nothing, if you are on your guard, is to be feared, nothing, if you are negligent, goes as you desire. Take for example the strength of the Spartans then, which you overcame by attention to your duties, and the insolence of this man now, by which through neglect of our interests we are confounded. But if there are any among you, men of Athens, who think Philip hard to be conquered in view of the magnitude of his existing power and the loss by us of all our strongholds, they reason rightly. But they should remember that once we held Pydna and Potidaea and Methone and all the region round about [Macedonia] as our own, and that many of the tribes now leagued with him were then independent and free and preferred our friendship to his. Had Philip then concluded that it was difficult to contend with Athens, when she had so many strong outposts on his borders and he was destitute of allies, he would never have gained his recent successes nor acquired his present power. But he saw clearly, men of Athens, that all these outposts were the open prizes of war, that by natural right the possessions of the absent belong to those on the spot and the possessions of the negligent to those who will venture and toil. Acting on this principle, he has won these places and holds them, either by right of conquest or by means of friendship and alliance — for all men will side with and respect those whom they see prepared and willing to take action.

Men of Athens, if you will adopt this principle now, though you did not do so before, and if each citizen who can and ought to give his service to the state is ready to give it without excuse, the rich to contribute, the able-bodied to enlist; if, put bluntly, you will become your own masters and each cease expecting to do nothing himself while his neighbor does everything for him, then, God willing, you will recover your own, get back what has been frittered away, and turn the tables on Philip. Do not imagine that his power is everlasting like that of a god. There are those who hate and fear and envy him, men of Athens, even among those who now seem most friendly. We can assume that all the feelings that are in other men belong also to his adherents. But now they are all cowed, having no refuge because of your apathy and indolence, which I urge you to abandon at once. For you see, men of Athens, to what pitch of arrogance the man has advanced: he leaves you not even the choice of action or inaction, he threatens and uses outrageous language, he cannot rest content in possession of his conquests but continually widens their circle, and, while we dally and delay, he throws his net around us.

When, then, Athenians, when will you act as becomes you? What are you waiting for? When it is necessary, I suppose. And how should we regard what is happening now? Surely, to free men the strongest necessity is the disgrace of their condition. Or tell me, do you like walking about and asking one another, "Is there any news?" Could there be more startling news than that a Macedonian is subduing Athenians and directing the affairs of Greece? "Is Philip dead?" you ask. "No, but he is sick." What difference does it make? Should anything happen to this man, you will soon create a second Philip if that is the way you attend to affairs. For this Philip has grown great not so much by his own strength as by our negligence. . . .

"BE IN ADVANCE OF CIRCUMSTANCES"

Shameful it is, men of Athens, to delude ourselves, and by putting off everything unpleasant to miss the time for action and be unable even to understand that skillful makers of war should not follow circumstances, but be in advance of them; for just as a general may be expected to lead his armies, so statesmen must guide circumstances if they are to carry out their policies and not be forced to follow at the heels of events. Yet you, men of Athens, with greater resources than any people — ships, infantry, cavalry, revenue — have never up to this day made proper use of them; instead, your war with Philip differs in no respect from the boxing of barbarians. For among them the party struck moves his hands to the spot; strike him somewhere else, there go his hands again. He neither can nor will parry a blow or look his opponent in the face. So you, if you hear of Philip in the Chersonese, vote to send relief there, if at Thermopylae, the same; if anywhere else, you run up and down after his heels. You take your orders from him; no plan have you devised, no event do you forsee, until you learn that something has happened or is about to happen. Formerly perhaps this was tolerable; now it is come to a crisis and is tolerable no longer. It seems to me, men of Athens, as if some god, ashamed for us because of our conduct, has inspired this activity in Philip. For if he were willing to remain at peace in possession of his conquests and prizes, attempting nothing further, some of you, I think, would be satisfied with a state of things which brands our nation with shame, cowardice, and deep disgrace. But by continually encroaching and grasping after more, he may possibly rouse you, if you have not completely abandoned hope. . . .

One thing is clear: he will not stop, unless someone stops him. Are we to wait for this? Do you think all is well if you dispatch empty ships and the vague hope of some deliverer? Shall we not man the fleet? Shall we not sail with at least a part of our troops, now if never before? Shall we not make a landing on his coast? "Where, then, shall we land?" someone asks. The war itself, men of Athens, will uncover the weak parts of his empire, if we make the effort; but if we sit at home listening to the orators accuse and malign one another, no good can ever be achieved. I believe that wherever you send a force of our own citizens — or even partly ours — there Heaven will bless us and Fortune will aid our struggle; but where you send out a general and an empty decree and high hopes from the debate, nothing that you desire is achieved; your enemies scoff, and your allies die of fright. . . .

"THE FUTURE DEPENDS ON OURSELVES"

Some of us go about saying that Philip is negotiating with Sparta for the destruction of Thebes and the dissolution of the free states; some say that he has sent envoys to the king [of Persia]; others say that he is fortifying cities in Illyria — thus do we wander about, each inventing his own story. For my part, men of Athens, I solemnly believe that Philip is intoxicated with the magnitude of his exploits and has many such dreams in his mind, for he sees the absence of opponents and is elated by his successes. But most certainly he has no such plan of action as to let the most foolish among us know what his intentions are, and the most foolish are these newsmongers. Let us dismiss such talk and remember only that Philip is our enemy, that he has long been robbing and insulting us, that wherever we have expected aid from others we have found hostility, that the future depends on ourselves, and that unless we are willing to fight him there we shall perhaps be forced to fight here. This let us remember, and then we shall decide wisely and be done with idle conjectures. You need not speculate about the future except to assure yourselves that it will be disastrous unless you face the facts and are willing to do your duty.

◆B◆ ISOCRATES, ADDRESS TO PHILIP

"A champion powerful in action."

By some Isocrates is praised as a man of statesmanlike vision who "saw far into the future" and "grasped the situation in its ecumenical aspect," while by others he is condemned as a traitorous visionary whose naïve idealism paved the way for the Macedonian conquest of Greece and the loss of Greek liberty. There are facts to support both estimates.

Isocrates' internationalism was based upon a realistic appraisal of the economic and political conditions of his time. He saw that only the removal of economic distress could bring an end to social and political disturbances in the Greek world. To solve this underlying economic problem he urged the Greeks to form a union under the leadership of Athens and Sparta for the purpose of waging war on the Persian Empire and opening Asia to Greek colonization. This program of imperialistic expansion to solve the ills of Greece was first expressed in 380 B.C. in his Panegyric oration:

> We cannot enjoy a sure peace unless we join together in a war against the barbarians, nor can the Greeks achieve concord until we wrest our material advantages from the same source and wage war against the same enemy. When these things are achieved, when we have been freed from the poverty surrounding our lives — which breaks up friendships, perverts to enmity the ties of kindred, and throws all mankind into wars and seditions — then surely we shall enjoy a spirit of concord and our mutual good-will will be real.

Years later, in his Address to Philip (346 B.C.), Isocrates' views had undergone one important change. He was now convinced that the Greeks were incapable of voluntarily forming themselves into a union, and he placed the blame

From "The Philippus," Chs. 8, 9, 12–16, 30, 31, 36–45, 72–75, 89, 120, 121, 152–155, based on the translation by J. H. Freese in *Orations of Isocrates*, Vol. I. By permission of G. Bell & Sons, Ltd.

squarely upon the excesses of democracy and the fickleness of the voters who preferred the harangues of demagogues to the reasoned arguments of statesmen. He complains that democracy has become so corrupt that "violence is regarded as democracy, lawlessness as liberty, impudence of speech as equality, and license to act in this manner as happiness." The only possible solution is to put the direction of affairs into the capable hands of a strong and wise leader.

We can trace Isocrates' growing disillusionment with democracy in his speeches. He first proposed to stem its radicalism and instability at Athens by a return to the limited democracy of the time of Solon. Then the state had been governed, he declared in his Areopagiticus oration (about 358 B.C.), "not by appointing magistrates from the general body of citizens by lot, but by selecting the best and most capable to fill each office." This, he argued, would put the direction of affairs where it belonged, in the hands of the aristocrats of birth and wealth, for only "those who are able to enjoy ease and who possess sufficient means should attend to public affairs." Security and stability must inevitably follow from the rule of such men, for "their only care was to avoid abolishing any of the institutions of their forefathers."

But all this was wishful thinking, and Isocrates turned gradually to the idea of one-man rule and proceeded to publish three tracts favoring the monarchical principle. Above all he became convinced that only through the efforts of a strong man, and not by such constitutional schemes as he had advocated earlier, could the unification of Greece and the conquest of Asia be accomplished. "Great and melancholy indeed is the change which has come over the old age of Isocrates," wrote the ninetenth-century liberal historian Grote in describing Isocrates' search for a strong man, a search which ended with the appearance of Philip of Macedon. The Address to Philip sets forth Isocrates' views in their final form. It contains a good deal of sound political and economic insight mixed with a naïve idealization of Philip's character and his future relations with the Greek states.

> By intrigue and aggression Philip had expanded southward with only inadequate and tardy Athenian resistance, despite Demosthenes' fervid warnings. In 346 this undeclared war was temporarily ended by a peace treaty — the "False Peace" as the Athenians later called it — and Isocrates refers to this peace in the opening selection from his Address to Philip, composed immediately thereafter.

Rejoicing at the resolutions which were adopted concerning peace, and thinking that they would be to your advantage and to that of all the rest of Hellas as well as to us, I was unable to divert my thoughts from the possibilities connected with it and was in a frame of mind to set to work immediately to consider how to give permanence to what we had achieved and to prevent our state from again, after a short interval, desiring other wars. An examination of these questions in my own mind led me to the conclusion that there was no other way for her to remain at peace except by the determination of the leading states of Hellas to put an end to mutual quarrels and carry the war into Asia, resolving to win from the barbarians the selfish advantages which they now look for at the expense of Hellenes. This was, indeed, the policy I had already advised in the *Panegyric* oration. . . .

"SPEECHES ARE INEFFECTUAL, TAKE THE LEAD"

To trouble the great festivals with oratory, addressing the crowds that come there, is really to speak without an audience; speeches of that kind are as ineffectual as laws and constitutions drawn up by the sophists. Those who wish, on the contrary, to do some practical good instead of idly chattering, and who think they have formed ideas of value to the community, must leave it to others to orate at the festivals while they seek a champion for their cause from among those who are powerful in speech and action and have great reputations — if, that is to say, anyone is to pay attention to them.

With this in mind, I chose to address my discourse to you, not making this choice to win your favor, although it is true that I should consider it of great importance to speak in a manner acceptable to you, but it was not to this end that I came to this decision. It was because I saw that all the other men of high repute were living under the rule of states and laws, without power to do anything but obey orders, and besides were far too weak for the enterprise which I shall propose, while to you alone had Fortune granted full power to send ambassadors to whomsoever you chose and to receive them from whomsoever you pleased, and to say whatever you thought it expedient to say, and besides this, that you were the possessor to a greater degree than any man in Hellas of wealth and power, the only two things in existence which can both persuade and compel — things which I think will also be required by the enterprise which I am going to propose. For my intention is to advise you to take the lead both in securing the harmony of Hellas and in conducting a campaign against the barbarians; and as persuasion is expedient in dealing with the Greeks, so force is useful in dealing with the barbarians. Such, then, is the general scope of my discourse. . . .

"APPEAR AS A BENEFACTOR"

I will now direct my remarks to the subject at hand. I say that, while neglecting none of your own interests, you ought to try to reconcile Argos, Sparta, Thebes, and our state; for if you are able to bring these together you will have no difficulty in uniting the others as well, for they are all under the influence of those that I have mentioned and when alarmed take refuge with one or the other of those states and depend on their aid. So if you can persuade four states only to act wisely, you will also release the rest from many evils. . . .

And you have a good opportunity, for . . . it is a good thing to appear as the benefactor of the leading states and at the same time to be furthering your own interests no less than theirs. Besides this, you will remove any unpleasant relations that you have had with any of them, for services rendered in the present crisis will cause all of you to forget the wrongs you have committed against each other in the past. Moreover, it is also beyond question that there is nothing which all men remember so well as benefits received in times of trouble. And you can see how they have been reduced to distress by war. . . .

Now perhaps someone will venture to oppose what I have said on the ground that I am endeavoring to persuade you to undertake an impossible task. He may say that the Argives can never be friends with the Lacedaemonians, or the Lacedaemonians with the Thebans, nor, in a word, can those who have been accustomed always to seek their selfish interests ever cast their lot with one another. I think that nothing of this kind could have been accomplished when our state, or again when Lacedaemon, was supreme in Hellas, for either of them could easily have blocked the attempt; but now I no longer have the same opinion of them. For I know that they have all been brought down to the same level by their misfortunes, so that I think they will much prefer the benefits of union to the selfish advantages of their former policy.

Furthermore, while I admit that there is no one else who could reconcile these states, to you such an undertaking is not difficult. For I see that you have accomplished many things which others considered hopeless and beyond expectations, and that therefore it would not be strange if you alone should be able to effect this union. In fact, men of high aspirations and eminent position should not attempt enterprises which any ordinary man could carry out, but should confine themselves to those which no one could attempt except men of abilities and power like yours.

Now I am surprised that those who consider it impossible that any such policy could be carried out do not know from their own experience, or have not heard from others, that there have been indeed many terrible wars after which the participants have been reconciled and done each other great services. What could exceed the enmity between Xerxes and the Hellenes? Yet everyone knows that both we and the Lacedaemonians were more pleased with the friendship of Xerxes than of those who helped us to found our respective empires. And need we refer to ancient history or to our relations with the barbarians? . . . When the Lacedaemonians made war against the Thebans with the intention of ravaging Boeotia and breaking up its league of cities, we gave our help and thwarted their desires; and when fortune changed again and the Thebans and all the Peloponnesians attempted to lay Sparta in ruins, we alone in Hellas made an alliance even with our ancient foes and contributed to their preservation. A man then would be full of folly who could observe such great reversals and see that states care nothing for former enmities or oaths or anything else save what they suppose to be for their advantage, caring only for what is expedient and devoting all their energies to that end, and still suppose that they would be of the same mind now as they always have been, especially with you to preside over the settlement of their disputes, which expediency recommends and present necessity compels. For I think that with these influences fighting on your side everything will turn out as it should. . . .

I should be satisfied with what I have already said on this subject had I not omitted one point, not from forgetfulness, but from a certain unwillingness to mention it. However, I think I ought to disclose it now, for I am of the opinion that it is as much to your advantage to hear what I have to say concerning it as it is becoming to me to speak with my accustomed freedom.

I perceive that you are being slandered by those who are jealous of you and are accustomed to throw their own cities into confusion — men who regard the peace which is for the good of all as a war against their own selfish interests. Unconcerned about everything else, they speak of nothing but your power, asserting that its growth is not for the interests of Hellas but against them, and that you have been already for a long time plotting against us all, and that, while you pretend to be anxious to assist the Messenians as soon as you have settled with the Phocians, you are in reality endeavoring to get the Peloponnesus into your power. . . . By talking such nonsense and pretending that they possess an accurate knowledge of affairs, and by predicting a speedy overthrow of the whole world, they persuade many. . . .

"CONCERNING THE EXPEDITION TO ASIA"

On these points no sensible man would venture to contradict me. And I think that it would occur to any others who should propose to advise in favor of the expedition to Asia to point out that all whose lot it has been to undertake war against the Persian king have risen from obscurity to renown, from poverty to wealth, and from low estate to the ownership of many lands and cities. . . .

What opinion must we think all will have of you if you actually do this; above all, if you endeavor to conquer the whole Persian empire, or at least to take from it a vast territory, what some call "Asia from Cilicia to Sinope," and in addition to build cities throughout this region and send there as colonists those who are now wanderers from want of their daily bread and who harass all whom they meet? For if we do not stop these men from joining together by providing them with sufficient to live upon, they will before we realize it become so numerous that they will be as great a cause of alarm to the Hellenes as to the barbarians. We, however, pay no attention to them; we ignore the existence of a terrible menace that threatens us all and is increasing day by day. . . .

CONCLUSION

. . . When Fortune honorably leads the way, it is a disgrace to lag behind and show yourself unready to advance in whatever direction she wishes.

I think that, while you ought to honor all those who speak well of what you have done, you ought to consider that the most honorable eulogy is that of those who consider your talents worthy of still greater deeds than those which you have already accomplished, great as they are, and who express themselves grateful to you, not only in the present, but who will cause posterity to admire your acts beyond those of all who have lived in former times. . . .

It remains to summarize what I have said in this discourse in order that, in as few words as possible, you may understand the chief point of my advice. I say that you ought to be the benefactor of the Hellenes, the king of Macedonia, and the ruler over as many barbarians as possible. If you succeed in this, all will be grateful to you — the Hellenes by reason of advantages enjoyed; the Macedonians, if you govern them like a king and not like a tyrant; and the rest of mankind, if they are freed by you from barbarian despotism and gain the protection of Hellas. How far my composition is well proportioned in style and in expression, I may reasonably expect to learn from my hearers; but that no one could give you advice that is better than this, or more suited to present circumstances, of that I feel convinced.

◆ C ◆ DEMOSTHENES, ON THE CROWN

"You took the most glorious course in pursuance of my counsels."

It is ironic that the most important speech by the greatest ancient orator should today be looked upon as the funeral oration on Greek freedom. Demosthenes delivered his oration On the Crown in 330 B.C., eight years after Philip had defeated and united the Greeks, as a defense of his unsuccessful policy of opposition to Philip. A member of Demosthenes' democratic party had proposed a law stating that Demosthenes should be "rewarded by the people with a golden crown for his integrity ... and because he had ever both by word and deed promoted the interests of the people and been zealous to do all the good in his power." The conservative party, whose policy of collaboration with Philip had been championed by Isocrates, was now in power under the leadership of Aeschines who promptly claimed the bill to be unconstitutional and brought suit against its proposer in the manner sanctioned by Athenian law. This gave Demosthenes an opportunity to justify his policy on the grounds of patriotism and devotion to the cause of Greek freedom against the foreign tyrant of a less civilized people. His impassioned plea easily convinced the judges, and although it is one of the verdicts of history that Demosthenes was "the man least capable of understanding his time of all that figured in antiquity as statesmen," yet most observers will agree with A. A. Trever that "such criticism is always academic, for with their high traditions the Athenians could do no other, and any self-respecting people today, in a similar situation, would do the same. Their fight for a losing cause must enlist sympathy and admiration wherever the spirit of liberty still lives. It is one of the tragic but inspiring chapters in the history of the human struggle for freedom." [1]

Chs. 60–69, 70–72, 196, 198–205, 208, based on the translation by Charles R. Kennedy.
[1] *History of Ancient Civilization*, 2 vols. (New York: Harcourt, Brace & Co., 1936), I, 402.

"PHILIP STARTED WITH A GREAT ADVANTAGE"

The conquests which Philip seized and held before I commenced life as a statesman and orator, I shall pass over, as I do not think they concern me. But what
he was prevented from doing from the day of my entering public life, I will call
to your mind and give a full account of them, premising one thing only —
Philip started, men of Athens, with a great advantage. It happened that among
the Greeks — not some, but all alike — there sprang up a crop of traitors and
venal wretches such as the memory of man had never known before. These he
got for his agents and supporters. The Greeks, already quarrelsome and un-
friendly to each other, he brought into a still worse condition. By deceiving
some, bribing some, and corrupting others in every way possible, he split the
Greeks into many factions when they all had one common interest — to prevent his aggrandizement. When the Greeks were in such a condition, all ignorant of the gathering and growing danger, you should consider, men of Athens,
what was the right policy for our city to adopt. And on this question I ought to
be called to account, for I was the man who took a firm position in that area of
public affairs.

"WHAT SHOULD ATHENS HAVE DONE?"

Should Athens, Aeschines, have cast off her spirit and dignity, and, in the style
of Thessalians and Dolopians, helped Philip to acquire the domination of
Greece and extinguish the honors and rights of our ancestors? Or, if she did not
do this — which indeed would have been shameful — was it right that what
she saw would happen if unprevented, and was for a long time aware of, she
should allow to happen?

I would now like to ask the severest critic of our acts which party he would
have wished Athens to join: those who contributed to the disgraces and disasters
of the Greeks (the party of the Thessalians and their followers), or those who
permitted it all for the hope of selfish advantage (here we may put the Arcadi-
ans, Messenians, and Argives)? But many of them, or rather all, have fared
worse than we. If Philip after his victory had immediately departed and kept
the peace without molesting any of his own allies or the Greeks, there might
have been some grounds for blaming and reproaching those who opposed his
enterprises. But when he has stripped all alike of their dignity, their authority,
their liberty — even their constitutions, where he was able — can it be doubted
that you took the most glorious course in pursuance of my counsels?

But I return to the question: What should Athens, Aeschines, have done
when she saw Philip establishing an empire and dominion over Greece? What
was I, a statesman at Athens, to advise or move — for this is fundamental — I
who knew that from the earliest time, until the day of my own mounting the
platform, our country had ever striven for preeminence in honor and renown,
and had expended more blood and treasure for the sake of glory and the interest of all Greece than the rest of the Greeks had expended in their own interests; who saw that Philip himself, with whom we were contending, had, in

the struggle for power and empire, had his eye cut out, his collarbone fractured, his hand and leg mutilated, and was ready and willing to sacrifice any part of his body that Fortune chose to take provided he could live with the remainder in honor and glory? Surely no one will venture to say this — that it was fitting for a man born at Pella, then an obscure and insignificant place, to possess such inborn spirit as to aspire to the mastery of Greece and form the project in his mind, while you, who are Athenians, day after day in speeches and in dramas reminded of the courage of your ancestors, should have been so naturally base as of your own free will and accord to surrender to Philip the liberty of Greece. No man will say this!

"THE ONLY COURSE THAT REMAINED"

The only course then that remained was a just resistance to all his unjust actions against you. Such a course you took from the beginning, properly and fittingly, and I assisted by motions and counsels during the period of my political life — I acknowledge it. . . . But I ask — the man who was annexing Euboea and making it a fortress against Attica, attacking Megara, seizing Oreus, razing Porthmus, setting up Philistides as tyrant in Oreus and Clitarchus in Eretria, subjugating the Hellespont, beseiging Byzantium, destroying some Greek cities and restoring exiles to others — was he by all these acts committing injustice, breaking the truce, violating the peace, or not? Was it right that any of the Greeks should rise up to prevent these actions, or not? If not, if Greece was to present the spectacle of a proverbial [cowardly and non-resisting] Mysian prey, while Athenians still lived and breathed, then I have exceeded my duty in speaking on the subject, and Athens has exceeded her duty in following my counsels — I admit that every measure has been a misdeed, a blunder of mine. But if someone ought to have arisen to prevent these things, who but the Athenian people should it have been? Such was my policy. I saw Philip reducing all men to subjection, and I opposed him; I continued warning and exhorting you not to surrender. . . .

"A RATHER PARADOXICAL ASSERTION"

All this, at such length, have I addressed to you, men of the jury, and to the outer circle of spectators; as for this contemptible fellow, a short and plain answer is enough. If the future were revealed to you alone, Aeschines, when the state was deliberating, you ought to have forewarned us at the time. If you did not foresee it, you are responsible for the same ignorance as the rest. Why then do you accuse me rather than I you? . . . Is anything going on that appears good for the people? Aeschines is silent. Has anything regrettable happened or gone amiss? Forth comes Aeschines, just as old fractures and sprains become active when the body is attacked by some disease.

But since he insists so strongly on results, I will make a rather paradoxical assertion, and I beg of you not to marvel at its boldness but to consider what I say with good will. If the outcome had been completely clear, if all had foreseen it and you, Aeschines, had foretold it and protested with clamor and out-cry — you who never opened your mouth — not even then should the city have abandoned her policy if she had any regard for glory, or ancestry, or the future. As it is, she appears to have failed, a thing to which all men are liable if the gods so decide. But if Athens, claiming to be the leader of Greece, had abandoned her claim, she would have incurred the charge of betraying all to Philip. Why, had we resigned without a struggle that which our ancestors had encountered every danger to win, who would not have spit upon you, Aeschines? Not on the city, not on me! With what countenance could we have looked on strangers visiting the city if the result had been what it is, and Philip had been chosen master of all Greece and others apart from us had made the struggle to prevent it, especially since in former times our country had never preferred an ignominious security to the battle for honor? For what Greek or what barbarian does not know that the Thebans, or the Spartans who were supreme before them, or the Persian king, would gratefully and gladly have allowed Athens to take what she pleased and hold what she had provided she obey their will and allow another power to be the leader of Greece? But it seems that to the Athenians of that day such conduct would not have been national, or natural, or endurable; no one could at any period of time persuade the city to attach herself to the security of slavery to the powerful and unjust; through every age has she persevered in a perilous struggle for first place in honor and glory. And this you esteem so noble and consistent with your character that among your ancestors you honor most those who acted in such a spirit. And rightly so. For who would not admire the courage of those men who resolutely embarked in their warships and left country and home rather than obey another's orders, choosing Themistocles, who gave such counsel, for their general, and stoning Cyrsilus to death for advising submission — not only Cyrsilus; your wives stoned his wife as well. The Athenians of that day looked not for an orator or a general who would lead them to a pleasant servitude; they scorned to live if it could not be in freedom. Each of them considered that he was not born to his father or mother only, but also to his country. What is the difference? He who thinks himself born for his parents only is satisfied to wait for his fated and natural end; he who thinks himself born for his country as well will sooner die than see her in slavery, and he will regard the insults and indignities which must be borne in a city enslaved as more to be feared than death itself. . . .

"NEVER CAN YOU HAVE DONE WRONG, MEN OF ATHENS!"

But never, never can you have done wrong, men of Athens, in undertaking the battle for the freedom and safety of all! I swear it by your ancestors — those who met the peril at Marathon, those who took the field at Plataea, those in the sea battles at Salamis and Artemisium, and many other brave men who re-pose in the public monuments, all of whom alike, as being worthy of the same honor, the country buried, Aeschines, not the successful and victorious alone! For the duty of brave men has been done by all; their fortune has been such as heaven assigned to each.

32

Alexander the Great

"Divinely sent to govern the world"

The amazing conquests of Alexander the Great (356–323 B.C.), who in ten short years brought under his sway a vast empire stretching from Greece to India, ushered in a new epoch in history, the Hellenistic Age. With the barriers between East and West removed, Greek and oriental cultures met and in time produced a cultural amalgam. The long range significance of Alexander's conquests becomes apparent when we consider that much of Roman culture was borrowed from the Hellenistic world — Christianity being an outstanding example — and that Rome in turn handed on this Hellenistic heritage to the Germanic West.

To many who lived in the cosmopolitan atmosphere of the Hellenistic and Roman periods, the union of East and West in one world was thought to have been planned by Alexander even before he set foot on the soil of Asia. Various of Alexander's later military and administrative policies were cited in support of this view: the blending of orientals with Greeks and Macedonians in his army and administration; the founding of "seventy cities" in the East, in which he settled many Greek and Macedonian veterans; his marriages to two oriental princesses, and the encouraging of his officers and men to take foreign wives; the promotion of empire-wide trade by the opening of new trade routes, the founding of port cities, and the minting of a standard coinage; and the demand that the Greek city-states accord him "divine honors" in the manner of an oriental monarch. Especially significant was the dramatic incident at Opis in Babylonia where, following his return from India, Alexander ordered the dismissal of his over-aged and maimed Macedonian veterans and their replacement by Persians. We are told that the aggrieved veterans mutinied after shouting at Alexander, "You have made Persians your kinsmen!" When order was restored, Alexander held a feast of reconciliation, attended by nine thousand Macedonians and Persians, and solemnized by Greek seers and Magian priests. Alexander himself capped the ceremonies with a prayer that one modern scholar has called a revolution in human thought — he prayed "for concord and partnership in the empire between Macedonians and Persians."

Plutarch's "On the Fortune or the Virtue of Alexander the Great" is a youthful and idealized essay written to refute the argument that Alexander's

Reprinted with permission of The Macmillan Company from *De Alexandri Magni Fortuna aut Virtute, Oratio i*, by Plutarch, tr. Truesdell S. Brown, *Sources in Western Civilization: Ancient Greece*, pp. 194–200, 202. Copyright © The Free Press of Glencoe, a Division of The Macmillan Company, 1965.

campaign, like the one planned by his father Philip, was intended only to avenge the harm done to Greece by Xerxes' invasion of 480 B.C. (Selection 23), and that his conquest of a vast empire was the unforeseen result of chance and luck. Some modern scholars, no doubt reflecting the cosmopolitan spirit of our present age, have found in Plutarch's essay much support for the view that it was Alexander's considered policy over many years to create a world state founded, as one historian has put it, on his "dream of the brotherhood of man, a dream of peace and union between Greek and barbarian, . . . that mankind should contemplate not exclusive, 'national' societies, but universalism, the idea of the oecumene, or 'inhabited world,' where all men are indeed sons of one Father." [1]

"FORTUNE WAS MY ADVERSARY"

Now Fortune argues that Alexander belongs to her and to her alone. However, this ought to be denied in the name of philosophy and even more so because of the wrath and indignation of Alexander at the notion that he received as a gift of Fortune that empire which he purchased with a copious expenditure of his blood and repeated wounds,

> And many sleepless nights he spent
> And bloody days consumed while making war,

contending with invincible forces, nations without number, impassable rivers, and rocks above the range of bow and arrow, helped only by good judgment, perseverance, courage and self-control.

And I imagine he might address Fortune when she claimed these deeds for herself in these words: "Do not depreciate my honor, or strip me of my fame . . . my body bears many indications that Fortune was my adversary, not my ally. First I was struck in the head by a stone and clubbed on the neck in the Illyrian land. Later, at the Granicus, my head was broken by the lone knife of a barbarian, and at Issus my thigh was gashed with a sword. Before Gaza my ankle was pierced by an arrow, when I fell heavily, dislocating my shoulder. At Maracanda my shin was broken by an arrow. Then came blows and the ravages of famine in the Indian lands. Among the Aspasians I was shot in the shoulder by an arrow; in the land of the Gandridae in the leg; among the Malli a missile from a bow reached me, burying its iron point in my breast, and when I had also been struck by a club along the neck, the ladders that had been raised against the walls gave way, and Fortune, taking delight in such a deed, penned me up there alone, not to contend with famous adversaries but with unknown barbarians. And if Ptolemy had not covered me with his shield and if Limnaeus had not died in front of me after intercepting countless missiles, and if the Macedonians had not torn down the walls in their rage, then that nameless barbarian village would have been Alexander's tomb."

And in this same expedition gales, droughts, deep rivers, rocks higher than

[1] Charles Alexander Robinson, Jr., *Alexander the Great: The Meeting of East and West in World Government and Brotherhood* (New York: E. P. Dutton and Co., 1947), p. 225.

a bird can fly, monstrous beasts, savage customs, a succession of petty rulers and constant betrayals were also encountered. But even before the expedition itself, Greece fought back after the ways of Philip. The Thebans shook the dust of Chaeronea from their weapons, rising up after disaster while Athens extended a helping hand. All Macedon was ripe for rebellion, looking secretly to Amyntas and the sons of Aeropus. The Illyrians erupted and the state of affairs in Scythia threatened her troubled neighbors. Persian gold, diffused in every direction by popular orators, stirred up the Peloponnese. Philip's treasury was empty and there was even a deficit of two hundred talents, as Onesicritus relates. With such an appalling lack of money and with the government still in confusion a young man just barely beyond boyhood had the audacity to entertain thoughts of Babylon and Susa, and even of an empire embracing all mankind — and this, mind you, with thirty thousand foot and four thousand horse. Those at least are the figures given by Aristobulus; according to King Ptolemy there were thirty thousand foot and five thousand horse, while Anaximenes gives 43,500 foot and 5,500 horse. The great and magnificent sum which Fortune had provided for his traveling chest was seventy talents, as Aristobulus tells it, but Duris says he had only supplies for thirty days.

"ALEXANDER REVEALED AS A PHILOSOPHER"

Then Alexander must have been an unthinking hothead to challenge such a formidable power with his meager resources? Not at all. Did anyone ever start out for war with greater or better preparation for succeeding than nobility of character, intelligence, self-mastery and courage — with which philosophy had equipped him for his journey? He crossed over against the Persians with greater resources furnished by his teacher Aristotle than by his father Philip. In fact there are writers who allege that Alexander once said that he had brought the *Iliad* and the *Odyssey* along as a provision for the army; and we believe them, honoring Homer. And if anyone maintains that he only used Homer for relaxation after toil and as a pleasant way of diverting his leisure moments, but that his real provision for the journey lay in the philosophic doctrines, in discourses on fearlessness and valor, on self-mastery and on high-mindedness we look on this with scorn. For obviously Alexander wrote nothing about syllogisms or propositions, and he never held forth in the Lyceum or presented a thesis for debate in the Academy, while such a view would restrict philosophy to things of this sort as though it were made up of words rather than deeds. Yet there were famous philosophers like Pythagoras, or Socrates, or Arcesilaus or Carneades who wrote nothing. And these men were not occupied with such great wars, or civilizing barbarian princes, or establishing Greek cities among savage peoples, nor did they continue pressing on against lawless and ignorant tribes in order to instruct them in law and peace. Instead, though they did have the time, they abandoned writing to the sophists. Then why are they believed to have been philosophers? Because of what they said, how they lived and what they taught. Then let Alexander be judged on the same basis and he will be revealed as a philosopher by what he said, by what he did and by what he taught.

But first and, if you will, most surprising, look at Alexander's pupils and compare them with those of Socrates and Plato. Now they were teaching adaptable scholars who spoke the same language, for even if they knew nothing else they all understood Greek. Despite this, there were many of them whom they failed to convince: the Critiases, Alcibiadeses and Clitophons went astray, spitting out their doctrines as a horse gets rid of a bit. But then look at Alexander's instruction: he taught marriage to the Hyrcanians, he showed the Arachosians how to farm, he persuaded the Sogdianians to support their fathers instead of killing them, and induced the Persians to respect their mothers and not to marry them. What an admirable philosophy, which caused the Indians to bow down before the gods of Greece, the Scythians to bury their dead instead of devouring them! We are astonished at the ability of Carneades if he hellenizes Clitomachus, who was a Carthaginian by birth formerly named Hasdrubal, and we also admire Zeno for his skill if he induces Diogenes of Babylon to become a philosopher. But thanks to Alexander Homer was read in Asia, and the sons of Persia, Susiana, and Gedrosia sang the choruses of Euripides and Sophocles. Now Socrates was brought to judgment for introducing foreign gods by informers in Athens, but Alexander caused Bactra and the Caucasus to worship the gods of Greece. While Plato drew up a single form of government which was so strict he could induce no one to adopt it, Alexander, by founding more than seventy cities among the barbarian tribes, and seeding Asia with Greek outposts, suppressed their savage and uncivilized customs. Although a few of us read about the laws of Plato, countless numbers have adopted and continue to use the laws of Alexander. Those whom Alexander conquered were more fortunate than those who escaped, because there was no one to correct their foolish way of life, while the conquerer forced his subjects to live in prosperity. Therefore Themistocles' remark when he received munificent gifts from the king during his exile and obtained three tribute-paying cities — one to furnish him with grain, one with wine and the other with condiments: "Oh, my children, had we not been ruined, we would have been ruined indeed!" — was a remark that might have been made even more appropriately by those whom Alexander conquered. For they would not have been civilized unless they had been conquered. And Egypt would not have had its Alexandria, or Mesopotamia its Seleuceia, or India its Bucephalia, nor would the Caucasus have had a Greek city founded there, yet it is by means of such cities that savagery is gradually extinguished and bad customs changed into good ones. Now if philosophers really set such store by refining and altering rough and ignorant dispositions then Alexander, who is seen transforming countless races and natural savages, ought truly to be regarded as a very great philosopher.

"MAKING ALL MANKIND A SINGLE PEOPLE"

Now the much-admired *Republic* of Zeno, the founder of the Stoic school, adds up to this one thing: that we ought not to live in cities or in demes, each distinguished by its own regulations, but we should look on all men as fellow citizens and demesmen, having one life and one world, feeding together like a single herd sharing a common pasture. Zeno, however, wrote this as a dream, a philosophic image of a well-governed state, while Alexander expressed his views by deeds. He did not follow Aristotle's advice to treat the Greeks as a leader, the barbarians as a master, cultivating the former as friends and kinsmen, and treating the latter as animals or plants. Had he done so his kingdom would have been filled with warfare, banishments and secret plots, but he regarded himself as divinely sent to mediate and govern the world. And those whom he failed to win over by persuasion he overpowered in arms, bringing them together from every land, combining, as it were in a loving cup, their lives, customs, marriages and manner of living; he bade them all look on the inhabited world as their native land, on his camp as their citadel and protection, on good men as their kinsmen and evil doers as aliens, and not to distinguish Greek from barbarian by the chlamys, or the shield, or the sword, or the sleeved tunic but to associate Hellenism with virtue and barbarism with evil doing; and to regard their clothing, food, marriages and manners as common to all, blended together by their blood and their children.

Now Demaratus of Corinth, the mercenary and a friend of Philip's, wept tears of joy when he saw Alexander in Susa, exclaiming that those Greeks who had died earlier had been robbed of great happiness since they had not seen Alexander sitting on Darius' throne. But I, by Zeus, do not envy those who saw a spectacle which is associated with Fortune and lesser kings, but I think I would have been more pleased at the fair and blessed sight of the marriage procession when, bringing together one hundred Persian brides and one hundred Greek and Macedonian grooms into a single tent bedecked with gold, with a single hearth and a single table, he was the first, crowned with flowers, to raise the hymeneal song, singing as it were a song of friendship, while he joined together the greatest and most powerful peoples into one community by wedlock: the bridegroom of one, but for everyone at once a bride-giver, a father and a sponsor. I would gladly have said: "O barbarous and foolish Xerxes, your great efforts in putting a bridge across the Hellespont were wasted, for intelligent rulers do not join Asia to Europe in this way with planks, or floats or lifeless and unfeeling fetters; but they unite the races by true laws, and chaste marriages and common offspring." ...

... For he did not cross Asia like a robber, nor did he have it in mind to ravage and despoil it for the booty and loot presented by such an unheard-of stroke of fortune — the way Hannibal treated Italy later on, or the way the Treres acted earlier in Ionia or the Scythians in Media. Instead he conducted himself as he did out of a desire to subject all the races in the world to one rule and one form of government, making all mankind a single people. Had not the divinity that sent Alexander recalled his soul so soon, there would have been a single law, as it were, watching over all mankind, and all men would have looked to one form of justice as their common source of light. But now, that portion of the world that never beheld Alexander has remained as if deprived of the sun.

Now, at the outset, the very purpose of his expedition commends the man as a philosopher for aiming not at wealth and luxury for himself but at bringing peace, harmony and mutual fellowship to all men. Secondly, let us examine what he said, since other kings and rulers reveal their character by the spirit of their pronouncements. . . . When he talked to Diogenes himself, in Corinth, he was so captivated and overwhelmed by the man's way of life and reputation that he would often refer to him later, saying: "If I were not Alexander, I would like to be Diogenes!" By this he meant: . . . "If I did not intend to blend the customs of the Greeks and the barbarians; to cross every continent and tame it; to search out the farthest points of land and sea; to make Ocean the boundary of Macedon; and if I did not mean to transplant the peace and the justice of Greece to every people, even then I would not waste my energies in useless luxury, but I would emulate the frugality of Diogenes. But now, Diogenes, excuse me. I am imitating Heracles, rivalling Perseus and following in the footsteps of Dionysus, the ancestor of my line. I wish to bring the chorus of victorious Greeks to India once more, and to renew the memory of Bacchic revels among the wild mountainous peoples beyond the Caucasus. And there are said to be holy men in those parts who live under laws of their own, a rough and naked sect devoting their lives to the god. They are even more self-denying than Diogenes, in that they require no wallet, for they do not save any food since the land continually provides them with a fresh supply. Flowing rivers furnish them with drink, trees shed their foliage over them and herbs of the field serve them as a bed. Thanks to me they will come to know of Diogenes, and Diogenes of them. I, too, must coin money, and stamp the form of a Greek constitution on a barbarian mold."

Well, then, do his deeds appear to be primarily the result of chance? Power in war? Government by force? Do they not rather suggest the great courage and justice, the great self-control and mildness of one who does everything in an orderly and intelligent manner and in accordance with a sober and sagacious plan?

------------------------ 33 ------------------------

Hellenistic Philosophy: The Cynic Counter-Culture

Soon after the death of Socrates, his pupils began to differ radically from one another concerning the content of his teaching, and a number of different Socratic schools eventually arose. Plato held that Socrates was a systematic philosopher who created the theory of Ideas, the doctrine of the immortality

From Lucian, "The Cynic." Reprinted by permission of the publishers and The Loeb Classical Library from Lucian, *Dialogues*, Vol. VIII, tr. by M. D. MacLeod. Cambridge, Mass.: Harvard University Press, © 1967 by the President and Fellows of Harvard College.

of the soul, and the concept of an ideal state. Other pupils, influenced by the impact of Socrates' teaching on their own lives, argued that he was not a philosopher in that sense at all, but a moral hero whose character and manner of living should be emulated. While Plato held that Socrates' pretense of knowing nothing was only the first step on the way to a knowledge of the eternal Ideas that were preexistent in the soul, Antisthenes, who together with his more radical disciple Diogenes is considered the founder of the Cynic school of philosophy, denied that it was possible to know anything. And while Plato went on to develop Socrates' basic assumption that all education must be political, training Athenians to be either good rulers or good subjects, Antisthenes preached the need to be a "citizen of the world" (kosmopolites) in a new society free of the conventional laws and mores of the Greek city-states. Diogenes, who was an older contemporary of Alexander the Great, ex-aggerated Socrates' criticism of the values pursued by his fellow citizens (see Selection 28B) and his ideal of frugality and independence of external things — autarky, or self-sufficiency. Frugality in Diogenes became asceticism — he looked and acted the part of a beggar and lived in a large wine cask — and self-sufficiency meant the severence of all human ties. He and many other Cynics were exhibitionists who dramatized their counter-culture and scandalized sober citizens by their biting attacks on the Establishment and by their unconventional appearance and behavior. ("When my body needs sexual satisfaction," Antisthenes once said, "whatever lies close to hand is good enough for me. So the women I associate with are exceedingly grateful to me, for no one else will approach them.")

Like the other major Hellenistic philosophies — Skepticism (Selection 44A), Epicureanism (Selection 46), and Stoicism (Selection 51) — Cynicism later spread through much of the Roman world when conditions similar to those of the Hellenistic Age appeared. The second century A.D. in particular witnessed large numbers of Cynic philosophers crisscrossing the Empire and preaching and actively demonstrating the Cynic ideal of the virtuous wise man who has achieved perfect happiness by freeing himself from the external world. The Syrian-born and Greek-educated Lucian of Samosata (ca. 120–190 A.D.), rhetorician and man of letters, rationalist and skeptic, frequently excoriated those Cynic philosophers he considered to be charlatans. But in his dialogue "The Cynic," which purports to be a conversation between himself ("Lycinus") and a Cynic philosopher, Lucian presents a sympathetic picture of the Cynic wise man whose patron saint is that energetic battler against overwhelming odds, the mythical hero Heracles, and who has achieved true self-sufficiency by rejecting the values and conventions of society. He is most like the gods be-cause he, too, needs nothing.

Lycinus. You there, why in heaven's name have you the beard and the long hair, but no shirt? Why do you expose your body to view, and go barefooted, adopting by choice this nomadic anti-social and bestial life? Why unlike all others do you abuse your body by ever inflicting on it what it likes least, wan-dering around and prepared to sleep anywhere at all on the hard ground, so that your old cloak carries about a plentiful supply of filth, though it was never fine or soft or gay?

Cynic. I need no such cloak. Mine is the kind that can be provided most easily and affords least trouble to its owner. Such a cloak is all I need. But *you* tell *me* something, I beg you. Don't you think that there's vice in extravagance?

Lycinus. Yes indeed.

Cynic. And virtue in economy?

Lycinus. Yes indeed.

Cynic. Why, then, when you see me living a more economical life than the average man, and them living a more extravagant life, do you find fault with me rather than with them?

Lycinus. Because — by Zeus! — I do not think your manner of life more economical than that of the average man, but more wanting — or rather completely wanting and ill-provided. For you're no better than the paupers who beg for their daily bread. . . .

Cynic. Do you think that Heracles, the best of all mankind, a godlike man and rightly considered a god, was compelled by an evil star to go around naked, wearing only a skin and needing none of the same things as you do? No, *he* was not ill-starred, he who brought the rest of men relief from their banes, nor was *he* destitute who was the master of both land and sea; for no matter what he essayed, he prevailed over all everywhere, and never encountered his equal or superior, till he left the realm of men. Do you think that *he* couldn't provide blankets and shoes, and that was why he went around in the state he did? No one could say that; no, he had self-control and hardness; he wished to be powerful, not to enjoy luxury. . . . These men of old therefore are the ones that *I* admire and should like to emulate, but the men of today I do not admire for the "wonderful" prosperity they enjoy in the matter of food and clothing, and when they smooth and depilate every part of their bodies, not even allowing any of their private parts to remain in its natural condition.

I pray that I may have feet no different from horses' hooves, as they say were those of Chiron [the Centaur], and that I myself may not need bedclothes any more than do the lions, nor expensive fare any more than do the dogs. But may I have for bed to meet my needs the whole earth, may I consider the universe my house, and choose for food that which is easiest to procure, gold and silver may I not need, neither I nor any of my friends. For from the desire for these grow up all men's ills — civic strife, wars, conspiracies and murders. All these have as their fountainhead the desire for more. But may this desire be far from us, and never may I reach out for more than my share, but be able to put up with less than my share.

Such, you see, are our wishes, wishes assuredly far different from those of most men. Nor is it any wonder that we differ from them in dress when we differ so much from them in principles too. But you surprise me by the way that you think that a lyre-player has a particular uniform and garb, and, by heavens, that a piper has his uniform, and a tragic actor his garb, but, when it comes to a good man, you don't think that he has his own dress and garb, but should wear the same as the average man, and that too although the average man is depraved. If good men need one particular dress of their own, what one would be more suitable than this dress which seems quite shameless to debauched men and which they would most deprecate for themselves?

Therefore my dress is, as you see, a dirty shaggy skin, a worn cloak, long hair and bare feet, but yours is just like that of the sodomites and no one could tell yours from theirs either by the color of your cloaks, or by the softness and number of your tunics, or by your wraps, shoes, elaborate hair-styles, or your scent. For nowadays you reek of scent just like them — you, who are the most fortunate of men! Yet of what value can one think a man who smells the same as a sodomite? So it is that you are no more able to endure hardships than they are, and no less amenable to pleasures than they. Moreover, your food is the same as theirs, you sleep like them and walk like them — or rather just like them prefer not to walk but are carried like baggage, some of you by men, others by beasts. But I am carried by my feet wherever I need to go, and I am able to put up with cold, endure heat and show no resentment at the works of the gods, because I am unfortunate, whereas you, because of your good fortune, are pleased with nothing that happens, and always find fault, unwilling to put up with what you have, but eager for what you have not, in winter praying for summer, and in summer for winter, in hot weather for cold, and in cold weather for hot, showing yourselves as hard to please and as querulous as invalids. But whereas the cause of *their* behavior is illness, the cause of *yours* is your character.

Again you would have us change and you would reform our manner of life for us because we often are ill-advised in what we do, though you yourselves bestow no thought on your own actions, basing none of them on rational judgment, but upon habit and appetite. Therefore you are exactly the same as men carried along by a torrent; for they are carried along wherever the current takes them, and you wherever your appetites take you. Your situation is just like what they say happened to the man who mounted a mad horse. For it rushed off, carrying him with it; and he couldn't dismount again because the horse kept running. Then someone who met them asked him where he was off to, and he replied, "Wherever this fellow decides," indicating the horse. Now if anyone asks you where you're heading for, if you wish to tell the truth, you will say simply that it's where your appetites choose, or more specifically where pleasure chooses, or now where ambition, or now again where avarice chooses; and sometimes temper, sometimes fear, or sometimes something else of the sort seems to carry you off. For you are carried along on the back not of one but of many horses, and different ones at different times — but all of them mad. As a result they carry you away towards cliffs and chasms. But before you fall you are quite unaware of what is going to happen to you.

But this worn cloak which you mock, and my long hair and my dress are so effective that they enable me to live in peace of mind doing what I want to do and keeping the company of my choice. For the fools and the uninstructed do not wish to associate with one who dresses as I do, while the fops turn away while they're still a long way off. But my associates are the most intelligent and decent of men, and those with an appetite for virtue. These men are my particular associates, for I rejoice in the company of men like them. But I dance no attendance at the doors of the so-called fortunate, but consider their golden crowns and their purple robes mere pride, and I laugh at the fellows who wear them.

And I'd have you know that my style of dress becomes not only good men but also gods, though you go on to mock it; and so consider the statues of the gods. Do you think they are like you or like me? And don't confine your attentions to the statues of the Greeks, but go round examining foreigners' temples too, to see whether the gods themselves have long hair and beards as I do, or whether their statues and paintings show them close-shaven like you. What's more, you will see they are just like me not only in these respects but also in having no shirt. How then can you still have the effrontery to describe my style of dress as contemptible, when it's obvious that it's good enough even for gods?

34

Hellenistic Literature: Theocritus

Hellenistic literature can best be understood in relation to the environment of the new age (following the conquests of Alexander) out of which it grew. The Greek city-state was now dwarfed and largely dominated by the Hellenistic empires, and the creativeness it had helped to inspire and sustain in its citizens dried up. Just as Hellenistic philosophy — and religion — centered attention upon the individual person and not upon society, so the literature of the age reflected an extreme individualism. Two general types of Hellenistic literature flourished. One represents the activity of a large number of individual scholars who directed their energies to criticizing, summarizing, and interpreting the creative work of the past. They secluded themselves in vast libraries and wrote books about books. To them we owe the preservation of much of Greek classical literature in the form in which it has come down to us. The other type was written for a larger audience by poets whose reaction to life was either to escape from it by immersing themselves romantically in love and in nature, or to face it and depict a "slice of life" in all its naked reality. In general, Hellenistic literature lacks deep insight into the meaning of life. Most of it is second- or third-rate, but among the exceptions the Idyls ("little pictures") of Theocritus of Syracuse (about 315–250 B.C.) stand out.

◆A◆ IDYL XI

Romanticized love and nature

It would be difficult to find a better illustration of the contrast between the Hellenic and the Hellenistic spirit than is provided by the following lines. The first was written in the fifth century on the tomb of Aeschylus:

> This tomb hides Aeschylus, Athenian born,
> Euphorion's son, amid far Gela's corn —
> How good a fighter, Marathon could tell,
> The long-haired Persian knows it but too well! [1]
>
> Trans. Alfred Zimmern

Here there is no element of subjectivity or individualism; Aeschylus and his contemporaries recognized that meaning in life was to be found chiefly in man's activity in peace and war as a citizen. Thus there is no mention of the fact that Aeschylus was a supreme dramatic poet; in Alfred Zimmern's words, "the poet is swallowed up in the citizen."

The second selection is by Moschus, a younger contemporary of Theocritus, and it affords a vivid and instructive contrast:

> Would that my father had taught me the craft of a keeper of sheep,
> For so in the shade of the elm-tree, or under the rocks on the steep,
> Piping on reeds I had sat, and had lulled my sorrow to sleep.
>
> Trans. Ernest Myers

Here there is displayed no zest for life arising out of a deep social consciousness, but only an extreme individualism seeking release from world-weariness by a romantic escape into a sentimentalized dream-world of nature.

Theocritus' pastoral idyls are the first of this romantic literary type and are clearly superior, in their spontaneity, naturalness, and musical style to their later imitations in Hellenistic, Roman, and early modern times. In his eleventh idyl he romanticizes an old myth and uses it as a vehicle to idealize the simple life of shepherds and to portray the tribulations of romantic love.

THE CYCLOPS IN LOVE

Nicias, the physician and poet, being in love, Theocritus reminds him that in song lies the only remedy. It was by song, he says, that the Cyclops, Polyphemus, got him some ease, when he was in love with Galatea, the sea-nymph.

The idyl displays, in the most graceful manner, the Alexandrian taste

---

[1] From Alfred Zimmern, *The Greek Commonwealth*, 5th ed., 1931, p. 70. By permission of the Oxford University Press, Oxford.

for turning Greek mythology into love stories. No creature could be more remote from love than the original Polyphemus, the cannibal giant of the Odyssey.

There is none other medicine, Nicias, against Love, neither unguent, methinks, nor salve to sprinkle — none, save the Muses of Pieria! Now a delicate thing is their minstrelsy in man's life, and a sweet, but hard to procure. Methinks thou know'st this well, who art thyself a leech, and beyond all men art plainly dear to the Muses nine.

'Twas surely thus the Cyclops fleeted his life most easily, he that dwelt among us — Polyphemus of old time — when the beard was yet young on his cheek and chin; and he loved Galatea. He loved, not with apples, not roses, nor locks of hair, but with fatal frenzy, and all things else he held but trifles by the way. Many a time from the green pastures would his ewes stray back, self-shepherded, to the fold. But he was singing of Galatea, and pining in his place he sat by the sea-weed of the beach, from the dawn of day, with the direst hurt beneath his breast of mighty Cypris's sending — the wound of her arrow in his heart!

Yet this remedy he found, and sitting on the crest of the tall cliff, and looking to the deep, 'twas thus he would sing:

> "O whitest Galatea, can it be
>   That thou shouldst spurn me off who love thee so?
> More white than curds, my girl, thou art to see,
> More meek than lambs, more full of leaping glee
>   Than kids, and brighter than the early glow
> On grapes that swell to ripen — sour like thee!
> Thou comest to me with fragrant sleep,
>   And with the fragrant sleep thou goest from me; . . .
> Come up, O Galatea, from the ocean,
>   And, having come, forget again to go!
> As I, who sing out here my heart's emotion,
>   Could sit forever. Come up from below!
> Come, keep my flocks beside me, milk my kine;
>   Come, press my cheese, distrain my whey and curd! . . .
>   O Cyclops, Cyclops! whither has thou sent
>   Thy soul on fluttering wings? If thou wert bent
> On turning bowls, or pulling green and thick
>   The sprouts to give thy lambkins, thou wouldst make thee
>   A wiser Cyclops than for what we take thee.
> Milk dry the present! Why pursue too quick
> That future which is fugitive aright?
> Thy Galatea thou shalt haply find,

Prose portion translated by Andrew Lang; poetry by Elizabeth Barrett Browning.

Or else a maiden fairer and more kind;
For many girls do call me thro the night,
    And, as they call, do laugh out silvery.
    I, too, am something in the world, I see!"
While thus the Cyclops love and lambs did fold,
Ease came with song, he could not buy with gold.

◆B◆ IDYL XV

Realism

Among Theocritus' idyls are several mimes — playlets written to be read rather than acted — which seek to mimic life. Most famous is the fifteenth idyl which presents a cross section of real life in Alexandria, the great cosmopolitan metropolis of the Hellenistic age. It illustrates the realism, found in much of Hellenistic literature, which began to predominate in the late fourth century in the comedies of Menander of Athens and led a contemporary to exclaim, "Oh Menander and life, which of you copied from the other?"

This mime includes a hymn to Adonis which throws light on the character and tendencies of popular religion in the Hellenistic age. Already in the earlier Hellenic period the common people of Greece had turned to the Orphic and Eleusinian mystery cults which promised a blessed and happy life hereafter to the initiate who became identified with the dying god or goddess (Dionysus or Persephone) worshipped by the cult. "Happy and blessed one!" states a typical Orphic inscription, "Thou shalt be god instead of mortal." Now that the Greek and oriental worlds were mingled, many Greeks were drawn to the various ancient but still flourishing mystery cults of Egypt and Mesopotamia. The Adonis ("lord"), whose festival celebrating his annual resurrection is described in this mime, is none other than the old Sumerian dying god, Tammuz ("Lord Tammuz"), whose cult still flourished in the ancient Orient. His consort, Ishtar, whose wailings had returned him to life after death, is here identified with Aphrodite, the old Homeric goddess of love. This process of religious borrowing and mixing, called syncretism, is characteristic of Hellenistic religion. Thus the hymn refers to Aphrodite — here called Cypris, an indication of her connection with the Near East — as "the Goddess of many names and many temples."

TWO SYRACUSAN WOMEN OF ALEXANDRIA

This famous idyl should rather, perhaps, be called a mime. It describes the visit paid by two Syracusan women residing in Alexandria, to the festival of the resurrection of Adonis. The festival is given by Arsinoe, wife and sister of Ptolemy II Philadelphus, and the poem cannot have been written earlier

Based on the translation by Andrew Lang in *Theocritus, Bion and Moschus* (London: Macmillan and Co., Ltd., 1911), pp. 76–84.

than his marriage, in 276 B.C. Nothing can be more gay and natural than the chatter of the women, which has changed no more in two thousand years than the song of birds. . . .

Gorgo. Is Praxinoe at home?

Praxinoe. Gorgo darling! She *is* at home! How long it's been! It's a wonder you got here at last. Eunoe, get her a chair. And throw a cushion on it.

Gorgo. It's fine as it is.

Praxinoe. Do sit down.

Gorgo. How foolish I am! I barely got here alive, Praxinoe! With all these crowds and chariots! Cavalry boots and men in uniform all over the place! And the street is endless — you really live *too* far away!

Praxinoe. It's all the fault of that madman of mine. He came to the ends of the earth and bought this rathole — some house! — to prevent us being neighbors. The jealous brute, always the same, always for spite.

Gorgo. Don't talk about your Dinon like that, darling, before the little boy — look how he's staring at you. Never mind, Zopyrion, honey, she's not talking about daddy.

Praxinoe. Heavens! The child understands.

Gorgo. Nice daddy!

Praxinoe. Well that daddy of his the other day — it was just the other day — went to get soap and rouge at the shop, and back he came with salt — the overgrown boob!

Gorgo. Mine's the same. Diocleides throws money away! Yesterday he went to buy five fleeces, and paid seven drachmas apiece for — what do you suppose? — dogskins, shreds of old bags, mere trash — trouble on trouble! But come, put on your dress and shawl. Let's go to the palace of rich King Ptolemy to see the Adonis. I hear the Queen has provided a grand show.

Praxinoe. Grand folks do everything grandly.

Gorgo. And the sights you see are worth telling those who haven't seen them. Come, it's time to go.

Praxinoe. Every day's a holiday for those with nothing to do. Eunoe, you lazy good-for-nothing, pick up the spinning. Lazy cats are always asleep. Come, hustle, bring the water — quickly! I want water first and she brings soap! Very well, let me have it. Don't pour so much, you spendthrift! Idiot! Why are you wetting my robe? That'll do. I've washed as well as heaven allows. Where's the key to the big chest? Bring it here.

Gorgo. That full dress suits you wonderfully, Praxinoe. Tell me, how much did the stuff cost you off the loom?

Praxinoe. Don't remind me, Gorgo. More than two minas in hard cash — and the work on it! I slaved my soul over it.

Gorgo. Well, it's *most* successful. All you could wish.

Praxinoe. How sweet of you to say so. (*To a slave.*) Bring my shawl and set my hat on my head, the fashionable way. No, child, I wont take you. Boo! Bogies! Bad horsey bites! Bawl as much as you please, but I won't have you crippled. Let's be going. Phrygia, take the child and keep him amused. Call in the dog and lock the front door.

(They go into the street.)

Heavens, what a crowd! How on earth are we ever to get through this mob? They're like ants — no one can count them. Ptolemy, you've done many good things since your father joined the immortals. No more hoods creep up on you nowadays and do you in — an old Egyptian habit. The tricks those scoundrels used to play! They're all alike — dirty, lazy, good-for-nothings! Gorgo, darling, look! What shall we do? It's the Royal Cavalry. My dear sir, don't run over me! Look, the bay's rearing, what a temper! Eunoe, you foolish girl, keep out of the way! That beast will kill the man leading him. Lucky I left my brat at home.

Gorgo. It's all right, Praxinoe, we're past them now. They've gone to their station.

Praxinoe. Good! I'm beginning to feel better. Ever since I was a child I've been scared of horses and chilly snakes. Let's hurry, this mob will crush us.

Gorgo (to an old woman). Are you coming from the palace, mother?

Old woman. Yes, my child.

Praxinoe. Is it easy to get in?

Old woman. The Achaeans got into Troy by trying, my pretty one. Where there's a will there's a way!

Gorgo. The old girl has spoken her oracles and off she goes.

Praxinoe. Women know everything — even how Zeus got married!

Gorgo. Look, Praxinoe, what a crowd there is at the doors!

Praxinoe. Horrible! Gorgo, give me your hand. Eunoe, catch hold of Eutychis' and don't get separated. Now let's all go in together. Eunoe, hold tight to me. Oh, how awful! My shawl is torn in two! For heaven's sake, sir, if you know what's good for you, watch out for my shawl!

Man. I'm helpless myself, but I'll do my best.

Praxinoe. What a mob! Pushing like a herd of pigs!

Man. Cheer up, lady, we're in the clear now.

Praxinoe. And may *you* always be in the clear, dear sir, for looking after us. A real gentleman! Eunoe's getting squeezed — come, you idiot, push your way in. Finally! "All inside" quoth the bridegroom as he shut himself in with his bride.

Gorgo. Come here, Praxinoe. Look first at these embroidered robes. How delicate and charming! They're garments fit for the gods.

Praxinoe. Lady Athene! What weavers wove them, what artists designed them, they're so lifelike! The figures stand and move like real people, not woven patterns. How clever man is! Ah, and Adonis himself — how beautiful he lies on his silver couch, with the first down on his cheeks. Thrice-loved Adonis, loved even among the dead.

Second man. You tiresome women! Stop your endless cooing! A couple of turtledoves! They'll bore you to death with all their broad vowels.

Praxinoe. Well! And where did this person come from? What's it to you if we do chatter? Boss your own slaves, sir. Do you think you can give orders to ladies of Syracuse? If you must know, we are Corinthians by descent, just like Bellerophon, and we speak Peloponnesian. Dorians may speak Doric, I suppose? By heaven, one husband is enough! So there — I'm not afraid of your threats!

Gorgo. Hush, Praxinoe! The Argive woman's daughter, the famous singer, is going to sing the *Adonis.* She won the prize last year for dirge-singing. I'm sure she'll give us something lovely. See, she's clearing her throat.

THE HYMN TO ADONIS

O Queen that lovest Golgi, and Idalium, and the steep of Eryx, O golden Aphrodite, see how from the stream eternal of Acheron they have brought back to thee Adonis — after the twelfth month they have brought him, the dainty-footed Hours. Tardiest of the Immortals are the beloved Hours, but dear and desired they come, for always, to all mortals, they bring some gift with them. O Lady of Cypris, daughter of Dione, from mortal to immortal, so men tell, thou hast changed Bernice, dropping sweet Ambrosia in her woman's breast. Therefore, for thy sake, O Goddess of many names and many temples, doth the daughter of Bernice, Arsinoe, lovely as Helen, honor Adonis with all things beautiful.

Beside him lie all ripe fruits that the tall trees bear, and delicate gardens, arrayed in baskets of silver, and the golden flasks are full of incense of Syria. And all the dainty cakes that women fashion in the kneading-tray, mingling colors manifold with the white wheat flour, and those they make of sweet honey and soft oil. . . .

In Adonis' rosy arms the Lady of Cypris lies, and he in hers. A bridegroom of eighteen or nineteen years is he, his kisses are not rough, the golden down being still upon his lips. And now good-night to Cypris, in the arms of her lover. But in the morning we will all of us gather with the dew, and carry him forth among the waves that break upon the beach, and with hair unloosed, bosoms bare, and robes falling to the ankles, will we begin our shrill sweet song.

Thou only, dear Adonis, so men tell, thou only of the demigods dost visit both this world and the stream of Acheron. For Agamemnon had no such lot, nor Aias, that mighty lord of the terrible anger, nor Hector, the eldest born of the twenty sons of Hecube, nor Patroclus, nor Pyrrhus, when he returned from Troy, nor the heroes of yet more ancient days, the Lapithae and Deucalion's sons, nor the sons of Pelops, and the chiefs of Pelasgian Argos. Be gracious to us now, dear Adonis, and throughout the coming year. Dear to us has thine advent been, Adonis, and dear shall it be when thou comest again.

Gorgo. Isn't she wonderful, Praxinoe? Happy woman to know so much, and happier still to have so sweet a voice. But it's time to head for home. Diocleides hasn't had his dinner, and the man's all vinegar — don't go near him when he's kept waiting for dinner. Farewell, beloved Adonis, I hope you'll find us happy when you return!

35

Hellenistic Science: Archimedes

Science and mathematics reached their highest point of development in ancient times during the Hellenistic Age. The debt of Western civilization to the Hellenistic workers in medicine, botany, geography, astronomy, physics, and mathematics is incalculable. In all antiquity the greatest name in mathematics — which was the most extensive and enduring contribution of the Hellenistic scientists — and physics is Archimedes of Syracuse (ca. 287–212 B.C.). Everyone has heard of his famous boast on discovering the principle of the lever, "Give me a place to stand, and I will move the earth"; and of his rushing naked from his bath with the cry, "Eureka!" on discovering the principle of specific gravity.

Archimedes was killed during an incident in the Second Punic War when the Romans under Marcellus besieged and sacked Syracuse after it had sided with the Carthaginians. Plutarch's "Life of Marcellus" contains a description of this event along with an account of Archimedes' scientific genius. Here one finds a striking statement of the Greek devotion to knowledge for its own sake, typical of both Hellenic and Hellenistic times. But the achievements of Archimedes show that the Greeks could, when they wished, make practical application of their theoretical knowledge. Their failure to achieve the spectacular material progress more characteristic of the Roman and especially of our own modern civilization is here attributed to a disdainful regard for "the whole business of mechanics and the useful arts as base and vulgar."

14. . . . He [Marcellus] now attacked the city both by sea and land, Appius commanding the land forces, while Marcellus directed a fleet of sixty quinqueremes full of armed men and missile weapons. He raised a vast engine upon a raft made by lashing eight ships together, and sailed with it to attack the wall, trusting to the numbers and excellence of his siege engines and to his own personal prestige. But Archimedes and his machines cared nothing for this, though he did not speak of any of these engines as being constructed by serious labor, but as the mere holiday sports of a geometrician. He would not indeed have constructed them but at the earnest request of King Hiero [of Syracuse], who entreated him to leave the abstract for the concrete and bring his ideas within the comprehension of the people by embodying them in tangible forms.

Eudoxus and Archytas were the first who began to treat of this renowned science of mechanics, cleverly illustrating it, and proving such problems as were

From Plutarch, *Parallel Lives*, "Marcellus," tr. Aubrey Stewart and George Long.

hard to understand, by means of solid and actual instruments. . . . Plato was much vexed at this, and inveighed against them for destroying the real excellence of geometry by making it leave the region of pure intellect and come within that of the senses, and become mixed up with bodies which require much base servile labor. So mechanics became separated from geometry, and, long regarded with contempt by philosophy, was reckoned among the military arts.

However Archimedes, who was a relative and friend of Hiero, wrote that with a given power he could move any given weight whatever, and, as if rejoicing in the strength of his demonstration, he is said to have declared that if he were given another world to stand upon, he could move this upon which we live. Hiero wondered at this, and begged him to put this theory into practice and show him something great moved by a small force. Archimedes took a three-masted ship, a transport in the king's navy, which had just been dragged up on land with great labor and many men; in this he placed her usual complement of men and cargo, and then sitting at some distance, without any trouble, by gently pulling with his hand the end of a system of pullies, he dragged it towards him with as smooth and even a motion as if it were passing over the sea. The king wondered greatly at this, and perceiving the value of his arts, prevailed upon Archimedes to construct for him a number of machines, some for the attack and some for the defence of a city, of which he himself did not make use, as he spent most of his life in unwarlike and literary leisure, but now these engines were ready for use in Syracuse, and the inventor also was present to direct their working.

15. So when the Romans attacked by sea and land at once, the Syracusans were at first terrified and silent, dreading that nothing could resist such an armament. But Archimedes opened fire from his machines, throwing upon the land forces all manners of darts and great stones, with an incredible noise and violence, which no man could withstand; but those upon whom they fell were struck down in heaps, and their ranks thrown into confusion, while some of the ships were suddenly seized by iron hooks, and by a counter-balancing weight were drawn up and then plunged to the bottom. Others they caught by irons like hands or claws suspended from cranes, and first pulled them up by their bows till they stood upright upon their sterns, and then cast down into the water, or by means of windlasses and tackles worked inside the city, dashed them against the cliffs and rocks at the base of the walls, with terrible destruction to their crews. Often was seen the fearful sight of a ship lifted out of the sea into the air, swaying and balancing about, until the men were all thrown out or overwhelmed with stones from slings, when the empty vessel would either be dashed against the fortifications or dropped into the sea by the claws being let go.

The great engine which Marcellus was bringing up on the raft, called the Harp from some resemblance to that instrument, was, while still at a distance, struck by a stone of ten talents weight [about 830 pounds], and then another and another, which fell with a terrible crash, breaking the platform on which the machine stood, loosening its bolts, and tearing asunder the hulks which supported it. Marcellus, despairing of success, drew off his ships as fast as possible and sent orders to the land forces to retreat. In a council of war, it was determined to make another assault by night; for they argued that the straining cords which Archimedes used to propel his missiles required a long distance to work in, and would make the shot fly over them at close quarters, and be practically useless, as they required a long stroke. But he, it appears, had long before prepared engines suited for short as well as long distances, and short darts to use in them; and from many small loop-holes pierced through the wall small scorpions, as they are called, stood ready to shoot the enemy, though invisible to them.

16. When they attacked, expecting that they would not be seen, they again encountered a storm of blows from stones which fell perpendicularly upon their heads and darts which were poured from all parts of the wall. They were forced to retire, and when they came within range of the larger machines missiles were showered upon them as they retreated, destroying many men and throwing the ships into great disorder, without their being able to retaliate. For most of the engines on the walls had been devised by Archimedes, and the Romans thought that they were fighting against gods and not men, as destruction fell upon them from invisible hands.

17. However, Marcellus escaped unhurt, and sarcastically said to his own engineers: "Are we to give in to this Briareus of a geometrician, who sits at his ease by the sea-shore and plays at upsetting our ships, to our lasting disgrace, and surpasses the hundred-handed giant of fable by hurling so many weapons at us at once?" For indeed all the other Syracusans were merely the limbs of Archimedes, and his mind alone directed and guided everything. All other arms were laid aside and the city trusted to his weapons solely for defence and safety. At length Marcellus, seeing that the Romans had become so scared that if only a rope or small beam were seen over the wall they would turn and fly, crying out that Archimedes was bringing some engine to bear upon them, ceased assaulting the place, and trusted to time alone to reduce it.

Yet Archimedes had so great a mind and such immense philosophic speculations that although by inventing these engines he had acquired the glory of a more than human intellect, he would not condescend to leave behind him any writings upon the subject, regarding the whole business of mechanics and the useful arts as base and vulgar, but placed his whole study and delight in those speculations in which absolute beauty and excellence appear unhampered by the necessities of life, and argument is made to soar above its subject matter, since by the latter only bulk and outward appearance, but by the other accuracy of reasoning and wondrous power, can be attained: for it is impossible in the whole science of geometry to find more difficult hypotheses explained on clearer or more simple principles than in his works. Some attribute this to his natural genius, others say that his indefatigable industry made his work seem as though it had been done without labor, though it cost much. For no man by himself could find out the solution of his problems, but as he reads, he begins to think that he could have discovered it himself, by so smooth and easy a road does he lead one up to the point to be proved.

One cannot therefore disbelieve the stories which are told of him: how he seemed ever bewitched by the song of some indwelling siren of his own so as to forget to eat his food, and neglect his person, and how, when dragged forcibly to the baths and perfumers, he would draw geometrical figures with the ashes on the hearth, and when his body was anointed would trace lines on it with his finger, absolutely possessed and inspired by the joy he felt in his art. He discovered many beautiful problems, and is said to have begged his relatives and friends to place upon his tomb when he died a cylinder enclosing a sphere, and to write on it the proof of the ratio of the containing solid to the contained.

Such was Archimedes, who at this time rendered himself, and as far as lay in him, the city, invincible. . . .

[*The city is finally taken and plundered.*]

19. . . . Marcellus was especially grieved at the fate of Archimedes. He was studying something by himself upon a figure which he had drawn, to which he had so utterly given up his thoughts and his sight that he did not notice the assault of the Romans and the capture of the city, and when a soldier suddenly appeared before him and ordered him to follow him into the presence of Marcellus, he refused to do so before he had finished his problem and its solution. The man hereupon in a rage drew his sword and killed him. Others say that the Roman fell upon him at once with a sword to kill him, but he, seeing him, begged him to wait for a little while, that he might not leave his theorem imperfect, and that while he was reflecting upon it, he was slain. A third story is that he was carrying into Marcellus's presence his mathematical instruments, sundials, spheres, and quadrants, by which the eye might measure the magnitude of the sun, some soldiers met with him, and supposing that there was gold in the boxes, slew him. But all agree that Marcellus was much grieved, that he turned away from his murderer as though he were an object of abhorrence to gods and men, and that he sought out his family and treated them well.

By the prosperity and order of eight hundred years has this fabric of empire been consolidated.

— TACITUS (see p. 383)

Roman Civilization

"**A Roman Triumph**" — in the Vatican Museum.
Photo courtesy of Anderson–Giraudon.

Western civilization rests upon a continuity of history that moves from the ancient Near East through Greece and Rome to the Germanic West. The role of Rome is largely that of a transmitter, a bridge over which the heritage of Greece and the Near East moved on to the West. This resulted from the lateness of Rome's emergence, for from the very beginnings of her development she could and did avail herself of the achievements of the more advanced peoples with whom she came into contact — Etruscans, Greeks, Carthaginians, and Orientals. In this process "Rome conquered the world, but lost her own soul," for much of Roman thought, religion, art, and literature was taken over from the conquered. Rome's main contribution was this conquest, the unification of the ancient world which made possible, in the words of Vergil, "a new hope for the human race, a hope of peace, of order, of civilization." The ancient world was given one last opportunity to create an Earthly City devoted to the peace and prosperity of man and founded upon human reason and equity. By the end of the second century A.D. this ideal seemed realized, and the Greek orator Aelius Aristides could address the Romans thus: "Before the establishment of your empire the world was in confusion, upside down, adrift and out of control; but as soon as you Romans intervened the turmoils and factions ceased, and life and politics were illumined by the dawn of an era of universal order." This "Roman peace" collapsed in the following century, but it has remained one of the greatest of purely human ideals, perhaps never more so than today in our own larger world, also "in confusion, upside down, adrift and out of control."

To Edward Gibbon, eighteenth-century rationalist and author of the *Decline and Fall of the Roman Empire*, the fall of Rome was the result of "the triumph of barbarism and religion [Christianity]," but this view confuses results with causes. The German barbarians overran the western half of the Roman Empire only after it had been enfeebled beyond the possibility of successful resistance by internal collapse, and Christianity triumphed only after paganism had grown world-weary and was already turning from materialism and rationalism to the spiritualism and mysticism of other-wordly philosophies. Indeed, it can be argued that Christianity brought a renewal of creativity to the ancient world which, had it come earlier, might have reversed this decline. The Christian polemicist Lactantius in his *Divine Institutes,* addressed to the emperor Constantine in the early fourth century, argued that what the world needed to save it from collapse was the reformation of individual character which only Christianity could give. The initial error of paganism, he insisted, was its "separation of reason from faith"; the consequent materialism and essential self-centeredness of its way of life had brought the world to a state of collapse. A spiritual revival was needed that would reform human character through the realization that all men were sons of God and therefore brothers. Thus through the love of God and all His creatures men would be inspired to create a true commonwealth based on justice and bring about the rejuvenation of human society. These views and hopes do not sound very different from those expressed by Arnold J. Toynbee in our present "age of anxiety."

36

Polybius, The Histories

The constitution of the Roman Republic

Second only to Thucydides among Greek historians was Polybius (ca. 200–ca. 117 B.C.). He witnessed and speculated upon the events which marked the expansion of Rome in the Mediterranean area from Spain to Asia Minor, and he grasped the fact that Hellenistic history was passing over into Roman history. He spent sixteen years in Rome as one of a thousand Greek hostages brought to Rome in 167 B.C. to insure the good behavior of their compatriots at home. Here he became a firm admirer of the character and the political and social institutions of his Roman captors. Above all, he became convinced that the expansion of Rome was natural and inevitable, and he undertook to write a history of his own times in order to reconcile the Greek world to the reality of Roman domination. He chose the year 220 B.C. as his starting point because, as he put it, "since that time history has been a kind of organic whole, and the affairs of Italy and Africa have been interconnected with those of Asia and Greece, all moving toward one end," the Roman world-state. He closed his history with the events of 146 B.C., the year in which the Third Punic War was ended with the complete destruction of Carthage, and the year in which the final step in the subjugation of Greece and Macedonia was signaled by an equally ruthless destruction of Corinth.

Polybius was particularly interested in discovering causes and in seeing the interrelation of events, without which history is but a rope of sand with no meaning or value: "Neither the writer nor the reader of history, therefore, should confine his attention to a bare statement of facts. . . . For if you take from history all explanation of cause, principle, and motive, and of the adaptation of the means to the end, what is left is a mere panorama without being instructive, and though it may please for the moment, has no abiding value."

He attributed Rome's rise to the superior qualities of its citizens and the perfection of its institutions, all of which he contrasted with those of other peoples in the Mediterranean area. His famous description of the Roman constitution of the third century B.C. is a case in point. Influenced by Aristotle, he divided good governments into three types — monarchy, aristocracy, and democracy — and he attributed the excellence of the Roman constitution to the fact that it contained elements of these three types in equilibrium. His emphasis upon the checks and balances of the Roman constitution influenced

From Polybius, *The Histories*, Book VI, tr. Evelyn S. Shuckburgh.

eighteenth-century French political thinkers and through them entered into the American constitution.

1. I am aware that some will be at a loss to account for my interrupting the course of my narrative for the sake of entering upon the following disquisition of the Roman constitution. But I think that I have already in many passages made it fully evident that this particular branch of my work was one of the necessities imposed on me by the nature of my original design; and I pointed this out with special clearness in the preface which explained the scope of my history. I there stated that the feature of my work which was at once the best in itself, and the most instructive to the students of it, was that it would enable them to know and fully realize in what manner, and under what kind of constitution, it came about that nearly the whole world fell under the power of Rome in somewhat less than fifty-three years — an event certainly without precedent. This being my settled purpose, I could see no more fitting period than the present for making a pause, and examining the truth of the remarks about to be made on this constitution. In private life if you wish to satisfy yourself as to the badness or goodness of particular persons, you would not, if you wish to get a genuine test, examine their conduct at a time of uneventful repose, but in the hour of brilliant success or conspicuous reverse. For the true test of a perfect man is the power of bearing with spirit and dignity violent changes of fortune. An examination of a constitution should be conducted in the same way; and therefore being unable to find in our day a more rapid or more signal change than that which has happened to Rome, I reserved my disquisition on its constitution for this place. . . .

3. Of the Greek republics, which have again and again risen to greatness and fallen into insignificance, it is not difficult to speak, whether we recount their past history or venture an opinion on their future. For to report what is already known is an easy task, nor is it hard to guess what is to come from our knowledge of what has been. But in regard to the Romans it is neither an easy matter to describe their present state, owing to the complexity of their constitution; nor to speak with confidence of their future, from our inadequate acquaintance with their peculiar institutions in the past whether affecting their public or their private life. It will require then no ordinary attention and study to get a clear and comprehensive conception of the distinctive features of this constitution.

Now, it is undoubtedly the case that most of those who profess to give us authoritative instruction on this subject distinguish three kinds of constitutions, which they designate *kingship, aristocracy, democracy*. But in my opinion the question may be fairly put to them, whether they name these as being the *only* ones, or as the best. In either case I think they are wrong. For it is plain that we must regard as the *best* constitution that which partakes of all these three elements. And this is no mere assertion, but has been proved by the example of Lycurgus, who was the first to construct a constitution — that of Sparta — on this principle. . . .

11. . . . I will now endeavor to describe [the constitution] of Rome at the period of their disastrous defeat at Cannae [216 B.C.].

I am fully conscious that to those who actually live under this constitution I shall appear to give an inadequate account of it by the omission of certain details. Knowing accurately every portion of it from personal experience, and from having been bred up in its customs and laws from childhood, they will not be struck so much by the accuracy of the description as annoyed by its omissions; nor will they believe that the historian has purposely omitted unimportant distinctions, but will attribute his silence upon the origin of existing institutions or other important facts to ignorance. What is told they depreciate as insignificant or beside the purpose; what is omitted they desiderate as vital to the question: their object being to appear to know more than the writers. But a good critic should not judge a writer by what he leaves unsaid, but from what he says: if he detects misstatement in the latter, he may then feel certain that ignorance accounts for the former; but if what he says is accurate, his omissions ought to be attributed to deliberate judgment and not to ignorance. So much for those whose criticisms are prompted by personal ambition rather than by justice. . . .

Another requisite for obtaining a judicious approval for an historical disquisition, is that it should be germane to the matter in hand; if this is not observed, though its style may be excellent and its matter irreproachable, it will seem out of place, and disgust rather than please. . . .

THREE SOVEREIGN ELEMENTS

As for the Roman constitution, it had three elements, each of them possessing sovereign powers: and their respective share of power in the whole state had been regulated with such a scrupulous regard to equality and equilibrium, that no one could say for certain, not even a native, whether the constitution as a whole were an aristocracy or democracy or despotism. And no wonder: for if we confine our observation to the power of the Consuls we should be inclined to regard it as despotic; if on that of the Senate, as aristocratic; and if finally one looks at the power possessed by the people it would seem a clear case of democracy. What the exact powers of these several parts were, and still, with slight modifications, are, I will now state.

12. The Consuls, before leading out the legions, remain in Rome and are supreme masters of the administration. All other magistrates, except the Tribunes, are under them and take their orders. They introduce foreign ambassadors to the Senate; bring matters requiring deliberation before it; and see to the execution of its decrees. If, again, there are any matters of state which require the authorization of the people, it is their business to see to them, to summon the popular meetings, to bring the proposals before them, and to carry out the decrees of the majority. In the preparations for war, also, and in a word in the entire administration of a campaign, they have all but absolute power. It is competent to them to impose on the allies such levies as they think good, to appoint the Military Tribunes, to make up the roll for soldiers and select those that are suitable. Besides they have absolute power of inflicting punishment on

all who are under their command while on active service: and they have authority to expend as much of the public money as they choose, being accompanied by a quaestor who is entirely at their orders. A survey of these powers would in fact justify our describing the constitution as despotic, — a clear case of royal government. Nor will it affect the truth of my description, if any of the institutions I have described are changed in our time, or in that of our posterity: and the same remarks apply to what follows.

13. The Senate has first of all the control of the treasury, and regulates the receipts and disbursements alike. For the Quaestors cannot issue any public money for the various departments of the state without a decree of the Senate, except for the service of the Consuls. The Senate controls also what is by far the largest and most important expenditure, that, namely, which is made by the censors every *lustrum* [five years] for the repair or construction of public buildings; this money cannot be obtained by the censors except by the grant of the Senate. Similarly all crimes committed in Italy requiring a public investigation, such as treason, conspiracy, poisoning, or willful murder, are in the hands of the Senate. Besides, if any individual or state among the Italian allies requires a controversy to be settled, a penalty to be assessed, help or protection to be afforded — all this is the province of the Senate. Or again, outside Italy, if it is necessary to send an embassy to reconcile warring communities, or to remind them of their duty, or sometimes to impose requisitions upon them, or to receive their submission, or finally to proclaim war against them — this too is the business of the Senate. In like manner the reception to be given foreign ambassadors in Rome, and the answers to be returned to them, are decided by the Senate. With such business the people have nothing to do. Consequently, if one were staying at Rome when the Consuls were not in town, one would imagine the constitution to be a complete aristocracy: and this has been the idea entertained by many Greeks, and by many kings as well, from the fact that nearly all the business they had to do with Rome was settled by the Senate.

14. After this one would naturally be inclined to ask what part is left for the people in the constitution, when the Senate has these various functions, especially the control of the receipts and expenditures of the exchequer; and when the Consuls, again, have absolute power over the details of military preparation, and an absolute authority in the field? There is, however, a part left the people, and it is a most important one. For the people is the sole fountain of honor and of punishment; and it is by these two things and these alone that dynasties and constitutions and, in a word, human society are held together. . . . The people then are the only court to decide matters of life and death; and even in cases where the penalty is money, if the sum to be assessed is sufficiently serious, and especially when the accused have held the higher magistracies. And in regard to this arrangement there is one point deserving especial commendation and record. Men who are on trial for their lives at Rome, while sentence is in process of being voted — if even only one of the tribes whose votes are needed to ratify the sentence has not voted — have the privilege at Rome of openly departing and condemning themselves to a volun-

tary exile. Such men are safe at Naples or Praeneste or at Tibur, and at other towns with which this arrangement has been duly ratified on oath.

Again, it is the people who bestow offices on the deserving, which are the most honorable rewards of virtue. It has also the absolute power of passing or repealing laws; and, most important of all, it is the people who deliberate on the question of peace or war. And when provisional terms are made for alliance, suspension of hostilities, or treaties, it is the people who ratify them or the reverse.

These considerations again would lead one to say that the chief power in the state was the people's, and that the constitution was a democracy.

CHECKS AND BALANCES

15. Such, then, is the distribution of power between the several parts of the state. I must now show how each of these several parts can, when they choose, oppose or support each other.

The Consul, then, when he has started on an expedition with the powers I have described, is to all appearance absolute in the administration of the business in hand; still he has need of the support both of people and Senate, and, without them, is quite unable to bring the matter to a successful conclusion. For it is plain that he must have supplies sent to his legions from time to time; but without a decree of the Senate they can be supplied neither with corn, nor clothes, nor pay, so that all the plans of a commander must be futile, if the Senate is resolved either to shrink from danger or hamper his plans. And again, whether a Consul shall bring any undertaking to a conclusion or no depends entirely on the Senate: for it has absolute authority at the end of a year to send another Consul to supersede him, or to continue the existing one in his command. Again, even to the successes of the generals, the Senate has the power to add distinction and glory, and on the other hand to obscure their merits and lower their credit. For these high achievements are brought in tangible form before the eyes of the citizens by what are called "triumphs." But in these triumphs the commanders cannot celebrate with proper pomp, or in some cases celebrate at all, unless the Senate concurs and grants the necessary money. As for the people, the Consuls are preeminently obliged to court their favor, however distant from home may be the field of their operations; for it is the people, as I have said before, that ratifies, or refuses to ratify, terms of peace and treaties; but most of all because when laying down their office they have to give an account of their administration before it. Therefore in no case is it safe for the Consuls to neglect either the Senate or the good will of the people.

16. As for the Senate, which possesses the immense power I have described, in the first place it is obliged in public affairs to take the multitude into account, and respect the wishes of the people; and it cannot put into execution the penalty for offences against the republic, which are punishable with death, unless the people first ratify its decrees. Similarly even in matters which directly affect the senators — for instance, in the case of a law depriving senators of

certain dignities and offices, or even actually cutting down their property — even in such cases the people have the sole power of passing or rejecting the law. But most important of all is the fact that, if the Tribunes interpose their veto, the Senate not only are unable to pass a decree, but cannot even hold a meeting at all, whether formal or informal. Now, the Tribunes are always bound to carry out the decree of the people, and above all things to have regard to their wishes: therefore, for all these reasons the Senate stands in awe of the multitude, and cannot neglect the feelings of the people.

17. In like manner the people on its part is far from being independent of the Senate, and is bound to take its wishes into account both collectively and individually. For contracts, too numerous to count, are given out by the censors in all parts of Italy, for the repairs or construction of public buildings; there is also the collection of revenue from many rivers, harbors, gardens, mines, and land — everything, in a word, that comes under the control of the Roman government: and in all these the people at large are engaged; so that there is scarcely a man, so to speak, who is not interested either as a contractor or as being employed in the works. For some purchase the contracts from the censors for themselves; and others go partners with them; while others again go security for these contractors, or actually pledge their property to the treasury for them. Now over all these transactions the Senate has absolute control. It can grant an extension of time; and in case of unforeseen accident can relieve the contractors from a portion of their obligation, or release them from it altogether, if they are absolutely unable to fill it. And there are many details in which the Senate can inflict great hardships, or, on the other hand, grant great indulgences to the contractors: for in every case the appeal is to it. But the most important point of all is that the judges are taken from its members in the majority of trials, whether public or private, in which the charges are heavy. Consequently, all citizens are much at its mercy; and being alarmed at the uncertainty as to when they may need its aid, are cautious about resisting or actively opposing its will. And for a similar reason men do not rashly resist the wishes of the Consuls, because one and all may become subject to their absolute authority on a campaign.

18. The result of this power of the several estates for mutual help or harm is a union sufficiently firm for all emergencies, and a constitution than which it is impossible to find a better. For whenever any danger from without compels them to unite and work together, the strength which is developed by the State is so extraordinary, that everything required is unfailingly carried out by the eager rivalry shown by all classes to devote their whole minds to the need of the hour, and to secure that any determination come to should not fail for want of promptitude; while each individual works, privately and publicly alike, for the accomplishment of the business in hand. Accordingly, the peculiar constitution of the State makes it irresistible, and certain of obtaining whatever it determines to attempt. Nay, even when these external alarms are past, and the people are enjoying their good fortune and the fruits of their victories, and, as usually happens, growing corrupted by flattery and idleness, show a tendency to violence and arrogance — it is in these circumstances, more than ever, that

the constitution is seen to possess within itself the power of correcting abuses. For when any one of the three classes becomes puffed up, and manifests an inclination to be contentious and unduly encroaching, the mutual interdependency of all the three, and the possibility of the pretensions of any one being checked and thwarted by the others, must plainly check this tendency; and so the proper equilibrium is maintained by the impulsiveness of the one part being checked by its fear of the other.

───── 37 ─────

Livy: The Foreign Policy of the Roman Republic

"One people in the world which would fight for others' liberties."

Immediately following the victory over Hannibal (201 B.C.), which ended the Second Punic War and left the Roman Republic the dominant power in the western Mediterranean, the Romans were drawn into the maelstrom of eastern Mediterranean politics. By 189 B.C. Rome had fought and defeated in turn the two most powerful Hellenistic states, Macedon and the Seleucid Empire, thereby becoming the virtual master of the entire Mediterranean area.

The following selection from Livy's History of Rome, written in the reign of Augustus, supports the view held by most present-day historians that Rome's intervention in the East, like her expansion in the West, was motivated by fear rather than ambition. During the darkest days of the Second Punic War, Philip V of Macedon had threatened Rome by allying himself with Hannibal, and by 200 B.C., following an agreement with the Seleucid ruler Antiochus III to partition the outlying possessions of the declining Ptolemaic rulers of Egypt, he was advancing in the Aegean Sea region. The small states of Pergamum and Rhodes, already at war with Philip, asked Rome's aid in preserving the balance of power in the East, and the Senate decided to act. Philip's refusal to heed a Roman ultimatum was followed by a declaration of war, but only after the Senate had overcome the initial refusal of the popular assembly to sanction another war.

Reprinted by permission of the publishers and The Loeb Classical Library from Evan T. Sage's translation of Livy, *History of Rome*, Book XXXIII, Chs. 11–12, 30–33 (Cambridge, Mass.: Harvard University Press).

Supported by some Greek allies, notably the Aetolian League and Athens, the Roman commander Quinctius Flamininus routed the Macedonian army at Cynoscephalae in 197 B.C. Rome's lenient peace terms were designed to end Philip's dreams of empire while preserving his state as a buffer against barbarians to the north and Antiochus III to the east. The decision to end Macedon's long-standing attempt to dominate Greece, together with the philhellene sentiments of Flamininus and other leading Romans, led to the theatrical announcement of the freedom of Greece and the withdrawal of Roman forces. The delirious enthusiasm that this declaration evoked among the Greeks was quickly undermined, however, by misunderstandings between the liberators and the liberated. In time the paternalistic attitude of the Romans convinced most Greeks that the Romans were still semi-barbarians, and the Romans in turn lost their early philhellene idealism. In 146 B.C. the exasperated Romans placed Greece under the administrative authority of the Roman governor of Macedonia, which had been annexed two years earlier. Livy's account indicates that some Greeks became disillusioned with Roman policy immediately following the Battle of Cynoscephalae.

ROMAN POLICY VEXES THE AETOLIANS

11. Philip, having collected the straggling fugitives who had followed his trail after the changing fortunes of the battlefield, sent agents to Larisa to burn the royal records, in order to prevent their falling into the hands of the Romans, and retired into Macedonia. Quinctius [Flamininus] sold part of the prisoners and booty and gave part to the soldiers, and marched towards Larisa, still uncertain where the king had gone and what he was planning. There the king's herald met him, ostensibly to ask for a truce, that those who had fallen in the battle might be removed for burial, in reality to ask permission to send an embassy. Both requests were granted by the Roman. The consul, moreover, added that the king should take heart, a phrase which gave great offence to the Aetolians, who were already swollen with pride and complaining that victory had changed the general: before the battle he had been wont to discuss with the allies all matters great and small, but now they were excluded from all his deliberations, and he decided everything according to his own personal judgment, since he was trying to win a place of private influence with the king, in order that, although the Aetolians had endured the hardships and toils of the war, the Roman might take to himself the credit for the peace and the profits of victory. And beyond doubt something of their honorable position has been lost; but they did not see why they should be utterly ignored. They believed that the consul — a man of a soul unconquerable by such cupidity — was eager to receive gifts from the king; but he was in fact angry at the Aetolians, and with just cause, for their insatiable desire for booty and their arrogance in claiming the glory of the victory for themselves, while with their boasting they had offended the ears of everyone, and he saw that with Philip out of the way and the power of the Macedonian kingdom broken the Aetolians would be held the masters of Greece. For these reasons he deliberately took many steps to cause them to be and to seem of less moment and importance in the eyes of all men.

12. A truce of fifteen days had been granted to the enemy and a conference arranged with the king; but before the time for this arrived, he called a council of the allies and referred to them the terms of peace which they wished to be imposed. Amynander, king of the Athamanes, spoke briefly: the peace should be so arranged that Greece, even in the absence of the Romans, should be strong enough to maintain at once peace and liberty. The language of the Aetolians was more harsh; they said, after a brief preface, that the Roman commander was acting correctly and in order in discussing the conditions of peace with those whom he had had as his allies in the war; but that he was totally wrong if he thought that he would leave either assured peace to the Romans or liberty to the Greeks unless Philip were either killed or dethroned, either of which was easy if he were willing to follow up his good fortune.

In reply, Quinctius asserted that the Aetolians neither remembered Roman policy nor employed arguments consistent with themselves. On the one hand, in all previous conferences and conversations they had always spoken of conditions of peace and not of waging a war of extermination; on the other, the Romans, in addition to observing, from remote antiquity, their custom of sparing conquered peoples, had given striking proof of their mercifulness in the peace granted to Hannibal and the Carthaginians. He would say nothing about the Carthaginians: how often had conferences been held with Philip himself? Never was there any suggestion that he should give up his kingdom. Or, because he had been defeated in battle, did that make war an unpardonable offense? An armed enemy should be met in hostile mood; towards the conquered, the mildest possible attitude was the greatest thing. The Macedonian kings seemed a menace to Greek liberty; but if that kingdom and people were removed, the Thracians, the Illyrians, and then the Gauls, fierce and untamed peoples, would pour into Macedonia and into Greece. They should not, by breaking up all the nearest states, open the way to themselves for larger and more powerful tribes. Then, when Phaeneas, the Aetolian praetor, interrupted, reminding him that if Philip escaped this time he would soon cause a greater war, Quinctius replied, "Cease causing disturbance when we should be deliberating. The conditions by which the king will be bound will not be such that he will be able to start a war." . . .

PEACE TERMS IMPOSED ON PHILIP

30. . . . [T]en commissioners arrived from Rome, and with their approval peace was granted to Philip on these terms: that all the Greek cities which were in Europe or in Asia should enjoy their liberty and laws; that, whatever cities had been under the sway of Philip, from these Philip should withdraw his garrisons and should hand them over to the Romans, free of his troops, before the time of the Isthmian Games; that he should withdraw also from the following cities in Asia: Euromum and Pedasa and Bargyliae and Iasus and Myrina and Abydus and Thasos and Perinthus (for it was determined that these too should be free); that, regarding the liberation of the Ciani, Quinctius should write to Prusias, king of Bithynia, the decision of the senate and the ten commissioners; that Philip should turn over to the Romans the prisoners and de-

serters, all his warships except five, and one royal galley of almost unmanageable size, which was propelled by sixteen tiers of oars; that he should have a maximum of five thousand soldiers and no elephants at all; that he should wage no war outside Macedonia without the permission of the senate; that he should pay to the Roman people an indemnity of one thousand talents, half at once and half in ten annual instalments. Valerius Antias states that a tribute of four thousand pounds of silver annually for ten years was imposed upon the king; Claudius fixes the payments at four thousand two hundred pounds annually for thirty years and twenty thousand pounds immediately. The same writer mentions an explicit provision that he should not wage war with Eumenes, son of Attalus — he was the new king there [Pergamum]. Hostages were taken to insure performance, among them Demetrius, the son of Philip. Valerius Antias adds that the island of Aegina and the elephants were presented as a gift to Attalus, who was absent, that the Rhodians were given Stratonicea and other cities in Caria which Philip had held, and the Athenians the islands of Paros, Imbros, Delos, and Scyros.

GRUMBLINGS OF THE AETOLIANS

31. While all the Greek cities approved this settlement, only the Aetolians with secret grumblings criticized the decision of the ten commissioners: mere words had been trimmed up with the empty show of liberty; why were some cities delivered to the Romans without being named, others specified and ordered to be free without such delivery, unless the purpose was that those which were in Asia, being more secure by reason of their remoteness, should be set free, but those which were in Greece, not being named, should become Roman property, to wit, Corinth and Chalcis and Oreus along with Eretria and Demetrias? Their complaint was not altogether groundless. For there was some uncertainty with respect to Corinth and Chalcis and Demetrias, because in the decree of the senate, under which the ten commissioners were sent from Rome, the other cities of Greece and Asia were beyond question set free, but regarding these three cities the commissioners were instructed to take such action as the public interest should have proved to demand, in accordance with the general good and their own sense of honor. There was King Antiochus, who, there was no doubt, would invade Europe as soon as his forces seemed adequate; they did not wish to leave these cities, so favorably located, open to his occupancy. Quinctius with the ten commissioners moved from Elatia to Anticyra and thence to Corinth. There plans for the liberation of Greece were discussed almost every day at meetings of the ten commissioners. Quinctius urged repeatedly that all Greece should be set free, if they wished to stop the muttering of the Aetolians and to create genuine affection and respect for the Roman name among all the Greeks, and if they wished to convince them that they had crossed the sea to liberate Greece and not to transfer dominion from Philip to themselves. The others said nothing opposed to this as regards the freedom of the cities, but they believed it safer for the Greeks themselves to remain for a while under the protection of Roman garrisons than to receive Antiochus as lord in place of Philip. Finally, this decision was reached: Corinth should be

given over to the Achaeans, a garrison, however, to be retained in Acrocorinthus; Chalcis and Demetrias should be held until the anxiety about Antiochus should have passed.

THE LIBERATION OF GREECE

32. The appointed time of the Isthmian Games was at hand, a spectacle always, even on other occasions, attended by crowds, on account of the fondness, native to the race, for exhibitions in which there are trials of skill in every variety of art as well as of strength and swiftness of foot; moreover, they came because, on account of the favorable situation of the place, lying between the two opposite seas and furnishing mankind with abundance of all wares, the market was a meeting-place for Asia and Greece. But at this time they had assembled from all quarters not only for the usual purposes, but especially they were consumed with wonder what thenceforth the state of Greece would be, and what their own condition; they not only had their own silent thoughts, some believing one thing and others another, but discussed openly what the Romans would do; almost no one was convinced that they would withdraw from all Greece. They had taken their seats at the games and the herald with the trumpeter, as is the custom, had come forth into the midst of the arena, where the games are regularly opened with a ritual chant, and proclaiming silence with a trumpet-call, the herald read the decree: "The Roman senate and Titus Quinctius, *imperator*, having conquered King Philip and the Macedonians, declare to be free, independent, and subject to their own laws, the Corinthians, the Phocians, all the Locrians, the island of Euboea, the Magnesians, the Thessalians, the Perrhaebians, and the Phthiotic Achaeans." He had named all the states which had been subject to King Philip. When the herald's voice was heard there was rejoicing greater than men could grasp in its entirety. They could scarce believe that they had heard aright, and they looked at one another marvelling as at the empty vision of a dream; they asked their neighbors what concerned each one, unwilling to trust the evidence of their own ears. The herald was recalled, each one desiring not only to hear but to behold the man who brought the tidings of his freedom, and again the herald read the same decree. Then, when the ground for their joy was certain, such a storm of applause began and was so often repeated that it was easily apparent that a throng of good men values nothing more highly than liberty. The contests were then rapidly finished, no man's eyes or thoughts being fixed upon the sight; joy alone had so completely replaced their perception of all other delightful things.

33. When the games were over, almost everyone rushed towards the Roman commander, so that he was endangered by the crowd that rushed to one place, desiring to draw near him, to touch his hand, and showering garlands and chaplets upon him. But he was only about thirty-three years old, and both the vigor of youth and the joy he felt at so remarkable a reward of fame gave him strength. Nor did the rejoicing spend itself at once, but was renewed for many days in thoughts and expressions of gratitude: there was one people in the world which would fight for others' liberties at its own cost, to its own

peril and with its own toil, not limiting its guarantees of freedom to its neighbors, to men of the immediate vicinity, or to countries that lay close at hand, but ready to cross the sea that there might be no unjust empire anywhere and that everywhere justice, right, and law might prevail. By the single voice of a herald, they said, all the cities of Greece and Asia had been set free; to conceive hopes of any such thing as this required a bold mind; to bring it to pass was the proof of immense courage and good fortune as well.

———————— 38 ————————

Cato the Elder

Traditional standards in a new age

The Romans of the early Republic attributed their military successes, along with the stability of their whole society, to the qualities of character instilled in them by the mos majorum — their ancestral way of life which subordinated the individual to the religious and social traditions of family, state, and gods. Yet, ironically, it was continued military success that did much to destroy the hold of the mos majorum. As one crisis followed another and Rome expanded within and outside Italy, new situations arose that required a new type of leadership which could only come from self-confident individuals who did not feel tightly bound by tradition. The career of Scipio Africanus (ca. 236–ca. 183 B.C.) illustrates the emergence of this new type of highly individualistic leader. In the darkest days of Roman defeats inflicted by Hannibal in the Second Punic War, Scipio arose to shatter all precedents of caution and restraint and, while often acting contrary to the orders of the Senate, turned the tide of war against the Carthaginians. Conservatives like Cato the Elder (234–149 B.C.) were keenly aware that such individualism was a challenge to the old Roman traditions, and they retaliated later by accusing and convicting Scipio on trumped-up charges of irregularities in military expenditures. Scipio scornfully refused to defend himself and chose to remain in voluntary exile from his "thankless city" for the remainder of his life.

It is significant that Scipio was also one of the earliest Romans to embrace enthusiastically the study of Greek literature. This contributed to the suspicion

Reprinted by permission of the publishers and The Loeb Classical Library from Bernadotte Perrin's translation of Plutarch, *Parallel Lives*, "Marcus Cato," Chs. 1, 2, 4, 19–23 (Cambridge, Mass.: Harvard University Press).

held by his conservative opponents that Greek thought was subversive of the established order. Did not much Greek literature celebrate a romantic individualism that rejected all standards of truth and action? Did not the Hellenistic philosophies, with their emphasis on reason and individual happiness, undermine the traditional subordination of the individual to family, state and gods? It is no wonder that strenuous attempts were made by Roman conservatives, led by Cato, to prevent the advance of Greek culture. In 181 B.C. the Senate ordered the public burning of a treatise on Pythagorean philosophy. Again, in 173 B.C., two Epicurean philosophers were ordered out of Rome, and a more general decree twelve years later expelled all Greek teachers and philosophers. But all such efforts were futile, and by the end of the second century the cosmopolitan culture of Greece had absorbed and transformed the ancestral Roman way of life. In Horace's well-known line, "Captive Greece captured in turn her untutored conqueror."

The following selection from Plutarch's "Life of Marcus Cato" illustrates two main reasons for Cato's claim to fame: his personification of early Roman character, and his leadership in the struggle against Greek learning. He fought hard for an old ideal he realized was fast slipping away, and in one of his last speeches he finally and sadly acknowledged that his cause was lost. "It is hard," he said, "to have to give an account of your life to men of another age than that in which you have lived."

CATO, A "NEW MAN"

1. The family of Marcus Cato, it is said, was of Tusculan origin, though he lived, previous to his career as soldier and statesman, on an inherited estate in the country of the Sabines. His ancestors commonly passed for men of no note whatever, but Cato himself extols his father, Marcus, as a brave man and good soldier. He also says that his grandfather, Cato, often won prizes for soldierly valor, and received from the state treasury, because of his bravery, the price of five horses which had been killed under him in battle. The Romans used to call men who had no family distinction, but were coming into public notice through their own achievements, "new men," and such they called Cato. But he himself used to say that as far as office and distinction went, he was indeed new, but having regard to ancestral deeds of valor, he was oldest of the old. . . .

2. Near his fields was the cottage which had once belonged to Manius Curius, a hero of three triumphs. To this he would often go, and the sight of the small farm and the mean dwelling led him to think of their former owner, who, though he had become the greatest of the Romans, had subdued the most warlike nations, and driven Pyrrhus out of Italy, nevertheless tilled this little patch of ground with his own hands and occupied this cottage, after three triumphs. Here it was that the ambassadors of the Samnites once found him seated at his hearth cooking turnips, and offered him much gold; but he dismissed them, saying that a man whom such a meal satisfied had no need of gold, and for his part he thought that a more honorable thing than the possession of gold was the conquest of its possessors. Cato would go away with his

mind full of these things, and on viewing again his own house and lands and servants and mode of life, would increase the labors of his hands and lop off his extravagancies. . . .

4. The influence which Cato's oratory won for him waxed great, and men called him a Roman Demosthenes; but his manner of life was even more talked about and noised abroad. For his oratorical ability only set before young men a goal which many already were striving eagerly to attain; but a man who wrought with his own hands, as his fathers did, and was contented with a cold breakfast, a frugal dinner, simple raiment, and a humble dwelling — one who thought more of not wanting the superfluities of life than of possessing them — such a man was rare. The commonwealth had now grown too large to keep its primitive integrity; the sway over many realms and peoples had brought a large admixture of customs, and the adoption of examples set in new modes of life of every sort. It was natural, therefore, that men should admire Cato, when they saw that, whereas other men were broken down by toils and enervated by pleasures, he was victor over both, and this too, not only while he was still young and ambitious, but even in his hoary age, after consulship and triumph. Then, like some victorious athlete, he persisted in the regimen of his training, and kept his mind unaltered to the last.

He tells us that he never wore clothing worth more than a hundred drachmas; that he drank, even when he was praetor or consul, the same wine as his slaves; that as for fish and meats, he would buy thirty asses' worth for his dinner from the public stalls, and even this for the city's sake, that he might not live on bread alone, but strengthen his body for military service; that he once fell heir to an embroidered Babylonian robe, but sold it at once; that not a single one of his cottages had plastered walls; that he never paid more than fifteen hundred drachmas for a slave, since he did not want them to be delicately beautiful, but sturdy workers, such as grooms and herdsmen, and these he thought it his duty to sell when they got oldish, instead of feeding them when they were useless; and that in general, he thought nothing cheap that one could do without, but that what one did not need, even if it cost but a penny, was dear; also that he bought lands where crops were raised and cattle herded, not those where lawns were sprinkled and paths swept.

5. These things were ascribed by some to the man's parsimony; but others condoned them in the belief that he lived in this contracted way only to correct and moderate the extravagance of others. However, for my part, I regard his treatment of his slaves like beasts of burden, using them to the uttermost, and then, when they were old, driving them off and selling them, as the mark of a very mean nature, which recognizes no tie between man and man but that of necessity. . . .

CATO AS CENSOR: "STILL MORE STRICT"

19. . . . [After being elected censor, Cato] grew still more strict. He cut off the pipes by which people conveyed part of the public water supply into their private houses and gardens; he upset and demolished all buildings that encroached on public land; he reduced the cost of public works to the lowest,

and forced the rent of public lands to the highest possible figure. All these things brought much odium upon him. . . .

Still, it appears that the people approved of his censorship to an amazing extent. At any rate, after erecting a statue to his honor in the temple of Health, they commemorated in the inscription upon it, not the military commands nor the triumph of Cato, but, as the inscription may be translated, the fact "that when the Roman state was tottering to its fall, he was made censor, and by helpful guidance, wise restraints, and sound teachings, restored it again." And yet, before this time he used to laugh at those who delighted in such honors, saying that, although they knew it not, their pride was based simply on the work of statuaries and painters, whereas his own images, of the most exquisite workmanship, were borne about in the hearts of his fellow citizens. And to those who expressed their amazement that many men of no fame had statues, while he had none, he used to say: "I would much rather have men ask why I have no statue, than why I have one." In short, he thought a good citizen should not even allow himself to be praised, unless such praise was beneficial to the commonwealth. . . .

"GOOD FATHER, HUSBAND, ECONOMIST"

20. He was also a good father, a considerate husband, and an economist of no mean talent, nor did he give only a fitful attention to this, as a matter of little or no importance. Therefore I think I ought to give suitable instances of his conduct in these relations. He married a wife who was of gentler birth than she was rich, thinking that, although the rich and the high-born may be alike given to pride, still, women of high birth have such a horror of what is disgraceful that they are more obedient to their husbands in all that is honorable. He used to say that the man who struck his wife or child, laid violent hands on the holiest of holy things. Also that he thought it more praiseworthy to be a good husband than a great senator, nay, there was nothing else to admire in Socrates of old except that he was always kind and gentle in his intercourse with a shrewish wife and stupid sons. After the birth of his son, no business could be so urgent, unless it had a public character, as to prevent him from being present when his wife bathed and swaddled the babe. For the mother nursed it herself, and often gave suck also to the infants of her slaves, that so they might come to cherish a brotherly affection for her son. As soon as the boy showed signs of understanding, his father took him under his own charge and taught him to read, although he had an accomplished slave, Chilo by name, who was a school-teacher, and taught many boys. Still, Cato thought it not right, as he tells us himself, that his son should be scolded by a slave, or have his ears tweaked when he was slow to learn, still less that he should be indebted to his slave for such a priceless thing as education. He was therefore himself not only the boy's reading-teacher, but his tutor in law, and his athletic trainer, and he taught his son not merely to hurl the javelin and fight in armor and ride the horse, but also to box, to endure heat and cold, and to swim lustily through the eddies and billows of the Tiber. His History of Rome, as he tells us himself, he wrote out with his own hand and in large characters, that his son

might have in his own home an aid to acquaintance with his country's ancient traditions. He declares that his son's presence put him on his guard against indecencies of speech as much as that of the so-called Vestal Virgins, and that he never bathed with him. This, indeed, would seem to have been a general custom with the Romans, for even fathers-in-law avoided bathing with their sons-in-law, because they were ashamed to uncover their nakedness. Afterwards, however, when they had learned from the Greeks their freedom in going naked, they in turn infected the Greeks with the practice even when women were present.

So Cato wrought at the fair task of molding and fashioning his son to virtue. . . .

21. . . . However, as he applied himself more strenuously to money-getting, he came to regard agriculture as more entertaining than profitable, and invested his capital in business that was safe and sure. He bought ponds, hot springs, districts given over to fullers, pitch factories, land with natural pasture and forest, all of which brought him in large profits, and "could not," to use his own phrase, "be ruined by Jupiter." He used to loan money also in the most disreputable of all ways, namely, on ships, and his method was as follows. He required his borrowers to form a large company, and when there were fifty partners and as many ships for his security, he took one share in the company himself, and was represented by Quintio, a freedman of his, who accompanied his clients in all their ventures. In this way his entire security was not imperilled, but only a small part of it, and his profits were large. He used to lend money also to those of his slaves who wished it, and they would buy boys with it, and after training and teaching them for a year, at Cato's expense, would sell them again. Many of these boys Cato would retain for himself, reckoning to the credit of the slave the highest price bid for his boy. He tried to incite his son also to such economies, by saying that it was not the part of a man, but of a widow woman, to lessen his substance. But that surely was too vehement a speech of Cato's, when he went so far as to say that a man was to be admired and glorified like a god if the final inventory of his property showed that he had added to it more than he had inherited.

"HE MADE MOCK OF ALL GREEK CULTURE"

22. When he was now well on in years, there came as ambassadors from Athens to Rome, Carneades the Academic, and Diogenes the Stoic philosopher. . . . Upon the arrival of these philosophers, the most studious of the city's youth hastened to wait upon them, and became their devoted and admiring listeners. The charm of Carneades especially, which had boundless power, and a fame not inferior to its power, won large and sympathetic audiences, and filled the city, like a rushing mighty wind, with the noise of his praises. Report spread far and wide that a Greek of amazing talent, who disarmed all opposition by the magic of his eloquence, had infused a tremendous passion into the youth of the city, in consequence of which they forsook their other pleasures and pursuits and were "possessed" about philosophy. The other Romans were pleased at this, and glad to see their young men lay hold of Greek culture and consort

with such admirable men. But Cato, at the very outset, when this zeal for discussion came pouring into the city, was distressed, fearing lest the young men, by giving this direction to their ambition, should come to love a reputation based on mere words more than one achieved by martial deeds. And when the fame of the visiting philosophers rose yet higher in the city, and their first speeches before the Senate were interpreted, at his own instance and request, by so conspicuous a man as Gaius Acilius, Cato determined, on some decent pretext or other, to rid and purge the city of them all. So he rose in the Senate and censured the magistrates for keeping in such long suspense an embassy composed of men who could easily secure anything they wished, so persuasive were they. "We ought," he said, "to make up our minds one way or another, and vote on what the embassy proposes, in order that these men may return to their schools and lecture to the sons of Greece, while the youth of Rome give ear to their laws and magistrates, as heretofore."

23. This he did, not, as some think, out of personal hostility to Carneades, but because he was wholly averse to philosophy, and made mock of all Greek culture and training, out of patriotic zeal. He says, for instance, that Socrates was a mighty prattler, who attempted, as best he could, to be his country's tyrant, by abolishing its customs, and by enticing his fellow citizens into opinions contrary to the laws. He made fun of the school of Isocrates, declaring that his pupils kept on studying with him till they were old men, as if they were to practise their arts and plead their cases before Minos in Hades. And seeking to prejudice his son against Greek culture, he indulges in an utterance all too rash for his years, declaring, in the tone of a prophet or a seer, that Rome would lose her empire when she had become infected with Greek letters. But time has certainly shown the emptiness of this ill-boding speech of his, for while the city was at the zenith of its empire, she made every form of Greek learning and culture her own.

39

Tiberius Gracchus:
The Roman New Deal

It is an ironic but outstanding lesson of history that the Roman constitution of the middle of the second century B.C., whose stability and permanence seemed so apparent to Polybius (see Selection 36), was soon to weaken and collapse. Polybius' verdict on the history of the Greek states, that "while they

From Plutarch, *Parallel Lives*, "Tiberius Gracchus," based on the translation by John Dryden and revised by Arthur H. Clough.

still thought themselves prosperous, and likely to remain so, they found themselves involved in circumstances completely the reverse," can be applied equally well to the events of the last century of the Roman Republic.

The hundred years preceding 31 B.C. witnessed great changes not only in Rome's political institutions, but in every other important aspect of Roman civilization as well. Historians have aptly named the period the "Roman Revolution," for at its end Cicero could sadly contemplate the radical changes it had brought and ask, "What remains of the old ways in which Ennius [239–169 B.C., whose poetry celebrated the old traditions] said the Roman state stood rooted?" The forces that destroyed the old ways came out of the new environment produced by Rome's expansion in the Mediterranean area. The political, economic, social, and cultural ideas and institutions which had served well a small city-state underwent radical change when Rome emerged as a world power.

The impact of the new forces that were destined to change Roman civilization was manifested in politics for the first time during the tribunate of Tiberius Gracchus in 133 B.C. Tiberius was a young aristocrat in whom the influence of the liberal learning of Greece, newly imported and popular in the best-educated circles of Roman higher society, combined with an awareness that the old Roman way of life was fast slipping away and inspired him to become a reformer. He proposed an agrarian reform law aimed at solving all the problems that had arisen out of the new environment created by Rome's expansion; he hoped to recapture the traditional Roman ways by restoring the old environment which had originally produced them. By breaking up the newly-formed large estates worked by a slave-labor force plentifully provided by Rome's wars, he would reverse the trend of events that had brought troubles to the Roman state: the dangerous and still growing proletariat of the city would be dispersed to become again a middle class of small landowners, the old Roman morale and traditional ideals would reappear, a citizen-army of sturdy yeomen would be possible as of old, and a stable foundation for the revival of democratic government would be provided. In his hopes for these beneficial results of land reform, Tiberius reflected a traditional Roman viewpoint; Marcus Cato the Elder (see the preceding selection), for example, had written of the old Romans that "when they praised a man as good, they called him 'a good farmer' and 'a good tiller of the soil,'" and he had insisted that "from among the tillers of the soil both the strongest men and the most efficient soldiers come, and that way of gaining a livelihood carries with it beyond all others fidelity to gods and men, and stability and freedom from envy, and those occupied in it are least liable to evil thoughts."

The opposition to Tiberius' agrarian law centered in the Senate, not only because its members constituted the great landholding class whose economic interests were threatened, but above all because the political supremacy of that body was challenged by the tactics used by the reformer. Since the passage of the Hortensian Law in 287 B.C., Rome had been a democracy with an unwritten constitution of checks and balances which had aroused the admiration of Polybius. But Polybius had failed to notice that, in the unsettled period following the passage of the Hortensian Law, Rome had in fact but not in theory become an oligarchy in which the senatorial nobility ruled. During these critical years Rome fought the Punic Wars and expanded in Italy and the Mediterranean, and the Roman populace willingly allowed the Senate, composed largely of experienced ex-magistrates, to take over all administrative and legislative authority. When Tiberius Gracchus revived the democratic power of the popular assembly in order to bypass his opposition in the Senate, the supremacy of the senatorial oligarchy was threatened.

In the ensuing struggle it is difficult to determine the degree of guilt or innocence of the rival factions, for both resorted to illegal or ill-considered measures; but certainly the use of violence by the senatorial faction was the great error which ultimately reaped the whirlwind of civil war and led to the fall of the Republic. Yet the lesson found here has rarely been learned, and history is filled with similar instances in which men blinded by fear and hate have unwittingly destroyed that which they sought to preserve. It was the head of the Roman state religion, the pontifex maximus Nasica, who incited the mob to kill Tiberius and his followers, and he did so with a cry that marks the epitome of misguided patriotism: "Let those who would save our country follow me!"

The selections which follow are from Plutarch's "Life of Tiberius Gracchus," generally considered to favor the reform party.

THE LAND PROBLEM

8. Of the land which the Romans gained by conquest from their neighbors, part they sold and part they added to the public domain. This latter common land they assigned to those of the citizens who were poor and landless, on payment of a small rent into the public treasury. But when the wealthy began to offer larger rents and to drive the poorer people out, a law was enacted [367 B.C.] that no person could hold more than three hundred acres of public land. This act for some time checked the avarice of the rich and aided the poor, who retained the land they had rented in the past. Later, however, the rich men of the neighborhood managed to get these lands into their possession by using fictitious names, and finally they claimed most of the public land as their own. The poor, who were thus deprived of their farms, no longer registered for service in war, nor did they care about the education of their children. In a short time there were comparatively few free laborers left in Italy, which swarmed with gangs of foreign slaves. These the rich used in cultivating the lands from which they had driven the free citizens. Gaius Laelius, the close friend of Scipio, tried to reform this abuse; but meeting with opposition from men of influence he soon desisted, fearing a disturbance; as a result he received the name of "the Wise" or "the Prudent," both meanings belonging to the Latin word *Sapiens*.

TIBERIUS' LAND LAW

Tiberius, however, being elected tribune of the people, embarked on the same venture without delay, at the instigation, most people say, of Diophanes the rhetorician and Blossius the philosopher. Diophanes was a refugee from Mitylene, the other was an Italian from Cumae. . . . Some have also charged that Cornelia, the mother of Tiberius, was partly responsible because she frequently upbraided her sons by saying that the Romans called her the daughter of Scipio rather than the mother of the Gracchi. Others say that Spurius Postumius was to blame. He was a man of the same age as Tiberius and his rival as a public speaker. When Tiberius returned from the army he found that Postumius had far outdistanced him in fame and influence and was much looked up to. Tiberius thought to outdo him by promoting a political measure of great daring and great consequence for the people. But his brother Gaius stated in one of his writings that when Tiberius went through Tuscany to Numantia and found the country almost depopulated, there being hardly any free farmers or shepherds but for the most part only imported barbarian slaves, he then first conceived the public policy which in its sequel proved so fatal to his family. However, it is very certain that the people themselves did most to kindle his zeal and determination by writing appeals on porticoes, walls, and monuments, calling upon him to return the public lands to the poor.

9. He did not, however, draw up his law without the advice and assistance of those citizens who were most eminent for their virtue and reputation, among whom were Crassus the *pontifex maximus*, Mucius Scaevola the jurist, who was then consul, and Appius Claudius, his father-in-law. Never did any law appear more moderate and mild, especially in view of such great injustice and avarice. For men who ought to have been punished for transgressing the law, and who should at least have lost title to lands which they illegally enjoyed, were nevertheless to receive compensation for quitting their unlawful claims and giving up the lands to those citizens who needed help. But even though this reform was very moderate — the people were satisfied and ready to forget the past if they could prevent abuses of like nature in the future — the rich hated the law because of their greed and the lawgiver because of their anger and party spirit. They therefore endeavored to confuse the people, declaring that Tiberius was designing a general redivision of lands in order to overthrow the government and put all things in confusion.

But they had no success. For Tiberius, supporting an honorable and just measure with an eloquence sufficient to make a far less credible cause appear plausible, was quite invincible. Whenever the people crowded around the rostra, he would take his place there and speak on behalf of the poor. "The wild beasts of Italy," he would say, "have their own dens as places of repose and refuge, but the men who fight and die for their country enjoy nothing more in it than the air and light; having no houses or settlements of their own, they must wander from place to place with their wives and children. The army commanders are guilty of a ridiculous error when they exhort the common soldiers to defend their sepulchers and altars, for not one among so many Romans has an ancestral altar or tomb. They fight and die to maintain the luxury and wealth of other men. They are called the masters of the world, but they have not one foot of ground to call their own."

10. Eloquence of this nature, spoken to an enthusiastic and sympathetic audience by a person of commanding spirit and genuine feeling, none of the opponents of Tiberius could successfully oppose. Abandoning therefore all discussion and debate, they turned to Marcus Octavius, one of the tribunes, a young man of steady and orderly character and a close friend of Tiberius. For this reason Octavius at first declined the task of opposing him; but finally, under pressure from numerous influential people, he was prevailed upon to do so by vetoing the bringing of the law to a vote. (It is the law that any tribune has the power to veto an act, and that all the other tribunes can do nothing if one of them dissents.) Angered by this procedure, Tiberius withdrew his mild bill and introduced another which was more pleasing to the common people and more severe against the wrongdoers, since it ordered the latter to immediately surrender without compensation all lands which they held contrary to former laws. . . .

Observing that Octavius himself would be an offender against this law, for he held a great deal of public land, Tiberius begged him to stop his opposition, offering to pay the price of Octavius' land out of his own pocket, although he was not rich. But when Octavius refused this offer, Tiberius issued an edict prohibiting all magistrates from exercising their public functions until such time as his law was voted on. . . .

11. When the appointed day came and Tiberius was summoning the people to vote, the rich men carried off the voting urns and thus caused great confusion. But when Tiberius' party appeared strong enough to oppose the other faction and banded together with the intention to do so, Manlius and Fulvius, men of consular rank, threw themselves before Tiberius, took him by the hand, and with tears in their eyes begged him to desist. Tiberius, considering the dangers that were now threatening and having great respect for two such eminent men, asked them what they would advise him to do. They acknowledged themselves unfit to advise on a matter of so great importance, and earnestly entreated him to refer the question to the senate. He agreed; but when the senate assembled it could accomplish nothing, owing to the influence of the rich faction. Tiberius then resorted to a course neither legal nor fair, the removal of Octavius from his tribunate, for it was impossible for him in any other way to bring his law to a vote. . . .

12. When the people again met, Tiberius mounted the rostra and tried a second time to persuade Octavius. But when Octavius could not be persuaded, Tiberius referred the whole matter to the people, calling on them to vote at once on whether Octavius should be deposed or not. When seventeen of the thirty-five tribes had already voted against Octavius and there was needed only the votes of one more tribe for his deposition, Tiberius called a halt to the proceedings and once more renewed his entreaties, embracing and kissing Octavius before the assembly, earnestly begging him not to allow himself to be so dishonored or force Tiberius to be known as the promoter of so severe and odious

a measure. Octavius, we are told, did seem a little softened and moved by these entreaties; his eyes filled with tears and he stood silent for a long time. But when he looked toward the men of wealth and substance who stood gathered in a body together, partly for shame and partly for fear of disgracing himself with them, he boldly bid Tiberius to do what he pleased. The law was passed and Tiberius ordered one of his freedmen to remove Octavius from the rostra. This use of a freedman as a public official made the action seem all the sadder — Octavius being dragged out in such an ignominious manner. The people immediately assaulted him, while the rich men ran to his assistance. With some difficulty, Octavius was snatched away and safely conveyed out of the crowd; though one of his faithful slaves, who had placed himself in front of his master to protect him, had his eyes torn out, much to the displeasure of Tiberius who, when he perceived the disturbance, ran with all haste to stop the violence.

13. The land law was then passed, and three commissioners were appointed to make a survey and distribute the public land. These were Tiberius himself, his father-in-law Appius Claudius, and his brother Gaius, who was not in Rome but in the army serving with Scipio against Numantia. These appointments Tiberius arranged quietly and without disturbance; in addition he had a new tribune chosen, not a person of distinction but a certain Mucius, one of his own clients. The great men of the city resented all this and, fearing lest he grow even more powerful, they took every opportunity to insult him in the senate. When he requested to have the customary tent provided at public expense for his use while dividing the land, though it was a favor commonly granted to persons employed in business of much less importance, it was refused him; and the allowance made him for his daily expenses was fixed at nine sesterces [about fifty cents]. The chief promoter of these affronts was Publius Nasica, who completely surrendered himself to his hatred of Tiberius, for he was a large holder of public lands and greatly resented being forced to give them up. The people, on the other hand, became more and more excited. . . .

THE SENATE'S CONTROL OF FOREIGN POLICY ENDANGERED

14. About this time Attalus Philometor [the last king of Pergamum] died, and Eudemus of Pergamum brought his will to Rome. In it the king had made the Roman people his heirs. Tiberius courted popular favor by immediately proposing a law to distribute the money of Attalus among the citizens who were receiving public land, to enable them to stock and cultivate their farms. As for what was to be done with the cities in the kingdom of Attalus, he declared that this matter did not belong to the senate but to the people, and that he would refer to the judgment of the people. By this proposal he offended the senate more than ever, and Pompeius arose and told that body that he was a neighbor of Tiberius and so he knew that Eudemus the Pergamenian had presented Tiberius with a royal diadem and a purple robe, since he intended to be king of Rome. . . .

15. Tiberius soon realized that the action he had taken against Octavius had alarmed not only the nobility, but the people as well, because they felt that the dignity of the tribunes, so carefully guarded up to that time, had been insulted and destroyed. He therefore made a speech to the people, from which it may be proper to quote some of the argument to illustrate his force and persuasiveness as a speaker. He admitted that a tribune was sacred and inviolable because he was consecrated to be the guardian and protector of the people, "but if he degenerates so far as to harm the people, reducing their power and taking away their right to vote, he stands deprived of his immunity by the neglect of the conditions on which it was bestowed upon him. Otherwise we should be obliged to allow a tribune to do what he wished, even though he should try to destroy the Capitol or set fire to the arsenal. He who attempts such acts would be a bad tribune; he who attacks the power of the people is no tribune at all. Is it not inconceivable that a tribune should have power to imprison a consul, while the people who gave him that power have no right to take it from him when he uses it to their detriment? For tribunes and consuls alike are elected by the people. The rule of a king, which embraces all power in itself, is also sanctified by the most solemn religious ceremonies. Yet the citizens deposed Tarquin when he acted wrongfully; because of one man's arrogance, the ancient government under which Rome was founded was abolished. What is there in all Rome so sacred and venerable as the Vestal Virgins, who tend the eternal fire? Yet if one of them breaks her vows, she is buried alive; the sanctity granted her for the gods' sake is forfeited when she offends against the gods. So likewise a tribune loses his inviolability, which was granted him for the people's sake, when he offends against the people by attacking that very power from which he derives his own. We consider him to be a legally chosen tribune who is elected by a majority of votes; is it not equally legal to depose him by a unanimous vote? Nothing is so sacred and inviolable as religious offerings; yet the people were never prohibited from using them, or removing and carrying them wherever they pleased. So, just like some sacred object, they have the power to transfer the tribunate from one man to another. Nor can that office be considered inviolable and irremovable which so many of those who have held have of their own accord asked to be discharged from."

A SECOND TERM AND OTHER PROPOSALS

16. These were the principal points of Tiberius' defense. But his friends, discerning the threats and the hostile combination against him, were of the opinion that the safest way would be for him to be reelected tribune for the following year. Accordingly he again sought to secure popular support with fresh laws: reducing the term of military service, granting the right of appeal from the judges to the people, and adding to the judges, who at that time were all senators, an equal number of citizens of the equestrian order. Indeed, he endeavored as much as possible to weaken the power of the senate, being influ-

enced more by passion and partisanship than by any regard for justice and the public good. . . .

17. . . . Several men ran to Tiberius with a message from his friends on the Capitol, saying that all things there went according to expectation. And indeed Tiberius' appearance there went well at first, for as soon as he appeared the people welcomed him with loud cheers, and as he went up the hill they repeated their expressions of joy, gathering around him so that no stranger might approach.

18. Mucius then began again to call the roll of the tribes, but he could do nothing in proper order because a disturbance caused by those who were on the edge of the crowd, where there was a struggle going on with those of the opposite party who were pushing and trying to force their way in. In the midst of this confusion, Flavius Flaccus, a senator . . . finally reached Tiberius and informed him that the rich men, having failed to win over the consul in a meeting of the senate, had decided among themselves to assassinate him, and for that purpose had armed a great number of their clients and slaves.

19. Tiberius reported this to those around him, and they immediately tucked up their togas and seized the fasces with which the officers keep back the crowd. These they broke and distributed the pieces to use against attack. Those who stood at a distance wondered at this and asked what was going on. Tiberius, knowing that they could not hear him at that distance, lifted his hand to his head to indicate the great danger he was in. His opponents, noticing this, ran off at once to the senate house and reported that Tiberius desired the people to bestow a crown upon him, claiming this was the meaning of his touching his head. This news enraged the senators, and Nasica demanded that the consul should rescue the state and destroy the tyrant. The consul quietly replied that he would resort to no violence, nor would he allow any citizen to be put to death without a trial; neither would he allow any measure to go into effect, if by persuasion or compulsion on the part of Tiberius the people voted to do anything illegal. Thereupon Nasica jumped from his seat and cried out: "Since the consul has betrayed the state, let those who would save our country follow me!" He then threw the edge of his toga over his head and ran to the Capitol. Those who followed him wrapped their togas around their left arms and forced their way through the crowd. Since they were men of great dignity, the common people did not obstruct their passing; instead they pushed one another aside and fled. . . . Tiberius tried to save himself by flight. As he was running he was stopped by a senator who caught hold of his toga, but he threw it off and fled in his tunic. Then he stumbled and fell over the bodies of those who had been knocked down. As he struggled to rise, everyone saw Publius Satureius, one of his fellow tribunes, give him the first fatal blow by hitting him on the head with the leg of a bench. Lucius Rufus claimed the second blow, as though it had been a deed to be proud of. And of the rest more than three hundred were killed with clubs and stones, but not one with a sword.

20. This, we are told, was the first disturbance at Rome since the expulsion of the kings to end in bloodshed and the murder of citizens. All others — neither small nor about trivial matters — were amicably settled by mutual concessions, the senate yielding for fear of the commons, and the commons out of respect for the senate. And it is probable that Tiberius could easily have been persuaded to compromise, and he certainly would have yielded if his opponents had not resorted to violence and bloodshed, since he had not more than three thousand followers. It is probable that this rising against him was fomented more out of the hatred and anger of the rich than for the reasons they alleged. In support of this we may cite the barbarous and inhuman treatment of his dead body: they would not allow his own brother to bury it at night, as he requested, but they threw it, along with the other corpses, into the river. Nor was this all; they banished some of his friends without trial, and they arrested and killed others. . . . Blossius of Cumae was brought before the consuls, and when he was asked about what had happened, he admitted that he had done whatever Tiberius requested. "What," cried Nasica, "then if Tiberius had ordered you to burn the Capitol, would you have burned it?" His first answer was that Tiberius never would have given such an order; but being pressed with the same question by several others, he declared: "If Tiberius had ordered it, it would have been right for me to do it, for he never would have given such an order if it had not been for the peoples' good." Blossius was acquitted. . . .

Gaius Gracchus: The Roman New Deal, Continued

To an even greater degree than his older brother, Gaius Gracchus labored to bring government back to the people. He was elected tribune in 124 B.C., and until he failed to be reelected for a third term he consistently ignored the Senate in presenting his comprehensive program of legislation before the popular assembly. When the use of legitimate but quite unethical means of stopping him failed, the senatorial oligarchy contributed to the precedent of force,

From Plutarch, *Parallel Lives*, "Gaius Gracchus," based on the translation by John Dryden and revised by Arthur H. Clough.

which it had already established in dealing with his elder brother, by forcing Gaius' death and decreeing death without trial for some three thousand of his supporters. After this there remained little hope of solving Rome's problems by democratic and constitutional means.

Although mixed with an amount of political opportunism, Gaius Gracchus' legislative program was far more constructive and statesmanlike than the simple land law of his more visionary brother. Where Tiberius hoped to eliminate present problems in one fell swoop with the restoration of the old Roman agricultural society, Gaius realistically sought to solve each specific problem by remedial legislation fitted to the demands of the situation.

Men will always debate the validity of much of Gaius Gracchus' major legislation, but few will doubt, after reading Plutarch's account of the constructive energy with which he faced Rome's problems, that he deserves the name of statesman. It should not be difficult to understand why the Roman people, as Plutarch reports, "looked with amazement at the man himself, seeing him attended by crowds of building contractors, artisans, ambassadors, magistrates, soldiers, and learned men, to all of whom he was of easy access."

CHARACTER AND POPULARITY

1. Gaius Gracchus at first, either for fear of his brother's enemies or because he wanted to make them more odious to the people, withdrew from public life and lived quietly at home like a humbled man who wanted to pass his life in inaction. Some, indeed, went so far as to say that he disliked his brother's program and had repudiated it. He was also still a youth, being nine years younger than his brother, and Tiberius was not yet thirty when he was slain. In time, however, his true character asserted itself — an utter aversion to indolence, effeminacy, drinking, and moneymaking. And it became clear from the emphasis he placed on the study of oratory as wings upon which he might aspire to public office, that he did not intend to pass his days in obscurity. . . .

3. . . . Gaius now came forward to ask for the tribuneship. Though he was universally opposed by all men of distinction, so many people from all parts of Italy came to vote for him that lodgings for many could not be supplied in the city; and the Campus Martius not being large enough to contain the assembly, many climbed upon the roofs and the tilings of the houses to shout their support. However, the nobility so far forced the people to their will and disappointed Gaius' hopes that he was not returned the first, as was expected, but the fourth tribune. But after entering into his office, he quickly made himself first tribune, for he was a better orator than any of his contemporaries, and the passion with which he still lamented his brother's death made him bold in speaking. . . .

LEGISLATIVE PROGRAM

5. Of the laws which he introduced to win the favor of the people and undermine the power of the senate, the first concerned the public lands, which

were to be divided among the poor citizens; another concerned the soldiers, who were to be clothed at public expense without any deduction from their pay, and no one was to be conscripted into the army who was under seventeen years old; another gave Italians the same voting rights as the citizens of Rome; a fourth related to the supply of grain and the lowering of its price to the poor; and a fifth regulated the courts of justice. This last law greatly reduced the power of the senators. Hitherto they alone sat as judges and were therefore much feared by the common people and the equestrian order. Gaius added three hundred citizens of equestrian rank to the senators, who also numbered three hundred, and entrusted the judicial authority to the whole six hundred.

In arguing for this law he showed in many ways unusual earnestness; whereas other popular leaders had always turned their faces toward the senate and the place called the *comitium*, he now for the first time turned the other way, toward the people, and he continued to do so thereafter — an insignificant change of posture, yet it marked no small revolution in state affairs, in a way transforming the constitution from an aristocracy to a democracy, his action implying that speakers should address themselves to the people and not to the senate.

6. When the people not only ratified this law but gave him power to select the equestrians of his choice to be judges, he acquired almost kingly power, and even the senate listened to his advice. Nor did he advise any measure that might lessen the honor of that body. For example, his decree concerning the grain which the propraetor Fabius sent from Spain was very just and honorable; for he persuaded the senate to sell the grain and return the money to the Spanish provinces, and also to censure Fabius for making the Roman government odious and burdensome to its subjects. This earned him great respect and good will in the provinces.

He also introduced bills to found colonies, construct roads, and establish public granaries. He himself undertook the management and superintendence of all these works and was never too busy to attend to the execution of all these different and great undertakings, in each instance doing so with wonderful rapidity and industry as though it were his only task. Even those who hated or feared him were astonished to see what a capacity he had for effecting and completing all he undertook. As for the people themselves, they looked with amazement at the man himself, seeing him attended by crowds of building contractors, artisans, ambassadors, magistrates, soldiers, and learned men, to all of whom he was of easy access. Yet he preserved his dignity while being affable, and he adapted his own nature to those who addressed him. Thus he demonstrated that those who had represented him as a terrible, overbearing, and violent person, were ugly slanderers. He was thus a more skillful popular leader in his private conduct and dealings with men than in his public speeches.

7. He was especially interested in constructing roads, laying stress on beauty and grace as well as utility. They were carried through the country in a perfectly straight·line, and were paved with hewn stone laid upon solid masses

of gravel. Depressions were filled and intersecting watercourses were bridged; and the roads were so well-levelled — being of equal height on both sides — that the work presented a uniform and beautiful sight. In addition, he had the roads measured in miles . . . , and erected stone pillars to mark the distance. He placed other stones at short intervals on both sides of the road to help travellers mount their horses without needing a groom.

TACTICS OF THE SENATE

8. When the people praised him for these services and were ready to express their affection for him in any way, he said in a speech that he had one favor to ask, which, if it were granted, he would value greatly, but if it were denied he would not blame them. This statement led people to believe that his ambition was to be consul, and everyone expected that he would be a candidate for the consulship and the tribunate at the same time. But when the day for the election of consuls was at hand and everyone was in great expectation, he appeared in the Campus Martius with Gaius Fannius, canvassing for him with his friends. This turned the tide in Fannius' favor. He was chosen consul, and Gaius was elected tribune for the second time on a wave of popular enthusiasm, though he was not a candidate and did not seek the office. But when he saw the senate openly hostile and Fannius weakening in his friendship toward him, he again wooed the people with other laws. He proposed that colonists be sent to repeople Tarentum and Capua, and that the Latins should enjoy the same privileges as Roman citizens. The senate, fearing that he would become invincible, made a new and unusual attempt to alienate the people from him by playing the demagogue and offering them favors contrary to the best intertests of the state. One of Gaius' fellow tribunes was Livius Drusus, a man of as good a family and as well-educated as any Roman, and the equal in eloquence and wealth to the most honored and powerful men of the time. To him the nobles turned, urging him to attack Gaius and join them against him, not by resorting to violence or clashing with the people, but by using his office to gratify and please them. . . .

9. So Livius devoted his tribunate to the senate's interests, introducing laws that were neither honorable nor advantageous but had one purpose only, to outdo Gaius in winning the favor of the mob, as in a comedy. The senate thus showed clearly that it was not angry with Gaius' program but desired to destroy him completely — or at least to humble him. For when Gaius proposed to found two colonies, to which he would admit only the better class of citizens, they accused him of being a demagogue. But when Livius proposed to found twelve colonies, each to consist of three thousand poor citizens, they supported him. When Gaius divided the public land among the needy and charged each of them a small rent to be paid into the treasury, they were angry and accused him of truckling to the mob. Yet they commended Livius when he proposed to exempt the allotment holders from paying any rent. They were angry with Gaius for offering the Latins equal voting rights, but when Livius proposed that it be made unlawful for a Roman to flog a Latin soldier, they

supported his law. In his speeches to the people, Livius always said that the laws he proposed were agreeable to the senate, which was concerned with the people's welfare. This really was the only good result of his political activities, for the people now looked more kindly on the senate. . . .

12. After Gaius' return to Rome [from Carthage, where he supervised the founding of a colony], he gave up his house on the Palatine hill and went to live near the forum, which he thought more democratic since most of the poor and humble citizens lived there. He then announced the rest of his laws, intending to have them ratified by popular vote. A vast number of people gathered from all parts, but the senate persuaded the consul Fannius to order out of the city all who were not Romans. Accordingly a new and unusual proclamation was made, prohibiting any of the allies and friends of Rome to appear in the city during that time. Gaius published a counter edict, denouncing the consul and promising the allies his support if they remained in Rome. However, he did not keep his word, for though he saw one of his friends and companions dragged to prison by Fannius' officers, he passed by without aiding him, either because he was afraid to put to test his power which was already on the decline, or because he was unwilling, as he said, to give his enemies the opportunity they were seeking of coming to a violent collision. He had also, for the following reason, incurred the anger of his fellow tribunes. An exhibition of gladiators was to be held for the people in the forum, and most of the magistrates had erected seats round about with the intention of renting them. Gaius ordered them to dismantle the seats so the poor might see the show without cost. When no one obeyed this order, he collected a group of city employees and removed the seats the night before the spectacle. By the next morning the forum was clear, and in accomplishing this the common people thought he had acted the part of a man. But he had annoyed his colleagues, who regarded him as audacious and violent.

LAST DAYS

This act, it was believed, cost him the election to the tribunate for the third time; although he received the most votes, his colleagues out of revenge caused false returns to be made. This story is disputed, however. It is certain that he greatly resented this failure and behaved with unusual arrogance toward some of his adversaries who exulted over his defeat, telling them that their laughter was a false sardonic mirth since they little realized how much his political measures threw them into obscurity.

13. After effecting the election of Opimius to the consulship, Gaius' enemies began to repeal many of his laws and to meddle with the organization of his colony at Carthage. They omitted nothing that was likely to irritate him, in order that his reaction might give them grounds to get rid of him. Gaius at first endured all this patiently; but finally, at the urging of his friends, especially Fulvius, he organized his supporters to oppose the consul. . . .

On the day when Opimius intended to repeal the laws of Gaius, both parties met very early on the Capitol. After the consul had offered sacrifice, one of his officers named Quintus Antyllius was carrying out the entrails of the sacrificed victim when he cried out to the partisans of Fulvius, "Make way for honest citizens, you rascals!" Some say that when he uttered these words he extended his bare arm in an insulting gesture. At any rate he was killed on the spot, stabbed with large writing styles said to have been made expressly for this purpose. The murder caused sudden panic in the assembly, and it produced exactly opposite effects on the leaders of the two parties. Gaius was much distressed and severely reprimanded his followers for providing their adversaries with a pretense for action which they had long awaited; but Opimius was elated, having found the opportunity he wanted, and he urged the people to get revenge. A shower of rain occurred just then, and the assembly was dissolved.

14. Early the next morning the consul convened the senate and proceeded to transact business. In the meantime the corpse of Antyllius was laid upon a bier and, as prearranged, carried through the forum and past the senate house with loud cries and lamentations. Opimius knew what was happening, but as he pretended to be surprised at the noise, the senate went out to investigate. . . . On returning to the senate house, they passed a decree investing the consul Opimius with extraordinary power to protect the state and suppress the tyrants. The consul immediately ordered the senators to arm themselves, and each member of the equestrian order was directed to appear early the next morning accompanied by two well-armed slaves. Fulvius also made his preparations and collected a rabble; but Gaius, as he left the forum, stopped in front of his father's statue and looked at it for some time without speaking, then he burst into tears and departed with a groan. . . .

16. When [next day] the people were assembled, Gaius advised Fulvius to send his youngest son to the forum with a herald's staff in his hand. He was a very handsome and modest youth, and with tears in his eyes he addressed conciliatory words to the consul and the senate. The majority of those present were inclined to come to terms; but Opimius declared that the petitioners should not send messengers in an attempt to persuade the senate, but should surrender themselves for trial, like law-abiding citizens, and then beg for mercy. He ordered the youth not to come back again unless he came on those terms. Gaius, it is reported, was willing to go and clear himself before the senate; but no one else agreed with him, so Fulvius sent his son a second time to plead in their behalf as before. But Opimius, who was eager for a fight, ordered the youth to be seized and imprisoned, and then he advanced on Fulvius' supporters with many legionary soldiers and Cretan archers. These archers inflicted so many wounds that panic and flight quickly followed. Fulvius fled into an unused bath where he was soon discovered and slain, together with his oldest son. Gaius was not observed taking part in the violence; greatly disturbed by what was happening, he withdrew into the Temple of Diana. There he attempted to kill himself, but was prevented by his faithful friends, Pomponius and Licinius, who took away his sword and urged him to fly. It is reported that,

falling upon his knees and lifting his hands to the goddess, he prayed that the Roman people might always remain in slavery as a punishment for their ingratitude and treachery, for a proclamation of amnesty had been announced and most of them were openly deserting him.

17. Gaius then fled, closely pursued by his enemies . . . . All the onlookers, as though at a race, urged him to run faster, but no one came to his aid, nor did anyone lend him a horse when he asked for one, for his pursuers were close behind him. He barely had time to hide in a sacred grove of the Furies. There he fell by the hand of his slave Philocrates, who then killed himself on the body of his master. . . .

They say that when Gaius' head had been cut off and was being carried away, a friend of Opimius named Septimuleius forcibly took it from him because, just as the fighting began, they had issued a proclamation that whoever brought in the head of Gaius or Fulvius would receive its weight in gold. So Septimuleius fixed Gaius' head on his spear and presented it to Opimius. Scales were brought in and it was found to weigh seventeen and two-thirds pounds. Septimuleius was as great a knave as he was a scoundrel, for he had taken out the brain and replaced it with lead. But those who brought in the head of Fulvius got nothing, because they belonged to the lower class. The bodies of Gaius and Fulvius and their followers — they numbered three thousand — were thrown into the Tiber. Their property was confiscated, their wives forbidden to go into mourning, and Gaius' wife Licinia was deprived of her widow's portion. Most inhumane of all was their treatment of Fulvius' youngest son. He had not taken up arms against them or been present at the fighting, but had only tried to effect an agreement; for this he was first imprisoned, then slain.

But what angered the common people most was that Opimius built a temple to Concord, which was viewed as evidence of his insolence and arrogance — a kind of triumph for the slaughter of so many citizens. One night someone added this verse under the inscription on the temple: "Folly and Discord Concord's temple built."

18. This Opimius, the first consul to exercise the power of a dictator, who condemned without trial three thousand citizens, among them Gaius Gracchus and Fulvius Flaccus, one of whom had been consul and had celebrated a triumph, while the other far excelled all his contemporaries in virtue and honor — this Opimius was afterwards incapable of keeping his hands from fraud. When he was sent as ambassador to Jugurtha, King of Numidia, he accepted bribes. On his return, he was found guilty of shameful corruption. He grew old in infamy, hated and insulted by the people, who, though humbled and frightened for a time, did not fail before long to let everybody know the respect and veneration they had for the memory of the Gracchi. They ordered statues of the brothers to be made and set up in public view, and they declared the places where they were slain to be holy ground and brought there the first-fruits of the season as offerings. Many came daily to worship there, as at a temple of the gods.

The Conspiracy of Catiline

The Roman Republic in decay

The sordid story of the conspiracy of Catiline (63 B.C.) is an excellent commentary on political, social, and moral conditions in the decaying Roman Republic. The prodigal living of the nobility, growing out of the taste for luxury that accompanied Roman expansion, and the enormous cost of campaigning for public office, caused by the prevalence of bribery and corruption, had created a chronic condition of debt and bankruptcy among many patrician families. The brilliant but dissolute Catiline became the leader of this group and, having failed three times to win the consulship by constitutional means — on his third attempt, in 63 B.C., he advocated a general cancellation of debts — he conspired to gain it by causing disruption and employing force. He may have been influenced by the example of Sulla, who in 82 B.C. had used his army to establish a dictatorship in the interest of the Optimates or "best people," as the senatorial oligarchy was now called. Catiline had served under Sulla, but now he posed as a leader of the Populares ("peoples' party") and successor to Gaius Gracchus, although his democratic sentiments appear to have been a sham to cover his own selfish interests and those of his followers, disreputable young nobles whose futures had been frustrated, and the city mob, now largely composed of non-Roman freedmen who equated democracy with governmental handouts. The corrupt character of the Roman masses and the nature of their interest in Catiline's program was noted by Plutarch who reports that in the year following the suppression of the conspiracy, "Cato [the Younger], seeing the people greatly stirred up by Caesar in the affair of Catiline and dangerously inclined toward a revolution, persuaded the Senate to vote a dole to the poor, and the giving of this halted the disturbance and checked the insurrection."

The following account of the conspiracy, written by Sallust (86–34 B.C.), is considered more reliable than that found in the famous Catilinarian Orations of Cicero, who as consul had suppressed Catiline. Yet neither was Sallust impartial, despite his claim to writing objective history with Thucydides as his model. He had been an active partisan of Julius Caesar and the popular party and, after Caesar's assassination, had turned to writing the history of his time in a manner which highlighted the incompetence and corruption of the Optimates. To some modern scholars, Catiline was motivated mainly by wounded pride and fierce ambition thwarted by the Establishment and the electoral

Based on the translation by John Selby Watson.

process; to Sallust he was a demagogue whose true character, typical of the whole aristocracy, was ultimately recognized by even the common people.

Sallust's view of Republican history, a story of degeneration and moral decay resulting from Roman expansion, became the favorite reading of the Romans of the later Empire, and especially of the Christians. The famous character sketch of the conspiratress Sempronia, the mother of Caesar's assassin Decimus Brutus, illustrates both Sallust's skill in depicting the vices of the nobility and the degree of his bias in favor of Caesar. His moving description of the death of Catiline contributes to the suspicion that Catiline may deserve better of history than ancient and unfavorable sources of information allow.

SALLUST'S PURPOSE

4. When I had found peace of mind after many troubles and trials and had determined to pass the remainder of my days unconnected with politics, it was not my intention to waste my valuable leisure in indolence and inactivity, or to engage in the slavish occupations of farming or hunting. Rather, I decided to return to those studies from which a misguided ambition had lured me — the writing of monographs on episodes worthy of record in the history of the Roman people, a task for which I felt myself well-qualified as my mind was uninfluenced by the hopes and fears of political partisanship. I shall accordingly give as true and brief an account as I can of the conspiracy of Catiline, for I think it a subject eminently deserving of record because of the unusual nature of the crime and its danger to the state. But before beginning my narrative, I must give a short description of the character of the man.

PERSONALITY AND MOTIVES OF CATILINE

5. Lucius Catiline was a man of noble birth and of eminent mental and physical endowments, but he had a vicious and depraved nature. From his youth he had delighted in civil war, bloodshed, pillage, and political strife, and in such activities he had spent his early manhood. His body could endure hunger, cold, and lack of sleep to an incredible degree. His mind was daring, crafty, versatile, and capable of any kind of pretense or cover-up. He was covetous of other men's property and prodigal of his own. A man of violent passions, he had abundant eloquence but little wisdom. His insatiable ambition was always pursuing objects extravagant, romantic, and unattainable.

After Sulla's dictatorship, a strong desire of seizing the government had possessed him, nor did he care by what means he might achieve it. His violent spirit was goaded more and more every day by poverty and a consciousness of guilt, both of which were aggravated by those evil practices which I have mentioned. He was spurred on, too, by the corrupt morals of society, which were thoroughly depraved by two pernicious and opposite vices, extravagance and avarice.

"THE CONDUCT OF OUR ANCESTORS"

Since the occasion has thus brought public morals to my attention, it seems appropriate to look back and briefly describe the conduct of our ancestors in peace and war, how they governed the state, which they made so great before leaving it to us, and how by gradual degeneration it changed from the most virtuous of states to the most vicious and corrupted. . . .

8. Surely Fortune rules all things; she makes all events famous or obscure according to caprice rather than merit. The exploits of the Athenians, as far as I can judge, were very great and glorious, but somewhat less important than her fame indicates. But because writers of great talent flourished there, the actions of the Athenians are celebrated over the world as the most splendid achievements. Thus the merit of men of action is rated as high as illustrious intellects exalt it in their writings. But the Romans never had that advantage, because with them the most able men were the most actively engaged in affairs. No one exercised the mind independently of the body; every man of ability preferred action to words and thought that his own deeds should be celebrated by others rather than that he should record theirs.

9. Good morals, accordingly, were cultivated at home and in the camp. There was the greatest possible harmony and the least possible avarice. Justice and probity prevailed, not so much from the influence of laws as from natural inclination. They displayed animosity, enmity, and resentment only against the enemy. Citizens contended with citizens in nothing but honor. They were lavish in their religious services, frugal in their homes, and loyal to their friends.

By these two virtues, boldness in war and justice in peace, they maintained themselves and their state. I consider the following to be convincing proof of this: in time of war punishment was more often inflicted on those who attacked an enemy contrary to orders and retired too slowly when commanded to retreat than on those who had dared to abandon their standards or give ground when pressed by the enemy; in time of peace they governed more by conferring benefits than by exciting terror, and when wronged they would rather pardon than avenge the injury.

"UNIVERSAL INNOVATION"

10. But when by perseverance and integrity the Republic had increased its power, when mighty kings had been vanquished in war, when barbarous tribes and populous states had been reduced to subjection, when Carthage, the rival of Rome's dominion, had been utterly destroyed and sea and land lay everywhere open, Fortune became unkind and introduced universal innovation. Those who had easily endured toil, danger, anxiety, and adversity had found leisure and wealth, the objects of desire to others, to be a burden and a curse. Now first the love of money, then of power, began to prevail, and these became the sources of every evil. For avarice destroyed honesty, integrity, and other honorable principles, and in their stead inculcated pride, inhumanity, contempt of religion, and the belief that everything has its price. Ambition prompted many to become deceitful, to keep one thing concealed in the breast and another ready on the tongue, to judge friendships and enmities not by merit but by profit, and to value a good front more than a good heart. These vices at first grew slowly and were sometimes punished. But later, when the infection had

spread like a plague, the state was entirely changed, and the government, once so just and admirable, became cruel and intolerable.

11. At first, however, it was ambition rather than avarice that influenced the minds of men. Ambition is a vice which comes nearer to being a virtue than avarice. For glory, honor, and power are desired by the worthy and the worthless; but the one pursues them by just methods, while the other, being destitute of honorable qualities, works with fraud and deceit. But avarice has only money for its object, which no wise man has ever desired. It is like a deadly poison, which enervates whatever is manly in body or mind. It is always unbounded and insatiable, and is abated neither by abundance nor by want.

But after Lucius Sulla, having taken over the state by force of arms, proceeded after a good beginning to a bad end, all became robbers and plunderers. Some coveted houses, others land. His victorious troops knew neither restraint nor moderation, but inflicted on the citizens disgraceful and inhuman outrages. Their rapacity was increased by the fact that Sulla had sought to secure the loyalty of the forces which he commanded in Asia by allowing them, contrary to the practice of our ancestors, extraordinary luxury and exemption from discipline, and pleasant resorts had easily enervated the warlike spirits of soldiers on leave. There it was that the army of the Roman people first became habituated to women and wine, and to admire statues, paintings, and sculptured vases which they stole from public edifices and private dwellings, plundering temples and lacking all respect for everything both sacred and profane. Such troops, accordingly, when once they obtained a victory, left nothing to the vanquished. Since success undermines the principles even of philosophers, how should these depraved men show moderation in victory?

12. As soon as wealth came to be considered an honor, and fame, privilege, and power depended on it, honesty lost its influence, poverty was thought a disgrace, and a blameless life was regarded as a sign of ill-nature. The result of the influence of riches was that high living, selfishness, and insolence began to prevail among the young. They stole and squandered, cared little for what was their own and coveted what was another's, set aside modesty and continence, lost all distinction between sacred and profane, and threw off all consideration of self-restraint.

It is worthwhile to compare our modern mansions and villas, some of which are the size of cities, with the temples which our god-fearing ancestors erected. Our forefathers adorned the temples of the gods with piety and their homes with their own glory, and they took nothing from those whom they conquered except the power of doing harm. Their base descendants, on the contrary, have even wrested from our allies, with the most flagrant injustice, whatever our brave and victorious ancestors had left them, as though the only use of power were to inflict injury.

13. Need I mention those displays of extravagance which can be believed only by those who have seen them? Mountains have been leveled and seas covered over by private citizens for their building operations. Such men I consider to have made a sport of their wealth, since they were impatient to squander shamelessly what they might have enjoyed with honor.

The passion for lust, vice, and all kinds of sensuality had spread with equal force. Men forgot their sex; women threw off all the restraints of modesty. To gratify their appetites, they sought out every kind of delicacy by land and by sea; they slept before there was any need for sleep; they did not wait to feel hunger, thirst, cold, or fatigue, but anticipated them all with decadent indulgence. Such practices drove the young, when their patrimonies were exhausted, to criminal practices, for minds impregnated with evil habits could not easily abstain from gratifying their passions, and so were even more recklessly devoted to all kinds of rapacity and extravagance.

"ACCOMPLICES AND ADHERENTS"

14. In so populous and so corrupt a city, Catiline could easily keep around him, like a bodyguard, gangs of the unprincipled and desperate. For all these shameless, libertine, and profligate characters who had dissipated their patrimonies by gambling, luxury, and sensuality; all who had contracted heavy debts to purchase immunity for their crimes or offenses; all assassins or sacrilegious persons from every quarter, convicted or dreading conviction for their evil deeds; all, in addition, who maintained themselves by perjury or civil bloodshed; all, in short, who were wicked, poor, or had a guilty conscience, were the associates and intimate friends of Catiline. And if anyone still innocent fell into his company, by daily contact and temptation he soon became similar to the rest. It was the young whose acquaintance he chiefly sought; their minds, being still impressionable and unsettled, were easily ensnared. In order to gratify their youthful desires, he furnished mistresses to some, bought horses and dogs for others, and spared neither his purse nor his honor to make them his devoted followers. Some, I know, have thought that the youth who frequented the house of Catiline were guilty of crimes against nature, but this report arose rather from other causes than from any evidence of the fact. . . .

16. . . . Depending on such accomplices and adherents, and knowing that the load of debt was everywhere great and that Sulla's veterans had spent their money too freely and, remembering the loot acquired from past victories, were longing for civil war, Catiline planned a revolution. There was no army in Italy; Pompey was fighting in a distant part of the world; he himself had great hopes of being elected consul; the senate was wholly off its guard; everything was quiet and tranquil — all these circumstances were exceedingly favorable for Catiline. . . .

AFTER HIS FAILURE AT THE POLLS, CATILINE ADDRESSES HIS COMRADES

20. ". . . What I have been planning you have already heard individually. My own ardor for action is daily more and more excited when I consider what our lot will be unless we ourselves assert our claims to liberty. Ever since the state has come under the power and jurisdiction of a few, foreign kings and princes have constantly paid them tribute and nations and tribes have paid them taxes. All the rest of us, however brave and worthy, whether noble or plebeian, have been regarded as a mere mob, without influence or authority, and subject to those who in a true state would be afraid of us. Thus all influ-

ence, power, honor, and wealth are in their hands or where they choose to bestow them; to us they leave only insults, dangers, persecutions, and poverty. How long, brave comrades, will you submit to such indignities? Is it not better to die in a glorious attempt, than, after having been the sport of other men's insolence, to lose a miserable and dishonored existence like cowards?

"But success — I call gods and men to witness! — is in our grasp. We are young and our spirit is unbroken, whereas our oppressors are enfeebled by age and wealth. We have only to make a start; the course of events will accomplish the rest.

"Who in the world who is a man at heart can endure that they should have a surplus of wealth to squander in building out over the seas and in leveling mountains, while we lack the means to buy even the necessities of life? They join together two houses or more, and we have not a home to call our own. Though they purchase paintings, statues, and sculptured vases, pull down new buildings to erect others, and lavish and abuse their wealth in every possible way, yet with all their extravagance they cannot exhaust it. But for us there is poverty at home and debts everywhere; our present circumstances are bad, our prospects much worse; what, in fact, have we left but a miserable existence?

"Wake up, then! Look! Liberty, that liberty of which you have so often dreamed is set before your eyes, together with wealth, honor, and glory. All these prizes Fortune offers to the victorious. Let the facts, the opportunity, your poverty, your peril, and the rich spoils of war animate you far more than my words. Use me as your leader or as your fellow-soldier; neither my heart nor my hand will ever desert you. These objects I hope to achieve with your help when I am consul — unless indeed my hopes deceive me and you prefer to be slaves rather than masters." . . .

THE CONSPIRATRESS SEMPRONIA

25. Among the number of female adherents was Sempronia, a woman who had committed many crimes with the spirit of a man. In birth and beauty, in her husband and her children, she was extremely fortunate. Well-educated in Greek and Roman literature, she could sing, play, and dance with greater skill than became a respectable woman, and she possessed many other accomplishments that tend to excite the passions. Nothing was of less value to her than honor or chastity. Whether she was more careless of her money or her reputation would have been difficult to decide. Her desires were so ardent that she more often made advances to men than waited for solicitation. She had frequently, before this period, broken her word, repudiated debts, been an accessory to murder, and been propelled into the utmost excesses by her extravagance and poverty. Yet her abilities were not to be despised; she could compose verses, jest, and join in conversation either modest, tender, or licentious. In a word, she was a woman of considerable wit and charm. . . .

"THE COMMON PEOPLE FAVORED CATILINE"

37. Nor was this madness confined only to the ringleaders of the conspiracy; the common people as a whole, in their eagerness for change, favored

the scheme of Catiline. This one would expect from their general character. In every state the poor envy the better class of citizens and make heroes of agitators; they hate the established order and long for something new; they are discontented with their own lot and desire a general upheaval; they can support themselves in the midst of tumult and revolution without worry, since poverty has nothing to lose.

The common people of the city had become disaffected for various reasons. Those who everywhere took the lead in crime and audacity, those who had wasted their substance in dissipation, and all whom vice and villainy had driven from their homes, had poured into Rome as though it were a sewer. Many, remembering the victory of Sulla, when they had seen some raised from common soldiers to senators and others so enriched as to live in luxury and pomp like kings, hoped for similar rewards of victory if they took up arms. Young men from the country, who barely earned a living by manual labor, had been attracted by public and private doles and preferred idleness in the city to hard labor in the field. These and all the others would benefit from public disorders. It is not at all surprising, therefore, that paupers with low principles and high hopes should have considered their country's interest subservient to their own. Those also whose parents had been proscribed by Sulla, whose property had been confiscated, and whose civil rights had been curtailed, looked forward to the event of a war with precisely the same feelings. Again, all the factions opposed to the senate preferred to see the government overturned than themselves out of power. Such was the evil which, after many years, again threatened the state. . . .

AFTER CICERO'S DISCLOSURE OF THE PLOT,
THE COMMON PEOPLE DESERT CATILINE

48. The disclosure of the plot caused the common people, who had at first, in their desire for a change in the government, been only too eager for war, to change their minds. They now cursed Catiline's scheme and praised Cicero to the skies, showing as much joy and happiness as if they had been rescued from slavery. Other acts of civil war they thought would bring gain rather than loss, but the proposed burning of the city they thought inhuman, outrageous, and especially ruinous to themselves, whose whole property consisted of articles of everyday use and the clothes they wore. . . .

DEFEAT AND DEATH OF CATILINE

60. . . . Catiline, when he saw his army routed and himself left with only a few supporters, remembering his birth and former dignity, rushed into the thickest of the enemy, where he was slain, fighting to the last.

61. When the battle was over it became plainly evident how boldly and courageously Catiline's army had fought. For almost every soldier covered with his body when he died the spot he had occupied when alive. A few in the center, whom the praetorian cohort had routed, had fallen some distance away,

but all had wounds in front. Catiline himself was found far in advance of his men among dead bodies of the enemy. He was not quite dead, his face expressing the spirit of haughty defiance that he had shown all his life. Of his whole army not one free-born citizen was taken prisoner either in battle or in flight, for they had spared their own lives no more than those of the enemy. Nor did the army of the Roman people obtain a joyful or bloodless victory; all the bravest men were either killed in the battle or left the field severely wounded. Many who went from the camp to view the ground or plunder the slain, in turning over the bodies of the enemy found a friend, an acquaintance, or a relative. Some also recognized an enemy. Thus gladness and sorrow, grief and joy, were variously felt throughout the whole army.

42

Julius Caesar: The Man and the Statesman

*"He doth bestride the narrow world like a
colossus." — Shakespeare*

Among the complex of problems that destroyed the Roman Republic, the immediate and most apparent one was the rise to supremacy of military leaders strong enough to defy constitution, Senate, and assembly alike. The deep-seated and largely unsolved issues that had arisen during more than a century of Roman expansion were fundamental to the decline of the Republic, but it was on the sword of the victorious and supremely powerful general that the Republic committed suicide.

The First Triumvirate (60–53 B.C.) was formed when three military leaders — Julius Caesar, Pompey, and Crassus — relinquished their rivalry in order to control Rome in their own interests and in defiance of the constitution. After the death of Crassus, however, the Senate, scheming to regain power, won over Pompey with the intent of using him against Caesar and then destroying him.

Reprinted by permission of the publishers and The Loeb Classical Library from J. C. Rolfe's translation of Suetonius, *The Lives of the Caesars*, "The Deified Julius," Book I, Chs. 40–47, 50–60, 62, 65, 67, 68, 74–80 (Cambridge, Mass.: Harvard University Press).

The results of the civil war that followed were not what the Senate had anticipated. Caesar emerged all-powerful and proceeded to manipulate the constitution to give himself absolute power for life. He was convinced that the events of the previous century had made the republican constitution unworkable, that, in his own words, "The republic is nothing but a name, without substance or reality."

During the short period of his dictatorship (46–44 B.C.), Caesar brought order throughout the Roman world. His constructive program of legislation and his vigorous personality are described in the following selections from The Lives of the Caesars by Suetonius (ca. 75–ca. 150 A.D.)

The son of an army officer of the equestrian (capitalist) class, Suetonius held various imperial posts, including that of secretary to the emperor Hadrian, before he retired to a life of study and writing. Of his voluminous writings, only the Lives — the biographies of Julius Caesar and the first eleven emperors (Augustus to Domitian) — has survived entire, an indication of its early and continuing popularity. It is also an outstanding source of information on the early Empire, for despite Suetonius' uncritical fondness for gossip and scandal he frequently quotes contemporary documents and uses other sources of great value to the historian.

CAESAR THE STATESMAN

40. Then [46 B.C.] turning his attention to the reorganization of the state, he reformed the calendar, which the pontiffs had long since so disordered, by neglecting to order the necessary intercalations, that the harvest festivals did not come in summer nor those of the vintage in the autumn. He adjusted the year to the sun's course by making it consist of 365 days, abolishing the intercalary month and adding one day every fourth year. Furthermore, that the correct reckoning of time might begin with the next Kalends of January, he inserted two additional months between November and December. Hence the year in which these arrangements were made was one of fifteen months, including the intercalary month which belonged to that year according to the former custom.

41. He filled the vacancies in the senate, enrolled additional patricians, and increased the number of praetors, aediles, and quaestors as well as of minor officials. He reinstated those who had been degraded by official action of the censors or found guilty of electoral bribery by verdict of the jurors. He shared the elections with the people on this basis: that except in the case of the consulship, half of the magistrates should be appointed by the people's choice while the rest should be those whom he personally had nominated. . . .

He made the enumeration of the people neither in the usual manner nor place, but from street to street aided by the owners of blocks of houses. He then reduced the number of those who received grain at public expense from 320,000 to 150,000, and to prevent the calling of additional meetings at any future time for purposes of enrollment, he provided that the places of such as died should be filled by lot each year by the praetor from those who were not on the list. . . .

42. Moreover, . . . he enacted a law . . . that those who made a business of grazing should have among their herdsmen at least one third who were men of free birth. He conferred citizenship on all who practiced medicine at Rome, and on all teachers of the liberal arts, to make them more desirous of living in the city and to induce others to resort to it.

As to debts, he disappointed those who looked for their cancellation, which was often agitated, but finally decreed that the debtors should satisfy their creditors according to a valuation of their possessions at the price which they paid for them before the civil war, deducting from principal any interest that had been paid in cash or assigned in writing — an arrangement which wiped out about a fourth part of their indebtedness. He dissolved all associations, except those of ancient foundation. He increased the penalties for crimes; and inasmuch as the rich involved themselves in guilt with less hesitation because they merely suffered exile without any loss of property, he punished murderers of freemen by confiscation of all their goods, and murderers of others by the loss of half.

43. He administered justice with the utmost conscientiousness and strictness. Those convicted of extortion he even expelled from the senatorial order. He annulled the marriage of an ex-praetor who had married a woman the very day after her divorce, although there was no suspicion of adultery. He imposed duties on foreign wares. He denied the use of litters and the wearing of scarlet robes or pearls to all except those of a designated position or age, and then only on fixed days. In particular he enforced the law against extravagance, setting watchmen in various parts of the market to seize and bring to him dainties which were exposed for sale in violation of the law; and sometimes he sent his lictors and soldiers to take from a dining room any articles which had escaped the vigilance of his watchmen, even after they had been served.

44. In particular, for the adornment and convenience of the city, also for the protection and extension of the Empire, he formed more projects and more extensive ones every day: first of all, to rear a temple to Mars, greater than any in existence, filling up and leveling the pool in which he had exhibited the sea-fight, and to build a theater of vast size, sloping down from the Tarpeian rock; to reduce the civil code to fixed limits, and of the vast and prolix mass of statutes to include only the best and most essential in a limited number of volumes; to open to the public the greatest possible libraries of Greek and Latin books, assigning to Marcus Varro the charge of procuring and classifying them; to drain the Pomptine marshes; to let out the water from Lake Fucinus; to make a highway from the Adriatic across the summit of the Apennines as far as the Tiber; to cut a canal through the Isthmus [of Corinth]; to check the Dacians, who had poured into Pontus and Thrace; then to make war on the Parthians by way of Lesser Armenia, but not to risk a battle with them until he had first tested their mettle.

All these enterprises and plans were cut short by his death. But before I speak of that, it will not be amiss to describe briefly his personal appearance, his dress, his mode of life, and his character, as well as his conduct in civil and military life.

CAESAR THE MAN

45. He is said to have been tall of stature, with a fair complexion, shapely limbs, a somewhat full face, and keen black eyes; sound of health, except that towards the end he was subject to sudden fainting fits and to nightmare as well. He was twice attacked by the falling sickness during his campaigns. He was somewhat overnice in the care of his person, being not only carefully trimmed and shaved, but even having superfluous hair plucked out, as some have charged; while his baldness was a disfigurement which troubled him greatly, since he found that it was often the subject of the gibes of his detractors. Because of it he used to comb forward his scanty locks from the crown of his head, and of all the honors voted him by the senate and people there was none which he received or made use of more gladly than the privilege of wearing a laurel wreath at all times. They say, too, that he was fantastic in his dress; that he wore a senator's tunic with fringed sleeves reaching to the wrist, and always had a girdle over it, though rather a loose one; and this, they say, was the occasion of Sulla's *mot*, when he often warned the nobles to keep an eye on the ill-girt boy.

46. He lived at first in the Subura in a modest house, but after he became pontifex maximus, in the official residence on the Sacred Way. Many have written that he was very fond of elegance and luxury; that having laid the foundations of a country-house on his estate at Nemi and finished it at great cost, he tore it all down because it did not suit him in every particular, although at the time he was still poor and heavily in debt; and that he carried tesselated and mosaic floors about with him on his campaigns.

47. They say that he was led to invade Britain by the hope of getting pearls, and that in comparing their size he sometimes weighed them with his own hand; that he was always a most enthusiastic collector of gems, carvings, statues, and pictures by early artists; also of slaves of exceptional figure and training at enormous prices, of which he himself was so ashamed that he forbade their entry in his accounts. . . .

50. That he was unbridled and extravagant in his intrigues is the general opinion, and that he seduced many illustrous women, among them Postumia, wife of Servius Sulpicius, Lollia, wife of Aulus Gabinius, Tertulla, wife of Marcus Crassus, and even Gnaeus Pompey's wife Mucia. At all events there is no doubt that Pompey was taken to task by the elder and the younger Curio, as well as by many others, because through a desire for power he had afterwards married the daughter of a man [Caesar] on whose account he divorced a wife who had borne him three children, and whom he had often referred to with a groan as an Aegisthus. But beyond all others Caesar loved Servilia, the mother of Marcus Brutus, for whom in his first consulship he bought a pearl costing six million sesterces. During the civil war, too, besides other presents, he

knocked down some fine estates to her in a public auction at a nominal price, and when some expressed their surprise at the low figure, Cicero wittily remarked: "It's a better bargain than you think, for there is a third off." And in fact it was thought that Servilia was prostituting her own daughter Tertia to Caesar.

51. That he did not refrain from intrigues in the provinces is shown in particular by this couplet, which was also shouted by the soldiers in his Gallic triumph:

Men of Rome, keep close your consorts, here's a bald adulterer.
Gold in Gaul you spent in dalliance, which you borrowed here in
    Rome.

52. He had love affairs with queens too, including Eunoe the Moor, wife of Bogudes, on whom, as well as on her husband, he bestowed many splendid presents, as Naso writes; but above all with Cleopatra, with whom he often feasted until daybreak, and he would have gone through Egypt with her in her state-barge almost to Aethiopia, had not his soldiers refused to follow him. Finally he called her to Rome and did not let her leave until he had ladened her with high honors and rich gifts, and he allowed her to give his name to the child which she bore. In fact, according to certain Greek writers, this child was very like Caesar in looks and carriage. Mark Antony declared to the senate that Caesar had really acknowledged the boy, and that Gaius Matius, Gaius Oppius, and other friends of Caesar knew this. Of these Gaius Oppius, as if admitting that the situation required apology and defense, published a book, to prove that the child whom Cleopatra fathered on Caesar was not his. Helvius Cinna, tribune of the commons, admitted to several that he had a bill drawn up in due form, which Caesar had ordered him to propose to the people in his absence, making it lawful for Caesar to marry what wives he wished, and as many as he wished, "for the purpose of begetting children." But to remove all doubt that he had an evil reputation both for shameless vice and for adultery, I have only to add that the elder Curio in one of his speeches calls him "every woman's man and every man's woman."

53. That he drank very little wine not even his enemies denied. There is a saying of Marcus Cato that Caesar was the only man who undertook to overthrow the state when sober. Even in the matter of food Gaius Oppius tells us that he was so indifferent, that once when his host served stale oil instead of fresh, and the other guests would have none of it, Caesar partook even more plentifully than usual, not to seem to charge his host with carelessness or lack of manners.

54. Neither when in command of armies nor as a magistrate at Rome did he show a scrupulous integrity; for as certain men have declared in their memoirs, when he was proconsul in Spain, he not only begged money from the allies, to help pay his debts, but also attacked and sacked some towns of the Lusitanians, although they did not refuse his terms and opened their gates

to him on his arrival. In Gaul he pillaged shrines and temples of the gods filled with offerings, and oftener sacked towns for the sake of plunder than for any fault. In consequence he had more gold than he knew what to do with, and offered it for sale throughout Italy and the provinces at the rate of three thousand sesterces the pound. In his first consulship he stole three thousand pounds of gold from the Capitol, replacing it with the same weight of gilded bronze. He made alliances and thrones a matter of barter, for he extorted from Ptolemy alone in his own name and that of Pompey nearly six thousand talents, while later on he met the heavy expenses of the civil wars and of his triumphs and entertainments by the most bare-faced pillage and sacrilege.

55. In eloquence and in the art of war he either equalled or surpassed the fame of their most eminent representatives. After his accusation of Dolabella, he was without question numbered with the leading advocates. At all events when Cicero reviews the orators in his *Brutus*, he says that he does not see to whom Caesar ought to yield the palm, declaring that his style is elegant as well as brilliant, even grand and in a sense noble. . . . He is said to have delivered himself in a high-pitched voice with impassioned action and gestures, which were not without grace. . . .

56. He left memoirs too of his deeds in the Gallic war and in the civil strife with Pompey. . . . With regard to Caesar's memoirs Cicero, also in the *Brutus* speaks in the following terms: "He wrote memoirs which deserve the highest praise; they are naked in their simplicity, straightforward yet graceful, stripped of all rhetorical adornment, as of a garment; but while his purpose was to supply material to others, on which those who wished to write history might draw, he haply gratified silly folk, who will try to use the curling-irons on his narrative, but he has kept men of any sense from touching the subject." Of these same memoirs Hirtius uses this emphatic language: "They are so highly rated in the judgment of all men, that he seems to have deprived writers of an opportunity, rather than given them one; yet our admiration for this feat is greater than that of others; for they know how well and faultlessly he wrote, while we know besides how easily and rapidly he finished his task." Asinius Pollio thinks that they were put together somewhat carelessly and without strict regard for truth; since in many cases Caesar was too ready to believe the accounts which others gave of their actions, and gave a perverted account of his own, either designedly or perhaps from forgetfulness; and he thinks that he intended to rewrite and revise them. . . .

57. He was highly skilled in arms and horsemanship, and of incredible powers of endurance. On the march he headed his army, sometimes on horseback, but oftener on foot, bareheaded both in the heat of the sun and in rain. He covered great distances with incredible speed, making a hundred miles a day in a hired carriage and with little baggage, swimming the rivers which barred his path or crossing them on inflated skins, and very often arriving before the messengers sent to announce his coming.

58. In the conduct of his campaigns it is a question whether he was more cautious or more daring, for he never led his army where ambuscades were

possible without carefully reconnoitering the country, and he did not cross to Britain without making personal inquiries about the harbors, the course, and the approach to the island. But on the other hand, when news came that his camp in Germany was beleaguered, he made his way to his men through the enemies' pickets, disguised as a Gaul. He crossed from Brundisium to Dyrrachium in wintertime, running the blockade of the enemy's fleets; and when the troops which he had ordered to follow him delayed to do so, and he had sent to fetch them many times in vain, at last in secret and alone he boarded a small boat at night with his head muffled up and he did not reveal who he was, or suffer the helmsman to give way to the gale blowing in their teeth, until he was all but overwhelmed by the waves.

59, No regard for religion ever turned him from any undertaking, or even delayed him. Though the victim escaped as he was offering sacrifice, he did not put off his expedition against Scipio and Juba. Even when he had a fall as he disembarked, he gave the omen a favorable turn by crying: "I hold thee fast, Africa." Furthermore, to make the prophecies ridiculous which declared that the stock of the Scipios was fated to be fortunate and invincible in that province, he kept with him in camp a contemptible fellow belonging to the Cornelian family, to whom the nickname Salvito had been given as a reproach for his manner of life.

60. He joined battle, not only after planning his movements in advance but on a sudden opportunity, often immediately at the end of a march, and sometimes in the foulest weather, when one would least expect him to make a move. It was not until his later years that he became slower to engage, through a conviction that the oftener he had been victor, the less he ought to tempt fate, and that he could not possibly gain as much by success as he might lose by a defeat. He never put his enemy to flight without also driving him from his camp, thus giving him no respite in his panic. When the issue was doubtful, he used to send away the horses, and his own among the first, to impose upon his troops the greater necessity of standing their ground by taking away that aid to flight. . . .

62. When his army gave way, he often rallied it single-handed, planting himself in the way of the fleeing men, laying hold of them one by one, and even catching them by the throat and forcing them to face the enemy; that, too, when they were in such a panic that an eagle-bearer made a pass at him with the point as he tried to stop him, while another left the standard in Caesar's hand when he would hold him back. . . .

65. He valued his soldiers neither for their personal character nor their fortune, but solely for their prowess, and he treated them with equal strictness and indulgence; for he did not curb them everywhere and at all times, but only in the presence of the enemy. Then he required the strictest discipline, not announcing the time of a march or a battle, but keeping them ready and alert to be led on a sudden at any moment wheresoever he might wish. He often called them out even when there was no occasion for it, especially on rainy days and holidays. And warning them every now and then that they must keep close

watch on him, he would steal away suddenly by day or night and make a longer march than usual, to tire out those who were tardy in following. . . .

67. He did not take notice of all their offenses or punish them by rule, but he kept a sharp lookout for deserters and mutineers, and chastised them most severely, shutting his eyes to other faults. Sometimes, too, after a great victory he relieved them of all duties and gave them full license to revel, being in the habit of boasting that his soldiers could fight well even when reeking of perfumes. In the assembly he addressed them not as "soldiers," but by the more flattering term "comrades," and he kept them in fine trim, furnishing them with arms inlaid with silver and gold, both for show and to make them hold faster to them in battle, through fear of the greatness of the loss. Such was his love for them that when he heard of the disaster to Titurius, he let his hair and beard grow long, and would not cut them until he had taken vengeance.

68. In this way he made them most devoted to his interests as well as most valiant. When he began the civil war, every centurion of each legion proposed to supply a horseman from his own allowance, and the soldiers one and all offered their service without pay and without rations, the richer assuming the care of the poorer. Throughout the long struggle not one deserted and many of them, on being taken prisoner, refused to accept their lives, when offered them on the condition of consenting to serve against Caesar. They bore hunger and other hardships, both when in a state of siege and when besieging others, with such fortitude, that when Pompey saw in the works at Dyrrachium a kind of bread made of herbs, on which they were living, he said that he was fighting wild beasts; and he gave orders that it be put out of sight quickly and shown to none of his men, for fear that the endurance and resolution of the foe would break their spirit.

How valiantly they fought is shown by the fact that when they suffered their sole defeat before Dyrrachium, they insisted on being punished, and their commander felt called upon rather to console than to chastise them. In the other battles they overcame with ease countless forces of the enemy, though decidedly fewer in number themselves. Indeed one cohort of the sixth legion, when set to defend a redoubt, kept four legions of Pompey at bay for several hours, though almost all were wounded by the enemy's showers of arrows, of which 130,000 were picked up within the ramparts. And no wonder, when one thinks of the deeds of individual soldiers, either of Cassius Scaeva the centurion, or of Gaius Acilius of the rank and file, not to mention others. Scaeva, with one eye gone, his thigh and shoulder wounded, and his shield bored through in a hundred and twenty places continued to guard the gate of a fortress put in his charge. Acilius in the sea-fight at Massilia grasped the stern of one of the enemy's ships, and when his right hand was looped off rivalling the famous exploit [at Marathon] of the Greek hero Cynegirus, boarded the ship and drove the enemy before him with the boss of his shield. . . .

74. Even in avenging wrongs he was by nature most merciful, and when he got hold of the pirates who had captured him, he had them crucified, since he had sworn beforehand that he would do so, but ordered that their throats be

cut first. He could never make up his mind to harm Cornelius Phagites, although when he was sick and in hiding, the man had waylaid him night after night, and even a bribe had barely saved him from being handed over to Sulla. The slave Philemon, his amanuensis, who had promised Caesar's enemies that he would poison him, he merely punished by death, without torture. When summoned as a witness against Publius Clodius, the paramour of his wife Pompeia, charged on the same count with sacrilege, Caesar declared that he had not evidence, although both his mother Aurelia and his sister Julia had given the same jurors a faithful account of the whole affair; and on being asked why it was then that he had put away his wife he replied; "Because I maintain that the members of my family should be free from suspicion, as well as from guilt."

75. He certainly showed admirable self-restraint and mercy, both in his conduct of the civil war and in the hour of victory. While Pompey threatened to treat as enemies those who did not take up arms for the government, Caesar gave out that those who were neutral and of neither party should be numbered with his friends. He freely allowed all those whom he had made centurions on Pompey's recommendation to go over to his rival. When conditions of surrender were under discussion at Ilerda, and friendly intercourse between the two parties was constant, Afranius and Petreius, with a sudden change of purpose, put to death all of Caesar's soldiers whom they found in their camp; but Caesar could not bring himself to retaliate in kind. At the battle of Pharsalus he cried out, "Spare your fellow citizens," and afterwards allowed each of his men to save any one man he pleased of the opposite party. And it will be found that no Pompeian lost his life except in battle, save only Afranius and Faustus, and the young Lucius Caesar; and it is believed that not even these men were slain by his wish, even though the two former had taken up arms again after being pardoned, while Caesar had not only cruelly put to death the dictator's slaves and freedmen with fire and sword, but had even butchered the wild beasts which he had procured for the entertainment of the people. At last, in his later years, he went so far as to allow all those whom he had not yet pardoned to return to Italy, and to hold magistracies and the command of armies: and he actually set up the statues of Lucius Sulla and Pompey, which had been broken to pieces by the populace. After this, if any dangerous plots were formed against him, or slanders uttered, he preferred to quash rather than to punish them. Accordingly, he took no further notice of the conspiracies which were detected, and of meetings by night, than to make known by proclamation that he was aware of them; and he thought it enough to give public warning to those who spoke ill of him, not to persist in their conduct, bearing with good nature the attacks on his reputation made by the scurrilous volume of Aulus Caecina and the abusive lampoons of Pitholaus.

"THIS MAN AT LAST IS MADE OUR KING"

76. Yet after all, his other actions and words so turn the scale, that it is thought that he abused his power and was justly slain. For not only did he

accept excessive honors, such as an uninterrupted consulship, the dictatorship for life, and the censorship of public morals, as well as the forename Imperator, the surname of Father of his Country, a statue among those of the kings, and a raised couch in the orchestra; but he also allowed honors to be bestowed on him which were too great for mortal man: a golden throne in the House and on the judgment seat; a chariot and litter in the procession at the circus; temples, altars, and statues beside those of the gods; a special priest, an additional college of the Luperci, and the calling of one of the months by his name. In fact, there were no honors which he did not receive or confer at pleasure.

He held his third and fourth consulships in name only, content with the power of the dictatorship conferred on him at the same time as the consulships. Moreover, in both years he substituted two consuls for himself for the last three months, in the meantime holding no elections except for tribunes and plebeian aediles, and appointing praefects instead of the praetors, to manage the affairs of the city during his absence. When one of the consuls suddenly died the day before the Kalends of January, he gave the vacant office for a few hours to a man who asked for it. With the same disregard of law and precedent he named magistrates for several years to come, bestowed the emblems of consular rank on ten ex-praetors, and admitted to the House men who had been given citizenship, and in some cases half-civilized Gauls. He assigned the charge of the mint and of the public revenues to his own slaves, and gave the oversight and command of the three legions which he had left at Alexandria to a favorite of his called Rufio, son of one of his freedmen.

77. No less arrogant were his public utterances, which Titus Ampius records: that the Republic was nothing, a mere name without body or form; that Sulla did not know his A. B. C. when he laid down his dictatorship; that men ought now to be more circumspect in addressing him, and to regard his word as law. So far did he go in his presumption, that when a soothsayer once reported direful innards without a heart, he said: "They will be more favorable when I wish it; it should not be regarded as a portent, if a beast has no heart."

78. But it was the following action in particular that roused deadly hatred against him. When the Senate approached him in a body with many highly honorary decrees, he received them before the temple of Venus Genetrix without rising. Some think that when he attempted to get up, he was held back by Cornelius Balbus; others, that he made no such move at all, but on the contrary frowned angrily on Gaius Trebatius when he suggested that he should rise. And this action of his seemed the more intolerable, because when he himself in one of his triumphal processions rode past the benches of the tribunes, he was so incensed because a member of the college, Pontius Aquila by name, did not rise, that he cried: "Come then, Aquila, take back the Republic from me, you mighty tribune"; and for several days he would not make a promise to anyone without adding, "That is, if Pontius Aquila will allow me."

79. To an insult which so plainly showed his contempt for the Senate he added an act of even greater insolence; for at the Latin Festival, as he was returning to the city, amid the extravagant and unprecedented demonstrations of the populace, someone in the press placed on his statue a laurel wreath with a

white fillet tied to it; and when Epidius Marullus and Caesetius Flavus, tribunes of the commons, gave orders that the ribbon be removed from the crown and the man taken off to prison, Caesar sharply rebuked and deposed them, either offended that the hint at regal power had been received with so little favor, or, as he asserted, that he had been robbed of the glory of refusing it. But from that time on he could not rid himself of the odium of having aspired to the title of monarch, although he replied to the commons, when they hailed him as king, "I am Caesar and no king," and at the Lupercalia, when the consul Antony several times attempted to place a crown upon his head as he spoke from the rostra, he put it aside and at last sent it to the Capitol, to be offered to Jupiter Optimus Maximus. Nay, more, the report had spread in various quarters that he intended to move to Ilium or Alexandria, taking with him the resources of the state, draining Italy by levies, and leaving it and the charge of the city to his friends; also that at the next meeting of the Senate Lucius Cotta would announce as the decision of the Fifteen [priests], that inasmuch as it was written in the books of fate that the Parthians could be conquered only by a king, Caesar should be given that title.

80. It was this that led the conspirators to hasten in carrying out their designs, in order to avoid giving their assent to this proposal. Therefore the plots which had previously been formed separately, often by groups of two or three, were united in a general conspiracy, since even the populace no longer were pleased with present conditions, but both secretly and openly rebelled at his tyranny and cried out for defenders of their liberty. On the admission of foreigners to the Senate, a placard was posted: "God bless the Commonwealth! let no one consent to point out the House to a newly made senator." The following verses too were sung everywhere: —

> Caesar led the Gauls in triumph, led them to the senate house;
> Then the Gauls put off their breeches, and put on the laticalve
> [senator's tunic].

When Quintus Maximus, whom he had appointed consul in his place for three months, was entering the theater, and his lictor called attention to his arrival in the usual manner, a general shout was raised: "He's no consul!" At the first election after the deposing of Caesetius and Marullus, the tribunes, several votes were found for their appointment as consuls. Some wrote on the base of Lucius Brutus' statue, "Oh, that you were still alive"; and on that of Caesar himself:

> First of all was Brutus consul, since he drove the kings from Rome;
> Since this man drove out the consuls, he at last is made our king.

More than sixty joined the conspiracy against him, led by Gaius Cassius and Marcus and Decimus Brutus.

43

The Assassination of Julius Caesar

"Liberty! Freedom! Tyranny is dead!" — Cinna

The assassination of Caesar on the Ides of March (March 15), 44 B.C., turned out to be an act of great folly that removed the only statesman capable of maintaining order in the dying Roman Republic. The conspirators had no program and little understanding of the needs of the time, and the result of their work was the renewal of anarchy and civil war.

While some of the sixty or more conspirators undoubtedly were motivated by selfish interests, many were genuinely alarmed over Caesar's too open disregard of republican forms and traditions. To them it seemed a simple solution to commit what Cicero afterwards called "a great and glorious deed" and in the name of liberty rid Rome of a tyrant. But this was idealism gone blind, for what was restored was the liberty of the privileged senatorial few to exploit the inhabitants of the provinces, and the liberty of the shiftless Roman mob to sell itself to the highest bidder. The folly of the deed and the anarchy that was to follow were foreshadowed when, immediately after the murder, Brutus addressed the Senate with an oration on liberty to which, as Plutarch recounts, no one paid any attention.

"THOSE WHO DESIRED A CHANGE"

57. . . . When Caesar's friends advised him to have a bodyguard, and many of them volunteered to serve in it, he would not allow it. It was better, he said, to die once than to live always in fear of death. He considered the good will of the people to be the best and surest guard, so he again sought popular support by providing feasts and distributions of grain for the people and by founding colonies for his soldiers. His most famous colonies were at Carthage and at Corinth. It is noteworthy that both these cities had been taken and destroyed at the same time, and now they were both restored at the same time.

58. He won over the nobility by promising some of them consulates and praetorships, and by giving others various offices and honors. To all he held out the prospects of hope, for he desired to rule over a willing people. Thus when Fabius Maximus died suddenly toward the end of his consulship, he appointed Caninius Rebilius consul for the day that remained. Many people went to pay

From Plutarch, *Parallel Lives*, "Julius Caesar," based on the translation by John and William Langhorne.

the usual respects to the new consul and to escort him to the senate house. This was the occasion on which Cicero made the remark: "Let us make haste, or his term of office will expire before we get there." . . .

62. In this state of affairs, many people turned their thoughts to Marcus Brutus, who, on his father's side, was thought to be a descendant of that ancient Brutus [who had overthrown the monarchy], and whose mother was of the illustrious house of the Servilii. He was also the nephew and son-in-law of Cato. No man was more inclined than he to lift his hand against monarchy, but he was held back by the honors and favors he had received from Caesar, who had not only spared his life after Pompey's defeat at Pharsalus, and pardoned many of his friends at his request, but had continued to honor him with a special trust. That very year Caesar had granted him the most important of the praetorships and had designated him for the consulship four years later — in preference to Cassius, who was Brutus' rival for the position. Caesar is reported to have said, "Cassius has the stronger claims, but I cannot refuse Brutus." Even after the conspiracy was formed and some people were accusing Brutus of complicity, Caesar placed his hand on his body and said to them, "Brutus will wait for this skin of mine" — implying that though Brutus' qualities made him worthy of power, he would not behave basely or ungratefully to obtain it.

However, those who desired a change looked to Brutus only, or at least principally; and as they dared not speak openly, night after night they left notes on the platform and the seat which he used as praetor. Most of the messages were of this sort: "You are asleep, Brutus," or "You are not really Brutus." When Cassius noticed that they were having some effect on Brutus' pride, he increased his efforts to spur him on. Cassius had his own reasons for hating Caesar; and Caesar, too, was suspicious of him and once said to his friends, "What do you think Cassius is aiming at? I do not like his pale looks." And another time, when Antony and Dolabella were accused of plotting against him, Caesar said, "I have no apprehensions about those fat and sleek men; I fear rather the pale and lean ones" — meaning Cassius and Brutus.

"STRANGE SIGNS AND APPARITIONS"

63. It seems, however, that fate is more unavoidable than unexpected, for we are told that there were strange signs and apparitions before the death of Caesar. As for the lights in the heavens, the strange noises heard in various directions at night, and the appearance of unusual birds in the forum, perhaps they do not deserve notice in connection with so great an event as this. But Strabo the philosopher tells us that a great many men, all on fire, were seen in the air fighting one another. . . . What is still more extraordinary, many report that a certain soothsayer warned Caesar against a great danger which threatened him on the Ides of March; and that when the day had come, Caesar, on his way to the senate house, called out to the soothsayer in jest, "The Ides of March have come!" to which the soothsayer replied in a soft voice, "Yes, but they have not gone."

On the previous evening Caesar dined with Marcus Lepidus, and he was signing letters, as was his custom, as he reclined at the table. While he was so engaged, the question arose as to what kind of death was best, and before anyone could answer Caesar cried out, "A sudden one." The same night, when he was in bed with his wife, the doors and windows of the room flew open all at once. Awakened by both the noise and the moonlight, Caesar observed that although Calpurnia was sound asleep she was uttering indistinct words and inarticulate groans. She was dreaming that she held his murdered body in her arms and was weeping over it. Others say she dreamed that the gable ornament on Caesar's house, which, Livy tells us, the senate had ordered to be erected as a mark of honor and distinction, had fallen, and that it was for this reason that she lamented and wept. Be that as it may, the next morning she implored Caesar not to go out that day if he could possibly avoid it, and to postpone the meeting of the senate; or, she said, if he had no confidence in her dreams, then he should inquire about his fate by sacrifices and other forms of divination. This caused Caesar some alarm; for he had never before noticed any womanish superstition in Calpurnia, whom he now saw in such great distress. He therefore ordered a number of sacrifices, and when the diviners reported unfavorable omens he decided to send Antony to dismiss the senate.

64. At this point Decimus Brutus, surnamed Albinus, came in. Caesar placed so much confidence in him that he had made him his second heir, yet he was engaged in the conspiracy with the other Brutus and Cassius. Now, fearing that if Caesar adjourned the senate to another day the plot might be discovered, he scoffed at the diviners and told Caesar he would be to blame if he gave the senate such a good reason to complain of being slighted by him. They were meeting, he said, at Caesar's summons, and they were ready to vote unanimously to honor him with the title of king in the provinces with the right to wear a diadem everywhere outside of Italy, on land and on sea. "But now when they are in session, if anyone were to go and tell them that they must disperse and return again when Calpurnia happens to have better dreams, what will your enemies say! If you are absolutely certain that this is an unlucky day, then it is certainly better to go yourself to the senate and personally adjourn the meeting." While he was saying this, he took Caesar by the hand and led him out the door.

Caesar had not gone far when a slave belonging to some other person tried to approach him, but finding it impossible because of the crowd that surrounded him, he made his way into the house and put himself in the hands of Calpurnia. He asked her to keep him safe until Caesar's return, because he had some very important information to give him.

65. Artemidorus the Cnidian, a teacher of Greek philosophy who had become acquainted with Brutus and his friends and so had learned of the conspiracy, approached Caesar with a note describing what he had discovered. But when he saw that Caesar gave all papers to his attendants as soon as he received them, he came as close as possible to him and said, "Caesar, read this to yourself and quickly; it contains matter of the greatest importance which concerns you personally." Caesar took it and attempted several times to read it, but was prevented from doing so by the many people who came to speak to him. How-

ever, he kept that paper, and he was still holding it in his hand when he came into the senate. (Some say that this note was delivered to him by another man, and that the crowd kept Artemidorus from approaching him all along the route.)

66. All these things could have happened by chance; but the fact that the place where the senate was meeting, which was destined to be the scene of the tragedy, not only contained a statue of Pompey but was a building that Pompey had erected and dedicated as an ornament to his theater, clearly shows that some supernatural power guided the action and directed that it should take place in that very spot. Even Cassius, though a follower of the doctrines of Epicurus, turned his eyes toward the statue of Pompey and silently invoked his aid just before the act. This crucial moment of imminent danger apparently overpowered his former rationalistic views and laid him open to the influence of nonrational emotion.

Antony, Caesar's faithful friend and a man of great physical strength, was detained outside the building by Brutus Albinus, who deliberately engaged him in a long conversation. When Caesar entered, the senate rose in his honor. Some of Brutus' accomplices stood behind his chair while others went to meet him, pretending to support the petition of Tillius Cimber for the recall of his brother from exile. They kept up their entreaties until he came to his chair. When he was seated he rejected their request, but they continued more and more urgently until he began to grow angry. Cimber then grasped his toga with both hands and pulled it off his neck, which was the signal for the attack. Casca struck the first blow, stabbing Caesar in the neck with his dagger. But the wound was not mortal or even dangerous, probably because at the beginning of so bold an action he was very nervous. Caesar therefore was able to turn around and grasp the dagger and hold on to it. At the same time they both cried out, Caesar in Latin, "Casca, you villain! What does this mean?" and Casca in Greek to his brother, "Brother, help!"

After such a beginning, those who were unaware of the conspiracy were so astonished and horrified that they could neither run away or assist Caesar, nor could they even utter a word. But all the conspirators now drew their daggers and hemmed Caesar in on every side. Whichever way he turned he met with blows and saw nothing but cold steel gleaming in his face. Like some wild beast attacked by hunters, he found every hand lifted against him, for they had agreed that all must share in this sacrifice and flesh themselves with his blood. For this reason Brutus also gave him a stab in the groin. Some say that Caesar resisted all the others, shifting his body to escape the blows and calling for help, but when he saw Brutus' drawn dagger he covered his head with his toga and sank to the ground. Either by chance or because he was pushed by his murderers, he fell against the pedestal of Pompey's statue and drenched it with his blood. So Pompey himself seemed to preside over this act of vengeance, treading his enemy under his feet and enjoying his agonies. Those agonies were great, for they say he received twenty-three wounds. And many of the conspirators wounded each other as they aimed their blows at him.

"AFTER CAESAR WAS KILLED"

67. After Caesar was killed, Brutus stepped forward to give reasons for what had been done, but the senators would not stay to hear him. They rushed out of the building, thus causing great alarm and confusion among the people. Some locked their doors; others left their shops and counters. All ran one way or another; some were running to see the place where the murder had occurred, while others were running back after having seen it. Antony and Lepidus, Caesar's principal friends, stole away and hid themselves in other people's houses. Meanwhile Brutus and his confederates, still on fire from the murder, marched in a body from the senate house to the Capitol, not like men thinking of escaping, but with an air of gaiety and confidence. They called on the people to resume their liberty, and they invited every man of consequence whom they met to join them. Some of these did join their procession as it moved toward the Capitol, pretending to have taken part in the deed and claiming a share of the glory. . . .

The next day Brutus and the rest of the conspirators came down from the Capitol and Brutus addressed the people. They listened without expressing either pleasure or resentment at what had been done. By their silence it appeared that they both pitied Caesar and respected Brutus. The senate passed a general amnesty and tried to reconcile all parties. It decreed that Caesar should be worshipped as a god and it confirmed all the acts of his dictatorship. At the same time it granted provincial governorships and other such suitable honors to Brutus and his friends. It was generally thought, therefore, that all things were firmly settled again, and in the best possible way.

68. But when Caesar's will was opened and it was found that he had left a considerable legacy to each Roman citizen, and when the people saw his body, all disfigured with wounds, being carried through the forum, they could not be kept within the bounds of discipline and order. They heaped benches, barricades, and tables into a pile and burned the corpse there. Then snatching flaming brands from the pile, some ran to set fire to the houses of the murderers, while others ranged the city trying to find the conspirators themselves to tear them to pieces. They, however, had provided for their security, and not one of them was caught by the mob.

They say that a man named Cinna, a friend of Caesar's, had a strange dream the preceding night. He dreamed that Caesar invited him to supper and he declined. Caesar then caught him by the hand and pulled him after him, despite all his reluctance. Hearing now that the body of Caesar was to be burned in the forum, Cinna got up and went there out of respect for his memory, though he had a fever and felt apprehensive as a result of his dream. One of the crowd who saw him there asked who he was and, having learned his name, told it to another. So the report spread quickly that he was one of Caesar's murderers, since one of the conspirators was indeed named Cinna. The crowd, thinking he was the man, rushed at him and tore him to pieces on the spot. Brutus and Cassius were so terrified by this that within a few days they left the city. What they did after that, and how they suffered and died, is described in my *Life of Brutus.*

69. Caesar died at the age of fifty-six, surviving Pompey by not much more than four years. His objective was sovereign power and authority, which he pursued through innumerable dangers, and which by prodigious efforts he gained at last. The only fruit he reaped from it was an empty title and an offensive glory. But that divine power, which had watched over him in life, remained active after death as his avenger, pursuing and tracking down the murderers over every sea and land, and not resting until there was not a man left, either of those who dipped their hands in his blood or of those who helped plan the deed.

Cicero

"An eloquent man who loved his country well."

The speeches and writings of Marcus Tullius Cicero (106–43 B.C.) contain numerous passages justifying the assassination of Julius Caesar as well as the role of the conservative party (Optimates, "best people") in Roman politics. Born near Rome into a non-noble equestrian family, Cicero achieved such great fame as a courtroom lawyer that in 63 B.C. he was elected to the consulship with the backing of the Optimates, who desired at all costs to defeat the bid of the radical Catiline for that office. Following his consulship, during which he suppressed the Catilinarian conspiracy (see Selection 41) and was eulogized as "father of his country" by the Senate, Cicero was unable to take an active part in the turbulent politics of the dying Republic, being but a parvenu among the senatorial nobility, and lacking the essential support of either great wealth or legions. In his desire "never to stop seeking the good of the community," he turned to the writing of popular treatises on political theory and moral philosophy. These treatises became the medium through which much of the best of Greek thought on these subjects was transmitted to the Romans.

Running as a thread through all of Cicero's writings and speeches is his concern for freedom and order in society and, conversely, his opposition to despotism. With such fervor and eloquence does he expound this theme, together with the Roman ideal of virtue as dedication to social and civic duty, that his views have become an integral part of the Western heritage. On the evidence of Plutarch's "Life of Cicero," it appears that even Caesar's heir and successor Augustus recognized Cicero's contribution: "I have heard that Caesar [Augustus] a long time after once went to see one of his daughter's sons, and as the youth had in his hands one of Cicero's writings, he was afraid and hid it in his vest; which Caesar observing took the book and read a good part of it while standing, and then returning the book said, 'An eloquent man, my son, and one who loved his country well.' "

◆A◆ ADVOCATE OF PROPERTY RIGHTS AND THE STATUS QUO

As shown by the following selections — the first from a courtroom speech delivered in 56 B.C., the second from his last treatise on philosophy written in 44 B.C. — Cicero's concern for freedom and order often took on a strong reactionary slant. On such occasions he is little more than a propagandist for vested interests, concerned with preserving property rights and the status quo, and not averse to slanting the evidence to serve his purpose. This narrowness of outlook is a reflection of Cicero's supposition that the Republic's ills were caused by the "seditious" activities of a few "mad revolutionaries." The second selection also includes Cicero's views on the value of philosophy and why he turned to it — in particular to the Academic school founded by Plato but which under the leadership of men like Carneades (see p. 300) had rejected Plato's dogmatism and adopted an attitude of detached skepticism concerning truth. Their liberal open-minded approach to truth required that it be tested by experience and exposed to the possibility of contradiction. As Cicero put it in another of his philosophical writings, "The only difference between us and the dogmatists is that they have no doubt of the truth of their case, whereas we consider many doctrines probable and are prepared to act on them, but hardly to affirm them as certain."

IN DEFENSE OF SESTIUS

You made a special point of asking me what was the meaning of our "breed of *optimates*," to use your own term. You ask about a matter which is vital for our younger generation to learn and not difficult for me to offer some instruction. . . .

There have always been two classes of men in this state eager to engage in politics and to distinguish themselves. One group wished to be known, by repute and in reality, as *populares*; the other, *optimates*. The *populares* were those who wished everything they did and said to be agreeable to the masses; the *optimates* acted so as to win by their policy the approval of the best people.

Adapted by permission of the publishers and The Loeb Classical Library from R. Gardner's translation of Cicero, *Pro Sestio*, 96–100, 102–103 (Cambridge, Mass.: Harvard University Press).

Who then are these "best people"? Their numbers, if you ask me, are infinite; for otherwise we could not survive in politics. They include the leaders of public opinion and those who follow their lead; they include men of the upper classes to whom the Senate is open; they include Romans living in municipal towns and in country districts; they include men of business, too, as well as freedmen — all these are "best people." In its numbers, I repeat, this class is spread far and wide and is variously composed. But, to prevent misunderstanding, the whole class can be summed up and defined in a few words. All are *optimates* who are neither criminal nor vicious in disposition, nor mad revolutionaries, nor embarrassed by their private life. It follows, then, that those who are upright, sound in mind, and good family men, belong to this so-called "breed." Those in the government who serve the wishes, the interests, and the principles of these men are called their champions and are regarded as the most influential of the *optimates*, the most eminent of our citizens, and the leaders of the state. What then is the goal to which those who guide the helm of state ought to direct their course? It is the best and noblest goal of all sound and good and prosperous men — civil peace with honor. Those who desire this are *optimates*; those who achieve it are considered the best of men and the saviors of the state. For just as it is wrong for men to be so carried away by the honor of public office that they are indifferent to civil peace, so too it is wrong for them to welcome a peace which is inconsistent with honor.

Now civil peace with honor has the following foundations and elements which our leaders ought to protect and defend even at the risk of life itself: religious observances, auspices, powers of the magistrates, authority of the Senate, laws and ancestral custom, criminal and civil justice, credit, our provinces and allies, the prestige of our government and its army and treasury. To be a defender and a protector of so many and so important interests requires great courage, great ability, and great resolution. For, in so large a body of citizens, there are great numbers of men who, either from fear of punishment, being conscious of their crimes, seek to cause chaos and revolution; or who, owing to a sort of inborn anarchistic madness, thrive on civil discord and sedition; or who, on account of private financial embarrassment, prefer a general conflagration to their own ruin. When such men as these have found advisers and leaders to suit their vicious aims, storms are aroused in the commonwealth, so that those who have hitherto been granted the helm of state must watch and strive with all their skill and devotion that they may be able, without any damage to those foundations and elements of which I have just spoken, to keep on their course and reach that haven of peace with honor. If I were to deny, gentlemen, that this course is stormy and difficult, perilous and treacherous, I should be telling a lie — especially since not only have I always understood it to be so, but experience has convinced me more than others.

There are greater forces and means for attacking than for defending the state. The reason is that reckless and depraved men need only a nod to set them moving, and their own natural disposition incites them against the state. But good men somehow show less activity, neglect the beginnings of movements, and are aroused to action at the last moment only by dire necessity. As a result, thanks to their hesitation and indolence, sometimes even when they wish to enjoy civil peace with the loss of honor, they lose both. . . .

It is a difficult task; I do not deny it. There are many risks; I confess it. Truly has it been said, "Many traps are set for the virtuous." . . . A law to provide for voting by secret ballot was proposed by Lucius Cassius [137 B.C.]. The people thought that their liberty was at stake. The leading men in the state held a different opinion; they were concerned over the interests of the *optimates* and they dreaded the irresponsibility of the masses and the license afforded by the secret ballot. Tiberius Gracchus proposed an agrarian law. The law was popular with the people, for it seemed to restore the fortunes of the poorer classes. The *optimates* vigorously opposed it, because they thought it would cause dissension and strip the state of its stoutest champions by evicting the rich from their long-established holdings. Gaius Gracchus brought forward a grain law. It delighted the masses, for it provided food in abundance without work. Good citizens were against it; they thought it was an invitation to the masses to desert work for idleness, and they saw it as a drain upon the treasury.

ON DUTY

"I advocate the study of philosophy"

My books have aroused in not a few men the desire not only to read but to write, and yet I sometimes fear that what we term philosophy is distasteful to certain worthy gentlemen and that they wonder that I devote so much time and effort to it.

As long as the state was administered by its own elected representatives, I devoted all my effort and thought to it. But when it passed under the absolute control of a despot [Julius Caesar] and there was no longer any room for my leadership and advice, and when I had lost the eminent friends who had been associated with me in the task of serving the interests of the state, I neither resigned myself to despair, which would have overwhelmed me had I not struggled against it, nor surrendered myself to a life of sensual pleasure unbecoming to a philosopher.

I would that the state had stood fast in its former position and had not fallen into the hands of men who desired not so much to reform as to abolish the constitution. For then, in the first place, I should now be devoting my energies more to politics than to writing, as I used to do when the Republic existed; and in the second place, I should be committing to written form not these present essays but my public speeches, as I often formerly did. But when the Republic, to which all my care and thought and effort used to be devoted, was no more, then, of course, my voice was silenced in the forum and in the senate. And since my mind could not be wholly idle, I thought, as I had been well-read along these lines of thought from my early youth, that the most

Adapted by permission of the publishers and The Loeb Classical Library from Walter Miller's translation of Cicero, *De Officiis*, II, 2–8, 73–74, 78–80, 83–85 (Cambridge, Mass.: Harvard University Press).

honorable way for me to forget my sorrows would be by turning to philosophy. As a young man, I had devoted a great deal of time to philosophy as a discipline; but after I began to fill the high offices of state and devoted myself heart and soul to the public service, there was only so much time for philosophical studies as was left over from the claims of my friends and of the state; all of this was spent in reading; I had no leisure for writing.

Therefore, amid all the present most awful calamities I yet flatter myself that I have won this good out of evil — that I may commit to written form matters not at all familiar to our countrymen but still very much worth their knowing. For what, in the name of heaven, is more to be desired than wisdom? What is more to be prized? What is better for a man, what more worthy of his nature? Those who seek after it are called philosophers; and philosophy is nothing else, if one will translate the word into our idiom, than "the love of wisdom." Wisdom, moreover, as the word has been defined by the philosophers of old, is "the knowledge of things human and divine and of the causes by which those things are controlled." And if the man lives who would belittle the study of philosophy, I quite fail to see what in the world he would see fit to praise. For if we are looking for mental enjoyment and freedom from care, what can be compared with the pursuits of those who are constantly searching for something that will tend toward and effectively promote a good and happy life? Or, if our concern is for strength of character and virtue, then this is the method by which we can attain to those qualities, or there is none at all. And to say that there is no "method" for securing the highest blessings, when none even of the least important concerns is without its method, is the language of people who talk without due reflection and who blunder in matters of the utmost importance. Furthermore, if there is really a way to learn virtue, where shall one look for it, when one has turned aside from this field of learning? When I advocate the study of philosophy, I usually discuss this subject at greater length, as I have done in another of my books. For the present I mean only to explain why, deprived of the tasks of public service, I have devoted myself to this particular pursuit.

But people raise other objections against me — and they are philosophers and scholars — asking whether I think I am quite consistent in that, although our school maintains that nothing can be known for certain, yet I make a habit of presenting my opinions on all sorts of subjects and at this very moment am trying to formulate rules of duty. I wish that they had a better understanding of our position. We Academics are not men whose minds wander in uncertainty and never know what principles to adopt. For what sort of mental habit, or rather what sort of life would that be which would dispense with all rules for reasoning or even for living? Not so with us. Other schools maintain that some things are certain, others uncertain; we, differing from them, say that some things are probable, others improbable.

What, then, is to prevent me from pursuing what seems to me to be probable and rejecting what seems to be improbable? Surely by shunning the presumption of dogmatism one keeps clear of that recklessness of assertion which is so far removed from true wisdom. And as to the fact that our school questions the certainty of everything, that is only because we could not get a clear view of what is "probable" unless a comparative analysis were made of all the arguments on both sides. . . .

"Undermining the Foundations of the Commonwealth"

Any man who holds a state office must make it his first care that everyone shall have what belongs to him and that private citizens shall suffer no invasion of their property rights by act of the state. It was a ruinous policy that Philippus proposed when in his tribuneship [104 B.C.] he introduced his agrarian bill. However, when his law was rejected, he took his defeat with good grace and displayed extraordinary moderation. But in his public speeches on the measure he often played the demagogue, and dangerously so when he said that owners of private property in the state numbered less than two thousand. That speech deserves unqualified condemnation, for it favored an equal distribution of property; and what more subversive policy than that can be conceived? For the chief purpose in the establishment of constitutional state and municipal governments was that individual property rights might be protected. Although by nature men are gregarious, it was in the hope of safeguarding their possessions that they sought the protection of cities.

The administration should also put forth every effort to prevent the levying of a property tax, and to this end precautions should be taken long in advance. Such a tax was often levied in the time of our forefathers on account of the depleted state of their treasury caused by incessant wars. But if any state . . . ever has to face a crisis requiring the imposition of such a burden, every effort must be made to let all the people realize that they must bow to the inevitable if they wish to survive the crisis. . . .

But they who pose as friends of the people and for that reason either attempt to have agrarian laws passed in order that the occupants may be driven out of their homes, or propose that money loaned should be remitted to the borrowers, are undermining the foundations of the commonwealth. First of all, they are destroying harmony, which cannot exist when money is taken away from one party and bestowed upon another; and second, they do away with equity, which is utterly subverted if the rights of property are not respected. For, as I said above, it is the peculiar function of the state and the city to guarantee to every man the free and undisturbed control of his own particular property. . . . And how is it fair that a man who never had any property should take possession of lands that had been occupied for many years or even generations, and that he who had them before should lose possession of them?

Now, it was on account of just this sort of wrongdoing that the Spartans banished their ephor Lysander, and put their king Agis to death — an act without precedent in the history of Sparta. From that time on — and for the same reason — dissensions so serious ensued that tyrants arose, the nobles were sent into exile, and the best-governed state in history crumbled to pieces. Nor did it fall alone; the contagion of the ills that originated in Sparta spread widely and dragged the rest of Greece down to ruin. What shall we say of our own Gracchi, the sons of that famous Tiberius Gracchus and grandson of Africanus? Was it not strife over the agrarian issue that caused their downfall and death? . . .

And this is the highest statesmanship and the soundest wisdom on the part of a good citizen, not to divide the interests of the citizens but to unite all on the basis of impartial justice. "Let them live in their neighbor's house rent-free." Why so? In order that, when I have bought, built, kept up, and spent my money upon a place, you may without my consent enjoy what belongs to me? What else is that but to rob one man of what belongs to him and to give to another what does not belong to him? And what is the meaning of an abolition of debts, except that you buy a farm with my money? You have the farm, and I have not my money.

We must, therefore, take measures that there shall be no indebtedness of a nature to endanger the public safety. It is a menace that can be averted in many ways; but should a serious debt be incurred, we are not to allow the rich to lose their property while the debtors profit by what is their neighbor's. For there is nothing that upholds a government more powerfully than its credit, and it can have no credit unless the payment of debts is enforced by law. Never were measures for the repudiation of debts more strenuously agitated than in my consulship. Men of every sort and rank attempted with arms and armies to force the project through. But I opposed them with such energy that this plague was wholly eradicated from the body politic. Indebtedness was never greater; yet debts were never liquidated more easily or more fully because the hope of defrauding the creditor was cut off and payment was enforced by law. . . .

Those, then, whose office it is to look after the interests of the state will refrain from that form of liberality which robs one man to enrich another. Above all, they will take particular care that everyone shall be protected in the possession of his own property by the fair administration of the law and the courts, that the poorer classes shall not be oppressed because of their helplessness, and that envy shall not stand in the way of the rich to prevent them from keeping or recovering possession of what is theirs.

◆ B ◆ CHAMPION OF LIBERTY

For a few months following the assassination of Julius Caesar in 44 B.C., the Senate reasserted a shaky and bumbling control of state affairs. With Cicero again playing a leading role, it first outmaneuvered Mark Antony (Marcus Antonius), Caesar's lieutenant and colleague in the consulship, and then, with the decisive assistance of the young Octavian (the future Augustus) and his legions, defeated him in battle and forced him to flee Italy. Exultant hopes for a new era of republican constitutionalism were short-lived, however. Once Antony no

From *Second Philippic*, 1, 25–30, 112–114, 116–119, based on the translation by C. D. Yonge.

longer seemed a danger, the Senate slighted Octavian — "The young man is to be praised, honored, and set aside," advised Cicero — with the result that he joined with Antony and Lepidus in forming a new military dictatorship, the Second Triumvirate.

During the struggle with Antony, Cicero assumed the role of a second Demosthenes fighting for liberty against another Philip. He denounced Antony in a series of fourteen Philippic Orations, thereby assuring his own death at the hands of Antony's agents during the proscriptions that followed the establishment of the Second Triumvirate. The following selection from the Second Philippic, the most famous of the series, is both a good example of the powerful invective directed at Antony (and at the late Julius Caesar as well), and a last eloquent statement of the higher ideals which underlay Cicero's attachment to the Republic. Because Cicero's career had ended as it had begun, fighting despotism, two generations later the historian Velleius Paterculus could confidently predict, in a passage directed against Mark Antony, "He lives and will live in the memory of all succeeding ages.... All posterity will admire his writings against you, and execrate your conduct toward him; and sooner shall the race of man fail in the world, than his name decay."

To what destiny of mine, gentlemen of the senate, shall I attribute it that no one for the last twenty years has been an enemy of the Republic without at the same time declaring war against me? Nor is there any necessity for naming any particular person; you yourselves recollect instances in proof of my statement. They have all suffered severer punishments than I could have wished for them; but I marvel that you, Antonius, do not shudder at the end of those men whose conduct you are imitating. And in the case of the others I had less cause for wonder. None of those men was a personal enemy of mine; all of them were attacked by me for the sake of the Republic. But you, who have never been injured by me, not even by a word, in order to appear more audacious than Catiline, more mad than Clodius, have of your own accord attacked me with abuse, and have considered that your break with me would be a recommendation of you to disloyal citizens.

What am I to think? That I am despised? I see nothing earlier in my life, or in my influence in the city, or in my exploits, or even in the moderate abilities with which I am endowed, which Antonius can despise. Did he think that it was easiest to slander me in the senate, a body which has borne testimony to many most illustrious citizens because they governed the Republic well, but to me alone of all men because I saved it? Or did he wish to contend with me in the field of oratory? That, indeed, is an act of generosity! For what could be a more fertile or richer subject for me than to speak in defense of myself and against Antonius? ...

Cicero next takes up various charges (omitted here) made by Antony against him, including the charge that Cicero caused the war between Caesar and Pompey.

But that is ancient history. This charge, however, is quite new, that Caesar was slain by my advice. I am afraid, gentlemen of the senate, lest I should appear to you to have planted a sham accuser against myself (which is a most disgraceful thing to do) — a man not only to distinguish me by the praises which are my due, but to load me also with those which do not belong to me. For who ever heard my name mentioned as an accomplice in that most glorious deed? And whose name has ever been concealed among the number of that gallant band? Concealed, did I say? Whose name was not at once made public? I would be more inclined to say that some had boasted in order to appear to have been members of that conspiracy, though they had really known nothing of it, than that anyone who had been an accomplice in it would have wished his name concealed. Moreover, how likely is it that among many men, some obscure, some young, all courting publicity, my name could possibly have escaped notice?

Indeed, if leaders were needed for the liberation of the country, what need was there of my instigating the Bruti, one of whom saw every day in his house the bust of Lucius Brutus and the other that of Ahala? Were these the men to seek counsel from the ancestors of others rather than their own, and from outside rather than at home? What? Caius Cassius, a man of that family which could not endure, I do not say the supremacy, but even the authority of others — he, I suppose, needed my encouragement? . . . Was Cnaeus Domitius spurred on to seek to recover his liberty, not by the death of his father, a most illustrious man, nor by the death of his uncle, nor by his own loss of office, but by my influence? Did I persuade Caius Trebonius? I would not have ventured even to suggest it. The Republic owes him even a greater debt of gratitude, because he preferred the liberty of the Roman people to the friendship of one man, and because he preferred overthrowing arbitrary power to sharing it. Was it my advice that Lucius Tillius Cimber followed? My surprise that he took part exceeded any expectation that he would. I was surprised that in remembering his country he forgot the favors received from Caesar. What do you say of the two Servilii? Shall I call them Cascas, or Ahalas? Do you think they were instigated by my influence rather than by their affection for the Republic? It would take a long time to go through all the rest; it is a glorious thing for the Republic, and a most honorable thing for themselves, that they were so numerous.

But consider how this shrewd fellow has convicted me. "When Caesar was slain," he says, "Marcus Brutus immediately lifted high his bloody dagger, called on Cicero by name, and congratulated him on the recovery of liberty." Why on me of all people? Because I knew of the plot? Consider whether this was not his reason for calling on me: when he had performed a deed very like those which I myself had done, he called me especially to witness that he had been an imitator of my glorious exploits. But, you stupid blockhead, do you not understand that if it is a crime to have wished for Caesar's death — which you accuse me of doing — it is also a crime to have rejoiced at his death? For what is the difference between a man who advises an action and one who approves it? Or what does it matter whether I wished it done or rejoiced that it was done? Is there anyone then, except those men who wished him to become a king, who was unwilling that the deed should be done or who disapproved of it after it was done? All men, therefore, are guilty. For all good men, to the best of their ability, had a part in the slaying of Caesar. Some had no plan, some had no courage, some had no opportunity — everyone had the desire.

But note the stupidity of this fellow — I should say, rather, this jackass. For this he said: "Marcus Brutus, whom I name to do him honor, holding aloft his bloody dagger, called out 'Cicero!' From this it must be understood that he was in on the plot." Am I then called a criminal by you because you suspect that I suspected something; and is Brutus who openly displayed his dripping dagger named by you that you may honor him? All right; let this stupidity exist in your language; how much greater is it in your actions and opinions! Make up your mind sometime, consul, what view you want held of the Bruti, of Caius Cassius, of Cnaeus Domitius, of Caius Trebonius and all the rest. Sleep off your hangover; sleep it off and breathe deeply. Must one use a torch to waken you while you are sleeping over such an important issue? Will you never understand that you have to decide whether those men who performed that deed are murders or asserters of freedom? . . .

However, we will say no more of what is past. But today, this very day that now is, this very moment while I am speaking, defend your conduct during this very moment, if you can. Why is the senate surrounded by a belt of armed men? Why are your henchmen listening to me sword in hand? Why are not the doors of the Temple of Concord open? Why do you bring Ityreans, the most barbarous of all tribes, into the forum armed with arrows? He says he does so as a guard. Is it not better to perish a thousand times than to be unable to live in one's own city without an armed guard? But believe me, there is no protection in that — a man must be defended by the affection and good will of his fellow-citizens, not by arms. The Roman people will take them from you, will wrest them from your hands — may it be while we are still safe! But however you treat us, as long as you follow your present policy it is impossible for you, believe me, to live long. . . . The Roman people still has men to whom it can entrust the helm of state; wherever they are, there is the defense of the Republic, or rather, there is the Republic itself, which as yet has only avenged, not reestablished, itself. Truly and surely the Republic has high-born youths ready to defend it. Though they may for a time keep in the background from a desire for tranquillity, they will be recalled by the Republic.

The name of peace is sweet, the thing itself is wholesome. But between peace and slavery there is a wide difference. Peace is liberty in tranquillity; slavery is the worst of all evils — to be repelled, if need be, not only by war but even by death. But if those liberators of ours have taken themselves away out of our sight, still they have left behind the example of their conduct. They have done what no one else had done. Brutus fought Tarquinius, who was a king when it was lawful for a king to exist in Rome; Spurius Cassius, Spurius Maelius, and Marcus Manlius were all slain because they were suspected of aiming at kingly power. These today are the first men who have ever ventured to attack, sword in hand, a man who was not aiming at kingly power but actually reigning. And their deed is not only a glorious and godlike exploit, but it is also one for us to imitate, especially since by it they have acquired such glory as appears hardly to be bound by heaven itself. . . .

But if you are not afraid of brave men and good citizens because they are prevented from attacking you by an armed guard, still, believe me, your own followers will not long put up with you. And what a life it is, day and night to fear danger from your own followers! Unless, of course, you have men who are bound to you by greater obligations than Caesar had from some of those by whom he was slain; or unless there are any aspects in which you can be compared with him.

In that man were combined genius, logic, memory, literary talent, prudence, deliberation, and industry. He had performed exploits in war which, though calamitous for the Republic, were nevertheless mighty deeds. Having for many years aimed at absolute power, he had with great labor and much personal danger accomplished what he intended. He had conciliated the ignorant crowd by shows, public works, gifts of food, and banquets; he had bound his own party to him by rewards, his adversaries by a show of clemency. In short, he had already brought to a free community the habit of slavery, partly out of fear, partly out of passiveness.

With him I can, indeed, compare you as to your passion for power, but in all other respects you are in no way comparable. But from the many evils which he has inflicted upon the Republic there is this good: the Roman people has learned how much to believe each man, to whom to entrust itself, and against whom to be on guard. Do you never think of these things? And do you not realize that it is enough for brave men to have learned how noble in act, how welcome in benefit, how glorious in fame, it is to slay a tyrant? Believe me, the time will come when men will compete with one another to do this deed, and when no one will wait for the tardy arrival of an opportunity.

Recover your senses sometime, I beg of you. Think of the family of which you are born, not of the men with whom you are living. Treat me as you will, but be reconciled to the Republic. But decide on your own conduct; I myself will declare what mine shall be. I defended the Republic in my youth, I will not desert it now that I am old. I scorned the sword of Catiline, I will not dread yours. No, I will gladly offer my body if the liberty of the state can be restored by my death and the pangs of the Roman people at last give birth to that which it has so long been in labor. Indeed, if twenty years ago in this very temple I asserted that death could not come prematurely to a man of consular rank, with how much more truth can I now say the same of an old man? To me, Conscript Fathers, death is now even desirable, after all the honors I have gained and the deeds I have done. I pray only for these two things: one, that dying I may leave the Roman people free — no greater boon than this can be granted me by the immortal gods. The other, that each man may meet with a fate suitable to his deserts and conduct toward the Republic.

◆ C ◆ THE LAWS

"Let us investigate the origins of justice."

It is generally held that Roman law (ius civile), because of its lasting influence on Western civilization, is the greatest achievement of the Romans. This influence stems from the universality of Roman law, the result of the efforts of Roman legal scholars to formulate abstract principles of law that would be generally applicable. These legal scholars, or jurisprudentes ("skilled in the law"), who worked chiefly during the "classical age" of Roman law from Trajan to Septimius Severus, "were conversant with the world of letters as well as with the world of politics, and so were able to find meaningful relationships between philosophical truths and empirical situations — an accomplishment illustrated, for example, by their imaginative adjustment of Stoicism to the ius civile." [1] This description of the jurisprudentes of the early Empire applies also to Cicero, whose concern for the reestablishment of order in the late Republic led him to view law as something based upon universal principles of right which it is the duty of philosophy to teach. Utilizing the Stoic formula of one God, one reason, one commonwealth, and one universal law, Cicero in The Laws expounds the theme that "Law is not a product of human thought, nor is it any enactment of peoples, but something eternal which rules the whole universe by its wisdom in command and prohibition." He explains the purpose of his work is "to promote the firm foundation of States, the strengthening of cities, and the curing of the ills of peoples."

Cicero wrote The Laws as a sequel to his Republic, an idealized account of the constitution of the early Republic — the "finished picture of another century" — which Polybius had described (see Selection 36). It is in the form of a Platonic dialogue, and the participants are Cicero (Marcus), his brother Quintus, and his good friend Pomponius Atticus.

Atticus. . . . Kindly begin without delay the statement of your opinions on the civil law.

Marcus. My opinions? Well then, I believe that there have been most eminent men in our State whose customary function it was to interpret the law to the people and answer questions in regard to it, but that these men, though they have made great claims, have spent their time on unimportant details. What subject indeed is so vast as the law of the State? But what is so trivial as the task of those who give legal advice? It is, however, necessary for the people.

Reprinted by permission of the publishers and The Loeb Classical Library from Clinton Walker Keyes' translation of Cicero, *De Legibus*, I, iv.14–vi.20; vii.22–23; x.28–30; xii.33–34; xiii.37, II, iv.8–v.13; vii.15–16 (Cambridge, Mass.: Harvard University Press). Bracketed insertions appear as in the original translation.

[1] Adda B. Bozeman, *Politics and Culture in International History* (Princeton, N.J.: Princeton University Press, 1960), p. 201.

But, while I do not consider that those who have applied themselves to this profession have lacked a conception of universal law, yet they have carried their studies of this civil law, as it is called, only far enough to accomplish their purpose of being useful to the people. Now all this amounts to little so far as learning is concerned, though for practical purposes it is indispensable. What subject is it, then, that you are asking me to expound? To what task are you urging me? Do you want me to write a treatise on the law of eaves and house walls? Or to compose formulas for contracts and court procedure? These subjects have been carefully treated by many writers, and are of humbler character, I believe, than what is expected of me.

A. Yet if you ask what I expect of you, I consider it a logical thing that, since you have already written a treatise on the constitution of the ideal State, you should also write one on its laws. For I note that this was done by your beloved Plato, whom you admire, revere above all others, and love above all others.

M. Is it your wish, then, that as he discussed the institutions of States and the ideal laws with Clinias and the Spartan Megillus in Crete on a summer day amid the cypress groves and forest paths of Cnossus, sometimes walking about, sometimes resting — you recall his description — we, in like manner, strolling or taking our ease among these stately poplars on the green and shady river bank, shall discuss the same subjects along somewhat broader lines than the practice of the courts calls for?

A. I should certainly like to hear such a conversation.

M. What does Quintus say?

Quintus. No other subject would suit me better.

M. And you are wise, for you must understand that in no other kind of discussion can one bring out so clearly what Nature's gifts to man are, what a wealth of most excellent possessions the human mind enjoys, what the purpose is, to strive after and accomplish which we have been born and placed in this world, what it is that unites men, and what natural fellowship there is among them. For it is only after all these things have been made clear that the origin of Law and Justice can be discovered.

A. Then you do not think that the science of law is to be derived from the praetor's edict, as the majority do now, or from the Twelve Tables, as people used to think, but from the deepest mysteries of philosophy?

M. Quite right; for in our present conversation, Pomponius, we are not trying to learn how to protect ourselves legally, or how to answer clients' questions. Such problems may be important, and in fact they are; for in former times many eminent men made a specialty of their solution, and at present one person performs this duty with the greatest authority and skill. But in our present investigation we intend to cover the whole range of universal Justice and Law in such a way that our own civil law, as it is called, will be confined to a small and narrow corner. For we must explain the nature of Justice, and this must be sought for in the nature of man; we must also consider the laws by which States ought to be governed; then we must deal with the enactments and decrees of nations which are already formulated and put in writing; and among these the civil law, as it is called, of the Roman people will not fail to find a place.

Q. You probe deep, and seek, as you should, the very fountainhead, to find what we are after, brother. And those who teach the civil law in any other way are teaching not so much the path of justice as of litigation.

M. There you are mistaken, Quintus, for it is rather ignorance of the law than knowledge of it that leads to litigation. But that will come later; now let us investigate the origins of Justice.

Well then, the most learned men have determined to begin with Law, and it would seem that they are right, if, according to their definition, Law is the highest reason, implanted in Nature, which commands what ought to be done and forbids the opposite. This reason, when firmly fixed and fully developed in the human mind, is Law. And so they believe that Law is intelligence, whose natural function it is to command right conduct and forbid wrongdoing. . . .

Now if this is correct, as I think it to be in general, then the origin of Justice is to be found in Law, for Law is a natural force; it is the mind and reason of the intelligent man, the standard by which Justice and Injustice are measured. But since our whole discussion has to do with the reasoning of the populace, it will sometimes be necessary to speak in the popular manner, and give the name of law to that which in written form decrees whatever it wishes, either by command or prohibition. For such is the crowd's definition of law. But in determining what Justice is, let us begin with that supreme Law which had its origin ages before any written law existed or any State had been established.

Q. Indeed that will be preferable and more suitable to the character of the conversation we have begun.

M. Well, then, shall we seek the origin of Justice itself at its fountainhead? For when that is discovered we shall undoubtedly have a standard by which the things we are seeking may be tested.

Q. I think that is certainly what we must do. . . .

M. I will not make the argument long. Your admission leads us to this: that animal which we call man, endowed with foresight and quick intelligence, complex, keen, possessing memory, full of reason and prudence, has been given a certain distinguished status by the supreme God who created him; for he is the only one among so many different kinds and varieties of living beings who has a share in reason and thought, while all the rest are deprived of it. But what is more divine, I will not say in man only, but in all heaven and earth, than reason? And reason, when it is full grown and perfected, is rightly called wisdom. Therefore, since there is nothing better than reason, and since it exists both in man and God, the first common possession of man and God is reason. But those who have reason in common must also have right reason in common. And since right reason is Law, we must believe that men have Law also in common with the gods. Further, those who share Law must also share Justice; and those who share these are to be regarded as members of the same commonwealth. If indeed they obey the same authorities and powers, this is true in a far greater degree; but as a matter of fact they do obey this celestial system, the divine mind, and the God of transcendent power. Hence we must now conceive of this whole universe as one commonwealth of which both gods and men are members. . . .

A. Ye immortal gods, how far back you go to find the origins of Justice! And you discourse so eloquently that I not only have no desire to hasten on to the consideration of the civil law, concerning which I was expecting you to speak, but I should have no objection to your spending even the entire day on your present topic; for the matters which you have taken up, no doubt, merely as preparatory to another subject, are of greater import than the subject itself to which they form an introduction.

M. The points which are now being briefly touched upon are certainly important; but out of all the material of the philosophers' discussions, surely there comes nothing more valuable than the full realization that we are born for Justice, and that right is based, not upon men's opinions, but upon Nature. This fact will immediately be plain if you once get a clear conception of man's fellowship and union with his fellowmen. For no single thing is so like another, so exactly its counterpart, as all of us are to one another. Nay, if bad habits and false beliefs did not twist the weaker minds and turn them in whatever direction they are inclined, no one would be so like his own self as all men would be like all others. And so, however we may define man, a single definition will apply to all. This is a sufficient proof that there is no difference in kind between man and man; for if there were, one definition could not be applicable to all men; and indeed reason, which alone raises us above the level of the beasts and enables us to draw inferences, to prove and disprove, to discuss and solve problems, and to come to conclusions, is certainly common to us all, and, though varying in what it learns, at least in the capacity to learn it is invariable. For the same things are invariably perceived by the senses, and those things which stimulate the senses, stimulate them in the same way in all men; and those rudimentary beginnings of intelligence to which I have referred, which are imprinted on our minds, are imprinted on all minds alike; and speech, the mind's interpreter, though differing in the choice of words, agrees in the sentiments expressed. In fact, there is no human being of any race who, if he finds a guide, cannot attain to virtue. . . .

The next point, then, is that we are so constituted by Nature as to share the sense of Justice with one another and to pass it on to all men. And in this whole discussion I want it understood that what I shall call Nature is [that which is implanted in us by Nature]; that, however, the corruption caused by bad habits is so great that the sparks of fire, so to speak, which Nature has kindled in us are extinguished by this corruption, and the vices which are their opposites spring up and are established. But if the judgments of men were in agreement with Nature, so that, as the poet says, they considered "nothing alien to them which concerns mankind," then Justice would be equally observed by all. For those creatures who have received the gift of reason from Nature have also received right reason, and therefore they have also received the gift of Law, which is right reason applied to command and prohibition.

And if they have received Law, they have received Justice also. Now all men have received reason; therefore all men have received Justice. . . .

Now all this is really a preface to what remains to be said in our discussion, and its purpose is to make it more easily understood that Justice is inherent in Nature. After I have said a few words more on this topic, I shall go on to the civil law, the subject which gives rise to all this discourse. . . .

But you see the direction this conversation is to take; our whole discourse is intended to promote the firm foundation of States, the strengthening of cities, and the curing of the ills of peoples. For that reason I want to be especially careful not to lay down first principles that have not been wisely considered and thoroughly investigated. . . .

Once more, then, before we come to the individual laws, let us look at the character and nature of Law, for fear that, though it must be the standard to which we refer everything, we may now and then be led astray by an incorrect use of terms, and forget the rational principles on which our laws must be based.

Q. Quite so, that is the correct method of exposition.

M. Well, then, I find that it has been the opinion of the wisest men that Law is not a product of human thought, nor is it any enactment of peoples, but something eternal which rules the whole universe by its wisdom in command and prohibition. Thus they have been accustomed to say that Law is the primal and ultimate mind of God, whose reason directs all things either by compulsion or restraint. Wherefore that Law which the gods have given to the human race has been justly praised; for it is the reason and mind of a wise lawgiver applied to command and prohibition.

Q. You have touched upon this subject several times before. But before you come to the laws of peoples, please make the character of this heavenly Law clear to us, so that the waves of habit may not carry us away and sweep us into the common mode of speech on such subjects.

M. Ever since we were children, Quintus, we have learned to call, "If one summon another to court," [2] and other rules of the same kind, laws. But we must come to the true understanding of the matter, which is as follows: this and other commands and prohibitions of nations have the power to summon to righteousness and away from wrong-doing; but this power is not merely older than the existence of nations and States, it is coeval with that God who guards and rules heaven and earth. For the divine mind cannot exist without reason, and divine reason cannot but have this power to establish right and wrong. No written law commanded that a man should take his stand on a bridge alone, against the full force of the enemy, and order the bridge broken down behind him; yet we shall not for that reason suppose that the heroic [Horatius] Cocles was not obeying the law of bravery and following its decrees in doing so noble a deed. Even if there was no written law against rape at Rome in the reign of Lucius Tarquinius, we cannot say on that account that Sextus Tarquinius did

---

[2] From the Twelve Tables. [Editor's note.]

not break that eternal Law by violating Lucretia, the daughter of Tricipitinus! For reason did exist, derived from the Nature of the universe, urging men to right conduct and diverting them from wrong-doing, and this reason did not first become Law when it was written down, but when it first came into existence simultaneously with the divine mind. Wherefore the true and primal Law, applied to command and prohibition, is the right reason of supreme Jupiter.

Q. I agree with you, brother, that what is right and true is also eternal, and does not begin or end with written statutes.

M. Therefore, just as that divine mind is the supreme Law, so, when [reason] is perfected in man [that also is Law; and this perfected reason exists] in the mind of the wise man; but those rules which, in varying forms and for the need of the moment, have been formulated for the guidance of nations, bear the title of laws rather by favor than because they are really such. . . .

What of the many deadly, the many pestilential statutes which nations put in force? These no more deserve to be called laws than the rules a band of robbers might pass in their assembly. For if ignorant and unskillful men have prescribed deadly poisons instead of healing drugs, these cannot possibly be called physicians' prescriptions; neither in a nation can a statute of any sort be called a law, even though the nation, in spite of its being a ruinous regulation, has accepted it. Therefore Law is the distinction between things just and unjust, made in agreement with that primal and most ancient of all things, Nature; and in conformity to Nature's standard are framed those human laws which inflict punishment upon the wicked but defend and protect the good. . . .

So in the very beginning we must persuade our citizens that the gods are the lords and rulers of all things, and that what is done, is done by their will and authority; that they are likewise great benefactors of man, observing the character of every individual, what he does, of what wrong he is guilty, and with what intentions and with what piety he fulfills his religious duties; and that they take note of the pious and impious. For surely minds which are imbued with such ideas will not fail to form true and useful opinions. Indeed, what is more true than that no one ought to be so foolishly proud as to think that, though reason and intellect exist in himself, they do not exist in the heavens and the universe, or that those things which can hardly be understood by the highest reasoning powers of the human intellect are guided by no reason at all? In truth, the man that is not driven to gratitude by the orderly courses of the stars, the regular alternation of day and night, the gentle progress of the seasons, and the produce of the earth brought forth for our sustenance — how can such an one be accounted a man at all? And since all things that possess reason stand above those things which are without reason, and since it would be sacrilege to say that anything stands above universal Nature, we must admit that reason is inherent in Nature. Who will deny that such beliefs are useful when he remembers how often oaths are used to confirm agreements, how important to our well-being is the sanctity of treaties, how many persons are deterred from crime by the fear of divine punishment, and how sacred an association of citizens becomes when the immortal gods are made members of it, either as judges or as witnesses?

There you have the proem to the law; for that is the name given to it by Plato.

45

The Poetry of Catullus

Romantic excitements

Gaius Valerius Catullus (ca. 84–ca. 54 B.C.) was one of the founders of a genre new to Latin literature — the emotional, spontaneous, and highly personal lyric. Although he was indebted to the Greeks, as were all Roman poets, for the metrical form of his poetry, he was nevertheless vigorously original in the personal thoughts and feelings which filled his lyrics. They reflect his short and stormy career in Rome to which he came in his early twenties from Verona in the north. He fell in with the dissipated youth of the corrupt capital who sought joy in life through the pursuit of varied excitements. Catullus forgot every excitement but love when he met the beautiful but unprincipled Clodia, a married woman ten years his senior whom Cicero once called "a two-bit harlot." He immortalized his love for her in verse (addressed to "Lesbia") containing the outpouring of every emotion from passionate devotion through jealousy and disillusionment to bitter hate.

All this contrasts sharply with the impersonal quality of earlier Roman literature, which stressed the subordination of the individual to the collective interests of the group, and took its inspiration from a patriotic devotion to the state. Like the Greek epics, it glorified the hero. In the words of Ennius (239–169 B.C.), the fragments of whose epic on the history of Rome constitute the only substantial remains we have of early Latin poetry, "Rome stands built upon the ancient ways of life (mos majorum) and upon her men." Catullus' lyrics are of another century and emphatically of a spirit totally at variance with the older Roman traditions.

TO CORNELIUS NEPOS

My little volume is complete,
Fresh pumice-polished and as neat
As book need wish to be;

And now, what patron shall I choose
For these gay sallies of my muse?
    Cornelius, whom but thee!

For though they are but trifles, thou
Some value didst to them allow,
    And that from thee is fame,
Who dared in thy three volumes' space,
Alone of all Italians, trace
    Our history and name.

Great Jove, what lore, what labor there!
Then take this little book, whate'er
    Of good or bad it store;
And grant, oh guardian Muse, that it
May keep the flavor of its wit
    A century or more!

Trans. Theodore Martin

MY SWEETEST LESBIA

My sweetest Lesbia, let us live and love
And though the sager sort our deeds reprove,
Let us not weigh them. Heaven's great lamps do dive
Into their west, and straight again revive,
But, soon as once set is our little light,
Then must we sleep one ever-during night.

If all would lead their lives in love like me,
Then bloody swords and armor should not be;
No drum nor trumpet peaceful sleeps should move,
Unless alarm came from the camp of Love:
But fools do live and waste their little light,
And seek with pain their ever-during night.

When timely death my life and fortune ends,
Let not my hearse be vext with mourning friends,
But let all lovers rich in triumph come
And with sweet pastimes grace my happy tomb:
And, Lesbia, close up thou my little light,
And crown with love my ever-during night.

Trans. Thomas Campion

LESBIA RAILING

Lesbia forever on me rails.
To talk of me she never fails.
Now, hang me, but for all her art,
I find that I have gained her heart.
My proof is this: I plainly see
The case is just the same with me;
I curse her every hour sincerely,
Yet, hang me, but I love her dearly.

Trans. Jonathan Swift

TRUE OR FALSE

None could ever say that she,
Lesbia! was so loved by me.
Never all the world around
Faith so true as mine was found.
If no longer it endures
(Would it did!) the fault is yours.
I can never think again
Well of you: I try in vain.
But . . . be false . . . do what you will —
Lesbia! I must love you still.

Trans. Walter Savage Landor

LOVE'S UNREASON

I hate and love — the why I cannot tell,
But by my tortures know the fact too well.

TO HIMSELF

Wretched Catullus, play the fool no more:
The lost is lost, the dead forever dead —
White were the suns that gleamed for you of yore,
When roamed your footsteps where your lady led,
O loved by us as none was loved before:
O then I spoke those playful words so dear

That then my lady loved so well to hear —
White were the suns that gleamed for you of yore.

She wishes them no more; and 'tis for you,
Poor weakling, now to cease to wish them too.
No longer strive to follow what will flee:
No longer live the wretch you've lived to be.
But now with steadfast mind, be calm and bear.
Farewell, my child, Catullus now is strong;
He will not ask or seek you anywhere
Unbidden more.

                But you shall grieve for long,
When none will ask. O what a life is there,
Miscreant woman. Who will come, ah who
Hereafter? Unto whom shall you be fair?
Who now will love? To whom shall you belong?
Whom will you kiss? and bite whose lips! —
                        But you,
Catullus, still remember to be strong.

Trans. William Ellery Leonard

HOME TO SIRMIO ON LAKE GARDA

Dear Sirmio, thou art the very eye
Of islands and peninsulas, that lie
Deeply embosomed in calm inland lake,
Or where the waves of the vast ocean break;
Joy of all joys, to gaze on thee once more!
I scarce believe that I have left the shore
Of Thynia, and Bithynia's parching plain,
And gaze on thee in safety once again!
Oh, what more sweet than when, from care set free,
The spirit lays its burden down, and we,
With distant travel spent, come home and spread
Our limbs to rest along the wished-for bed!
This, this alone, repays such toils as these!
Smile, then, fair Sirmio, and thy master please, —
And you, ye dancing waters of the lake,
Rejoice; and every smile of home awake!

Trans. Theodore Martin

46

Lucretius, On the Nature of Things

Epicurean philosophy at Rome

Titus Lucretius Carus (ca. 99–55 B.C.) was born of aristocratic parents amidst the social and spiritual decline of the Roman Republic's fatal last century. He saw his fellow citizens, he tells us, "in their greed for gain swelling their possessions out of civil war, doubling their wealth by piling murder on murder, and welcoming a brother's tragic death with heartless glee." He rejected the normal political career open to men of his class, "for to seek power, an empty thing which is never gained, and ever to labor sore in that pursuit, is but struggling to push up a mountain a stone which rolls back from the very top and rushes down to the level of the open plain." Thoroughly disillusioned with life, Lucretius withdrew into the seclusion of what he called the "ivory tower" ("quiet citadel" in the translation presented here).

But retreat from the world did not mean for Lucretius an indifference to the welfare of his fellow citizens. There had come to him, as a sudden revelation of truth comes to one who has long been without truth, a new faith and a new ideal. With the impassioned enthusiasm of a prophet he presented his views in a long didactic poem, On the Nature of Things (De rerum natura). His new faith was founded on the belief that science could destroy ignorance, from which came all the evil in the world; and his new ideal was the tranquility which men could achieve in their lives if they would only be guided by reason.

The source of this revelation was the Hellenistic philosophy of Epicurus (ca. 342–270 B.C.), who taught that the happiness sought after by man consisted simply of being free from pain in body and mind. ("By pleasure we mean the absence of pain in the body and of trouble in the soul.") Epicurus, in turn, based his simple ethical philosophy upon the physics of Democritus (fifth century B.C.), who taught that the universe is composed of tiny particles of matter called atoms which come together and then fall apart, thus providing the constant flux and change that is characteristic of all material things and all life. There is, according to Epicurus, no meaning or purpose to be found in the workings of the natural world. Although people have free will — this is the result of the ability of atoms to "swerve," a concept added by Epicurus to

Reprinted by permission of the publisher from Ronald Latham's translation of Lucretius: On the Nature of the Universe, I, 62–126, 136–158, 215–224, 265–297; II, 1–52, 62–128, 216–293; III, 417–458, 784–805, 830–869, 912–930, 964–977; IV, 1058–1070, 1089–1192. (Penguin Books Ltd.: 1951).

Democritus' atomic theory — they are still a part of nature. Their birth and death represent the temporary coalescence and final disintegration of a group of atoms. The gods, if they exist, do not concern themselves with mundane affairs but spend their time pursuing happiness, like good Epicureans. When people understand that the world has no purpose, they can be freed from the fears, the errors, and the vain pursuits (including love) which produce unhappiness.

All this Lucretius expounds to his friend Memmius with the fervor of a convert to a new faith, enriching the dry arguments of Epicurus with a wealth of illustrations and a poetic enthusiasm. The result is both a work of art and the best existing description of Epicurean philosophy.

THE NATURE OF HAPPINESS

What joy it is, when out at sea the stormwinds are lashing the waters, to gaze from the shore at the heavy stress some other man is enduring! Not that anyone's afflictions are in themselves a source of delight; but to realize from what troubles you yourself are free is joy indeed. What joy, again, to watch opposing hosts marshalled on the field of battle when you have yourself no part in their peril! But this is the greatest joy of all: to stand aloof in a quiet citadel, stoutly fortified by the teaching of the wise, and to gaze down from that elevation on others wandering aimlessly in a vain search for the way of life, pitting their wits one against another, disputing for precedence, struggling night and day with unstinted effort to scale the pinnacles of wealth and power. O joyless hearts of men! O minds without vision! How dark and dangerous the life in which this tiny span is lived away! Do you not see that nature is clamoring for two things only, a body free from pain, and a mind released from worry and fear for the enjoyment of pleasurable sensations?

So we find that the requirements of our bodily nature are few indeed, no more than is necessary to banish pain. To heap pleasure upon pleasure may heighten man's enjoyment at times. But what matter if there are no golden images of youths about the house, holding flaming torches in their right hands to illumine banquets prolonged into the night? What matter if the hall does not sparkle with silver and gleam with gold, and no carved and gilded rafters ring to the music of the lute? Nature does not miss these luxuries when men recline in company on the soft grass by a running stream under the branches of a tall tree and refresh their bodies pleasurably at small expense. Better still if the weather smiles upon them and the season of the year stipples the green herbage with flowers. Burning fevers flee no swifter from your body if you toss under figured counterpanes and coverlets of crimson than if you must lie in rude homespun.

If our bodies are not profited by treasures or titles or the majesty of kingship, we must go on to admit that neither are our minds. Or tell me, Memmius, when you see your legions thronging the Campus Martius in the ardor of mimic warfare, supported by ample auxiliaries, magnificently armed and fired by a common purpose, does that sight scare the terrors of superstition from your mind? Does the fear of death retire from your breast and leave it carefree at the moment when you sight your warships ranging far and wide? Or do we not find such resources absurdly ineffective? The fears and anxieties that dog the human breast do not shrink from the clash of arms or the fierce rain of missiles. They stalk unabashed among princes and potentates. They are not awe-struck by the gleam of gold or the bright sheen of purple robes.

Can you doubt then that this power rests with reason alone? . . .

When human life lay grovelling in all men's sight, crushed to the earth under the dead weight of superstition whose grim features lowered menacingly upon mortals from the four quarters of the sky, a man of Greece was first to raise mortal eyes in defiance, first to stand erect and brave the challenge. Fables of the gods did not crush him, nor the lightning flash and the growling menace of the sky. Rather, they quickened his manhood, so that he, first of all men, longed to smash the constraining locks of nature's doors. The vital vigor of his mind prevailed. He ventured far out beyond the flaming ramparts of the world and voyaged in mind throughout infinity. Returning victorious, he proclaimed to us what can be and what cannot: how a limit is fixed to the power of everything and an immovable frontier post. Therefore superstition in its turn lies crushed beneath his feet, and we by his triumph are lifted level with the skies.

"SUPERSTITION IS THE MOTHER OF SINFUL DEEDS"

One thing that worries me is the fear that you may fancy yourself embarking on an impious course, setting your feet on the path of sin. Far from it. More often it is this very superstition that is the mother of sinful and impious deeds. Remember how at Aulis the altar of the Virgin Goddess was foully stained with the blood of Iphigeneia by the leaders of the Greeks, the patterns of chivalry. The headband was bound about her virgin tresses and hung down evenly over both her cheeks. Suddenly she caught sight of her father standing sadly in front of the altar, the attendants beside him hiding the knife and her people bursting into tears when they saw her. Struck dumb with terror, she sank on her knees to the ground. Poor girl, at such a moment it did not help her that she had been first to give the name of father to a king. Raised by the hands of men, she was led trembling to the altar. Not for her the sacrament of marriage and the loud chant of Hymen. It was her fate in the very hour of marriage to fall a sinless victim to a sinful rite, slaughtered to her greater grief by a father's hand, so that a fleet might sail under happy auspices. Such are the heights of wickedness to which men are driven by superstition.

You yourself, if you surrender your judgment at any time to the blood-curdling declamations of the prophets, will want to desert our ranks. Only think what phantoms they can conjure up to overturn the tenor of your life and wreck your happiness with fear. And not without cause. For, if men saw that a term was set to their troubles, they would find strength in some way to withstand the hocus-pocus and intimidations of the prophets. As it is, they have no power of resistance, because they are haunted by the fear of eternal punishment after death. They know nothing of the nature of the spirit. Is it born, or is it implanted in us at birth? Does it perish with us, dissolved by death, or does it visit the murky depths and dreary sloughs of Hades? Or is it transplanted by divine power into other creatures, as described in the poems of our own Ennius, who first gathered on the delectable slopes of Helicon an ever-green garland destined to win renown among the nations of Italy? Ennius indeed in his immortal verses proclaims that there is also a Hell, which is peopled not by our actual spirits or bodies but only by shadowy images, ghastly pale. It is from this realm that he pictures the ghost of Homer, of unfading memory, as appearing to him, shedding salt tears and revealing the nature of the universe. . . .

FIRST PRINCIPLES

I am well aware that it is not easy to elucidate in Latin verse the obscure discoveries of the Greeks. The poverty of our language and the novelty of the theme compel me often to coin new words for the purpose. But your merit and the joy I hope to derive from our delightful friendship encourage me to face any task however hard. This it is that leads me to stay awake through the quiet of the night, studying how by choice of words and the poet's art I can display before your mind a clear light by which you can gaze into the heart of hidden things.

This dread and darkness of the mind cannot be dispelled by the sunbeams, the shining shafts of day, but only by an understanding of the outward form and inner workings of nature. In tackling this theme, our starting-point will be this principle: *Nothing can ever be created by divine power out of nothing.* The reason why all mortals are so gripped by fear is that they see all sorts of things happening on the earth and in the sky with no discernible cause, and these they attribute to the will of God. Accordingly, when we have seen that nothing can be created out of nothing, we shall then have a clearer picture of the path ahead, the problem of how things are created and occasioned without the aid of the gods. . . .

The second great principle is this: *nature resolves everything into its component atoms and never reduces anything to nothing.* If anything were perishable in all its parts, anything might perish all of a sudden and vanish from sight. There would be no need of any force to separate its parts and loosen their links. In actual fact, since everything is composed of indestructible seeds, nature obviously does not allow anything to perish till it has encountered a force that shatters it with a blow or creeps into chinks and unknits it. . . .

Well, Memmius, I have taught you that things cannot be created out of nothing nor, once born, be summoned back to nothing. Perhaps, however, you are becoming mistrustful of my words, because these atoms of mine are not visible to the eye. Consider, therefore, this further evidence of *bodies whose existence you must acknowledge though they cannot be seen.* First, wind, when its force is roused, whips up waves, founders tall ships and scatters cloud-rack. Sometimes scouring plains with hurricane force it strews them with huge trees and batters mountain peaks with blasts that hew down forests. Such is wind in its fury, when it whoops aloud with a mad menace in its shouting. Without question, therefore, there must be invisible particles of wind which sweep sea and land and the clouds in the sky, swooping upon them and whirling them along in a headlong hurricane. In the way they flow and the havoc they spread they are no different from a torrential flood of water when it rushes down in a sudden spate from the mountain heights, swollen by heavy rains, and heaps together wreckage from the forest and entire trees. Soft though it is by nature, the sudden shock of oncoming water is more than even stout bridges can withstand, so furious is the force with which the turbid, storm-flushed torrent surges against their piers. With a mighty roar it lays them low, rolling huge rocks under its waves and brushing aside every obstacle from its course. Such, therefore, must be the movement of blasts of wind also. When they have come surging along some course like a rushing river, they push obstacles before them and buffet them with repeated blows; and sometimes, eddying round and round, they snatch them up and carry them along in a swiftly circling vortex. Here then is proof upon proof that winds have invisible bodies, since in their actions and behavior they are found to rival great rivers, whose bodies are plain to see. . . .

. . . It follows that nature works through the agency of invisible bodies. . . .

"ALL PARTICLES OF MATTER ARE ON THE MOVE"

And now to business. I will explain *the motion by which the generative bodies of matter give birth to various things*, and, after they are born, dissolve them once more; the force that compels them to do this; and the power of movement through the boundless void with which they are endowed. It is for you to devote yourself attentively to my words.

Be sure that matter does not stick together in a solid mass. For we see that everything grows less and seems to melt away with the lapse of time and withdraw its old age from our eyes. And yet we see no diminution in the sum of things. This is because the bodies that are shed by one thing lessen it by their departure but enlarge another by their coming; here they bring decay, there full bloom, but they do not linger there. So the sum of things is perpetually renewed. Mortals live by mutual interchange. One race increases by another's decrease. The generations of living things pass in swift succession and like runners hand on the torch of life.

If you think that the atoms can stop and by their stopping generate new motions in things, you are wandering far from the path of truth. Since the atoms are moving freely through the void, they must all be kept in motion either by their own weight or on occasion by the impact of another atom. For it must often happen that two of them in their course knock together and immediately bounce apart in opposite directions, a natural consequence of their hardness and solidity and the absence of anything behind to stop them.

As a further indication that all particles of matter are on the move, remember that the universe is bottomless: there is no place where the atoms could come to rest. As I have already shown by various arguments and proved conclusively, space is without end or limit and spreads out immeasurably in all directions alike.

It clearly follows that no rest is given to the atoms in their course through the depths of space. Driven along in an incessant but variable movement, some of them bounce far apart after a collision while others recoil only a short distance from the impact. From those that do not recoil far, being driven into a closer union and held there by the entanglement of their own interlocking shapes, are composed firmly rooted rock, the stubborn strength of steel and the like. Those others that move freely through larger tracts of space, springing far apart and carried far by the rebound — these provide for us thin air and blazing sunlight. Besides these, there are many other atoms at large in empty space which have been thrown out of compound bodies and have nowhere even been granted admittance so as to bring their motions into harmony.

This process, as I might point out, is illustrated by an image of it that is continually taking place before our very eyes. Observe what happens when sunbeams are admitted into a building and shed light on its shadowy places. You will see a multitude of tiny particles mingling in a multitude of ways in the empty space within the light of the beam, as though contending in everlasting conflict, rushing into battle rank upon rank with never a moment's pause in a rapid sequence of unions and disunions. From this you may picture what it is for the atoms to be perpetually tossed about in the illimitable void. To some extent a small thing may afford an illustration and an imperfect image of great things. Besides, there is a further reason why you should give your mind to these particles that are seen dancing in a sunbeam: their dancing is an actual indication of underlying movements of matter that are hidden from our sight. . . .

"THE ATOMS SWERVE"

In this connection there is another fact that I want you to grasp. *When the atoms are traveling straight down through empty space by their own weight, at quite indeterminate times and places they swerve ever so little from their course,* just so much that you can call it a change of direction. If it were not for this swerve, everything would fall downwards like raindrops through the abyss of space. No collision would take place and no impact of atom on atom would be created. Thus nature would never have created anything.

If anyone supposes that heavier atoms on a straight course through empty space could outstrip lighter ones and fall on them from above, thus causing impacts that might give rise to generative motions, he is going far astray from the path of truth. The reason why objects falling through water or thin air vary in speed according to their weight is simply that the matter composing water or air cannot obstruct all objects equally, but is forced to give way more speedily to heavier ones. But empty space can offer no resistance to any object in any quarter at any time, so as not to yield free passage as its own nature demands. Therefore, through undisturbed vacuum all bodies must travel at equal speed though impelled by unequal weights. The heavier will never be able to fall on the lighter from above or generate of themselves impacts leading to that variety of motions out of which nature can produce things. We are thus forced back to the conclusion that the atoms swerve a little — but only a very little, or we shall be caught imagining slantwise movements, and the facts will prove us wrong. For we see plainly and palpably that weights, when they come tumbling down, have no power of their own to move aslant, so far as meets the eye. But who can possibly perceive that they do not diverge in the very least from a vertical course?

Again, if all movement is always interconnected, the new arising from the old in a determinate order — if the atoms never swerve so as to originate some new movement that will snap the bonds of fate, the everlasting sequence of cause and effect — what is the source of the free will possessed by living things throughout the earth? What, I repeat, is the source of that willpower snatched from the fates, whereby we follow the path along which we are severally led by pleasure, swerving from our course at no set time or place but at the bidding of our hearts? There is no doubt that on these occasions the will of the individual originates the movements that trickle through his limbs. Observe, when the starting barriers are flung back, how the racehorses in the eagerness of their strength cannot break away as suddenly as their hearts desire. For the whole supply of matter must first be mobilized throughout every member of the body: only then, when it is mustered in a continuous array, can it respond to the prompting of the heart. So you may see that the beginning of movement is generated by the heart; starting from the voluntary action of the mind, it is then transmitted throughout the body and the limbs. Quite different is our experience when we are shoved along by a blow inflicted with compulsive force by someone else. In that case it is obvious that all the matter of our body is set going and pushed along involuntarily, till a check is imposed through the limbs by the will. Do you see the difference? Although many men are driven by an external force and often constrained involuntarily to advance or to rush headlong, yet there is within the human breast something that can fight against this force and resist it. At its command the supply of matter is forced to take a new course through our limbs and joints or is checked in its course and brought once more to a halt. So also in the atoms you must recognize the same possibility: besides weight and impact there must be a third cause of movement, the source of this inborn power of ours, since we see that nothing can come out of nothing. For the weight of an atom prevents its movements from being completely determined by the impact of other atoms. But the fact that the mind itself has no internal necessity to determine its every act and compel it to suffer in helpless passivity — this is due to the slight swerve of the atoms at no determinate time or place. . . .

"SPIRIT IS MORTAL"

My next point is this: you must understand that the *minds of living things and the light fabric of their spirits are neither birthless nor deathless.* To this end I have long been mustering and inventing verses with a labor that is also a joy. Now I will try to set them out in a style worthy of your career.

Please note that both objects are to be embraced under one name. When, for instance, I proceed to demonstrate that "spirit" is mortal, you must understand that this applies equally to "mind" since the two are so conjoined as to constitute a single substance.

First of all, then, I have shown that spirit is flimsy stuff composed of tiny particles. Its atoms are obviously far smaller than those of swift-flowing water or mist or smoke, since it far outstrips them in mobility and is moved by a far slighter impetus. Indeed, it is actually moved by images of smoke and mist. So, for instance, when we are sunk in sleep, we may see altars sending up clouds of steam and giving off smoke; and we cannot doubt that we are here dealing with images. Now, we see that water flows out in all directions from a broken vessel and the moisture is dissipated, and mist and smoke vanish into thin air. Be assured, therefore, that spirit is similarly dispelled and vanishes far more speedily and is sooner dissolved into its component atoms once it has been let loose from the human frame. When the body, which served as a vessel for it, is by some means broken and attenuated by loss of blood from the veins, so as to be no longer able to contain it, how can you suppose that it can be contained by any kind of air, which must be far more tenuous than our bodily frame?

Again, we are conscious that mind and body are born together, grow up together and together decay. With the weak and delicate frame of wavering childhood goes a like infirmity of judgment. The robust vigor of ripening years is accompanied by a steadier resolve and a maturer strength of mind. Later, when the body is palsied by the potent forces of age and the limbs begin to droop with blunted vigor, the understanding limps, the tongue falters and the mind totters: everything weakens and gives way at the same time. It is thus natural that the vital spirit should all evaporate like smoke, soaring into the gusty air, since we have seen that it shares the body's birth and growth and wearies with the weariness of age. . . .

A tree cannot exist high in air, or clouds in the depths of the sea, as fish cannot live in the fields, or blood flow in wood or sap in stones. There is a determined and allotted place for the growth and presence of everything. So mind cannot arise alone without body or apart from sinews and blood. If it could do this, then surely it could much more readily function in head or shoulders or the tips of the heels and be born in any other part, so long as it was held in the same container, that is to say in the same man. Since, however, even in the human body we see a determined and allotted place set aside for the growth and presence of spirit and mind, we have even stronger grounds for denying that they could survive or come to birth outside the body altogether. You must admit, therefore, that when the body has perished there is an end also of the spirit diffused through it. It is surely crazy to couple a mortal object with an eternal and suppose that they can work in harmony and mutually interact. What can be imagined more incongruous, what more repugnant and discordant, than that a mortal object and one that is immortal and everlasting should unite to form a compound and jointly weather the storms that rage about them? . . .

"NOTHING TO FEAR IN DEATH"

From all this it follows that *death is nothing to us* and no concern of ours, since our tenure of the mind is mortal. In days of old, we felt no disquiet when the hosts of Carthage poured in to battle on every side — when the whole earth, dizzied by the convulsive shock of war, reeled sickeningly under the high ethereal vault, and between realm and realm the empire of mankind by land and sea trembled in the balance. So, when we shall be no more — when the union of body and spirit that engenders us has been disrupted — to us, who shall then be nothing, nothing by any hazard will happen any more at all. Nothing will have power to stir our senses, not though earth be fused with sea and sea with sky.

If any feeling remains in mind or spirit after it has been torn from our body, that is nothing to us, who are brought into being by the wedlock of body and spirit, conjoined and coalesced. Or even if the matter that composes us should be reassembled by time after our death and brought back into its present state — if the light of life were given to us anew — even that contingency would still be no concern of ours once the chain of our identity had been snapped. We who are now are not concerned with ourselves in any previous existence: the sufferings of those selves do not touch us. When you look at the immeasurable extent of time gone by and the multiform movements of matter, you will readily credit that these same atoms that compose us now must many a time before have entered into the self-same combinations as now. But our mind cannot recall this to remembrance. For between then and now is interposed a breach in life, and all the atomic motions have been wandering far astray from sentience.

If the future holds travail and anguish in store, the self must be in existence, when that time comes, in order to experience it. But from this fate we are redeemed by death, which denies existence to the self that might have suffered these tribulations. Rest assured, therefore, that we have nothing to fear in death. One who no longer is cannot suffer, or differ in any way from one who has never been born, when once this mortal life has been usurped by death the immortal. . . .

Here, again, is the way men often talk from the bottom of their hearts when they recline at a banquet, goblet in hand and brows decked with garlands: "How all too short are these good times that come to us poor creatures! Soon they will be past and gone, and there will be no recalling them." You would think the crowning calamity in store for them after death was to be parched and shrivelled by a tormenting thirst or oppressed by some other vain desire. But even in sleep, when mind and body alike are at rest, no one misses himself or sighs for life. If such sleep were prolonged to eternity, no longing for ourselves would trouble us. And yet the vital atoms in our limbs cannot be far removed from their sensory motions at a time when a mere jolt out of sleep enables a man to pull himself together. Death, therefore, must be regarded, so far as we are concerned, as having much less existence than sleep, if anything can have less existence than what we perceive to be nothing. For death is followed by a far greater dispersal of the seething mass of matter: once that icy breach in life has intervened, there is no more waking.

. . . The old is always thrust aside to make way for the new, and one thing must be built out of the wreck of another. There is no murky pit of Hell awaiting anyone. There is need of matter, so that later generations may arise; when they have lived out their span, they will all follow you. Bygone generations have taken your road, and those to come will take it no less. So one thing will never cease to spring from another. To none is life given in freehold; to all on lease. Look back at the eternity that passed before we were born, and mark how utterly it counts to us as nothing. This is a mirror that Nature holds up to us, in which we may see the time that shall be after we are dead. Is there anything terrifying in the sight — anything depressing — anything that is not more restful than the soundest sleep? . . .

"THE THING CALLED LOVE — BE ON YOUR GUARD!"

This, then, is what we term Venus. This is the origin of the thing called love — that drop of Venus' honey that first drips into our heart, to be followed by numbing heartache. Though the object of your love may be absent, images of it still haunt you and the beloved name chimes sweetly in your ears. If you find yourself thus passionately enamoured of an individual, you should keep well away from such images. Thrust from you anything that might feed your passion, and turn your mind elsewhere. Vent the seed of love upon other objects. By clinging to it you assure yourself the certainty of heartsickness and pain. . . .

This is the one thing of which the more we have, the more our breast burns with the evil lust of having. Food and fluid are taken into our body: since they can fill their allotted places, the desire for meat and drink is thus easily appeased. But a pretty face or a pleasing complexion gives the body nothing to enjoy but insubstantial images, which all too often fond hope scatters to the winds.

When a thirsty man tries to drink in his dreams but is given no drop to quench the fire in his limbs, he clutches at images of water with fruitless effort and while he laps up a rushing stream he remains thirsty in the midst. Just so in the midst of love Venus teases lovers with images. They cannot glut their eyes by gazing on the beloved form, however closely. Their hands glean nothing from those dainty limbs in their aimless roving over all the body. Then comes the moment when with limbs entwined they pluck the flower of youth. Their bodies thrill with the presentiment of joy, and it is seed-time in the fields of Venus. Body clings greedily to body; moist lips are pressed on lips, and deep breaths are drawn through clenched teeth. But all to no purpose. One can glean nothing from the other, nor enter in and be wholly absorbed, body in body; for sometimes it seems that that is what they are craving and striving to do, so hungrily do they cling together in Venus' fetters, while their limbs are unnerved and liquefied by the intensity of rapture. At length, when the spate of lust is spent, there comes a slight intermission in the raging fever. But not for long. Soon the same frenzy returns. The fit is upon them once more. They ask themselves what it is they are craving for, but find no device that will master their malady. In aimless bewilderment they waste away, stricken by an unseen wound.

Add to this that they spend their strength and fail under the strain. Their days are passed at the mercy of another's whim. Their wealth slips from them, transmuted to Babylonian brocades. Their duties are neglected. Their reputation totters and goes into a decline. It is all very well for dainty feet to sparkle with gay slippers of Sicyon; for settings of gold to enclasp huge emeralds aglow with green fire, and sea-tinted garments to suffer the constant wear and stain of Venus. A hard-won patrimony is metamorphosed into bonnets and tiaras or, it may be, into Grecian robes, masterpieces from the looms of Elis or of Ceos. No matter how lavish the décor and the cuisine — drinking parties (with no lack of drinks), entertainments, perfumes, garlands, festoons and all — they are still to no purpose. From the very heart of the fountain of delight there rises a jet of bitterness that poisons the fragrance of the flowers. Perhaps the unforgetting mind frets itself remorsefully with the thought of life's best years squandered in sloth and debauchery. Perhaps the beloved has let fly some two-edged word, which lodges in the impassioned heart and glows there like a living flame. Perhaps he thinks she is rolling her eyes too freely and turning them upon another, or he catches in her face a hint of mockery.

And these are the evils inherent in love that prospers and fulfills its hopes. In starved and thwarted love the evils you can see plainly without even opening your eyes are past all counting. How much better to be on your guard beforehand, as I have advised, and take care that you are not enmeshed!

To avoid enticement into the snares of love is not so difficult as, once entrapped, to escape out of the toils and snap the tenacious knots of Venus. And yet, be you never so tightly entangled and embrangled, you can still free yourself from the curse unless you stand in the way of your own freedom. First, you should concentrate on all the faults of mind or body of her whom you covet and sigh for. For men often behave as though blinded by love and credit the beloved with charms to which she has no valid title. How often do we see blemished and unsightly women basking in a lover's adoration! One man scoffs at another and urges him to propitiate Venus because he is the victim of such a degrading passion; yet as like as not the poor devil is in the same unhappy plight himself, all unaware. A sallow wench is acclaimed as a nut-brown maid. A sluttish slattern is admired for her "sweet disorder." Her eyes are never green, but grey as Athene's. If she is stringy and woody, she is lithe as a gazelle. A stunted runt is a sprite, a sheer delight from top to toe. A clumsy giantess is "a daughter of the gods divinely tall." She has an impediment in her speech — a charming lisp, of course. She's as mute as a stockfish — what modesty! A waspish, fiery-tempered scold — she "burns with a gem-like flame." She becomes "svelte" and "willowy" when she is almost too skinny to live; "delicate" when she is half-dead with coughing. Her breasts are swollen and protuberant: she is "Ceres suckling Bacchus." Her nose is snub — "a Faun," then, or "a child of the Satyrs." Her lips bulge: she is "all kiss." It would be a wearisome task to run through the whole catalogue. But suppose her face in fact is all that could be desired and the charm of Venus radiates from her whole body. Even so, there are still others. Even so, we lived without her before. Even so, in her physical nature she is no different, as we well know, from the plainest of her sex. She is driven to use foul-smelling fumigants. Her maids keep well away from her and snigger behind her back. The tearful lover, shut out from the presence, heaps the threshold with flowers and garlands, anoints the disdainful doorposts with perfume, and plants rueful kisses on the door. Often enough, were he admitted, one whiff would promptly make him cast round for some decent pretext to take his leave. His fond complaint, long-pondered and far-fetched, would fall dismally flat. He would curse himself for a fool to have endowed her with qualities above mortal imperfection.

To the daughters of Venus themselves all this is no secret. Hence they are at pains to hide all the back-stage activities of life from those whom they wish to keep fast bound in the bonds of love. But their pains are wasted, since your mind has power to drag all these mysteries into the daylight and get at the truth behind the sniggers.

47

Augustus' Reconstruction of the Roman World

Contrasting estimates

The murder of Julius Caesar was in part a reaction to his growing leanings toward oriental despotism, and, although it led to a resumption of civil war, it was not wholly in vain. It demonstrated the tenacity with which republican traditions still held on at Rome, and so helped to determine the final settlement established by Augustus after his victory over Antony and Cleopatra at Actium (31 B.C.). That decisive battle, in fact, was pictured by Romans as a victory of Latin civilization over the autocratic forces of orientalism. Accordingly, Augustus claimed that his system of government, known in history as the Principate, was in essence a restoration of the Republic. "May it be my privilege to establish the Republic safe and sound on its foundations," Suetonius reports him as saying, "gathering the fruit of my desire to be known as the author of the ideal constitution, and taking with me to the grave the hope that the basis which I have laid will be permanent."

The nature of this "ideal constitution" has been the subject of debate ever since. Were Augustus' words sincerely uttered and was he really a true republican who reluctantly kept for himself only such power as would insure the continued operation of the constitution and prevent a return to anarchy? Or was he at heart a tyrant who skillfully camouflaged his autocratic powers under republican forms? Modern scholars are still debating the question in much the same fashion as did the ancient Romans whose divergent views are indicated in the following selections.

◆A◆ DIO CASSIUS, ROMAN HISTORY

The "true democracy" of the Roman Empire

In attempting to understand the constitutional settlement which Augustus imposed upon Rome at the end of the civil wars, the remarkable document which purports to be the advice given to Augustus by Maecenas, the richest capitalist in Rome, deserves study. It is found in the Roman History of Dio Cassius (ca. 155–235 A.D.), a Greek from Nicaea in Asia Minor who had a long career in governmental service both at Rome and in the provinces. The speech of Maecenas is Dio's own invention, a favorite device of ancient historians since Herodotus and Thucydides. But because of Dio's insight into political and constitutional matters, even though the words and ideas expressed are his, there is little reason to doubt that they were, in substance, the views of men like Maecenas. No one in Roman times seems to have doubted their appropriateness, and the reforms of Augustus were in line with such views.

The essence of Maecenas' argument is that the old-style democracy is to be distrusted and should be replaced by the joint rule of Augustus and "the best men." The constitution will continue to be called a democracy and the emphasis will still be upon liberty, but this will be the "true" democracy and liberty that can guarantee order and the welfare of all classes in the state.

The more significant of Maecenas' views and recommendations, all of which were put into effect by Augustus, are given in the following selection. Various questions should suggest themselves to the reader: Are the arguments for this "true" democracy and liberty justified? Is Maecenas concerned more with the general welfare or with the welfare of one class?

"PUT AN END TO THE INSOLENCE OF THE POPULACE"

14. . . . If you feel any concern at all for your country, for which you have fought so many wars and would so gladly give even your life, reorganize it and regulate it in the direction of greater moderation. For while the privilege of doing and saying precisely what one pleases becomes, in the case of sensible persons, if you examine the matter, a cause of the highest happiness to them all, yet in the case of the foolish it becomes a cause for disaster. For this reason he who offers this privilege to the foolish is virtually putting a sword in the hands of a child or a madman; but he who offers it to the prudent is not only preserving all their other privileges but is also saving these men themselves even in spite of themselves. Therefore I ask you not to fix your gaze upon the specious terms applied to these things and thus be deceived, but to weigh carefully the results which come from the things themselves and then put an end to the insolence of the populace and place the management of public affairs in the

Reprinted by permission of the publishers and The Loeb Classical Library from Earnest Cary's translation of Dio Cassius, Roman History, Book LII, Chs. 14–19, 23, 27, 28–30, 34, 39, 40 (Cambridge, Mass.: Harvard University Press).

hands of yourself and the other best citizens, to the end that the business of deliberation may be performed by the most prudent and that of ruling by those best fitted for command, while the work of serving in the army for pay is left to those who are strongest physically and most needy. In this way each class of citizens will zealously discharge the duties which devolve upon them and will readily render to one another such services as are due, and will thus be unaware of their inferiority when one class is at a disadvantage as compared with another, and all will gain the true democracy and the freedom which does not fail. For the boasted freedom of the mob proves in experience to be the bitterest servitude of the best element to the other and brings upon both a common destruction; whereas this freedom of which I speak everywhere prefers for honor the men of prudence, awarding at the same time equality to all according to their deserts, and thus gives happiness impartially to all who enjoy this liberty.

15. For I would not have you think that I am advising you to enslave the people and the senate and then set up a tyranny. This is a thing I should never dare suggest to you nor would you bring yourself to do it. The other course, however, would be honorable and expedient both for you and for the city — that you should yourself, in consultation with the best men, enact all the appropriate laws, without the possibility of any opposition or remonstrance to these laws on the part of anyone from the masses; that you and your counsellors should conduct the wars according to your own wishes, all other citizens rendering instant obedience to your commands; that the choice of the officials should rest with you and your advisers; and that you and they should also determine the honors and the punishments. The advantage of all this would be that whatever pleased you in consultation with your peers would immediately become law; that our wars against our enemies would be waged with secrecy and at the opportune time; that those to whom any task was entrusted would be appointed because of their merit and not as the result of the lot or rivalry for office; that the good would be honored without arousing jealousy and the bad punished without causing rebellion. Thus whatever business was done would be most likely to be managed in the right way, instead of being referred to the popular assembly, or deliberated upon openly, or entrusted to partisan delegates, or exposed to the danger of ambitious rivalry; and we should be happy in the enjoyment of the blessings which are vouchsafed to us, instead of being embroiled in hazardous wars abroad or in unholy civil strife. For these are the evils found in every democracy — the more powerful men, namely, in reaching out after the primacy and hiring the weaker, turn everything upside down — but they have been most frequent in our country, and there is no other way to put a stop to them than the way I propose. And the evidence is, that we have now for a long time been engaged in wars and civil strife. The cause is the multitude of our population and the magnitude of the business of our government; for the population embraces men of every kind, in respect both to race and to endowment, and both their tempers and their desires are manifold; and the business of the state has become so vast that it can be administered only with the greatest difficulty.

16. Witness to the truth of my words is borne by our past. For while we were but few in number and differed in no important respect from our neighbors, we got along well with our government and subjugated almost all Italy; but ever since we were led outside the peninsula and crossed over to many continents and many islands, filling the whole sea and the whole earth with our name and power, nothing good has been our lot. At first it was only at home and within our walls that we broke up into factions and quarrelled, but afterwards we even carried this plague out into the legions. Therefore our city, like a great merchantman manned with a crew of every race and lacking a pilot, has now for many generations been rolling and plunging as it has drifted this way and that in a heavy sea, a ship as it were without ballast. Do not, then, allow her to be longer exposed to the tempest; for you see that she is waterlogged. And do not let her be pounded to pieces upon a reef; for her timbers are rotten and she will not be able to hold out much longer. But since the gods have taken pity on her and have set you over her as her arbiter and overseer, prove not false to her, to the end that, even as now she has revived a little by your aid, so she may survive in safety for the ages to come.

"ACCEPT THE LEADERSHIP"

17. Now I think you have long since been convinced that I am right in urging you to give the people a monarchical government; if this is the case, accept the leadership over them readily and with enthusiasm — or rather do not throw it away. For the question we are deliberating upon is not whether we shall take something, but whether we shall decide not to lose it and by so doing incur danger into the bargain. Who, indeed, will spare you if you thrust the control of the state into the hands of the people, or even if you entrust it to some other man, seeing that there are great numbers whom you have injured, and that practically all these will lay claim to the sovereignty, and yet no one of them will wish either that you should go unpunished for what you have done or that you should be allowed to survive as his rival? Pompey, for example, once he had given up the supreme power, became the object of scorn and of secret plotting and consequently lost his life when he was unable to regain his power. Caesar also, your father, lost not only his position but also his life for doing precisely what you are proposing to do. And Marius and Sulla would certainly have suffered a like fate had they not died first. And yet some say that Sulla, fearing this very fate, forestalled it by making away with himself; at any rate, much of his legislation began to be undone while he was yet alive. Therefore you also must expect that there will be many a man who will prove a Lepidus to you and many a man who will prove a Sertorius, a Brutus, or a Cassius.

18. Looking then, at these facts and reflecting upon all the other considerations involved, do not abandon yourself and your country merely in order to avoid giving impression to some that you deliberately sought the office. For, in the first place, even if men do suspect this, the ambition is not inconsistent

with human nature and the risk involved is a noble one. Again, what man is there who does not know the circumstances which constrained you to assume your present position? Hence, if there be any fault to find with these compelling circumstances, one might with entire justice lay it upon your father's murderers. For if they had not slain him in so unjust and pitiable a fashion, you would not have taken up arms, would not have gathered your legions, would not have made your compact with Antony and Lepidus, and would not have had to defend yourself against these men themselves. That you were right, however, and were justified in doing all this, no one is unaware. Therefore, even if some slight error has been committed, yet we cannot at this time with safety undo anything that has been done. Therefore, for our own sake and for that of the state let us obey Fortune, who offers you the sole rulership. And let us be very grateful to her that she has not only freed us from our domestic troubles, but has also placed in your hands the organization of the state, to the end that you, by bestowing due care upon it, may prove to all mankind that those troubles were stirred up and that mischief wrought by other men, whereas you are an upright man.

"ADMINSTER AS I SHALL ADVISE"

And do not, I beg you, be afraid of the magnitude of the empire. For the greater its extent, the more numerous are the salutary elements it possesses; also, to guard anything is far easier than to acquire it. Toils and dangers are needed to win over what belongs to others, but a little care suffices to retain what is already yours. Moreover, you need not be afraid, either, that you will live quite safely in that office and enjoy all the blessings which men know, provided that you will consent to administer it as I shall advise you. And do not think that I am shifting the discussion from the subject in hand if I speak to you at considerable length about the office. For of course my purpose in doing this will be, not to hear myself talk, but that you may learn by a strict demonstration that it is both possible and easy, for a man of sense at least, to rule well and without danger.

19. I maintain, therefore, that you ought first and foremost to choose and select with discrimination the entire senatorial body, inasmuch as some who have not been fit have, on account of our dissensions, become senators. Such of them as possess any excellence you ought to retain, but the rest you should erase from the roll. Do not, however, get rid of any good man because of his poverty, but even give him the money he requires. In the place of those who have been dropped introduce the noblest, the best, and the richest men obtainable, selecting them not only from Italy but also from the allies and the subject nations. In this way you will have many assistants for yourself and will have in safekeeping the leading men from all the provinces; thus the provinces, having no leaders of established repute, will not begin rebellions, and their prominent men will regard you with affection because they have been made sharers in your empire.

Take these same measures in the case of the knights also, by enrolling in the equestrian order such men as hold second place in their several districts as regards birth, excellence and wealth. Register as many new members in both classes as you please, without being over-particular on the score of their number. For the more men of repute you have as your associates, the easier you will find it, for your own part, to administer everything in time of need and, so far as your subjects are concerned, the more easily will you persuade them that you are not treating them as slaves or as in any way inferior to us, but that you are sharing with them, not only all the other advantages which we ourselves enjoy, but also the chief magistracy as well, and thus make them as devoted to that office as if it were their own. And so far am I from retracting this last statement as rashly made, that I declare that the citizens ought every one actually to be given a share in the government, in order that, being on an equality with us in this respect also, they may be our faithful allies, living as it were in a single city, namely our own, and considering that this is in very truth a city, whereas their own homes are but the countryside and the villages. . . .

23. Let all these men to whom the commands outside the city are assigned receive salaries, the more important officers more, the less important less, and those between an intermediate amount. For they cannot live in a foreign land upon their own resources, nor should they indulge, as they do now, in unlimited and indefinite expenditure. They should hold office not less than three years, unless they are guilty of misconduct, nor more than five. The reason is that offices held for only one year or for short periods merely teach the officials their bare duties and then dismiss them before they can put any of their acquired knowledge into use, while, on the other hand, the longer terms of many years' duration somehow have the effect, in many cases, of filling the officials with conceit and encouraging them to rebellion. Hence, again, I think that the more important posts ought in no case to be given consecutively to the same man. . . .

27. Let this be your procedure, then, in the case of the senators and the knights. A standing army also should be supported, drawn from the citizens, the subject nations, and the allies, its size in the several provinces being greater or less according as the necessities of the case demand; and these troops ought always to be under arms and to engage in the practice of warfare continually. They should have winter-quarters constructed for them at the most advantageous points, and should serve for a stated period, so that a portion of life may still be left for them between their retirement from service and old age. The reason for such a standing army is this: far removed as we are from the frontiers of the empire, with enemies living near our borders on every side, we are no longer able at critical times to depend upon expeditionary forces; and if, on the other hand, we permit all the men of military age to have arms and to practice warfare, they will always be the source of seditions and civil wars. . . .

28. From what source, then, is the money to be provided for these soldiers and for the other expenses that will of necessity be incurred? . . . My proposal, therefore, is that you shall first of all sell the property that belongs to the state, — and I observe that this has become vast on account of the wars, — reserving only a little that is distinctly useful or necessary to you; and that you lend out all the money thus realized at a moderate rate of interest. In this way not only will the land be put under cultivation, being sold to owners who will cultivate

it themselves, but also the latter will acquire a capital and become more prosperous, while the treasury will gain a permanent revenue that will suffice for its needs. . . . The next step is to provide for any deficiency by levying an assessment upon absolutely all property which produces any profit for its possessors, and by establishing a system of taxes among all the peoples we rule. For it is but just and proper that no individual or district be exempt from these taxes, inasmuch as they are to enjoy the benefits derived from the taxation as much as the rest. And you should appoint tax-collectors to have supervision of this business in each district, and cause them to exact the entire amount that falls due during the term of their supervision from all the sources of revenue. This plan will not only render the work of collection easier for these officials, but will in particular benefit the tax-payers, inasmuch, I mean, as these will bring in what they owe in the small installments appointed, whereas now, if they are remiss for a brief period, the entire sum is added up and demanded of them in a single payment.

I am not unaware that some will object if this system of assessments and taxes is established. But I know this, too — that if they are subjected to no further abuses and are indeed convinced that all these contributions of theirs will make for their own security and for their fearless enjoyment of the rest of their property, and that, again, the larger part of their contributions will be received by none but themselves, as governors, procurators, or soldiers, they will be exceedingly grateful to you, since they will be giving but a slight portion of the abundance from which they derive the benefit without having to submit to abuses. Especially will this be true if they see that you live temperately and spend nothing foolishly. For who, if he saw that you were quite frugal in your expenditures for yourself and quite lavish in those for the commonwealth, would not willingly contribute, believing that your wealth meant his own security and prosperity?

30. So far as funds are concerned, therefore, a great abundance would be supplied from these sources. And I advise you to conduct as follows the administration of such matters as have not yet been mentioned. Adorn this capital with utter disregard of expense and make it magnificent with festivals of every kind. For it is fitting that we who rule over many people should surpass all men in all things, and brilliance of this sort, also, tends in a way to inspire our allies with respect for us and our enemies with terror. The affairs of the other cities you should order in this fashion: In the first place, the populace should have no authority in any matter, and should not be allowed to convene in any assembly at all; for nothing good would come out of their deliberations and they would always be stirring up a good deal of turmoil. . . .

None of the cities should be allowed to have its own separate coinage or system of weights and measures; they should all be required to use ours. . . .

34. . . . You should, of course, supervise the lives of your subjects, but do not scrutinize them with too much rigor. . . .

36. Therefore, if you desire to become in very truth immortal, act as I advise; and, furthermore, do you not only yourself worship the Divine Power everywhere and in every way in accordance with the traditions of our fathers,

but compel all others to honor it. Those who attempt to distort our religion with strange rites you should abhor and punish, not merely for the sake of the gods (since if a man despises these he will not pay honor to any other being), but because such men, by bringing in new divinities in place of the old, persuade many to adopt foreign practices, from which spring up conspiracies, factions, and cabals, which are far from profitable to a monarchy. Do not, therefore, permit anybody to be an atheist or a sorcerer. . . . For such men, by speaking the truth sometimes, but generally falsehood, often encourage a great many to attempt revolutions. The same thing is done also by many who pretend to be philosophers; hence I advise you to be on your guard against them, too. Do not, because you have had experience of good and honorable men like Areius and Athenodorus, believe that all the rest who claim to be philosophers are like them; for infinite harm, both to communities and to individuals, is worked by certain men who but use this profession as a screen. . . .

"A SUMMARY"

39. These are the things I would have you do — these and others of like nature; for there are many which I must pass over, since it is impossible to include them all in a single discussion. There is, however, one statement which will serve as a summary with respect both to what has been said and to what has been left unsaid: if you of your own accord do all that you would wish another to do if he became your ruler, you will err in nothing and succeed in everything, and in consequence you will find your life most happy and utterly free from danger. For how can men help regarding you with affection as father and savior, when they see that you are orderly and upright in your life, successful in war though inclined to peace; when you refrain from insolence and greed; when you meet them on a footing of equality, do not grow rich yourself while levying tribute on them, do not live in luxury yourself while imposing hardships upon them, are not licentious yourself while reproving licentiousness in them — when, instead of all this, your life is in every way and manner precisely like theirs? Therefore, since you have in your own hands a mighty means of protection — that you never do wrong to another — be of good courage and believe me when I tell you that you will never become the object of hatred or of conspiracy. And since this is so, it follows of necessity that you will also lead a happy life; for what condition is happier, what more blissful, than, possessing virtue, to enjoy all the blessings which men can know and to be able to bestow them upon others?

Think upon these things and upon all that I have told you, and be persuaded of me, and let not this fortune slip which has chosen you from all mankind and has set you up as their ruler. For, if you prefer the monarchy in fact but fear the title of "king" as being accursed, you have but to decline this title and still be sole ruler under the appellation of "Caesar." And if you require still other epithets, your people will give you that of "*imperator*" as they gave it to your father; and they will pay reverence to your august position by still another term of address, so that you will enjoy fully the reality of the kingship without the odium which attaches to the name of "king."

◆ B ◆ TACITUS, ANNALS

"It was really from a lust for power."

The greatest Roman writer of history was Tacitus (d. ca. 120 A.D.), whose *Annals* and *Histories* cover the period of the early Empire from the death of Augustus to that of Domitian (96 A.D.) in his own day. He is outstanding for his ability to evaluate and criticize the facts which he carefully collected and verified, and his unique style is characterized by its biting irony and its epigrammatic sentences filled with a world of meaning. Like Thucydides and other great historians, he sought after the lessons which he believed history provided. To Tacitus, these were moral lessons, and he defined the object of history to be "to ensure that merit shall not lack its record and to hold before the vicious word and deed the terrors of posterity and infamy." He idealized the freedom of the old Republic and overemphasized the tyrannical behavior of the early emperors after Augustus. In the following selection from the *Annals*, Tacitus reports two opposing estimates of Augustus, and although he does not choose between them, it is not difficult to ascertain his own conclusion: Augustus had fatally undermined republican liberty.

"WITHOUT BITTERNESS OR PARTIALITY"

1. Rome at the beginning was ruled by kings. Freedom and the consulship were established by Lucius Brutus. Dictatorships were held for a temporary crisis. The power of the decemvirs did not last beyond two years, nor was the consular jurisdiction of the military tribunes of long duration. The despotisms of Cinna and Sulla were brief; the rule of Pompy and of Crassus soon yielded before Caesar; the arms of Lepidus and Antony yielded before Augustus; who, when the world was wearied by civil strife, subjected it to empire under the title of *princeps*. The successes and reverses of the old Roman people have been recorded by famous historians; and fine intellects were not wanting to describe the times of Augustus, till growing sycophancy scared them away. The histories of Tiberius, Caius, Claudius, and Nero, while they were in power, were falsified through terror, and after their death were written under the irritation of a recent hatred. Hence my purpose is to relate a few facts about Augustus — more particularly his last acts, then the reign of Tiberius, and all which follows, without either bitterness or partiality, from any motives to which I am far removed.

"AUGUSTUS WON OVER ALL MEN"

2. When after the destruction of Brutus and Cassius there was no longer any army of the Republic, . . . then, dropping the title of triumvir, and giving out that he was a consul, and was satisfied with a tribune's authority for the protection of the people, Augustus won over the soldiers with gifts, the populace with cheap grain, and all men with the allurements of peace, and so grew

From Book I, based on the translation by A. J. Church and W. J. Brodribb.

greater by degrees, while he concentrated in himself the functions of the Senate, the magistrates, and the laws. He was wholly unopposed, for the boldest spirits had fallen in battle, or in the proscription, while the remaining nobles, the readier they were to be slaves, were raised the higher by wealth and promotion, so that, aggrandized by revolution, they preferred the safety of the present to the dangerous past. Nor did the provinces dislike that condition of affairs, for they distrusted the government of the Senate and the people, because of the rivalries between the leading men and the rapacity of the officials, while the protection of the laws was unavailing, as they were continually deranged by violence, intrigue, and finally by corruption.

THE SUCCESSION: "SAFEGUARDS TO REST ON"

3. Augustus meanwhile, as supports to his despotism, raised to the pontificate and curule aedileship Marcellus, his sister's son, while a mere stripling, and Marcus Agrippa, of humble birth, a good soldier, and one who had shared his victory, to two consecutive consulships, and as Marcellus soon afterwards died, he also accepted him as his son-in-law. Tiberius and Drusus, his stepsons, he honored with imperial titles, although his own family was as yet undiminished. For he had admitted the children of Agrippa, Caius and Lucius, into the house of the Caesars; and before they had yet laid aside the dress of boyhood he had most fervently desired, with an outward show of reluctance, that they should be entitled "leaders of the youth," and be consuls-elect. When Agrippa died, and Lucius Caesar as he was on his way to our armies in Spain, and Caius while returning from Armenia, still suffering from a wound, were prematurely cut off by destiny, or by their step-mother Livia's treachery, Drusus too having long been dead, Tiberius remained alone of the stepsons, and in him everything tended to center. He was adopted as a son, as a colleague in empire and a partner in the tribunitian power, and paraded through all the armies, no longer through his mother's secret intrigues, but at her open suggestion. For she had gained such a hold on the aged Augustus that he drove out as an exile into the island of Planasia, his only grandson, Agrippa Postumus, who, though devoid of worthy qualities, and having only the brute courage of physical strength, had not been convicted of any gross offense. And yet Augustus had appointed Germanicus, Drusus's offspring, to the command of eight legions on the Rhine, and required Tiberius to adopt him, although Tiberius had a son, now a young man, in his house; but he did it that he might have several safeguards to rest on. He had no war at the time on his hands except against the Germans, which was rather to wipe out the disgrace of the loss of Quintilius Varus and his army than out of an ambition to extend the empire, or for any adequate recompense.

"HOW FEW WERE LEFT WHO HAD SEEN THE REPUBLIC!"

At home all was tranquil, and there were magistrates with the same title as before; there was a younger generation, sprung up since the victory of Actium, and even many of the older men had been born during the civil wars. How few were left who had seen the republic!

4. Thus the state had been revolutionized, and there was not a vestige

left of the old sound morality. Stripped of equality, all looked up to the commands of a *princeps* without the least apprehension for the present, while Augustus in the vigor of life, could maintain his own position, that of his house, and the general tranquillity. When in advanced old age, he was worn out by a sickly frame, and the end was near and new prospects opened, a few spoke in vain of the blessings of freedom. . . .

"MEN SPOKE VARIOUSLY OF HIS LIFE"

8. . . . On the day of the funeral [of Augustus] soldiers stood round as a guard, amid much ridicule from those who had either themselves witnessed or who had heard from their parents of the famous day when slavery was still something fresh, and freedom had been resought in vain by the slaying of Caesar, the dictator — to some the vilest, to others the most glorious of deeds. Now, they said, an aged autocrat, whose power has lasted long, who has provided his heirs with abundant means to coerce the state, seems to require the defense of soldiers that his burial may be undistrubed.

9. Then followed much talk about Augustus himself, and many expressed an idle wonder that the same day marked the beginning of his assumption of empire and the close of his life, and, again, that he had ended his days at Nola in the same house and room as his father Octavius. People extolled too the number of his consulships, in which he had equalled Valerius Corvus and Caius Marius combined, the continuance for thirty-seven years of the tribunician power, the title of Imperator twenty-one times earned, and his other honors which had been either frequently repeated or were wholly new. Sensible men, however, spoke variously of his life with praise and censure. Some said that dutiful feeling towards a father, and the necessities of the state in which laws had then no place, drove him into civil war, which can neither be planned nor conducted on any right principles. . . . the only remedy for his distracted country was the rule of a single man. Yet the state had been organized under neither the name of a kingdom nor a dictatorship, but under that of a *princeps*. The ocean and remote rivers were the boundaries of the empire; the legions, provinces, fleets, all things were linked together; there was law for the citizens; there was respect shown to the allies. The capital had been embellished on a grand scale; only in a few instances had he resorted to force, simply to secure general tranquillity.

10. It was said, on the other hand, that filial duty and state necessity were merely assumed as a mask. It was really from a lust for power that he had excited the veterans by bribery, had, when only a youth and without official status, raised an army, tampered with the consul's legions, and feigned an attachment to the faction of Sextus Pompeius. Then, when by a decree of the Senate he had usurped the high functions and authority of praetor, . . . he wrested the consulate from a reluctant Senate, and turned against the state the arms with which he had been intrusted against Antony. Citizens were proscribed and lands distributed, without the approval even of those who carried out these deeds. Even granting that the deaths of Cassius and Brutus were sacrifices to an inherited feud (though duty requires us to waive private animosities for the

sake of the public welfare), still Sextus Pompeius had been deluded by the phantom of peace, and Lepidus by the mask of friendship. Subsequently, Antony had been lured on by the treaties of Tarentum and Brundisium, and by the marriage to his sister, and had paid by his death the penalty of a treacherous alliance. No doubt, there was peace after all this, but it was a peace stained with blood . . . .

The domestic life too of Augustus was not spared — how he had abducted Nero's wife . . . Livia, terrible to the state as a mother, terrible to the house of the Caesars as a stepmother. No honor was left for the gods when Augustus chose to be himself worshipped with temples and statues, like those of the deities, and with flamens and priests. He had not even adopted Tiberius as his successor out of affection or any regard to the state, but, having thoroughly seen his arrogant and savage temper, he had sought glory for himself by a contrast of extreme wickedness. . . .

However, after the funeral rites had been duly performed, a temple and divine worship was decreed him.

—————————— 48 ——————————

The Pax Romana

Divergent views

The Augustan reorganization of the Roman world lasted without major change through the death of Marcus Aurelius in 180 A.D. These two centuries of peace and security, the Pax Romana, constitute the longest period of tranquillity known in the history of the Western world. It is the judgment of many modern historians that the ideals and practices of Roman imperial administration were generally successful, and that modern states can learn much from them: "Particularly happy was Rome in her methods of Romanization and civilization of backward peoples in Western Europe. By her spirit of practical realism, wise compromise, generous grants of citizenship, and development of local, tribal, or municipal autonomy, she inspired a feeling of loyalty in the Western provinces." [1]

To many of Rome's high-spirited neighbors, however, the prospect of Roman domination was unattractive, to say the least. The writings of Tacitus throw light on both sides of the matter.

[1] Albert A. Trever, *History of Ancient Civilization*, 2 vols. (New York: Harcourt, Brace and Co., 1936), II, 748.

◆A◆ TACITUS, HISTORIES

*"By the prosperity and order of eight hundred years
has this empire been consolidated."*

The year 69 A.D., known as the "Year of the Four Emperors," witnessed a temporary breakdown of the Pax Romana after the death of Nero when a series of civil wars were fought by rival frontier armies seeking to elevate their respective commanders to imperial power. "The secret of empire was now disclosed," wrote Tacitus, "that an emperor could be made elsewhere than at Rome," and the resulting anarchy encouraged a revolt of subject peoples along the lower Rhine. The leader of the revolt was a German Batavian chieftain named Julius Civilis, who had served with his troops in the Roman auxiliary armies for twenty-five years and was a Roman citizen. He and his people had been aroused by Nero's high-handed arrest of their officers on the charge of treason, and he now urged other German tribes in the area to join him in forming an independent German kingdom. Inspired by this German example, Belgian tribes in northeastern Gaul, led by the Treveri and the Lingones (the latter having recently received Roman citizenship), also revolted and proclaimed a Gallic national state. The revolts collapsed early in 70 A,D. when a strong Roman expedition arrived on the scene. Tacitus reports in his Histories the substance of the speech delivered to the Treveri and Lingones by the Roman commander Cerialis after their surrender. It sums up bluntly and realistically the Roman Empire's policy of "submission and safety" as the alternative to "petty kingdoms and intestine wars."

73. Cerialis then convoked an assembly of the Treveri and Lingones, and thus addressed them: "I have never cultivated eloquence; it is by my sword that I have asserted the excellence of the Roman people. Since, however, words have very great weight with you, since you estimate good and evil, not according to their real value, but according to the representations of seditious men, I have resolved to say a few words, which, as the war is at an end, it may be useful for you to have heard rather than for me to have spoken. Roman generals and emperors entered your territory, as they did the rest of Gaul, with no ambitious purposes, but at the solicitation of your ancestors, who were wearied to the last extremity by intestine strife, while the Germans, whom they had summoned to their help, had imposed their yoke alike on friend and foe. How many battles we have fought against the Cimbri and Teutones, at the cost of what hardships to our armies, and with what result we have waged our German wars, is perfectly well known. It is not to defend Italy that we occupied the borders of the Rhine, but to insure that no second Ariovistus should seize Gaul. . . . There have ever been the same causes at work to make the Germans cross over into Gaul, lust, avarice, and the longing for a new home, prompting them to leave

From Book IV, tr. A. J. Church and W. J. Brodribb.

their own marshes and deserts, and to possess themselves of this most fertile soil and of you its inhabitants. Liberty, indeed, and the like specious names are their pretexts; but never did any man seek to enslave his fellows and secure dominion for himself without using the very same words.

74. "Gaul always had its petty kingdoms and intestine wars, till you submitted to our authority. We, though so often provoked, have used the right of conquest to burden you only with the cost of maintaining peace. For the tranquillity of nations cannot be preserved without armies; armies cannot exist without pay; pay cannot be furnished without tribute; all else is common among us. You often command our legions. You rule these and other provinces. There is no privilege, no exclusion. From worthy Emperors you derive equal advantage, though you dwell so far away, while cruel rulers are most formidable to their neighbors. Endure the passions and rapacity of your masters, just as you bear barren seasons and excessive rains and other natural evils. There will be vices as long as there are men. But they are not perpetual, and they are compensated by the occurrence of better things. . . .

"Should the Romans be driven out (which God forbid) what can result but wars between all these nations? By the prosperity and order of eight hundred years has this fabric of empire been consolidated, nor can it be overthrown without destroying those who overthrow it. Yours will be the worst peril, for you have gold and wealth, and these are the chief incentives to war. Give therefore your love and respect to the cause of peace, and to that capital in which we, conquerors and conquered, claim an equal right. Let the lessons of fortune in both its forms teach you not to prefer rebellion and ruin to submission and safety." With words to this effect he quieted his audience, who feared harsher treatment.

◆B◆ TACITUS, AGRICOLA

"They create a desolation and call it peace"

Shortly after the suppression of the Rhineland revolt, Cerialis was appointed governor of Britain by Vespasian, who had emerged victorious out of the "Year of the Four Emperors." The conquest of Britain was only half-completed; Claudius had begun it in 43 A.D., but under Nero the Romans had been set back by a revolt under famed Queen Boudicca. Cerialis and his successors now resumed the northward march of Roman conquest which was completed by Agricola, Vespasian's third governor of Britain (78-83 A.D.), who conquered Caledonia (Scotland). But during Domitian's reign Rome's legions were needed on the Rhine and Danube frontiers; Agricola was recalled and Caledonia abandoned. Tacitus, who was Agricola's son-in-law, wrote a biography of him which is at once a eulogy to a noble Roman, a description of Britain and its conquest, and a case study of Roman imperialism in action. The last point is

Chs. 30–32; based on the translation by A. J. Church and W. J. Brodribb.

illustrated by the following selection, the speech which Tacitus attributes to the Caledonian chieftain Calgacus just before his final defeat by the Romans. A description of Roman imperialism as it appeared to freedom-loving people, it balances the Roman picture of the Pax Romana.

Whenever I consider the causes of this war and the circumstances of our position, I have sure confidence that this day, and our united efforts, will be the beginning of freedom for the whole of Britain. To all of us slavery is a thing unknown; there are no lands beyond us, and even the sea is not safe, menaced as we are by a Roman fleet. And thus war and battle, in which the brave find glory, offers the only safety even to cowards. Former battles, in which, with varying fortune, the Romans were resisted, still left us as a last hope, because we, being the most renowned nation of Britain, dwelling in the very heart of the country, and out of sight of the shores of the conquered, could keep even our eyes unpolluted by the contagion of slavery. To us who dwell on the uttermost confines of the earth and of freedom, this remote sanctuary of Britain's glory has up to this time been a defense. Now, however, the furthest limits of Britain are thrown open, and the unknown always passes for the marvellous. But there are no tribes beyond us, nothing indeed but waves and rocks, and the yet more terrible Romans, from whose oppression escape is vainly sought by obedience and submission. Robbers of the world, having by their universal plunder exhausted the land, they rifle the deep. If the enemy be rich, they are rapacious; if he be poor, they lust for dominion; neither East nor West has been able to satisfy them. Alone among men they covet with equal eagerness the poor and the rich. To robbery, slaughter, plunder, they give the lying name of empire; they create a desolation and call it peace.

Nature has willed that every man's children and kindred should be his dearest objects. Yet these are torn from us by conscriptions to be slaves in foreign lands. Our wives and our sisters, even though they may escape being raped by the enemy, are seduced under the names of friendship and hospitality. Our goods and fortunes they collect for their tribute, our harvests for their granaries. Our very hands and bodies, under the lash and in the midst of insult, are worn down by the toil of clearing forests and swamps. Creatures born to slavery are sold once for all, and are, moreover, fed by their masters; but Britain is daily purchasing, is daily feeding, her own enslaved people. And as in a household the last comer among the slaves is always the butt of his companions, so we in a world long used to slavery, as the newest and the most contemptible, are marked for destruction. For we have neither fruitful plains, nor mines, nor harbors, for the working of which we may be spared. Valor, too, and high spirit in subjects, are offensive to rulers; besides, remoteness and seclusion, while they give safety, provoke suspicion. Since then you cannot hope for mercy, at least take courage, whether it be safety or renown that you hold most precious. Under a woman's leadership the Brigantes were able to burn a colony, to storm a camp, and had not success made them careless, might have thrown off the yoke. Let us, then, a fresh and unconquered people, eager to maintain our freedom, show at the very first encounter what heroes Caledonia has held in reserve.

Do you suppose the Romans will be as brave in war as they are licentious in peace? To our strifes and discords they owe their fame, and they turn the errors of an enemy to the renown of their own army, an army which, composed as it is of every variety of nations, is held together by success and will be broken up by disaster. These Gauls and Germans, and, I blush to say, these numerous Britons, who, though they lend their lives to support a stranger's rule, have been its enemies longer than its subjects, you cannot really believe to be bound by loyalty and affection. Fear and terror are feeble bonds of attachment; remove them, and those who have ceased to fear will begin to hate. All the incentives to victory are on our side. The Romans have no wives to kindle their courage; no parents to taunt them if they run away; many have either no country or one far away. Few in number, ignorant of the country, looking around upon a sky, a sea, and forests which are unfamiliar to them, the gods have delivered them, like caged prisoners, into our hands. Be not frightened by outward show, by the glitter of gold and silver, which can neither protect nor wound. In the very ranks of the enemy we shall find hands to help us. The Britons will recognize their own cause; the Gauls will remember their former freedom; the rest of the Germans will desert them, as the Usipi recently did. Behind them there is nothing to dread. The forts are ungarrisoned; the colonies are in the hands of aged men; the towns with their disloyal subjects and oppressive rulers are ill-affected and rife with discord. Here before you is their general and his army; behind are the tribute, the mines, and all the other penalties of an enslaved people. Whether you endure these for ever, or instantly avenge them, this field is to decide. Think, therefore, as you advance to battle, of your ancestors and of your posterity.

———— 49 ————

Capitalism in the Early Empire

From free enterprise to state intervention

One of the major characteristics of capitalism is that by its very nature — wealth invested to produce yet more wealth — it is a dynamic economic system. As long as opportunities for continued expansion exist, capitalism works well, but when economic contraction sets in, surpluses accumulate and the system begins to falter. The role of the state in a capitalistic society generally moves from a policy of laissez-faire to one of increasing state intervention and control. What is known concerning the Roman economy during the early Empire illustrates this two-phased development.

◆ A ◆ PETRONIUS, THE SATYRICON

A self-made millionaire

The Augustan era saw many aspects of Roman civilization, including its economy, enter a golden age. The new security, together with the laissez-faire policy of Augustus (foreshadowed in the advice given him by Maecenas in Selection 47A) led to a remarkable expansion of large-scale agriculture, commerce, and industry, particularly in Italy. Abundant capital circulated freely, large fortunes were easily made, and a new class of bourgeois rich men, many of whom started life as slaves, arose to rival the old aristocracy. Typical of this *nouveau riche* class is the fictional character Trimalchio, whose swift rise to riches and bourgeois outlook on life were amusingly satirized in the picaresque novel the Satyricon, written by Gaius Petronius (d. 65 A.D.), a member of the old aristocracy and arbiter of taste at the court of the Emperor Nero. Like many other self-made men of this and similar ages, Trimalchio accumulated his first fortune by shrewd trading, then turned to money-lending and the purchase of numerous estates. Lacking culture and good breeding, he sought compensation in a vulgar and ostentatious display of his wealth.

The setting of the following selection from the Satyricon is a banquet given by Trimalchio and attended by some of his newly rich fellow capitalists, their wives, and a professor of rhetoric who has brought along two rapscallion students, one of whom narrates the scene. Professor William Arrowsmith's translation employs contemporary American idiom and clearly achieves his aim to "persuade the willing reader to forget for a little while that Rome is dead and that Trimalchio spoke Latin (more or less)."

At last we took our places. Immediately slaves from Alexandria came in and poured ice water over our hands. These were followed by other slaves who knelt at our feet and with extraordinary skill pedicured our toenails. Not for an instant, moreover, during the whole of this odious job, did one of them stop singing. This made me wonder whether the whole menage was given to bursts of song, so I put it to the test by calling for a drink. It was served immediately by a boy who trilled away as shrilly as the rest of them. In fact, anything you asked for was invariably served with a snatch of song, so that you would have thought you were eating in a concert-hall rather than a private dining room.

Now that the guests were all in their places, the *hors d'oeuvres* were served, and very sumptuous they were. Trimalchio alone was still absent, and the place of honor — reserved for the host in the modern fashion — stood empty. But I was speaking of the *hors d'oeuvres*. On a large tray stood a donkey made of rare Corinthian bronze; on the donkey's back were two panniers, one holding green olives, the other, black. Flanking the donkey were two side dishes, both engraved with Trimalchio's name and the weight of the silver, while in dishes shaped to resemble little bridges there were dormice, all dipped in honey and rolled in poppyseed. Nearby, on a silver grill, piping hot, lay small sausages, while beneath the grill black damsons and red pomegranates had been sliced up and arranged so as to give the effect of flames playing over charcoal.

We were nibbling at these splendid appetizers when suddenly the trumpets blared a fanfare and Trimalchio was carried in, propped up on piles of miniature pillows in such a comic way that some of us couldn't resist impolitely smiling. His head, cropped close in a recognizable slave cut, protruded from a cloak of blazing scarlet; his neck, heavily swathed already in bundles of clothing, was wrapped in a large napkin bounded by an incongruous senatorial purple stripe with little tassels dangling down here and there. On the little finger of his left hand he sported an immense gilt ring; the ring on the last joint of his fourth finger looked to be solid gold of the kind the lesser nobility wear, but was actually, I think, an imitation, pricked out with small steel stars. Nor does this exhaust the inventory of his trinkets. At least he rather ostentatiously bared his arm to show us a large gold bracelet and an ivory circlet with a shiny metal plate.

He was picking his teeth with a silver toothpick when he first addressed us. "My friends," he said, "I wasn't anxious to eat just yet, but I've ignored my own wishes so as not to keep you waiting. Still, perhaps you won't mind if I finish my game." At these words a slave jumped forward with a board of juniper wood and a pair of crystal dice. I noticed one other elegant novelty as well: in place of the usual black and white counters, Trimalchio had substituted gold and silver coins. His playing, I might add, was punctuated throughout with all sorts of vulgar exclamations. . . .

By this time Trimalchio had finished his game. He promptly sent for the same dishes we had had and with a great roaring voice offered a second cup of mead to anyone who wanted it. Then the orchestra suddenly blared and the trays were snatched away from the tables by a troupe of warbling waiters. But in the confusion a silver side dish fell to the floor and a slave quickly stooped to retrieve it. Trimalchio, however, had observed the accident and gave orders that the boy's ears should be boxed and the dish tossed back on the floor. Immediately the servant in charge of the dishware came pattering up with a broom and swept the silver dish out the door with the rest of the rubbish. Two curly-haired Ethiopian slaves followed him as he swept, both carrying little skin bottles like the circus attendants who sprinkle the arena with perfume, and poured wine over our hands. No one was offered water.

We clapped enthusiastically for this fine display of extravagance. "The god of war," said Trimalchio, "is a real democrat. That's why I gave orders that each of us should have a table to himself. Besides, these stinking slaves will bother us less than if we were all packed in together."

Glass jars carefully sealed and coated were now brought in. Each bore this label:

GENUINE FALERNIAN WINE
GUARANTEED ONE HUNDRED YEARS
OLD!
BOTTLED
IN THE CONSULSHIP
OF
OPIMIUS.

While we were reading the labels, Trimalchio clapped his hands for attention. "Just think, friends, wine lasts longer than us poor suffering humans. So soak it up, it's the stuff of life. I give you, gentlemen, the genuine Opimian vintage. Yesterday I served much cheaper stuff and the guests were much more important." While we were commenting on it and savoring the luxury, a slave brought in a skeleton, cast of solid silver, and fastened in such a way that the joints could be twisted and bent in any direction. The servants threw it down on the table in front of us and pushed it into several suggestive postures by twisting its joints, while Trimalchio recited this verse of his own making:

Nothing but bones, that's what we are.
Death hustles us humans away.
Today we're here and tomorrow we're not,
So live and drink while you may! . . .

Suddenly the orchestra gave another flourish and four slaves came dancing in and whisked off the top of the tray. Underneath, in still another tray, lay fat capons and sowbellies and a hare tricked out with wings to look like a little Pegasus. At the corners of the tray stood four little gravy boats, all shaped like the satyr Marsyas, with phalluses for spouts and a spicy hot gravy dripping down over several large fish swimming about in the lagoon of the tray. The slaves burst out clapping, we clapped too and turned with gusto to these new delights. Trimalchio, enormously pleased with the success of his little *tour de force*, roared for a slave to come and carve. The carver appeared instantly and went to work, thrusting with his knife like a gladiator practicing to the accompaniment of a water-organ. But all the time Trimalchio kept mumbling in a low voice, "Carver, carver, carver carver. . ." I suspected that this chant was somehow connected with a trick, so I asked my neighbor, an old hand at these party surprises. "Look," he said, "you see that slave who's carving? Well, he's called Carver, so every time Trimalchio says 'Carver,' he's also saying 'Carve'er!' and giving him orders to carve."

This atrocious pun finished me: I couldn't touch a thing. So I turned back to my neighbor to pick up what gossip I could and soon had him blabbing away, especially when I asked him about the woman who was bustling around the room. "Her?" he said, "why, that's Fortunata, Trimalchio's wife. And the name couldn't suit her better. She counts her cash by the cartload. And you know what she used to be? Well, begging your Honor's pardon, but you wouldn't have taken bread from her hand. Now, god knows how or why, she's sitting pretty: has Trimalchio eating out of her hand. If she told him at noon it was night, he'd crawl into bed. As for him, he's so loaded he doesn't know how much he has. But that bitch has her finger in everything — where you'd least expect it too. A regular tightwad, never drinks, and sharp as they come. But she's got a nasty tongue; get her gossiping on a couch and she'll chatter like a parrot. If she likes you, you're lucky; if she doesn't, god help you.

"As for old Trimalchio, that man's got more farms than a kite could flap over. And there's more silver plate stuffed in his porter's lodge than another man's got in his safe. As for slaves, whoosh! So help me, I'll bet not one in ten has ever seen his master. Your ordinary rich man is just peanuts compared to him; he could knock them all under a cabbage and you'd never know they were gone.

"And buy things? Not him. No sir, he raises everything right on his own estate. Wool, citron, pepper, you name it. By god, you'd find hen's milk if you looked around. Now take his wool. The home-grown strain wasn't good enough. So you know what he did? Imported rams from Tarentum, bred them into the herd. Attic honey he raises at home. Ordered the bees special from Athens. And the local bees are better for being crossbred too. And, you know, just the other day he sent off to India for some mushroom spawn. Every mule he owns has a wild ass for a daddy. And you see those pillows there? Every last one is stuffed with purple or scarlet wool. That boy's loaded!

"And don't sneer at his friends. They're all ex-slaves, but every one of them's rich. You see that guy down there on the next to last couch? He's worth a cool half-million. Came up from nowhere. Used to tote wood on his back. People say, but I don't know, he stole a cap off a hobgoblin's head and found a treasure. He's the god's fair-haired boy. That's luck for you, but I don't begrudge him. Not so long ago he was just a slave. Yes sir, he's doing all right. Just a few days ago he advertised his apartment for rent. The ad went like this:

APARTMENT FOR RENT AFTER THE FIRST OF JULY.
AM BUYING A VILLA. SEE G. POMPEIUS DIOGENES.

"And you see that fellow in the freedman's seat? He's already made a pile and lost it. What a life! But I don't envy him. After the first million the going got sticky. Right now I'll bet he's mortgaged every hair on his head. But it wasn't his fault. He's too honest, that's his trouble, and his crooked friends stripped him to feather their own nests. One thing's sure: once your little kettle stops cooking and the business starts to slide, you get the brushoff from your friends. And, you know, he had a fine, respectable business too. Undertaking. Ate like a king: boars roasted whole, pastry as tall as buildings, pheasants, chefs, pastrycooks — the whole works. Why, he's had more wine spilled under his table than most men have in their cellars. Life? Hell, it was a dream! Then when things started sliding, he got scared his creditors would think he was broke. So he advertised an auction:

GAIUS JULIUS PROCULUS
WILL HOLD
AN AUCTION
OF HIS
SPARE FURNITURE! . . .

"For god's sake," the ragseller Echion broke in, "cut out the damned gloom, will you? 'Sometimes it's good, sometimes it's bad,' as the old peasant said when he sold the spotted pig. Luck changes. If things are lousy today, there's always tomorrow. That's life, man. Sure, the times are bad, but they're no better anywhere else. We're all in the same boat, so what's the fuss? If you lived anywhere else, you'd be swearing the pigs here went waddling around already roasted. And don't forget, there's a big gladiator show coming up the day after tomorrow. Not the same old fighters either; they've got a fresh shipment in and there's not a slave in the batch. You know how old Titus works. Nothing's too good for him when he lets himself go. Whatever it is, it'll be something special. I know the old boy well, and he'll go whole hog. Just wait. There'll be cold steel for the crowd, no quarter, and the amphitheater will end up looking like a slaughterhouse. He's got what it takes too. . . .

"Well, Agamemnon, I can see you're thinking, 'What's that bore blabbing about now?' You're the professor here, but I don't catch you opening your mouth. No, you think you're a cut above us, don't you, so you just sit there and smirk at the way we poor men talk. Your learning's made you a snob. Still, let it go. I tell you what. Someday you come down to my villa and look it over. We'll find something to nibble on, a chicken, a few eggs maybe. This crazy weather's knocked everything topsy-turvy, but we'll come up with something you like. Don't worry your head about it, there'll be loads to eat.

"You remember that little shaver of mine? Well, he'll be your pupil one of these days. He's already doing division up to four, and if he comes through all right, he'll sit at your feet someday. Every spare minute he has, he buries himself in his books. He's smart all right, and there's good stuff in him. His real trouble is his passion for birds. . . . The older boy now, he's a bit slow. But he's a hard worker and teaches the others more than he knows. Every holiday he spends at home, and whatever you give him, he's content. So I bought him some of those big red lawbooks. A smattering of law, you know, is a useful thing around the house. There's money in it too. He's had enough literature, I think. But if he doesn't stick it out in school, I'm going to have him taught a trade. Barbering or auctioneering, or at least a little law. The only thing that can take a man's trade away is death. But every day I keep pounding the same thing into his head: 'Son, get all the learning you can. Anything you learn is money in the bank. Look at Lawyer Phileros. If he hadn't learned his law, he'd be going hungry and chewing on air. Not so long ago he was peddling his wares on his back; now he's running neck and neck with old Norbanus. Take my word for it, son, there's a mint of money in books, and learning a trade never killed a man yet.' "

Conversation was running along these lines when Trimalchio returned, wiping the sweat from his brow. He splashed his hands in perfume and stood there for a minute in silence. "You'll excuse me, friends," he began, "but I've been constipated for days and the doctors are stumped. I got a little relief from a prescription of pomegranate rind and resin in a vinegar base. Still, I hope my tummy will get back its manners soon. Right now my bowels are bumbling around like a bull. But if any of you has any business that needs attending to, go right ahead; no reason to feel embarrassed. There's not a man been born yet with solid insides. And I don't know any anguish on earth like trying to hold it in. Jupiter himself couldn't stop it from coming — what are you giggling about, Fortunata? You're the one who keeps me awake all night with your trips to the potty. Well, anyone at table who wants to go has my permission, and the doctors tell us not to hold it in. Everything's ready outside — water and pots and the rest of the stuff. Take my word for it, friends, the vapors go straight to your brain. Poison your whole system. I know of some who've died from being too polite and holding it in." We thanked him for his kindness and understanding, but we tried to hide our snickers in repeated swallows of wine.

As yet we were unaware that we had slogged only halfway through this "forest of refinements," as the poets put it. . . .

By now Trimalchio was drinking heavily and was, in fact, close to being drunk. "Hey, everybody!" he shouted, "nobody's asked Fortunata to dance. Believe me, you never saw anyone do grinds the way she can." With this he raised his hands over his forehead and did an impersonation of the actor Syrus singing one of his numbers, while the whole troupe of slaves joined in on the chorus. He was just about to get up on the table when Fortunata went and whispered something in his ear, probably a warning that these drunken capers were undignified. Never was a man so changeable: sometimes he would bow down to Fortunata in anything she asked; at other times, as now, he went his own way.

But it was the secretary, not Fortunata, who effectively dampened his desire to dance, for quite without warning he began to read from the estate records as though he were reading some government bulletin.

"Born," he began, "on July 26th, on Trimalchio's estate at Cumae, thirty male and forty female slaves.

"Item, 500,000 bushels of wheat transferred from the threshing rooms into storage.

"On the same date, the slave Mithridates crucified alive for blaspheming the guardian spirit of our master Gaius.

"On the same date, the sum of 300,000 returned to the safe because it could not be invested.

"On the same date, in the gardens at Pompeii, fire broke out in the house of the bailiff Nasta . . ."

"What?" roared Trimalchio. "When did I buy any gardens at Pompeii?"

"Last year," the steward replied. "That's why they haven't yet appeared on the books."

"I don't care what you buy," stormed Trimalchio, "but if it's not reported to me within six months, I damn well won't have it appearing on the books at all!" . . .

. . . Trimalchio suddenly . . . ordered his will brought out and read aloud from beginning to end while the slaves sat there groaning and moaning. At the close of the reading, he turned to Habinnas. "Well, old friend, will you make me my tomb exactly as I order it? First, of course, I want a statue of myself. But carve my dog at my feet, and give me garlands of flowers, jars of perfume and every fight in Petraites' career. Then, thanks to your good offices, I'll live on long after I'm gone. In front, I want my tomb one hundred feet long, but two hundred feet deep. Around it I want an orchard with every known variety of fruit tree. You'd better throw in a vineyard too. For it's wrong, I think, that a man should concern himself with the house where he lives his life but give no thought to the home he'll have forever. But above all I want you to carve this notice:

THIS MONUMENT DOES NOT PASS INTO
THE POSSESSION OF MY HEIRS.

In any case I'll see to it in my will that my grave is protected from damage after my death. I'll appoint one of my ex-slaves to act as custodian to chase off the people who might come and crap on my tomb. Also, I want you to carve me several ships with all sail crowded and a picture of myself sitting on the judge's bench in official dress with five gold rings on my fingers and handing out a sack of coins to the people. For it's a fact, and you're my witness, that I gave a free meal to the whole town and a cash-handout to everyone. Also make me a dining room, a frieze maybe, but however you like, and show the whole town celebrating at my expense. On my right I want a statue of Fortunata with a dove in her hand. And oh yes, be sure to have her pet dog tied to her girdle. And don't forget my pet slave. Also I'd like huge jars of wine, well-stoppered so the wine won't slosh out. Then sculpt me a broken vase with a little boy sobbing out his heart over it. And in the middle stick a sundial so that anyone who wants the time of day will have to read my name. And how will this do for the epitaph?

HERE LIES GAIUS POMPEIUS TRIMALCHIO
MAECENATIANUS,
VOTED IN ABSENTIA AN OFFICIAL OF THE
IMPERIAL CULT.
HE COULD HAVE BEEN REGISTERED
IN ANY CATEGORY OF THE CIVIL SERVICE AT ROME
BUT CHOSE OTHERWISE.
PIOUS AND COURAGEOUS,
A LOYAL FRIEND,
HE DIED A MILLIONAIRE,
THOUGH HE STARTED LIFE WITH NOTHING.

LET IT BE SAID TO HIS ETERNAL CREDIT
THAT HE NEVER LISTENED TO PHILOSOPHERS.
PEACE TO HIM
FAREWELL. . . .

At this moment an incident occurred on which our little party almost foundered. Among the incoming slaves there was a remarkably pretty boy. Trimalchio literally launched himself upon him and, to Fortunata's extreme annoyance, began to cover him with rather prolonged kisses. Finally, Fortunata asserted her rights and began to abuse him. "You turd!" she shrieked, "you hunk of filth." At last she used the supreme insult: "Dog!" At this Trimalchio exploded with rage, reached for a wine cup and slammed it into her face. Fortunata let out a piercing scream and covered her face with trembling hands as though she'd just lost an eye. Scintilla, stunned and shocked, tried to comfort her sobbing friend in her arms, while a slave solicitously applied a glass of cold water to her livid cheek. Fortunata herself hunched over the glass heaving and sobbing.

But Trimalchio was still shaking with fury. "Doesn't that slut remember what she used to be? By god, I took her off the sale platform and made her an honest woman. But she blows herself up like a bullfrog. She's forgotten how lucky she is. She won't remember the whore she used to be. People in shacks shouldn't dream of palaces, I say. By god, if I don't tame that strutting Cassandra, my name isn't Trimalchio. And to think, sap that I was, that I could have married an heiress worth half a million. And that's no lie. Old Agatho, who sells perfume to the lady next door, slipped me the word: 'Don't let your line die out, old boy,' he said. But not me. Oh no, I was a good little boy, nothing fickle about me. And now I've gone and slammed the axe into my shins good and proper — but someday, slut, you'll come scratching at my grave to get me back! And just so you understand what you've done, I'll remove your statue from my tomb. That's an order, Habinnas. No sir, I don't want any more domestic squabbles in my grave. And what's more, just to show her I can dish it out too, I won't have her kissing me on my deathbed. . . .

"But the hell with her. Friends, make yourselves comfortable. Once I used to be like you, but I rose to the top by my ability. Guts are what make the man; the rest is garbage. I buy well, I sell well. Others have different notions. But I'm like to bust with good luck — you slut, are you still blubbering? By god, I'll give you something to blubber about.

"But like I was saying, friends, it's through my business sense that I shot up. Why, when I came here from Asia, I stood no taller than that candlestick there. In fact, I used to measure myself by it every day; what's more, I used to rub my mouth with lamp oil to make my beard sprout faster. Didn't do a bit of good, though. For fourteen years I was my master's pet. But what's the shame in doing what you're told to do? But all the same, if you know what I mean, I managed to do my mistress a favor or two. But mum's the word: I'm none of your ordinary blowhards.

"Well, then heaven gave me a push and I became master in the house. I was my master's brains. So he made me joint heir with the emperor to everything he had, and I came out of it with a senator's fortune. But we never have enough, and I wanted to try my hand at business. To cut it short, I had five ships built. Then I stocked them with wine — worth its weight in gold at the time — and shipped them off to Rome. I might as well have told them to go sink themselves since that's what they did. Yup, all five of them wrecked. No kidding. In one day old Neptune swallowed down a cool million. Was I licked? Hell, no. That loss just whetted my appetite as though nothing had happened at all. So I built some more ships, bigger and better and a damn sight luckier. No one could say I didn't have guts. But big ships make a man feel big himself. I shipped a cargo of wine, bacon, beans, perfume and slaves. And then Fortunata came through nicely in the nick of time: sold her gold and the clothes off her back and put a hundred gold coins in the palm of my hand. That was the yeast of my wealth. Besides, when the gods want something done, it gets done in a jiffy. On that one voyage alone, I cleared about five hundred thousand. Right away I bought up all my old master's property. I built a house, I went into slave-trading and cattle-buying. Everything I touched just grew and grew like a honeycomb. Once more I was worth more than all the people in my home town put together, I picked up my winnings and pulled out. I retired from trade and started lending money to ex-slaves. To tell the truth, I was tempted to quit for keeps, but on the advice of an astrologer who'd just come to town, I decided to keep my hand in. He was a Greek, fellow by the name of Serapa, and clever enough to set up as consultant to the gods. Well, he told me things I'd clean forgotten and laid it right on the line from A to Z. Why, that man could have peeked into my tummy and told me everything except what I'd eaten the day before. You'd have thought he'd lived with me all his life.

"Remember what he said, Habinnas? You were there, I think, when he told my fortune. 'You have bought yourself a mistress and a tyrant,' he said, 'out of your own profits. You are unlucky in your friends. No one is as grateful to you as he should be. You own vast estates. You nourish a viper in your bosom'. There's no reason why I shouldn't tell you, but according to him, I have thirty years, four months, and two days left to live. And soon, he said, I am going to receive an inheritance. Now if I could just add Apulia to the lands I own, I could die content.

"Meanwhile, with Mercury's help, I built this house. As you know, it used to be a shack; now it's a shrine. It has four dining rooms, twenty bedrooms, two marble porticos, an upstairs dining room, the master bedroom where I sleep, the nest of that viper there, a fine porter's lodge, and guestrooms enough for all my guests. In fact, when Scaurus came down here from Rome, he wouldn't put up anywhere else, though his father has lots of friends down on the shore who would have been glad to have him. And there are lots of other things I'll show you in a bit. But take my word for it: money makes the man. No money and you're nobody. But big money, big man. That's how it was with yours truly: from mouse to millionaire."

◆ B ◆ EMERGENCY MEASURES TO DEAL WITH DEPRESSION

One of Tacitus' somewhat malicious verdicts on the early Empire, "the public welfare is sacrificed to private profit" (Annals VI, 16), was made in reference to the laissez-faire economic policy of Augustus and his Julio-Claudian successors. So flourishing was the economy that state intervention was unnecessary except to eliminate major obstacles standing in the way of capitalistic expansion. To this end, for example, Augustus sent a naval expedition into the Red Sea to gain control of this important trade route to the Far East and break the monopoly held by the Arabs of the Aden region. Again, Tiberius in 33 A.D. set up a "land bank" which issued interest-free loans for three years to Italian landowners, enabling them to survive a financial panic caused by a temporary shortage of capital. More drastic action was taken by the Flavian emperor Domitian (81–96 A.D.) to aid Italian wine producers plagued by competition from new vineyards in the western provinces. Domitian sought to create an artificial scarcity by forbidding the planting of new vineyards in Italy and by decreeing the plowing-under of half the existing vineyards in the provinces. But by this time the Italian economy was under sufficient strain as to cause many people, Tacitus among them, to become concerned about "public welfare." An important result of this concern was state inauguration of the alimentary, or child-assistance, program, begun by Nerva in 97 A.D. The program was partly modeled after foundations already established by private philanthropists alarmed at the increase of poverty among the masses. Under this program the state loaned money to ailing landowners at five percent annual interest, with the interest to be paid into the treasuries of Italian municipalities and earmarked "for girls and boys of needy parents to be supported at public expense." In the second century this method of subsidizing both producers and consumers was extended to the provinces, and it was of increasing importance until the collapse of the Roman economy in the third century culminated in large-scale state control under Diocletian (see Selection 56B).

The selections that follow illustrate the growing concern for "public welfare" as opposed to "private profit" on the part of both private individuals and the state.

1. *Apollonius of Tyana and The Grain Dealers*

Late in the first century A.D., during the reigns of Domitian and Nerva, a growing popular interest in mysticism and morality produced a wide variety of wandering saints and charlatans. Whether he was a saint or a charlatan — Christians vehemently insisted on the latter — Apollonius of Tyana in Asia

Reprinted by permission of the publishers and The Loeb Classical Library from F. C. Conybeare's translation of Philostratus, *Life of Apollonius of Tyana*, I, Ch. 15, pp. 39, 41, 43 (Cambridge, Mass.: Harvard University Press).

Minor was a notable example of these wandering evangelists. Born about the same time as Christ, he spent his long life wandering from Spain to India, performing miracles, practicing asceticism (including a five-year period of silence), and preaching to commoners and emperors alike on the immortality and transmigration of souls, communion with God, and man's duty to God and to his fellowman. After his death he was regarded as divine, and the emperor Hadrian built a temple and endowed a priesthood for his worship at Tyana. In the third century the emperor Severus Alexander (222–235 A.D.) placed the image of Apollonius in his private chapel beside those of Abraham, Orpheus, Alexander the Great, and Christ. Earlier in the same century the empress Julia Domna, wife of Septimius Severus, had commissioned the Greek rhetorician Philostratus to write a life of Apollonius based largely on the memoirs of a disciple and companion of the prophet. The following incident, reported by Philostratus, occurred during the period when Apollonius was adhering to his vow of complete silence.

These years of silence he spent partly in Pamphylia and partly in Cilicia; and though his paths lay through such effeminate races as these, he never spoke nor was even induced to murmur. Whenever, however, he came on a city engaged in civil conflict (and many were divided into factions over spectacles of a low kind), he would advance and show himself, and by indicating part of his intended rebuke by manual gesture or by look on his face, he would put an end to all the disorder, and people hushed their voices, as if they were engaged in the mysteries. Well, it is not so very difficult to restrain those who have started a quarrel about dances and horses, for those who are rioting about such matters, if they turn their eyes to a real man, blush and check themselves and easily recover their senses; but a city hard pressed by famine is not so tractable, nor so easily brought to a better mood by persuasive words and its passion quelled. But in the case of Apollonius, mere silence on his part was enough for those so affected. Anyhow, when he came to Aspendus in Pamphylia . . . , he found nothing but vetch [plants used for animal fodder] on sale in the market, and the citizens were feeding upon this and on anything else they could get; for the rich men had shut up all the grain and were holding it up for export from the country. Consequently an excited crowd of all ages had set upon the governor, and were lighting a fire to burn him alive, although he was clinging to the statues of the Emperor, which were more dreaded at that time and more inviolable than the Zeus in Olympia; for they were statues of Tiberius, in whose reign a master is said to have been held guilty of impiety, merely because he struck his own slave when he had on his person a silver drachma coined with the image of Tiberius. Apollonius then went up to the governor and with a sign of his hand asked him what was the matter; and he answered that he had done no wrong, but was indeed being wronged quite as much as the populace; but, he said, if he could not get a hearing, he would perish along with the populace. Apollonius then turned to the bystanders, and beckoned to them that they must listen; and they not only held their tongues from wonderment at him, but they laid the fire they had kindled on the altars which were there. The governor then plucked up courage and said: "This man and that man," and he named several, "are to blame for the famine which has arisen; for they have taken away the grain and are keeping it, one in one part of the country and another in another." The inhabitants of Aspendus thereupon passed the word to one another to make for these men's estates, but Apollonius signed with his head, that they should do no such thing, but rather summon those who were to blame and obtain the grain from them with their consent. And when, after a little time the guilty parties arrived, he very nearly broke out in speech against them, so much was he affected by the tears of the crowd; for the children and women had all flocked together, and the old men were groaning and moaning as if they were on the point of dying by hunger. However, he respected his vow of silence and wrote on a writing board his indictment of the offenders and handed it to the governor to read out aloud; and his indictment ran as follows: "Apollonius to the grain-dealers of Aspendus. The earth is mother of us all, for she is just; but you, because you are unjust have pretended that she is your mother alone; and if you do not stop, I will not permit you to remain upon her." They were so terrified by these words, that they filled the market-place with grain and the city revived.

2.   State Regulation of Grain Dealers and Bakers

In the first of the following edicts the governor of the province of Galatia orders the sale of surplus grain in a famine area and fixes a ceiling price. In the second, the proconsul of Asia steps in to end a bakers' strike with which the city authorities were unable to cope after apparently provoking it by their exacting demands. To assure the steady production of "the staff of life" some towns operated municipal bakeries.

ANTIOCH, PISIDIA, A.D. C.93

Lucius Antistius Rusticus, legate with rank of praetor of the Emperor Caesar DOMITIAN Augustus Germanicus, declares:

Whereas the duovirs and decurions of the most illustrious colony of Antioch has written to me that on account of the severity of the winter the price of grain has soared, and they have petitioned that the populace be given an opportunity to buy;

Therefore — may good fortune attend! — all who are either citizens or residents of the colony of Antioch shall declare before the duovirs of the colony of Antioch, within thirty days after this edict of mine is posted in public, how much grain each has and in what place, and how much he deducts for seed or for the year's supply of food for his household; and he shall make all the remaining grain available to purchasers of the colony of Antioch. Furthermore, I fix next August 1 as the date of the sale. And if anyone fails to comply, let

Reprinted by permission of the publishers from Naphtai Lewis and Meyer Reinhold, eds., *Roman Civilization*, Vol. II: *The Roman Empire*, pp. 339–340. (New York: Columbia University Press, 1955).

him know that I shall claim for confiscation whatever is withheld contrary to my edict, reserving a one-eighth share as a reward for informers.

Whereas, furthermore, I am assured that before this prolonged severe winter a *modius* of grain in the colony cost eight or nine *asses*, and it is most unjust for anyone to profiteer from the hunger of his fellow citizens, I forbid the price of grain to exceed one *denarius* per *modius*.[1]

EPHESUS, ASIA, SECOND CENTURY

... Thus it happens at times that the populace is plunged into disorder and riots by the inexcusable audacity of the bakers' agitation in the market place. Under these circumstances they should by now have been hailed into court and have paid the penalty. But since it is necessary to prefer the welfare of the city to the punishment of these individuals, I thought it best to bring them to their senses by an edict. Wherefore, I forbid the bakers to assemble in association[2] and their officers to make inflammatory speeches, and I order them to give complete obedience to those in charge of the community's welfare and to provide the city fully with the necessary production of bread. If any of them is caught from this time on either meeting contrary to my orders or leading any riot or agitation, he shall be hailed into court and suffer the appropriate punishment; and if anyone dares to hide and continue disrupting the city, he shall in addition be branded on the foot with the word *decuria*,[3] and anyone who harbors any such person shall thereby become liable to the same punishment. [The rest is here omitted.]

Juvenal: The Emancipated Women of the Early Empire

Those who feel that the troubled era in which we are living today approximates conditions to be found in Greece and Rome find support in the poetry of Juvenal (ca. 55–ca. 140 A.D.), who has been called "the greatest satiric poet who

---

[1] At that, the governor is permitting a maximum price of about twice the pre-famine normal price.

[2] The governor by this act suspends the right of association which the bakers had apparently enjoyed.

[3] "City council," indicating presumably that he was branded by its order.

From Peter Green, trans., Juvenal: *The Sixteen Satires* (Penguin Classics, 1967), pp. 142–144. Copyright © Peter Green, 1967. Reprinted by permission of Penguin Books Ltd.

ever lived," and whose sixteen Satires luridly reveal the glaring vices and follies of Roman society at the end of the first century A.D. Juvenal was a relatively well-off member of the Roman middle class with a good start on a career in the Imperial civil service until his property was confiscated and he was exiled in 92 A.D. for lampooning the political influence of a foreign ballet dancer in the entourage of the emperor Domitian. Four years later political exiles were recalled by Nerva, the first of the Five Good Emperors whose last member was Marcus Aurelius (see Selection 51), and a penniless and embittered Juvenal returned to Rome where he set himself the task of denouncing his age. He saw himself as a member of the silent majority of thrifty, hard-working, patriotic, and virtuous citizens speaking out against those who were disrupting the old pattern of society — those of the upper class who lowered their standards and neglected their traditional duties, and those of the mob who demanded and received free "bread and circuses" or rose "from the gutter" to become "top people." To Juvenal, all this was the result of too many years of debilitating peace, the influx of foreign customs, and the corrupting power of wealth. He was convinced that money had corroded everything, particularly social conventions and morality, and that moral degeneracy had reached its zenith in the Rome of his day.

In his Sixth Satire, Juvenal denounces the emancipated upper-class women of Rome for breaching social conventions and moral standards. Because of the resulting collapse of sexual morality and family life, a good woman is a rara avis (rare bird), as "uncommon as a black swan." To prove his case, he sets forth a series of horrid examples of ruthless, strong-willed women motivated by ambition, selfishness, and lust. The two examples given below illustrate Juvenal's strong tendency to exaggerate and caricature — corrupt women are bitches and virtuous women are bores — and his use of violent invective and overloaded repulsive detail, which has not always been to the taste of modern readers. The fact that readers today may not find Juvenal's coarse realism shocking is another illustration of how contemporary conditions approximate those of ancient Rome.

> Yet a musical wife's not so bad as some presumptuous
> Flat-chested busybody who rushes around the town
> Gate-crashing all-male meetings, talking back straight-faced
> To a uniformed general — *and* in her husband's presence.
> She knows all the news of the world, what's cooking in Thrace
> Or China, just what the stepmother did with her stepson
> Behind closed doors, who's fallen in love, which gallant
> Is all the rage. She'll tell you who got the widow
> Pregnant, and in which month; she knows each woman's
> Pillow endearments, and all the positions she favors.
> She's the first to spot any comet presaging trouble
> For some eastern prince, in Armenia, maybe, or Parthia.

She's on to the latest gossip and rumors as soon as
They reach the city-gates, or invents her own, informing
Everyone she meets that Niphates has overflowed
And is inundating whole countries — towns are cut off,
She says, and the land is sinking: flood and disaster!
     Yet even this is not so insufferable
As her habit, when woken up, of grabbing some poor-class
Neighbor and belting into him with a whip. If her precious
Sleep is broken by barking, 'Fetch me the cudgels,'
She roars, 'and be quick about it!' The dog gets a thrashing,
But its master gets one first. She's no joke to cross,
And her face is a grisly fright. Not till the evening
Does she visit the baths: only then are her oil-jars and
The rest of her clobber transferred there. First she works out
With the weights and dumb-bells. Then, when her arms are aching,
The masseur takes over, craftily slipping one hand
Along her thigh, and tickling her up till she comes.
Lastly she makes for the sweat-room. She loves to sit there
Amid all that hubbub, perspiring. Meanwhile at home
Her unfortunate guests are nearly dead with hunger.
At last she appears, all flushed, with a three-gallon thirst,
Enough to empty the brimming jar at her feet
Without assistance. She knocks back two straight pints
On an empty stomach, to sharpen her appetite: then
Throws it all up again, souses the floor with vomit
That flows in rivers across the terrazzo. She drinks
And spews by turns, like some big snake that's tumbled
Into a wine-vat, till her gilded jordan brims
Right over with sour and vinous slops. Quite sickened,
Eyes shut, her husband somehow holds down his bile.

     Worse still is the well-read menace, who's hardly settled for dinner
Before she starts praising Virgil, making a moral case
For Dido (death justifies all), comparing, evaluating
Rival poets, Virgil and Homer suspended
In opposite scales, weighed up one against the other.
Critics surrender, academics are routed, all
Fall silent, not a word from lawyer or auctioneer —
Or even another woman. Such a rattle of talk,
You'd think all the pots and bells were being clashed together
When the moon's in eclipse. . . .
                So avoid a dinner-partner
With an argumentative style, who hurls well-rounded
Syllogisms like slingshots, who has all history pat:

Choose someone rather who doesn't understand *all* she reads.
I hate these authority-citers, the sort who are always thumbing
Some standard grammatical treatise, whose every utterance
Observes all the laws of syntax, who with antiquarian zeal
Quote poets I've never heard of. Such matters are men's concern.
If she wants to correct someone's language, she can always
Start with her unlettered girl-friends.

--5 I--

Marcus Aurelius, To Himself

"Either atoms or providence"

When Marcus Aurelius died in 180 A.D. at Vindobona (Vienna) on the
Danube frontier, he had completed thirteen successful years of campaigning
against the first great wave of Germanic penetration into the Empire. As a
Roman emperor he had fought hard to maintain the security of the state, and
as a Roman intellectual he had written on the values which sustained him in
the face of a world beginning to grow turbulent and weary. These thoughts,
set down at odd moments late in life under the simple heading of To Himself,
constitute the last great expression of the classical viewpoint, centered in
Stoicism, that human reason is an adequate guide to the good life. His basic
view is that there is not to be found "in human life anything better than justice,
truth, temperance, fortitude, and, in a word, anything better than your own
mind's satisfaction in the things which it enables you to do according to right
reason." Yet in the writings of the later Roman Stoics — Seneca, Epictetus, and
Marcus Aurelius — it is possible to detect an underlying pessimism about man's
ability to save himself by his own resources. When we see Marcus Aurelius
choosing to rely on "Providence" rather than the "atoms" of the scientific
Epicurean outlook, and rejecting the classical "city of Athens" for a spiritual
"city of God," we see pagan thought moving in the direction of religion and
the ultimate triumph of Christianity.

Based on the translation by George Long.

II, 1. Begin the morning by saying to yourself, I shall meet with the busy-body, the ungrateful, arrogant, deceitful, envious, unsocial. All these things happen to them by reason of their ignorance of what is good and evil. But I who have seen the nature of the good that it is beautiful, and of the bad that it is ugly, and the nature of him who does wrong, that it is akin to me, not only of the same blood or seed, but that it participates in the same intelligence and the same portion of the divinity, I can neither be injured by any of them, for no one can fix on me what is ugly, nor can I be angry with my kinsman, nor hate him. For we are made for cooperation, like feet, like hands, like eyelids, like the rows of the upper and lower teeth. To act against one another then is contrary to nature; and it is acting against one another to be vexed and to turn away. . . .

17. Of human life the time is a point, and the substance is in a flux, and the perception dull, and the composition of the whole body subject to putre-faction, and the soul a whirl, and fortune hard to divine, and fame a thing devoid of judgment. And, to say all in a word, everything which belongs to the body is a stream, and what belongs to the soul is a dream and vapor, and life is a warfare and a stranger's sojourn, and after-fame is oblivion. What then is that which is able to conduct a man? One thing and only one, philosophy. But this consists in keeping the demon within a man free from violence and unharmed, superior to pains and pleasures, doing nothing without a purpose, nor yet falsely and with hypocrisy, not feeling the need of another man's doing or not doing anything; and besides, accepting all that happens, and all that is allotted, as coming from thence, wherever it is, from whence he himself came; and, finally, waiting for death with a cheerful mind, as being nothing else than a dissolution of the elements of which every living being is compounded. But if there is no harm to the elements themselves in each continually changing into another, why should a man have any apprehension about the change and dissolution of all the elements? For it is according to nature, and nothing is evil which is according to nature. . . .

IV, 23. Everything harmonizes with me, which is harmonious to you, O Universe. Nothing for me is too early nor too late, which is in due time for you. Everything is fruit to me which your seasons bring, O Nature; from you are all things, in you are all things, to you all things return. The poet says, Dear city of Athens; and will you not say, Dear city of God?

41. You are a little soul carrying a corpse, as Epictetus used to say. . . .

48. Think continually how many physicians are dead after often contract-ing their eyebrows over the sick; and how many astrologers after predicting with great pretentions the deaths of others; and how many philosophers after endless discourses on death or immortality; how many heroes after killing thou-sands; and how many tyrants who have used their power over men's lives with terrible insolence as if they were immortal; and how many cities are entirely dead, so to speak, Helice and Pompeii and Herculaneum, and others innumer-able. Add to the reckoning all whom you have known, one after another. One man after burying another has been laid out dead, and another buries him;

and all this in a short time. To conclude, always observe how ephemeral and worthless human beings are, and what was yesterday a little mucus, tomorrow will be a mummy or ashes. Pass then through this little space of time conformably to nature and end your journey in content, just as an olive falls off when it is ripe, blessing nature who produced it, and thanking the tree on which it grew. . . .

V, 27. Live with the gods. And he does live with the gods who constantly shows to them that his own soul is satisfied with that which is assigned to him, and that it does all that the demon wishes, which Zeus has given to every man for his guardian and guide, a portion of himself. And this is every man's understanding and reason. . . .

VI, 7. Take pleasure in one thing and rest in it, in passing from one social act to another social act, thinking of God. . . .

10. Either a confusion of alternate combination and dispersion of atoms, or a unity of order and Providence. If the former, why do I desire to tarry in a random combination of things and such a disorder? And why do I care about anything else than how I shall at last become earth? And why be disturbed, for the dispersion of my atoms will happen whatever I do? But if the latter, then I venerate, and I am content, and I trust in the power that governs. . . .

44. . . . My nature is rational and social; and my city and country, so far as I am Antoninus, is Rome, but so far as I am a man, it is the world. The things then which are useful to these cities are alone useful to me. . . .

54. That which is not good for the swarm, neither is it good for you. . . .

VII, 18. Is any man afraid of change? Why, what can take place without change? What then is more pleasing or more suitable to the universal nature? And can you take a bath unless the wood undergoes a change? And can you be nourished, unless the food undergoes a change? And can anything else that is useful be accomplished without change? Do you not see then that for yourself also to change is just the same, and equally necessary for the universal nature? . . .

28. Retire into yourself. The rational principle which rules has this nature, that it is content with itself when it does what is just, and so secures tranquillity. . . .

49. Consider the past, such great changes of political supremacies. Thou mayest foresee also the things which will be. For they will certainly be of like form, and it is not possible that they should deviate from the order of the things which take place now; accordingly to have contemplated human life for forty years is the same as to have contemplated it for ten thousand years. For what more wilt thou see? . . . ˙

VIII, 16. Remember that to change thy opinion and to follow him who corrects your error is as consistent with freedom as it is to persist in your error. For it is your own, the activity which is exerted according to your own movement and judgment, and indeed according to your own understanding too. . . .

59. Men exist for the sake of one another. Teach them then or bear with them. . . .

IX, 23. As you yourself are a component part of a social system, so let every act of yours be a component part of social life. Whatever act of yours then has no reference either immediately or remotely to a social end, this tears asunder your life, and does not allow it to be one, and it is of the nature of a mutiny, just as when in a popular assembly a man acting by himself stands apart from the general agreement. . . .

X, 10. A spider is proud when it has caught a fly, and a man when he has caught a hare, and another when he has taken a little fish in a net, and another when he has taken wild boars, and another when he has taken bears, and another when he has taken Germans. Are not these bandits, when you examine their principles? . . .

XI, 3. What an admirable soul that is which is ready, if at any moment it must be separated from the body, and ready for extinction, or dispersal, or survival. This readiness must come from a man's own judgment, not from mere obstinacy, as with the Christians, but with reason and dignity if it is to persuade another, and without tragic show.

·4. Have I done something for the general interest? Well than I have had my reward. Let this always be present to your mind, and never stop. . . .

XII, 26. When you are troubled about anything, you have forgotten this, that all things happen according to the universal nature; and forgotten this, that a man's wrongful act is nothing to you; and further you have forgotten this, that everything which happens, always happened so and will happen so, and now happens so everywhere; forgotten this too, how close is the kinship between a man and the whole human race, for it is a community, not of a little blood or seed, but of intelligence. And you have forgotten this too, that every man's intelligence is a god, and is an efflux of the deity; and forgotten this, that nothing is a man's own, but that his child and his body and his very soul came from the deity; forgotten this, that everything is opinion; and lastly you have forgotten that every man lives the present time only, and loses only this. . . .

32. How small a part of the boundless and unfathomable time is assigned to every man? for it is very soon swallowed up in the eternal. And how small a part of the whole substance? and how small a part of the universal soul? and on what a small clod of the whole earth you creep? Reflecting on all this consider nothing to be great, except to act as your nature leads you, and to endure that which the common nature brings. . . .

36. Man, you have been a citizen in this great state, the world; what difference does it make to you whether for five years or fifty? For that which is conformable to the laws is just for all. Where is the hardship then, if no tyrant nor yet an unjust judge send you away from the state, but nature who brought you into it, the same as if a praetor who has employed an actor dismisses him from the stage — "But I have not finished the five acts, but only three of them" — you say well, but in life the three acts are the whole drama; for what shall be a complete drama is determined by him who was once the cause of its composition, and now of its dissolution: but you are the cause of neither. Depart then satisfied, for he also who releases you is satisfied.

52

Apuleius, The Golden Ass

The cult of Isis and religious syncretism

In a famous passage, Gilbert Murray has characterized the growing religiosity evident in the Roman Empire as "a failure of nerve":

> It is a rise of asceticism, of mysticism, in a sense, of pessimism; a loss of self-confidence, of hope in this life and of faith in normal human effort; a despair of patient inquiry, a cry for infallible revelation; an indifference to the welfare of the state, a conversion of the soul to God.[1]

This attraction to the certitude and security to be found in religion is well-illustrated in the life of Lucius Apuleius, a contemporary of Marcus Aurelius. The son of a wealthy Greek family living in North Africa, he received his higher education first at Carthage and later at Athens. He lived the typical life of the dissolute youth of his day, and he soon squandered his patrimony on drink, women, and evil associates. This life was changed by his initiation into the mystery cult of Isis, after which he became a follower of the Platonic philosophy and spent the rest of his life as a traveling orator and lecturer. A number of his writings have survived, notably The Golden Ass (also called Metamorphoses), a semi-autobiographical account of man's rise from evil days to a new life under the inspiration of religion. The story is based upon an older Greek romance which told how a man named Lucius, dabbling in magic in order to further his immoral desires, carelessly used the wrong ointment and was transformed into an ass, the personification of lust and wickedness. He had many adventures, both ribald and sordid, until he regained his human form by means of a magical antidote. Apuleius has changed this ending, his Lucius being transformed through the ministrations of the goddess Isis, and the story becomes an allegory of human life moving from the sensual to the spiritual. A similar progression was recorded two centuries later by St. Augustine in his spiritual autobiography, the Confessions (see Selection 54C).

The following selections from The Golden Ass describe how Lucius is re-

Reprinted by permission of the publishers and The Loeb Classical Library from W. Aldington's translation of Apuleius, *The Golden Ass*, revised by S. Gaselee, Book XI (Cambridge, Mass.: Harvard University Press).

[1] Gilbert Murray, *Five Stages of Greek Religion* (New York: Columbia University Press, 1925), p. 155.

stored to human form by Isis' providence, becomes a convert to her cult, and visits her temple in the "holy city" of Rome. Also evident is the syncretism — the assimilation and combination of common elements from many religions — which characterized religious practice during the Roman Empire.

5. Thus the divine shape, breathing out the pleasant spice of fertile Arabia, disdained not with her holy voice to utter these words unto me:

"Behold, Lucius, I am come; thy weeping and prayer hath moved me to succor thee. I am she that is the natural mother of all things, mistress and governess of all the elements, the initial progeny of worlds, chief of the powers divine, queen of all that are in hell, the principal of them that dwell in heaven, manifested alone and under one form of all the gods and goddesses. At my will the planets of the sky, the wholesome winds of the seas, and the lamentable silences of hell be disposed; my name, my divinity is adored throughout all the world, in divers manners, in variable customs, and by many names. For the Phrygians that are the first of all men call me the Mother of the gods at Pessinus; the Athenians, which are sprung from their own soil, Cecropian Minerva; the Cyprians, which are girt about by the sea, Paphian Venus; the Cretans, which bear arrows, Dictynnian Diana; the Sicilians, which speak three tongues, infernal Proserpine; the Eleusians their ancient goddess Ceres; some Juno, other Bellona, other Hecate, other Rhamnusia, and principally both sort of the Ethiopians which dwell in the Orient and are enlightened by the morning rays of the sun, and the Egyptians, which are excellent in all kind of ancient doctrine, and by their proper ceremonies accustom to worship me, do call me by my true name, Queen Isis. Behold I am come to take pity of thy fortune and tribulation; behold I am present to favor and aid thee; leave off thy weeping and lamentation, put away all thy sorrow, for behold the heathful day which is ordained by my providence. . . .

6. . . . Thou shalt live blessed in this world, thou shall live glorious by my guide and protection, and when after thine allotted space of life thou descendest to hell, there thou shalt see me in that subterranean firmament shining (as thou seest me now) in the darkness of Acheron, and reigning in the deep profundity of Styx, and thou as a dweller in the Elysian Fields shalt worship me as one that hath been favorable to thee. And if I perceive that thou art obedient to my commandment and addict to my religion, meriting by thy constant chastity my divine grace, know thou that I alone may prolong thy days above the time that the fates have appointed and ordained." . . .

LUCIUS IS RESTORED TO HUMAN SHAPE

15. The priest, looking upon me with a sweet and benign countenance, began to say in this sort:

"O my friend Lucius, after the endurance of so many labors and the escape of so many tempests of fortune, thou are now at length come to the port and haven of rest and mercy. Neither did thy noble lineage, thy dignity, neither thy excellent doctrine anything avail thee; but because thou didst turn to servile pleasures, by a little folly of thy youthfulness, thou hast had a sinister reward of thy unprosperous curiosity. But howsoever the blindness of fortune tormented thee in divers dangers, so it is now that by her unthoughtful malice thou art come to the present felicity of religion. Let fortune go and fume with fury in another place; let her find some other matter to execute her cruelty; for fortune hath no puissance against them which have devoted their lives to serve and honor the majesty of our goddess. For what availed the thieves? The beast savage? Thy great survitude? The ill, toilsome, and dangerous ways? The fear of death every day? What availed all those, I say, to cruel fortune? Know thou that now thou art safe, and under the protection of that fortune that is not blind but can see, who by her clear light doth lighten the other gods: wherefore rejoice, and take a convenable countenance to thy white habit, and follow with joyful steps the pomp of this devout and honorable procession. Let the irreligious see, let them see and learn how wrong they are: 'Behold here is Lucius that is delivered from his former so great miseries by the providence of the goddess Isis, and rejoiceth therefore and triumpheth of victory over his fortune.' And to the end thou mayest live more safe and sure, make thyself one of this holy order, to which thou wast but a short time since pledged by oath, dedicate thy mind to the obeying of our religion, and take upon thee a voluntary yoke of ministry: for when thou beginnest to serve and honor the goddess, then shalt thou feel the more the fruit of thy liberty." . . .

HE IS INITIATED INTO THE CULT OF ISIS

22. . . . When I had heard these and other divine commandments of the high goddess, I greatly rejoiced, and arose before day to speak with the great priest, whom I fortuned to espy coming out of his chamber. Then I saluted him, and thought with myself to ask and demand with a bold courage that I should be initiate, as a thing now due; but as soon as he perceived me, he began first to say: "O Lucius, now know I well that thou art most happy and blessed, whom the divine goddess doth so greatly accept with mercy. Why dost thou stand idle and delay? Behold the day which thou didst desire with prayer, when as thou shalt receive at my hands the order of most secret and holy religion, according to the divine commandment of this goddess of many names." Thereupon the old man took me by the hand, and led me courteously to the gate of the great temple, where, after that it was religiously opened, he made a solemn celebration, and after the morning sacrifice was ended, he brought out of the secret place of the temple certain books written with unknown characters, partly painted with figures of beasts declaring briefly every sentence, partly with letters whose tops and tails turned round in fashion of a wheel, joined together above like unto the tendrils of a vine, whereby they were wholly strange and impossible to read of the profane people; thence he interpreted to me such things as were necessary to the use and preparation of mine order.

23. This done, I diligently gave in charge to certain of my companions to

buy liberally whatsoever was needed and convenient; but part thereof I bought myself. Then he brought me, when he found that the time was at hand, to the next baths, accompanied with all the religious sort, and demanding pardon of the gods, washed me and purified my body according to the custom; after this, when two parts of the day were gone, he brought me back again to the temple and presented me before the feet of the goddess, giving me a charge of certain secret things unlawful to be uttered, and commanding me generally before all the rest to fast by the space of ten continual days, without eating of any bread or drinking of any wine; which things I observed with a marvellous continency. Then behold the day approached when as the sacrifice of dedication should be done; and when the sun declined and evening came, there arrived on every coast a great multitude of priests, who according to their ancient order offered me many presents and gifts. Then was all the laity and profane people commanded to depart, and when they had put on my back a new linen robe, the priest took my hand and brought me to the most secret and sacred place of the temple.

Thou wouldst peradventure demand, thou studious reader, what was said and done there; verily, I would tell thee if it were lawful for me to tell, thou wouldst know if it were convenient for thee to hear; but both thy ears and my tongue should incur the like pain of rash curiosity. Howbeit I will not long torment thy mind, which peradventure is somewhat religious and given to some devotion; listen therefore, and believe it to be true. Thou shalt understand that I approached near unto hell, even to the gates of Proserpine, and after that I was ravished throughout all the elements. I returned to my proper place; about midnight I saw the sun brightly shine, I saw likewise the gods celestial and the gods infernal, before whom I presented myself and worshipped them. Behold now have I told thee, which although thou hast heard, yet it is necessary that thou conceal it; wherefore this only will I tell, which may be declared without offence for the understanding of the profane. . . .

TO ROME, THE "HOLY CITY"

26. . . . And so within a short while after, by the exhortation of the goddess I made up my packet and took shipping towards the city of Rome, and I voyaged very safely and swiftly with a prosperous wind to the port of Augustus, and thence travelling by chariot, I arrived at that holy city about the twelfth day of December in the evening. And the greatest desire which I had there was daily to make my prayers to the sovereign goddess Isis, who, by reason of the place where her temple was builded, was called Campensis, and continually is adored of the people of Rome; her minister and worshipper was I, a stranger to her church, but not unknown to her religion.

53

The New Testament

The beginnings of Christianity

The New Testament, an anthology comprising the four Gospels (Mark, Matthew, Luke, and John), the Acts of the Apostles, twenty-one Epistles, and the Book of Revelation, is the record of the career and teaching of Jesus of Nazareth and the founding of a new religion by his followers. The growth and spread of Christianity from an obscure Jewish sect in Palestine to the official religion of the Roman Empire is one of the most fascinating dramas in history. The New Testament recounts the first hundred years of this story.

◆A◆ THE TEACHINGS OF JESUS

"Turn away from your sins! The Kingdom of heaven is near!"

The life and teachings of Jesus form the central theme of the New Testament. He followed in the tradition of the Hebrew prophets in denouncing the empty legalism and formalism of the established religion and in emphasizing a renovation of the inner spiritual and ethical content of that religion. His struggle to reform Judaism by breathing new life into old forms led to the conflict with priestism which in turn led to his tragic death. An integral part of Jesus' teachings consists of the growing apocalyptic (see p. 105) and eschatological (from the Greek word for "end" or "final") ideas of his day concerning resurrection of the dead, last judgment, angels, devils, hell, and the Messiah or Christ, the "Anointed One" of God who will carry out His purposes. The following selections from the Gospels (from the Greek word for "good news") illustrates the mingling of ethical and eschatological elements in the teachings of Jesus. They are taken from Good News for Modern Man, a completely new translation into "today's English" prepared by the American Bible Society. It "attempts to follow, in this century, the example set by the authors of the New Testament books who, for the most part, wrote in the standard, or common [koinē] form of the Greek language used throughout the Roman Empire."

From *Good News for Modern Man: The New Testament in Today's English Version,* copyright American Bible Society, 1966. Reprinted by permission of the American Bible Society.

1. *John The Baptist and The Sermon on the Mount*

Following his baptism by John the Baptist, a fiery prophet who proclaimed the imminent coming of the Kingdom of God and whose act gave assurance of Jesus' divine appointment as Messiah, Jesus began his ministry which was to culminate on the cross. One of the great moments in Jesus' messianic ministry was his preaching of the Sermon on the Mount, which has been called the Magna Carta of Christian ethics. It established for Christians a sublime — and largely unattainable — ideal of universal brotherhood and love. An indication of the new and radical nature of Jesus' teaching is the frequent use of the phrase, "You have heard that men were told in the past, . . . but now I tell you . . . ." The sermon on the Mount is reported in the two Gospels of Matthew and Luke, both, along with that of Mark, composed during the last three decades of the first century A.D.

THE PREACHING OF JOHN THE BAPTIST

At that time John the Baptist came and started preaching in the desert of Judea. "Change your ways," he said, "for the Kingdom of heaven is near!" John was the one that the prophet Isaiah was talking about when he said:

> Someone is shouting in the desert:
> "Get the Lord's road ready for him,
> Make a straight path for him to travel!"

John's clothes were made of camel's hair; he wore a leather belt around his waist, and ate locusts and wild honey. People came to him from Jerusalem, from the whole province of Judea, and from all the country around the Jordan river. They confessed their sins and he baptized them in the Jordan.

When John saw many Pharisees and Sadducees coming to him to be baptized, he said to them: "You snakes — who told you that you could escape from God's wrath that is about to come? Do the things that will show that you have changed your ways. And do not think you can excuse yourselves by saying, 'Abraham is our father.' I tell you that God can take these rocks and make children for Abraham! The ax is ready to cut the trees at the roots; every tree that does not bear good fruit will be cut down and thrown in the fire. I baptize you with water to show that you have repented; but the one who will come after me will baptize you with the Holy Spirit and fire. He is much greater than I am; I am not good enough even to carry his sandals. He has his winnowing-shovel with him to thresh out all the grain; he will gather his wheat into his barn, but burn the chaff in a fire that never goes out!"

THE BAPTISM OF JESUS

At that time Jesus went from Galilee to the Jordan, and came to John to be baptized by him. But John tried to make him change his mind. "I ought to

Matthew 3:1–17, 4:17–5:48, 6:5–15.

be baptized by you," John said, "yet you come to me!" But Jesus answered him, "Let it be this way for now. For in this way we shall do all that God requires." So John agreed.

As soon as Jesus was baptized, he came up out of the water. Then heaven was opened to him, and he saw the Spirit of God coming down like a dove and lighting on him. And then a voice said from heaven, "This is my own dear Son, with whom I am well pleased." . . .

From that time Jesus began to preach his message: "Turn away from your sins! The Kingdom of heaven is near!"

JESUS CALLS FOUR FISHERMEN

As Jesus walked by Lake Galilee, he saw two brothers who were fishermen, Simon (called Peter) and his brother Andrew, catching fish in the lake with a net. Jesus said to them, "Come with me and I will teach you to catch men." At once they left their nets and went with him.

He went on and saw two other brothers, James and John, the sons of Zebedee. They were in their boat with their father Zebedee, getting their nets ready. Jesus called them; at once they left the boat and their father, and went with Jesus.

THE SERMON ON THE MOUNT

Jesus went all over Galilee, teaching in their meeting houses, preaching the Good News of the Kingdom, and healing people from every kind of disease and sickness. The news about him spread through the whole country of Syria, so that people brought him all those who were sick with all kinds of diseases, and afflicted with all sorts of troubles: people with demons, and epileptics and paralytics — Jesus healed them all. Great crowds followed him from Galilee and the Ten Towns, from Jerusalem, Judea, and the land on the other side of the Jordan.

Jesus saw the crowds and went up a hill, where he sat down. His disciples gathered around him, and he began to teach them:

> "Happy are those who know they are spiritually poor:
>   the Kingdom of heaven belongs to them!
> "Happy are those who mourn:
>   God will comfort them!
> "Happy are the meek:
>   they will receive what God has promised!
> "Happy are those whose greatest desire is to do what
>   God requires:
>   God will satisfy them fully!
> "Happy are those who show mercy to others:
>   God will show mercy to them!
> "Happy are the pure in heart:
>   they will see God!

"Happy are those who work for peace among men:
  God will call them his sons!
"Happy are those who suffer persecution because they
  do what God requires:
  the Kingdom of heaven belongs to them!

"Happy are you when men insult you and mistreat you and tell all kinds of evil lies against you because you are my followers. Rejoice and be glad, because a great reward is kept for you in heaven. This is how men mistreated the prophets who lived before you.

"You are like salt for the earth. If the salt loses its taste, there is no way to make it salty again. It has become worthless, and so it is thrown away where people walk on it.

"You are like the light for the world. A city built on a high hill cannot be hid. Nobody lights a lamp to put it under a bowl; instead he puts it on the lamp-stand, where it gives light for everyone in the house. In the same way your light must shine before people, so that they will see the good things you do and give praise to your Father in heaven.

"Do not think that I have come to do away with the Law of Moses and the teaching of the prophets. I have not come to do away with them, but to give them real meaning. Remember this! As long as heaven and earth last, the least point or the smallest detail of the Law will not be done away with — not until the end of all things. Therefore, whoever breaks even the smallest of the commandments, and teaches others to do the same, will be least in the Kingdom of heaven. On the other hand, whoever obeys the Law, and teaches others to do the same, will be great in the Kingdom of heaven. I tell you, then, you will be able to enter the Kingdom of heaven only if your standard of life is far above the standard of the teachers of the Law and the Pharisees.

"You have heard that men were told in the past, 'Do not murder; anyone who commits murder will be brought before the judge.' But now I tell you: whoever is angry with his brother will be brought before the judge; whoever calls his brother "You good-for-nothing!' will be brought before the Council; and whoever calls his brother a worthless fool will be in danger of going to the fire of hell. So if you are about to offer your gift to God at the altar and there you remember that your brother has something against you, leave your gift there in front of the altar and go at once to make peace with your brother; then come back and offer your gift to God. . . .

"You have heard that it was said, 'Do not commit adultery.' But now I tell you: anyone who looks at a woman and wants to possess her is guilty of committing adultery with her in his heart. So if your right eye causes you to sin, take it out and throw it away! It is much better for you to lose a part of your body than to have your whole body thrown into hell. If your right hand causes you to sin, cut it off and throw it away! It is much better for you to lose one of your limbs than to have your whole body go off to hell.

"It was also said, 'Anyone who divorces his wife must give her a written notice of divorce.' But now I tell you: if a man divorces his wife, and she has not been unfaithful, then he is guilty of making her commit adultery if she marries again; and the man who marries her also commits adultery.

"You have also heard that men were told in the past, 'Do not break your promise, but do what you have sworn to do before the Lord.' But now I tell you: do not use any vow when you make a promise; do not swear by heaven, because it is God's throne; nor by earth, because it is the resting place for his feet; nor by Jerusalem, because it is the city of the great King. Do not even swear by your head, because you cannot make a single hair white or black. Just say 'Yes' or 'No' — anything else you have to say comes from the Evil One.

"You have heard that it was said, 'An eye for an eye, and a tooth for a tooth.' But now I tell you: do not take revenge on someone who does you wrong. If anyone slaps you on the right cheek, let him slap your left cheek too. And if someone take you to court to sue you for your shirt, let him have your coat as well. And if one of the occupation troops forces you to carry his pack one mile, carry it another mile. When someone asks you for something, give it to him; when someone wants to borrow something, lend it to him.

"You have heard that it was said, 'Love your friends, hate your enemies.' But now I tell you: love your enemies, and pray for those who mistreat you, so that you will become the sons of your Father in heaven. For he makes his sun to shine on bad and good people alike, and gives rain to those who do right and those who do wrong. Why should you expect God to reward you, if you love only the people who love you? Even the tax collectors do that! And if you speak only to your friends, have you done anything out of the ordinary? Even the pagans do that! You must be perfect — just as your Father in heaven is perfect. . . .

"And when you pray, do not be like the show-offs! They love to stand up and pray in the meeting houses and on the street corners so that everybody will see them. Remember this! They have already been paid in full. But when you pray, go to your room and close the door, and pray to your Father who is unseen. And your Father, who sees what you do in private, will reward you.

"In your prayers do not use a lot of words, as the pagans do, who think that God will hear them because of their long prayers. Do not be like them; God is your Father and he already knows what you need before you ask him. This is the way you should pray:

Our Father in heaven:
May your name be kept holy,
May your Kingdom come,
May your will be done on earth as it is in heaven.
Give us today the food we need;
Forgive us what we owe you as we forgive what others owe us;
Do not bring us to hard testing, but keep us safe from the Evil One.

For if you forgive others the wrongs they have done you, your Father in heaven will forgive you. But if you do not forgive others, then your Father in heaven will not forgive the wrongs you have done."

2. *Parables of the Kingdom*

A favorite teaching device used by Jesus is the parable, a humble story of every-day life containing a profound truth. The first three Gospels contain almost fifty parables dealing with such subjects as humility, sympathy, forgiveness, and, above all, the nature of the Kingdom of God.

THE PARABLE OF THE SOWER

That same day Jesus left the house and went to the lakeside, where he sat down to teach. The crowd that gathered around him was so large that he got into a boat and sat in it, while the crowd stood on the shore. He used parables to tell them many things.

"There was a man who went out to sow. As he scattered the seed in the field, some of it fell along the path, and the birds came and ate it up. Some of it fell on the rocky ground, where there was little soil. The seeds soon sprouted, because the soil wasn't deep. When the sun came up it burned the young plants, and because the roots had not grown deep enough the plants soon dried up. Some of the seed fell among thorns, which grew up and choked the plants. But some seeds fell in good soil, and bore grain: some had one hundred grains, others sixty, and others thirty." And Jesus said, "Listen, then, if you have ears!"

THE PURPOSE OF THE PARABLES

Then the disciples came to Jesus and asked him, "Why do you use parables when you talk to them?" "The knowledge of the secrets of the Kingdom of heaven has been given to you," Jesus answered, "but the man who has nothing will have taken away from him even the little he has. This is the reason that I use parables to talk to them: it is because they look, but do not see, and they listen, but do not hear or understand. So the prophecy of Isaiah comes true in this case:

> You will listen and listen, but not understand;
> You will look and look, but not see.
> Because this people's mind is dull;
> They have stopped up their ears,
> And they have closed their eyes.
> Otherwise, their eyes might see,
> Their ears might hear,
> Their minds might understand
> And they might turn to me, says God,
> And I would heal them.

As for you, how fortunate you are! Your eyes see and your ears hear. Remember this! Many prophets and many of God's people wanted very much to see what you see, but they could not, and to hear what you hear, but they did not."

Matthew 13:1–58; Luke 10:25–37.

JESUS EXPLAINS THE PARABLE OF THE SOWER

"Listen, then, and learn what the parable of the sower means. Those who hear the message about the Kingdom but do not understand it are like the seed that fall along the path. The Evil One comes and snatches away what was sown in them. The seed that fell on rocky ground stands for those who receive the message gladly as soon as they hear it. But it does not sink deep in them, and they don't last long. So when trouble or persecution comes because of the message, they give up at once. The seed that fell among thorns stands for those who hear the message, but the worries about this life and the love for riches choke the message, and they don't bear fruit. And the seed sown in the good soil stands for those who hear the message and understand it: they bear fruit, some as much as one hundred, others sixty, and others thirty."

THE PARABLE OF THE WEEDS

Jesus told them another parable: "The Kingdom of heaven is like a man who sowed good seed in his field. One night, when everyone was asleep, an enemy came and sowed weeds among the wheat, and went away. When the plants grew and the heads of grain began to form, then the weeds showed up. The man's servants came to him and said. 'Sir, it was good seed you sowed in your field; where did the weeds come from?' 'It was some enemy who did this,' he answered. 'Do you want us to go and pull up the weeds?' they asked him. 'No,' he answered, 'because as you gather the weeds you might pull up some of the wheat along with them. Let the wheat and the weeds grow together until harvest, and then I will tell the harvest workers: Pull up the weeds first and tie them in bundles to throw in the fire; then gather in the wheat and put it in my barn.' " . . .

JESUS EXPLAINS THE PARABLE OF THE WEEDS

Then Jesus left the crowd and went indoors. His disciples came to him and said, "Tell us what the parable of the weeds in the field means." Jesus answered: "The man who sowed the good seed is the Son of Man; the field is the world; the good seed is the people who belong to the Kingdom; the weeds are the people who belong to the Evil One; and the enemy who sowed the weeds is the Devil himself. The harvest is the end of the age, and the harvest workers are angels. Just as the weeds are gathered up and burned in the fire, so it will be at the end of the age: the Son of Man will send out his angels and they will gather up out of his Kingdom all who cause people to sin, and all other evildoers, and throw them into the fiery furnace, where they will cry and gnash their teeth. Then God's people will shine like the sun in their Father's Kingdom. Listen, then, if you have ears!" . . .

JESUS REJECTED AT NAZARETH

When Jesus finished telling these parables, he left that place and went back to his home town. He taught in their meeting house, and those who heard him were amazed. "Where did he get such wisdom?" they asked. "And what about his miracles? Isn't he the carpenter's son? Isn't Mary his mother, and aren't

James, Joseph, Simon, and Judas his brothers? Aren't all his sisters living here? Where did he get all this?" And so they rejected him. Jesus said to them: "A prophet is respected everywhere except in his home town and by his own family." He did not perform many miracles there because they did not have faith. . . .

THE PARABLE OF THE GOOD SAMARITAN

Then a certain teacher of the Law came up and tried to trap him. "Teacher," he asked, "what must I do to receive eternal life?" Jesus answered him, "What do the Scriptures say? How do you interpret them?" The man answered: " 'You must love the Lord your God with all your heart, and with all your soul, and with all your strength, and with all your mind'; and, 'You must love your neighbor as yourself.' " "Your answer is correct," replied Jesus; "do this and you will live."

But the teacher of the Law wanted to put himself in the right, so he asked Jesus, "Who is my neighbor?" Jesus answered: "A certain man was going down from Jerusalem to Jericho, when robbers attacked him, stripped him and beat him up, leaving him half dead. It so happened that a priest was going down that road; when he saw the man he walked on by, on the other side. In the same way a Levite also came there, went over and looked at the man, and then walked on by, on the other side. But a certain Samaritan who was traveling that way came upon him, and when he saw the man his heart was filled with pity. He went over to him, poured oil and wine on his wounds and bandaged them; then he put the man on his own animal and took him to an inn, where he took care of him. The next day he took out two silver coins and gave them to the innkeeper. 'Take care of him,' he told the innkeeper, 'and when I come back this way I will pay you back whatever you spend on him.' " And Jesus concluded, "Which one of these three seems to you to have been a neighbor to the man attacked by the robbers?" The teacher of the Law answered, "The one who was kind to him." Jesus replied, "You go, then, and do the same."

3. *Jesus' Instructions To His Disciples*

The following passages throw light on Jesus' own conception of his mission. It is to be preached solely among the Jews of "the house of Israel," and he has no illusions concerning the deep cleavage it will produce between those who accept his teachings and those who cling to the established orthodox position. Furthermore, while Jesus accepts the belief of his disciples that he is the Messiah, he adds the novel view that he must suffer, die, and be resurrected as a prelude to the coming of the Kingdom.

THE MISSION OF THE TWELVE

Jesus called his twelve disciples together and gave them power to drive out the evil spirits and to heal every disease and every sickness. These are the names of

Matthew 10:1–42, 16:13–28, 24:3–31, 25:31–46.

the twelve apostles: first, Simon (called Peter) and his brother Andrew; James and his brother John, the sons of Zebedee; Philip and Bartholomew; Thomas and Matthew, the tax collector; James, the son of Alphaeus, and Thaddaeus; Simon, the patriot, and Judas Iscariot, who betrayed Jesus.

Jesus sent these twelve men out with the following instructions: "Do not go to any Gentile territory or any Samaritan towns. Go, instead, to the lost sheep of the people of Israel. Go and preach, 'The Kingdom of heaven is near!' Heal the sick, raise the dead, make the lepers clean, drive out demons. You have received without paying, so give without being paid. Do not carry any gold, silver, or copper money in your pockets; do not carry a beggar's bag for the trip, or an extra shirt, or shoes, or a walking stick. A worker should be given what he needs.

"When you come to a town or village, go in and look for someone who is willing to welcome you, and stay with him until you leave that place. When you go into a house say, 'Peace be with you.' If the people in that house welcome you, let your greeting of peace remain; but if they do not welcome you, then take back your greeting. And if some home or town will not welcome you or listen to you, then leave that place and shake the dust off your feet. Remember this! On the Judgment Day God will show more mercy to the people of Sodom and Gomorrah than to the people of that town!

"Listen! I am sending you just like sheep to a pack of wolves. You must be as cautious as snakes and as gentle as doves. Watch out, for there will be men who will arrest you and take you to court, and they will whip you in their meeting houses. You will be brought to trial before rulers and kings for my sake, to tell the Good News to them and to the Gentiles. When they bring you to trial, do not worry about what you are going to say or how you will say it; when the time comes, you will be given what you will say. For the words you speak will not be yours; they will come from the Spirit of your Father speaking in you.

"Men will hand over their own brothers to be put to death, and fathers will do the same to their children; children will turn against their parents and have them put to death. Everyone will hate you, because of me. But the person who holds out to the end will be saved. And when they persecute you in one town, run away to another one. I tell you, you will not finish your work in all the towns of Israel before the Son of Man comes. . . .

"Do not think that I have come to bring peace to the world; no, I did not come to bring peace, but a sword. I came to set sons against their fathers, daughters against their mothers, daughters-in-law against their mothers-in-law; a man's worst enemies will be the members of his own family.

"Whoever loves his father or mother more than me is not worthy of me; whoever loves his son or daughter more than me is not worthy of me. Whoever does not take up his cross and follow in my steps is not worthy of me. Whoever tries to gain his own life will lose it: whoever loses his life for my sake will gain it.

"Whoever welcomes you, welcomes me; and whoever welcomes me, welcomes the one who sent me. Whoever welcomes God's messenger because he is

God's messenger will share in his reward; and whoever welcomes a truly good man, because he is that, will share in his reward. And remember this! Whoever gives even a drink of cold water to one of the least of these my followers, because he is my follower, will certainly receive his reward." . . .

PETER'S DECLARATION ABOUT JESUS

Jesus went to the territory near the town of Caesarea Philippi, where he asked his disciples, "Who do men say the Son of Man is?" "Some say John the Baptist," they answered. "Others say Elijah, while others say Jeremiah or some other prophet." "What about you?" he asked them. "Who do you say I am?" Simon Peter answered, "You are the Messiah, the Son of the living God." "Simon, son of John, you are happy indeed!" answered Jesus. "For this truth did not come to you from any human being, but it was given to you directly by my Father in heaven. And so I tell you: you are a rock, Peter, and on this rock I will build my church. Not even death will ever be able to overcome it. I will give you the keys of the Kingdom of heaven: what you prohibit on earth will be prohibited in heaven; what you permit on earth will be permitted in heaven." Then Jesus ordered his disciples that they were not to tell anyone that he was the Messiah.

JESUS SPEAKS ABOUT HIS SUFFERING AND DEATH

From that time on Jesus began to say plainly to his disciples: "I must go to Jerusalem and suffer much from the elders, the chief priests, and the teachers of the Law. I will be put to death, and on the third day I will be raised to life." Peter took him aside and began to rebuke him. "God forbid it, Lord!" he said. "This must never happen to you!" Jesus turned around and said to Peter: "Get away from me, Satan! You are an obstacle in my way, for these thoughts of yours are men's thoughts, not God's!"

Then Jesus said to his disciples: "If anyone wants to come with me, he must forget himself, carry his cross, and follow me. For the man who wants to save his own life will lose it; but the man who loses his life for my sake will find it. Will a man gain anything if he wins the whole world but loses his life? Of course not! There is nothing a man can give to regain his life. For the Son of Man is about to come in the glory of his Father with his angels, and then he will repay everyone according to his deeds. Remember this! There are some here who will not die until they have seen the Son of Man come as King." . . .

TROUBLES AND PERSECUTIONS

As Jesus sat on the Mount of Olives, the disciples came to him in private. "Tell us when all this will be," they asked, "and what will happen to show that it is the time for your coming and the end of the age."

Jesus answered: "Watch out, and do not let anyone fool you. Because many men will come in my name, saying, 'I am the Messiah!' and fool many people. You are going to hear the noise of battles close by and the news of battles far away; but, listen, do not be troubled. Such things must happen, but they do not mean that the end has come. One country will fight another country, one kingdom will attack another kingdom. There will be famines and earthquakes everywhere. All these things are like the first pains of childbirth.

"Then men will arrest you and hand you over to be punished, and you will be put to death. All mankind will hate you because of me. Many will give up their faith at that time; they will betray each other and hate each other. Then many false prophets will appear and fool many people. Such will be the spread of evil that many people's love will grow cold. But the person who holds out to the end will be saved. And this Good News about the Kingdom will be preached through all the world, for a witness to all mankind — and then will come the end.

"You will see 'The Awful Horror,' of which the prophet Daniel spoke [see p. 105, Introduction], standing in the holy place." (Note to the reader: understand what this means!) . . .

THE COMING OF THE SON OF MAN

"Soon after the trouble of those days the sun will grow dark, the moon will no longer shine, the stars will fall from heaven, and the powers in space will be driven from their course. Then the sign of the Son of Man will appear in the sky; then all the tribes of earth will weep, and they will see the Son of Man coming on the clouds of heaven with power and great glory. The great trumpet will sound, and he will send out his angels to the four corners of the earth, and they will gather his chosen people from one end of the world to the other. . . .

THE JUDGMENT OF THE NATIONS

"When the Son of Man comes as King, and all the angels with him, he will sit on his royal throne, and all the earth's people will be gathered before him. Then he will divide them into two groups, just as a shepherd separates the sheep from the goats: he will put the sheep at his right and the goats at his left. Then the King will say to the people on his right: 'You who are blessed by my Father: come! Come and receive the kingdom which has been prepared for you ever since the creation of the world. I was hungry and you fed me, thirsty and you gave me drink; I was a stranger and you received me in your homes, naked and you clothed me; I was sick and you took care of me, in prison and you visited me.' The righteous will then answer him: 'When, Lord, did we ever see you hungry and feed you, or thirsty and give you drink? When did we ever see you a stranger and welcome you in our homes, or naked and clothe you? When did we ever see you sick or in prison, and visit you?' The King will answer back, 'I tell you, indeed, whenever you did this for one of these poorest brothers of mine, you did it for me!'

"Then he will say to those on his left: 'Away from me, you who are under God's curse! Away to the eternal fire which has been prepared for the Devil and his angels! I was hungry but you would not feed me, thirsty but you would not give me drink; I was a stranger but you would not welcome me in your homes, naked but you would not clothe me; I was sick and in prison but you would not take care of me.' Then they will answer him: 'When, Lord, did we ever see you hungry, or thirsty, or a stranger, or naked, or sick, or in prison, and we would not help you?' The King will answer them back, 'I tell you, indeed, whenever you refused to help one of these poor ones, you refused to help me.' These, then, will be sent off to eternal punishment; the righteous will go to eternal life."

◆ B ◆ THE WORK OF PAUL

"Jews and Gentiles are all one in union with Christ Jesus."

Paul of Tarsus (ca. 10–ca. 65 A.D.), a Hellenized Jew of the Diaspora, has been called the second founder of Christianity. He played a crucial role in the initial spreading of Christianity among the Gentiles of the Roman world and in establishing the fundamental Christian doctrines of Jesus as the crucified Christ, the incarnation of God, whose death was an atonement for the sins of the whole world and whose resurrection assured immortality to those who entered into a mystical union with his Spirit. There will always be much debate as to the extent to which Pauline Christianity is an elaboration on the teachings of Jesus to meet Gentile needs, but there is complete agreement that Paul was a genius whose work was of epochal significance for the history of Western civilization.

1. Paul's Address to the Athenians

"What is this ignorant show-off trying to say?"

Paul's missionary activities took him into the leading cities of Asia Minor, Macedonia, and Greece, seeking converts among both Jews and Gentiles. Our knowledge of this work is derived from the Acts of the Apostles, thought to be the work of Luke, and Paul's own Epistles. Paul's visit to Athens (ca. 51 A.D.) is of great interest, even though largely unsuccessful. His failure with one exception to convert the Athenian intellectuals, who are seen still maintaining the famed Greek curiosity about any "new thing," is typical of the failure of early Christianity to attract the educated classes; it took the more philosophical approach of the later Apologists to win them over (see Selection 54).

While Paul was waiting in Athens for Silas and Timothy, he was greatly upset when he noticed how full of idols the city was. So he argued in the meeting house with the Jews and the Gentiles who worshiped God, and in the public square every day with the people who happened to come by. Certain Epicurean and Stoic teachers also debated with him. Some said, "What is this ignorant show-off trying to say?" Others said, "He seems to be talking about foreign gods." They said this because Paul was preaching about Jesus and the resurrection. So they took Paul, brought him before the meeting of the Areopagus, and said: "We would like to know this new teaching that you are

Acts 17:16–34.

talking about. Some of the things we hear you say sound strange to us, and we would like to know what they mean." (For all the people of Athens and the foreigners who lived there liked to spend all their time telling and hearing the latest new thing.)

Paul stood up in front of the meeting of the Areopagus and said: "Men of Athens! I see that in every way you are very religious. For as I walked through your city and looked at the places where you worship, I found also an altar on which is written, 'To an Unknown God.' That which you worship, then, even though you do not know it, is what I now proclaim to you. God, who made the world and everything in it, is Lord of heaven and earth, and does not live in temples made by men. Nor does he need anything that men can supply by working for him, since it is he himself who gives life and breath and everything else to all men. From the one man he created all races of men, and made them live over the whole earth. He himself fixed beforehand the exact times and the limits of the places where they would live. He did this so that they would look for him, and perhaps find him as they felt around for him. Yet God is actually not far from any one of us; for

In him we live and move and are.

It is as some of your poets have also said,

We too are his children.

Since we are his children, we should not suppose that God's nature is anything like an image of gold or silver or stone, shaped by the art and skill of man. God has overlooked the times when men did not know, but now he commands all men everywhere to turn away from their evil ways. For he has fixed a day in which he will judge the whole world with justice, by means of a man he has chosen. He has given proof of this to everyone by raising that man from death!"

When they heard Paul speak about a raising from death, some of them made fun of him, but others said, "We want to hear you speak about this again." And so Paul left the meeting. Some men joined him and believed; among them was Dionysius, a member of the Areopagus, a woman named Damaris, and some others.

2.   *Paul's Epistles*

"His letters, say they, are weighty and powerful." — II Corinthians 10:10

Paul's failure at Athens, where he stayed only a few days, contrasts sharply with his success at the populous commercial city of Corinth, where he remained eighteen months and to whose congregation he later wrote two of his most important Epistles. The New Testament contains fourteen of Paul's letters, undoubtedly only a portion of those he wrote to instruct and encourage the infant Christian communities. Altogether, as the following passages illustrate, they are a primary source for our knowledge of early Christian theology and they form a body of devotional literature that has continuously inspired Christian readers.

a. PAUL'S ANSWER TO INTELLECTUALS

Christ did not send me to baptize. He sent me to tell the Good News, and to tell it without using the language of men's wisdom, for that would rob Christ's death on the cross of all its power.

For the message about Christ's death on the cross is nonsense to those who are being lost; but for us who are being saved, it is God's power. For the scripture says,

> I will destroy the wisdom of the wise,
> I will set aside the understanding of the scholars.

So then, where does that leave the wise men? Or the scholars? Or the skillful debaters of this world? God has shown that this world's wisdom is foolishness!

For God in his wisdom made it impossible for men to know him by means of their own wisdom. Instead, God decided to save those who believe, by means of the "foolish" message we preach. Jews want miracles for proof, and Greeks look for wisdom. As for us, we proclaim Christ on the cross, a message that is offensive to the Jews and nonsense to the Gentiles; but for those whom God has called, both Jews and Gentiles, this message is Christ, who is the power of God and the wisdom of God. For what seems to be God's foolishness is wiser than men's wisdom, and what seems to be God's weakness is stronger than men's strength.

Now remember what you were, brothers, when God called you. Few of you were wise, or powerful, or of high social status, from the human point of view. God purposely chose what the world considers nonsense in order to put wise men to shame, and what the world considers weak in order to put powerful men to shame. He chose what the world looks down on, and despises, and thinks is nothing, in order to destroy what the world thinks is important. . . .

When I came to you, my brothers, to preach God's secret truth to you, I did not use long words and great learning. For I made up my mind to forget everything while I was with you except Jesus Christ, and especially his death on the cross. So when I came to you I was weak and trembled all over with fear, and my speech and message were not delivered with skillful words of human wisdom, but with convincing proof of the power of God's Spirit. Your faith, then, does not rest on man's wisdom, but on God's power.

I Corinthians 1:17–2:8.

Yet I do speak wisdom to those who are spiritually mature. But it is not the wisdom that belongs to this world, or to the powers that rule this world — powers which are losing their power. The wisdom I speak is God's secret wisdom, hidden from men, which God had already chosen for our glory, even before the world was made. None of the rulers of this world knew this wisdom. If they had known it, they would not have nailed the Lord of glory to the cross.

b. FAITH AND THE LAW

You must remember this, my brothers: many times I have planned to visit you, but something has always kept me from doing so. I have wanted to win converts among you, too, as I have among other Gentiles. For I have an obligation to all peoples, to the civilized and to the savage, to the educated and to the ignorant. Therefore, I am eager to preach the Good News to you also who live in Rome.

For I have complete confidence in the gospel: it is God's power to save all who believe, first the Jews and also the Gentiles. For the gospel reveals how God puts men right with himself: it is through faith alone, from beginning to end. As the scripture says, "He who is put right with God through faith shall live." . . .

But now God's way of putting men right with himself has been revealed, and it has nothing to do with law. The Law and the prophets gave their witness to it: God puts men right through their faith in Jesus Christ. God does this to all who believe in Christ, for there is no difference at all: all men have sinned and are far away from God's saving presence. But by the free gift of God's grace they are all put right with him through Christ Jesus, who sets them free. God offered him so that by his death he should become the means by which men's sins are forgiven, through their faith in him. God offered Christ to show how he puts men right with himself. In the past, God was patient and overlooked men's sins; but now in the present time he deals with men's sins, to prove that he puts men right with himself. In this way God shows that he himself is righteous and that he puts right everyone who believes in Jesus.

What, then, is there to boast about? Nothing! For what reason? Because a man obeys the Law? No, but because he believes. For we conclude that a man is put right with God only through faith, and not by doing what the Law commands. Or is God only the God of the Jews? Is he not the God of the Gentiles also? Of course he is. God is one, and he will put the Jews right with himself on the basis of their faith, and the Gentiles right through their faith. Does this mean that we do away with the Law by this faith? No, not at all; instead, we uphold the Law. . . .

It is just as the scripture says about Abraham: "He believed God, and be-

Romans 1:13–17, 3:21–31; Galatians 3:15–29.

cause of his faith God accepted him as righteous." You should realize, then, that the people who have faith are the real descendants of Abraham. The scripture saw ahead of time that God would put the Gentiles right with himself through faith. Therefore the scripture preached the Good News to Abraham ahead of time: "Through you God will bless all the people on earth." Abraham believed and was blessed; so all who believe are blessed as he was.

Those who depend on obeying the Law live under a curse. For the scripture says, "Whoever does not always obey everything that is written in the book of the Law is under the curse!" . . .

But Christ has set us free from the curse the Law brings by becoming a curse for us. As the scripture says, "Anyone who is hanged on a tree is under the curse." Christ did so in order that the blessing God promised Abraham might be given to the Gentiles by means of Christ Jesus, that we, through faith, might receive the Spirit promised by God.

Brothers, I am going to use an everyday example: when two men agree on a matter and sign a covenant, no one can break that covenant or add anything to it. Now, God made his promises to Abraham and to his descendant. It does not say, "and to his descendants," meaning many people. It says, "and to your descendant," meaning one person only, who is Christ. This is what I mean: God made a covenant and promised to keep it. The Law, which came four hundred and thirty years later, cannot break that covenant and cancel God's promise. For if what God gives depends on the Law, then it no longer depends on his promise. However, God gave it to Abraham because he had promised it to him.

Why was the Law given, then? It was added in order to show what wrongdoing is, and was meant to last until the coming of Abraham's descendant, to whom the promise was made. The Law was handed down by angels, with a man acting as a go-between. But a go-between is not needed when there is only one person; and God is one.

Does this mean that the Law is against God's promises? No, not at all! For if a law had been given that could give life to men, then man could be put right with God through law. But the scripture has said that the whole world is under the power of sin, so that those who believe might receive the promised gift that is given on the basis of faith in Jesus Christ.

Before the time for faith came, however, the Law kept us all locked up as prisoners, until this coming faith should be revealed. So the law was in charge of us, to be our instructor until Christ came, so that we might be put right with God through faith. Now that the time of faith is here, the instructor is no longer in charge of us.

For it is through faith that all of you are God's sons in union with Christ Jesus. For all who are baptized into union with Christ have taken upon themselves the qualities of Christ himself. So there is no difference between Jews and Gentile, between slaves and free men, between men and women: you are all one in union with Christ Jesus. If you belong to Christ, then you are the descendants of Abraham, and will receive what God has promised.

c. FLESH AND THE SPIRIT

My inner being delights in the law of God. But I see a different law at work in my body — a law that fights against the law that my mind approves of. It makes me a prisoner to the law of sin which is at work in my body. What an unhappy man I am! Who will rescue me from this body that is taking me to death? Thanks be to God, through our Lord Jesus Christ!

This, then, is my condition: by myself I can serve God's law only with my mind, while my human nature serves the law of sin.

There is no condemnation now for those who live in union with Christ Jesus. For the law of the Spirit, which brings us life in union with Christ Jesus, has set me free from the law of sin and death. What the Law could not do, because human nature was weak, God did. He condemned sin in human nature by sending his own Son, who came with a nature like man's sinful nature to do away with sin. God did this in order that we who live according to the Spirit, and not according to human nature, might fully obey the righteous demands of the Law. For those who live as their human nature tells them to live, have their minds controlled by what human nature wants. Those who live as the Spirit tells them to live, have their minds controlled by what the Spirit wants. To have your mind controlled by what human nature wants will result in death; to have your mind controlled by what the Spirit wants will result in life and peace. And so a man becomes an enemy of God when his mind is controlled by what human nature wants; for he does not obey God's law, and in fact he cannot obey it. Those who obey their human nature cannot please God.

But you do not live as your human nature tells you to; you live as the Spirit tells you to — if, in fact, God's Spirit lives in you. Whoever does not have the Spirit of Christ does not belong to him. But if Christ lives in you, although your body is dead because of sin, yet the Spirit is life for you because you have been put right with God. If the Spirit of God, who raised Jesus from death, lives in you, then he who raised Christ from death will also give life to your mortal bodies by the presence of his Spirit in you.

So then, my brothers, we have an obligation, but not to live as our human nature wants us to. For if you live according to your human nature, you are going to die; but if, by the Spirit, you kill your sinful actions, you will live. Those who are led by God's Spirit are God's sons. For the Spirit that God has given you does not make you a slave and cause you to be afraid; instead, the Spirit makes you God's sons, and by the Spirit's power we cry to God, "Father! my Father!" God's Spirit joins himself to our spirits to declare that we are God's children. Since we are his children, we will possess the blessings he keeps for his people, and we will also possess with Christ what God has kept for him; for if we share Christ's suffering, we will also share his glory.

Romans 7:22–8:17.

d. THE RESURRECTION OF CHRIST AND THE FAITHFUL

And now I want to remind you, brothers, of the Good News which I preached to you, which you received, and on which your faith stands firm. That is the gospel, the message that I preached to you. You are saved by the gospel if you hold firmly to it — unless it was for nothing that you believed.

I passed on to you what I received, which is of the greatest importance: that Christ died for our sins, as written in the Scriptures; that he was buried and raised to life on the third day, as written in the Scriptures; that he appeared to Peter, and then to all twelve apostles. Then he appeared to more than five hundred of his followers at once, most of whom are still alive, although some have died. Then he appeared to James, and then to all the apostles.

Last of all he appeared also to me — even though I am like one who was born in a most unusual way. For I am the least of all the apostles — I do not even deserve to be called an apostle, because I persecuted God's church. But by God's grace I am what I am, and the grace that he gave me was not without effect. On the contrary, I have worked harder than all the other apostles, although it was not really my own doing, but God's grace working with me. So then, whether it came from me or from them, this is what we all preach, this is what you believe.

Now, since our message is that Christ has been raised from death, how can some of you say that the dead will not be raised to life? If that is true, it means that Christ was not raised; and if Christ has not been raised from death, then we have nothing to preach, and you have nothing to believe. More than that, we are shown to be lying against God, because we said of him that he raised Christ from death — but he did not raise him, if it is true that the dead are not raised to life. For if the dead are not raised, neither has Christ been raised. And if Christ has not been raised, then your faith is a delusion and you are still lost in your sins. It would also mean that the believers in Christ who have died are lost. If our hope in Christ is good for this life only, and no more, then we deserve more pity than anyone else in all the world.

But the truth is that Christ has been raised from death, as the guarantee that those who sleep in death will also be raised. For just as death came by means of a man, in the same way the rising from death comes by means of a man. For just as all men die because of their union to Adam, in the same way all will be raised to life because of their union to Christ. . . .

Brothers, I face death every day! The pride I have in you in our life in Christ Jesus our Lord makes me declare this. If I have fought "wild beasts" here in Ephesus, as it were, simply from human motives, what have I gained? As the saying goes, "Let us eat and drink, for tomorrow we will die" — if the dead are not raised to life. . . .

I Corinthians 15:1–55.

Someone will ask, "How can the dead be raised to life? What kind of body will they have?" You fool! When you plant a seed in the ground it does not sprout to life unless it dies. And what you plant in the ground is a bare seed, perhaps a grain of wheat, or of some other kind, not the full-bodied plant that will grow up. God provides that seed with the body he wishes; he gives each seed its own proper body. . . .

This is how it will be when the dead are raised to life. When the body is buried it is mortal; when raised, it will be immortal. When buried, it is ugly and weak; when raised, it will be beautiful and strong. When buried, it is a physical body; when raised, it will be a spiritual body. There is, of course, a physical body, so there is bound to be a spiritual body. For the scripture says: "The first man, Adam, was created a living being"; but the last Adam is the lifegiving Spirit. It is not the spiritual that comes first, but the physical, and then the spiritual. The first Adam was made of the dust of the earth; the second Adam came from heaven. Those who belong to the earth are like the one who was made of earth; those who are of heaven are like the one who came from heaven. Just as we wear the likeness of the man made of earth, so we will wear the likeness of the Man from heaven.

This is what I mean, brothers: what is made of flesh and blood cannot share in God's Kingdom, and what is mortal cannot possess immortality.

Listen to this secret: we shall not all die, but in an instant we shall all be changed, as quickly as the blinking of an eye, when the last trumpet sounds. For when it sounds, the dead will be raised immortal beings, and we shall all be changed. For what is mortal must clothe itself with what is immortal: what will die must clothe itself with what cannot die. So when what is mortal has been clothed with what is immortal, and when what will die has been clothed with what cannot die, then the scripture will come true: "Death is destroyed: victory is complete!"

"Where, O Death, is your victory?
Where, O Death, is your power to hurt?"

e. PREDESTINATION

I consider that what we suffer at this present time cannot be compared at all with the glory that is going to be revealed to us. All of creation waits with eager longing for God to reveal his sons. For creation was condemned to become worthless, not of its own will, but because God willed it to be so. Yet there was this hope: that creation itself would one day be set free from its slavery to decay, and share the glorious freedom of the children of God. For we know that up to the present time all of creation groans with pain like the pain of childbirth. But not just creation alone; we who have the Spirit as the first of God's gifts, we also groan within ourselves as we wait for God to make us his sons and set our whole being free. For it was by hope that we were saved; but if we

Romans 8:18–31; 9:14–22.

see what we hope for, then it is not really hope. For who hopes for something that he sees? But if we hope for what we do not see, we wait for it with patience. . . .

For we know that in all things God works for good with those who love him, those whom he has called according to his purpose. For those whom God had already chosen he had also set apart to share the likeness of his Son, so that the Son should be the first among many brothers. And so God called those whom he had set apart; not only did he call them, but he also put them right with himself; not only did he put them right with himself, but he also shared his glory with them.

Faced with all this, what can we say? If God is for us, who can be against us? . . .

What shall we say, then? That God is unjust? Not at all. For he said to Moses, "I will have mercy on whom I wish, I will take pity on whom I wish." So then, it does not depend on what man wants or does, but only on God's mercy. For the scripture says to Pharaoh, "I made you king for this very purpose, to use you to show my power, and to make my name known in all the world." So then, God has mercy on whom he wishes, and he makes stubborn whom he wishes.

One of you, then, will say to me, "If this is so, how can God find fault with any man? For who can resist God's will?" But who are you, my friend, to talk back to God? A clay pot does not ask the man who made it, "Why did you make me like this?" After all, the man who makes the pots has the right to use the clay as he wishes, and to make two pots from the same lump of clay, an expensive pot and a cheap one. And the same is true of what God has done.

f. LOVE

I may be able to speak the languages of men and even of angels, but if I have not love, my speech is no more than a noisy gong or a clanging bell. I may have the gift of inspired preaching; I may have all knowledge and understand all secrets; I may have all the faith needed to move mountains — but if I have not love, I am nothing. I may give away everything I have, and even give up my body to be burned — but if I have not love, it does me no good.

Love is patient and kind; love is not jealous, or conceited, or proud; love is not ill-mannered, or selfish, or irritable; love does not keep a record of wrongs; love is not happy with evil, but is happy with the truth. Love never gives up: its faith, hope, and patience never fail.

Love is eternal. There are inspired messages, but they are temporary; there are gifts of speaking, but they will cease; there is knowledge, but it will pass. For our gifts of knowledge and of inspired messages are only partial; but when what is perfect comes, then what is partial disappears.

I Corinthians 13:1–13.

When I was a child, my speech, feelings, and thinking were all those of a child; now that I am a man, I have no more use for childish ways. What we see now is like the dim image in a mirror; then we shall see face to face. What I know now is only partial; then it will be complete, as complete as God's knowledge of me.

Meanwhile these three remain: faith, hope, and love; and the greatest of these is love.

54

Christianity and Greco-Roman Thought

"Whatever has been uttered aright by any men in any place belongs to us Christians." — Justin

To the intellectuals of the Greco-Roman world early Christianity appeared to be just another mystery cult of interest only to the uneducated lower classes; in the words of Tacitus, it was a "pernicious superstition," particularly unattractive because of its "hatred for the whole human race." On the other hand, the earliest Christians were equally hostile to pagan philosophy, and they agreed with St. Paul that God had "made foolish the wisdom of this world." Before Christianity could spread triumphantly through the whole classical world, taking into its fold men on all levels of learning, some solution to this conflict had to be achieved. We have seen that in the early Roman Empire Greek philosophy, notably Stoicism and a revived Platonism, became increasingly imbued with religious values (see Selection 51 and the Introduction to Selection 52); consequently, when men trained in Greek learning began to accept Christianity, an amalgamation of philosophy and Christianity was not difficult to bring about. This process, the work of intellectual Christians known as Apologists and Church Fathers, began in the second century in the more Christian East and culminated in the work of St. Augustine at the end of the fourth century in the West.

Various methods were used in giving an intellectual tone to Christianity. The personal God of the Jews and Christians was identified with the abstract god of the Greek philosophers — a pure, invisible, incorporeal intelligence. The literal interpretation of the Old Testament was replaced by an allegorical one in which a deeper symbolical and spiritual meaning was found to lie behind the simple words of the text. Biblical truth, wrote Origen, one of the outstanding third-century Greek Apologists, "is sometimes conveyed in what one might call literal falsehood." Above all, use was made of the Logos doctrine, which explained how God was the source of all truth, both pagan and Christian. "Logos" was a term used in Greek philosophy to signify the powers of reason. It is translated variously as "word," "argument," and "reason." Plato and other Greek thinkers referred to the Logos as eternal and divine, and the Christian Apologists adopted the term for the divine principle regulating all things and bridging the gap between God and man. They taught that the Logos (reason) of the Greek philosophers was one means by which God sought to enlighten and save mankind, but that when this attempt failed He then sent the Logos in the form of his Only-Begotten Son, Jesus. "Thus philosophy was a preparation," wrote Clement, Origen's predecessor as head of the Christian school at Alexandria, "paving the way towards perfection in Christ." A better-known statement of the Logos doctrine and the incarnation of this divine force in Jesus is found in the Gospel of John: "In the beginning was the Word, and the Word was with God, and the Word was God.... And the light shineth in darkness; and the darkness comprehended it not.... And the Word was made flesh and dwelt among us, (and we beheld his glory, the glory as of the only begotten of the Father,) full of grace and truth."

◆A◆   JUSTIN, APOLOGY

"Those who lived according to reason are Christians."

The first important Christian Apologist was Justin, whose Apology was addressed to the emperor Antoninus Pius about the middle of the second century. Although a Greek, he spent much time in Rome, where he conducted a school and where he ultimately suffered martyrdom. His conversion to Christianity from Stoicism and Platonism illustrates the strong appeal of what he called "the noble precepts of Christ" over the pagan way of life, a view he summarizes in the first selection given below. The second selection is an excellent short statement illustrating the attitude of the majority of Church Fathers towards pagan learning.

CHRISTIANITY AND MORAL REGENERATION

Since our conversion to Christianity, we who formerly delighted in debauchery, now rejoice in purity of life; we who formerly used magical arts, dedicate ourselves to the good and unbegotten God; we who valued above all things the acquisition of wealth and possessions, now bring together all that we have and share it with those who are in need. Formerly, we hated and destroyed one an-

From Justin, I, 14, 46; II, 13; based on the translation by Marcus Dods in *The Ante-Nicene Fathers* (Buffalo, 1885), Vol. I.

other and, because of differences in nationality and customs, would not allow strangers to live with us. Now, since the coming of Christ, we live familiarly with them, and pray for our enemies, and endeavor to persuade those who hate us unjustly to live according to the good precepts of Christ, to the end that they may become partakers with us of the same joyful hope of a reward from God the ruler of all. . . .

CHRISTIANITY AND PAGAN LEARNING

Lest some should assert, unreasonably and to turn men from what we teach, that we say that Christ was born one hundred and fifty years ago under Cyrenius, and subsequently, in the time of Pontius Pilate, taught what we say He taught, and then accuse us of saying that all men who were born before Him were irresponsible — let us anticipate and solve this difficulty. We have been taught that Christ is the first-born of God, and we have declared above that He is the Word [reason] of whom every race of men were partakers. Those who lived according to reason are Christians, even though they have been thought atheists — such as, among the Greeks, Socrates and Heraclitus, and men like them; and among barbarians, Abraham, and Ananias . . . .

For each man spoke rightly in proportion to the share he had of the seminal Word [reason], seeing what was related to it. . . . Whatever things were rightly said among all men in all places belong to us Christians. For next to God we worship and love the Word who is from the unbegotten and ineffable God, since also He became man for our sakes, that, becoming a partaker of our sufferings, He might also bring us healing. For all the writers were able to see realities darkly through the sowing of the implanted Word that was in them.

◆ B ◆ TERTULLIAN, AGAINST HERETICS

"What is there in common between Athens and Jerusalem?"

Justin had called Heraclitus "a Christian before Christ" and this liberal attitude towards pagan philosophers soon became dominant in Eastern Christianity. In the Latin West, however, this point of view did not find great favor until the appearance of St. Augustine in the late fourth century. The outstanding opponent of classical philosophy among the Latin Apologists was Tertullian, who died at Carthage about 222 A.D. He was trained in Roman law, and his view of Christianity was a legalistic one. To him Christianity was essentially a legal and moral code established by God and revealed through Christ. Sin and salvation were based on adherence to the Divine Law as judged by Christ. The subtleties of Greek philosophy were not only unnecessary to Tertullian; they were absurd and dangerous. He preached a "simple faith," for "to know nothing against the rule of faith is to know everything." The truest Christian was "the

From Tertullian, *Against Heretics*, Ch. 7, based on the translation by Peter Holmes in *The Ante-Nicene Fathers* (Buffalo, 1885), Vol. III.

simple and uncultivated soul, whose whole experience has been gleaned on street-corners and cross-roads and in the factory." Such a man, Tertullian boasted, could answer all the questions that had puzzled the minds of the greatest philosophers.

These are "the doctrines" of men and "of demons" produced for itching ears of the spirit of this world's wisdom: this the Lord called "foolishness" and "chose the foolish things of the world" to confound even philosophy itself. For philosophy it is which is the material of the world's wisdom, the rash interpreter of the nature and the dispensation of God. Indeed heresies are themselves instigated by philosophy. From this source came the "Aeons," and I know not what "infinite forms" and the "trinity of man" in the system of Valentinus, who was of Plato's school. From the same source came Marcion's better god, with all his tranquillity; he came of the Stoics. Then, again, the opinion the the soul dies is held by the Epicureans; while the denial of the restoration of the body is taken from the aggregate school of all the philosophers; also, when matter is made equal to God, then you have the teaching of Zeno; and when any doctrine is alleged touching a god of fire, then Heraclitus comes in. The same subject matter is discussed over and over again by the heretics and the philosophers; the same arguments are involved. Whence comes evil? Why is it permitted? What is the origin of man? and in what way does he come? Besides the questions which Valentinus has very lately proposed — Whence comes God? Which he settles with the answer: From *enthymesis* and *ectroma*. Unhappy Aristotle! who invented for these men dialectics, the art of building up and pulling down; an art so evasive in its propositions, so far-fetched in its conjectures, so harsh in its arguments, so productive of contentions — embarrassing even to itself, retracting everything, and really treating of nothing! . . . What is there in common between Athens and Jerusalem? What concord is there between the Academy and the Church? what between heretics and Christians? . . . Away with all attempts to produce a mottled Christianity of Stoic, Platonic, and dialectic composition! We want no curious disputation after possessing Christ Jesus, no inquisition after enjoying the gospel! With our faith, we desire no further belief.

✦ C ✦ ST. AUGUSTINE, CONFESSIONS

"Our heart is restless until it rests in You."

Frequently when reading the works of the Church Fathers one comes across the statement, "Christians are not born but made." This cogently expressed the fact that Christianity came to these Greco-Roman intellectuals as a final and satisfying answer to their long search for truth and meaning. The classical em-

From St. Augustine I, 9, 13, 14; II, 1, 3, 4, 6, 9; III, 1–7; IV, 3; V, 10, 13, 14; VII, 9, 20; VIII, 3, 4, 6, 8, 11, 12; based on the translation by E. B. Pusey.

phasis on rationalistic humanism was no longer satisfying, and men turned from it to the spiritual truths of Christianity. This story is best told in the intellectual and spiritual autobiography of St. Augustine (354–430 A.D.), bishop of Hippo in North Africa. We see the picture of a man akin to ourselves in his gropings after truth in an age grown weary from disorder and anxiety.

As a boy, Augustine tells us, he thought of God in childish terms, as one who could hear such petitions as would help him to escape punishment in school. As he grew older and attended the university at Carthage, he discarded such simple beliefs and, plunging into a life of romantic excitements, "walked the streets of Babylon and wallowed in the mire thereof." But university life also marked an important advance toward maturity in that it turned him from the pursuit of sensual pleasures to a love of wisdom, a transformation he attributed to the writings of Cicero. Yet this new love was barren of permanently satisfying results, and a similar discouragement resulted when he turned to religion. The Christian Scriptures repelled him; he could not accept the immoralities and anthropomorphism of the Old Testament, and he saw only a deficiency of style and charm in the New Testament. The Manichaean heresy interested him for a number of years before it was revealed to be a tissue of sham and imposture. Then he "despaired of finding the truth" and found congenial the dictum of the Skeptic philosophers that "no truth can be comprehended by man." The major barriers to his conversion to Christianity were removed by Ambrose, who gave him the allegorical method of interpreting the Scriptures, and by Neo-Platonism, which taught him the immateriality of God. He felt that the affinities between Christianity and Platonism were so close that, as he stated later in his essay Of True Religion, all that was needed to convert Platonists was the modification of a few words and formulae. Like Platonism, too, which Plato said could be accepted only by "some few who are able ... to find it out for themselves," Augustine's Christianity is a way of life that cannot be taught by one man to another. The real significance of Christianity can only be grasped by one who has experienced much, suffered much, and thought much; and such is the final message of the Confessions: "You, O God, are the Good, which is in need of no other good. ... What man shall teach another to understand this? Or what angel another angel? Or what angel man? This must be asked of you, sought in you, knocked for at you: thus only shall it be received, thus shall it be found, thus shall it be opened to us. Amen." (XIII, 38)

The final step for Augustine is a wrenching free from a confused rationalism by a deliberate act, inspired by the example of the unlearned, of reaching up to "take heaven by force." Once more, in this final mystical step, we find an echo of Plato's words: "suddenly a light, as it were, is kindled in one soul by a flame that leaps to it from another, and thereafter sustains itself." (See page 216.)

SCHOOLDAYS

O God, my God, what miseries and mockeries did I now experience, when obedience to my teachers was proposed to me as proper in a boy in order that in this world I might prosper and excel in rhetorical learning, which would obtain for me the praise of men and deceitful riches. Then I was put to school to get learning, in which I (poor wretch) knew not what use there was; and yet, if idle in learning, I was beaten. For this was considered right by our forefathers; and many, passing the same way before us, had built for us a weary path along which we were compelled to go, multiplying toil and grief upon the sons of Adam.

Yet we noticed, Lord, that men prayed to You, and we learned from them to think of You (according to our capacities) as some great One, who, though hidden from our senses, could hear and help us. So as a boy I began to call upon You, my Aid and Refuge; though small, yet with no small earnestness, I broke the fetters of my tongue to call on You, praying to You that I might not be beaten at school. And when You did not hear me (not thereby encouraging my folly), my elders, yes, even my parents, who yet wished me no harm, laughed at my stripes, which were a great and grievous ill to me. . . .

It was not that we lacked, O Lord, memory or capacity; You gave us enough of these for our age. But our sole delight was play, and for this we were punished by those who were themselves doing the same thing. But older folks' idleness is called "business"; the idling of boys, though really the same, is punished by these older folks; and no one is sorry for either boys or men. For will anyone of sound discretion approve of my being beaten as a boy because, by playing ball, I made less progress in studies which, by learning, I might as a man play some more unbecoming game? . . .

Why I so much hated Greek, which I had to study as a boy, I do not fully understand. For I loved Latin; not the elementary grammar, but the literature. As for the rudiments — reading, writing, and arithmetic — I found them as hard and hateful as Greek. . . .

Why then did I hate Greek literature? . . . The difficulty of learning a foreign language sprinkled bitterness over all the sweetness of the Greek stories. For not one word of it did I understand, and to make me understand I was urged vehemently with cruel threats and punishments. There was a time also (as an infant) when I knew no Latin; but I learned it without fear or suffering, by mere observation, amid the caresses of my nurses and the jests of friends, whose smiles and laughter encouraged me. I learned it without any pressure or punishment to urge me on, for my heart urged me to give birth to thoughts which I could only do by learning words not from instructors but from those who talked with me and for whom I was able to express what I was feeling. There is no doubt, then, that free curiosity has more value in learning languages than harsh enforcement. . . .

"TO WHOM AM I TELLING THIS? AND TO WHAT PURPOSE?"

I will now call to mind my past foulness and the carnal corruptions of my soul, not because I love them but that I may love You, O my God. For love of Your love I do it, reviewing my most wicked ways in the very bitterness of my remembrance, that You may grow sweet to me (O sweetness never failing, blissful and assured sweetness). And I gather myself together out of that dissipated state, in which I was torn to pieces while turned from You, the One Good, while losing myself among a multiplicity of things.

Having arrived at adolescence, I was on fire to take my fill of hell. I became like an animal, pursuing various and shady lusts: *my beauty consumed away* and I stank in Your sight; pleasing myself and desirous to please in the sight of men. . . .

To whom am I telling this? Not to You, my God, but in Your presence to my own kind, to that small portion of mankind as may come upon these writings of mine. And to what purpose? Simply that I and whoever reads this may think *out of what depths we are to cry unto Thee*. For what is nearer to Your ears than a confessing heart and a life of faith? . . .

AN ACT OF VANDALISM: "SEEKING ONLY TO BE WICKED"

Theft is punished by Your law, O Lord, and the law written in the hearts of men . . . . Yet I wanted to steal, and did steal, compelled not by hunger or poverty but because I lacked a sense of justice and was filled with iniquity. For I stole that of which I had plenty, and of much better quality. Nor cared I to enjoy what I stole; I enjoyed the theft itself, and the sin.

There was a pear tree near our vineyard, laden with fruit but tempting neither in color or taste. To shake it and rob it, I and some lewd young fellows went late one night (having according to our depraved custom prolonged our sports in the street till then) and took huge loads, not for eating — we barely tasted them — but to fling to the hogs. Our real pleasure in doing this was that it was forbidden. Such was my heart, O God, such was my heart which You had pity on when it was at the bottom of the bottomless abyss. Now let my heart tell You what it sought there, when I was evil for no purpose, having no reason for wrongdoing except wrongdoing itself. It was foul, and I loved it; I loved destroying myself; I loved my sin, not the thing for which I had sinned but the sin itself. Foul soul, falling from Your firmament to utter destruction; not seeking profit from wickedness, but seeking only to be wicked! . . .

Did I find pleasure in appearing to break Your law, doing so by stealth since I had no real power to do so? Was I, like a prisoner, making a small show of liberty by doing unpunished what I was not allowed to do and so getting a false sense of omnipotence? Behold Your servant, fleeing from his Lord and pursuing a shadow! What rottenness! What monstrosity of life and abyss of death! Could I enjoy what was forbidden only because it was forbidden? . . .

See, my God, this vivid memory of my soul. Yet I could not have committed that theft alone. . . . When someone cries "Come on, let's do it," we are ashamed to be ashamed. . . .

"LOVING A VAGRANT LIBERTY"

I came to Carthage, where there sang all around me in my ears a cauldron of unholy loves. I was not yet in love, yet I loved the idea of love, and out of a deep-seated want I hated myself for not wanting more. I sought for something to love, being in love with loving, and I hated security and a life without snares. For within me was a famine of that spiritual food, Yourself, my God . . . . To love then, and to be loved, was sweet to me; but more so when I obtained the enjoyment of the body of the person I loved. Thus I defiled the spring of friendship with the filth of physical desire and beclouded its brightness with the hell of lust . . . .

Stage plays also carried me away, full of images of my miseries and of fuel for my fire. Why is it that man desires to be made sad, beholding miserable and tragic things which he himself would by no means wish to suffer? Yet he desires as a spectator to feel sorrow, and this sorrow is his pleasure. . . .

O my God, my exceeding great mercy, my refuge from those terrible destroyers, among whom I wandered in my arrogance, withdrawing further from You, loving my own ways and not Yours, loving a vagrant liberty.

"AROUSED TO SEEK WISDOM WHATEVER IT MIGHT BE"

These studies of mine also, which were considered commendable, were designed to fit me to excel in the law courts — the more craftier I was, the more famous I should become. Such is men's blindness, that blindness itself should become a source of pride! And by now I was a leader in the school of rhetoric, which I proudly enjoyed, swelling with arrogance, though (Lord, You know) I was far quieter and entirely removed from the subvertings of those "Subverters" (for this cruel and devilish name was their badge of sophistication) among whom I lived, with a shameless shame that I was not like them. With them I went about and sometimes I enjoyed their friendship, although I always hated their actions — that is, their "subvertings," when they wantonly persecuted the modesty of freshmen whom they disturbed by mocking and jeering for no reason whatever, feeding thereby their own malicious mirth. Nothing can be more like the behavior of devils than this. They were rightly called "subverters," being themselves subverted and perverted by the same deceiving spirits which secretly derided and seduced them when they amused themselves by jeering and deceiving others.

Among such companions, in that unsettled age of mine, I studied books of eloquence, wherein I desired to be eminent for a damnable and vainglorious end — joy in human vanity. In the normal course of study I fell upon a certain book by Cicero, whose style almost all admire, though not his heart. This book of his contains an exhortation to philosophy, and is called *Hortensius*. But this book altered my mind; it turned my prayers to You, O Lord, and gave me other purposes and desires. Every vain hope suddenly became worthless to me; I longed with an incredibly burning desire for an immortality of wisdom, and I began now to rise, so that I might return to You. For not to sharpen my tongue (which was the goal of the education I was purchasing with my mother's allowances, in my nineteenth year, my father having died two years before), not to sharpen my tongue did I use that book; what moved me was not its style, but its content.

How did I burn then, my God, how did I burn to fly from earthly things to You. But I did not know what You would do with me; for with You is wisdom. But the love of wisdom is in Greek called "philosophy," and it was with wisdom that that book inflamed me. . . . And since at that time (You, O light of my heart, know this) Apostolic Scripture was not known to me, the one thing that delighted me in Cicero's exhortation was that I was greatly aroused, kindled, and inflamed to love, seek, obtain, hold, and embrace not this sect but wisdom itself, whatever it might be. And this alone checked my ardent desire, that the name of Christ was not there. For this name, O Lord, this name of my Savior, Your Son, had my tender heart, even with my mother's milk, devoutly drunk in and deeply treasured; and whatsoever was without that name, however learned, polished, or true, could not hold me entirely.

"THE HOLY SCRIPTURES SEEMED TO ME UNWORTHY"

I resolved then to direct my attention to the Holy Scriptures, that I might see what they were like. And what I saw was something not understood by the proud nor laid open to children; and I was not one who could enter into it, or stoop my neck to follow its path. For not as I now write did I feel when I first turned to those Scriptures; they seemed to me unworthy to be compared to the stateliness of Cicero. My swelling pride shunned their style, nor could my sharp wit pierce their depths. Yet they were such as would grow up with a little child; but I disdained to be a little child, and, swollen with pride, took myself to be grown-up.

THE MANICHAEANS: "FOOLISH DECEIVERS"

Therefore I fell among men who were proudly raving, exceedingly carnal and wordy, in whose mouths were the snares of the Devil, smeared with a mixture of the syllables of Your name and of our Lord Jesus Christ and of the Holy Ghost, the Paraclete, our Comforter. These names were always in their mouths, but only as sounds and the noise of the tongue, for their hearts were void of truth. Yet they cried out "Truth, Truth" and spoke much thereof to me, yet the truth was not in them. . . . Yet because I thought them to be You, I fed upon them; not eagerly, for You did not in them taste to me as You are; for You are not these empty falsehoods, nor was I nourished by them, but exhausted rather. . . .

For that which really is, I knew not; and I was through my sharpness of wit persuaded to assent to foolish deceivers when they asked me, "What is the origin of evil?" "Is God bounded by a bodily shape and has he hair and nails?" "Are those [patriarchs of the Old Testament] to be esteemed righteous who had many wives at the same time and killed men and sacrificed living creatures?" At which I, in my ignorance, was much troubled and, while departing from the truth, seemed to myself to be drawing towards it. This was because as yet I did not know that evil is nothing but an absence of good. . . . I did not even know that God is a spirit, having no parts extended in length and breadth. . . .

"THOSE IMPOSTERS CALLED ASTROLOGERS"

Thus I did not hesitate to consult those imposters called astrologers, because they offered no sacrifices and prayed to no spirit to assist their divinations. Yet true Christian piety necessarily rejects and condemns their art. For *it is a good thing to confess unto Thee*, and to say, *Have mercy upon me, heal my soul, for I have sinned against Thee*, and not to misuse Your mercy as a license, but to remember the Lord's words, *Behold, thou art made whole, sin no more, lest a worse thing happen to thee.* All this wholesome truth the astrologers strive to destroy, saying: "The cause of your sin is inevitably determined in the heavens" and "This did Venus do, or Saturn or Mars." As though man, who is flesh and blood and proud corruption, should be blameless, while the Creator and Ruler of heaven and the stars is to bear the blame. And who is He but our God? ...

The governor of the province in those days was a wise man, skillful and renowned in medicine. ... When I told him that I was much given to reading the books of the horoscope-casters, he kindly and in a fatherly way advised me to throw them away and not to waste on such nonsense care and attention that could be put to better use. ... When I asked him why it was that many things were foretold by astrology, he reasoned that it was due to the force of chance, which is diffused throughout the whole order of things. Thus while haphazardly paging through a book of poetry, one often comes upon a line which is wondrously appropriate to some matter on one's mind, though the poet was singing and thinking of something quite different. So, he said, it is not to be wondered at if a man's mind should unconsciously by some instinct, and by chance rather than by art, produce an answer that would seem to correspond with the affairs and actions of the inquirer. ...

SKEPTICISM: "MEN OUGHT TO DOUBT EVERYTHING"

At Rome I again associated with those false and deceiving "holy ones" [Manichaeans], not only with the "hearers" (one of whom was the man in whose house I had fallen sick and recovered), but also with those whom they call "the elect." For I still held the belief that it is not we who sin but some other nature sinning in us; it gratified my pride to think myself free of blame when I had done anything evil. ... However, I now despaired of finding any profit in that false doctrine, and I began to hold laxly and carelessly even those ideas with which I had decided to rest content if I could find nothing better.

The thought occurred to me that those philosophers whom they call Academics were wiser than the rest because they held that men ought to doubt everything and had concluded that no truth can be comprehended by man [see p. 343]. For so I was clearly convinced that they thought (as is commonly believed), though I did not yet understand their real meaning. And I did openly discourage my host from that overconfidence which I perceived him to have in those fables of which the books of Manes are full. Yet I lived on more friendly terms with them than with others who were not of this heresy. I no longer defended it with my former eagerness; still my friendship with that sect (Rome secretly harboring many of them) made me slower to seek any other belief, especially since I despaired of finding the truth in Your Church, O Lord of heaven and earth, Creator of all things visible and invisible. For they had turned me against it, and it seemed to me degrading to believe that You had the shape of human flesh and were bounded by the bodily outlines of our limbs. . . .

AMBROSE

To Milan I came, to Ambrose the bishop, known to the whole world as among the best of men, Your devout servant whose eloquence did then plentifully dispense to *Thy people the fatness of Thy wheat, the gladness of Thy oil and the sober intoxication of Thy wine.* To him was I unknowingly led by You, that I might knowingly be led to You by him. That man of God received me as a father, and as bishop welcomed my coming. I began to love him, at first indeed not as a teacher of the truth (which I utterly despaired of finding in Your Church), but as a person who was kind to me. I listened diligently to him preaching to the people, not with the right intent but, as it were, judging his eloquence, whether it was equal to his fame or flowed higher or lower than was reported. So I hung intently on his words, but of what he said I was a careless and scornful onlooker. I was delighted with the charm of his discourse; it was more learned, yet less winning and harmonious than that of Faustus. Of the actual matter, however, there was no comparison; Faustus was merely wandering amid Manichaean delusions, while Ambrose was soundly teaching salvation. But salvation is far from sinners such as I then was. Yet I was drawing nearer little by little, though unconsciously.

For though I took no pains to learn what he said but only to hear how he said it, . . . yet together with the words which I liked came also into my mind the subject matter to which I was indifferent, for I could not separate them. And while I opened my heart to admit how eloquently he spoke, it also occurred to me gradually how truly he spoke. The things he said now began to appear to me capable of being defended. The Catholic faith, for which I had thought nothing could be said against the Manichaean objections, I now thought might be maintained on sound grounds — especially after I had heard one or two passages of the Old Testament explained figuratively, which, when I had taken them literally, I was slain spiritually. Many passages then of those books having been explained in a spiritual sense, I now blamed my conceit for having believed that no answer could be given to those who hated and scoffed at the Law and the Prophets. Yet I did not then feel that the Catholic way was to be followed merely because it also could find learned maintainers who could at length and with some show of reason answer objections, nor that the faith which I held was to be condemned because both faiths could be defended. Thus the Catholic cause seemed to me not vanquished, nor not as yet victorious.

Then I earnestly bent my mind to see if in any way I could by any certain proof convict the Manichaeans of falsehood. Could I only have been able to conceive of a spiritual substance, all their strongholds would have collapsed and been cast out of my mind. But I could not. However, concerning the body of this world and the whole of nature which our senses can reach to, as I more and more considered and compared things, I judged the views of most of the philosophers to be much more probable. So then after the supposed manner of the Academics, doubting everything and wavering between all, I decided that I must leave the Manichaeans. I judged that, while in a state of doubt, I could not continue in that sect to which I now preferred some of the philosophers. These philosophers, however, because they were without the saving name of Christ, I utterly refused to commit the cure of my sick soul. I determined therefore to be a catechumen in the Catholic Church, which my parents had encouraged me to join, until something certain should dawn upon me by which I might steer my course. . . .

"SOME BOOKS OF THE PLATONISTS"

By means of a man puffed up with the most exaggerated pride, You brought to my attention some books of the Platonists translated from Greek into Latin. And therein I read, not of course in the same words but to the very same effect and supported by many sorts of reasons, that *In the beginning was the Word, and the Word was with God, and the Word was God: the same was in the beginning with God. All things were made by Him, and without Him was nothing made: that which was made by Him is life, and the life was the light of men, and the light shineth in the darkness, and the darkness comprehended it not.* And that the soul of man, though it *bears witness to the light,* yet itself *is not that light;* but the Word of God, being God, *is that true light that lighteth every man that cometh into the world.* Also that *He was in the world, and the world was made by Him, and the world knew Him not.* But I did not read there that *He came unto His own, and His own received Him not; but as many as received Him, to them gave He power to become the sons of God, as many as believed in His name.*

I also read there that *God the Word was born not of flesh, nor of blood, nor of the will of man, nor of the will of the flesh, but of God.* But I did not find there that *the Word was made flesh, and dwelt among us.* . . .

And You have called the Gentiles into Your inheritance. I myself had come to You from the Gentiles, and I set my mind upon the gold which You willed Your people to take from Egypt, since it was Yours, wherever it was. And to the Athenians You said by Your Apostle, that in You we live, move, and have our being, as one of their own poets had said. And certainly these books came from Athens. . . .

Having then read those books of the Platonists, which taught me to search for incorporeal truth, I came to see Your *invisible things, understood by those things which are made.* And though I fell back from this point, I still perceived what that was which, through the darkness of my mind, I was unable to contemplate; I was certain that You are and that You are infinite, yet not being diffused in space whether finite or infinite: that You truly are and are ever the same, in no part or motion varying; and that all other things are from You, as is proved by the sure fact that they exist. . . . I believe it was Your will that I should come upon these books before I studied Your Scriptures, that it might be imprinted on my memory how I was affected by them; and that afterwards when my spirits were tamed through Your books, and my wounds dressed by Your healing fingers, I might be able to distinguish between presumption and confession, between those who see the goal but not the way — the way that leads us not only to see but to dwell in the country of blessedness. . . .

CHRISTIANS ARE MADE, NOT BORN

Good God! what takes place in man that he should more rejoice at the salvation of a soul despaired of or freed from a great peril, than if there had always been hope or the peril had been less? . . .

What is it in the soul, then, which makes it more delighted at finding or recovering the things it loves than if it had always had them? Indeed, other creatures bear the same witness; everywhere all things cry out, "So it is." The conquering general has his triumph; yet he would not have conquered if he had not fought; and the more peril there was in the battle, the more joy there is in the triumph. The storm tosses the sailors and threatens shipwreck; all are pale at the approach of death; then the sky and sea are calmed, and they are as exceedingly joyful as they had been fearful. A friend is sick and his pulse threatens danger; all who long for his recovery are sick in mind with him. He recovers, though as yet he walks not with his former strength; yet there is more joy than there was before when he walked sound and strong. Even the ordinary pleasures of human life men acquire through pain, not only those pains which fall upon us unlooked for and against our will, but also self-chosen and pleasure-seeking pain. Eating and drinking give no pleasure unless they are preceded by the pains of hunger and thirst. Drunkards eat certain salty things to procure an uncomfortable dryness which drink alleviates, thus causing pleasure. It is also customary that the engaged girl should not at once give herself, lest the husband later should hold her cheap whom, as betrothed, he no longer sighed after. . . .

Do not many, out of a deeper hell of blindness . . . , come back to You and are enlightened by that light which *they who receive, receive power from Thee to become Thy sons?*" . . .

ANTONY THE EGYPTIAN MONK

One day there came to see Alypius and me a certain Ponticianus, our countryman, an African holding high office in the emperor's court. What he wanted of us I did not know, but we sat down to converse. It chanced that he noticed a book on a gaming table beside us. He took it, opened it, and contrary to his expectation — he thought it would be one of those books which I was wearying myself in teaching — found that it was the Apostle Paul. Smiling and looking at me, he expressed his joy and wonder that he had come suddenly upon this book, and only this book, beside me. For he was a Christian, and baptized. He often bowed himself before You, our God, in Church, in long and frequent prayers. When I then told him that I gave great attention to these works of Scripture, a conversation began, suggested by him, about Antony the Egyptian monk, whose name was very well known among Your servants, though up to that hour unknown to Alypius and me. When he discovered this he talked all the more about him, informing us and wondering at our ignorance of one so eminent. And we were amazed to hear of Your wonderful works so fully attested in times so recent — almost in our own time — and done in the true

Faith and Catholic Church. All three of us were filled with wonder; we because the deeds were so great, and he because they had not reached us.

He spoke next of the flocks of men in the monasteries, of their holy ways full of the sweet fragrance of You, and of the fruitul deserts in the wilderness, about which we knew nothing. There was actually a monastery at Milan outside the walls, full of good brothers under the care of Ambrose, and we knew nothing of it. He went on speaking, and we listened in intense silence. He told us how one afternoon at Triers, when the emperor was at the chariot races in the Circus, he and three companions went for a walk in the gardens near the city walls. They happened to walk in pairs, one of the three going with him and the other two wandering off by themselves. As the latter two strolled along, they came upon a cottage inhabited by some of Your servants, *poor in spirit, of whom is the kingdom of heaven,* and there they found a little book containing the life of Antony. This one of them began to read. He became full of wonder and excitement, and as he read on he began to think of taking up such a life, giving up his secular service to serve You. For these two men were state officials called "agents for public affairs." Then, suddenly filled with a holy love and a sober shame, in anger with himself he turned to his friend and said: "Tell me now, what do we expect to attain by all these labors of ours? What do we aim at? Why do we serve the state? Can our hopes at court rise higher than to be the emperor's favorites? And is that not a difficult position to hold, and full of dangers? And how many dangers must we survive before we reach a position that is even more dangerous? And how long before we arrive there? But a friend of God, if I wish it, I can become now at once." So he spoke. And in pain with the birth of a new life, he turned his eyes again upon the book. He read on and was changed inwardly, where You alone could see; and his mind, it soon appeared, threw off the burden of the world. For as he read and the waves of his heart rolled up and down, he stormed at himself awhile, then saw the better course and chose it for his own. Being now Yours, he said to his friend, "Now I have broken loose from those hopes we had and have decided to serve God; and I begin this service at this moment, in this place. If you do not wish to imitate me, at least do not oppose me." The other answered that he would stay with him and be his comrade in so glorious a service and for so glorious a reward. . . . This was the story Ponticianus told us. . . .

"SICK AT HEART AND TORMENTED"

Then in this great tumult of my inner dwelling, which I had stirred up against my soul in the chamber of my heart, troubled in mind and countenance, I turned toward Alypius. "What ails us?" I exclaimed. "What is this that you have just heard? The unlearned rise up and take heaven by force, and we with all our learning wallow in flesh and blood! Are we ashamed to follow because others have gone before us? And do we feel no shame at not following?" Some such words I uttered, and then my feverish mind tore me away from him while he stared silently at me in astonishment. For it was not my usual voice; my forehead, cheeks, eyes, color, and tone of voice spoke my mind more than the words I uttered.

There was a garden next to our lodging, and we used it as well as the whole house; for the owner of the house, our landlord, did not live there. The tumult in my breast drove me into this garden, for there no one could intervene in this ardent suit I had brought against myself until it should end as You knew, but I did not. But there I was, going mad in order to become sane, dying in order to have life, knowing how evil I was, not knowing how good I was soon to become. I retired then into the garden, Alypius following my steps. . . .

Thus was I sick at heart and tormented, accusing myself much more bitterly than ever, rolling and turning in my chain till I could break free. I was held only slightly, but I was still held. . . . I kept saying within myself, "Let it be done now, let it be done now!" and as I spoke the words I began to do it. I almost made it, but not quite. . . .

Those toys and trifles and vanities of vanities, my old mistresses, held me back. They pulled at my garment of flesh and whispered softly: "Are you casting us off?" and "From this moment shall we be no more with you forever?" and "From this moment shall you not be allowed to do this or that forever?" . . . What defilements did they suggest! What shame! And now I only half heard them; they no longer openly showed themselves to contradict me, but they were muttering behind my back and stealthily pulling on me, as I departed, to make me look back at them. Yet they did retard me, so that I hesitated to tear myself free from them and leap in the direction I was called; and the strong force of habit kept saying to me, "Do you think you can live without them?" . . .

"ALL THE DARKNESS OF DOUBT VANISHED AWAY"

But when my searching thought had from the secret depths of my soul drawn up all my misery and heaped it in the sight of my heart, a mighty storm rose up within me, bringing a mighty shower of tears. I stood up and left Alypius so that I might weep and cry to my heart's content, solitude seeming more suited for the business of weeping. I moved away far enough so that his presence would not embarrass me. . . . Somehow I flung myself down under a fig tree and gave way to my tears. . . . And in my misery I kept crying, "How long shall I go on saying 'tomorrow, tomorrow'? Why not now? Why not make an end of my ugly sins at this moment?"

Such things I said, weeping all the while with the most bitter sorrow in my heart. Suddenly I heard the sing-song voice of a child in a nearby house. Whether it was the voice of a boy or a girl I cannot say, but again and again it repeated the refrain, "Take it and read, take it and read." Instantly I looked up, thinking hard whether there was any kind of game in which children chanted such words, but I could not remember ever hearing anything like it before. I checked my tears and stood up, telling myself that this could only be a command from God to open my book of Scripture and read the first passage I should find. For I had heard the story of Antony, and I remembered how he had entered a church during the reading of the Gospel and had taken it as an admonition addressed to him when he heard the words: Go, *sell all that thou hast, and give to the poor, and thou shalt have treasure in heaven, and come* and follow me. And by such an oracle he had been immediately converted to You. Eagerly then I returned to the place where Alypius was sitting, for there I had put down the volume of the Apostle Paul when I arose. I snatched it up, opened it, and in silence read the first passage on which my eyes fell: *Not in rioting and drunkenness, not in chambering and wantonness, not in strife and envying, but put ye on the Lord Jesus Christ, and make not provision for the flesh, to fulfill the lusts thereof.* I had no wish to read more and no need to do so. For instantly, as I came to the end of that sentence, it was as though the light of confidence streamed into my heart, and all the darkness of doubt vanished away.

55

The Persecution of Christians

"Amid the ruins of a falling age, our spirit remains erect." — Bishop Cyprian, 3rd century

Both for its subjects and for later ages the most attractive features of the Roman Empire and the Pax Romana were three: a law that stood above the private interests of individuals (see Selection 44C), a citizenship open to men of all races (see Selection 48A), and religious toleration. This last assertion appears contradicted by Roman persecution of the Christians; yet hindsight supports the conclusion that the clash could have been avoided, that it was the product of mutual misunderstandings which led to fear, hysteria, intransigence, and the use of force. As the Roman state saw it, the Christians failed to satisfy the terms on which toleration could be granted in that they appeared to be subversive of the moral, political, and social order and refused to tolerate other religions. According to Tacitus (Annals XV, 44), as early as 64 A.D., when Nero persecuted the Christians in Rome, a general fear and hatred of Christians existed:

> Nero falsely shifted the guilt [for the great fire at Rome] on those people commonly called "Christians" who were hated for their abominations, and inflicted on them the most exquisite tortures. Christus, from whom the name had its origin, suffered the extreme penalty during the reign of Tiberius at the hands of one of our procurators, Pontius Pilate, and a most mischievous superstition, thus checked for the moment, again broke out not only in Judea, the first source of the evil, but even in Rome, where all things hideous and shameful from every part of the world find their center and become popular. Accordingly, an arrest was made of all who pleaded guilty; then, upon their information, an immense multitude was convicted, not so much of the crime of firing the city, as of being haters of the human race.

Such hostility embittered the Christians and turned them away from the position announced by Jesus ("Render unto Caesar the things which are Caesar's") and Paul ("The powers that be are ordained by God"). But by keeping themselves aloof from pagan society the Christians contributed to the suspicion of subversion and treason.

◆A◆ PLINY, LETTERS

Trajan's enlightened policy

There is no evidence of an official state pronouncement regarding Christianity before the early second century A.D. Persecutions were sporadic and local, being the product of popular hostility and action. They were handled by provincial governors (with the exception of Nero's persecution at Rome), who based their action on the laws against secret societies and the refusal of the Christians to demonstrate their loyalty to the state by the purely political gesture of sacrificing to the emperor. This is referred to in the famous letter written about 112 A.D. by Pliny the Younger, Governor of Bithynia in Asia Minor, to the Emperor Trajan. Pliny asked for more definite instructions with regard to the Christians, and Trajan's reply established an official policy based upon precedents set by earlier governors. This policy, which placed the label of traitor upon convicted Christians but also protected them against both sporadic and systematic persecution, continued until the Empire began to disintegrate in the last half of the third century. Measures to wipe out Christianity as a danger to the unity and security of a troubled state culminated in the Great Persecution (303–311 A.D.) under Diocletian. When this failed, Constantine's proclamation of toleration in 313 A.D. became the established policy.

PLINY TO TRAJAN

It is my custom, my lord, to refer to you all things concerning which I am in doubt. For who can better guide my indecision or enlighten my ignorance?

I have never taken part in the trials of Christians; hence I do not know for what crime or to what extent it is customary to punish or investigate. I have been in no little doubt as to whether any consideration should be given to age, or should the treatment of the young differ from that of the old; whether pardon is granted in case of repentance, or should a man who was once a Christian gain nothing by having ceased to be one; whether the name itself without the proof of crimes, or only the crimes associated with the name, are to be punished.

Meanwhile I have followed this procedure in the case of those who have been brought before me as Christians. I asked them whether they were Christians; those who confessed I questioned a second and a third time, threatening them with punishment; those who persisted I ordered executed. For I did not doubt that, whatever it was that they had confessed, their stubbornness and

X, 96, 97; adapted from *Translations and Reprints from the Original Sources of European History*, Vol. IV, No. 1, eds. D. C. Munro and Edith Bramhall (Philadelphia, 1898.)

inflexible obstinacy ought certainly to be punished. There were others of similar madness; but because they were Roman citizens, I signed an order sending them to Rome.

Soon, the crime spreading, as is usual when attention is called to it, more cases arose. An anonymous accusation, containing many names, was presented. Those who denied that they were or had been Christians, ought, I thought, to be dismissed since they repeated after me a prayer to the gods and made supplication with incense and wine to your image, which I had ordered to be brought for the purpose together with the statues of the gods, and since besides they cursed Christ, not one of which things they say those who are really Christians can be compelled to do. Others, accused by the informer, said that they were Christians and afterwards denied it; in fact, they had been but had ceased to be, some many years ago, some even twenty years before. They all worshipped your image and the statues of the gods, and cursed Christ. They maintained that the substance of their fault or error had been that on a fixed day they were accustomed to come together before daylight and sing by turns a hymn to Christ as though he were a god, and to bind themselves by oath, not for some crime, but not to commit robbery, theft, or adultery, nor to betray a trust or deny a deposit when called upon. After this it was customary to disperse and to come together again to partake of food of an ordinary and harmless kind. Even this they ceased to do after the publication of my edict in which, according to your orders, I had forbidden associations. Hence I believed it the more necessary to examine two female slaves, who were called deaconesses, in order to find out what was true, and to do it by torture. I found nothing but a vicious, extravagant superstition.

Consequently I postponed the examination and hastened to consult you. For it seemed to me that the subject would justify consultation, especially on account of the number of those involved. For many of all ages, of every rank, and even of both sexes are and will be endangered. The infection of this superstition has not only spread to the cities but also to the villages and country districts. But it seems possible to check it and cure it. It is plain enough that the temples, which had been almost deserted, have begun to be frequented again, that the sacred rites, which had been neglected for a long time, have begun to be restored, and that food for sacrifices, for which until now there was scarcely a purchaser, is sold. From this it is easy to imagine what a multitude of people can be reclaimed if repentance is permitted.

TRAJAN TO PLINY

You have followed the correct procedure, my dear Pliny, in conducting the cases of those who were accused before you as Christians, for no general rule can be laid down as a set form. They are not to be sought out; if they are brought before you and convicted, they ought to be punished, with the proviso that whoever denies that he is a Christian and proves it by worshipping our gods, even though he may have been under suspicion in the past, shall obtain pardon on repentance. In no case should attention be paid to anonymous charges, for they afford a bad precedent and are not worthy of our age.

◆ B ◆ TERTULLIAN, APOLOGY

The Christian view of the persecutions

Tertullian, Latin Christianity's first great writer and its outstanding opponent of classical thought (see Selection 54B), wrote an Apology (197 A.D.) for Christianity which is an eloquent defense against attacks by both the hostile provincial governments and the ill-informed populace. Mixing passion with irony, he attacks the illegality of judicial procedures where Christians are involved, castigates the unreasoning hatred shown them, and refutes the numerous charges, from treason to drunkenness, leveled at them. Indeed, "the Apology is one of those works which survive the circumstances which gave them birth and which enter into the common treasury of civilized nations. Nowhere shall we listen to more fervid demands for justice, tolerance, or the rights of an accused man; to more vivid protestations against the tyranny of unjust laws assumed to be irrevocable; lastly, to a more eloquent defense of Christianity [and] of its moral nobility...." [1]

"LET THE TRUTH REACH YOUR EARS"

1. Magistrates of the Roman Empire, seated as you are before the eyes of all, in almost the highest position in the state to pronounce judgment: if you are not to conduct an open and public examination and inquiry as to what the real truth is with regard to the Christians; if, in this case alone your authority fears or blushes to conduct a public investigation with the diligence demanded by justice; if, in fine — as happened lately in the private courts — hatred of this group has been aroused to the extent that it actually blocks their defense, then let the truth reach your ears by the private and quiet avenue of literature.

Truth makes no appeal on her own behalf, because she does not wonder at her present condition. She knows that she plays the role of an alien on earth, that among strangers she readily discovers enemies, but she has her origin, abode, hope, recompense, and honor in heaven. Meanwhile, there is one thing for which she strives: that she be not condemned without a hearing....

This, then, is the first grievance we lodge against you, the injustice of the hatred you have for the name of Christian. The motive which appears to excuse this injustice is precisely that which both aggravates and convicts it; namely, ignorance. For, what is more unjust than that men should hate what they do not know, even though the matter itself deserves hatred? Only when one knows whether a thing deserves hatred does it deserve it. But, when there is no knowledge of what is deserved, how is the justice of hatred defensible? Justice must be proved not by the fact of a thing's existence, but by knowledge of it. When

From Sister Emily Joseph Daly, C. S. J., tr., *Tertullian: Apologetical Works, and Minucius Felix Octavius* (New York: Fathers of the Church, 1950), Vol. X: *The Fathers of the Church,* Reprinted by permission of The Catholic University of America Press.

[1] P. de Labriolle, *History and Literature of Christianity* (New York: Alfred A. Knopf, 1924), p. 70.

men hate because they are in ignorance of the nature of the object of their hatred, what is to prevent that object from being such that they ought not to hate it? Thus we counterbalance each attitude by its opposite: men remain in ignorance as long as they hate, and they hate unjustly as long as they remain in ignorance.

The proof of their ignorance, which condemns while it excuses their injustice, is this: In the case of all who formerly indulged in hatred [of Christianity] because of their ignorance of the nature of what they hated, their hatred comes to an end as soon as their ignorance ceases. From this group come the Christians, as a result, assuredly, of their personal experience. They begin now to hate what once they were and to profess what once they hated; and the Christians are really as numerous as you allege us to be. Men cry that the city is filled with Christians; they are in the country, in the villages, on the islands; men and women, of every age, of every state and rank of life, are transferring to this group, and this they lament as if it were some personal injury. . . .

2. If, then, it is decided that we are the most wicked of men, why do you treat us so differently from those who are on a par with us, that is, from all other criminals? The same treatment ought to be meted out for the same crime. When others are charged with the same crimes as we, they use their own lips and the hired eloquence of others to prove their innocence. There is full liberty given to answer the charge and to cross-question, since it is unlawful for men to be condemned without defense or without a hearing. Christians alone are permitted to say nothing that would clear their name, vindicate the truth, and aid the judge to come to a fair decision. One thing only is what they wait for; this is the only thing necessary to arouse public hatred: the confession of the name of Christian, not an investigation of the charge. Yet, suppose you are trying any other criminal. If he confesses to the crime of murder, sacrilege, incest, or treason — to particularize the indictments hurled against us — you are not satisfied to pass sentence immediately; you weigh the attendant circumstances, the character of the deed, the number of times it was committed, the time, the place, the witnesses, and the partners-in-crime. In our case there is nothing of this sort. No matter what false charge is made against us, we must be made to confess it; for example, how many murdered babies one has devoured, how many deeds of incest one has committed under cover of darkness, what cooks and what dogs were on hand. Oh, what glory for that governor who should have discovered someone who had already consumed a hundred infants!

TRAJAN'S LETTER: "HOW AMBIGUOUS WAS THAT DECISION!"

On the other hand, we find that it has been forbidden to search us out. For when Pliny the Younger was in charge of his province and had condemned certain Christians and had driven others from their established position, he was so disturbed because of the numbers involved that he consulted Trajan, emperor at the time, as to what he should do thereafter. He explained that, except for their obstinate refusal to offer sacrifice, he had learned nothing else about their religious rites except that they met before daybreak to sing to Christ and to God and to bind themselves by oath to a way of life which forbade murder, adultery, dishonesty, treachery, and all other crimes. Trajan wrote back that men of this kind should not be sought out, but, when brought to court, they should be punished.

Oh, how unavoidably ambiguous was that decision! He says that they should not be sought — as though they were innocent; then prescribes that they should be punished — as though they were guilty! He spares them, yet vents his anger upon them; he pretends to close his eyes, yet directs attention toward them! Judgment, why do you thus ensnare yourself? If you condemn them, why not also search for them? If you do not search for them, why not also acquit them? Throughout the provinces troops of soldiers are assigned to track down robbers. Against traitors and public enemies each individual constitutes a soldier: the search is extended even to comrades and accomplices. Only the Christian may not be sought out — but he may be brought to court. As though a search were intended to bring about something else than his appearance in court! So, you condemn a man when he is brought into court, although no one wanted him to be sought out. He has earned punishment, I suppose, not on the ground that he is guilty, but because he was discovered for whom no search had to be made. . . .

"SUCH HATRED OF THE NAME"

3. What should one say of the fact that many shut their eyes and force themselves to such hatred of the name that, even when they speak favorably of someone, they insert some hateful remark about this name? "Caius Seius is a good man, except that he is a Christian." Similarly, someone else says: "I am surprised that Lucius Titius, otherwise a man of sense, has suddenly become a Christian!" No one stops to think whether Caius is good and Lucius sensible because he is a Christian, or is a Christian because he is sensible and good! Men praise what they know and find fault with what they do not know. They contaminate their knowledge with their ignorance, although it would be more correct to form a preconceived idea with regard to what is unknown from what is known than to condemn beforehand what is known because of what is unknown.

Others censure those whom they knew in the past, before they acquired this name, as vagrant, good-for-nothing scoundrels, and they censure them in the very act of praising them. In the blindness of their hatred they stumble into favorable criticism. "That woman! How dissolute and frivolous she was! And that young man, how much more prodigal and debauched he used to be! They have become Christians." Thus, the name which was responsible for their reformation is set down as a charge against them. Some, even, at the expense of their own advantage, bargain with their hatred, satisfied to suffer a personal loss, provided that their home be freed from the object of their hatred. A wife who has become chaste is cast out by her husband now that he is relieved of his jealous suspicions of her. A son, now docile, is disowned by a father who was patient with him in the past. A servant, now trustworthy, is banished from the sight of a master who was formerly indulgent. To the degree that one is reformed under the influence of the name he gives offense. The Christians' goodness is outweighed by the hatred borne them. . . .

4. Now that I have set down these remarks as a preface, as it were, to stigmatize the injustice of the public hatred against us, I shall take the stand to defend our innocence. Not only shall I refute the charges which are brought against us, but I shall even hurl them back upon those who make them, so that men may thereby know that among the Christians those crimes do´ not exist which they are not unaware exist among themselves; and that, at the same time, they may blush when, as utter reprobates, they accuse — I do not say the most righteous of men — but, as they themselves would have it, their equals. We shall reply to each charge individually: to those which we are said to commit in secret, and to those which we are found to be committing before the eyes of all — charges on the basis of which we are held to be criminals, deceivers, reprobates, and objects of ridicule. . . .

7. We are spoken of as utter reprobates and are accused of having sworn to murder babies and to eat them and of committing adulterous acts after the repast. Dogs, you say, the pimps of darkness, overturn candles and procure license for our impious lusts. We are always spoken of in this way, yet you take no pains to bring into the light the charges which for so long a time have been made against us. Now, either bring them into the light, if you believe them, or stop believing them, inasmuch as you have not brought them to light! Because of your hypocrisy, the objection is made against you that the evil does not exist which you yourselves dare not bring to light. Far different is the duty you enjoin upon the executioner against the Christians, not to make them state what they do, but to make them deny what they are.

The origin of this religion, as we have already said, dates from the time of Tiberius. Truth and hatred came into existence simultaneously. As soon as the former appeared, the latter began its enmity. It has as many foes as there are outsiders, particularly among Jews because of their jealousy, among soldiers because of their blackmailing, and even among the very members of our own household because of corrupt human nature. Day by day we are besieged; day by day we are betrayed; oftentimes, in the very midst of our meetings and gatherings, we are surprised by an assault. Who has ever come upon a baby wailing, as the accusation has it? Who has ever kept for the judge's inspection the jaws of Cyclopes and Sirens, bloodstained as he had found them? Who has ever found any traces of impurity upon [Christian] wives? Who has discovered such crimes, yet concealed them or been bribed to keep them secret when dragging these men off to court? If we always keep under cover, whence the betrayal of our crimes?

Rather, who could have been the traitors? Certainly not the accused themselves, since the obligation of pledged silence is binding upon all mysteries by their very nature. The mysteries of Samothrace and of Eleusis are shrouded in silence; how much more such rites as these which, if they were made public, would provoke at once the hatred of all mankind — while God's wrath is reserved for the future? If, then, Christians themselves are not the betrayers, it follows that outsiders ate. Whence do outsiders get their knowledge, since even holy initiation rites always ban the uninitiated and are wary of witnesses? . . .

Rumor, a word designating uncertainty, has no place where there is certainty. But does anyone except the unthinking believe rumor? One who is wise surely does not heed uncertainty. Everyone can reflect that however great the zeal with which the tale has been spread, however strong the assertion with which it was fabricated, it necessarily started at some time or other from one source. Thence it creeps gradually along the grapevine of tongues and ears, and a defect in the tiny seedlings so overshadows the other details of the rumor that no one reflects whether the first mouth sowed the seed of falsehood, as often happens, from a spirit of envy or a suspicious thought or from the pleasure some derive from lying — a pleasure not new-born, but inborn.

It is well that time brings all things to light; as even your own proverbs and sayings testify, in accordance with the design of nature which has so ordained things that nothing remains a secret for long, even though rumor has not spread it abroad. Rightly, then, is rumor alone for so long a time aware of the crimes of Christians; this is the witness you bring forth against us. What it has sometime or other spread abroad and over such an interval of time hardened into a matter of opinion, it has not yet been able to prove, so that I call upon the steadfastness of nature itself against those who assume that such accusations are credible. . . .

"THE CHIEF ACCUSATION AGAINST US"

10. "You do not worship the gods," you say, "and you do not offer sacrifice for the emperors." It follows that we do not offer sacrifices for others for the same reason that we do not do it even for ourselves — it follows immediately from our not worshipping the gods. Consequently, we are considered guilty of sacrilege and treason. This is the chief accusation against us — in fact, it is the whole case — and it certainly deserves investigation, unless presumption and injustice dictate the decision, the one despairing of the truth, the other refusing it.

We cease worshipping your gods when we find out that they are nonexistent. This, then, is what you ought to demand, that we prove that those gods are non-existent and for that reason should not be worshipped, because they ought to be worshipped only if they were actually gods. Then, too, the Christians ought to be punished if the fact were established that those gods do exist whom they will not worship because they consider them nonexistent. "But, for us," you say, "the gods do exist." We object and appeal from you to your conscience. Let this pass judgment on us, let this condemn us, if it can deny that all those gods of yours have been mere men. But, if it should deny this, it will be refuted by its own documents of ancient times from which it has learned of the gods. Testimony is furnished to this very day by the cities in which they were born, and the regions in which they left traces of something they had done and in which it is pointed out that they were buried. . . .

12. ... As for your gods, then, I see in them merely the names of certain men long dead. I hear their stories and recognize the sacred rituals arising from these myths. As for their statues, I find no fault with them, except that the material used in them matches that in common pots and household utensils. Or if you will, they exchange their destiny, as it were, with those same pots and pans by being consecrated. The free hand of art transforms them and treats them thereby with utmost insult, adding sacrilege in the very act of transformation. Actually, for us who are beaten because of these very gods, it could be a particular source of comfort in our punishments that they themselves, in order to become gods, undergo the same harsh treatment as ourselves. ...

28. ... We have come, then, to the second charge alleged against us, that of offending a more august majesty. You pay your obeisance to Caesar with greater fear and craftier timidity than to Olympian Jupiter himself. And rightly so, if you but knew it! For, what living man — whoever he may be — is not more powerful than any of your dead ones? But you do this, not for any logical reason, but out of regard for his manifest and perceptible power. In this point, too, it will be seen that you are lacking in religious feeling towards your gods, since you show more fear to a human lord. Finally, one is more ready among you to take a false oath by all the gods together than by the lone genius of Caesar. ...

"WE PRAY FOR THE WELFARE OF THE EMPERORS"

30. For, in our case, we pray for the welfare of the emperors to the eternal God, the true God, the living God, whom even the emperors themselves prefer to have propitious to them before all other gods. They know who has given them power; they know — for they are men — who has given them life; they feel that He is the only God in whose power alone they are, commencing with whom they are second, after whom they stand first, who is before all and above all gods. ... Looking up to Him, we Christians — with hands extended, because they are harmless, with head bare because we are not ashamed, without a prayer leader because we pray from the heart — constantly beseech Him on behalf of all emperors. We ask for them long life, undisturbed power, security at home, brave armies, a faithful Senate, an upright people, a peaceful world, and everything for which a man or a Caesar prays. ...

31. Well, now, we have been flattering the emperor and have lied about the prayers we said just to escape rough treatment! That ingenious idea of yours is certainly of advantage to us, for you permit us to prove whatever we allege in our defense. If you think that we have no interest in the emperor's welfare, look into our literature, the Word of God. We ourselves do not keep it concealed; in fact, many a chance hands it over to outsiders. Learn from this literature that it has been enjoined upon us, that our charity may more and more abound, to pray to God even for our enemies, and to beg for blessings for our persecutors. Now, who are any greater enemies and persecutors of Christians than those on whose account we are charged with the crime of treason? But it is clearly and expressly said: "Pray for kings, for princes and for rulers, that all may be peaceful for you!" For, when the empire is shaken, and its other mem-

bers are shaken, we, too, although we are considered outsiders by the crowd, are naturally involved in some part of the disaster.

32. There is also another, even greater, obligation for us to pray for the emperors; yes, even for the continuance of the empire in general and for Roman interests. We realize that the tremendous force which is hanging over the whole world, and the very end of the world with its threat of dreadful afflictions, is arrested for a time by the continued existence of the Roman Empire. This event we have no desire to experience, and, in praying that it may be deferred, we favor the continuance of Rome. . . .

"POLITICS AND PUBLIC SHOWS"

38. Accordingly, ought not this religion to be regarded with somewhat milder judgment among those societies which cannot legally exist? Its members commit no such crimes as are regularly feared from illegal associations. For, unless I am mistaken, the motive for prohibiting associations rests on the prudent care of public order, lest the state be split into parties, a situation which would easily disturb voting assemblies, council meetings, the Senate, mass meetings, and even public entertainments by the clash of rival interests, since by now men have even begun to make a business of their violence, offering it for sale at a price. But, for us who are indifferent to all burning desire for fame and honor, there is no need of banding together. There is nothing more unfamiliar to us than politics. There is only one state for all which we acknowledge — the universe.

Likewise, we renounce your public shows just as we do their origins which we know were begotten of superstition, while we are completely aloof from those matters with which they are concerned. Our tongues, our eyes, our ears have nothing to do with the madness of the circus, the shamelessness of the theater, the brutality of the arena, the vanity of the gymnasium. How, then, do we offend you? If we prefer different pleasures, if, in fine, we do not want to be amused, that is our loss — if loss there be — not yours. . . .

"THE PRACTICES OF THE CHRISTIAN CHURCH"

39. Now I myself will explain the practices of the Christian Church, that is, after having refuted the charges that they are evil, I myself will also point out that they are good. We form one body because of our religious convictions, and because of the divine origin of our way of life and the bond of common hope. We come together for a meeting and a congregation, in order to besiege God with prayers, like an army in battle formation. Such violence is pleasing to God. We pray, also, for the emperors, for their ministers and those in power, that their reign may continue, that the state may be in peace, and that the end of the world may be postponed. We assemble for the consideration of the Holy Scriptures, [to see] if the circumstances of the present times demand that we look ahead or reflect. Certainly, we nourish our faith with holy conversation, we uplift our hope, we strengthen our trust, intensifying our discipline at the same time by the inculcation of moral precepts. At the same occasion, there are words of encouragement, of correction, and holy censure. Then, too, judg-

ment is passed which is very impressive, as it is before men who are certain of the presence of God, and it is a deeply affecting foretaste of the future judgment, if anyone has so sinned that he is dismissed from sharing a common prayer, assembly, and all holy intercourse. Certain approved elders preside, men who have obtained this honor not by money, but by the evidence of good character. For, nothing that pertains to God is to be had for money.

Even if there is some kind of treasury, it is not accumulated from a high initiation fee as if the religion were something bought and paid for. Each man deposits a small amount on a certain day of the month or whenever he wishes, and only on condition that he is willing and able to do so. No one is forced; each makes his contribution voluntarily. These are, so to speak, the deposits of piety. The money therefrom is spent not for banquets or drinking parties or good-for-nothing eating houses, but for the support and burial of the poor, for children who are without their parents and means of subsistence, for aged men who are confined to the house; likewise, for shipwrecked sailors, and for any in the mines, on islands or in prisons. Provided only it be for the sake of fellowship with God, they become entitled to loving and protective care for their confession. The practice of such a special love brands us in the eyes of some. "See," they say, "how they love one another" (for they hate one another), "and how ready they are to die for each other." (They themselves would be more ready to kill each other.)

Over the fact that we call ourselves brothers, they fall into a rage — for no other reason, I suppose, than because among them every term of kinship is only a hypocritical pretense of affection. But, we are your brothers, too, according to the law of nature, our common mother, although you are hardly men since you are evil brothers. But, with how much more right are they called brothers and considered such who have acknowledged one father, God, who have drunk one spirit of holiness, who in fear and wonder have come forth from the one womb of their common ignorance to the one light of truth! Perhaps this is why we are considered less legitimate brothers, because no tragic drama has our brotherhood as its theme, or because we are brothers who use the same family substance which, among you, as a rule, destroys brotherhood.

So, we who are united in mind and soul have no hesitation about sharing what we have. Everything is in common among us — except our wives. . . .

Why wonder, then, if such dear friends take their meals together? You attack our modest repasts — apart from saying that they are disgraced by crimes — as being extravagant. . . .

Our repast, by its very name, indicates its purpose. It is called by a name which to the Greeks means "love." Whatever it costs, it is gain to incur expense in the name of piety, since by this refreshment we comfort the needy, not as, among you, parasites contend for the glory of reducing their liberty to slavery for the price of filling their belly amidst insults, but as, before God, greater consideration is given to those of lower station. If the motive of our repast is honorable, then on the basis of that motive appraise the entire procedure of our discipline. What concerns the duty of religion tolerates no vulgarity, no immorality. No one sits down to table without first partaking of a prayer to God. They eat as much as those who are hungry take; they drink as much as temperate people need. They satisfy themselves as men who remember that they must worship God even throughout the night; they converse as men who know that the Lord is listening. After this, the hands are washed and lamps are lit, and each one, according to his ability to do so, reads the Holy Scriptures or is invited into the center to sing a hymn to God. This is the test of how much he has drunk. Similarly, prayer puts an end to the meal. From here they depart, not to unite in bands for murder, or to run around in gangs, or for stealthy attacks of lewdness, but to observe the same regard for modesty and chastity as people do who have partaken not only of a repast but of a rule of life.

Such is the gathering of Christians. There is no question about it — it deserves to be called illegal, provided it is like those which are illegal; it deserves to be condemned, if any complaint is lodged against it on the same ground that complaints are made about other secret societies. But, for whose destruction have we ever held a meeting? We are the same when assembled as when separate; we are collectively the same as we are individually, doing no one any injury, causing no one any harm. When men who are upright and good assemble, when the pious and virtuous gather together, the meeting should be called not a secret society but a senate.

40. On the other hand, those men deserve the name of a secret society who band together in hatred of good and virtuous men, who cry out for the blood of the innocent, at the same time offering as a justification of their hatred the idle plea that they consider that the Christians are the cause of every public calamity and every misfortune of the people. If the Tiber rises as high as the city walls, if the Nile does not rise to the fields, if the weather will not change, if there is an earthquake, a famine, a plague — straightway the cry is heard: "Toss the Christians to the lion!" So many of them for just one beast?

56

The Reforms of Diocletian

"By whose virtue and foreseeing care
all is being reshaped for the better"

As we have seen, Augustus hoped that his settlement of Roman affairs would be permanent. It lasted for some two hundred years before collapsing in the third century and was perhaps as permanent as purely human institutions can ever hope to be. In 284 A.D. Diocletian was thus faced by the necessity of reconstructing the Roman state. His reforms — the embodiment of tendencies already evident — were more extreme than those of Augustus, no doubt because the decline had been far greater, and he substituted a regime of oriental despotism for the constitutional monarchy of the Principate. This late Roman Empire was relatively as totalitarian as some twentieth-century dictatorships; the state imposed a pattern of regimentation on all aspects of life, including religion — hence Diocletian's ruthless persecution of Christianity. The verdict of Aurelius Victor (late fourth century A.D.) indicates, however, that although Diocletian's rule was strong, it was not harsh: "Diocletian's faults were counterbalanced by good qualities; for even if he took the title of 'lord' (dominus), he did act [toward the Romans] as a father." His system of bureaucratic controls, completed by Constantine, remained characteristic of the succeeding thousand-year history of the East Roman (or Byzantine) Empire and was undoubtedly a major factor in its longevity.

◆ A ◆ ADMINISTRATIVE REORGANIZATION

"This man overturned the Roman Empire."

The essence of Diocletian's cure for the chronic ills of the third-century Roman world can be simply put — more government. Since the problems of empire had proved too great for one man, the Empire was divided into four parts, each under an emperor (the Tetrarchy). The provinces were reduced in size and more than doubled in number. The 120 provincial governors were supervised by twelve vicars, whose unit of administration was called a diocese. The vicars in turn were controlled by four prefects who served directly under the four emperors. Civil and military functions were separated, and a different hierarchy of officials exercised military authority within these numerous administrative units. Secret agents, called "agents for public affairs," kept watch over the efficiency of the entire administration. To support this enormous bureaucratic machine, citizens were burdened with new and higher taxes and strict economic controls.

Did Diocletian's reforms stabilize the Empire or contribute further to its decline? The latter view was held by Diocletian's contemporary, the Christian polemicist Lactantius, whose account of the reforms is given below. It is taken from On the Deaths of the Persecutors, which Lactantius wrote so "that all who are afar off, and all who shall arise hereafter, may learn how the Almighty manifested His power and sovereign greatness in rooting out and utterly destroying the enemies of His name."

From Lactantius, *On the Deaths of the Persecutors*, Ch. 7, based on the translation by William Fletcher in *The Ante-Nicene Fathers* (Buffalo, New York, 1886), Vol. VII.

While Diocletian, that author of ill, and deviser of misery, was ruining all things, he could not withhold his insults even against God. This man, by avarice partly, and partly by timid counsels, overturned the Roman empire: for he made choice of three persons to share the government with him; and thus, the empire having been quartered, armies were multiplied, and each of the four princes strove to maintain a much more considerable military force than any sole emperor had done in times past. There began to be fewer men who paid taxes than there were who received wages [from the state]; so that the means of husbandmen being exhausted by enormous assessments, farms were abandoned, cultivated grounds became wilderness, and universal dismay prevailed. Besides, the provinces were divided into minute portions, and many governors and a multitude of inferior officers lay heavy on each territory, and almost on each city. There were also many procurators of different degrees, and deputies of prefects. Very few civil cases came before them: but there were condemnations daily, and forfeitures frequently inflicted; taxes on numberless commodities, and those not only often repeated, but perpetual, and, in exacting them, intolerable wrongs.

Whatever was laid on for the maintenance of the soldiery might have been endured; but Diocletian, through his insatiable avarice, would never allow the sums of money in his treasury to be diminished; he was constantly heaping together extraordinary aids and free gifts, that his original hoards might remain untouched and inviolable. He also, when by various extortions he had made all things exceedingly dear, attempted by an ordinance to limit their prices. Then much blood was shed for the veriest trifles; men were afraid to expose aught to sale, and the scarcity became more excessive and grievous than ever, until, in the end, the ordinance, after having proved destructive to multitudes, was from mere necessity abrogated. To this there were added a certain endless passion for building, and, on that account, endless exactions from the provinces for furnishing wages to laborers and artificers, and supplying carriages and whatever else was requisite to the works which he projected. Here public halls, there a circus, here a mint, and there a shop for making implements of war; in one place a house for his empress, and in another for his daughter. Presently a great part of the city [Nicomedia, Diocletian's capital] was quitted, and all men removed with their wives and children, as from a town taken by enemies; and when those buildings were completed to the destruction of whole provinces, he said, "They are not right, let them be done on another plan." Then they were to be pulled down, or altered, to undergo perhaps a future demolition. By such folly was he continually endeavoring to equal Nicomedia with the city Rome in magnificence.

I omit mentioning how many perished on account of their possessions or wealth; for such evils were exceedingly frequent, and through their frequency appeared almost lawful. But this was peculiar to him, that whenever he saw a field remarkably well cultivated, or a house of uncommon elegance, a false accusation and capital punishment were straightway prepared against the proprietor; so that it seemed as if Diocletian could not be guilty of rapine without also shedding blood.

◆ B ◆ EDICT OF PRICES

The controlled economy of the late Roman empire

The collapse of the Roman economy in the third century called for drastic action. In 301 A.D. Diocletian issued an edict of prices which sought to stabilize the economy by fixing a scale of maximum prices and salaries ranging from "peas, not split" to haircuts. Despite the death penalty for violators, the edict apparently proved unworkable and was rescinded, a fact sometimes cited by those today who are opposed to similar economic controls.

In the following preamble to his edict, Diocletian describes the evils he sought to remedy and the social philosophy which inspired his actions. It serves well to illustrate the paternalistic character of the late Roman Empire, and it helps us to understand why a contemporary North African inscription should honor Diocletian as one "by whose virtue and foreseeing care all is being reshaped for the better."

That the fortune of our state — to which, after the immortal gods, as we recall the wars which we have successfully fought, we must be grateful for a world that is tranquil and reclining in the embrace of the most profound calm, and for the blessings of a peace that was won with great effort — be faithfully disposed and suitably adorned, is the demand of public opinion and the dignity and majesty of Rome; therefore, we, who by the gracious favor of the gods have repressed the former tide of ravages of barbarian nations by destroying them, must guard by the due defences of justice a peace which was established for eternity. If, indeed, any self-restraint might check the excesses with which limitless and furious avarice rages — avarice which with no thought for mankind hastens to its own gain and increase, not by years or months or days but by hours and even minutes — or, if the general welfare could endure undisturbed the riotous license by which it, in its misfortune, is from day to day most grievously injured, there would perhaps be left some room for dissimulation and silence, since human forbearance might alleviate the detestable cruelty of a pitiable situation. Since, however, it is the sole desire of unrestrained madness to have no thought for the common need and since it is considered among the unscrupulous and immoderate almost the creed of avarice, swelling and rising with fiery passions, to desist from ravaging the wealth of all through necessity rather than its own wish; and since those whom extremes of need have brought to an appreciation of their most unfortunate situation can no longer close their eyes to it, we — the protectors of the human race — viewing the situation, have agreed that justice should intervene as arbiter, so that the long-hoped-for solution which mankind itself could not supply might, by the remedies of our foresight, be applied to the general betterment of all. . . .

Reprinted by permission of the publishers from the translation by E. R. Graser in Tenney Frank ed., *An Economic Survey of Ancient Rome*, 6 vols. (Baltimore, 1940), V, pp. 311–317. Copyright 1940, The Johns Hopkins Press.

We, therefore, hasten to apply the remedies long demanded by the situation, satisfied that there can be no complaints that the intervention of our remedy may be untimely or unnecessary, or trivial or unimportant among the unscrupulous who, in spite of perceiving in our silence of so many years a lesson in restraint, have been unwilling to copy it. For who is so insensitive and so devoid of human feeling that he cannot know, or rather, has not perceived, that in the commerce carried on in the markets or involved in the daily life of cities immoderate prices are so widespread that the uncurbed passion for gain is lessened neither by abundant supplies nor by fruitful years. . . . Who, therefore, does not know that insolence, covertly attacking the public welfare — wherever the public safety demands that our armies be directed, not in villages or towns only, but on every road — comes to the mind of the profiteer to extort prices for merchandise, not fourfold or eightfold, but such that human speech is incapable of describing either the price or the act; and finally that sometimes in a single purchase a soldier is deprived of his bonus and salary, and that the contribution of the whole world to support the armies falls to the abominable profits of thieves, so that our soldiers seem with their own hands to offer the hopes of their service and their completed labors to the profiteers, with the result that the pillagers of the nation constantly seize more than they know how to hold.

Aroused justly and rightfully by all the facts which are detailed above, and with mankind itself now appearing to be praying for release, we have decreed that there be established, not the prices of articles for sale — for such an act would be unjust when many provinces occasionally rejoice in the good fortune of wished-for low prices and, so to speak, the privilege of prosperity — but a maximum, so that when the violence of high prices appears anywhere — may the gods avert such a calamity! — avarice which, as if in immense open areas, could not be restrained, might be checked by the limits of our statute or by the boundaries of a regulatory law. It is our pleasure, therefore, that the prices listed in the subjoined summary be observed in the whole of our empire in such fashion that every man may know that while permission to exceed them has been forbidden him, the blessing of low prices has in no case been restricted in those places where supplies are seen to abound, since special provision is made for these when avarice is definitely quieted. . . .

Since, therefore, it is agreed that even in the time of our ancestors it was customary in passing laws to restrain insolence by attaching a prescribed penalty — since it is indeed rare for a situation tending to the good of humanity to be embraced spontaneously, and since, as a guide, fear is always found the most influential preceptor in the performance of duty — it is our pleasure that anyone who shall have resisted the form of this statute shall for his daring be subject to a capital penalty. And let no one consider the penalty harsh since there is at hand a means of avoiding the danger by the observance of moderation. To the same penalty, moreover, is he subject who in the desire to buy shall have conspired against the statute with the greed of the seller. Nor is he exempt from the same penalty who, although possessing necessities of life and business, believes that subsequent to this regulation he must withdraw them from the general market, since a penalty should be even more severe for him who introduces poverty than for him who harasses it against the law. We, therefore, urge upon the loyalty of all our people that a law constituted for the public good may be observed with willing obedience and due care; especially since in such a statute provision has been made, not for single states and peoples and provinces, but for the whole world, to whose ruin very few are known to have raged excessively, whose avarice neither fullness of time nor the riches for which they strive could lessen or satisfy.

—————— *57* ——————

Tacitus, Germania

The early Germans

When Tacitus wrote his essay "On the Origins, Geography, and Customs of the Germans" (usually called the *Germania*) in 98 A.D., the Germans had become something of a problem to the Romans. The Emperior Trajan was encamped along the Rhine frontier, and there was some talk that he might revive Augustus' ill-fated plan to conquer Germany, which had ended ingloriously in 9 A.D., when three legions were ambushed and destroyed by a German chieftain named Hermann (Arminius). Tacitus wrote to satisfy Roman curiosity concerning the barbarians of the North for whose martial abilities he had a healthy respect. Nor could he refrain from his inclination to moralize by frequently contrasting the virtues of the Germans with the moral laxity of the Romans of his own day.

This work is of inestimable historical value. All modern accounts of the early Germans are largely based upon it, and medieval civilization was a fusion of the Germanic ideas and institutions described here and those appropriated from the Romans. Similarities with the ideas and institutions of the early Sumerians (see Selection 1) and Greeks (see Selection 17) will be apparent.

ORIGIN AND PHYSICAL CHARACTERISTICS

2. I regard the Germans themselves as an indigenous people, without any subsequent mixture of blood through immigration or friendly intercourse; for

Adapted from Arthur C. Howland, ed., *Translations and Reprints from the Original Sources of European History*, Vol. VI, No. 3 (Philadelphia, 1900).

in ancient times it was by sea and not by land that those who wished to change their homes wandered, and the boundless and, so to speak, hostile sea beyond us, is rarely traversed by ships from our part of the world. And not to mention the danger of the terrible and unknown sea, who indeed would leave Asia or Africa or Italy to seek Germany with its wild scenery, its harsh climate, its sullen manners and aspect, unless, indeed, it were his native country? They tell in their ancient songs, the only kind of tradition and history that they have, how Tuisto, a god sprung from the earth and his son Mannus were the originators and founders of their race. . . .

4. I myself subscribe to the opinion of those who hold that the German tribes have never been contaminated by intermarriage with other nations, but have remained peculiar and unmixed and wholly unlike the other people. Hence, the physical type is the same among them all, despite the vastness of their population. They all have fierce blue eyes, reddish hair and large bodies fit only for sudden exertion; they do not submit patiently to work and effort and cannot endure thirst and heat at all, though cold and hunger they are accustomed to because of their climate. . . .

KINGS AND LEADERS

7. They choose their kings on account of their ancestry, their leaders for their valor. The kings do not have free and unlimited power and the leaders lead by example rather than command, winning great admiration if they are energetic and fight in plain sight in front of the line. But no one is allowed to put a culprit to death or to imprison him, or even to beat him with stripes except the priests, and then not by way of a punishment or at the command of the leader but as though ordered by the god who they believe aids them in their fighting. Certain figures and images taken from their sacred groves they carry into battle, but their greatest incitement to courage is that a division of horse or foot is not made up by chance or by accidental association but is formed of families and clans; and their dear ones are close at hand so that the wailings of the women and the crying of the children can be heard during the battle. These are for each warrior the most sacred witnesses of his bravery, these his dearest applauders. They carry their wounds to their mothers and their wives, nor do the latter fear to count and examine their wounds while they bring them food and urge them to deeds of valor. . . .

RELIGION

9. Among the gods they worship Mercury most of all, to whom it is lawful to offer human sacrifices also on stated days. Hercules and Mars they placate by the sacrifice of worthy animals. Some of the Suebi sacrifice to Isis. The reason for this foreign rite and its origin I have not discovered, except that the image fashioned like a galley shows that the cult has been introduced from abroad. On the other hand they hold it to be inconsistent with the sublimity of the celestials to confine the gods in walls made by hands, or to liken them to the form of any human countenance. They consecrate woods and sacred groves to

them and give the names of the deities to that hidden mystery which they perceive by faith alone.

10. They pay as much attention as any people to augury and lots. The method of casting lots is uniform. They cut off a branch from a fruitbearing tree and divide it into small wands marked with certain characters. These they throw at random on a white cloth. Then the priest of the tribe, if it is a matter concerning the community, or the father of the family in case it is a private affair, calling on the gods and keeping his eyes raised toward the sky, takes up three of the lots, one at a time, and then interprets their meaning according to the markings before mentioned. If they have proven unfavorable there can be no further consultation that day concerning that particular matter. . . .

COUNCIL OF CHIEFS AND POPULAR ASSEMBLY

11. Concerning minor matters the chiefs deliberate, but in important affairs all the people are consulted, although the subjects referred to the common people for judgment are discussed beforehand by the chiefs. Unless some sudden and unexpected events calls them together they assemble on fixed days either at the new moon or the full moon, for they think these the most auspicious times to begin their undertakings. . . . When the crowd is sufficient they take their places fully armed. Silence is proclaimed by the priests, who have on these occasions the right to keep order. Then the king or a chief addresses them, each being heard according to his age, noble blood, reputation in warfare and eloquence, though more because he has the power to persuade than the right to command. If an opinion is displeasing they reject it by shouting; if they agree to it they clash their spears. The most complimentary form of assent is that which is expressed by means of their weapons.

LAW [See also Ch. 21, below.]

12. It is also allowable in the assembly to bring up accusations, and to prosecute capital offenses. Penalties are distinguished according to crime. Traitors and deserters are hung to trees. Weaklings and cowards and those guilty of infamous vices are cast into the mire of swamps with a wattled hurdle placed over their heads. This difference of penalty indicates that violent crimes should be punished publicly while shameful acts should be hidden out of sight. Lighter offenses also are punished according to their degree, the guilty parties being fined a certain number of horses or cattle. A part of the fine goes to the king or the tribe, part to the injured party or his relatives. In these same assemblies are chosen the magistrates who decide suits in the cantons and villages. Each one has a hundred associates, chosen from the people, who support them with their advice and influence.

THE "FOLLOWING" (COMITATUS)

13. They undertake no public or private business without being armed. But it is not customary for anyone to bear arms until the tribe has recognized his competence to use them. Then in a full assembly some one of the chiefs or

the father or relatives of the youth invest him with shield and spear. This is the sign that the lad has reached the age of manhood; this is his first honor. Before this he was only a member of a household, hereafter he is a member of the tribe. Distinguished rank or the great services of their parents secure even for lads the rank of chief. They attach themselves to certain more experienced chiefs of approved merit; nor are they ashamed to be looked upon as belonging to their followings. There are even different grades among the followers, assigned by the judgment of its leader. There is a great rivalry among these companions as to who shall rank first with the chief, and among the chiefs as to who shall have the most and the bravest followers. It is an honor and a source of strength always to be surrounded by a great band of chosen youths, for they are an ornament in peace and a defense in war. It brings reputation and glory to a leader not only in his own tribe but also among the neighboring peoples if his following is superior in numbers and courage: for he is courted by embassies and honored by gifts, and often the fame attached to his name decides wars.

VALUES

14. When they go into battle it is a disgrace for the chief to be outdone in deeds of valor and for the following not to match the courage of their chief; furthermore for any one of the followers to have survived his chief and come unharmed out of a battle is life-long infamy and shame. It is in accordance with their most sacred oath of allegiance to defend and protect him and to ascribe their bravest deeds to his renown. The chief fights for victory; the men of his following for their chief. If the tribe to which they belong sinks into the lethargy of long peace and quiet many of the noble youth voluntarily seek other tribes that are still carrying on war, because a quiet life is irksome to the Germans and they gain renown more readily in the midst of perils, and a large following cannot be maintained except by violence and war. For they look to the generosity of their chief for their war-horse and their deadly and victorious spear; the feasts and entertainments, however, furnished them on a homely but liberal scale, they count as mere pay. The means for this bounty are acquired through war and plunder. Nor could you persuade them to till the soil and await the yearly produce as easily as you could induce them to stir up an enemy and earn glorious wounds. They think it tame and stupid to acquire by sweat what they can win by their blood.

15. In the intervals of peace they spend some time in hunting but more in idleness, giving themselves over to sleep and eating. All the bravest and most warlike do nothing, while the hearth and home and the care of the fields is given over to the women, the old men, and the weakest members of the family. The warriors lie buried in sloth because of that strange contradiction in their nature that causes them to love indolence and hate peace. . . .

CUSTOMS

16. It is well known that none of the German tribes live in cities, nor even allow their dwellings to be set close together. They live separated and in various

places, as a spring or a meadow or a grove strikes their fancy. They lay out their villages not as with us in connected or closely-jointed houses, but each one surrounds his dwelling with an open space, either as a protection against fire or because of their ignorance of the art of building. They do not even make use of rough stones or tiles. They use for all purposes undressed timber, giving no beauty or comfort. Some parts they plaster carefully with earth of such purity and brilliancy as to form a substitute for painting and designs in color. . . .

19. Thus they live in well-protected virtue, uncorrupted by the allurements of public shows or the enticement of banquets. Men and women alike know nothing of clandestine love letters. Though the nation is so populous, adultery is very rare, its punishment being immediate and inflicted by the injured husband. He cuts off the woman's hair in the presence of her kinsfolk, drives her naked from his house and flogs her through the whole village. Indeed, the loss of chastity meets with no mercy; neither beauty, youth, nor wealth can procure the guilty woman a husband, for no one there laughs at vice, nor is corrupting and being corrupted spoken of as the way of the world. Those tribes do better still where only the virgins marry and where the hopes and aspirations of a bride are settled once and for all. They accept one husband, just as they have one body and one life; they must have no thought beyond this, no further desire. Their love must not be for the married state itself but for the husband. To limit the number of children or to put any late children to death is considered a crime, and with them good customs are more effective than good laws elsewhere.

20. In every household the children grow up naked and dirty with those stout bodies and sturdy limbs that we admire. Each mother nurses her own children; they are not handed over to servants and paid nurses. The master and the slave are in no way to be distinguished by the quality of their upbringing. They live among the same flocks and lie on the same ground until age separates them and valor distinguishes the free born. The young men marry late and their vigor is thereby unimpaired. Nor is the marriage of girls hastened. They have the same youthful vigor, the same stature as the young men. Thus well-matched and strong when they marry, the children reproduce the robustness of their parents. . . . A man's heirs and successors are his own children; there is no such thing as a will. If there are no children the next heirs are the brothers, then come the paternal and maternal uncles. The more relatives a man has and the greater the number of his relations by marriage, the more honored is his old age. Childlessness in Germany has no advantages.

21. A German is required to adopt not only the feuds of his father or of a relative, but also their friendships, though feuds are not irreconcilable. Even homicide is expiated by the payment of a certain number of cattle, and the whole family accepts the satisfaction — a useful practice for the community because feuds are more dangerous where there is much freedom.

No other nation indulges more freely in entertainment and hospitality. It is considered a crime to turn any man away from one's door. According to his means each one receives those who come with a well-furnished table. When all his food has been eaten, he who had been the host becomes the guide and companion of his guest to the next house, which they enter uninvited. It does not matter; they are received just as warmly. No one distinguishes between friend and stranger so far as concerns the right of hospitality. If the departing guest asks for any gift, it is customary to grant it to him. The host, too, feels the same freedom in making a request. They take great pleasure in presents, but they ask no favor for giving them, nor do they feel any obligation in accepting them.

22. As soon as they awake from sleep, which they generally prolong until late in the day, they bathe, usually in warm water as their winter lasts a great part of the year. After the bath they take food, each sitting in a separate seat and having a table to himself. Then they proceed to their business or not less often to feasts, fully armed. It is no disgrace to spend the whole day and night in drinking. Quarreling is frequent enough as is natural among drunken men, though their disputes are rarely settled by mere wrangling but oftener by blood-shed and wounds. Yet it is at their feasts that they consult about reconciling enemies, forming family alliances, electing chiefs, and even regarding war and peace, as they think that at no other time is the mind more open to fair judgment or more inflamed to mighty deeds. . . .

23. A liquor for drinking bearing a certain resemblance to wine is made by the process of fermentation from barley or other grain. Those next the border also buy wine. Their food is of a simple kind — wild fruit, fresh game, or curdled milk. They satisfy their hunger without elaborate preparation and without the use of condiments. In the matter of thirst they do not use the same moderation. If you indulge their love of drink by furnishing them as much as they wanted, they will be conquered as easily by their vices as by your arms.

26. Loaning money at interest and increasing it by compound interest is unknown, and so it is ignorance rather than legal prohibition that protects them. Land is held by the villages as communities according to the number of the cultivators, and is then divided among the freemen according to their rank. The vast extent of their territories makes this partition easy. They cultivate fresh fields every year and there is still land to spare. . . .

27. There is no pomp in the celebration of their funerals. The only custom they observe is that the bodies of illustrious men should be burned with certain kinds of wood. They do not heap garments and perfumes upon the funeral pile. In every case a man's arms are burned with him, and sometimes his horse also. They believe that stately monuments and sculptured columns oppress the dead with their weight; a mound of turf covers their graves. Tears and lamentations are quickly laid aside; sadness and grief linger long. It is fitting for women to mourn, for men to remember.

Such in general are the facts I have obtained concerning the origin and customs of the Germans as a whole.

Ausonius: Twilight in the Roman West

The third and fourth centuries A.D. witnessed the end of the Pax Romana and its replacement by recurrent civil wars, barbarian invasions, galloping inflation, and personal insecurity. This material instability was accompanied by a change in people's outlook on the world: "Men were ceasing to observe the external world and to try to understand it, utilize it or improve it. They were turning away from nature .... The idea of the beauty of the heavens and of the world went out of fashion and was replaced by that of the Infinite." [1] Evidence of the spiritual instability of this "age of anxiety," as it has been called, can be seen in various of the reading selections above. Although many were like the man described in St. Augustine's Confessions who "threw off the burden of the world" (p. 443) after reading the life of Antony the Egyptian monk, there were still some who clung to the old sentiments concerning life's pleasures. One such was St. Augustine's older contemporary, Ausonius (ca. 310–ca. 395 A.D.), who, after a long career as professor of rhetoric in Romanized Gaul, tutor to the emperor's son, and holder of high administrative offices, retired to his estate near Bordeaux to live the life of a cultivated country gentleman. In the twilight world of the Roman West, about to be overrun by waves of German invaders, Ausonius tended his vineyards and rose garden and composed charming and sensitive poems which reflect his feeling for the beauties of this world and what seems to be his only message. It is the same sad yet defiant message that has been expressed by people of similar mood in our own "age of anxiety": "This world in which an unresolvable discord is the fundamental fact is the world in which we must continue to live, and for us wisdom must consist, not in searching for a means of escape which does not exist but in making such peace with it as we may." [2]

ON NEWBLOWN ROSES

Spring, and the sharpness of the golden dawn.
Before the sun was up a cooler breeze

From Helen Waddell, trans., *Mediaeval Latin Lyrics* (Penguin Books, 1952), pp. 37, 39. Reprinted by permission of Constable and Company Limited.

[1] J. Bidez in *The Cambridge Ancient History*, Vol. XII (London: Cambridge University Press, 1939), p. 629.

[2] Joseph Wood Krutch, *The Modern Temper: A Study and a Confession* (New York: Harcourt, Brace & World, 1929), pp. 167–168.

Had blown, in promise of a day of heat,
And I was walking in my formal garden,
To freshen me, before the day grew old.

I saw the hoar frost stiff on the bent grasses,
Sitting in fat globes on the cabbage leaves,
And all my Paestum roses laughing at me,
Dew-drenched, and in the East the morning star,
And here and there a dewdrop glistening white,
That soon must perish in the early sun.

Think you, did Dawn steal color from the roses,
Or was it new-born day that stained the rose?

. . .

One moment, all on fire and crimson glowing,
All pallid now and bare and desolate.
I marvelled at the flying rape of time;
But now a rose was born: that rose is old.
Even as I speak the crimson petals float
Down drifting, and the crimsoned earth is bright.

So many lovely things, so rare, so young,
A day begat them, and a day will end.
O Earth, to give a flower so brief a grace!
As long as a day is long, so long the life of a rose.
The golden sun at morning sees her born,
And late at eve returning finds her old.
Yet wise is she, that hath so soon to die,
And lives her life in some succeeding rose.
O maid, while youth is with the rose and thee,
Pluck thou the rose: life is as swift for thee.